THE
COMPLETE CHRONICLE
OF THE
EMPERORS
OF
ROME

THE
COMPLETE CHRONICLE
OF THE
EMPERORS
OF
ROME

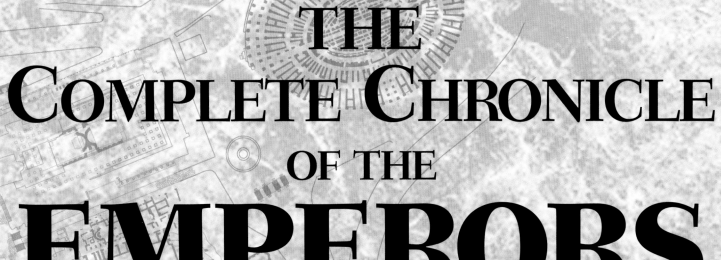

Roger Michael Kean
& Oliver Frey

THALAMUS

CONTENTS

Thalamus Publishing
is an imprint of
International Media Solutions Limited
4 Attorney's Walk, Bull Ring,
Ludlow, Shropshire SY8 1AA
England
01584 874977

British Library Cataloguing in Publication Data
A CIP Data Record for this book
is available from the British Library
ISBN 1-902886-05-4

Project editor: Warren Lapworth
Maps and design: Roger Kean
Illustrations: Oliver Frey

Typeset in Fairfield and Helvetica Neue Condensed

Printed and bound in Singapore
This book is printed on acid-free paper

10 9 8 7 6 5 4 3 2 1

**This book is dedicated to
Colleen McCulloch
and in fond memory of
Wallace Breem (1926–1990),
who rekindled the passion.**

LIST OF MAPS

Small maps for the ease of locating places mentioned in the text are not included in this listing

COMMON ABBREVIATIONS IN THE TEXT

BC   before the Christian era
AD   Christian era (*Anno Domini*)
c.   *circa*, about
(b.) ministry of bishop
(d.) died
(g.) governed
(p.) ministry of pope or patriarch
(r.) rule of Augustus, Caesar or king
(u.) rule of usurper
lit.   literally (means...)
q.v. cross reference (used in the Glossary)

PREFACE BY THE AUTHORS

Winston S Churchill in *A History of the English-Speaking Peoples* notes that we cannot understand history without continually relating the long periods mentioned to the experiences of our own short lives. 'Five years is a lot,' he writes. 'Twenty years is the horizon to most people. Fifty years is antiquity.'

In an age when the world's governments are not much older than two hundred years, and expectations of consistent political structures are limited to a few generations, the course of the Roman empire over eight hundred years† seems astonishing. That this is due in no small part to the concept of 'emperor' is not to be doubted. A 'family' – what we have come to recognise as a 'mafia', albeit not necessarily linked by heredity or even by dynasty – ensured a constancy by being imbued with the very nature of the position and duties of leadership. The empire's longevity indicates just how few emperors were the 'lazy no-nos' of popular imagination, but were in fact individuals doing their best at maintaining the welfare of Rome.

In the institutional rule of ancient Rome, what we witness is unlike a monarchy as we have come to understand the concept since medieval times; this was an obligation attached to the position and status of emperor that continued beyond dynastic bounds. Being emperor of Rome was both the supreme goal, but also in itself the assumption of a colossal duty, of which most incumbents were aware – though they might not live up to it in the course of their reigns.

However, there is another interesting factor in Rome's constancy, and that is the Romans' general awareness of their own history. 'Fifty years' may be 'antiquity', but it is clear that the Romans were very well aware of the past through mountains of the written word. In the age of Constantine, the antics of a Caligula or Commodus would still have been well known, either through the written or the spoken word. Some three hundred years after his death, Trajan was fondly remembered in the prayer that greeted a new emperor: 'More fortunate than Augustus, better than Trajan'. Even during the worst of times, the average Roman citizen could take comfort from knowing who he was, where he came from, and hope that the shining example of the past would inspire his rulers to restore order to the world – exactly as it should be.

This is a personal view, a voyage of discovery to fill in those gaps that years of gathered understanding had still left vague. Histories – unless concentrating on particular individuals – tend to portray an array of rulers through such a long passage of time as though each sprang fully formed into their imperial roles. Yet even in the most anarchic of times, Rome's Caesars and Augusti were known quantities as they rose through the ranks towards power. In researching this book it has been fascinating to see how many have a recorded history prior to their elevation, and to uncover the peculiar logic of the time that led each one to the imperial diadem.

Although the book concentrates on the emperors and their lives, it is not possible to separate a ruler from the consequences of his actions. So the larger, changing phases of socio-political history emerge; and at a more intimate level so do many interesting subsidiary people – wives, children, companions, adversaries.

My interest in ancient Rome came early. It sprang from an illustration in the children's *Newnes Pictorial Encyclopedia* that depicted in vibrant colour a Roman centurion shouting harsh instructions at his toiling soldiers as they built Hadrian's Wall. Everything was in that image to conjure up Rome – industry, discipline, military might – at once familiar and yet so seemingly alien to modern thinking. The impact the picture had then on my six-year-old mind has never left me.

However, the idea of writing this book came not from me but from my collaborator, the illustrator Oliver Frey. With Herculean fortitude he has uncovered just about every single major person mentioned in this chronicle – and a few who, through pressure on space, are not – to feature them from either their coins or their busts. The illustrations give a feel for the people, and this is entirely possible because, with a few exceptions, Roman portraiture was obsessed with visual accuracy, sometimes to the point that we might consider to be caricature.

In addition to the illustrations, colour maps feature prominently, placed beside the relevant text, not inconveniently at the front or back. I hope this will encourage even the least geographically minded to become involved in the places where events happen. The maps, too, are intended to add a ready sense of place and scale to the story and a feel for the perspectives of time.

It is worth drawing attention to the naming on the maps of the Mediterranean Sea. In pre-imperial times,

A barbarous habit
The Romans were insistent that their culture was far superior to that of the lesser races, the barbarians. And yet the ancient texts make continual mention of decapitation and of heads being dispatched to distant parts – to modern thinking a very barbarous thing. However, this was not simply a barbaric custom of triumphalism but – in a pre-photographic era – the only means of proving execution of a well-known personality to the authorities and the public.

† Counting from the end of the First Punic War in 241 BC (after which the Roman commonwealth can be considered an 'empire') to the conclusion of Justinian's reign in AD 565.

and after the Punic Wars, Romans called it *Mare Nostrum*, 'Our Sea', for indeed, it was theirs by conquest. But by the imperial period, written references suggest it had come to be known as the *Mare Internum*, since it sat at the heart of the empire. The terminology *Mare Mediterraneum* did not become currency until the mid-sixth century and at a point in time after this story has concluded.

Although Latin is used in the text for place names, I have excepted Rome, Constantinople and Athens because they are so well known by their English spelling that the Latin might intrude. Readers are frequently exercised over the use of capitalisation, so I lay out my reasoning in certain cases. I have referred to the Roman empire, not Empire, because to the Romans first there was the Republic (capital R), then there was the Roman state, for many still the RES PUBLICA, as epigraphic evidence proves. Since the word *imperator*, while it came to represent the ruler, did not really mean 'emperor', it follows that his hegemony was not an Empire. By the same logic, I have not used a capital E for the word emperor either. Senate or senate? I have adopted the lower-case spelling in keeping with modern conventions for most generic institutions; if this offends, I apologise.

A passion for Roman history might seem sufficient reason to write about the Roman emperors and their often grim but always fascinating lives. But there is another. Surprisingly, there are few books offering a coherent, chronological narrative account of the emperors from Augustus to Justinian, arguably the last classical Roman emperor.

Many are familiar with the period stretching from Augustus to the Antonines, but then events become hazy; and many Roman students have particular emperors or periods they know well, but little idea as to how the entire imperial train fits together. The Internet has boosted interest in Roman history, but too much of the available material ranges from the stuffily academic to the downright fictional; much is undigested, badly written and contradictory. Of course, contradiction is the staple of history – the trick is to consider the options and make a decision as to what seems most plausible; and if all else fails, admit the alternative. I hope I have managed to do this, and at the same time write a gripping story in which emotion, a sense of passing time, the ennui of fighting a battle well lost, and the passions of all the characters involved emerge alongside the chronicle of the emperors' histories.

Roger Kean
May 2005

Picturing the protagonists

We both felt, in this age of photography, when we are used to *seeing* famous people rather than just reading about them, that portraits of the emperors would add to the sense of the human beings behind the names and bridge the long distance that separates us from their lifetimes. Surprisingly, history has preserved images of all the emperors, well-nigh all the usurpers, and many of their wives and children. Most portraits are on coins, but busts are plentiful. The quality of the likenesses varies considerably, and can be said to generally deteriorate as the empire progresses, with the virtuosity of documentary realism of the early centuries giving way to less skilful workmanship, and then the intentional Byzantine stylisation of the twilight years; on the whole, however, distinct characterisation is in evidence throughout.

All portraits are deemed to be authenticated likenesses of the persons shown, unless we raise doubts in the caption, Helpfully, busts can be readily compared for authenticity to complementary images on coins which bear the personality's name – fortuitous in the case of the co-Augustus Balbinus who reigned in early 238 (*see page 130*): the Antalya Museum, Turkey, claims to own a bust of him, which bears no real semblance to the face on the many coins issued by him (*see page 315*, Getting it right, *for the comparison*).

We know that the Romans painted their sculpted busts elaborately to resemble the living person, right down to the colour of their eyes and hair (*you can see what effect this might have had on page 315*, Colouring a Roman), and a range of materials were used to fashion them. For the purposes of this book all bust-based portraits have been rendered in a uniform colour throughout to enhance the look of impartial 'photographic' documentation. Similarly the coins depicted, while accurate in detail and generally so in colouring, are used for portraiture only, and no attempt has been made to replicate their actual size, let alone relative scale – what would be a numismatist's delight would have resulted in severe eye-strain for the general reader more interested in the look of the protagonist, as in reality most of the coins are a great deal smaller than seen here! (*For a comparison, see the example on page 315*).

We hope you enjoy the long procession of characters great and insignificant, good and bad, fortunate or just plain unlucky, who bestrode the tumultuous stage of the Roman empire's long story.

Oliver Frey
June 2005

It is a testament to Roman pragmatism and love of civilised comfort that the longest-lived working survivor of the archaic, Republican, and imperial periods is Rome's city drainage system. The earliest sewer, the Cloaca Maxima, which drained the Subura district, still exists today, as do many subsidiary drains. Its exit into the Tiber between the Sublican and Aemilian bridges was only covered over by the embankment in recent times. Rome's modern manhole covers still bear the legend S.P.Q.R. – SENATUS POPULUSQUE ROMANUS, meaning 'the senate and the people of Rome'.

PROLOGUE: END OF THE REPUBLIC

The scholar M. Terentius Varro, who lived for eighty-eight years towards the end of the Republican period (c.115 BC–27 BC), established the date of 753 BC for the founding of Rome. Whether or not he was accurate – there were several other favoured dates either side – it became the officially accepted year that the city came into being. For some two hundred and forty years the small archaic Latin settlement on the east bank of the Tiberis was ruled by a series of kings, followed by a little under five centuries of Republican government, during which time Rome expanded exponentially from a mere city to a Mediterranean-wide commonwealth.

From this point, for a period of just over half a millennium, the Roman state was governed by a series of emperors – more than a hundred of them. The word 'governed' is employed loosely in this context, since the capabilities and behaviour of many left much to be desired. The first key moment in this long history came during the lifetime of Julius Caesar (12/13 July 100 BC to 15 March 44 BC), the figure most responsible for the final undoing of the Republic and the creation of a political environment in which autocracy was bound to prevail. As with most socio-political changes, this sweeping alteration in the Roman state did not happen overnight, nor was it a simple matter of an ambitious man overturning the rules that governed the Roman people. In fact Republican Rome enjoyed the most sophisticated form of government of any ancient Western civilisation, a complex interweaving of constitutional and legal statutes, political protections and counterbalances to elected authority. Caesar, and subsequently his adopted son Octavian, used the very substance of Roman law to bend the state to their will; although both also bent the rules whenever it suited, setting a precedent that many of their successors would follow.

There are as many theories behind the fall of the Roman Republic as there are historians to put them forward. However, certain assumptions can be made with some safety. By the middle of the first century BC Rome had become a victim of its own success. Conquests to the west in Hispania, to the east beyond Macedonia into Asia Minor and across the Mare Internum (Mediterranean) in North Africa had made the senatorial governing system unsustainable. Even this may have worked for some longer time, were it not for the fact that the senate – the body of three hundred most senior Romans – had grown both complacent and fractious. For several decades prior, it had been riven with factional conflicts that often centred on the ambitions of the ancient aristocratic families on the one hand and those of the 'new men', politicians arising from the rural Italian provinces, on the other. These two social groups broadly, but not exclusively, divided themselves between the OPTIMATES party, conservatives who put the rule of the senate first, and the POPULARES, reformers who worked through the people rather than the senate. The division of opinion was almost exclusively concerned with the benefits of the city of Rome and its immediate hinterland, not really with the greater matter of empire. Put simply, the Roman state had become too large and encompassed too many different peoples with varying needs for the existing government by senatorial and public committee to cope. Rome might have been the centre of the world, but its plutocrats acted more like parochial land-owners than the governors of an empire.

Rome itself had also swelled to bursting point, filled with a mass of indolent citizens who paid no taxes, thanks to recent conquests, and who constantly demanded free food and public entertainment. The mob was bored and happily exchanged yesterday's allegiance for today's, swayed by the next clever orator to come along. Street violence and open rioting was symptomatic of the factional crises facing the Republic, and in so many aspects it was writ large that Rome needed a strong man to guide the empire's fortunes. Before Caesar came to public notice, there had indeed been a string of such men, all of them with the loyalty of one or more of the Roman legions behind them. They owed their positions to a gradual erosion of the traditional constitution.

In earlier times, two senior senators were elected as consuls for each year. They were effectively the army's generals for their term. In theory each in turn, month by month, was active while his colleague looked on – one of the first checks and balances of power. In practice this was confused by the consul's military duties, especially in times of extended war, when both consuls would be in the field with their legions at the same time. There was a proper age for a senator to become a consul (forty-two), but this was increasingly ignored, as was the tradition that a consul should only serve once in his lifetime. Periods of extended conflict, such as the Punic Wars, made it desirable that the consuls should have their year-long term prolonged to provide a continuity of military leadership.

This finally led to the inevitable situation that an ambitious consul would find good reasons to request either a prolonged term or repeated consulships. The first to do both successfully was Gaius Marius (157–86 BC). He had himself elected consul first in 108 BC, again in 104, and then every year – first warring against Jugurtha in North Africa, and then against Germans invading Italia – until his sixth consulship in 100. This was contrary to all law and precedent. But he was outdone by his erstwhile lieutenant, Lucius Cornelius Sulla (138–78 BC). After what was virtually a civil war between the supporters of the two former colleagues, Sulla marched on Rome and declared himself dictator in 81. The role of dictator was constitutionally allowed for in times of great danger to the state. In effect, a senior senatorial magistrate was elected dictator and given absolute single-handed power to govern until such time as the danger had passed. He was then expected to stand down in return for an indemnity against the results of his actions. Sulla's unilateral assumption of the dictatorship was unprecedented too, and it would not be the last. Sulla ruled Rome without limitation to the

Gaius Marius is credited with creating the first professional Roman army, the men serving as salaried soldiers in permanent legions. In so doing, he swept away the democratic citizen-army and laid the foundations for a military that was loyal to its paymasters – the aristocratic LEGATI – rather than to the state. Marius was a practical man, who must have thought he was doing the best for Rome, given the circumstances, but he proved to be as unprincipled as his former comrade Sulla when the two clashed. Each claimed the loyalty of the legions they commanded and used Rome as a pawn in their struggle for supreme power. It set the pattern for the future empire and sowed the seeds of its ultimate destruction.

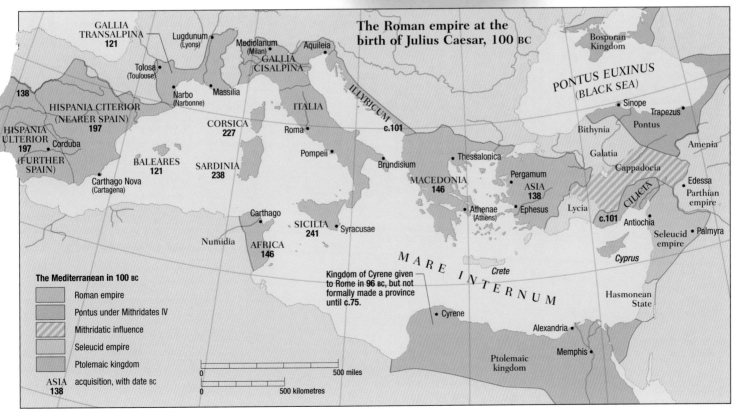

The Roman empire at the birth of Julius Caesar, 100 BC

The Mediterranean in 100 BC
- Roman empire
- Pontus under Mithridates IV
- Mithridatic influence
- Seleucid empire
- Ptolemaic kingdom
- ASIA 138 acquisition, with date BC

term of his office. However, it turned out to be a short period, but one notable for its cruelty as he 'purged' any who had not supported him – thousands died, including senators and men of the equestrian order, Rome's middle class businessmen. When, to everyone's surprise, he laid down the dictatorship at the end of the year he left behind a power vacuum into which stepped ambitious young men like Pompeius, Crassus and Caesar.

The new professional Roman army

None of these had any hope of gaining or retaining power without the backing of the Roman army, and this had changed greatly since the early and middle Republican periods. Previously, it had been an essentially unprofessional institution, manned by civilian conscripts who gave their time as part of the duty expected of every Roman citizen. This tradition dated back to archaic times when the tiny city-state was surrounded on all sides by foes and all male inhabitants of suitable age were called on to defend it

Lucius Cornelius Sulla adopted the COGNOMEN Felix (fortunate); and in general he did live up to his nickname. His enemies were less so after he was made dictator in 82 BC – their properties were confiscated and their lives forfeit in the worst reign of terror Rome had witnessed. Notwithstanding his bloodthirsty actions, Sulla's reforms led to the restoration of constitutional government, but also pointed the way of 'might is right' to his ambitious lieutenants. And in his private life his penchant for depravity foreshadowed the behaviour of many later emperors.

in times of war. History shows what an effective fighting force the later Republican army was, but it suffered from a major drawback in the new era of growing empire and extended conquest. Tradition required legionaries to be at least ADSIDUI, that is citizens who owned the minimum amount of property to be classed as land-owners. Since campaigning usually only took place between the spring to autumn seasons, a consul's legion was dismissed from service at the end of the campaigning year. This was necessary because the men had to get back to their farms at the conclusion of a period of service. Legions were, therefore, dissolved annually only to be reinvented in the following campaign season.

When he was elected consul in 108, Gaius Marius faced a war in Numidia against King Jugurtha, who had been fighting Rome since 112. But he encountered a serious shortage of manpower. Over the previous four decades the Italian peninsula – heartland of the ADSIDUI – had become depopulated of farming citizens. In part this was due to the seductive draw of Rome; with its corn dole and bright lights, the city naturally acted as a magnet for many rural citizens. As happens today, the young were particularly inclined to leave the land for a supposedly easier and more exciting urban lifestyle. But more importantly, laws and reforms had failed to prevent agrarian land from falling into the hands of a very few wealthy families, which they combined into giant estates called LATIFUNDIA. The satisfactory conclusion of the Punic Wars and Macedonian conquest had provided plenty of cheap labour in the form of slaves, and so the original citizen-farmers were not only dispossessed of their property, they were not even granted the right of tenancy or menial labour. This inevitably led to a great migration to Rome of men no longer considered eligible to serve in the army because they were no longer ADSIDUI; they had become part of the un-landed proletariat.

Faced by this situation, Marius simply abandoned the traditional practice of raising troops from among the ADSIDUI, and instead enlisted volunteers from the proletariat. However, these unmonied soldiers needed increases in the regular military stipend to afford their arms and armour and, more essentially, they expected to be kept in service to the end of their useful lives, and then settled on a smallholding for their old age. In effect, the legion had become a permanent organisation into which new recruits could be added. It was also one that owed allegiance to its commander, a man now more than likely to lead them for much longer than the traditional year. The legions under first Marius, then Sulla, Pompeius, Crassus and Caesar had effectively become their general's private force.

Young Julius Caesar

With cracks appearing in the Republic at every turn, the existence of large, powerful armies loyal to their leader, and men with the will to govern – if necessary by force – everything was in place for the final collapse of Republican government. And Gaius Julius Caesar was the Roman to give it the push. Genius military commander, gifted orator, prolific writer and law-maker, Caesar was a man of many parts. Famous for his clemency – he pointedly spared the lives of political enemies – he was cruel in his treatment of the Celts in Gallia. He spoke the language of the common legionary, but moved among Rome's elite on equal terms – at least as regards his patrician status; the OPTIMATES feared his popularist stance. His championing of the proletariat while accruing all honours he felt were owed to him made many of his aristocratic colleagues rightly suspicious of his motives. Julius Caesar had no time for nostalgic Republican sentiment.

From the ancient patrician GENS Julii, the young Julius was instilled with pride in Roman history, which must have been shaken when his father became a victim of political scheming and fell from grace, losing the family wealth along the way. From this point on Caesar was raised in Rome's poor Subura quarter, and until his middle adult years he remained immured in poverty. This may have contributed to his famous frugality. As the Roman historian Suetonius (c.AD 69–122) wrote: 'That he drank very little wine not even his enemies denied.' There is a saying of his bitterest political enemy Marcus Cato that Caesar was the only man who undertook to overthrow the state when sober. Even in the matter of food Gaius Oppius tells us that 'he was so indifferent…'.

At the age of fifteen, on the death of his father, Caesar joined the army. Four years spent on hectic military campaigns in Asia Minor earned him a reputation for valour and physical strength that belied the epilepsy from which he occasionally suffered. Aged twenty, he won the CORONA CIVICA (civic crown) for saving a fellow soldier's life in the storming of Mytilene on the Aegean island of Lesbos.

He first came to prominent political notice as a client of the fabulously wealthy Marcus Licinius Crassus (115–53 BC) – thus apparently hitching himself to the Sullan OPTIMATES party. But his

marriage to Cornelia, daughter of eminent Marian supporter Cinna, and the fact that Gaius Marius was his uncle by marriage, tied him to the democratic POPULARES cause. Marius rated Caesar a fellow radical – in this he was only partly correct, although Caesar was to use radical tactics during much of his later life. He remained constant to the POPULARES and all his life was an opponent of the senate, although he managed to maintain good relations with aristocratic Crassus.

In order to succeed in the Republican world, a young man with political ambitions had to have wealth, and while he had the former in abundance, Caesar had none of the latter. However, his problems were eased when, at thirty-six, he was elected PONTIFEX MAXIMUS, the supreme priest of Rome. This unexpected appointment gave him funds, an official residence and enhanced prestige. While financial concerns were uppermost, Caesar's desire for AUCTORITAS superseded anyone's and often amounted to an obsession. AUCTORITAS literally means 'authority', but in Latin the word meant much more, with overtones of eminence, public leadership and the ability to influence events through sheer personality. It was a quality important to any Roman aristocrat, but to Caesar, the seeking of it was almost a religion.

Caesar's first senior administrative posting was as

As a young man, Gnaeus Pompeius (Magnus) was Sulla's most devoted officer. His provincial background prevented his holding any significant political office in his early career, but his military reputation and his supreme skill as a self-publicist made him a power in later life. Plutarch wrote of him: 'Pompeius had a very engaging countenance, which spoke for him before he opened his lips.'

In 80 BC the governor of Spain, a democrat named Quintus Sertorius, rebelled against Sulla, refusing to acknowledge the senate's supremacy. He took to the hills with some 8,000 men, and accepted the offer of the Lusitanian tribes to become their leader. After successfully holding at bay the legions sent to destroy him, he faced Pompeius in 76. Over another three years, Pompeius wore down the rebel and his army of Roman refugees and Spanish guerrillas. The revolt collapsed when Sertorius was assassinated in 72, and Pompeius was given the credit and the hero worship of the nation. In seizing the military initiative, Sertorius became the first in a long line of rebels and usurpers of imperial power.

Impoverished aristocrat, Gaius Julius Caesar remained frugal throughout his life but greedy for power. When the two most powerful men in the empire came to blows, it spelled the end of the Republic. Pompeius gambled on his military prowess, Caesar on his genius for strategy. Having defeated his opponent, Caesar embarked on a massive construction programme, especially in the Forum Romanum. He also built himself an impregnable position of absolute rule. Despite showing clemency to former enemies, his moderation did little to dispell growing fears that Caesar had become a tyrant in the despised oriental manner.

propraetor of Hispania Citerior (Nearer Spain, later Tarraconensis), recently subdued by Pompeius after a rebellion, for which action the upstart general became known as Magnus, the 'Great'. Here, Caesar distinguished himself sufficiently to stand for the consular elections on his return to Rome. He needed a consulship desperately so that he could be given a proconsular governorship of a province afterwards – his only chance of accumulating wealth. It would also put him in command of an army of his own, which would increase his AUCTORITAS greatly. But his chances of election were poor – he still lacked the money, and the OPTIMATES majority in the senate detested him. Fortunately, he was able to rely on financial support from Crassus, but he knew that in order to win he also needed the backing of Pompeius Magnus, who was approved of by the senate for his military successes and Republican adherence (but disapproved of for his provincial background). Crassus and Pompeius stood

at opposite poles of Roman nobility – Crassus of established senatorial lineage, an OPTIMATE; Pompeius one of the new men from rural Picenum. Their politics and characters clashed, and Crassus was jealous of Pompeius's military acclaim. Their joint consulship of 70 BC had only served to divide them further.

Caesar had a valuable weapon in his armoury, his daughter Julia, of whom Pompeius was enamoured. Her marriage to the great soldier cemented relations between the two men, and drew Pompeius into negotiations with Crassus. Caesar employed all his charm and courtesy and was able to persuade the two bitter enemies to become reconciled to the inalienable fact that combined they were strong enough to command the senate to abide by their wishes. With their joint support, Caesar was elected one of the consuls for the year of 59, and their partnership was later known as the First Triumvirate. In this, Julius Caesar was the junior partner, but it was a status he did not tolerate for long. Crassus had the money; Caesar was a patrician with a common touch – he was at home with ordinary folk – but Pompeius had little to offer the triumvirate except his immense popularity among the legions. Even Cicero, one of his most adamant supporters, said Pompeius was 'nothing great, nothing outstanding, nothing that is not low and popular'.

The arrangement was not a legally constituted one, it was a private agreement assuring its members of co-operation. Each acted ostensibly in the interests of the others, while in reality they worked to secure increased power and wealth for themselves. The busiest was Caesar, who, after his election, acted on behalf of the triumvirs from a position of consular strength. The three men exerted influence on the government apparatus, despite senatorial attempts to thwart them at every turn. They pursued policies that would win them popular support, including the presentation of free games and extra grain rations. All this was costly, so Caesar ensured that the triumvirate secured the overseas posts for the following year that would replenish their fortunes. Pompeius returned to Hispania, Crassus pitched himself and his forces into Syria, while Caesar sought his destiny beyond the Alps in unconquered Gallia Comata (Gaul of the Long Hairs).

Although his task kept Caesar away from Rome for the better part of six years, he still returned from time to time to look after his own affairs and those of the triumvirate. The strain of this unnatural bonding soon became intolerable. Emergency talks dubbed the Luca Conference took place in 56 to avoid a falling out. The triumvirate was endorsed in 55 when Pompeius and

Crassus were once again consuls. But in 54, the link that kept Caesar and Pompeius allied was severed when Julia died. A year later Crassus was killed in battle at Carrhae (Harran) in Mesopotamia. Pompeius and Caesar were left tentatively circling one another, waiting and watching.

Caesar dictator

Caesar's conquest of Gallia in 58–51 BC was a remarkable achievement, even in a time of extraordinary men. It is not within the scope of this book to enter into any detail about the campaign. Suffice it to say that in the first three years he overran most of Gallia and Belgica, and then went on to subdue the German tribes living in the north of the region and push them back across the Rhenus. He even crossed to the island of Britannia, but gave up his limited invasion when fresh trouble broke out behind him in Gallia under the leadership of the charismatic Vercingetorix. Through brilliant strategic planning, the legions finally cornered the Avernian prince at Alesia, and by 58 all of Gallia was thoroughly under Roman rule. Of more importance to him personally, Caesar now had a large, highly trained force of seven legions, whose soldiers adored him without reservation. Caesar now looked to Rome for his reward.

In 52, a reluctant senate had given Pompeius a third consulship with the purpose of his quelling the eternal political street fighting, but without a colleague to hinder him. This virtual dictatorship was more than the Luca Conference had allowed for between the triumvirs, and left Caesar with the suspicion that Pompeius was conspiring against him. Caesar needed to be elected consul while still propraetor of Gallia, thus continuing his IMPERIUM and its automatic immunity to legal prosecution for any illegal acts he may have carried out in his province – of which, according to his political enemies, there were plenty. The senate insisted on the statutes, that he enter Rome as a PRIVATUS to canvas for the election. Although Pompeius agreed to use his position to waive the regulations, Caesar no longer trusted him, or he may have not believed that Pompeius could carry the senate with him. In any event, Caesar invaded Italia at the beginning of 49, crossing the Rubicon river – the boundary between Cisalpine Gallia and Italia – at the head of his devoted legions, and occupied Ariminum. He seems to have striven for a peaceful situation, if one was possible on his own terms. One source tells how he pondered the alternatives: 'To refrain from crossing will bring me misfortune; but to cross will

bring misfortune to all men.' But he would not lose the initiative through caution, and it was clear he had taken his erstwhile triumvir completely by surprise. Pompeius chose not to face him, and instead withdrew across the Mare Adriaticum to begin marshalling his forces in the Balkans.

Rome and all Italia fell to Caesar with scarcely any fighting, but the city had been emptied of most of its magistrates. His first task, therefore, was to provide some sort of government. However, he did this without entering the city, thus still adhering to constitutional form. The first act of the civil war took place in Hispania, where Pompeius still had a powerful army. Hoping to deal with this before Pompeius had time to raise a second army in the Balkans, Caesar dashed overland to Hispania. In his brief absence Marcus Antonius (Mark Antony), who as a young TRIBUNUS MILITUM had won his favour in Gallia, was appointed Caesar's MAGISTER EQUITUM (master of the horse) and left in charge of Italia. Antonius ensured that the compliant senate named Caesar dictator. Pompeius's cause fell rapidly in the hands of his poorly chosen generals, Lucius Afranius and Marcus Petreius. They surrendered in return for a pardon and the disbandment of the Pompeian legions. Caesar hurried back to Rome, where he was elected consul for a second time, to begin a round of diplomatic missions to help restore proper government. And then, at the end of a very hectic 49 BC, he set off to confront the Republicans.

After failing to dislodge Pompeius's well-entrenched forces at Dyrrachium, Caesar marched into Thessalia to intercept Metellus Scipio, the proconsular governor of Syria, who was coming overland to join the Pompeian army. Pompeius followed Caesar, and the three forces finally clashed in the summer of 48 at Pharsalus, in northern Greece. Despite being outnumbered two to one, Caesar's foot soldiers broke the massed Pompeian cavalry and then pressed the infantry to the point of routing it completely. Pompeius fled to the coast and took ship to Aegyptus in the hope that the children of King Ptolemy Auletes, Cleopatra and Ptolemy XII, would remember that when he was alive their father owed his throne to Pompeius's generosity. They did not – perhaps they feared Caesar more. When he landed, Pompeius Magnus was treacherously murdered on the beach, and his pickled head handed to a horrified Caesar on his arrival in Alexandria early in 47.

When news of the victory at Pharsalus reached

No authenticated bust of Publius Licinius Crassus exists. When he minted the coin below in 55 BC, he identified himself by name on the reverse as the moneyer, alongside the figure of a female warrior leading a horse; featuring actual portraits on the obverse would only begin a decade later.

Rome, Caesar's dictatorship was renewed. Now undisputed ruler of the Roman world, he mediated between the squabbling factions at the Alexandrian court, eventually siding with Cleopatra, and then returned to Rome. The sojourn was brief; in 46, he went to Africa and defeated Pompeius's remaining Republican forces at Thapsus. Among those there, Marcus Cato committed suicide, but the sons of Pompeius, Gnaeus and Sextus, fled to Hispania. Caesar pursued them and the war was soon ended by the battle of Munda (45 BC). Gnaeus was killed shortly after the

battle, but his younger brother Sextus made good his escape. Although the refugee could do nothing of consequence while Caesar lived, after the dictator's assassination he was able to make serious trouble.

Julius Caesar Rex

Having laboured long and hard for this cherished position of power, Caesar set about enjoying the rewards. In 46 his dictatorship was renewed again, this time for ten years, but two years later he was given the office for life. Honours were heaped on him by

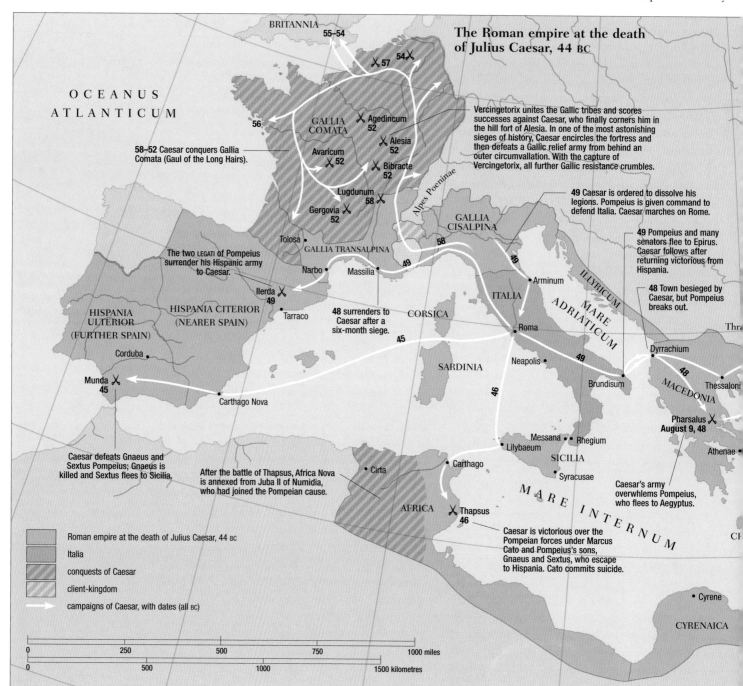

The Roman empire at the death of Julius Caesar, 44 BC

58–52 Caesar conquers Gallia Comata (Gaul of the Long Hairs).

Vercingetorix unites the Gallic tribes and scores successes against Caesar, who finally corners him in the hill fort of Alesia. In one of the most astonishing sieges of history, Caesar encircles the fortress and then defeats a Gallic relief army from behind an outer circumvallation. With the capture of Vercingetorix, all further Gallic resistance crumbles.

49 Caesar is ordered to dissolve his legions. Pompeius is given command to defend Italia. Caesar marches on Rome.

49 Pompeius and many senators flee to Epirus. Caesar follows after returning victorious from Hispania.

48 Town besieged by Caesar, but Pompeius breaks out.

The two LEGATI of Pompeius surrender his Hispanic army to Caesar.

48 surrenders to Caesar after a six-month siege.

Caesar defeats Gnaeus and Sextus Pompeius; Gnaeus is killed and Sextus flees to Sicilia.

After the battle of Thapsus, Africa Nova is annexed from Juba II of Numidia, who had joined the Pompeian cause.

Caesar's army overwhelms Pompeius, who flees to Aegyptus.

Caesar is victorious over the Pompeian forces under Marcus Cato and Pompeius's sons, Gnaeus and Sextus, who escape to Hispania. Cato commits suicide.

Roman empire at the death of Julius Caesar, 44 BC

Italia

conquests of Caesar

client-kingdom

campaigns of Caesar, with dates (all BC)

obsequious senators trying to outdo one another. His birthday became a public holiday. The month of his birth was renamed 'Julius' (July) after him. There seemed no end to his exaltation.

Although he refused the title REX (king), and rejected the crown Antony offered him in 44 at the Lupercalia, Caesar adopted many kingly trappings. He took to wearing a purple toga, the regal colour. He was awarded the right to sit on a golden chair during senate meetings, wearing a golden wreath. The final acts of his life effectively dismantled the last vestiges of the Republic. Caesar made no secret of his contempt for the institution and those constitutional forms that he had adhered to during his rise to power. He ignored the role of the various COMMITIAE, nominating magistrates himself; held consular elections for several years in advance after informing the senate of who would be elected; summoned the senate only to tell its members of his decisions; and silenced TRIBUNI who opposed him. When Queen Cleopatra of Aegyptus, with Caesarion, her son by Caesar, came to reside outside Rome's walls as his mistress, patrician, senatorial and equestrian disquiet turned to open rebellion. Rome still did not take kindly to monarchs and princes with a possible hereditary right.

According to Cicero, the conspiracy was contrived by people with 'the courage of men but the understanding of boys' – in other words, they were naïve if they believed the death of Caesar would restore the Republic. On the agreed day, the Ides (15th) of March, 44, Caesar went to the senate at its appointed place for that day, the meeting hall in the Porticoes of Pompeius. There, at the foot of Pompeius's oversize statue (which Caesar had allowed to remain), the large group of conspirators murdered him. Perhaps Caesar knew it was coming for he made little attempt to defend himself – he had even dismissed his lictors earlier. He succumbed to twenty-three stab wounds. After his death, Cleopatra returned with Caesar's son to Aegyptus, vituperatively declaiming that the conspirators were traitors. Although there were certainly lofty as well as less noble motives for the murder, this cruel and senseless act unleashed a civil war worse than any in Rome's history and ensured the end of the Republic forever.

What is important in the rise of Octavian, Caesar's adopted son and the future Augustus, is the Julian blood line; he was the son of Caesar's niece. As far into the future as the accession of Vespasian in AD 70, Roman soldiers would only accept a new emperor who had a hereditary link to the Julii, such was their veneration of Julius Caesar. Indeed, would-be emperors for two hundred years would cite their hereditary ties to the first Caesar, which soon ceased to be a name and became a title. Caesar himself had not become an emperor, but he had made it possible – even inevitable – that his successor Octavian would.

First, however, Octavian had a civil war to prosecute. Marcus Antonius had assumed that Caesar's mantle would fall on his own shoulders and not on those of the young man he contemptuously referred to as 'the boy'.

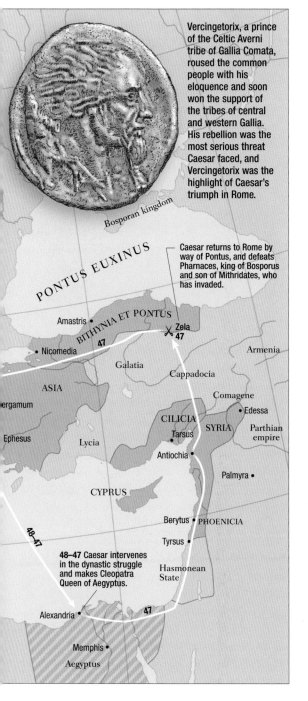

Vercingetorix, a prince of the Celtic Averni tribe of Gallia Comata, roused the common people with his eloquence and soon won the support of the tribes of central and western Gallia. His rebellion was the most serious threat Caesar faced, and Vercingetorix was the highlight of Caesar's triumph in Rome.

Bosporan kingdom

PONTUS EUXINUS

Caesar returns to Rome by way of Pontus, and defeats Pharnaces, king of Bosporus and son of Mithridates, who has invaded.

Amastris

BITHYNIA ET PONTUS

Zela 47

47

Nicomedia

Galatia

Armenia

Cappadocia

ASIA

Comagene

ergamum

Edessa

CILICIA

Tarsus

SYRIA

Parthian empire

Ephesus

Lycia

Antiochia

Palmyra

CYPRUS

Berytus PHOENICIA

48–47

Tyrsus

48–47 Caesar intervenes in the dynastic struggle and makes Cleopatra Queen of Aegyptus.

Hasmonean State

Alexandria

47

Memphis

Aegyptus

CHAPTER ONE   63 BC–AD 68
THE JULIO-CLAUDIAN DYNASTY

AUGUSTUS

Gaius (Julius Caesar) Octavianus / Imperator Caesar Augustus (r.16/1/27 BC–AD 19/8/14)

The future Augustus was born on 23 September 63 BC in the Palatine district of Rome according to one account, or at the family estate in Velitrae according to another. This was during the consulships of the orator Marcus Tullius Cicero and Gaius Antonius, father of Marcus Antonius. On his father's side, according to Suetonius, the Octavians were famous only in ancient Velitrae. At some previous point in time, a certain Gaius Rufus had become the first Octavian to gain office by a popular vote, winning a quaestorship. His sons Gaius and Gnaeus fathered two very different branches of the family. Gnaeus's descendants all held high office, including in 87 BC the consulship for Gnaeus Octavius (together with Lucius Cornelius Cinna, an opponent of Gaius Marius) and again in 76, and also for Lucius Octavius in the following year. Gaius's branch, however, remained lowly EQUITES until the entry into the senate of Gaius Octavius, who became famous as the father of Augustus. However, the father's influence was cut short by his death when his son was aged four, and it was Julius Caesar who was to become the greater imperative in the young Octavius's life.

The boy evidently made a good impression on Caesar, whom he would have met at family gatherings, since he was the grandson of Caesar's younger sister. At the age of twelve, he received his first taste of public speaking at the funeral of Caesar's daughter Julia, who had been married to Pompeius. At his coming of age at sixteen, he was awarded military decorations when Caesar celebrated his African triumph over the Pompeians, although he was still too young to have seen actual service. But when Caesar went to Hispania to fight the sons of Pompeius, Octavius followed with a small escort. Despite suffering from an illness, he fought his way with his men along enemy-held roads and survived a shipwreck – a spirited action that delighted Caesar. It was in Gallia Narbonensis that Octavius first met Marcus Vipsanius Agrippa, a junior TRIBUNUS on Caesar's staff, who was to remain Octavius's lifelong companion and supporter.

Caesar now appointed his great-nephew a TRIBUNUS and, on the recovery of Hispania, sent him ahead to Apollonia in Epirus, to begin planning a war against the Parthian empire. In his spare time, Octavius studied Greek literature and continued a lengthy correspondence with his patron as Caesar pursued his reforms of the government in Rome. Octavius was nineteen when the news of Caesar's assassination reached him. Since – to almost everyone's surprise – he was named as Caesar's heir in the will, he ignored his mother's pleas to stay away from politically dangerous Rome. The will, read at Caesar's funeral, gave the bulk of his fortune to Octavius, whom he posthumously adopted as his son. If Octavius were to refuse the adoption Decimus Junius Brutus was named in his place, which was ironical since Brutus had agreed to join the conspiracy, albeit in an insignificant way. For Marcus Antonius, who had commanded Italia as MAGISTER EQUITUM for three years until 47 and was Caesar's

Octavius, the boy: having lost his father when he was four, his great-uncle Julius Caesar (coin, below) became a much-admired influence on him.

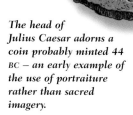

The head of Julius Caesar adorns a coin probably minted 44 BC – an early example of the use of portraiture rather than sacred imagery.

colleague in the consulship at the time of the dictator's murder, there was nothing of consequence. This was something of a blow, since Antonius had assumed to be named Caesar's heir; and his dissolute, profligate lifestyle and political ambitions certainly required the support of Caesar's fortune.

The problem for both the senate and Octavius was that much of Caesar's wealth and the loyalty of his legions were in Antonius's hands, and the surviving consul had ensured the support of the current MAGISTER EQUITUM, Marcus Aemilius Lepidus, by securing him the office of PONTIFEX MAXIMUS left vacant by Caesar's death. In addition he was effectively signalling his intention to assume the role of dictator. This the senate was robustly resisting as Octavius arrived in Rome. Antonius was unsurprisingly cool in his reception of 'the boy'. Meanwhile, thanks to Antonius playing both ends against the middle, Marcus Junius Brutus and Gaius Cassius Longinus, the most distinguished of Caesar's assassins, had been allowed to leave Rome free men, and had fled to Macedonia and Syria to begin raising a Republican army.

The underlying motive in all of Octavius's actions was to avenge Caesar's murder and to keep his laws and decrees in force. Unable at once to punish the leading assassins, he sought election as a TRIBUNUS PLEBIS to give him the authority required in order to carry out his plans. Antonius used his consular powers to oppose Octavius's candidacy on the grounds that although a plebeian by birth he was now an adoptive Julian, therefore a patrician and ineligible to be a tribune; though he was understood to have suggested to Octavius that a hefty bribe might make him change his mind. Octavius had better things to spend his money on, and Antonius's attitude drove him into the hands of the OPTIMATES who – seeking any advantage – wanted to use his name against Antonius's naked ambition. Cicero – so opposed to the Caesarian faction – now sought to gather Caesar's young heir into his Republican camp, and Octavius compliantly

Marcus Junius Brutus had this coin bearing his portrait minted to mark the assassination of the 'tyrant' Julius Caesar on the Ides of March 44 BC.

agreed to be guided in all things by the great rhetorician. For his own part, Octavius needed Cicero's powerful voice in his battle against Antonius, but was never tricked into believing that Cicero held him in high esteem. The great man was not fooled either, and summed up senatorial feelings when he said 'praise [Octavius], honour him, then get rid of him'.

In 43 BC Antonius, feeling a cold wind blowing, left Rome for the proconsular command of Gallia Cisalpina, which he had awarded himself by passing a law that overturned Caesar's appointment of Decimus Junius Brutus to the province. Cisalpina's advantage lay in being outside Italia, but close enough for him to influence events in Rome. However, Brutus refused to give up his rightful command, and war threatened. Cicero then began a series of impassioned speeches (the *Philippics*) against Antonius, and in one called him one of 'the very blackest and foulest monsters that have ever lived since the birth of man', worse even, he railed, than a Marius or a Sulla. Under the consuls for 43, Aulus Hirtius and Gaius Vibius Pansa, the senate sent an army north to aid Brutus, to which Octavius attached himself. Lepidus, whom Cicero had failed to suborn to the OPTIMATES' cause, offered support to his former colleague, and thus strengthened, Antonius attempted the expulsion of Brutus from Mutina (Modena). But Antonius lost two battles around the city and withdrew to the safety of Lepidus's camp. However, both Hirtius and Pansa were killed during the action, and Octavius seized control of the situation by demanding one of the vacant consulships. The soldiers of the legions would follow any with the name Caesar (Octavius had assumed it even though it was not yet legally his†) so when the senate refused, Octavius marched on Rome and secured the consulship by force. He now styled himself Gaius Julius Caesar Octavianus (Octavian), and basked in his unparalleled popularity among the Italian armies and the plebs as Caesar's true heir.

The Second Triumvirate

The last opportunity to restore the Republic was gone. Rome's own obsession with personal ambition had undone it, and Cicero's heroic efforts to revive it had turned into little more than hot air. However, now only in his twenty-first year, Octavian still had much to achieve before he was to become Rome's sole master. Financially and militarily unready to tackle Antonius and Lepidus, Octavian revealed his shrewd grasp of realpolitik by combining forces with his enemies.

---

† The adoption needed formal confirmation in the old COMITIA CENTURIATA, and Antonius was able to prevent this for some time.

Marcus Tullius Cicero's (106–43 BC) obdurate defence of the Republic ultimately cost him his life, when the triumvirs initiated a purge of their opponents.

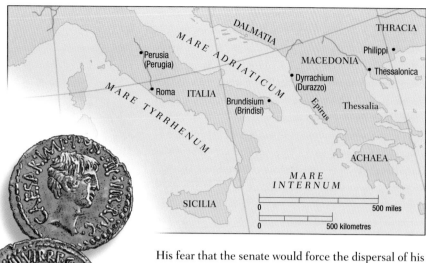

The members of the Second Triumvirate (from top): Octavian, Marcus Antonius and Marcus Aemilius Lepidus. Note the inscription III.V for TRIUM VIRI.

His fear that the senate would force the dispersal of his legions to avoid paying the veterans was well founded, so he laid aside his differences with Antonius and Lepidus, and the three most powerful Romans met at Bononia (Bologna) in 43. The result, intended to present a united front against the senate and the assassins, was the TRIUMVIRI REIPUBLICAE CONSTITUENDAE (Triumvirs for the Regulation of the Republic). Unlike the First Triumvirate, the Second was set up by law, and was effectively a joint dictatorship. Virtually at sword point, the senate granted the triumvirs draconian powers to hunt down Caesar's killers. In the ensuing purge, more than two thousand were proscribed and executed, including the too-voluble Cicero – on whom Octavian was bloodily willing to turn his back in return for Antonius sacrificing some of his own favourites. However, the real enemy was massing to the east under the banners of Marcus Brutus and Cassius.

The triumvirs crossed the sea in 42 and were victorious against the assassins' seventeen rebel legions at Philippi in Macedonia. Rather than risk capture, Brutus and Cassius committed suicide. In the same year, Julius Caesar was deified and Octavian basked in the great man's reflected glory – the adopted son of a god. Antonius and Octavian now redistributed the empire between them. Octavian received Italia and the western provinces, which included the command against Sextus, the surviving son of Pompeius Magnus. Antonius took the East and Lepidus was sidelined by being given only Africa.

Back in Rome, Octavian faced a new conflict. Known as the Perusine War, it was sparked when he attempted to settle the Philippi veterans on confiscated land. Antonius's brother Lucius, one of the consuls, backed by Antonius's wife Fulvia, took up arms on behalf of the dispossessed Italians. After months of desultory skirmishing, Lucius surrendered at Perusia (Perugia). Fulvia died shortly after. The conflict might have spiralled into full-scale civil war when Antonius hurried back and landed at Brundisium in 40, but both armies – all from Caesar's old legions – forced the two men to make peace. The triumvirate was re-established and the east-west division between the two principals confirmed. To secure the partnership, Octavian married off his sister Octavia to Antonius.

In the confusion after Caesar's murder, Sextus Pompeius had occupied Sicilia, still the principal provider of grain to Rome. When he cut off the supply, the threatened famine brought the triumvirs to the table in 39. However, the complex peace overtures failed, and Antonius left the matter in Octavian's hands to set off again for his triumviral oriental command in 37 BC.

During the peace discussions with Sextus Pompeius Octavian had agreed to marry Scribonia, a Pompeian relative. This expedient was doomed to failure since the two were ill-matched, and as war seemed shortly inevitable the union was politically pointless. He divorced Scribonia in 38, when she was pregnant with his daughter Julia, and married Livia Drusilla (58 BC–AD 29). A member of the powerful and ancient Claudian family, when she was sixteen Livia had married her cousin, Tiberius Claudius Nero, and bore him one son, Tiberius; and was pregnant with Drusus when she divorced her husband to marry Octavian. The abruptness of the wedding, only days after her divorce, caused a scandal that Octavian never quite lived down. Although she was not to bear him any children, which partly explains the succession problems that followed, the marriage lasted, spanning fifty-two turbulent years until Augustus's death in AD 14.

With Scribonia put aside, Octavian now set about dealing with Sextus Pompeius. Well served by his friend Marcus Vipsanius Agrippa, Octavian invaded Sicilia. Agrippa's massive fleet swung the balance when it annihilated the Pompeians at Naulochus in September 36. Sextus fled to Antonius (where he was soon executed on conspiracy charges) while Octavian confronted Lepidus. His fellow triumvir had brought his army from Africa for the campaign and now claimed Sicilia for himself. The situation was critical, but Octavian gambled that the Caesarian legionaries had little love for Lepidus. He persuaded the soldiers to desert, deposed Lepidus from the triumvirate and sent him into exile.

In the East, Antonius's campaign against the Parthians – the one Caesar had been planning at the

Pompeius Magnus's son Sextus Pompeius honoured his dead father and brother on the reverse of a coin issued in 42 BC.

time of his murder – ended in failure in 36, and he returned to Alexandria and his mistress, queen of Aegyptus, Cleopatra. This affair had started in 41 BC, when Antonius had summoned her to Tarsus to explain her actions since Caesar's death. Plutarch wrote of her exotic arrival: *'She came sailing up on a galley whose stern was golden; the sails were purple and the oars silver. The queen, in a dress and character of Aphrodite, lay on a couch of gold brocade, as though in a picture, while about her were pretty boys like cupids who fanned her.'*

Her effect on Antonius may have been erotic, but a more plausible explanation lies in politics. At some point after 37 BC Antonius put aside Octavia and married Cleopatra. This foreign wedding was not recognised in Rome, but to Egyptians, Marcus Antonius had become their king. For Cleopatra, first Julius Caesar, now Antonius, represented the power of Rome. But Rome was a force that had undercut the traditional means of maintaining Ptolemaic power in Aegyptus, which relied on an army of Greek mercenaries to keep the native population in subjection. These were raised in the Greek dominions, over which Rome was now master, and as a result Egyptian military strength had declined. Using her charms on Caesar and Antonius was a sensible way of influencing Rome to give back some of her country's old recruiting grounds.

For Antonius, he had a choice: stay in the East and found an oriental Roman empire with Cleopatra, or invade the West and deal with Octavian. Being

Antonius, he wanted both, on the grounds that if he failed in the West, he could always fall back on the East and hold it against Octavian. But whatever residual affection he had enjoyed as a protégé of Caesar had been thrown away: by (illegally) marrying a reigning monarch; by holding a sacred Roman triumph in Alexandria; by declaring Julius Caesar's son Caesarion to be the true heir of the West; by humiliating his virtuous wife, Octavia. In Rome, Octavian had cleared the senate of the small Antonian faction, and so found little difficulty in arousing war talk. Antonius's actions left himself vulnerable to his rival, who ably portrayed his former triumvir as either blind to reason or plain mad. Octavian determined to redeem Rome's honour and forced Italian citizens to swear allegiance to his cause (the COIURATIO ITALIAE). Antonius tried to enlist the support of Roman allies and client states, but he could not overcome the difficulty of being so far from the recruiting

Above: Octavian's sister Octavia, whom Marcus Antonius (left) had married to cement the triumvirate, was set aside by him when he illegally took Cleopatra (seen here on a coin) as wife and effectively became king of Aegyptus. The famous pair's campaign for domination of Rome was quickly crushed by Octavian.

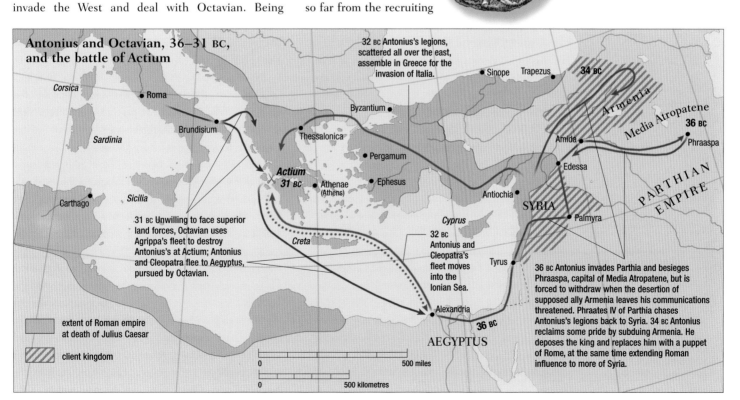

Antonius and Octavian, 36–31 BC, and the battle of Actium

32 BC Antonius's legions, scattered all over the east, assemble in Greece for the invasion of Italia.

34 BC

Corsica

Roma

Sardinia

Brundisium

Carthago

Sicilia

Sinope Trapezus

Byzantium

Thessalonica

Actium 31 BC

Athenae (Athens)

Pergamum

Ephesus

Antiochia

SYRIA

Amida

Edessa

Armenia

Media Atropatene 36 BC

Phraaspa

PARTHIAN EMPIRE

Palmyra

Cyprus

Creta

Tyrus

31 BC Unwilling to face superior land forces, Octavian uses Agrippa's fleet to destroy Antonius's at Actium; Antonius and Cleopatra flee to Aegyptus, pursued by Octavian.

32 BC Antonius and Cleopatra's fleet moves into the Ionian Sea.

Alexandria

36 BC

AEGYPTUS

extent of Roman empire at death of Julius Caesar

client kingdom

36 BC Antonius invades Parthia and besieges Phraaspa, capital of Media Atropatene, but is forced to withdraw when the desertion of supposed ally Armenia leaves his communications threatened. Phraates IV of Parthia chases Antonius's legions back to Syria. 34 BC Antonius reclaims some pride by subduing Armenia. He deposes the king and replaces him with a puppet of Rome, at the same time extending Roman influence to more of Syria.

0   500 miles

0   500 kilometres

Marcus Vipsanius Agrippa, admiral, governor and administrator, was Octavian's close friend and, in effect, second man in Rome.

A bust of Juba II shows him in his youth while living in Rome.

grounds in and around Rome, where the best soldiers were to be found.

War was declared late in 32 BC and after much manoeuvering the rival fleets finally clashed at Actium in the Mare Ionium on 2 September 31. Under Agrippa's naval command, Octavian's fleet was swiftly triumphant. Immediately, Octavian established his control over Antonine Achaea and Asia. He then invaded Aegyptus. Cornered in 30, Antonius and Cleopatra committed suicide. Although he took Antonius's children by Cleopatra under his protection and gave them the education their rank deserved (*see side panel below*), he ordered the death of Caesarion, thereby removing a legitimate contender for Roman rule.

Aegyptus lost its independent status and became a Roman province, and Octavian set his troops to cleaning out the irrigation canals of the Nilus (Nile), which had silted up from years of neglect. This was aimed to improve productivity and provide another valuable source of grain for Rome, alleviating the city's reliance on Sicilia and a still uncertain Africa. He also visited the sarcophagus of Alexander the Great and showed his veneration by covering the mummy's head with a golden crown. According to Suetonius, when he was then asked if he would like to visit the tombs of the royal Ptolemies, he replied: 'I came to see a king, not a row of corpses.' It cannot have escaped his attention that he, Gaius Octavianus at the age of thirty-two, was in reality the king of the Roman empire.

First emperor of Rome

The invention of Augustus, the first emperor of Rome, was an insidiously gradual process. However, early in 30 BC Octavian was not yet Augustus; that was an event three years in the future. There was much to be done after the fall of Antonius and Cleopatra, their removal left the whole eastern half of the empire in

ANTONIUS fathered three children by Cleopatra and these were sent by Octavian to Rome to be raised by his sister Octavia. The history of the two boys is unknown, but the young Cleopatra Selene married Juba II, king of Numidia and Mauretania. Juba's father had backed the Pompeians against Caesar and committed suicide after the battle of Thapsus (46 BC). Juba II (c.52 BC–AD 23) went as a hostage to Rome, where he was educated as a Roman and eventually granted citizenship. He was reinstated as a client king in 25 BC.

much confusion. Octavian kept many of Antonius's arrangements in place, as long as old loyalties were suitably redirected, a show of trust that earned him the gratitude of many former opponents. Meanwhile, he received news of the adulation being heaped on him back in Rome. The reorganisation took up most of the next year and a half, and Octavian only returned to the capital – amid tumultuous celebrations – in August of 29. He celebrated three triumphs over three days: for Dalmatia, Actium and Aegyptus. Perhaps as many as twenty-five legions totalling forty thousand men were then settled on land both in Italia and the adjacent provinces, this time without the unrest that had led to the Perusine War, since the vast wealth of Aegyptus allowed for ample compensation.

Nevertheless, despite the welcoming attitude of the senate and the people, Octavian's position was not clearly defined, least of all legally. It was clear that with the overwhelming support of every legion in the empire he was the *de facto* ruler of Rome, but there was no legal warrant for his power base. In short order after his final victory over Antonius, the senate bypassed some of the more obvious problems by allowing Octavian a continuous consulship that lasted from 29 to 23 BC. The constitutional process that followed was not instantaneous, nor did it adhere to a single agenda. Instead, it evolved piecemeal over time, with two key events – the 'Constitutional Settlements' of 27 and 23 BC – some refinements in 19, and sporadic assignments of numerous rights and privileges down to the granting of the ultimate title, PATER PATRIAE (Father of his Country) in 2 BC.

As Augustus, he was to later refer to the non-legal basis for his dominance as 'universal consent'. He explained this as being 'in complete control of [the empire's] affairs' precisely because everyone wanted him to be and, rather more significantly, because he was the last powerful man standing. There was also some justification for this, in that he had ended the civil wars, and all hopes for a peaceful future now rested with him alone. However, holding continuous consulships would hardly be sufficient as a method of administration in the long term, especially if, as he intended, the old order should be seen to be restored; as he portrayed it he was not overthrowing the Republic, he was strengthening it. Octavian was content to make haste slowly, preferring the inevitability of gradualness from one precedent to another. He had learned the lesson of Caesar's fall from grace by too hasty reform. This no doubt explains the eighteen-month gap between his return to Rome in August 29 BC and the First Constitutional Settlement at

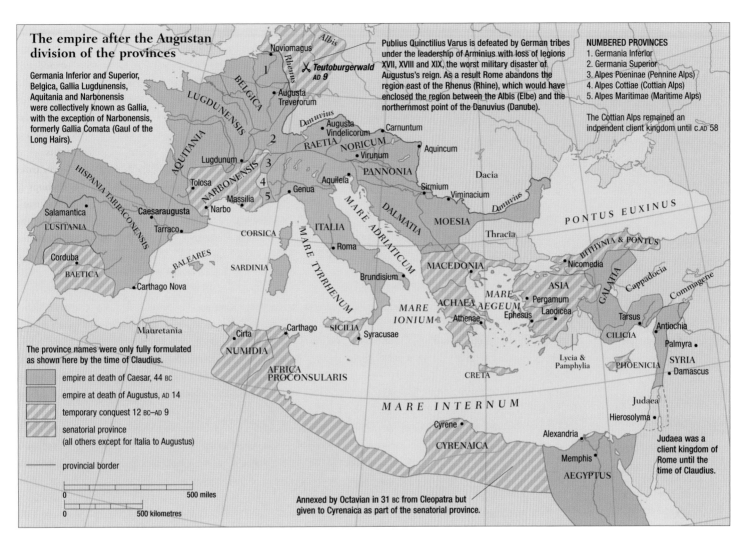

The empire after the Augustan division of the provinces

Germania Inferior and Superior, Belgica, Gallia Lugdunensis, Aquitania and Narbonensis were collectively known as Gallia, with the exception of Narbonensis, formerly Gallia Comata (Gaul of the Long Hairs).

Publius Quinctilius Varus is defeated by German tribes under the leadership of Arminius with loss of legions XVII, XVIII and XIX, the worst military disaster of Augustus's reign. As a result Rome abandons the region east of the Rhenus (Rhine), which would have enclosed the region between the Albis (Elbe) and the northernmost point of the Danuvius (Danube).

NUMBERED PROVINCES
1. Germania Inferior
2. Germania Superior
3. Alpes Poeninae (Pennine Alps)
4. Alpes Cottiae (Cottian Alps)
5. Alpes Maritimae (Maritime Alps)

The Cottian Alps remained an indpendent client kingdom until c.AD 58

The province names were only fully formulated as shown here by the time of Claudius.

- empire at death of Caesar, 44 BC
- empire at death of Augustus, AD 14
- temporary conquest 12 BC–AD 9
- senatorial province (all others except for Italia to Augustus)
- provincial border

0 — 500 miles
0 — 500 kilometres

Annexed by Octavian in 31 BC from Cleopatra but given to Cyrenaica as part of the senatorial province.

Judaea was a client kingdom of Rome until the time of Claudius.

---

the beginning of 27. He also recognised – as Caesar had not – the inherent danger of alienating the aristocracy, and did everything to appease the sensibilities of the elite by appearing modest in his ambitions.

He certainly achieved this aim on 13 January 27 when he entered the senate and, to general shock, announced that he planned to surrender his powers and retire to private life. The surprise was not universal. His particular supporters, who had presumably been warned beforehand, led the mounting cries of alarm and offered a solution that did not insult the constitution. This was to grant him proconsular command of approximately half of all the provinces – Hispania (except Baetica), Gallia, Syria, Cyprus and Aegyptus, while the senate and people controlled the remaining provinces. After a show of reluctance, Octavian graciously accepted. His were all provinces that his LEGATI were already governing and which in effect he had placed at the disposal of the senate and people. And he could point to legal precedents – the extended commands granted to Pompeius and Caesar

in the late Republic, for instance (although neither of these was as extensive in scope) – which appealed to Octavian's desire to appear to be maintaining traditions while doing nothing alarmingly new or innovative. This IMPERIUM PROCONSULARE was granted to him for a period of ten years, but as with many term-condition privileges given him, no one attempted to take them back when they expired. In consequence, Octavian was free to appoint LEGATI to administer the provinces on his behalf, with the exception of all-important Aegyptus, which remained effectively a private imperial fief, governed by an equestrian prefect.

There was a theoretical drawback to Octavian's new powers: by ancient law the IMPERIUM of a proconsul could not be exercised inside the city of Rome. But in practice this was not a problem – for as long as he was also a consul he was effectively the most distinguished of the urban magistrates.

More honours were forthcoming. At a second meeting on 16 January, Octavian was named Augustus, a word ringing with religious significance

Octavian, now become Caesar Augustus, and his second wife, Livia Drusilla (below). She had two sons from a previous marriage, Tiberius and Drusus, but bore Augustus no children. Their often turbulent union was to last 52 years until his death.

(AUGUR) and social meaning (AUCTORITAS) but falling well short of suggesting overt political dominance. Gaius Julius Caesar Octavianus now became Imperator Caesar Augustus. 'Augustus' was only a COGNOMEN, but he came to be known by it, and after his death it was granted the status of a title. At the time there was no word 'emperor' in Latin, which is derived from the word IMPERATOR, a title given by his soldiers to a successful general after a victory but who had not yet entered Rome to celebrate a triumph. In time, since the power of the army made its IMPERATOR the sole ruler of Rome, the word came to be associated with the absolute ruler of the empire. Augustus was content to adopt the title of PRINCEPS (first or leading citizen), from which we derive the word 'prince'. This leads to the use of the word 'principate' to describe the rule of the Roman emperors.† Augustus was said to be fond of voicing the opinion that he was no Caesar, meaning he was not a dictator or tyrant, merely the first man of Rome. It was a nicely modest attribute, familiar to Roman ears for centuries, which suited his subtle but relentless method of gaining total control by stealth.

Other honours carrying more symbolic meanings were heaped on him that helped establish Augustus's pre-eminent position in the state. By means of the First Settlement, Augustus was simultaneously commander, leader and saviour, yet no one of his privileges was inconsistent with those given to earlier Republican leaders, it was their concatenation that was unique. As a further mark of respect, the month Sextilis was renamed 'Augustus'. Humble Octavius had achieved much, and he was not yet thirty-six. He wasted no time in demonstrating that his great powers could be used to benefit Italia by ordering the repair of all the main arterial highways that had fallen into a sad state during the years of civil war. With this task under way, Augustus left Rome because he felt that his presence was needed in the western provinces, taking with him his nephew Gaius Claudius Marcellus and

his stepson Tiberius, both of them strapping youths of fifteen. The tour of Gallia and Hispania, which kept him away from Rome until 24 BC, was probably a sensible move in that it gave him a low profile out of the public eye while the arrangements of the First Settlement took root. During his absence, his aides Agrippa and Maecenas supervised matters in Rome.

On his return in the spring of 24, it was evident that the settlement of 27 had failed to win over the conservative constitutionalists, who continued to believe that Augustus had not returned the Republic to them. He began planning to modify elements of the settlement. Whether rumours of his intentions led to the conspiracy of the Republicans Fannius Caepio and Varro Murena, or whether they reacted to the Second Constitutional Settlement, is not known, but in c.23 Augustus suspected both men, and they were tried and executed. Nothing was solved by this, for deep in senatorial sentiment it rankled that Augustus had monopolised the office of consul, debasing what had hitherto been the highest position to which a Roman could aspire. However, as has been shown, should he lay down his perpetually renewable consulship he would render illegal his exercise of power within Rome itself. The provisions of the Second Constitutional Settlement were designed to get around this conundrum. By relinquishing the consulship in future years, he not only removed a source of senatorial annoyance but also made available an extra post to qualify men for administrative appointments; and the expanding empire needed capable administrators.

Augustus announced that he would give up the consulship (and was only to take it up for dynastic reasons on two further occasions in the rest of his life). In return, he received an empire-wide grant of IMPERIUM PROCONSULARE for five years. By virtue of this extensive gift, Augustus could intervene in the affairs of *any* province in the empire. Unlike other governors, he was also given dispensation to retain his power within the city limits of Rome. This was at the heart of what he needed in order to enlarge his powers, but it could be dressed up in a purely rational way for practical reasons: otherwise, every time he left the city, his proconsular power would need to be renewed.

In abrogating his earlier given right to the consulship, there was one further and very important hurdle in his way — the question of succession. When Augustus fell seriously ill in 23 BC and was expected to die, the problem came into sharp focus. His successor would have to be of Julian blood, the army would agree to nothing less, which ruled out his close friend

---

† 'Princeps' and 'principate' become less appropriate by the middle of the third century AD, as the nature of absolute rule changed to a greater despotism.

Agrippa (but who would have to take charge if he did die). So he turned to his nephew Marcellus, a young man with much to recommend him.

Marcellus – son of Augustus's adored sister Octavia by her first marriage to Gaius Claudius Marcellus (after his death she wed Marcus Antonius) and granddaughter of Julius Caesar's sister Julia – was technically a Claudian, but also with Julian blood. In marking Marcellus out for the succession, Augustus revealed the central strategy for the perpetuation of the principate, one that would be employed by many future emperors: a series of stepping stones were laid out that indicated the princeps' preference. Although there was no obligation on the people or the senate to accept what the 'signs' meant, few dared oppose Augustus's clear wishes. The steps consisted of allying the chosen to the imperial family through marriage and promoting the would-be successor through the CURSUS HONORUM at a pace far in advance of the traditional age requirements.

And so: in 25 BC Marcellus married fourteen-year-old Julia, Augustus's only child, whose mother had been Scribonia; in 24 the senate granted Marcellus the right to hold magistracies at an earlier age than normal; in 23 he became an aedile without having first been a quaestor, and was permitted to stand for consular election ten years before the traditional age. None of this, however, made his succession inevitable. After all, Augustus only held a special commission from the people and senate, it was not something he could will to anyone else. He needed a solution that not only retained his power but also perpetuated it for his successor.

The answer lay in the tribunes' powers. They were enabled to transact business with both the senate and the people, and could enact or veto legislation. On 26 June 23 BC the senate conferred on Augustus the TRIBUNICIA POTESTAS (tribunician power), which was ratified by the people through a special assembly (COMITIA TRIBUNICIAE POTESTATIS). It combined all the ordinary and some extraordinary prerogatives of the TRIBUNUS, most importantly that it was for life. (In fact, it was granted on an annual basis, but on the understanding that it would be perpetually renewed.) He was able to show this very unrepublican innovation in a positive light: since TRIBUNI traditionally safeguarded citizens against the unjust use of a magistrate's power, Augustus could claim he was associated with the *protection* of citizens, not their *repression*.

In addition to disguising the military basis of his position through the tribunes' legal trappings, the TRIBUNICIA POTESTAS rendered his nomination of a successor more feasible. Since it was within his gift to

confer the power on another man, that individual would be designated as his successor because he would be the equal of Augustus. With both his tribunician and proconsular powers, Augustus now had the ability to direct affairs in every wing of domestic and foreign administration. These two powers were long to remain the twin pillars of the Roman emperors' legal position. However, Augustus was unable to avoid the tragedy of his nephew's untimely death at the end of 23. With Marcellus gone, Augustus selected Agrippa, not as his successor, but as a regent until another Julian appeared.

The succession question

The informal nature of Augustus's succession arrangements laid his family open to perpetual domestic turmoil and proved the most consistently destabilising political factor in his reign; and those of future emperors. At least the granting of signs of preference to favoured individuals – in this case drawn largely from within the princeps' own house – had become accepted. In selecting members of his extended family, Augustus was behaving entirely within the ethos of the Roman aristocracy, for whom family was paramount. It also ensured that the name Caesar, so vital in establishing his own control over the army, remained at the head of the state. The thorny problem was who should be preferred.

Shortly before Marcellus's death, Agrippa had left for the Orient. Some accounts suggest that Augustus's closest friend went in a high dudgeon, annoyed at being passed over for the nineteen-year-old Marcellus. The stripling, basking in imperial favour, had found it hard to hide his contempt for the older man, even though in his late thirties Agrippa was hardly in his dotage. Undoubtedly irritated at Marcellus's attitude, it is unlikely that Agrippa extended his annoyance towards Augustus, in view of the fact that he went east with a grant of IMPERIUM PROCONSULARE, a share in Augustus's own powers. Augustus would not have given this if he suspected his friend's motives for wanting to leave Rome. In the event, with Marcellus dead, Agrippa was recalled to marry widowed Julia, a sign that he was marked for the succession in some form. After the marriage, Agrippa resumed his command of the Orient, and then in 18 BC Augustus made him his colleague in the TRIBUNICIA POTESTAS, which meant that if Augustus were suddenly to die Agrippa would automatically become princeps. But the principate did not become a dyarchy, for Agrippa's TRIBUNICIA POTESTAS was limited to five years, whereas that of Augustus was both annual and perpetual.

Marcellus, Augustus's 19-year-old nephew, was earmarked for succession, and married to the emperor's only daughter Julia – only to suffer an early death in 23 BC. Augustus, deeply upset by his nephew's untimely end, dedicated a large new theatre on the bank of the Tiberis to Marcellus.

The Julio-Claudian Dynasty

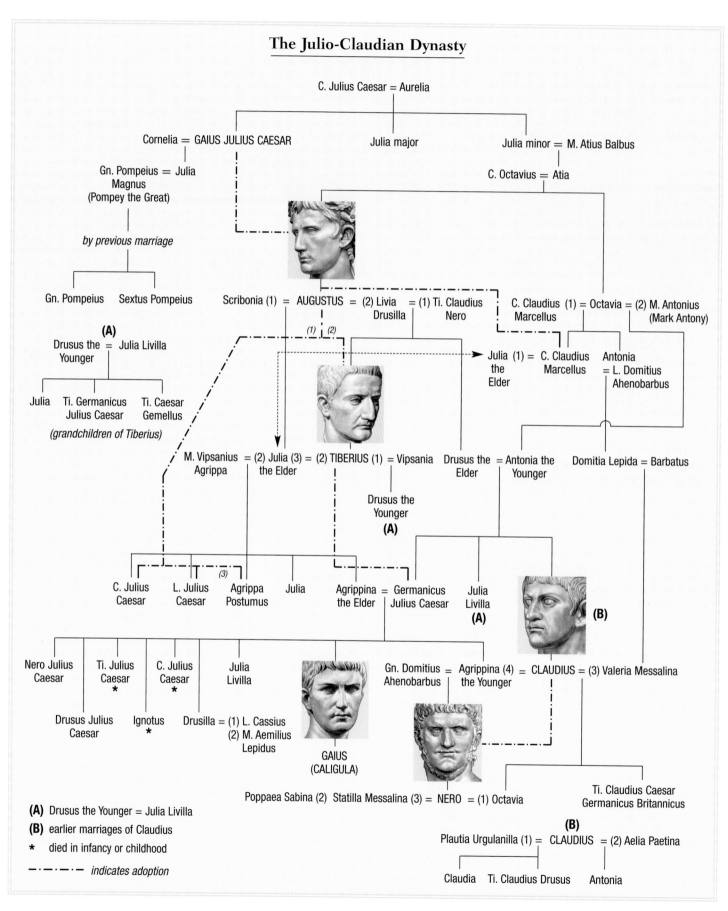

C. Julius Caesar = Aurelia

Cornelia = GAIUS JULIUS CAESAR

Julia major

Julia minor = M. Atius Balbus

Gn. Pompeius = Julia
Magnus
(Pompey the Great)

C. Octavius = Atia

by previous marriage

Gn. Pompeius   Sextus Pompeius

Scribonia (1) = AUGUSTUS = (2) Livia = (1) Ti. Claudius
Drusilla   Nero

C. Claudius (1) = Octavia = (2) M. Antonius
Marcellus   (Mark Antony)

(A)
Drusus the = Julia Livilla
Younger

Julia   Ti. Germanicus   Ti. Caesar
        Julius Caesar   Gemellus

(grandchildren of Tiberius)

(1) (2)

Julia (1) = C. Claudius
the   Marcellus
Elder

Antonia
= L. Domitius
Ahenobarbus

M. Vipsanius = (2) Julia (3) = (2) TIBERIUS (1) = Vipsania
Agrippa   the Elder

Drusus the = Antonia the
Elder   Younger

Domitia Lepida = Barbatus

Drusus the
Younger
(A)

(3)

C. Julius   L. Julius   Agrippa   Julia
Caesar   Caesar   Postumus

Agrippina = Germanicus
the Elder   Julius Caesar
(A)

Julia
Livilla

(B)

Nero Julius   Ti. Julius   C. Julius   Julia
Caesar   Caesar   Caesar   Livilla
              *   *

Gn. Domitius = Agrippina (4) = CLAUDIUS = (3) Valeria Messalina
Ahenobarbus   the Younger

Drusus Julius   Ignotus   Drusilla = (1) L. Cassius
Caesar   *   (2) M. Aemilius
                                        Lepidus

GAIUS
(CALIGULA)

Ti. Claudius Caesar
Germanicus Britannicus

Poppaea Sabina (2)   Statilla Messalina (3) = NERO = (1) Octavia

(B)

(A) Drusus the Younger = Julia Livilla

(B) earlier marriages of Claudius

★   died in infancy or childhood

—·—·—·— *indicates adoption*

Plautia Urgulanilla (1) = CLAUDIUS = (2) Aelia Paetina

Claudia   Ti. Claudius Drusus   Antonia

Julia's marriage to Agrippa was fruitful and she bore him three sons, Gaius in 20, Lucius in 17, and Agrippa Postumus in 12 BC. There were also two daughters – Julia the Younger, and Agrippina. Julian blood was again in the ascendancy, and Augustus now concentrated his hopes for the succession on his grandsons, making his point unmistakably in 17 by adopting Gaius and Lucius, who both became Caesars. It was a signal honour for Agrippa to have his sons adopted into the imperial family and made him at the very least the father of the next emperor.

Because his grandsons were only infants, Augustus decided to appoint two further guardians. This office fell to the two Claudian stepsons Livia had brought him, Drusus and Tiberius. History leaves us no indication of how Drusus felt about what was in effect a demotion in the hereditary line. He had an easy-going, open nature and, while never discourteous to his stepfather, made little secret of his opposition to the principate and his dreams for a full restoration of the Republic. Tiberius, naturally inclined to keep his Republican thoughts to himself, was clearly disgruntled at being passed over for two children, and his relations with them were never good. Both stepsons accepted their guardianship, for there was little alternative, and went on to serve Augustus well in military commands during the next four years.

In the spring of 12 BC, shortly after returning to Rome, Agrippa died, not only robbing Augustus of a trusted friend, but also of a regent in the event of his own death. Agrippa's sons were still too young to be successors (the third was only born after his father's death, hence his COGNOMEN Postumus). Augustus now forced Tiberius to divorce the wife he loved, Agrippa's daughter by a previous marriage named Vipsania, and marry the once-more widowed Julia in 11 BC. This was clearly not intended as a sign that Tiberius stood next in line for the succession, only that he was intended to replace Agrippa as the regent-guardian to the two young Caesars in the event of Augustus's death. Besides, his dour countenance and reportedly boorish conversation did not endear him to Augustus. Despite his open Republicanism, Augustus preferred the younger Drusus, who was still allowed the freedom of a military life, while Tiberius was now palace-bound by his duties. Unfortunately, Drusus was killed in 9 BC after a fall from his horse during a brilliant campaign that had taken his legions as far north as the Albis (River Elbe).

In 6 BC, having just been granted a share of the TRIBUNICIA POTESTAS by Augustus, Tiberius unexpectedly retired to Rhodus, despite his prominent public position

(*see page* 35). Augustus, infuriated by Tiberius's defection, had little choice but to rely on his own still-robust health to see his adopted sons Gaius and Lucius Caesar to their maturity. But fate intervened once more and both young men died: Lucius of an illness at Massilia in AD 2 and Gaius two years later of a wound received during a siege in Armenia. Augustus bowed to the inevitable and in AD 2 restored Tiberius to Rome as the only member of his household with the experience to help him, or carry on in the event of his death.

But Augustus still wished to ensure ultimate succession to a Julian, so at the same time he adopted his surviving grandson, the young Agrippa Postumus, and obliged Tiberius to adopt his dead brother Drusus's son, his nephew Julius Caesar Germanicus. This relegated Tiberius's own son, also named Drusus, to the position of second choice. Although he was technically a Claudian, Germanicus had Julian blood on his mother's side and moreover had married Agrippina, Augustus's granddaughter. Tiberius was once again relegated to the role of emperor-regent. The symbolism was clear – ultimately Julians, not Claudians, would inherit the principate. Unfortunately, the teenaged Postumus was a brutal lout, who in AD 7 Augustus was obliged to banish to the small coastal island of Planasia. Whether he liked it or not, up to the time of his death in AD 14 Augustus came to rely more and more on dour, grumbling and disillusioned Tiberius.

The succession question, then, was a difficult one for Augustus, and his solutions only perpetuated the problem for all future emperors. Despite the principal family's internal difficulties, Augustus – who stood forcefully for a return to old Roman moral virtues of the family – was keen to present a united image of the imperial house to the populace. We have been left a superb example of this family-values propaganda in the southern frieze of the ARA PACIS AUGUSTAE (Altar of the Augustan Peace), dedicated in January 9 BC. It depicts the imperial family parading as a dignified and corporate entity. The message is one of dynastic harmony and the promise of future stability. The reality, clearly, was rather different.

Gilding the empire

While Augustus spent a deal of time during his reign accruing power while seeming not to, and perpetuating the principate, he also concerned himself with the regeneration of the Roman State. Given that he had restored peace and prosperity, and that he reigned unchallenged for forty-five years, he had plenty of time

Augustus's youngest stepson through Livia, Drusus, brother of Tiberius.

Below: Gaius and Lucius Caesar, Agrippa's sons whom Augustus adopted as potential successors, but who both died young. Their youngest brother, Agrippa Postumus (bottom), whom Augustus adopted after their deaths, grew up to be an adolescent lout who in AD 7 had to be banished.

to transform the city of Rome and influence the improvement of towns and cities throughout the colonies and provinces of the whole empire.

As the empire's pre-eminent patron of the arts, his hand is most clearly seen in the field of architecture. Agreeing with Julius Caesar that Rome's buildings were unworthy of the city's position as capital of the empire, Augustus set about embellishing them. He was the first to use a new source of white marble from Luna (Carrara) in northern Italia. He also imported coloured marbles from all over the provinces, which added lustre to new Roman public buildings, as well as adorning older ones in need of repair. He claimed to have repaired no less than eighty-two temples during 28 BC alone. During his reign Augustus so improved the city's appearance that he justifiably boasted: 'I found Rome built of sun-dried bricks; I leave her clothed in marble.'

On the Campus Martius (Field of Mars), he repaired Pompeius's Theatre and two new ones were built, those of Marcellus and Balbus. In the same district, Agrippa built the Pantheon (later completely rebuilt under Hadrian), the first of Rome's great public baths, the Stagnum and Euripus, and the Saepta Julia. Among his many civil projects, Agrippa repaired the old aqueducts and built a new one, the Aqua Virgo. Augustus also built an aqueduct, the Aqua Alsietina, constructed to supply an artificial lake for naval displays. The Temple of Apollo on the Palatine, and the Temple of Mars Ultor (Avenging Mars) were only the most obvious of his prestige buildings. The latter was part of his great Forum, built because the two already in existence (Romanum and Julian) were no longer able to cope with the recent great increase in the number of lawsuits caused by a corresponding increase in population. In fact, its need was so pressing that he had it opened before work on Mars Ultor had been completed.

There is no evidence of careful town planning in Rome, nor of a systematic housing programme to cope with the swelling population, such as is evident in many other Italian towns like Augusta Praetoria (Aosta). Any major reorganisation of Rome's crowded districts would have to wait until the great fire during Nero's reign (and then, that was not much to the benefit of the citizens). Rome and the larger urban centres of the early imperial period were packed with tenement blocks called INSULAE (lit. islands). Built around a courtyard, with shops fronting the street, they were typically of three floors, although in Rome's poor Subura district they reached to six or seven stories. Each INSULA housed several families in cramped conditions, without the benefits of any sanitation. Augustus limited the height of INSULAE to five floors or a maximum height of sixty-eight feet. Fire from cooking was a continual hazard. An INSULA was constructed of timber frames and perishable mud bricks, which meant that they burned easily, and their height made them prone to disastrous collapse, burying the hapless victims of lower floors under tons of burning debris.

Augustus tackled the problem of essential services by dividing the city into fourteen districts under the control of magistrates elected annually by lot. The districts were further divided into wards under supervisors locally elected. Each district had its own administrative and technical services, and access to its own VIGILES (fire fighters); the total for the whole city numbered seven thousand.

Augustus and the army

The real base of the principate was the emperor's military power. Concern for its proper maintenance and for the effective channelling of its loyalties was, therefore, one of the chief goals of the Augustan settlement. Augustus continued the ongoing professionalisation of the Roman military begun under Marius by establishing a standing field army comprised of twenty-eight legions (three were to be lost in Germany in AD 9), made up of volunteer recruits. Service was for a prescribed period (first sixteen, then twenty years), on a regular wage, and with fixed rewards on discharge. After 14 BC, land grants were discontinued in favour of cash pension payments funded, after AD 6, by a new treasury, the AERARIUM MILITARE. Under the reforms of

The 14 Augustan districts of Rome

ancient Servian wall

IX — Circus Flaminius
VII — Via Lata
VI — Alta Semita
V — Esquiliae
Tiberis
Forum Romanum
IV — Templum Pacis
VIII
III — Isis et Serapis
XIV — Trans Tiberim
X — Palatium
XI — Circus Maximus
II — Caelimontium
XIII — Aventinus
XII — Piscina Publica
I — Porta Capena

Not all the district names were in use at the time of Augustus

Marius, military service had become a career choice in and of itself, but there were still uncertainties for citizen-soldiers. Under Augustus, these uncertainties were removed, and the greater intake of citizenry to leaven the mass of proletarian troops improved the overall quality of the soldiers enormously.

Augustus was careful to channel the loyalties of this new army in his direction. He achieved this by a number of methods. Since the founding of the Roman army in the time of the kings, recruits swore an oath of obedience at their induction, but in typically efficient Roman style, this was sworn in full by only one recruit, with the others saying IDEM IN ME (the same for me) after him. Augustus now changed this, and for the first time the troops were obliged to take a personal oath of loyalty to the princeps instead, to be renewed annually at the start of each new year. With this oath the troops recognised Augustus as their sole paymaster and guarantor of their discharge rewards.

The army's commanders were handpicked LEGATI of Augustus and its generals were members of Augustus's own family, men such as Agrippa, Tiberius or Germanicus. He followed Julius Caesar's precept that an idle army is not only useless but also dangerous – boredom breeds disobedience. Therefore, Augustus kept the legionaries busy in major campaigns in Hispania, the Alpine regions, along the Danuvius and Rhenus rivers, across the Rhenus into Germanic tribal areas, and in numerous small-scale actions all along the empire's frontiers.

Despite Germanic activity across the Rhenus, this was a period of relative peace, and Augustus never established permanent legionary garrisons on the frontiers. However, he at least removed the army from the centre of power and began the process of keeping the legions in the vicinity of the frontiers – that is, essentially, out of the hands of potential political troublemakers in Rome. There is no evidence to suggest that he pursued an expansionist foreign policy. Indeed, he seems to have reacted only as circumstances and local conditions dictated, and preferred the traditional methods of making other nations 'friends and allies of Rome', rather than setting out to conquer. The bounds of the empire were not conceived as a bulwark against hostiles on the other side, they were simply the almost insurmountable obstacles presented by the two massive European rivers, the Mare Britannicum (English Channel), and the African and Syrian deserts.

The monopolisation of army loyalty forced an important change in military tradition. As father of the state and commander-in-chief of the army, it followed that the glory of the triumph should be the princeps' and the triumphing IMPERATOR was merely his junior partner. Anything exceeding this was an affront to the emperor's AUCTORITAS. Two incidents as early in his reign as 27 BC reveal the new order of things. Marcus Licinius Crassus, grandson of Caesar's co-triumvir, had undertaken successful campaigns in 29–8 as governor of Macedonia. Awarded a triumph in 27, he went further in claiming the ancient honour of SPOLIA OPTIMA (the most honourable spoils), awarded to a Roman commander who had slain his counterpart with his own hand. Earned only on three prior occasions in Rome's history, the honour raised its recipient to the uppermost echelons of military glory. For Augustus it represented a potential challenge to his monopoly of the army's loyalty, so he blocked the award on a technicality. Crassus was allowed his triumph but promptly vanished from the records.

In the same year the PRAEFECTUS AEGYPTI, Gaius Cornelius Gallus – an Augustan appointment – tried something similar. Having successfully suppressed a serious revolt in the province, he celebrated his successes with statues of himself and bragging inscriptions. Enraged, Augustus let it be known that he no longer considered Gallus his friend. His social status and political career in ruins, his very life perhaps in danger, Gallus committed suicide (possibly in 26 BC). Both men had behaved fully within the boundaries of Republican precedent but had failed to appreciate a fundamental rule of the new order: there was to be no military glory but that of Augustus. In contrast, Agrippa, for so long Augustus's right-hand man, repeatedly refused the ovations and triumphs granted to him; all his victories were celebrated by Augustus. And during his reign, although more than thirty triumphs were granted, it was always known that they were his jointly with the triumphing commander – invariably one of the Augustan inner circle.

A military reorganisation that would prove to have a profound impact on the future was that of the

Augustus in full military regalia: throughout his long rule the princeps would always be depicted in the full vigour of youth.

COHORS PRAETORIA (praetorian guard, *see side panel below*). Augustus made a radical change to this institution by elevating the praetorians to a pivotal position within the military hierarchy. He combined the praetorian guard of his defeated opponent Antonius with his own to form a total of nine cohorts consisting of four thousand five hundred men, with a small mounted contingent. These were stationed in towns around Rome to be deployed immediately in the event of civil unrest. They only entered the city in small units as protection for the emperor and members of the imperial family. To encourage loyalty, Augustus reduced their length of service by a quarter (twelve years, as opposed to the initial sixteen in the legions), and by AD 14 he was paying them treble the standard annual wage of 225 DENARII. It is little surprise that the praetorians soon recognised the strength of their bargaining position.

Loyalty to Augustus was strengthened through daily contact. At first there was no overall command other than that of the principate. In 2 BC Augustus appointed two equestrian PRAEFECTI PRAETORIO (praetorian prefects) to take joint control. Every afternoon one PRAEFECTUS received the day's watchword from the emperor in person at his DOMUS on the Palatine. When he had business in the city, units of the guard escorted him and his family, mingling with the crowds, ready to quash trouble. At this point they rarely appeared in armour – a sop to old Republican sentiments – but were easily identifiable from the formal cut of their tunics. As an imperial bodyguard, the praetorians wore, and used, their arms within the POMERIUM of Rome – something denied any common legionary. This advantage catapulted the praetorians to an elite in the military close to the seat of power. While, during the life of Augustus, they acted as a bodyguard, after his death the praetorians became the most formidable force in the making and breaking of emperors; as subsequent events will show.

The origin of the praetorian guard

The first mention of the praetorians is in 133 BC. Scipio Aemilianus – the man who finally destroyed Carthage in the Third Punic War – formed a personal bodyguard that became known as the COHORS PRAETORIA, after the PRAETORIUM, the area of a Roman military camp in which the consul-general's tent was pitched. By the fall of the Republic it was customary for all generals to have a cohort of praetorian guards, usually raised specifically for the campaign in hand and dismissed at its conclusion. Most were drawn from the infantry, although the more experienced could apply to become members of the ORDO EQUESTER (order of equestrian knights).

Augustus's administration

If the army was the real basis of the princeps' power, the legal foundation was Augustus's special commission from the senate and people of Rome. In theory the senate appointed the emperor, with the people ratifying the senate's choice. In reality, it was the other way around. Augustus promoted the notion that the senate governed the empire with the princeps as guide and friend, but after 23 BC his IMPERIUM exceeded that of any senatorial magistracy. However, Augustus set about increasing the powers of the senate in a way Julius Caesar would have never permitted. The senate became one of the two high courts from whose verdict there was no appeal, and it possessed legislative powers that had once belonged to the COMITIA CENTURIATA, COMITIA TRIBUTA and the CONCILIUM PLEBIS. New legislation was issued in the form of SENATUS CONSULTA. As the title suggests, these were not strictly speaking laws, but resolutions passed by way of consultations, or advice, to magistrates. Since they were never ignored, they were *de facto* laws, and soon the senate acquired the right in full to make laws directly. However, the term continued in use, and later emperors usually issued their legislation in the form of a SENATUS CONSULTUM. The transfer to Augustus of the traditional powers of veto of the TRIBUNUS PLEBIS and the virtual removal of the TRIBUNI from the legislative process further enhanced the senate's authority; but the ancient institution did not have it all its own way.

While refusing the office of censor – traditionally a whip-hand over the senate's composition and an overt image he wished to avoid – as a consul Augustus revived the ancient practice of CENSORIA POTESTAS to order the senate's structure to his own design. He increased membership to as much as six hundred, then a thousand, then cut it back again to six hundred. He established the practice of bringing in new men from all walks of life – as long as they were financially eligible. From 13 BC onward the minimum qualification was a million sesterces, but by imperial grant a poor but worthy EQUES could be adlected by the princeps and take his place in the senate. The enlarged senate provided more capable men to run the empire's huge administration – and as with the army, Augustus liked to keep its members busy. He appointed senators to newly created offices dealing with finances, the upkeep of public buildings, the roads and aqueducts, and the clearing of the Tiberis.

Augustus also drew administrators from the non-senatorial section of the elite, the EQUITES. Posts created exclusively for equestrians included the command of the COHORS PRAETORIO and of the VIGILES, and a prefecture to administer the corn dole (PRAEFECTUS ANNONAE). Accordingly, the ORDO EQUESTER benefited enormously from Augustus's rule, and that of future emperors. Throughout his reign, Augustus consulted the senate frequently and treated it with respect. More significantly, he formed an inner cabinet, or CONSILIUM, from the two presiding consuls, a representation of minor magistrates and fifteen senators chosen by lot. Nevertheless, as the historian Cassius Dio wrote 'nothing was done that did not please Caesar'.

Augustus was assiduous in the administration of justice, often remaining in court until nightfall – a long day during the summer months, since year-long the Roman working day lasted from sunrise to sunset. The existing laws that he revised and the new ones he enacted dealt largely with public extravagance, adultery, licentious behaviour, bribery and the encouragement of marriage in the senatorial and equestrian orders. The latter grew into an obsession with him. In 18 and 17 BC he imposed penalties on the PLEBS and especially the EQUITES for remaining unmarried. There were financial benefits for those couples who produced children. These marriage laws may have been designed to counter a worrying drop in the birth rate of Roman citizens, but it is more probable that they were intended to regulate the lifestyle of the aristocrats, whose decadent ways in the late Republic had become notorious. However, his marriage legislation did not go unopposed. On one occasion, when there was open rebellion among some EQUITES at a public entertainment, Augustus paraded the numerous children of Germanicus and Agrippina and made it clear that it would be a good thing if the knights imitated the young man's example (see side panel right).

Augustus's concern with a return to older Roman morals and virtues sponsored a religious revival. He resurrected festivals that had fallen into disuse, filled the gaping vacancies in the priesthoods and repaired Rome's sacred buildings. In all this he was careful to avoid popular acclaim turning into worship of his person, even though this would have been a useful political adjunct. Ruler-worship was a common eastern practice, but Augustus knew the Romans would never accept it. Instead – in a move that would have lasting consequences for future emperors – he hit on the notion of combining the eastern practice with the western tendency to revere dead ancestors, such as Julius Caesar. This was expanded to permit the worship of the imperial house in conjunction with the worship of the goddess Roma. So in the provinces the people worshipped 'Rome and Augustus', while in Rome citizens bowed before 'Rome and the Deified Julius'. In 12 BC there was a rapid extension to this Caesar-worship when the ex-triumvir Marcus Lepidus died. Augustus had allowed him to remain in his office of PONTIFEX MAXIMUS, despite his living in exile, but now Augustus succeeded him, thus combining his secular powers with that of Rome's most senior religious figure. The invention of the principate was now complete and formed the basis of absolute power for all subsequent Roman emperors.

Augustus the man

Character portraits grow thinner on the ground in the later imperial period, but we have been left a wealth of detail on Augustus. We are told that he was a remarkably handsome man and 'of very graceful gait even as an old man'. Even allowing for a modicum of sycophancy, his many statues bear this out (although none are known of him in older age...). On the other hand he was notoriously uncaring of his personal appearance, which may have been a natural tendency, but perhaps it was also a long-term reaction to the taunts of 'pretty boy' that were thrown at him in his youth. As a young man there had been rumours of homosexuality, albeit from his enemies. Sextus Pompeius sneered at his effeminate behaviour; Marcus Antonius alleged that Julius Caesar made him willingly submit to sodomy as the price of adoption; and Antonius's brother Lucius claimed Augustus had sold his favours to Aulus Hirtius, the governor of Hispania Tarraconensis, for three hundred thousand sesterces. However, the same persons were eager enough to accuse Augustus of immodesty

The model Roman father

Born Nero Claudius Drusus on 24 May 15 BC, Germanicus earned his COGNOMEN for a victory against the Germans in AD 13, and became Julius Caesar Germanicus on his adoption by his uncle Tiberius. He married young and became a favourite of Augustus because of the number of children he and Agrippina produced – nine in all. Three boys died in childhood, but the eldest, Nero Julius Caesar and Drusus Julius Caesar, later became heirs-apparent, and the youngest, Gaius (Caligula), became emperor after Claudius. Two sisters, Drusilla and Livilla, were involved in several scandals (not least being Drusilla's suspected incest with Gaius) and conspiracy plots with ambitious senators; the third, Agrippina the Younger, was to become mother of Nero and wife of Claudius. The popular adulation heaped on Germanicus's shoulders was never entirely deserved. While a capable military commander, he frequently showed poor strategic judgement and resorted to over-emotional blackmail in his dealings with mutinous soldiers. Happier in the field, he was poorly suited to be a diplomat and was to stir up trouble in the East when sent there by Tiberius.

Augustus in the apparel of PONTIFEX MAXIMUS, *the office he assumed after the death of exiled Marcus Aemilius Lepidus in 12 BC.*

with women. Antonius made much of the indecent haste with which Augustus had snatched Livia Drusilla from her husband, and also of his hauling an ex-consul's wife from the dining room into the bedroom before her husband's very eyes. Suetonius quotes from what he describes as 'a racy letter' written by Antonius to Augustus before the two had quarrelled, defending his sexual relations with Cleopatra:

'And what about you? Are you faithful to Livia Drusilla? My congratulations if, when this letter arrives, you have not been in bed with Tertullia, or Terentilla, or Rufilla, or Salvia Titiseia – or all of them. Does it really matter so much where, or with whom, you fuck?'

As we have seen, Augustus was a man to proceed cautiously in everything he did (apart from marrying Livia, which, however, he did not repent at leisure). He regarded haste and recklessness as sins in his military commanders, and was fond of quoting proverbs such as 'More haste, less speed', and homilies like 'Give me a safe commander, not a rash one'. It was a principle that he never fought a battle unless more could be gained by victory than lost by defeat. We know from his letters that he enjoyed gambling with dice, and he remained a womaniser into old age. But in almost every other respect, his habits were modest.

Unlike his successors, Augustus was content to live in a small DOMUS on the Palatine. His first home disappeared under the Temple of Apollo, and the senate voted him a new house beside it and behind Livia's. It was called a 'palace', but the compact rooms were unadorned by either the marble he was so fond of or tessellated floors. Even his holiday homes at Lanuvium and Tibur (Tivoli) were unpretentious, furnished by couches and tables 'hardly considered fit for a PRIVATUS'. He liked to give dinner parties, but always in the strict Roman tradition, and ate and drank sparingly himself. His favourite food was that of the common people: coarse bread, whitebait fish, fresh hand-pressed cheese, and green figs ('of the second crop'). The dinners were, however, jolly affairs because of his talent for bringing the shy into the conversation, and his own natural good humour.

He was also a noted scholar and writer, having studied rhetoric with great eagerness in his youth. He wrote numerous pieces of prose and poetry to general acclaim, and was happy to act as patron to other writers (*see side panel below*). Augustus sponsored a great flowering of writing activity generated by the development of literary circles of patronage that had been mostly in abeyance since the second century BC. Most famous among these patrons was Gaius Maecenas, a close associate of Augustus from the very beginning but one who never played an active role in politics. Among others, he supported the careers of Virgil and Horace until his death in 8 BC. Another circle of patronage formed around Marcus Valerius Messalla Corvinus, who promoted the careers of Tibullus and Ovid. While it should be accepted that this literary upsurge was a natural consequence of the new peace and prosperity, it is equally likely that Augustus – never a man to waste good talent – would have expected the writers to toe the political line. And there is the evidence of Ovid – banished for affronting the new Augustan morality – in comparison to Virgil and Livy, who both prospered. Virgil's *Eclogues* and *Georgics* wax lyrical on the Augustan restoration of peace to the Italian countryside, while the Republican sentiments of Livy's *Histories* could be so pronounced that Augustus jokingly referred to him as 'my Pompeian'. But this attitude towards Livy also suggests that, as with his political machinations, Augustus had no desire to exert overt influence over writers – such interference did not fit his careful policies – he much preferred to provide 'encouragement' from the top.

While a naturally thrifty person, Augustus spent lavishly on public entertainments and encouraged the members of his family and inner circle to do the same, as was their Roman duty whenever they were elevated to some high office. He enjoyed cheerful people and often sought the company of small boys with whom he could enjoy a game of marbles. He particularly liked

Augustan literary giants

The Augustan literary scene was exceptionally vibrant. This was the era of some of Rome's most famous and influential writers, including Publius Vergilius Maro (Virgil, 70–19 BC), Quintus Horatius Flaccus (Horace, 65–8 BC), Publius Ovidius Naso (Ovid, 43 BC–AD 17), and other lesser lights, such as the poets Propertius and Tibullus.

Virgil's works include the *Georgics* (poems about farming), and the legendary life of Aeneas, the *Aeneid* – a new national epic for the Romans, which quickly came to replace Ennius's *Annales* as the poem every schoolchild learned by heart.

Horace was Rome's greatest poet and satirist, and all his published work has survived, due to his wide contemporary popularity. His best known works include the short poems in *Epodi*, the *Carmina* (Odes), *Ars Poetica* (Art of Poetry), and the *Carmen Saeculare* (Secular Hymn), a long ode written for Augustus welcoming the return of ancient virtues. Horace, whose biography was written by Suetonius, had a great influence on Renaissance authors.

Ovid was a prolific poet whose irreverence resulted in his banishment by Augustus, probably after he offended the new Augustan morality by publishing *Ars Amorata* (Art of Love), which deals with the strategies of seduction. Ovid continued to write in exile, and his numerous poems exercised a great influence on generations of Romans and post-Renaissance Europeans.

Moors and Syrians for their happy appearance, and loathed people who were dwarfish or in any way deformed, regarding them as freaks and bringers of bad luck. This predilection explains his treatment of his grandnephew, the future emperor Claudius, who of all his handsome family was the most ill-favoured in stance and appearance.

Augustus passed away at his country villa at Nola in the afternoon of 19 August AD 14 at the age of seventy-five. In his long life he had totally transformed the Roman State and secured a hereditary succession. In his funeral oration, Tiberius compared Augustus to the hero Hercules; and in September – his birth month – he was voted the status of a god. From this time on he was known as DIVUS AUGUSTUS, the Deified Augustus, and joined his adoptive father Julius Caesar among the leading divinities of the Roman pantheon.

His testament proved that he had named his stepson Tiberius and his wife Livia as his heirs. It directed that Tiberius should take two-thirds of his estate and adopt the name Augustus, while Livia should take the balance and adopt the title Augusta – a division that was to cause some fractious problems between them. On the other hand, Tiberius was bequeathed an empire that enjoyed external security and internal peace, a constitution that Romans found acceptable and an army that (not all willingly) hailed him as their commander because of his adoptive link to the sacred Julian bloodline.

TIBERIUS

Tiberius Claudius Nero Caesar
(r.AD 19/8/14–16/3/37)

There is some doubt as to when Tiberius was born; some accounts give it as the year of the consuls Marcus Aemilius Lepidus and Lucius Munatius Plancus, which would put it in 43 BC – they shared office with Octavian's brief seizure of the consulship after the battles around Mutina. But Suetonius cites the bulk of trustworthy opinion as preferring two years later, on 16 November, on the Palatine hill in Rome (although his father Tiberius Claudius Nero would not have been present, since he was on campaign with Antonius). The Claudian GENS, of which he was a member, had an ancient lineage that, according to one legend, dated back to the time of Romulus, the founder of Rome. Another puts the family settling in Rome at a later time, a few years after the expulsion of the kings in 509 BC. At the time of Tiberius, the Claudians had amassed twenty-eight consulships, six triumphs and two ovations.

Although several COGNOMINA were used by the Claudians, the most popular were the Sabine word 'Nero', meaning 'strong and energetic', and 'Drusus', dating from 283 BC, when its first holder killed an enemy chieftain called Drausus in single combat.

As a quaestor, Tiberius's father Nero brilliantly commanded Julius Caesar's fleet during the Alexandrine conflict of 48 BC (that settled the Ptolemaic dynastic conflict in favour of Cleopatra). Caesar rewarded Nero by appointing him to the high office of PONTIFEX MAXIMUS, and granting him the right to found the colonies of Narbo (Narbonne) and Arelate (Arles) in Gallia. Later, we find him supporting Marcus Antonius's brother Lucius during the Perusine War. When Perusia fell to Octavian, only Nero scorned to capitulate. In the slaughter that followed, he managed to escape and eventually took refuge in Sicilia. However, the island was in the hands of Sextus Pompeius, who spurned Nero as an ex-Caesarean. So he crossed to Italia and joined Marcus Antonius. When peace came, he returned to Rome in Antonius's company. Octavian's forgiveness of his former enemy almost certainly carried a price. With Nero came his wife Livia Drusilla, who had borne him Tiberius Claudius Nero and was pregnant with Drusus Claudius Nero. Octavian determined to marry Livia, and it seems that Nero – not exactly in any position to argue – surrendered her and the children to him, and apparently died soon after.

For Tiberus it was a difficult childhood, being dragged from town to town when Nero and Livia fled from Octavian's forces. His young life was almost snuffed out on several occasions: in Neapolis, Sicilia and even as far away as Sparta in Greek Achaea. However, as stepson of Octavian, soon to be Augustus, things looked up for Tiberius. He was honoured at the age of fourteen by taking part in Octavian's triumph of 29 BC after Actium. Octavian sat him on the left-hand horse of the triumphator's chariot, while he placed his favourite, Marcellus, astride the more auspicious right-hand horse (Marcellus would soon be dead, so it was not such a good omen after all).

Tiberius and the princeps were to have a long, uneasy association. By all accounts Tiberius was an enigmatic and darkly complex figure, intelligent and

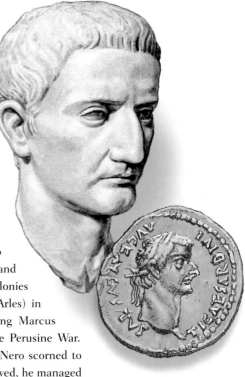

Tiberius Claudius Nero Caesar was 53 when he acceeded to the principate.

Bust of Tiberius in early adolescence.

cunning, but given to bouts of severe depression and grim moods. In this, he was the opposite of his stepfather, and his repressed Republican sentiments hardly helped their relationship. Nevertheless, Augustus did his traditional fatherly duty when Tiberius attained his majority, by leading him clad in his TOGA VIRILIS into the Forum Romanum. At the age of seventeen, he became a quaestor and was given the Augustan privilege of standing for the praetorship and consulship years in advance of the age prescribed by law.

As was customary for young aristocrats, Tiberius soon began appearing in the law courts as an advocate. His civil career started with the successful defence of Archelaus, the Jewish king, at a court presided over by Augustus. He next appeared before the senate as advocate of three cities in the province of Asia that were appealing for public relief after an earthquake. Tiberius also acted as the prosecutor in the conspiracy case in c.23 BC against Fannius Caepio and Varro Murena, securing their convictions for treason.

At about this time, when he would have been about eighteen, he married Vipsania Agrippina, a union that seemed full of promise. On the political side, she was the daughter of Marcus Agrippa by his previous marriage to Pomponia, daughter of Cicero's friend Pomponius Atticus. But what was more important, the couple loved each other passionately – a rare occurrence in a world of arranged marriages. Soon after his wedding, Tiberius was sent to the Orient in 20 BC to evict the Parthians from Armenia and restore

Tiberius's beloved first wife Vipsania, daughter of Marcus Agrippa, as identified in a group of portraits on the Ara Pacis in Rome.

Tigranes, the Roman client king, to his throne. Next, he oversaw one of his stepfather's proudest successes. The Parthians, who had captured the eagles of the legions lost in the failed campaigns of Marcus Crassus (53 BC), Decidius Saxa (40 BC), and Marcus Antonius (36 BC), formally handed them back.

On his return to Rome Tiberius assumed praetorian rank before leaving to undertake the more senior service that was expected of a consul-to-be. For a year or so he governed Gallia Lugdunensis (probably still known as Gallia Commata, Gaul of the Long Hairs), late in 19 BC, where barbarian raids and feuds between Gallic chieftains had caused unrest. He also served with his brother Drusus in campaigns in the Alps, Pannonia and in Germany. Tiberius proved to be a thoroughgoing if not inspired commander, and earned the respect of his troops – not that this would bring him much benefit at the time of his accession.

In 13 BC he became consul for the first time at the age of twenty-eight (some thirteen years before the traditional legal age for the office). His colleague, Publius Quinctilius Varus, was a relative of Augustus by marriage, but more famously the general who was to lose three of Augustus's legions to German raiders at the Teutoberg Forest in AD 9. Tiberius also became a father when Vipsania gave birth to a son they named Drusus.

However, personal disaster struck in the following year as a consequence of Marcus Agrippa's death. Augustus forced Tiberius to divorce Vipsania in order to marry Agrippa's widow, Julia. As Augustus's daughter, Julia was also Tiberius's stepsister (not to say also his recent stepmother-in-law) – the kind of tangled web so typical of the dynastic Roman families. After a short honeymoon period of mutual, if distant, contempt, they came to loathe each other bitterly, and Julia made little attempt to hide her ridicule of him as a man. Tiberius continued to moon about Rome after Vipsania until Augustus had to ban him from ever seeing her again. For her part, Julia suffered no such constraints and began a series of scandalous affairs with handsome young men that were eventually to lead to her downfall.

Augustus put Tiberius back to work by giving him important military commissions in Pannonia and Germania in 12–6 BC, when he was successful in the field; although any glory was marred by the tragic death of his brother in 9 BC. Tiberius brought the body of Drusus back to Rome himself. He was consul for the second time in 7 BC together with Gnaeus Calpurnius Piso, and granted the TRIBUNICIA POTESTAS in the following year. In essence, Tiberius had replaced Agrippa as Augustus's successor, but still only as the guardian of

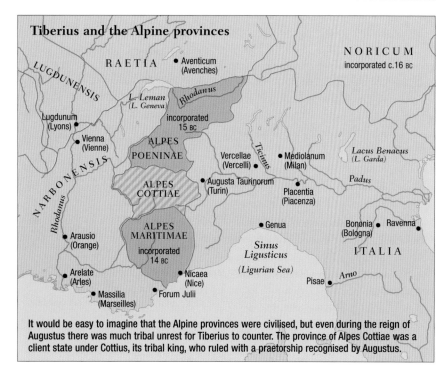

Tiberius and the Alpine provinces

RAETIA
- Aventicum (Avenches)

NORICUM
incorporated c.16 BC

LUGDUNENSIS

L. Leman (L. Geneva)
Rhodanus
incorporated 15 BC

Lugdunum (Lyons)
Vienna (Vienne)

NARBONENSIS

ALPES POENINAE

Vercellae (Vercelli)
Ticinus
Mediolanum (Milan)

Lacus Benacus (L. Garda)

ALPES COTTIAE

Augusta Taurinorum (Turin)

Placentia (Piacenza)

Padus

Rhodanus

Arausio (Orange)

ALPES MARITIMAE
incorporated 14 BC

Genua

Bononia (Bologna)
Ravenna

ITALIA

Arelate (Arles)

Sinus Ligusticus
(Ligurian Sea)

Nicaea (Nice)

Pisae
Arno

Massilia (Marseilles)

Forum Julii

It would be easy to imagine that the Alpine provinces were civilised, but even during the reign of Augustus there was much tribal unrest for Tiberius to counter. The province of Alpes Cottiae was a client state under Cottius, its tribal king, who ruled with a praetorship recognised by Augustus.

Agrippa's young sons, the Caesars Gaius and Lucius. At this point, he flung all his honours in Augustus's face, announced his withdrawal from public life, and went to live on the island of Rhodus with a small retinue of close friends and his personal astrologer Thrasyllus.

His reasons for this potentially dangerous move are unclear but there were several possible contributory factors. Julia's immoral behaviour disgusted him, not least because she made him such an obvious cuckold (except to Augustus, who remained either paternally blind or blissfully ignorant of her sexual indiscretions). His relationship with the young Caesars Gaius and Lucius was poor, and the precocious Gaius, half his age, made him out as a slow-witted boor, much as had the arrogant Marcellus made Agrippa feel at the end of his useful life. And then there was the influence of his domineering mother Livia, whose ambitions for her son far outstripped his. She had no time for Tiberius's Republican sentiments, nor his frequent brooding moods. His sadness at the loss first of Vipsania and then his light-hearted brother must have made the burden of coping with palace intrigue unbearable. Perhaps his apparent reluctance to succeed Augustus should also be taken into account. Although contemporary histories paint this as a fake sentiment to hide his real ambition, there were many occasions during his reign when he was unwilling to exercise power. His self-imposed exile to Rhodus could therefore be viewed as a sulky demonstration at being passed over, a retirement to mourn the death of his brother and his estrangement from Vipsania, or indeed a combination of all the above reasons. In any event, Tiberius soon came to regret his decision. But he was to be left in the wilderness for seven years.

Never particularly fond of his stepson, Augustus's opinion of Tiberius now deteriorated and henceforwards he seems to have had little patience with the exile. When he could no longer ignore it, Augustus is even said to have blamed Tiberius for Julia's unacceptable behaviour on the grounds that he should have paid her more attention and produced some children. Something of Augustus's irritation is revealed by his repeated refusal to allow Tiberius to return to Rome after the latter realised the delicacy of his position on Rhodus; and this in spite of pressure brought to bear on Augustus by the persuasive Livia. To this point, Tiberius had been protected by his tribunician power, but when its term expired in 1 BC, it was pointedly not renewed. He now began feeling vulnerable, and with good cause. In Rome, Gaius Caesar was beginning to stretch his political muscle. When

Tiberius's name cropped up at a private dinner party attended by Gaius, a guest rose to say that if he [Gaius] gave the order he would sail to Rhodus and 'fetch back the Exile's head'.

Eventually, Livia's arguments won the day, and Augustus gave his consent to Tiberius's return to Rome when Lucius Caesar died in Massilia in AD 2. The story is told that his astrologer Thrasyllus, in whom Tiberius had lost all faith, was about to be pushed over a cliff by his irate patron when a ship was sighted sailing towards the island. Thrasyllus swore it brought good news. Tiberius decided to spare the astrologer's life until the nature of the news had been discovered, although he was quietly resigned to being ordered to take his life. Thrasyllus, therefore, was not the only reprieved exile when the ship put into port. Tiberius returned to Rome, but he was not immediately reinstated in Augustus's affections. Gaius Caesar had only given his assent to the return as long as Tiberius was kept out of the political sphere. And this remained the state of affairs until Gaius died in AD 4.

Once more Augustus turned to his dour stepson, with the adoption arrangements outlined in the section on Augustus (*see page 27*). Considering the nature of their relations over the years, it may be difficult to see why Augustus eventually relented and allowed Tiberius to become his nominated successor. Anecdotes of Augustus's impatience at Tiberius abound in the histories. He is quoted as saying: 'Poor Rome, doomed to be masticated by those slow-moving jaws!' Yet the same man wrote to his stepson at the front with the words: 'Your summer campaigns, my dear Tiberius, deserve my heartiest praise; I am sure that no other man alive could have conducted them more capably than yourself....'

For such a cautious and prudent man as Augustus to make a mistake in his choice seems unlikely. Perhaps he weighed up the good and bad in Tiberius and reckoned that the good tipped the scale. In the summer of AD 14, when Tiberius was fifty-three, it was time to find out what Augustus's long planning had wrought.

Tiberius princeps

The reign got off to a poor start with a murder, a confused senate, a suicide and an army mutiny. The exiled young Agrippa Postumus posed a dynastic threat, and there are differing perspectives on his death. Tacitus makes Tiberius responsible for his execution, without specifically blaming him. Suetonius says that the officer appointed to guard Postumus received a written

Coin of Tiberius's younger brother Drusus. His death on campaign in Pannonia and Germania in 9 BC badly affected Tiberius, who was still smarting from an enforced divorce from his wife Vipsania.

order from Tiberius for the boy's execution, but allows that Augustus might have written it or even Livia in his name. Whether he knew about the execution or not, when the officer arrived to report that he had done his duty, Tiberius threatened to make him answerable for the unauthorised killing. On the other hand, Tiberius shelved the inquiry and the matter was forgotten, so perhaps he did have a hand in it. That Augustus himself ordered the execution of Agrippa and Julia's last-born son is perfectly possible. Even though the emperor had adopted him, he may have feared that leaving the exiled loutish Postumus alive would face Tiberius with a rival pretender. And Livia? Some sources go so far as to suggest she was behind the unfortunate deaths of so many Augustan favourites as far back as Marcellus. If so, it was all to see her son Tiberius on the throne, and Postumus would simply have been the last in a long line of nuisances.

Only after the matter of Postumus was resolved did Tiberius inform the senate of Augustus's death. He returned to Rome in the company of a cohort of praetorian guards to be greeted by the consuls Sextus Appuleius and (another) Sextus Pompeius, who were swift to swear an oath of loyalty and then administer the same to the senate, EQUITES and people. The senate convened on 18 September to inaugurate the new reign. Such a transfer of power had never happened before and nobody, including Tiberius, appears to have known what to do. Both Tacitus and Suetonius agree in general if not in detail on what happened next. Tiberius professed great reluctance to assume the office. He even scolded his closest supporters for suggesting he should become emperor. The confused and probably alarmed senators lost their patience. According to Suetonius, many thought Tiberius was a dissembling hypocrite, and one senator was heard to cry out: 'Some people are slow to do what they promise; you are slow to promise what you have already done.'

Perhaps Tiberius was genuinely reluctant to become the princeps. He had never enjoyed the cloying offices of Roman administration over the freedom of military life. Perhaps he genuinely wanted to leave the senate free to make its own decision on the grounds that it would at least provide a proper precedent for the succession. In any case, he was doing no more than had Augustus in 27 BC, when he had to be 'persuaded' to accept the imperial powers. Unfortunately, where Augustus used tact, Tiberius came across as obdurate.

Nevertheless, he finally acceded to the senate's wishes and accepted the title because there was no other suitable candidate for the job. However, he added that he reserved the right to resign later. This first meeting between the senate and Tiberius established a pattern for their later interaction. Throughout his reign, Tiberius was to confuse and frighten the senators. His actions and edicts seem to suggest that he wanted the senate to act on his implicit desires rather than on his explicit requests. If this was another attempt to imitate Augustus's careful wielding of his AUCTORITAS, it back-fired and eventually turned into a farce. And for his part, Tiberius held no high opinion of his senatorial colleagues: 'Men fit only to be slaves,' he said of them.

The rise and fall of Germanicus

Tiberius's disgraced wife Julia, despairing that her ban-ishment would never be revoked now her last son Postumus was dead, committed suicide on the island of Pandateria to which Augustus had exiled her. But Postumus – living up to his name – had a sting in his tail. One of his loyal slaves almost persuaded the German legions to mutiny in his master's memory. Although he failed, military unrest did not subside.

The long reign of Augustus had accustomed people to the concept of a sole ruler, but there had never been a succession, and the change of emperors prompted the soldiers to demand a pay rise. Mutinies broke out in Germania and in Pannonia. Tiberius had asked the senate to confer an IMPERIUM PROCONSULARE on his popular nephew and adopted son Germanicus, and put him in command of the armies of both Germania Inferior and Superior, each of four legions. Those in Germania Inferior mutinied and even begged Germanicus – a man of Julian blood – to become emperor, which he flatly refused to do. In Pannonia the three legions were finally brought under control by Tiberius's son Drusus, and Germanicus eventually managed the same on the Rhenus. There were genuine grievances underlying these revolts that stemmed from under-payment of the legionaries (especially in con-trast to the 'pampered' praetorians), being retained long after terms of service had expired, and bullying by their officers. In the event, the troops received assur-ances that their complaints would be addressed.

With the immediate anxieties of the first succession in Rome's history put aside, Tiberius's early years were generally good. He remained true to Augustus's plans for the succession by favouring Germanicus over his natural son, Drusus. He behaved with discretion in his dealings with magistrates and the senate as a whole.

The prison islands

Elba

Planasia (Pianosa)

ITALIA

Corsica

• Roma

Sardinia

Pandateria (Ventotene)

• Neapolis

MARE TYRRHENUM

He rejected any overtly sycophantic honours, such as the dedication of temples to his divinity. He declined to set the title princeps before his name or PATER PATRIAE after; and even refrained from adding the name Augustus to his own. His notorious parsimony resulted in legislation to cut down waste. He cut the expense of public entertainment by setting limits on the number of gladiatorial combats at many festivals; introduced price controls on household furniture; set an annual regulation on market values; and restricted the wasteful amount of food offered for sale in cook-shops. To set an example, he frequently served guests half-eaten dishes left over from the day before – which rendered an invitation to dinner a dubious treat.

Augustus's foreign policy had been one of conciliation, and Tiberius adhered to it resolutely. He refused to allow any extension of the frontiers, although Germanicus defied him in a series of trans-Rhenic campaigns in AD 14–16. In his defence, it might be said that Germanicus needed to take the soldiers' minds off the recent mutiny. But he was also in search of military glory unavailable on the mostly peaceful Gallic side of the Rhenus. Besides, the loss by Varus in AD 9 of three legions still rankled. There was little Tiberius could do. As a Julian, Germanicus was popular not only with the German troops but also with the Roman populace; and he was son of the much-lamented Drusus (the elder). The emperor finally brought his nephew to book by recalling him to celebrate a triumph on 26 May 17 and to load him with honours, including a consulship shared with Tiberius himself. Then, as soon as possible in 18, he packed Germanicus off to the eastern provinces with a MAIUS IMPERIUM.

The task Germanicus faced was a diplomatic one, that of installing a Roman appointee in Armenia without damaging friendly relations with the Parthian empire. Tiberius had no high hopes of the heir-apparent's abilities in this respect, but was aware that sending someone of lesser rank would have been an affront to Germanicus. Accordingly he sent his trusted former consular colleague Gnaeus Calpurnius Piso to be governor of Syria with, Tacitus tells us, secret instructions to restrain Germanicus from any serious indiscretions. Technically, Piso was Germanicus's inferior and should have contented himself with offering advice. Unfortunately, he began meddling in arrangements already made by Germanicus and refused him military aid when it was requested. Piso may have thought he was acting rationally in the face of some very unwise and sometimes overbearing actions of Germanicus, not to mention with the support of the emperor.

The upshot was that Germanicus ordered Piso out of Syria, but fell sick a few days after Piso had taken ship, and died on 10 October 19. With his last words he accused Piso of having poisoned him.

When Germanicus's widow Agrippina returned to Rome carrying her publicly adored husband's ashes, she declared Piso guilty of murder and hinted at Tiberius and Livia's involvement, claiming that they wanted his natural son Drusus to be his successor. Piso was put on trial by the senate, where he easily cleared himself of the charge of poisoning, but failed to get an acquittal on the charge of misconduct in his province and inciting the Syrian troops against his superior. In this, not even Tiberius could help him. Unable to see a way out, Piso committed suicide together with his wife Plancina. While the death of Germanicus could certainly be seen as fortuitous for Tiberius, Agrippina's accusations seem preposterous. Tiberius had always acted properly towards Germanicus, and if he had reservations about his headstrong but affable nephew, son – after all – of his own beloved brother Drusus, they certainly did not extend as far as having him murdered. Unfortunately, Piso's suicide – presumably to save the rest of his family and his estate – convinced many that he was guilty of poisoning Germanicus. Tiberius remained aloof from the proceedings, as did his mother Livia although she was a close associate of Plancina. It was an absence that was also interpreted as the action of guilty parties.

Sejanus and praetorian power

With Germanicus dead, Tiberius began, through the familiar Augustan methods, to elevate his own son. Drusus had married Julia Livilla, a daughter of Germanicus, so the twin sons she bore him in 19 (Tiberius Germanicus Caesar and Tiberius Caesar Gemellus) did have some Julian blood. Nevertheless, Drusus was, like his father, forced to recognise the prior right of succession of Germanicus and Agrippina's sons. A consulship came in 21 and in the next year the grant of TRIBUNICIA POTESTAS. The year also marks the moment when Tiberius – now in his sixty-first year – began making long absences from the capital, leaving the administration in the hands of Drusus and the PRAEFECTUS PRAETORIO, Sejanus, in whom Tiberius placed unbounded confidence. In a

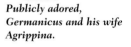

Publicly adored, Germanicus and his wife Agrippina.

A bust thought to be the likeness of Lucius Aelius Sejanus.

Tiberius's son Drusus and his wife Julia Livilla, the sister of Germanicus and Claudius.

long catalogue of rapacious men, Lucius Aelius Sejanus certainly qualifies as a nasty piece of work.

His date of birth is not recorded, but we know that Sejanus came from Volsinii in Etruria. On his mother's side he was descended from the old nobility and his father, Lucius Seius Strabo, was a wealthy equestrian. Sejanus first appears as a companion to Gaius Julius Caesar on his eastern mission of 1 BC–AD 4. Tiberius made Strabo and his son joint PRAEFECTI on his accession, and they shared the command until AD 15 when Tiberius appointed Strabo to the equestrian office of PRAEFECTUS AEGYPTI, leaving Sejanus as the sole PRAEFECTUS PRAETORIO. Through a combination of energetic efficiency, fawning sycophancy and outward displays of loyalty, he gained the position of Tiberius's closest friend and advisor. Tiberius openly praised him as 'the partner of my labours'.

Drusus, however, did not find co-operation with Sejanus easy. Agrippina's Julian party was agitating continuously against the Claudians, and Sejanus capitalised on the tensions for his own gain. Doubtless, Drusus would have foiled his intentions, but he died suddenly on 14 September 23, quickly followed by his one of his sons, Tiberius Germanicus. Sejanus's wife Apicata later asserted that her husband had seduced Drusus's wife Livilla and persuaded her to poison Drusus. The seduction story, at least, seems true, for within two years Sejanus had divorced Apicata and asked Tiberius if he could marry Livilla. Tiberius refused to take this last step to ally Sejanus to the imperial family, but in every other respect he left the PRAEFECTUS a free hand. It was Sejanus who induced Tiberius to concentrate all nine cohorts of the praetorian guards into a single camp – the CASTRA PRAETORIA

just beyond the old Servian wall, a process that began in AD 23. Augustus had billeted the praetorians in small towns around Rome, but now Sejanus commanded some nine thousand troops stationed on the city's edge. As Sejanus's public profile became more pronounced, he even had statues of himself erected in the Forum Romanum and other public places.

Tacitus dates the rapid degeneration of the reign to the death of Drusus; Tiberius's visits to his island retreat on Capreae (Capri), encouraged by Sejanus, became more prolonged. In contrast, Suetonius claims that Drusus's vicious and dissolute habits offended his father, and that Tiberius was unconcerned at his son's death; he even cut the official mourning period before going back to business as usual. In 26 Tiberius left Rome for Capreae, never again to visit the capital. His mother Livia was another cause for his retirement. Always the dominant force in his life, Tiberius resented her treating him as if he were still a child. She vexed him by meddling in the administration, which she saw as her right not only as the Augusta but by virtue of being the brains of the imperial family; and there was no denying that it was her house that was the centre of life in the court, with her many young favourites such as Servius Sulpicius Galba. When, angered by his obduracy, Livia produced some of Augustus's old letters and read out his unflattering comments on Tiberius's sour and stubborn character, the two parted in bitterness. Tiberius was only to visit Livia once more in the last three years of her life. He refused to attend her funeral in 29, withheld the bequests of her will and vetoed her deification on the untrue grounds that she had forbidden it.

With Tiberius out of the way on Capreae, Sejanus was now the only route of access to the ageing emperor, and acted as his voice in the senate. Any who dared question the PRAEFECTUS had only to glance over his shoulder at the menace of the praetorian guard. Sejanus began a regular persecution of the friends and family of Germanicus. Agrippina's never-ending fulminations gave him plenty of excuses. Tiberius seems to have approved; he too was tired of Agrippina's waspish tongue and fed up with the adulation of the senate and people for her sons, the two eldest of whom – the Caesars Nero and Drusus – would be the heirs apparent until Tiberius's remaining grandson Gemellus grew up. In rapid succession Nero and Agrippina were arrested and imprisoned on the island of Pandateria, and Drusus – for whom there should be little sympathy because he conspired with Sejanus in his older brother's downfall – found himself in turn arrested

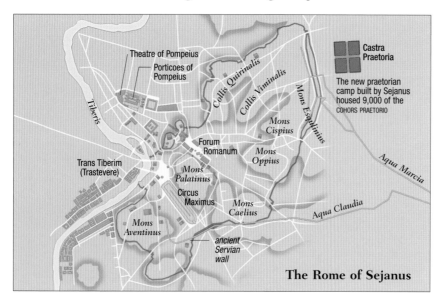

Theatre of Pompeius
Porticoes of Pompeius

Collis Quirinalis

Collis Viminalis

Mons Esquilinus

Tiberis

Mons Cispius

Forum Romanum

Mons Oppius

Trans Tiberim (Trastevere)

Mons Palatinus

Circus Maximus

Mons Caelius

Mons Aventinus

ancient Servian wall

Castra Praetoria

The new praetorian camp built by Sejanus housed 9,000 of the COHORS PRAETORIO

Aqua Marcia

Aqua Claudia

The Rome of Sejanus

and imprisoned in the gloomy Palatine palace. These events took place in 27; Nero and Agrippina died in captivity in 31, and Drusus only survived them by two years; apparently expiring from deliberate starvation.

By the end of 27 Sejanus had reached the pinnacle of his power, and his actions to that time clearly point to a desire to become the princeps in place of Tiberius. However, the young princes of the imperial house were a major impediment in achieving his ambition. These were now Tiberius's grandson, Tiberius Gemellus, and Germanicus's remaining sons, Drusus Julius Caesar and the young Gaius. Drusus, of course was imprisoned, and the problem was solved by his death in 33. This left Gaius as the eldest heir-apparent. Events now moved quickly. The voice of reason belonged to elderly Antonia, daughter of Marcus Antonius and Octavia, the emperor's sister-in-law and mother of Germanicus, with whom Tiberius had remained on good terms. When the stately matron told him of Sejanus's plotting Tiberius believed her, and acted. The problem was clear: on Capreae Tiberius had no forces, while in Rome Sejanus had the COHORS PRAETORIO. Clandestine planning was essential. In 31 Tiberius granted Sejanus an IMPERIUM CONSULARE and became his colleague in the consulship, the two honours that marked him out in the same way Augustus had Agrippa. The nineteen-year-old Gaius was called to Capreae for his safety, and in October Tiberius dispatched the EQUES Maevius Sutorius Macro, commander of the VIGILES, to Rome with the secret commission to replace Sejanus as PRAEFECTUS PRAETORIO.

When Sejanus was summoned to a meeting of the senate on 18 October, he probably expected to receive a share of the TRIBUNICIA POTESTAS, the final seal of the emperor's approval. But in an unexpected turn of events, the letter sent by Tiberius from Capreae initially praised Sejanus extensively, and then suddenly denounced him as a traitor and demanded his arrest. Chaos ensued. Supporters of Sejanus headed for the exit, others were confused, fearing that this was another Tiberian test of their loyalty. At this point Macro, having replaced the praetorian guards, appeared with a cohort of VIGILES, arrested Sejanus, conveyed him to prison, and shortly after executed him. Sejanus's family was arrested and put to death in the witch-hunt that followed; followers and friends of Sejanus were denounced and imprisoned, or tried and executed; others committed suicide. As late as 33 a general massacre of all those in custody was still taking place. Livilla's end came when her grandmother imprisoned her in a room without food; noble Antonia paid her own penance by listening as her granddaughter died of starvation.

The last years of Tiberius

In 32 and again in 33 Tiberius left Capreae for Rome, but turned back before reaching the city; otherwise for the remaining years of his life he stayed on the island. Many are the stories of his depravity with youths and young children of both sexes, and of appalling casual cruelty to any who offended him. It is worth bearing in mind that many of the ancient texts (particularly Suetonius and Tacitus) were written by historians living in a later age, whose autocratic rulers aspired to a high moral tone by playing up the excesses of their predecessors (this was to happen frequently).

Suetonius cites an anecdote of a fisherman who had taken the trouble to haul a huge mullet up the precipitous rocks to the imperial residence to present it to his emperor. Tiberius was so frightened by his unexpected appearance that he ordered his guards to rub the poor man's face with the fish. The scales skinned him raw, and the fisherman shouted in his agony: 'Thank Heaven, I did not bring Caesar that huge crab I also caught!' Tiberius promptly sent for the crustacean and had it used in the same way. Tales like this may have come about as colourful explanations for the excesses of the DELATORES (*see side panel below*) and the ramping up of the treason trials that followed in the wake of Sejanus's downfall, which certainly marred the later years of Tiberius's reign.

However, the accounts of his sexual antics seem at variance with the certainty that Capreae was filled with scholars. Nor are they consistent with the extraordinary amount of hard administrative work that Tiberius put in right up until his death – even unloved Rome was well cared for. It was under Tiberius that the PRAEFECTUS URBI (city prefect) of Rome became a permanent and important official, responsible for maintaining law and order with the COHORTES

ITALIA

Roma

Beneventum

Neapolis

Capraea

UNDER TIBERIUS the role of the DELATORES (professional informers) expanded as a result of the revision to the law of treason made by Augustus, although he was reluctant to implement it. At first, many treason trials appear to have been test cases to see how the new laws should be interpreted, and were probably frivolous, since Tiberius quashed many. However, Sejanus found them useful in pursuing his ends, and gradually what amounted to a reign of terror developed, in which the DELATORES were allowed to run amok. The DELATORES were not confined to treason cases, but there was a personal advantage in them for the informer. After a successful prosecution, the informer was given at least a quarter of his 'treasonous' victim's property, and such easy gains attracted the most unscrupulous men to invent charges against the wealthy. In time the DELATORES blighted Tiberius's reign with their scandalous actions, as they would those of future emperors.

URBANAE, who policed the streets. This senatorial office eventually exceeded that of the urban magistrates, with his court supplanting theirs.

Tiberius created an efficient administration of the provinces through a series of prudent appointments. He extended the terms of governors, which lessened the temptation to get rich quick that had bedevilled the Republican period when governors only held the office for a year. Public building work may have been slack in Rome, but much was done in Hispania, Syria, Moesia, Dalmatia and Pannonia, including the construction of new roads, bridges and even whole cities.

Despite his aversion to spending, Tiberius showed generosity on several occasions. He provided large subsidies in 19 so that the price of grain could be lowered. When a financial crisis arose in 33 because of a shortage of coinage in circulation, he lent the AERARIUM a million sesterces, interest free, and spent a similar sum in 36 to repair the damage caused by a massive fire on the Aventine. In contrast, there was almost no spending on new public buildings apart from a restoration of Pompeius's Theatre, and a new temple to the Deified Augustus that went so slowly it remained unfinished at his death. He erected a huge palace on the Palatine, even though he spent almost no time in it and its fabric fell into disrepair.

Economies may have been forced on him because massive spending on military campaigns in the last years of Augustus's reign had left the AERARIUM depleted. Beyond the unauthorised trans-Rhenic campaigns of 14–16, Tiberius embarked on no wars of conquest. A Gallic national revolt under Julius Sacrovir was put down in 21–2, and North Africa obtained peace after seven years of guerrilla warfare between 17 and 24, caused by Tacfrarinas, a man who had served in the Roman army. This situation became so serious that – since Africa was a senatorial province – the senate appointed the Pannonian commander Julius Blaesus to handle the matter. For defeating Tacfarinas in 22, Blaesus won the title IMPERATOR – the last time anyone outside the imperial house was permitted to receive the honour. His army shattered, Tacfarinas ceased to be a nuisance, and was slain by a Roman force two years later.

In the matter of the succession, Tiberius was faced with a choice between his grandson Tiberius Gemellus, who at sixteen was too young, and his grandnephew Gaius, Germanicus's son. At twenty-three he was also young, but Gaius *was* of the Julian

Gaius Caligula, grand-nephew of Tiberius and son of the popular Germanicus, was only 25 when he succeeded Tiberius.

blood line. Tiberius, who held suspicions that Gemellus was actually the illegitimate offspring of Sejanus, solved the question by appointing both as his co-heirs. There are indications that he would have liked to pass over Gaius, whom he knew suffered from serious character flaws, but being a Julian made it unwise to do so. Tiberius gave Gaius no responsible offices and kept him at Capreae under his watchful eye. Thus it was that, in 37, when Tiberius fell ill and feared his death was imminent, Gaius was in his company. The court left Capreae for the mainland but had only reached Misenum when at seventy-eight Tiberius died on 16 March, and Gaius profited from it by being the heir on the spot.

GAIUS CALIGULA
Gaius Julius Caesar Germanicus
(r.AD 18/3/37–24/1/41)

Gaius was born on 31 August AD 12, probably at the Julio-Claudian resort of Antium (Anzio), although both Tibur (Tivoli), east of Rome, and Augusta Treverorum (Trier) are given as alternatives. His father Germanicus was in his first of two consulships so he would have been constantly on the move, which explains the confusion over his son's actual birthplace. As a child on campaign with Germanicus, Gaius was nicknamed Caligula (Bootikin), which is how history knows him, because he wore the miniature uniform of a private soldier, including the CALIGA, or half-boot, of the infantryman. He was the youngest of the six boys born to Augustus's adopted grandson, and Augustus's granddaughter, Agrippina. His childhood was not a happy one, spent amid an atmosphere of paranoia, suspicion and murder.

Instability within the Julio-Claudian house, generated by uncertainty over the succession, led to a series of personal tragedies. He was with his parents when his father died under suspicious circumstances in Syria in AD 19, after which relations between his mother and his granduncle, the emperor Tiberius, deteriorated. After Agrippina returned from Syria, Gaius lived with her in Rome until her arrest by Sejanus. The adolescent Gaius was then sent to live first with his great-grandmother Livia in AD 27 and then, following her death two years later, with his other grandmother Antonia. Shortly before the fall of Sejanus in 31 Gaius was summoned to join Tiberius on Capreae, while his two older brothers, Drusus and Nero, and his mother Agrippina suffered persecution and, eventually, violent deaths. At the time of his accession he had held only two minor offices, that of a PONTIFEX in 31 and an honorary quaestorship in 33, although ensconced on Capreae neither counted since he was unable to undertake any official duties. Shortly before he was promoted to the pontificate, Gaius married Junia Claudilla, daughter of the distinguished senator Marcus Silanus.

Inevitably, there were rumours that Gaius was involved in Tiberius's death – or at least helped him on the way. The newly promoted PRAEFECTUS PRAETORIO Macro, who had replaced Sejanus, was said to have connived, and this may have been true, although the allegations were probably voiced because of Gaius's fortuitous proximity to the emperor's deathbed, and later given strength by his unbalanced behaviour. Certainly, due largely to the efforts of Macro, Gaius's succession went smoothly and the senate voted him the imperial prerogatives on 18 March 37.

Of course, there was the obstacle of Tiberius's will, which named Gemellus as co-heir. Gaius wasted no time in having the will annulled on the grounds of the old emperor's insanity, which was not difficult in the light of the senate's suspicions of the austere and reclusive Tiberius and the popular glee that greeted the news of his death. This left Gemellus in an unenviable position, and his grandfather's bequest was to shorten his life considerably. Gaius entered Rome on 28 March amid scenes of extravagant rejoicing. For the Roman people this seemed like a dream come true. While the senatorial nobility was concerned at his youth and inexperience, having a true Julian as the head of state was more than compensation for the people and the EQUITES.

His first acts as princeps were generous in spirit. He honoured the bequests of Tiberius and those of Livia (which Tiberius had held up), ended the activities of the DELATORES and quashed any impending treason trials. He also paid a donative to the praetorian guard, the first they had received. This may well be viewed as a reward for not standing in his way to the principate; if it was, it was certainly not the last such gift from an emperor. He had the personal papers of Tiberius publicly destroyed, which no doubt implicated many of the Roman elite in the destruction of Gaius's own family, and then he gave Tiberius a splendid funeral. But when this was done, he had the ashes of his mother and brother Nero removed from Pandateria and brought to Rome. The most distinguished EQUITES available carried the urns to Augustus's mausoleum, and Gaius decreed an annual day of remembrance, to be marked by games at which Agrippina's image would be paraded. He honoured his father by renaming the month of September 'Germanicus'. His grandmother Antonia was granted all of the privileges Livia had received during her whole life (an irony, since the two had hated each other; she had once caught him in bed with his sisters). Gaius adopted Tiberius Gemellus and made him PRINCEPS IUVENTUTIS. This was an astute move because it established that he alone and not the will of Tiberius could elevate the youth; and it also implied that he could remove the office if it pleased him. Gaius recalled exiles and reimbursed those who had been wronged by the imperial tax system. Finally, he pulled his forty-seven-year-old uncle Claudius away from his comfortable life as a historian and made him his colleague in the consulship, as well as insisting on his marriage to Valeria Messalina, who was related to Augustus on both sides of her family.

In two policies diametrically opposed to his predecessor's methods, Gaius attempted to boost his popularity. First he lavished CONGIARA on the mob, gifts of money which he could well afford, since Tiberius had left the AERARIUM with plenty of funds. Second he announced his intention to conquer the island of Britannia. This vigorous foreign policy following the caution of Augustus and the sedentary Tiberius proved hugely popular with the Romans and was a precedent that many later emperors were to follow. The average Roman regarded bravery displayed in war as an emperor's most laudable quality. Young, generous and Julian, Gaius basked in the love of his people. Yet within four years he lay dead in a palace corridor, murdered by the very men entrusted to protect him.

The ancient histories are unanimously hostile towards Gaius, perhaps most eloquently summed up by a marvellous line from Suetonius: 'So much for Caligula the Emperor; the rest of this history must needs deal with Caligula the Monster.' This makes it difficult to distinguish between fictional invective, histrionic lampooning and possibly factual writing. It seems that within months of his accession in 37, Gaius fell seriously ill – probably from a nervous breakdown of some kind – and emerged from it a changed man. We are told that he insisted on being treated as a god, that he would stand beside the shrine of Castor and Pollux in the Forum Romanum to be worshipped by all visitors, and established his own shrine nearby. He had a life-sized golden image displayed, dressed in clothes identical with those he happened to be wearing. It was his habit to commit incest

Gemellus, grandson of Tiberius, and his joint-heir with Gaius Caligula, was quickly sidelined by the new emperor and finally executed on trumped-up treason charges in AD 38.

with each of his three sisters in turn, his favourite being Drusilla. When she suddenly died – he may have had a hand in it – Gaius had her deified. He used his two other sisters, Agrippina the Younger and Julia (usually known as Livilla), as prostitutes for his courtiers, and then had the nerve to banish the girls for committing immoral acts – although they were also accused of conspiring against him.

SUETONIUS tells us that Gaius was tall for his build, with a pallid complexion and a badly built, hairy body. His forehead was broad and forbidding and, despite his youth, he was almost bald on top, about which he was so self-conscious that he made it a capital offence for anyone to look down on him from above. With sunken eyes, hollow temples, a thin neck and spindly legs, Suetonius gives a splendidly vituperative portrait, which he may have garnered from contemporary writings, or merely elaborated on the several statues that survived Gaius's downfall. Given the propensity for Graeco-Roman sculpture of the period to favour accuracy (although a degree of sycophancy must have been present, especially with a mercurial personality like Gaius), the statues depict a young man of more general appeal. The best, however, wonderfully suggests the latent teenage bully, coupled with a grim determination. Perhaps Suetonius's description dates from the last year of his reign, when dissolute living and the ravages of Julian-inherited epilepsy that frequently struck him down had taken their toll.

Caligula's sisters Agrippinilla, Drusilla and Julia Livilla were all rumoured to have had incestuous relationships with him.

Too much may have been made of his illness, but by the end of 37 he had come to ignore the senate and its powers, and enjoyed humiliating senators and EQUITES alike. Gaius did away with the advisory senate committee, abrogated to the principate the senate's right to issue coinage, and even made senators prostrate themselves before him as if he were an oriental potentate. It seems as if he was justifying his behaviour by the divine right of his Julian blood, and notions of an oriental-style monarchy may not have been far from his thoughts, since his most intimate advisor was the Jewish prince Herod Agrippa I.

By early 38 there was much uneasiness among the aristocracy at the way Gaius was establishing an absolute monarchy. Men who traditionally had a share in the government could no longer even offer advice and those that presumed to do so were invariably executed on the flimsiest of excuses. This even included Macro, who found himself increasingly divorced from the affections of the princeps he had helped make. Eventually Macro was tricked into giving up his command of the praetorians and forced to take his own life.

Aware of the sentiments being muttered around him, Gaius resurrected the treason laws and used them to hunt down the most aristocratic Claudians, whom he suspected of fomenting rebellion. The obvious focus was Tiberius Gemellus, although a serious plan to elevate him in place of Gaius seems unlikely and it is more probable that Gaius's antics were promoting designs for a republican coup. In one anecdote, suspecting that Gemellus had been taking precautionary emetics against the poison Gaius intended to administer, he scoffed: 'Can there really be an antidote against Caesar?' Evidently not; Gemellus was executed in May 38.

Late in 39, Gaius returned to his military campaign plans and went north to the Rhenus frontier, scene of his father's victories. The excuse that he needed to strengthen the frontier was a plausible one. Uncharacteristically, Tiberius had made poor appointments to the governorships in the region and discipline had suffered. However, the real reason was to deal with a plot against him, instigated by Marcus Aemilius Lepidus (a twice-removed nephew of the triumvir), widower of Drusilla and lover of her sister Agrippina the Younger. Gaius's third sister, Livilla was also implicated. Lepidus had gained the support of the LEGATUS LEGIONIS of Germania Superior, Lentulus Gaetulicus, but in an unusually well timed move, Gaius arrived on the frontier before the two could join up. The appeal of the Julian Gaius worked its magic and the mass of legionaries rallied to him under the command of two praetors, the stern disciplinarian Servius Sulpicius Galba and the inspired thirty-year-old strategist Titus Flavius Vespasianus.

Gaius passed the winter of 39–40 in Gallia while the legions put a stop to tribal forays across the Rhenus, and then began the invasion of Britannia in the spring. The histories paint this campaign as a ludicrous farce. Having gathered his forces on the Gallic coast, Gaius had the legions drawn up in battle array on the beach facing the sea. No one had any idea what his intentions were, when he suddenly ordered the men to gather up shells – the 'plunder from the sea' – in their helmets. The resulting hoard was to be taken back to Rome and presented in his triumph. This absurd incident has taxed modern historians, for it seems unlikely that the hardened soldiers would have accepted such an affront to their dignity, even from the young Julian god. The historian J.P.V.D. Balsdon offered his own theory in 1934 as to what may have happened by positing that the Roman troops – ever fearful of the sea – simply refused to board the waiting galleys. The same thing was to happen to Claudius two years later, but unlike his uncle, Gaius had little time for the troops to recover their nerve because events in

Rome were overtaking him and he had to hurry back. Gaius was able to put a brave face on it, however. Good fortune placed in his hands Adminius, son of a British king, who had been banished by his father and came over to the Romans with a handful of followers. Gaius sent a dispatch to Rome that made it sound as though the entire island of Celts had surrendered to him.

On his return to Rome, he resurrected the DELATORES and treason trials became the order of the day, primarily intended to raise money. Tiberius had left Gaius a fortune, but three and a half years of extravagance had squandered it, and the military campaigns, far from bringing in any new revenue, had bankrupted the emperor's FISCUS. Accordingly he used the treason laws to secure convictions of wealthy senators and EQUITES, and to confiscate their property. Other methods of raising money included imposing swingeing taxes and using praetorian guards as tax-gatherers in place of the appointed officials. The emperor held auctions of theatrical props, for which senators were forced to bid ludicrous prices; he also taxed foodstuffs, porters and prostitutes. A favourite money-raising operation was to honour a wealthy man by appointing him to the college of priests to Gaius's own godhead and then charge him an exorbitant fee. Failure to comply resulted in execution and the confiscation of property. Gaius enjoyed inflicting great physical and mental pain on those he intended to execute, and in this his cruelty knew no bounds. He was particularly fond of inviting parents to witness their sons' executions, and when one father excused himself on grounds of ill-health, kindly provided a litter for him.

There was, however, some merit in Gaius Caligula's government of the provinces. He continued Tiberius's road-building programme in Gallia, Hispania and Dalmatia. But in general he proved to be as erratic abroad as at home. He particularly favoured Herod Agrippa I, granting the Jewish prince the tetrarchies of his uncles, Philip and Herod Antipas, an action that contributed to subsequent rebellions in Judaea. His ignorance – or complete disregard – of Jewish sensibilities stirred up trouble when he ordered that his statue be erected in the Temple at Jerusalem. Only the delaying tactics of the Syrian governor, Publius Petronius, and the tactful intervention of Herod Agrippa prevented riots and a potential uprising in Judaea. In the event Gaius was dead before the order could be carried out, but the damage had been done. Towards Armenia he showed weakness in allowing Parthian influence to spread, while in Africa he quickly stripped the province of its senatorial status –

the only public province that had a legion – which was then assigned to an imperial LEGATUS.

Gaius was now universally hated and no one was safe from his arbitrary actions. Only the praetorians held him in any affection because of the donation at his accession and subsequent extra benefits, and yet it was from this direction that his end was to come. Macro's death had created a vacancy, but Gaius had not appointed a new PRAEFECTUS PRAETORIO, and the acting commander, a veteran named Cassius Chaerea, had good reason to hate his emperor. Chaerea was the victim of Gaius's insults, teases that implied the tough old soldier was effeminate. On requesting the day's password, Gaius used to give him obscene words like 'Cock' or 'Cunt', and forced him to kneel as the emperor waggled his middle finger suggestively for a kiss. Gaius, too, had marginalised the elite of the praetorians by insisting on a personal bodyguard of captured German tribesmen, captained by Thracian officers.

On 24 January 41, just past midday, Gaius left a theatre performance for luncheon. Guided by friends to choose a narrow passage linking the theatre to the palace, the young emperor was separated momentarily from his Germans and Cassius Chaerea struck him down with a sword thrust to the neck, while another guards officer, Gaius Sabinus, stabbed him in the breast. Having ruled for only three years and ten months, at the age of twenty-eight Gaius Caligula died in a pool of his own blood. Frenzied praetorians then seized the empress Milonia Caesonia, whom Gaius had married (his fourth) in 39, killed her and snatched her infant girl child, and swung her by her little ankles to bash her brains out against a column.

There is evidence that the praetorian officers were not alone in the assassination plot; a group of senators, headed by the ex-consul Lucius Annius Vicinianus, was also behind them. The senate he had so humiliated and bullied took revenge by repealing all his acts, although his successor prevented them from damning his memory. The reign of Gaius may represent an endeavour to establish that his autocratic will was now the Roman law, and the more ludicrously insane of his actions – even if exaggerated by later historians – were little more than the petulant whims of a callow youth demonstrating that he could do whatever he liked. The claims that he had intended to make his favourite race horse Incitatus a consul smack more of an irresponsible adolescent prank aimed to prick senatorial pomposity than a really determined intention. But the bridge of ships he had built across the bay at Baiae in 39 was real. Dressed in Alexander the Great's

Herod Agrippa I, favoured by Gaius Caligula with power in Judaea.

breastplate, Gaius rode across the bay like a god, an extravagantly theatrical advertisement of his divine power. What the reign makes most clear is the degree to which the senate had come to depend on the emperor and the level of tyranny that was inherent in the Augustan model of the principate. After Gaius, the Roman State would always be at the mercy of the princeps, and the empire's fortunes would wax and wane as a direct consequence of the qualities of a single man.

CLAUDIUS
Tiberius Claudius Drusus Germanicus /
Tiberius Claudius Caesar Germanicus
(r.26/1/41–13/10/54)

Claudius's birthright reads like that of a crown prince. On his father Drusus's side he was the grandson of the Augusta Livia; his mother Antonia was the daughter of Marcus Antonius; his grandfather by marriage the emperor Augustus; his uncle the emperor Tiberius; and his older brother Germanicus was marked out for the succession. But Claudius was unfortunate in health. He was born on 1 August 10 BC at Lugdunum (Lyons). A serious illness in childhood accompanied by a period of paralysis left him with an unattractive appearance. He is said to have drooled, walked with a limp, had a runny nose, stammered and habitually trembled. Physical disabilities such as these were more than sufficient to make his handsome family think him mentally defective, and his embarrassed parents did everything to keep him out of the public eye. However, this seclusion afforded Claudius a rare luxury for one of his family: ample opportunity to study. He became an accomplished historian, producing books on Etruscan, Augustan and Carthaginian history. None has survived.

Antonia was ashamed to be seen with him, often calling him a monster and accusing others of stupidity by exclaiming: 'He is a bigger fool than even my son Claudius!' Livia treated him with scorn and Augustus worried constantly whether he would reflect badly on the imperial family. In a memorandum to Livia (which he intended she should pass on to Antonia) regarding the upcoming festival of Mars Ultor, he wrote: *'We both agreed that an immediate decision ought to be taken. The question is whether he has – shall I say it? – full command of his five senses. If so, I can see nothing against sending him through the same degrees of office as his brother [Germanicus]; but should he prove physically and mentally deficient, the public must not be given a chance to laugh at him and us.'*

Right: An unflattering likeness of Claudius, based on the fragment of a statue found in England, and now at the British Museum in London.

Due to these concerns Claudius remained under the same kind of guardianship as would a Roman daughter, even after he had reached his majority. There is evidence, however, that Augustus suspected there might be more to his 'idiot' grandson than met the eye. Again to Livia: *'I'll be damned if your grandson Tiberius Claudius hasn't given me a very pleasant surprise! How on earth anyone who talks so confusedly can nevertheless speak so well in public – with such clearness, saying all that needs to be said – I simply do not understand.'*

But Augustus, ever cautious of his image, nevertheless kept Claudius away from the important offices young males of his family usually enjoyed, so he spent his childhood and youth in almost complete isolation. When he assumed the TOGA VIRILIS, for instance, he was carried to the Capitol in a litter at night, instead of being led into the Forum Romanum by his father. Despite these impediments, it seems he was respected by those who knew him best both for his mind and a certain spirit of nobility. And he did fill some minor offices. Under Augustus he was made an augur and presided at several games. Under Tiberius he obtained the insignia of a consular (although when he pressed for the duties as well as the empty title, Tiberius replied that the forty gold AUREII he had sent were meant to be squandered on toys). His nephew Gaius made him his colleague in a two-month consulship, the senate had honoured him more than once, and he was fairly prominent in the ORDO EQUESTER.

Claudius had inherited some Julian blood from his grandmother Octavia, but he may well have escaped execution throughout the dynastic struggles because he was far more of a Claudian. Since only the Julian house could count on the support of provincial armies, his chances of becoming emperor had always seemed slight, and his threat negligible. Was he involved in the plot to kill Gaius? There is no evidence to prove or disprove his complicity, and it may merely be happenstance that he was in the same theatre as Gaius on that fateful day in January 41 and that he left only moments before the doomed emperor. To have been a partner in the conspiracy seems too bold a move for reclusive Claudius. And in the events that followed, he comes across as a passive participant.

In the aftermath of the assassination – the first open murder of a Roman emperor – there was widespread panic and confusion. The emperor's German bodyguard, fiercely loyal to the princeps, went on a killing spree. Fortunately, Claudius was discovered cowering behind a curtain in the palace by a praetorian guard. His colleagues (perhaps even those who had just murdered Caesonia and her daughter) gathered up the hapless Claudius and carried him off to the safety of the CASTRA PRAETORIA, where he was shortly proclaimed emperor. A republican at heart, Claudius was said to prefer this version of events because it made his accession an accident of fate, absolving him from accusations that he wanted to perpetuate the principate. Another version paints the praetorians in a more decisive role. Fearing that their beneficial terms of military service were in jeopardy because of a republican coup, they seized on forty-eight-year-old Claudius as the only surviving mature member of the Julio-Claudian house and sent out troops to find him. Either way, Claudius is portrayed as the reluctant partner in the whole process.

Meanwhile, the news of Gaius's death prompted a senatorial discussion about restoring the Republic and dispensing with the principate altogether. The heated debate was halted when the senators heard that the praetorians had made the decision for them. The senate was again obliged to recognise the impotence it had faced when dealing with the military dynasts of the late Republic, and the meeting dissolved with the empire's fate undecided.

At a later meeting in the Temple of Jupiter Victor senatorial numbers were depleted, since many had fled the city to their country estates. The senate had three or four COHORTES URBANAE under the command of the PRAEFECTUS URBI, numbering perhaps three thousand men. With these and some armed freedmen they occupied the Forum Romanum and Palatine, thus acknowledging that supreme power in post-Augustan Rome could be achieved only by military force. But the COHORTES URBANAE deserted to the praetorians, with whom they shared the CASTRA PRAETORIA. The outcome was inevitable, and on 25 January 41 a group of senior senators went to the camp to pay their respects to Claudius and formally invest him with all the powers of the princeps.

The basic fact of the principate – implicit in the Augustan settlement but always carefully disguised – was now made plain: the emperor's position ultimately rested on the sword and not on the consensus of the senate and people. As the remainder of this history will show, the sword was often double-edged. Forever afterwards, emperors ruled under the sufferance of the troops they commanded, and a loss of army loyalty necessarily entailed a forfeit of power, usually accompanied by the loss of the incumbent's life.

Passive and reluctant he may have been, but Claudius wasted no time in establishing his rule. The immediate concern was to identify himself with the Julii, and so he assumed the name of Caesar, a popular choice with the army, Roman mob and provincials but hated by the senatorial nobility. Since he had no legal right to claim it, the adoption of 'Caesar' marks the first step in the word's transmutation from a COGNOMEN to a title meaning ruler. He made the association stronger by having Gaius's murderers executed, but acted with generosity towards those senators implicated in the plot. The treason trials were stopped, and exiles, including Gaius's two sisters Agrippina and Livilla, were recalled. The absurd taxes introduced by Gaius to refurbish the FISCUS were abolished, and to further please the people vast spectacles were provided in the Circus Maximus. There were, however, at least six plots against his principate, and we are told that Claudius executed thirty-five senators and between two to three hundred EQUITES in the process of suppressing them. He probably survived these through a wise policy of courting the praetorian guard. In addition to the large donative on his accession, perhaps as much as twenty thousand sesterces to each soldier, he continued the annual top-up established by Gaius and expanded the number of cohorts from nine to twelve. Nor were the legions ignored. The soldiers were given more opportunities for booty, and awards were showered lavishly on many units.

In all, thanks to Claudius's decisive and coherent policy, which must have surprised his detractors, and a lack of cohesion among the senators, the brief

Claudius and his fourth wife Agrippina, sister of Gaius Caligula and mother of Nero by an earlier marriage.

chance of a restoration passed. And it speaks eloquently of how far seven decades of the Augustan principate had removed Rome from the possibility of a return to the so-called free Republic.

Britannia conquered

Claudius followed his nephew's example and wasted no time in pursuing a bold foreign policy to further popularise his new reign by announcing his intention to annex Britannia. While the campaign was being organised, Claudius ordered the suppression of a new revolt in Mauretania. Under the command of the LEGATI Suetonius Paulinus and Hosidius Geta, this was accomplished and Mauretania divided into two procuratorial provinces, Caesariensis and Tingitana.

A full-scale invasion of Britannia was presented as the completion of Julius Caesar's unfinished business (and probably a snub to his nephew's failure), and that it would give Rome unfettered access to important slave, hides and metal markets. In fact, these benefits were greatly exaggerated. The island was not an unknown quantity. Roman-style coinage was already in widespread use by the Belgic and Celtic tribes and trade between Britannia and Gallia well established. A generation earlier in his *Geographical Sketches*,

A mounted warrior of the Atrebates, armed with shield and spear decorates a coin minted by Roman client king Verica, whose ousting from Britannia offered Claudius a political excuse for an invasion.

Strabo had written: *'Though Rome could have taken Britannia she declined to do so. In the first place the Britons are no threat, having insufficient strength to cross over and attack us. In the second, there would be little to gain. It seems that we presently get more out of them in duty on their exports than we would by direct taxation, especially if the costs of an occupation army and of tax collecting be discounted.'*

Glossing over this, Claudius found a political excuse for action in 42. The Roman client king Verica was defeated by Caratacus and Togodumnus, sons of the British ruler Cynobelinus, and fled to Rome from his kingdom in what is now West Sussex. This left the whole of southeast Britannia under Cynobelinus's control, a theoretical challenge to the empire. Managing the northwestern colonies required a divide-and-rule strategy that insured the incessantly quarrelling barbarian tribes never became strong enough to make common cause and engage imperial forces. If Cynobelinus allied with the Gauls, argued Claudius's advisers, it would be a recipe for rebellion.

In 42, preparations for the invasion were complete, but delays occasioned by the troops' reluctance to embark – a replay of the same problem faced by Gaius two years earlier – meant that the actual crossing took place in the spring of 43. Under the command of Aulus Plautius Silvanus three legions of experienced Rhenus troops – *II Augusta, XIV Gemina* and *XX Valeria Victrix* – joined *IX Hispania*, which had been transported from Pannonia. The gap this created along the Rhenus was filled by raising two new legions: *XV Primigenia* and *XXII Primigenia*. With auxiliaries and units from other legions, the task force numbered some fifty thousand men.

The landing took place at Rutupiae (Richborough in Kent). From there the four legions fought their way north, halting at the Tamesis (Thames) to await the carefully stage-managed arrival of the emperor. It was eight weeks before the imperial bandwagon, complete with war elephants, caught up with them, by which time all immediate resistance had been crushed. Claudius continued unchallenged to Camulodunum (Colchester), Cynobelinus's capital, where he held a victory parade. Sixteen days later he left the new province in the hands of Plautius and returned to Rome.

Claudius celebrated his triumph in 44, his military credentials firmly established. He was keen to stress that his principate was one of military achievements. In addition to the annexations of Mauretania and Britannia, he extended Roman influence in the state of Palmyra, situated between Syria and the Euphrates,

The Claudian conquest of Britannia, AD 43–54

OCEANUS GERMANICUS (North Sea)

Deva (Chester)
Lindum (Lincoln)
Littlechester
Branodunum (Brancaster)
Viroconium (Wroxeter)
Bravonium (Leintwardine)
Ratae (Leicester)
Wales
BRITANNIA
Glevum (Gloucester)
Corinium (Cirencester)
Camulodunum (Colchester)
Londinium (London)
Aquae Sulis (Bath)
Caleva Atrebates (Silchester)
Durbrivae (Rochester)
Rutupiae (Richborough)
Dubris (Dover)
Lemanis (Lympne)
Isca Dumnoniorum (Exeter)
Dumnovaria (Dorchester)
Noviomagus (Chichester)
Gesoriacum (Boulogne)
Mare Britannicum (English Channel)
BELGICA
Samarobriva Ambionorum (Amiens)

Roman territory in Britannia by death of Claudius, AD 54
● major Roman fort established during conquest
● other Roman or tribal center

Rotomagus (Rouen)
Sequana (Seine)
Lutetia Parisiorum (Paris)
GALLIA LUGDUNENSIS

0   50   100   150 miles
0   50   100   150   200   250 kilometres

WHEN THE CONQUEST resumed in the spring of 44, it was the young LEGATUS Vespasianus (Vespasian), who had supported Gaius in 39, who claimed the glory, of which more in chapter 3. The rebel leader Caratacus was captured by Britain's second governor Scapula in 51, but it would be another century before the north and west of Britannia were fully brought under military domination, and Caledonia (Scotland) would remain largely free of Roman control. The bloodiest revolt was led by Boudicca (or Boadicea), Queen of the Iceni – 'tall, terrifying, with flashing eyes, menacing voice and a wild mass of yellowish hair falling to her waist', according to the historian Cassius Dio – who burned, hanged, crucified and slaughtered seventy thousand people in the romanised southeast. However, by Claudius's death in 54, the Romans controlled almost all of Britannia south of a line drawn from east to west through Lindum (Lincoln), excluding Wales.

Boudicca was eventually defeated by Suetonius Paulinus, governor from 58 to 61, and hers was the last great British challenge to Rome's superiority. Ultimately, the legions would be forced out not by rebellion, but through the inexorable structural decay of an embattled empire.

annexed Lycia in 43 and the allied client kingdoms of Judaea in 44, Thracia in 46, and Ituraea (an area between the north of Judaea and the plains of Damascus) in 49, which was incorporated into Syria.

In the case of Judaea, the actions of Herod Agrippa I led to the kingdom's incorporation. The client prince had grown up at Rome as a pampered princely hostage of Augustus and had been awarded tetrarchic lands in Galilee by Gaius Caligula. There is some indication that he was beneficial to Claudius during the days after Gaius's murder and he was rewarded by the additional grant of Judaea and Samaria. He fell from grace, however, when he suspiciously extended Jerusalem's walls and invited other oriental kings to a conference at Tiberias. When he died suddenly in 44, his former kingdom came under direct Roman rule. Claudius was not entirely opposed to the Augustan concept of client kingdoms, however, establishing some on the borders of the new British province and giving Comagene to Antiochus IV. But the relationship of these kings to the emperor was made clear by their official titles of LEGATUS (or PROCURATOR) AUGUSTI.

Claudius also continued the policies of Julius Caesar and Augustus of founding COLONIAE (colonies) to extend the romanisation process in the imperial provinces, which were lagging behind the senatorial ones. COLONIAE were established in Mauretania, along the Danuvius, and in the west, the most famous being Augusta Treverorum (Trier) and Colonia Agrippina† (Cologne) in Germania. Tiberius's road-building programme was also continued and extended all over the empire. Claudius encouraged further romanisation by beginning a process that would become a contentious feature of later principates, that of granting Latin rights to tribal groupings that were deemed ready for the benefits and the tax obligations.

One act that was to have far-reaching consequences was his ruling that wealthy Gallic noblemen were eligible for senate membership as long as they were Roman citizens. There was no immediate flood of tribal chieftains to Rome, however, since the mass granting of citizenship rights and extending the senate to non-Italians was deeply unpopular with the Roman senatorial nobility, and a deal of passive resistance towards the ruling was evident. But it is hard to put the genie back in the bottle, and it must have been self-evident that this generous extension to the tribal nobility of Gallia would soon apply to the local aristocracy of other regions of the empire.

The administration of Claudius

In Italia, Claudius was responsible for several major construction programmes, the most significant of which included a new harbour (Portus) to replace nearby Ostia, which had become too silted for use, and two new aqueducts for Rome, the Aqua Claudia and Aqua Anio Novus. It was also during his reign that new roads were built, the Via Claudia Valeria to the Adriaticum coast, and roads over the western and Julian (eastern) Alps. The biggest undertaking was the draining of Lacus Fucinus (Fucine Lake). Historical sources are at pains to highlight the almost catastrophic outcome of this brave but doomed project, but its scale cannot be denied. Intended to provide much needed farming land, thirty thousand men were employed in the work for eleven years. Suetonius's assessment that 'his public works were grandiose and necessary rather than numerous' is appropriate.

Claudius always emphasised his resemblance in efficiency and administration to Julius Caesar and Augustus. Unlike his immediate predecessor, he made

King Antiochus IV of the Seleucid dynasty, who in AD 44 Claudius gave Comagene to rule as LEGATUS AUGUSTI.

† The spelling used here is a shortened form of either Colonia Agrippinensis or more fully Colonia Claudia Ara Agrippinensium.

haste slowly, preferring evolution instead of revolution, which went a way to placating the senatorial class. His relations with the senate were generally cordial – at least on his side – and he treated its members with courtesy, and avoided parading his pre-eminence overtly. He only held the consulship four times during his reign (42, 43, 47, and 51), and did not demand divine honours, although he did not refuse permission for provincials, especially in Britannia, to worship him on the pragmatic grounds that they would anyway. Claudius strengthened the powers of the princeps in a low-key way in which he could point to both ancient and recent precedents to justify his actions. Because of his absences from Rome, Tiberius had been obliged to appoint various secretaries to look after administrative business, such as reading petitions and supervising inheritance tax. The annual appointment of magistrates under the Republic was a system of government for a simpler time; it could not supply a stream of trained and experienced men to administer the numerous adjuncts of business created by the expanding state. Claudius began to recruit a new civil service to help in his labours, a reform that inevitably centralised more power in the hands of the principate.

The most noticeable changes came in the area of public finance, which had hitherto been split between various financial bureaux. These were now united under one central FISCUS, or imperial treasury; even the AERARIUM SATURNII (public treasury) was brought under the emperor's domain in 44, by its removal from the control of senatorial propraetors and its restoration to equestrian quaestors. While this had ancient precedent, what was new was that the quaestors were the princeps' nominations and served for three years instead of the traditional one. Almost all forms of taxation were transferred to the FISCUS, and offices of state were created to organise every aspect of imperial policy, from the emperor's personal correspondence to the management of the State Library.

The recruits to the Imperial Civil Service came from the ranks of the EQUITES, but imperial freedmen held the most important posts. The histories are united in portraying Claudius as a dupe to his ex-slave secretaries (as well as to his wives). It is possible that Claudius's reliance on his freedmen may have stemmed from his suspicion that the aristocracy was untrustworthy. But it is more likely that he appreciated the native intelligence and experience of the

slaves with which he had earlier surrounded himself, and rated their abilities more highly than those of any aristocrat. For whatever reasons, there is no doubt that Claudius's reign is the first era of the great imperial freedman. This type of secretariat had existed before Claudius, but centralisation meant that freedmen now wielded more power than they would have done under Augustus or Tiberius. His closest advisors were Greeks: Pallas, financial secretary; Narcissus, secretary-general; Callistus, legal secretary (who had gained prominence under Gaius); and Polybius, the privy seal. On occasion, these men even sat in the senate to represent the emperor's interests. In this, we might see a further humbling of the senate, but Claudius's main concern appears to have been efficiency in government, and that is evident in all his widespread legislation, which he preferred to enact as SENATUS CONSULTA rather than by imperial fiat. The senate was again allowed its ancient right of issuing copper coinage and recovered the right to conduct the elections that Gaius had given to the people (which had replaced the defunct elections of the ancient COMITIAE years before).

The wives of Claudius

While Claudius the princeps was a considerable success, his domestic life was something of a shambles. One bride-to-be, Livia Medullina, died on her wedding day. Claudius then divorced his first two wives, Plautia Urgulanilla and Aelia Paetina (the sister of Sejanus, who bore him a daughter, *see the side panel*), had the third, Valeria Messalina, executed after she cuckolded him, and was poisoned by the fourth, his niece Agrippina the Younger. Messalina bore Claudius two children, a daughter, Octavia, in 39 and a son, Tiberius Claudius Caesar Germanicus, in 41, who was recognominated Britannicus in commemoration of his father's conquest of Britannia. The marriage, which had been arranged by Gaius Caligula for purely mischevious motives, was otherwise not a success.

Claudius already knew of Messalina's lax sexual reputation when he married her in 38, so it is unlikely that he was duped into the role of blissful cuckold that Suetonius and Tacitus suggest. The union was politically useful because she was of Julian stock and he no doubt tolerated her misplaced passions for that reason. What he was unable to overlook, however, was Messalina's proclivity for palace intrigue. While Claudius was visiting Ostia in 48, Messalina held a palace party in the course of which a form of marriage ceremony was performed (or play-acted) between herself and the consul-elect, Gaius Silius. Reminded of

THE SECOND wife of Claudius, Aelia Paetina, bore him a daughter, named Antonia after her grandmother. Her first husband, Cn. Pompeius, was executed by Claudius and her second, Faustus Cornelius Sulla, by Nero. The elder Pliny implicated Antonia in the Piso plot against Nero (*see page* 54), but since she was never punished this seems a fabrication. However, Nero later had her killed as a revolutionary – the daughter of Claudius would always pose a threat to childless Nero.

the similar conspiracy of Marcus Aemilius Lepidus and Agrippina the Younger in Gaius's reign, Claudius ordered their immediate executions, along with others implicated in the plot, including the PRAEFECTUS VIGILUM.

There is no clear record of Claudius's desire (or lack of it) to remarry, since at the age of fifty-seven he might be thought to have been content to remain single and name Britannicus as his heir. However, he was probably mindful of the need for someone with more Julian blood to succeed him. In any event, Messalina's death initiated a scramble among the freedmen, each wishing to place his preferred candidate at Claudius's side as the new empress. His intimate friend Lucius Vitellius argued for Agrippina the Younger, forcefully backed by his financial secretary – Pallas had good reason to support Agrippina for she was his mistress, and the union was unlikely to spoil their relationship, while at same time it would strengthen his position in the hierarchy. For Claudius, the infatuation for Agrippina suggested by the ancient histories seems improbable. As the daughter of Germanicus she was his niece, as sister to Gaius he was well aware of her reputation as one of her brother's court prostitutes and of her affair with Lepidus that had resulted in her banishment. Agrippina had been married to Gnaeus Domitius Ahenobarbus, scion of a powerful but dissolute Roman family, some thirty years her senior. By this marriage she had an eleven-year-old son, Lucius Domitius Ahenobarbus. Pallas waved aside the fact that under Roman law such a marriage would be incestuous – he got the appropriate statutes changed – and Claudius saw the sense in a union that brought to him a direct descendant of Augustus with strong Julian connections. However, Agrippina's ambitions for her son proved to be the undoing of Claudius.

Agrippina's powerful personality dominated Claudius's last years. She was the daughter, after all, of Germanicus's wife Agrippina the Elder, who had caused Tiberius so many headaches, and she had inherited her mother's volubly imperious temperament. In addition, she had survived the vicissitudes of her brother's arbitrary reign and probably felt that dealing with the ageing Claudius would be simple by comparison. The aim, of course, was to see her son on the throne in place of the younger Britannicus, but more than that to rule the empire through him. She began her campaign of personal advancement immediately after the marriage in 48 and, with the active help of Pallas, soon became influential enough that her image began to appear on official inscriptions and coins. In 50 the senate voted her the title Augusta, the second

prominent imperial woman so honoured since Livia; and Livia had only earned it after Augustus's death. Official documents prove that Agrippina even greeted foreign embassies to Rome from her own tribunal, and also wore a gold-embroidered military cloak at such functions. The extent of her influence can be seen in the naming of the new town in Germania Inferior that bore her name, Colonia Agrippina.

Shortly after her marriage to Claudius, Agrippina's son Lucius was betrothed to the emperor's daughter Octavia, and in 50 Claudius adopted the youth with priority over his own son Britannicus, who was five years the junior. There is every indication that Claudius loved his natural son, but the fact was that Lucius had more Julian blood in his veins. Lucius now took the Claudian names of Nero Claudius Caesar Drusus Germanicus as his own. In 51, when he was only fourteen, he assumed the TOGA VIRILIS, was named consul elect for the year 58, and was given the title of PRINCEPS IUVENTUTIS. In 52 he became PRAE-FECTUS URBI, made his first senate appearance in 53, and married Claudius's daughter Octavia later in the same year. Claudius also took the precaution – as Tiberius had done – of appointing a loyal man, Sextus Afranius Burrus, as PRAEFECTUS PRAETORIO to safeguard Nero's succession when the time came.

At this point Claudius was sixty-three, but seems to have been fit and well for a man whose mother – had she been a real ancient Roman matron – might have had him put down after his childhood sickness. For Agrippina this posed a problem. Were he to live for another ten years or so there would be sufficient time for Britannicus to grow up and Claudius to alter the priority of the succession. And this was not an empty threat, since the secretary-general Narcissus, in opposition to Pallas, was urging Claudius to designate Britannicus as his heir. But there was another possible motive for hurrying her husband to his grave. Nero at sixteen was beginning to show signs of intractability and if she had to wait much longer for him to become emperor he would no longer need nor heed his mother's advice and Agrippina would lose her hold over him.

On 13 October 54, a month into his sixty-fifth

Claudius's last two wives: Messalina (top), who was executed in 48 for plotting against him, and Agrippina, who would be suspected of murdering him to make way for her 16-year-old son Nero.

The growth of the empire during the reign of Claudius

Roman empire before Claudius
province annexed to empire by Claudius, with date
client kingdom before Claudius
client kingdom added by Claudius

1 ALPES POENINAE
2 ALPES COTTIAE
3 ALPES MARITIMAE

year, Claudius died of poisoning. Some said his personal taster, the eunuch Halotus, administered the fatal dose, but most fingers pointed in Agrippina's direction. According to the senator and author Gaius Plinius Secundus (Pliny the Elder), she supposedly paid a notorious poisoner called Locusta to doctor a dish of mushrooms, but Pliny loathed the Augusta, so his accusations are suspect. In his translation of Suetonius's *The Twelve Caesars* Robert Graves mentions a treatise by Gordon Wasson which claimed to prove conclusively that Claudius died from eating an edible *boletus* cooked in a sauce of a similar poison-

ous variety. Apparently he then vomited this up and was poisoned a second time with the juice of a *colocynth* (wild Palestinian gourd) administered both orally and as an enema. And then, just to make sure, he was smothered.

Claudius turned out to be the most enigmatic of

the Julio-Claudian emperors. His reign was graced by stability and good government at home and in the provinces, and the successful management of client kingdoms. He was careful, intelligent, aware and respectful of tradition, but given to bouts of rage and cruelty. He was willing to sacrifice precedent to expediency, while using precedent to justify his actions. And, despite an apparently amiable disposition, he was utterly ruthless in his treatment of those who crossed him. Augustus's suspicion that there was more to his 'idiot' step-grandson than met the eye was more than fully borne out by the events of his unexpected reign. In almost universal gratitude – there were some detractors, notably Nero's tutor Seneca – he was accorded divine honours after his death, the first since Augustus to be so distinguished.

NERO

Lucius Domitius Ahenobarbus / Nero Claudius Caesar Drusus Germanicus (r.13/10/54–9/6/68)

More than any imperial reign, Nero's provides the most fertile ground for dramatisation. Characterised by extravagance, despotism, promiscuity and madness, it ended the Julio-Claudian dynasty and plunged the Roman world into another civil war. In the areas of government and the economy little of merit was achieved and much damage done: insurrection in the provinces, rampant inflation, devaluation, the mass murder of Christians, to mention a few evils of the reign. Appropriately, history has left us with the image of the insane emperor, playing his harp while watching Rome burn.

Many of Nero's vices were probably inherited, although as a self-acclaimed artist-performer, he was more than capable of presenting them on a broad stage. In Rome's early history there were two branches of the GENS Domitii: the Calvini and the Ahenobarbi, the latter named by the founder, Lucius Domitius. Tradition has it that he was the first to know that the Romans had won the important battle of Lacus Regillus (498 BC), when two gods told him. To prove that they were gods, they stroked his black beard and turned it to the colour of bronze, after which the family always used the COGNOMEN Ahenobarbus (red- or bronze-bearded). The family was peculiar in only having two PRAENOMINA, sometimes repeating and sometimes alternating between Lucius and Gnaeus. Down the centuries the Ahenobarbi earned a reputation for rudeness, bad temper, casual cruelty and dissolute behaviour. The best of the bunch was Nero's great-grandfather – a Lucius – who commanded with great bravery the conspirators' fleet in opposition to Julius Caesar. His grandfather – another Lucius – was Augustus's chief executor, and noted for his extravagance and arrogant rudeness. His father Gnaeus, a cheat, liar and violent man, was simply regarded as despicable.

The future emperor was born at Antium (Anzio) on 15 December AD 37. Acknowledging

The face of Nero, last of the Julio-Claudian emperors: shaped by vice, despotism, extravagance and eccentricity.

Young Nero and his mother Agrippina, an eminence grise intent on eliminating any family rivals to his power.

Below: The boy Britannicus, Nero's brother-in-law, who was too young to pose any threat but succumbed to poisoning in one of many palace intrigues. The coin portrays him looking older than his 14 years.

the predicted nature of his newborn son, Gnaeus told a companion that any child born to him and Agrippina the Younger was bound to have a detestable nature and become a danger to the public. Lucius grew up in poor circumstances after losing his father at the age of three and seeing his mother banished by Gaius Caligula, who then seized the child's estate left him by his father. His aunt Domitia Lepida raised him and, according to Suetonius, she chose a dancer and a barber to be his tutors, which goes some way to explaining his obsession with performing music and dance, not to say with his appearance. In his adolescent years this unsuitable education was somewhat rectified when Claudius rescinded Agrippina's exile. On her return she appointed the stoic philosopher Lucius Annaeus Seneca to be his tutor. With the accession of Claudius, Lucius had his fortune restored to him, and with his mother's marriage to the emperor, he became Nero and the heir-apparent.

Over eighty years of the principate had accustomed the Roman State to an imperial succession, and Nero's went smoothly, thanks to Sextus Afranius Burrus, the PRAEFECTUS PRAETORIO, who ensured the acclamation of the praetorian guards, and a compliant senate voted the sixteen-year-old the imperial powers. The provincial armies were not expected to contest the accession of a great-great-grandson of Augustus, and none did. The praetorians were duly thanked for their loyalty with a donative no less than that of Claudius. Nero then spoke to the senate, promising to restore the Augustan principle of the division of powers between princeps and senate. Seneca, of course, wrote the speech for him.

For a while, these promises seemed to be observed, but largely because the youthful Nero was content to leave the boring matters of state to someone else, principally Seneca and Burrus. At the same time, Nero's mother Agrippina was busy eliminating any possible family rivals, including his aunt Domitia Lepida and the great-grandson of Augustus, Marcus Junius Silanus, who was proconsular governor of Asia. For his support of Britannicus, the

freedman Narcissus was driven to suicide rather than face inevitable execution. However, Tacitus observed that Nero was saddened by this because 'the greed of Narcissus and his extravagance harmonised admirably with his own still latent vices'. Britannicus was still too young to be considered an immediate threat and was spared; besides, he was the emperor's brother-in-law, which afforded him some comfort… temporarily.

Nero demonstrated all the usual indulgences of a privileged young aristocrat, who, after a deprived childhood, has suddenly come into a fortune. Besides his passion for all things aesthetic, he enjoyed the pleasures of alcohol and promiscuous sex. His close companions Annaeus Serenus, the PRAEFECTUS VIG-ILUM, and a young noble called Marcus Salvius Otho, joined him on nightly hunts through the streets of Rome in search of unwary young women. Once cornered, the maiden dared not refuse the advances of her emperor, even though – barely disguised – the pretense that it was not he was maintained.

His marriage to Claudius's daughter Octavia did not prevent him from having a freedwoman called Acte as his mistress. It would appear that Seneca, no longer able to exercise his duties as a tutor as he had when his charge was younger, found Nero's nocturnal frolics useful in keeping him out of the business of running the empire. Both Seneca and Burrus had supported Agrippina while Claudius was alive, but now they were less certain of her temper. Agrippina's ambition to be the sole regent was getting in their way, and having coinage struck showing her on the obverse in partnership with her son was going too far.

Degeneration of Nero's court

Nero was also tiring of his mother's presumption of power, for her portrait was banished to the reverse of later coins and then vanished altogether. This was the result of Burrus and Seneca working on Nero's morbid fear of rivals and their suggestion that, as master of the world, he had no need to share power with anyone. Agrippina's habit of sitting beside Nero to handle meetings with ambassadors on his behalf was curtailed, and her supporter Pallas was removed from office. As her power waned, Agrippina played her trump card and switched her allegiance to her stepson Britannicus. But it was a poor hand, and in 55 Britannicus died of poisoning – probably administered by the very Locusta that Agrippina had employed to get rid of Claudius. Agrippina was accused of treason but brazened it out, although Nero made his mother remove herself from Rome, leaving the government effectively in the hands

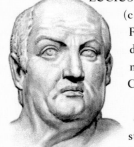

LUCIUS ANNAEUS SENECA (c.3 BC–AD 65) was a Roman philosopher, dramatist, and states- man. He was born in Corduba in Baetica but went to Rome as a child, where he later studied rhetoric and philosophy, earning renown as an orator when still a youth. Claudius exiled him in 41 because of his intimacy with Julia, the emperor's niece. Eight years later he returned under the patronage of Agrippina the Younger to become tutor to the young Nero. As a stoic, Seneca's writings take a high moral tone that contrast starkly with his own life, in which greed, expediency, and even connivance at murder figured. His best known works are his tragedies, which had a significant influence on Renaissance drama, although his later life proved fact more profound than fiction. After amassing a huge for- tune as Nero's co-regent, he was eventually deposed, accused of conspiracy and instructed to commit suicide. He carried out the order in true virtuous Roman tradition, by opening the veins in his wrist and dying slowly in his bath.

of Seneca and Burrus. For a period of five years after Agrippina's banishment, the empire's affairs went well and it was a time of general happiness and prosperity.

Little reference is made in the contemporary histo- ries to Nero's government of the provinces, and it is like- ly that he had no interest in them. The only item of note is that the Ligurian client kingdom of Alpes Cottiae was fully absorbed into the empire on the death of its ruler Cottius, probably in 58. That life in Rome was sweet was entirely due to the abilities of Seneca and Burrus, and the fact that Nero – so long as his regents assured him everything that was done extended from his divine beneficence – was happy playing the lyre and chasing young men and women around Rome with the worst of intentions. But baleful influences were at work in the form of Poppaea Sabina and Gaius Ofonius Tigellinus (he had been exiled in 39 by Gaius Caligula for adultery with Agrippina, but who returned to find preferment with Nero). The beautiful Poppaea Sabina's influence was the first to be felt. She was the wife of Nero's noc- turnal companion Otho (although the histories disagree

as to whether she was his wife or his mistress), but he had been conveniently sent to govern Lusitania†, and with him out of the way she became Nero's lover in 58.

Poppaea Sabina's first act was to persuade Nero to get rid of his mother, in whom she rightly perceived a dangerous rival. Seneca and Burrus had been busy hinting at the same end for some time, and Nero had developed a virulent hatred of Agrippina. After a foiled attempt to drown her – rather absurdly by making her sail on a ship designed to fall apart in the sea (a good swimmer, she was rescued by a fishing vessel) – the PRAEFECTUS of the Misenum fleet had her assassinat- ed. Seneca persuaded the senate that Agrippina had been plotting against her son's life. It is unlikely that anyone believed this fiction, but neither was anyone inclined to argue the point.

Having got away with matricide it seemed as though Nero could do anything, and shook off all restraints. These soon included Seneca and Burrus, with whose condescension and advice he had grown impatient. No doubt at Poppaea's urging he forced Seneca into retirement on the occasion of Burrus's death in 61. The young emperor, now twenty-four, had tired of his marriage to Octavia. He divorced her on the grounds that she was barren, which may have been true, and adulterous, which was unlikely, then exiled her. Octavia was executed shortly after and Nero married Poppaea. He then appointed his counsellor of the past months, Tigellinus, to the joint com- mand of the praetorians (with a cer- tain Faenius Rufus) from which position he exerted a further degenerat- ing influence on Nero.

Licentiousness, unbridled extravagance, and bisexual sensuality now became court features. Suetonius paints a lurid picture in which the emperor, not content with girls, seduced free-born boys and raped a Vestal Virgin. He tied men and women to stakes and attacked their genitals while dressed as a wild beast, and went through a sham wedding with a boy named Sporus, who was castrat- ed to make him into a 'girl' for the event.

Octavia (top), Claudius's daughter and Nero's first wife, was divorced by him and executed when he fell for devious Poppaea Sabina (bottom), wife of his friend Otho.

† Otho was only a quaestor, a rank below praetor or consul, the minimum requirement to be a provincial governor, which supports the claim that Nero conspired to get his former friend well away from Rome in order to pursue Poppaea.

For once, the ancient histories are probably right, if not in detail almost certainly in general. However, brutal gladiatorial sport – as often portrayed in Hollywood films – did not much feature because Nero was more interested in the games and athletics of the ancient Greeks. A lavish building programme began with the construction of Greek-style GYMNASIA on the Campus Martius and in the Vatican Valley. This un-Roman predilection for watching athletic sport was accompanied by a growing zeal for the performing arts. Actors of the age were considered lowly, vulgar types, but Nero seized any opportunity to perform in the theatre, prohibiting anyone to leave, or snooze, while he was playing or orating on the stage.

Towards civil war

Historically, the most famous event of Nero's reign is the great fire of Rome. The conflagration erupted on the night of 13 July 64, and over the period of almost a week it wiped out three of the fourteen regions and badly damaged a further seven. The legend that Nero 'fiddled' while Rome burned stems from a contemporary report that, after returning from Antium where he had been when the fire started, he watched the flames from the Tower of Maecenas and sang a composition of his own about the Sack of Troy. There was widespread belief that the emperor started the fire in order to clear space for a grandiose new palace. While this is understandable, because he did immediately begin construction of the Domus Aurea (Golden House), Rome's largest palace complex ever, it is contradicted by Nero's actions. The emperor dashed back to Rome, and was evident in his encouragement of the VIGILES. And new regulations that insisted on wide balconies to allow fire fighters access to large buildings date from Nero's time. However, the persistent rumours of arson only show how low in people's esteem the emperor had fallen, and Nero's massive spending on his new palace fuelled public hatred.

He decided to redirect speculation by making members of the Christian sect in Rome the scapegoats. Many Christians were rounded up, smeared with pitch, tied to stakes and set on fire. At a series of nocturnal games held in the Vatican Circus and the

This coin makes no attempt at flattery: the results of Nero's excessive lifestyle are all too apparent.

imperial palace grounds, blazing Christians were used as torches, while others were torn apart by wild beasts in the arena. But the exercise backfired. The public, even though hardened to scenes of gladiatorial death in the arena, were so sickened by such carnage that they turned their anger on Nero.

The costs of building the Domus Aurea and other similar projects spiralled out of control. The FISCUS became hard-pressed to cope, inflation increased. A devaluation of the gold AUREUS by reducing its weight by ten per cent proved to be only a temporary solution, so Nero resorted to the murder of men whose wealth he needed. Unbridled by any sensible advice, the treason trials began again, presided over by Tigellinus, who organised cohorts of the detested DELATORES to hasten charges and convictions against wealthy EQUITES and senators. Nero's readiness to eliminate opposition through murder rapidly created an atmosphere of paranoia. In 65 the pot boiled over and a conspiracy was hatched to replace Nero with Rome's most popular figure, the wealthy, charming senator Gaius Calpurnius Piso. But the plot was uncovered, thanks to the efforts of a praetor-designate named Marcus Cocceius Nerva, who had heard whispers of its imminence. The authorities tortured a few conspirators, who then revealed the names of their fellows. At least nineteen were either executed or driven to suicide, including the poet Marcus Annaeus Lucanus (Lucan), Nero's ex-tutor Seneca, and the co-PRAEFECTUS PRAETORIO Faenius Rufus.

Tigellinus continued with a free hand to suppress Nero's enemies, unhindered by his new colleague, Gaius Nymphidius Sabinus, who was appointed in the same year. Since opposition now existed in every sphere of the population, it only served to drive the emperor's unpopularity to a new high. Every class of citizen hated him, and in the provinces the neglected army had lost all faith in his rule. His habit of appointing his oriental freedmen as LEGATI did nothing to endear him to the common legionary, and in every sector there were continual rumblings of discontent. In the reign of terror that followed the Piso conspiracy, virtually all of Rome's remaining nobility was wiped out, obliging Nero's successors to create a new aristocracy. In an almost unending list of victims, one of the best known was Gaius Petronius, author of the *Satiricon*, whose louche description of *Trimalchio's Dinner* perfectly sums up the greedy, sexually lax atmosphere of Nero's court. Another was Annius Vinicianus, accused of leading a conspiracy aimed at replacing Nero with the celebrated LEGATUS Corbulo (*see side panel right*). Poppaea Sabina also died in 65 after receiving a bad-tempered kick in the stomach from Nero while she was pregnant; but this was obviously an accident.

In September 66 Nero decided to make himself scarce by travelling to Achaea, where his artistically Greek heart lay. However, the emperor's hasty departure did nothing to lessen the terror of Tigellinus, who unwisely eliminated some popular figures, most notably Corbulo, who was ordered to take his own life. To this point, the pogrom had mostly affected only the senatorial and wealthy equestrian classes. This senseless act caused the soldiers of legions on every front, disaffected by their treatment and angry at being ignored by their emperor, to raise their voices in outright hostility.

Nero – blissfully unaware that his henchman Tigellinus had quietly fled Rome in advance of a lynch mob – remained unconcerned. In Achaea he involved himself in a frenzied whirl of athletic competitions and musical diversions in which he always desired to be awarded the first prize. Reality was no longer a concept that Nero understood, so he did not care that in Greek competition merit, not social standing, was supposed to be rewarded; he even won the first prize in competitions he never attended. So overwhelmed was he by his adoring reception that, on 28 November 67, he proclaimed Achaea liberated. It was not free of the empire, but released from the province of Macedonia and received immunity from taxation. The liberation of Achaea had consequences in the west among the Gauls, who considered theirs the senior provinces of the empire. The affront to Gallic pride was sufficient for the standard of rebellion to be raised, and the insurgency soon spread to Hispania and Africa.

Nero's plans to travel further east to visit Aegyptus were halted when a serious revolt broke out in Judaea. And then to make matters worse, the rebellious proconsul of Africa, Clodius Macer, furious at Nero's tyranny, cut off the supply of grain to Rome. With supplies still coming from Aegyptus, this should not have been a disaster, but it was turned into one by the incompetent administration of a freedman named Helius, who had taken up the reins of government from Tigellinus. Thus was Nero's unwilling return to Rome forced on him at the beginning of 68. Abandoned by Tigellinus, odious to the mob for the innumerable executions and quite unable to disentangle the administrative chaos caused by Helius, Nero had run out of options.

His only hope of survival lay in the loyalty of the praetorian guards, but in this he was to be cheated. In the final act Sabinus, the remaining PRAEFECTUS PRAE-TORIO, promised the guards a massive donative of thirty thousand SESTERCES per head in the name of Galba, the LEGATUS PRO PRAETORE of Hispania Tarraconensis. With the populace set firmly against him and open mutiny among the legions, the senate declared Nero a public enemy and declared for Galba on 8 June 68. The shamed emperor fled to the suburbs where on the following day, lacking the courage to take his own life, he ordered his loyal freedman Epaphroditus to stab him. The Julio-Claudian dynasty ended as Nero fell, uttering the words, 'What an artist I die.' His long-suffering but faithful mistress Acte buried him anonymously in the Ahenobari mausoleum, just outside the Servian Wall on the side of the quiet Pincian Hill.

The great general Corbulo

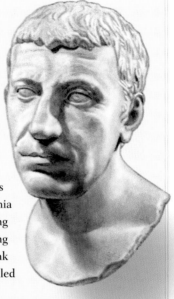

Gnaeus Domitius Corbulo (c.AD 7–66) was a scion of an Italian senatorial family. His early military career is unrecorded, but he was co-consul with Gaius Caligula in 40, his brother-in-law by the emperor's marriage with Milonia Caesonia, Corbulo's half-sister. He himself married Cassia Longina and their daughter Domitia Longina was to become wife of the emperor Domitian. In 47, Claudius appointed him LEGATUS PRO PRAETORE of Germania Inferior, where he was successful in supressing rebellions of the Cherusci and Chauci. During this time, Corbulo had a canal constructed to link the Rhenus to the Mosa (Maas/Meuse). Called 'Corbulus's canal', it is still visible today.

After a period spent in Rome, Corbulo was sent to govern Asia province in 52. In the previous year, the Parthian empire received a new king, Vologeses (Arsaces XXII), who established his brother Tiridates on the Armenian throne in place of the Roman client Radamistus. At first Nero's advisors Seneca and Burrus did nothing, but in 55 an opportunity presented itself when Vologeses faced a revolt inside Parthia by his own son Vardanes. Corbulo was dispatched to deal with Armenia, but took almost two years in recruiting new troops and knocking into shape the ill-disciplined legions (*III Gallica*, *VI Ferrata*, and *X Fretensis*) which had been sent to him from Syria. For five years Corbulo waged a series of successful campaigns that taught the Parthians respect for the might of Roman arms. In 63 Tiridates was persuaded to accept Nero as his nominal suzerain, and he visited Rome in 66 to receive his crown from the emperor. The terms of the peace, which were to last for half a century, established the courtesy of Parthia appointing the king of Armenia and Rome actually installing him as a client of the empire.

For his sweeping successes, Corbulo became a hero among his own troops, and his victories made him the most celebrated general of his day with the public. It was this eminence that led to his death.

CHAPTER TWO   AD 68–70
YEAR OF THE FOUR EMPERORS

GALBA
Servius Sulpicius Galba
(declared 6/4/68; princeps 8/6/68–15/1/69)

In the spring of 68, the governor of Gallia Lugdunensis, Gaius Julius Vindex, began canvassing provincial commanders to join him in open rebellion against Nero's rule. As a romanised Gaul he raised the standard for a nationalist movement, aiming to win for Gallia what Nero had bestowed on Achaea. However, his cry was also for freedom from tyranny. The local militia and Gallic tribes supported him with the exception of Lugdunum (Lyons), which remained loyal to Nero, and in March, Vindex besieged the wealthy colony. His appeal found support with the governor of Hispania Tarraconensis, seventy-year-old Galba, once a favourite of Livia. This was hardly surprising, for wealthy Galba had just received news that Nero had ordered his execution.

On 6 April, with the approval of Vindex, Galba proclaimed himself 'Legate of the Senate and Roman People', although his troops saluted him as princeps. The Tarraconensis garrison was limited to only one legion (*VI Victrix*) but Galba set about raising a second – *VII Galbiana*. He also received the support of Aulus Caecina Alienus, proconsular governor of Baetica, Marcus Salvius Otho, quaestor of Lusitania, and Aulus Vitellius, the latter soon being dispatched by Galba to command a legion in Germania Inferior. The governor of Germania Superior, Lucius Verginius Rufus, who refused to make cause with the others, marched against Vindex with his three legions – *IV Macedonica*, *XXI Rapax*, and *XII Primigenia* – and overwhelmed him in battle near Vesontio (Besançon) on 7 May. Despite the experience and strength of his forces, Verginius made no attempt to proclaim himself emperor, but he put his army at the senate's disposal, further weakening Nero's position.

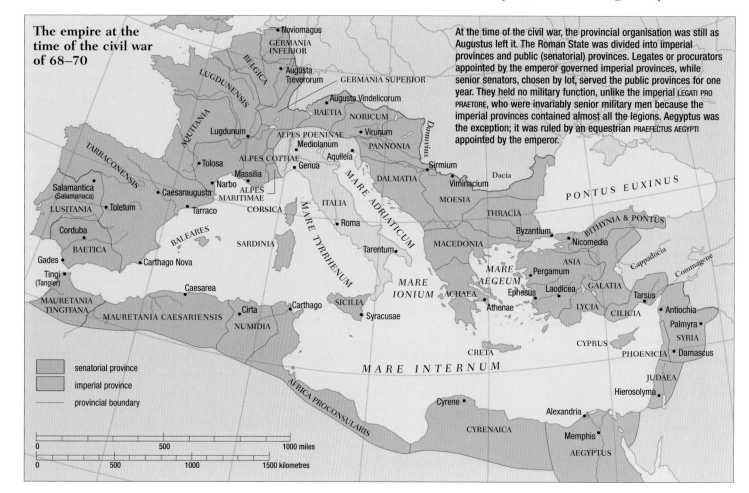

The empire at the time of the civil war of 68–70

At the time of the civil war, the provincial organisation was still as Augustus left it. The Roman State was divided into imperial provinces and public (senatorial) provinces. Legates or procurators appointed by the emperor governed imperial provinces, while senior senators, chosen by lot, served the public provinces for one year. They held no military function, unlike the imperial LEGATI PRO PRAETORE, who were invariably senior military men because the imperial provinces contained almost all the legions. Aegyptus was the exception; it was ruled by an equestrian PRAEFECTUS AEGYPTI appointed by the emperor.

senatorial province
imperial province
provincial boundary

0   500   1000 miles
0   500   1000   1500 kilometres

No foreigner to Roman politics, Galba had already canvassed for support in Rome and – more importantly – mollified the praetorian guard with a promised donative. The pledge, given on his behalf by the PRAEFECTUS PRAETORIO, Gaius Nymphidius Sabinus, was of vital importance. Galba knew he had to persuade the imperial bodyguard that the removal of a sitting princeps did not mean the loss of the reason for their existence. With events unfolding in Rome as detailed in the previous chapter, the senate declared for Galba on 8 June 68. It might seem precipitate of the senate to proclaim Galba, but he was a known quantity and, on the basis of ancestry, family tradition and service, arguably the most distinguished Roman noble still alive.

Galba was born on 24 December 3 BC in a hillside house on the Via Appia between Tarracina and Fundi some sixty-five miles south of Rome. The son of Gaius Sulpicius Galba, he was connected with the aristocratic house of Servii, which assured his acceptance among the highest levels of Roman society. As such, he owed much of his advancement through his adoption by Augustus's wife Livia. On her death, she bequeathed Galba fifty million SESTERCES, but Tiberius refused to hand it over. Galba outlived both his wife Lepida and their two sons and he remained a widower. His political career was typical of an ambitious Roman, beginning with a praetorship. Later, he served as governor of Aquitania, followed by a six-month consulship at the beginning of 33. He also served as governor in Germania Superior in 39–40, Africa (45–6) and Hispania Tarraconensis, starting in 61. He was honoured with triumphal insignia and three priesthoods during his career. And Nero's desire of his death probably proved Galba's worth to the state.

The praetorians, however, were not Galba's only military problem. The legionaries – notoriously restive as soon as it seemed that Rome might be ruled by any other than a man of the Julian house – disliked Galba's senatorial nobility. This is why he prudently claimed that he was seizing power in the name of the senate and the people. He showed decisiveness, too, in swiftly acting against the governor of Africa, Clodius Macer, who had also rebelled against Nero and cut off the grain supply to Rome. Galba needed no potential rivals at his back, and the single African legion (*III Augusta*) was insignificant in his overall plan. On Galba's orders, Macer was assassinated; any further unrest among the isolated African troops he intended to deal with at a later date.

After Nero's death Galba began his march from Tarraconensis to the capital in company with Otho.

Tacitus wrote: 'the secret of empire was revealed: an emperor could be made elsewhere than at Rome.' Now anyone with a provincial army to back him could aspire to the principate. By October 68, Galba was in Rome; however, his arrival was preceded by a degree of chaos. This was occasioned by the actions of Nymphidius Sabinus, who had orchestrated a demand from the praetorians to appoint him sole PRAEFECTUS PRAETORIO for life. But when it became clear that his real ambition was to take the throne, his troops backed the senate's choice and killed him. To make matters worse, Galba was met outside Rome by marines Nero had recruited to defend the city, who now demanded legionary standards and regular quarters. When they persisted, Galba's forces attacked, and many of the marines were killed.

Galba was resolute when he set his mind to solving problems, but not even his grasping years governing four provinces had prepared him for the deplorable state of the FISCUS. Since economies had to be made, everyone's pocket was hit: public shows were banned and promised donatives witheld – even from the praetorian guard. Stories of Galba's notorious inflexibility had preceded him to Rome, and they were soon confirmed as he had men of all ranks sentenced to death without trial on the scantiest evidence that they disapproved his administration. His popularity rapidly waned.

Galba, described by Tacitus as a 'mediocre genius' and 'capable of being emperor had he never ruled', tried to redeem cash from gifts given freely by Nero to his favourites, but it was a futile task. More essentially, his attempts to persuade the people that his reign had ushered in a return to Roman virtues were exploded by an obvious partiality to his immediate supporters. While it was to be expected that Vindex' supporters would receive preferment and punishment be handed out to his opponents, provincial unrest boiled over at the unbridled greed exhibited by many of Galba's appointees. Particularly, the soldiers of Germania could not forgive him his association with Vindex, against whom they had fought. Galba's attempts to restore discipline in the army proved to be clumsy from the start. The German troops had only acquiesced to Galba's accession with poor grace when their commander Verginius Rufus had pronounced in his favour. And yet Galba now recalled Verginius and replaced him with the elderly Hordeonius Flaccus. In Germania Inferior the troops became mutinous when the governor, Fonteius Capito, was murdered by Galba's creature Fabius Valens, commander of LEGIO *I Germana*, and replaced by Aulus Vitellius.

At the start of 69, the soldiers of Germania

Galba had been a favourite of the Augusta Livia, and in company with Vespasian later aided Gaius Caligula during the Rhenus army mutiny of 39. Galba's greed was said to know no bounds. According to Suetonius, when the people of Tarraco offered him a golden crown said to weigh 15lb (6.8kg), he had it melted down and made them supply the three ounces (85gm) needed to tip the scales to the advertised weight. In allowing favoured cronies to run their provinces according to their own benefit, Galba contributed to his own downfall.

Superior refused to take the annual oath to the emperor, and two days later joined the legions of Germania Inferior in proclaiming their new commander Vitellius as emperor. Valens supported Vitellius, as did Galba's treacherous former associate Caecina, the governor of Baetica, whom Galba had sent to command LEGIO V *Macedonica* in Germania Superior.

Despite these setbacks, Galba may still have held on to power, even though his parsimony had alienated the praetorian guard and made his position insecure. But his fatal mistake was to adopt Lucius Calpurnius Piso Frugi Licinianus – an inexperienced 30-year-old, whose mother was the great-grandaughter of Sextus Pompeius – as the person to support and eventually succeed him. This was the position that Otho had anticipated. Having nursed resentment against Nero for stealing his wife, this added act of imperial ingratitude from Galba spurred him to action. With promises of paying the withheld donative, Otho won over the praetorians, who proclaimed him emperor on 15 January 69. They then seized Galba in the Forum Romanum and murdered him. Among other supporters, the young Piso also met his fate at the point of a sword. As Galba's head was paraded on a pole around the city, the senate hastily ratified Otho's accession.

OTHO
Marcus Salvius Otho (r.15/1/69–16/4/69)

Otho was born at Ferentium on either 25 or 28 April AD 32, into a family that traced its origins back to an Etruscan royal house. His father, Lucius Otho, was consul in 33 and a trusted administrator under the emperors Tiberius, Gaius and Claudius. As recorded in the previous chapter, Otho's wildness as a youth brought him into Nero's circle and the two became close friends. Plutarch relates that Otho was so extravagant he was even able to tease Nero about his meanness. Ostensibly, Otho married the greatest beauty of her time, Poppaea Sabina, but there are conflicting accounts, some suggesting that the two lovers never actually married. However, it is generally accepted that Nero's taking her off him as a mistress and his 'banishment' to govern Lusitania, even though he was only a quaestor, severed their relationship and was sufficient reason for him to join the revolt against his former friend.

Otho immediately adopted the name Caesar and, unlike Galba, the troops and praetorians regarded him as the heir of the Julii and not another senatorial noble parading himself under the Julian name. It was not,

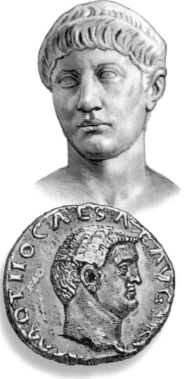

An early friend and confidant of Nero, Otho's cuckolding by the emperor in stealing away his wife, Poppaea Sabina, made Otho a willing conspirator in Nero's downfall.

however, enough for the troops of Germania, to whom he was a part of the hated Vindex-Galba axis. The combined nine legions had already declared Vitellius emperor on 3 January 69. Advance forces under Valens and Caecina were already moving south at the end of January and Vitellius was bringing the main army behind them for the invasion of Italia. Otho may have saved his position had he moved quickly and closed the Alpine passes, but he lost time in attempting to negotiate with Vitellius. Perhaps he was reluctant to commit his much smaller forces. He could count on the four legions of Pannonia and Dalmatia, and the three legions in Moesia. But the Illyrian army would need time to reach Italia, and in the meantime he only had his own imperial retinue of about nine thousand men. Vitellius's own troops numbered some thirty thousand, while those of Caecina and Valens were between fifteen and twenty thousand each. Any other support Otho could hope for was too far away to make any difference – in Syria under Gaius Licinius Mucianus and in Judaea under Vespasian.

Eventually, on 14 March, Otho moved north, deciding to hold the line along the Padus (Po) valley, to keep open communications with the Illyrian troops. He was barely in time. Caecina had crossed the Alps into Italia, and by the second week of March sat beside the Padus near Cremona, soon to be joined by Valens, who had swelled his force to some forty thousand. The two commanders were eager to bring Otho to battle and win the victory before Vitellius could arrive with the main force (now also swelling with new recruits).

Otho's strategy of making a diversionary strike with a force of COHORTES URBANAE, praetorians and marines in Narbonensis, in order to buy time for the Danuvian legions to reach him before engaging the enemy's vanguard, was successful. An advance guard sent to hold the line on the Padus also enjoyed initial success. Otho himself arrived at Bedriacum on about 10 April to meet his officers. It was agreed that the main concern was the bridge the Vitellian forces were building across the Padus in order to drive southward towards the Apennines and eventually to Rome. Otho ordered the larger part of his main force to advance from Bedriacum to interrupt its completion. While *en route* the Othonian forces, strung out along the Via Postumia amid baggage and supply trains, were attacked by Caecina and Valens near Cremona on 14 April. The battle of Bedriacum, as it became known, resulted in the defeat of the Othonians. Otho, who was at Brixellum with a force of infantry and cavalry to impede any Vitellian units that managed to cross the

Padus, realised that his strategy had proven too risky. Despite his profligacy and craven reliance on the praetorians, Otho's care for the empire showed in his noble refusal to pursue his cause and continue a protracted and bloody conflict. Two weeks short of his thirty-seventh birthday, on 16 April 69 he fell on his sword at dawn, ending a three-month rule.

VITELLIUS
Aulus Vitellius
(declared 3/1/69; princeps 19/4/69–20/12/69)

Vitellius was born in September AD 15, the son of Lucius Vitellius, one of the more successful public figures of the Julio-Claudian period and the confidant of Claudius who persuaded the emperor into marrying Agrippina. He held three consulships and was a fellow censor with Claudius. The younger Vitellius seems to have been equally at ease in aristocratic circles, successively winning the attention of the emperors Gaius, Claudius and Nero through flattery and political skill. Vitellius held the office of CURATOR OPERUM PUBLICO-RUM (public works) in Rome, and was proconsul of Africa in about 55. He was also a member of several priestly colleges, including one famous for its feasts, which it seems he enjoyed to the full. Twice married, he was involved in the death of his first son and the marriage ended in divorce; his second wife, Galeria Fundana, bore him a second son, who was killed by the Flavians after his father's overthrow.

When Galba appointed him governor of Germania Inferior late in 68, no one was probably more surprised than Vitellius, for he had almost no military skills. Perhaps wily Galba thought there would be little to fear in the way of rivalry from a man whose reputation for gluttony and gambling was notorious. If so, he was wrong. In the event, after his proclamation, Vitellius wisely relied on the superior skills of his generals Valens and Caecina, while following behind with the reserves. Caecina was already well on his way towards northern Italia when news reached him that Galba had been overthrown and Otho had taken his place as princeps. And Vitellius was still in Gallia when he heard that he had been granted the imperial powers on 19 April.

Unhindered, Vitellius now proceeded to Rome at the head of his troops, Roman and mercenary, plundering Gallia and Italia in a drunken orgy, and arriving in late June–early July. He dispersed Otho's legions back to their respective provinces and disbanded the existing praetorian guard, replacing them with cohorts of his own German troops. However, he made no move against the three Moesian legions, now sitting on Italia's northeastern border. On reaching the city, there was the familiar round of revenge killings with which Vitellius hoped to secure his position, although to his credit he was generally lenient to Otho's supporters, even pardoning Otho's brother Salvius Titianus, who had played a key role in the earlier regime. Vitellius also showed moderation in his transition to the principate.

He was too lazy to be brutal himself, but allowed Caecina and Valens to do the wet work. He assumed his powers gradually, participated in senate meetings, and put on games for the Roman mob. But no public display of either strength or modesty could mask the fact that he lacked talent. He had been one of Tiberius's young men on Capreae before emerging as a flattering courtier to each of his three successors. His highest achievements lay in gluttony and extravagance, in which he was said to be unmatched; and his days were numbered. By mid-July news arrived that the legions of Aegyptus had proclaimed a rival emperor, the popular general and governor of Judaea, Vespasian. The plan appeared to be that Vespasian would hold Aegyptus while his colleague Mucianus, governor of Syria, would invade Italia. However, before this transpired, the Illyrian legions, former supporters of Otho, joined Vespasian's cause and precipitated the next stage of the civil war.

Unusually, in a time of opportunist governors, this move did not come from the top. Lucius Tampius Flavianus of Pannonia, Marcus Pompeius Silvanus of Dalmatia, and Marcus Aponius Saturninus of Moesia preferred to sit on the fence and await the outcome of events. It was their subordinates who took the decision out of their vacillating hands, notably Cornelius Fuscus, procurator of Pannonia, and Marcus Antonius Primus, commander of Galba's recently raised LEGIO *VII Galbiana* (recruiting in Pannonia). The commanders of LEGIO *XI Claudia* in Dalmatia and LEGIO *VII Claudia* in Moesia also joined in. Under the overall command of Antonius what were now legions of the Flavian party began their march on northern Italia, while Antonius took a small advance force to seize the Julian Alpine passes before the Vitellians could reach them.

Vitellius had the numerical upper hand – at least until Vespasian's troops arrived – and decisive action could have saved the day, but like Otho before him, he dallied, preferring as usual to leave matters to Valens and Caecina. But Valens was ill, and Caecina was planning further treachery. Although his forces were only half of what Vitellius commanded in Italia, Antonius struck first before the emperor could muster additional

Vitellius, who always claimed that he was Nero's chosen successor, had been in close association with power from a young age. He was notorious for every sort of vice: Caligula admired his skill as a charioteer; Claudius, his skill at dice; Nero, for both of the above and his sycophancy in being the courtier who persuaded the 'reluctant' emperor to play his lute on public occasions. In turn, he adopted Nero's greed, Caligula's cruelty, and none of Claudius's common sense.

reinforcements from Germania, and raced across the Alpine passes to a bridge over the Athesis (Adige). Here they encountered some forty thousand Vitellian troops under Caecina, who was now consul, and Sextus Lucilius Bassus, PRAEFECTUS of the Ravenna fleet. They began secret negotiations with the Flavians, but while Bassus convinced his men to switch sides, Caecina's proved their mettle and refused. They arrested him at Hostilia near Cremona, and then joined the rest of the Vitellian forces trying to hold the line along the Padus.

With the Ravenna fleet in his pocket, Antonius was in a position to strike through the Padus line, which he did when the two arriving Pannonian legions, *VII Galbiana* and *XIII Gemima*, met him at Patavium (Padua). He led the reinforcements towards Verona, where they were joined by the three legions from Moesia, *III Gallicia*, *VII Claudia* and *VII Augusta*. This massing of the enemy forced the Vitellians to retreat from Hostilia towards Cremona, where two legions had been kept in reserve, and a race developed between the two sides to reach the city first. The Cremona garrison made a sortie against the onrushing Flavians in support of their retreating comrades, but were pushed back in what was called the second battle of Bedriacum. However, their spirited action enabled the troops from Hostilia to reach Cremona safely.

Having recovered from his illness, Valens had left

Progress and key events of the civil war, 68–70

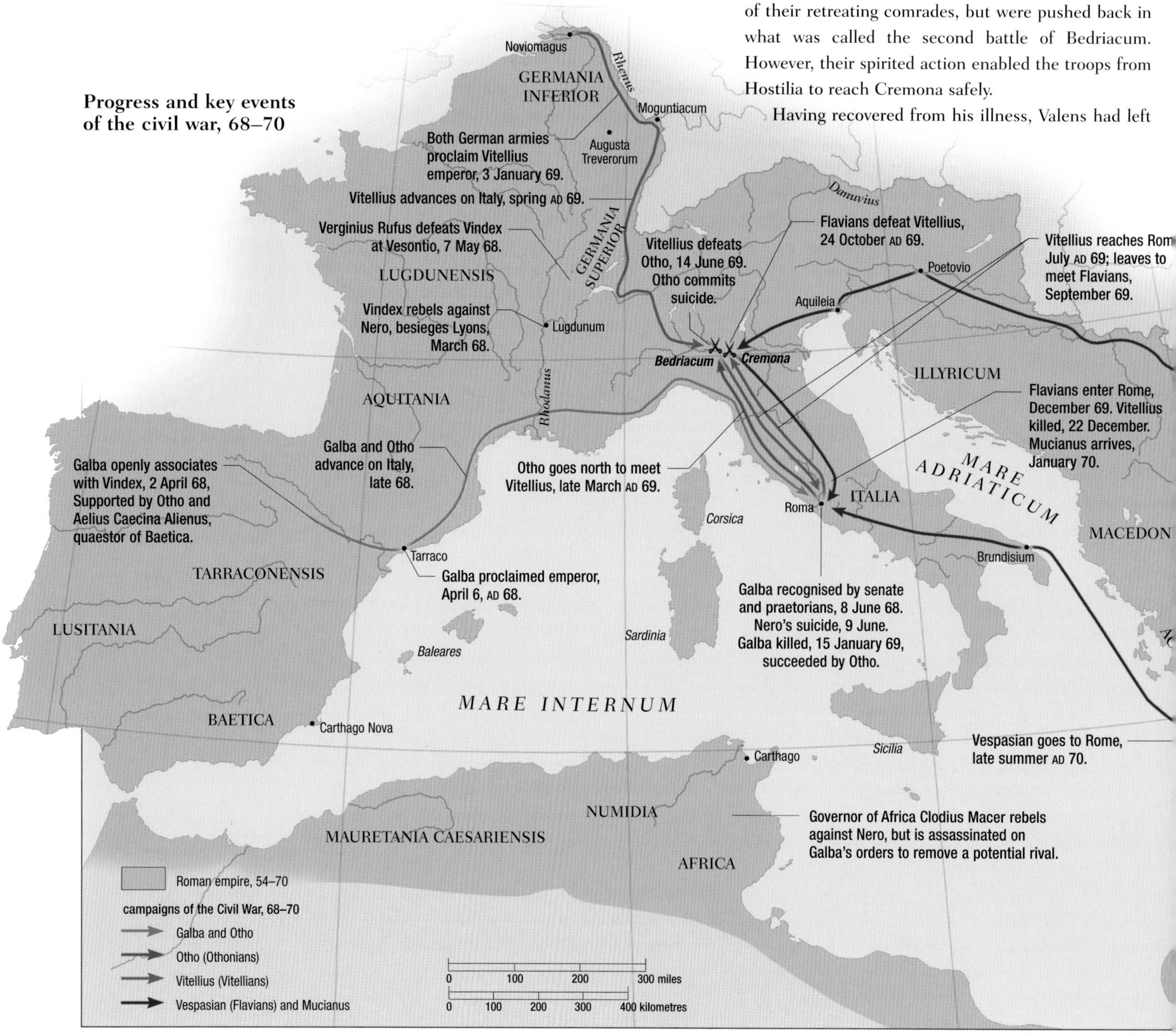

Both German armies proclaim Vitellius emperor, 3 January 69.

Vitellius advances on Italy, spring AD 69.

Verginius Rufus defeats Vindex at Vesontio, 7 May 68.

Vindex rebels against Nero, besieges Lyons, March 68.

Vitellius defeats Otho, 14 June 69. Otho commits suicide.

Flavians defeat Vitellius, 24 October AD 69.

Vitellius reaches Rom[e] July AD 69; leaves to meet Flavians, September 69.

Galba and Otho advance on Italy, late 68.

Otho goes north to meet Vitellius, late March AD 69.

Flavians enter Rome, December 69. Vitellius killed, 22 December. Mucianus arrives, January 70.

Galba openly associates with Vindex, 2 April 68, Supported by Otho and Aelius Caecina Alienus, quaestor of Baetica.

Galba proclaimed emperor, April 6, AD 68.

Galba recognised by senate and praetorians, 8 June 68. Nero's suicide, 9 June. Galba killed, 15 January 69, succeeded by Otho.

Vespasian goes to Rome, late summer AD 70.

Governor of Africa Clodius Macer rebels against Nero, but is assassinated on Galba's orders to remove a potential rival.

Map labels

Noviomagus
GERMANIA INFERIOR
Rhenus
Moguntiacum
Augusta Treverorum
GERMANIA SUPERIOR
Danuvius
LUGDUNENSIS
Lugdunum
Rhodanus
Poetovio
Aquileia
Bedriacum · Cremona
ILLYRICUM
AQUITANIA
ITALIA
MARE ADRIATICUM
Corsica
Roma
Brundisium
MACEDON[IA]
Tarraco
TARRACONENSIS
Sardinia
LUSITANIA
Baleares
MARE INTERNUM
BAETICA
Carthago Nova
Sicilia
Carthago
NUMIDIA
MAURETANIA CAESARIENSIS
AFRICA

Legend

Roman empire, 54–70

campaigns of the Civil War, 68–70

→ Galba and Otho
→ Otho (Othonians)
→ Vitellius (Vitellians)
→ Vespasian (Flavians) and Mucianus

0 100 200 300 miles
0 100 200 300 400 kilometres

Rome but did not make for Cremona. Instead, he went to Gallia in search of reinforcements, but was thwarted because the German legions were engaged in the suppression of a tribal uprising across the Rhenus that Antonius had arranged. Valens was captured later by Flavian forces and executed. This left the Vitellians in Cremona without any experienced leadership. Instead of remaining within the walls where they might have held on, they turned in force and, on the night of 27 October, engaged the Flavians. In the ensuing battle of Cremona, the Vitellians were soundly defeated and Cremona was brutally sacked by the victors. It is thought that as many as fifty thousand souls were slain in the four-day orgy of violence.

Vitellius had lost the north, but still held onto the peninsula with the praetorians, a newly raised legion and the COHORTES URBANAE. It is hard to understand why Vitellius had left the PRAEFECTUS URBI in office, for he was none other than Vespasian's older brother, Flavius Sabinus, appointed under Otho. And since he was the nominal commander of the COHORTES URBANAE, their reliability in Vitellius's cause must have been dubious. Nevertheless, in theory Vitellius had more

than enough troops to block the Flavian advance across the Appenines, and he took fourteen praetorian cohorts north to Mevania before Antonius could get through. But the anticipated battle never took place because Vitellius was forced to deal with a mutiny of the fleet at Misenum. He withdrew to Narnia and split his forces, sending some troops to Misenum, leaving detachments at Narnia, and went himself to Rome. The Narnia force promptly went over to the Flavians, and the way was open for Antonius to advance on Rome. Since Antonius did not expect further reinforcements from Mucianus, who was held up repelling a Dacian invasion of Moesia, he pressed on to the very walls of the city with his five legions.

When Vitellius's officers in Rome began deserting him, he accepted that the end was near, and negotiated terms with Flavius Sabinus. On 18 October 69 he agreed to abdicate. But events transpired differently when his troops, furious at their leader's desertion, attacked Sabinus, who retreated to the Capitol with units of the COHORTES URBANAE and Vespasian's youngest son, the eighteen-year-old Domitian. A fierce battle broke out, during which the Temple of Jupiter Optimus Maximus was destroyed. Domitian managed to escape, but Sabinus was cut down, and the Vitellians once more held Rome – for the day only. On the following morning of 20 December, the Flavian army assaulted Rome and fought its way into the city. Vitellius disguised himself in dirty clothing and hid in the imperial doorkeeper's quarters, leaning a couch and a mattress against the door for protection. Dragged from his hiding place by the Flavians, he was hauled off to the Forum Romanum, where he was tortured, killed and his body tossed into the Tiberis.

On 22 December, the senate recognised Vespasian, and voted him all the principate's powers and prerogatives. It was hoped that this would stop the Flavian army from sacking Rome, but neither Antonius nor Domitian – hailed as a Caesar to Vespasian's Augustus – could halt the disorder. The victorious soldiers continued the rampage until Mucianus arrived in January 70 and took the office of regent in Vespasian's name. Rome now awaited its new Augustus, who finally arrived in October. The civil wars were at an end and a new dynasty ruled the Roman empire.

Marcus Antonius Primus, born at Tolosa c.35, had been expelled from the senate on a charge of forging a will. Galba later reinstated him and placed him in command of VII Galbiana (later renamed VII Hispana). Described by Tacitus as 'greedy and extravagant, in peace a bad citizen, but brave in action, ready of speech, and in war an ally not to be despised', Antonius was poorly treated by Mucianus, who accused him of war atrocities. However, Vespasian discharged him honourably and Antonius returned to Tolosa. His end is not known, but the four epigrams addressed to him by the poet Martial suggest that he was still living in the reign of Domitian.

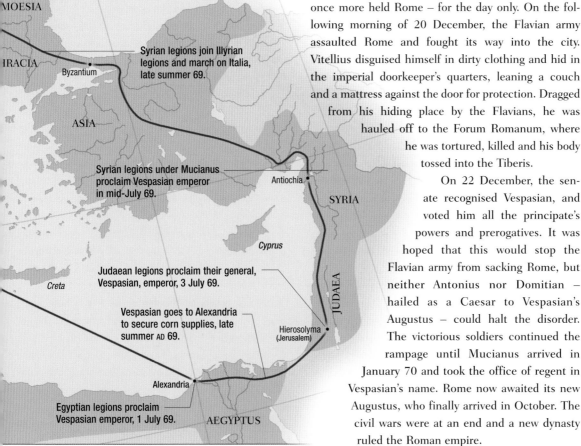

MOESIA

IRACIA

Byzantium

Syrian legions join Illyrian legions and march on Italia, late summer 69.

ASIA

Syrian legions under Mucianus proclaim Vespasian emperor in mid-July 69.

Antiochia

SYRIA

Cyprus

Creta

Judaean legions proclaim their general, Vespasian, emperor, 3 July 69.

JUDAEA

Vespasian goes to Alexandria to secure corn supplies, late summer AD 69.

Hierosolyma (Jerusalem)

Alexandria

Egyptian legions proclaim Vespasian emperor, 1 July 69.

AEGYPTUS

CHAPTER THREE   *AD 70–96*
THE FLAVIAN DYNASTY

VESPASIAN
Titus Flavius Vespasianus
(declared 1/7/69; princeps 22/12/69–23/6/79)

The Flavians were not of ancient Roman aristocracy, indeed their family history is obscure until Vespasian's father, Titus Flavius Petro, a citizen of Reate (Rieti) and a mule breeder, appears in the records as a centurion in the army of Pompeius, facing Caesar's at the battle of Pharsalus (9 August 48 BC). He secured an honourable discharge and went to Asia as a tax gatherer – apparently a rare one according to Suetonius, since statues were raised there to him inscribed 'To an Honest Tax-gatherer'. Flavius became a money-lender and then appears to have retired to Raetia, where he died, leaving his wife and two sons, Sabinus and Vespasian. Sabinus, the elder, went on to attain the rank of PRAEFECTUS URBI in Rome.

Vespasian was born on 17 November AD 9 in the hamlet of Falcrina, near Reate, in Sabine country. His mother, Vespasia Polla, had some aristocratic links through her brother, who entered the senate as a praetor, but otherwise the family was detached from events in Rome. Vespasian enjoyed a good education, and the financial help of his mother propelled him on the ladder of the CURSUS HONORUM. He was a TRIBUNUS MILITUM for three or four years in Thracia; held a quaestorship in Creta-Cyrenaica; and the offices of aedile and praetor, successively, under Gaius Caligula, the latter in Germania, where he helped the emperor put down a rebellion in 39. Later he was made proconsul of Africa and then governor of Judaea.

He gained valuable experience overseas, not only in military matters but also learning the value of providing housing, sanitation and an efficient tax-collecting system. In the process, he acquired a wife, Flavia Domitilla, who bore him two sons, Titus and Domitian, and a daughter, Domitilla. When Flavia died before his accession Vespasian returned to his former mistress, Caenis. Born a palace slave, Caenis had risen to become the Augusta Antonia's secretary and was later given her freedom, but the law that forbade senators to marry freedwomen meant she could never become his wife. Caenis, an intelligent, clear-headed person, exerted a beneficial influence over Vespasian.

His future seemed assured when the well-placed freedman Narcissus became his patron at Claudius's court. He was indebted to Narcissus for his command of a legion in Germania, and an army in Britannia (AD 44), where his brilliant record made him a popular figure. The historian Suetonius said of him: '*He went to Britannia, where he fought thirty battles, subjugated two tribes and took more than twenty oppida [hill forts], Vectis Insula [Isle of Wight] besides.*' This hardly does Vespasian justice. His mastery of artillery pieces such as the SCORPIO and BALLISTA allowed him to annihilate supposedly impregnable fortresses in Wessex and devastate native morale. With one quarter of the invasion force, his LEGIO *II Augusta* conquered three-quarters of the Romans' target territory, including a vast swathe across the south and southwest as far as Isca Dumnoniorum (Exeter). LEGIO IX *Hispania* pushed north as far as Lindum (Lincoln), while *XIV Gemima* and *XX Valeria Victrix* advanced to Ratae (Leicester). The line connecting them was the two-hundred-mile Fosse Way, the ancient limestone ridge between Devon and Lincolnshire that became the limit of the initial Claudian occupation. During this period Vespasian served at times under the consular commander Aulus Plautius, and at times reported directly to Claudius.

Vespasian was awarded the triumphal insignia, as well as a consulship for the last two months of (probably) AD 51. However, the death of Claudius and the

A naturalistic bust shows Vespasian as the bluff, down-to-earth country type he was; his smile, a surprise in Roman portraiture, imbues his features with human warmth.

accession of Nero – and specifically his mother Agrippina – cast Vespasian into the wilderness for some fifteen years. Agrippina showed animosity to any friend of Narcissus, even after the freedman had killed himself. Vespasian continued to serve on the periphery of the empire until Nero made him proconsul of Africa in about 63–4. On completion of his term, Vespasian returned to Rome where he seems to have gained the emperor's trust sufficiently to be included on Nero's tour of Achaea in 66–7. He was, therefore, the man on hand when a revolt broke out in Judaea, and Nero called on him to deal with the problem.

By spring of 67, with sixty thousand legionaries, auxiliaries and allies under his command, Vespasian in the company of Titus, the eldest of his two sons, set out to subdue Galilee and then to cut off Jerusalem. Success was quick and decisive. By October all of Galilee had been pacified and plans for the strategic circumvallation of Jerusalem were soon formed. It was in Judaea, he was to recall, that he came close to death for the second time, when he was narrowly rescued after being cornered by Jewish resistance fighters; the first time had been in Athens, when he fell asleep during one of Nero's interminable musical recitals. And it was from Judaea that Vespasian surveyed the fast-moving events of 68 and 69 in Italia.

He gave his short-lived approval to Galba as an alternative to Nero, but the new emperor was dead before Vespasian's goodwill message reached Rome. On hearing of the further deterioration of the situation, Vespasian determined to act. The idea of aspiring to the principate was not a new one. There had been omens in his childhood that predicted a great future. A popular story told of how, during his aedileship, Caligula – furious at Vespasian's failure to keep the streets of Rome clean – ordered soldiers to load the aedile down with mud[†]. This was interpreted to mean that one day the soil of Italia would be trampled on in a civil war, but that Vespasian would protect it.

However, it was luck that precipitated Vespasian's decision to do something. The two thousand men of the three legions in Moesia, one of them attached from Syria, had reached Aquileia in support of Otho, and remained there, despite news of his suicide. Seeing that other armies had declared their own emperors, these men decided to elect their own, and settled on Vespasian on the recommendation of the

Syrian contingent, who best knew Vespasian's record. When the news leaked out, the PRAEFECTUS AEGYPTI made his legions take the oath to Vespasian on 1 July 69, and the emperor-elect's own troops in Judaea were only too eager to follow suit days later. Swallowing his jealousy of Vespasian, Lucius Mucianus, governor of Syria, gave his support, and with a promise of forty thousand archers from Vologeses, king of the Parthians, Vespasian was ready to begin his campaign.

In this, as in everything he did, he showed the shrewdness of a Julius Caesar. Instead of marching directly on Rome, he directed Mucianus to take his two remaining Syrian legions west to support those of the Illyrian provinces that had proclaimed him. (Vespasian was not to know at this point that Marcus Antonius Primus was already advancing into northern Italia in his name). Vespasian then went to Alexandria to secure the grain supply and deny it to Vitellius. The threat of starvation in Rome did much to weaken Vitellius's standing in the eyes of the populace. Vespasian's delay also anticipated the fall of Jerusalem, which he needed since Jerusalem was wealthy and he knew that the FISCUS would be empty. However, the events in Rome of December 70 meant that he could no longer tarry in the east, so he left the investment of Jerusalem in the capable hands of his son Titus and left shortly before Jewish resistance finally crumbled. Pockets of Vitellian resistance held him up briefly, but the hindrance proved fortuitous in that on reaching Rome news of Jerusalem's fall had arrived, so the senate was able to decree their new Augustus a suitable triumph to greet him.

JOSEPH BEN MATTATHIAS (c.37–100), known to history as Josephus, became a close confidant of Vespasian. He had been the commander of a small Jewish force holding the small citadel of Jotapata in Galilee against Vespasian when it capitulated. At first Vespasian's prisoner, he became a valuable source of information on the Jews. More importantly, canny Josephus brought Vespasian's attention to an ancient eastern prophecy which foretold that the rulers of the world would arise from Judaea. Interpreting this to Vespasian's benefit, he was rewarded by being adopted as the emperor's son on Vespasian's accession. Josephus wrote a history of the war that served to flatter his patron and warn others against the folly of opposing Rome. Despite its partisan tone, the book's vivid prose earned Josephus a wide reputation as a historian. In one passage, he described the desperation of the Jews: 'Need drove the starving to gnaw at anything. Refuse which even animals would reject was collected and turned into food. In the end they were eating belts and shoes and the leather stripped off their shields.'

† The duty of maintaining Rome's streets fell to the lowliest rank of the CURSUS HONORUM the VINGTIVIRATE, not an aedile. Perhaps Suetonius, who tells this tale, confused the order of events in Vespasian's career, or he was making a point of Gaius's cruelty in forcing the senior aedile to do the junior vingtivirate's job.

Vespasian in office

At the age of sixty-one, Vespasian was now at the helm of an empire shattered by a year of anarchy. There had been an enormous loss of public confidence in the power of the Roman State, which the new princeps needed to heal. In this he enjoyed a natural advantage: a rustic, common-sense upbringing combined with a sterling military career. He brought to Rome the native shrewdness of an Italian farmer, rather than the intellectual brilliance of the city-dweller. He notoriously loathed any form of affectation – all too prevalent among the new nobility arising from the depradations of Nero. When a young man, reeking of perfume, approached him to give thanks for a promotion in rank, Vespasian turned away in disgust and cancelled the order, adding: 'I should not have minded so much if it had been garlic.'

Despite public acclamation, Vespasian faced immediate threats to his reign, among them the rebellion in Germania and Gallia of a Batavian auxiliary commander, Julius Civilis. This was swiftly suppressed, but it underlined the need for military reform. Like Augustus before him, Vespasian was well aware that an idle army is a dangerous one. Neither was the mistake Nero had made of remaining aloof from his troops lost on Vespasian, who assiduously cultivated the legions and so won their loyalty. In doing so, he and his sons finally weaned the provincial soldiers off their adherence to the Julii and gained from them the acceptance of the practice of succession in the principate. It was clear to Vespasian that the revolt of Civilis had succeeded due to the widespread support he found among the troops quartered in Gallia and along the Rhenus. Although called 'Roman', most were natives of their region and commanded by native officers. Vespasian took measures to ensure such a situation could not arise again. In future the auxiliaries were to serve in regions far away from the countries of their origin to avoid nationalistic sympathies colouring their loyalty to the state, nor were they allowed any longer to serve under native officers.

The emperor also wisely followed the Augustan principle of keeping the army busy. The failure of Augustus's major campaign of conquest, that of the extension of Gallia north to the line of the Albis (Elbe), meant that the Roman frontier followed the Rhenus south until it could cross to the upper Danuvius. This greatly extended the length of the line to be defended. In 73 Vespasian ordered the LEGATUS of Germania Superior, Gnaeus Cornelius Clemens to annex the triangular-shaped region between the rivers' headwaters known as the Agri Decumates, and this straightened out the frontier. While this proceeded without much hindrance from the tribes of the sparsely populated region – the modern Black Forest – it went slowly, since Clemens erected forts along his front lines as his troops pressed forward. But by 79 a line existed that at least stretched between Argentorate (Strasbourg) to Arae Flaviae (Rottweil), and from there to the edge of Lacus Venetus (Lake Constance); and Clemens may even have reached as far north as a line running from Aquae (Baden) to Guntia (Günzburg) on the Danuvius.

Vespasian also recognised another lesson in the revolts of Civilis and Vindex. The provinces, especially those of Gallia, had attained such a level of romanised development that they wanted to play an active part in the cultural, political and military life of the empire. Apart from Claudius opening up the senatorial order to Gallic nobles, little else had been done in this direction, and Vespasian feared that, denied participation, provincial energies would be diverted first towards nationalism and then separatism. In 73 he assumed the office of censor and used the position to fill the gaps in the senate with a new aristocracy drawn from the Italian MUNICIPIA. He then conferred Latin rights on Baetica and continued the programmes of Julius Caesar and Augustus in founding COLONIAE and granting municipal charters to provincial towns. Between 74–84 no fewer than three hundred and fifty Spanish towns received their MUNICIPIUM. Elsewhere in the empire numerous COLONIAE were also founded. Once made a Latin MUNICIPIUM, the local elite automatically acquired Roman citizenship and became eligible for high positions within the principate.

In this, he was quite open that, like Augustus, he intended to have a senate amenable to his actions – they should obey rather than just be co-operative. However, even those naturally opposed to him did not want to see a return to the spendthrift years of Caligula or Nero; Vespasian was famous for his parsimony. He made it the business of his reign to restore the moral foundation of the state and its economic stability before turning to artistic embellishment.

Among Vespasian's many achievements, a few stand out. In Rome, he expanded the city's POMERIUM to beyond the Servian Wall to help relieve crowding – an overt symbol of Rome's invulnerability to foreign attack that would remain until the later Aurelian Wall was

Vespasian (top) had little time for the trappings of imperial protocol with regard to himself, but was politically astute in allowing the senate to honour his wife Flavia Domitilla, who had died before his accession, by deifying her.

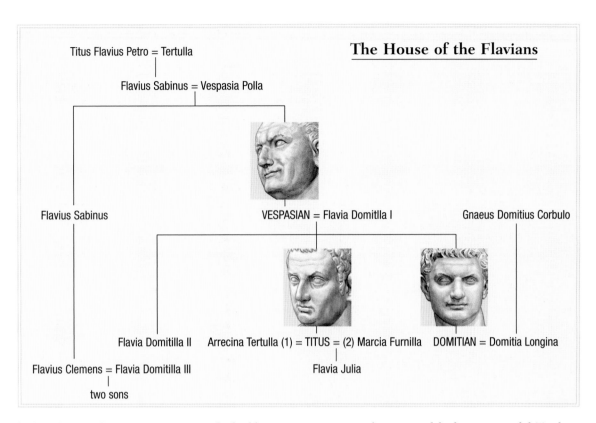

The House of the Flavians

Titus Flavius Petro = Tertulla

Flavius Sabinus = Vespasia Polla

Flavius Sabinus

VESPASIAN = Flavia Domitlla I

Gnaeus Domitius Corbulo

Flavia Domitilla II   Arrecina Tertulla (1) = TITUS = (2) Marcia Furnilla   DOMITIAN = Domitia Longina

Flavia Julia

Flavius Clemens = Flavia Domitilla III

two sons

built in less steady times. He encouraged rebuilding on vacated lots, restored the Capitol and the Temple of Jupiter Optimus Maximus destroyed in 69. Work began on three massive new monuments. On the Caelian Hill a temple was raised in honour of the deified Claudius, a project cannily designed to identify Vespasian as the legitimate heir to the Julio-Claudians, while distancing himself from Nero.[†] As a celebration of the tranquility Vespasian had brought to the empire the Templum Pacis (Temple of Peace) was built beside the Forum Romanum. On the Palatine, Vespasian pulled down Nero's palace and began construction of the extensive Domus Flavia that his younger son Domitian would complete. But above all, he began to build a massive amphitheatre on the site of the lake of Nero's Domus Aurea, known as the Amphitheatrum Flavium. We know it better today as the Colosseum.

Restoring the FISCUS to solvency after Nero and a year of civil strife was a monumental task, but by the end of his ten-year reign it was accomplished. This, of course, required numerous changes to taxation and many new ways of raising money, many of them unpopular. Cities that had been freed from paying tax in the past – Rhodus, Byzantium and Samos – now had to pay again. Achaea, freed by Nero, was returned

to provincial status and had to pay, as did Trachian (coastal) Cilicia and Comagene. No part of daily life escaped Vespasian's taxes, including the most basic production of human urine. This might seem odd, but it was collected for use by fullers in cleaning woollens. Titus – more fastidious than his gruff father – was said to have complained that taxing the contents of the public latrines was unsavoury. Vespasian held out a coin taxed on the first day and asked him to sniff it. When Titus complied and smelled nothing but its metallic odour, his father laughed and said that was odd, because it had come directly from a urinal.

The position of the principate in respect of the senate was quite clear. Vespasian held the office of consul in every year of his reign except 73 and 78, and made Titus his colleague on six occasions. In 71, Titus was given the IMPERIUM PROCONSULARE and the TRIBUNICIA POTESTAS, which firmly identified him as Vespasian's successor. However, to prevent repetition of praetorian meddling in the succession, he appointed Titus as sole PRAEFECTUS PRAETORIO (having reduced the guard from the sixteen cohorts of Vitellius to the Augustan number of nine). Nevertheless, Vespasian was courteous in his dealings with the senate – although it was clear to all who actually ruled the empire – and generous-spirited towards all men. As Suetonius says, his researches showed that Vespasian had no innocent party executed, and he went so far as

---

† The platform for this huge edifice had been begun during Nero's reign, but Nero appropriated it to become a raised garden for his Domus Aurea.

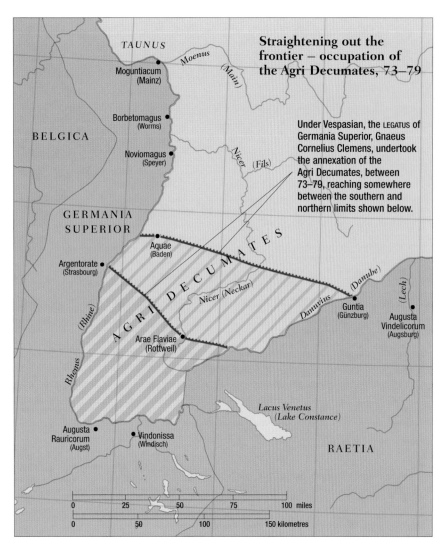

Straightening out the frontier – occupation of the Agri Decumates, 73–79

Under Vespasian, the LEGATUS of Germania Superior, Gnaeus Cornelius Clemens, undertook the annexation of the Agri Decumates, between 73–79, reaching somewhere between the southern and northern limits shown below.

TITUS
Titus Flavius Vespasianus (r.23/6/79–13/9/81)

Such was the care with which Vespasian had prepared for the succession, there was no question about the immediate elevation of Titus, who was in his fortieth year. There was, however, a great deal of unease. Titus had earned a reputation for extravagance and ruthlessness in his youth, and the senate – never well disposed towards the humbly-born Flavians – feared he might be another Nero. It turned out differently.

Titus was born on 30 December AD 39 in what was described as a small, dingy, slum bedroom in a Rome tenement block. But Vespasian's political ascent under Claudius meant that young Titus became a close companion to the emperor's son Britannicus, and the two studied together in the palace. Suetonius tells a story of how Narcissus called in a physiognomist to examine Britannicus's features and predict his future. The seer was emphatic that Britannicus would never become princeps, but that Titus would. The two boys remained close friends until Britannicus's cruel death in 55. In later years Titus erected statues of his dead friend in several locations and in the Domus Flavia.

At some point after 61, he served as a TRIBUNUS MILITUM in Germania Superior and Britannia before returning to Rome early in 64 to study law. His political career at this time is obscure, but on his return he married Arrecina Tertulla. We know little about her, and in any event, she died soon after. Titus then wed the daughter of a noble family, Marcia Furnilla, but later divorced her when the family fell into Nero's disfavour. There may have been a daughter called Julia, who was said to have died in her mid-twenties of an abortion forced on her by Titus's brother and successor, Domitian.

In 66 Nero appointed Titus as LEGATUS LEGIONIS to *XV Apollinaris* to accompany Vespasian in settling the revolt in Judaea, even though he had not yet been a praetor, the judicial post normally held by a senator before becoming a legionary commander. As the adopted son of Vespasian, Josephus was a writer with a strong Flavian bias, so his glowing account of Titus's contribution in the Jewish Wars may be suspect. Titus figured prominently in the subjugation of at least five rebel towns, but appears to have never completely taken any strongly defended citadels, until Jerusalem.

When Vespasian left for Alexandria in 69 and subsequently Rome, Titus was left in charge of reducing Jerusalem, the military exploit for which he is most remembered. It was a lengthy and bitter business in

to endow the daughter of his former enemy Vitellius for her marriage.

Unlike the majority of his predecessors, Vespasian died unmolested in his bed on 23 June 79, after contracting a brief illness; perhaps fortunate that his two ambitious sons Titus and Domitian were prepared to let nature take its course. At the age of seventy-eight, his life finished on an ironic note when Vespasian, who never mustered much faith in Roman religion or superstition, uttered, 'Woe is me, I think I am turning into a god.'

Of the three Flavian emperors, Vespasian was undoubtedly the greatest. Usually waspish Suetonius, writing in *The Life of Vespasian*, described his rule like this: *'The empire which for a long time had been unsettled and, as it were, drifting through the usurpation and violent death of three emperors, was at last taken in hand and given stability. This house was, it is true, obscure and without family portraits, yet it was one of which our country had no reason whatever to be ashamed....'*

which typical Roman discipline and sheer doggedness won the day. The city's fortifications were formidable. With four legions under his command, Titus began the assault in the spring of 70. In less than four weeks, the suburban walls were breached, leaving only the inner city and the Temple of Solomon in Jewish hands. The Romans built a siege wall around the citadel, and the circumvallation had the desired effect of inducing a famine within. By August, the outer Temple court had been breached and, in the ensuing attack, the Temple was burned to the ground and all the captives were butchered. Titus was hailed as IMPERATOR by his troops.

In this and the events that followed, Titus earned his reputation for cruelty. He went on a tour of the eastern provinces, parading his Judaean captives in public and throwing Jews to wild beasts in the arenas or forcing them to fight each other to the death. However, it should be remembered that in this he was only following Roman precedent, and – more importantly – demonstrating the price of rebelling against his father in a manner that was traditionally understood by the oriental population of the region. During this tour he fell in love with the Jewess Berenice, sister of Herod Agrippa II, and took her back to Rome with him in 71. The relationship between the heir-apparent and the formidable oriental princess spiked Roman prejudices and she was painted as another Cleopatra. It was with great reluctance that Titus eventually put her aside in 75. On his return to Rome he celebrated a lavish double-triumph with Vespasian (who would not waste the money on two separate events) for the fall of Jerusalem. A triumphal arch (now lost) was built into the eastern end of the Circus Maximus to mark the occasion. Shortly after, construction of a second arch was begun at the entrance to the Forum Romanum.

Titus demonstrated his administrative skills as his father's partner, politely attending senate meetings and asking advice of his elders. On the other hand Suetonius tells us that he was an adept forger who created evidence to win convictions, and was somewhat tyrannical in trying arraigned men in a theatre rather than a law court in the hope of winning a conviction by popular pressure rather than by reasoning. Titus was doing the regime's necessary dirty work, while leaving Vespasian on high moral ground. Set against this impression, Suetonius tells us that Titus was naturally kind-hearted.

Titus proceeded to disperse fears about the nature of his reign and increase his popularity the moment he became princeps. The better qualities noted by

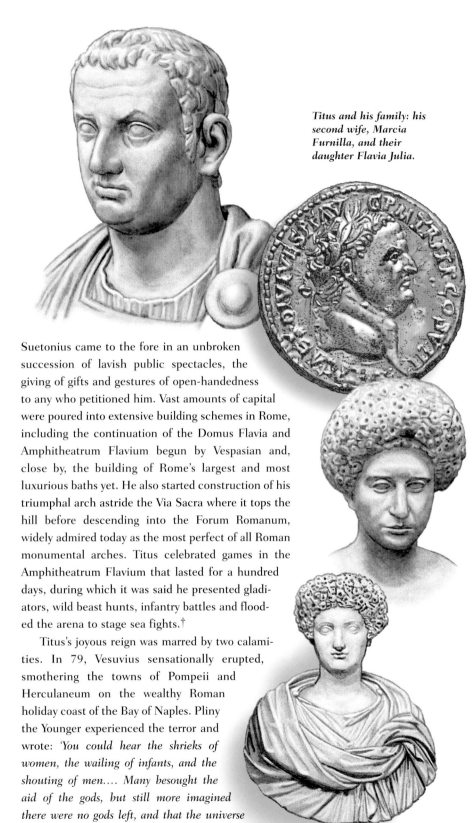

Titus and his family: his second wife, Marcia Furnilla, and their daughter Flavia Julia.

Suetonius came to the fore in an unbroken succession of lavish public spectacles, the giving of gifts and gestures of open-handedness to any who petitioned him. Vast amounts of capital were poured into extensive building schemes in Rome, including the continuation of the Domus Flavia and Amphitheatrum Flavium begun by Vespasian and, close by, the building of Rome's largest and most luxurious baths yet. He also started construction of his triumphal arch astride the Via Sacra where it tops the hill before descending into the Forum Romanum, widely admired today as the most perfect of all Roman monumental arches. Titus celebrated games in the Amphitheatrum Flavium that lasted for a hundred days, during which it was said he presented gladiators, wild beast hunts, infantry battles and flooded the arena to stage sea fights.†

Titus's joyous reign was marred by two calamities. In 79, Vesuvius sensationally erupted, smothering the towns of Pompeii and Herculaneum on the wealthy Roman holiday coast of the Bay of Naples. Pliny the Younger experienced the terror and wrote: *'You could hear the shrieks of women, the wailing of infants, and the shouting of men.... Many besought the aid of the gods, but still more imagined there were no gods left, and that the universe*

---

† This last would appear to be either a mistake or a silly exaggeration, because the wooden-floored construction of the Colosseum above three stories of underworks would have made flooding the arena an impossibility. On the other hand, there are still some modern historians who claim it could have been done, although no one to date has convincingly demonstrated how.

was plunged into eternal darkness for evermore.' One of the victims was his uncle, the prolific writer Pliny the Elder, the man who had so loathed Claudius's wife Agrippina. While Titus was visiting the disaster zone, a huge fire broke out in Rome, destroying the new Capitol, Agrippa's Pantheon and Baths, and a sizeable residential area. Titus responded by pouring money and resources into the stricken regions, even selling some of his own furniture to raise relief funds.

His death at Reate after reigning for only two years, two months and twenty days followed a short illness. Malaria was the probable cause, but because there was little love between Titus and his younger brother, suspicion also fell on Domitian. Titus, who had made no provision for the succession and did not have a son, was heard to say that Domitian was his appointed successor, but he never conferred the IMPERIUM PROCONSULARE or TRIBUNICIA POTESTAS on his brother. Fortunately for the empire, no one wanted a return to the horrors of 68–9, and when the praetorians immediately proclaimed Domitian emperor, the senate was hardly likely to demur. Gaius Caligula began a brightly starred reign and turned sour when the funds ran out; would Titus have been similar had he lived longer? Like James Dean in Hollywood history, bright, handsome Titus died before his star could fade, so that after his unexpectedly short reign he came to be regarded as Rome's most beloved emperor.

His brother Titus's popular image was a hard act for the self-reliant and autocratic Domitian (above) to follow. Despite a good reign with successful wars in the northern provinces, and a colossal building programme that transformed Rome, he would after his death be, rather unjustly, vilified by historians who picked on his negative traits to the exclusion of his positive achievements.

DOMITIAN
Titus Flavius Domitianus (r.13/9/81–18/9/96)

There was little doubt that Vespasian's remaining son would become princeps automatically, even though he had not been designated. In fact, in contrast to Titus, the thirty-year-old Domitian had no administrative experience to speak of. Neither his father nor his brother had seen fit to promote him to any offices, apart from some minor consulships, one as Vespasian's colleague. He had been styled PRINCEPS IUVENTUTIS and Caesar, but these were empty titles without sensible duties to go with them. However, Domitian's reign turned out to be a successful one by any standards. And yet the ancient histories vilified him as one of the cruellest and most despotic of tyrants.

Suetonius claimed that one of his favourite pastimes was catching flies and then stabbing them with a needle-sharp stylus, and that he regularly scorched his prisoners' testicles to make them reveal information. While there undoubtedly was a streak of Flavian cruelty in Domitian, as will become clear, the excesses attributed to him are largely the inventions of writers who shared the senatorial outlook of the Flavians as jumped-up rustics. More to the point, Domitian was succeeded by a new dynasty, and – as is usually the case – the new regime was anxious to portray itself in a good light by exaggerating the follies and wickedness of the previous. The senate, of whom Domitian remained openly contemptuous throughout his reign, eager to smear his name in any case, was officially encouraged to do so after his murder. However, given his character, he was touchy about any perceived affront to his dignity. While early in his reign he was content to be addressed as DOMINUS ET DEUS (Lord and God), he did nothing to have the title conferred on him officially. But towards the end Domitian's desire for deification during his lifetime was clearly apparent, and a refusal to worship him was taken as a sign of atheism, a sin that ended the careers and even lives of many.

Domitian was born in Rome on 24 October 51. Unlike Titus, Domitian was not educated in the palace, yet he received sound training in Rome in the same way as any member of the senatorial elite of his day. Domitian gave public recitals of his works, conversed elegantly, and was remembered for sound arguments in debate. With his mother Domitilla dead in his infant years, his brother the elder by ten years and not keen on a child tagging along after him, and a father constantly away in the provinces, Domitian's adolescence was marked by isolation. This seems to have bred within him a preference for seclusion similar to Tiberius; a need for self-reliance combined with tactlessness and an easily injured dignity characterised his autocratic reign. Tellingly, the writings of Tiberius were his favourite reading.

Domitian's movements during the upheavals of 68–70 are not known, other than that he was in Rome, in contact with his elderly uncle Flavius Sabinus. Suetonius tells us that he fled with Sabinus to the Capitol in the last tumultuous days, and when the Vitellians attacked, hid in the caretaker's quarters. In the morning he escaped, disguised as a follower of Isis, crossed the river to Trans Tiberim, and was hidden by the mother of a fellow-student from the agents sent to track him down. Emerging after the victory of the Flavian forces, Domitian was hailed as Caesar. In late 70 he married Domitia Longina, daughter of the legendary general, Gnaeus Domitius Corbulo, whom Nero had forced to commit suicide in 66. Corbulo's name was synonymous with the military achievement Domitian craved. Better still, the marriage brought with it the general's substantial base of clients, which improved Domitian's AUCTORITAS. However, the marriage was troubled. An only child died young, and Domitia was exiled by her husband c.83. Later, he recalled her to the palace, where she lived with him in some tumult until his death.

From the outset of his reign, Domitian made it clear that he wanted servants and not partners in the government. He held the consulship for the first eight years and a total of seventeen times in all, and only gave it up because he came to scorn such a lowly senatorial rank. In 85 he made himself CENSOR PERPETUUS instead of holding the office annually, as Vespasian had done. In this it was evident that he intended to control the make-up of the senate and dominate it. After first attending senate meetings he soon stopped, ignoring the body altogether and taking decisions in the style of an old dictator. Instead, he relied more on the aid of EQUITES and gave the order increased importance, and by placing knights in positions previously reserved for senators, he further earned the odium of the aristocracy. Only in one respect was an equestrian rank diminished – Domitian returned to the older practice of appointing two PRAEFECTI PRAETORIO, but he ensured they were not persons of influence or power, and he also changed them frequently to lessen the potential threat a prolonged term proffered.

Domitian's ambitious and spectacular building programme was unmatched by any other emperor since Augustus. After the great fire of 64, the civil wars of 68–9, and the devastating fire of 80, Rome was badly in need of repair. He began to erect, repair or complete some fifty structures, including the restored Temple of Jupiter Optimus Maximus on the Capitol. He finished the Amphitheatrum Flavium Vespasian had begun and Titus dedicated. He built structures in the Campus Martius for his LUDI CAPITOLINI (*see below*), an odeum, stadium and a new circus (still visible today as the Piazza Navona). On the Forum face of the Capitol he built a temple to his deified father and brother, and completed the Arch of Titus that celebrated the capture of Jerusalem. He raised a new shopping centre in the Saepta, and built granaries and water works. His most spectacular edifice was the vast palace on the Palatine, larger by far, in substance if not extent, than the Domus Aureus. Adjacent to the Domus Flavia, the Augustana was a continuation that fully covered Nero's extension on the Palatine as well as a considerable part of the Palace of Tiberius, and stretched from the ramparts above the Forum Romanum to the Circus Maximus, towering like a cliff above it.

Domitian's admiration for older Italian virtues was more pronounced than his father's. But more superstitious than Vespasian, he had brooded much on the subject of religion during his secluded adolescent years. Whereas Vespasian had evinced a return to simpler values by setting an example, Domitian legislated for morality. He curbed the licentiousness of stage performances, suppressed prostitution and revived the punishment of starvation to death for unchaste Vestal Virgins. Domitian closely identified himself with the ancient Roman gods Minerva and Jupiter, publicly linking the latter divinity to his regime through the LUDI CAPITOLINI (Capitoline Games) founded in 86. These were held every four years in the early summer, and consisted of chariot races, athletics and gymnastics, and music, oratory and poetry. Contestants came from many nations, and no expense was spared; the emperor himself awarded the prizes.

The huge building programme, the LUDI CAPITOLINI and many other lavish arena games, and the expense of several costly wars had a predictable effect on the economy. Free-giving Titus had not left the FISCUS in a particularly healthy state. However, Domitian left his successor a satisfactory public financial situation through a variety of means that did much to blacken his memory. The first was a good move. Shortly after taking office, Domitian restored the weight of the silver DENARIUS by about twelve per cent (to the earlier level of Augustus). Unfortunately, he was forced to debase it again in 85, when the imperial income proved insufficient to meet military and public expenditure. The rigorous collection of taxes soon became necessary, sparking a short-lived rebellion in Africa and rumblings elsewhere. Inevitably, confiscation and murder returned to the menu of money-raising methods, along with the reappearance of the hated DELATORES. He altered the law pertaining to RELEGATIO (a lighter form of banishment) to include the forfeiture of property as part of the sentence… and welcome extra income.

Domitian and his wife Domitia Longina, daughter of the famous general Corbulo. She would ultimately lead the plot that killed him.

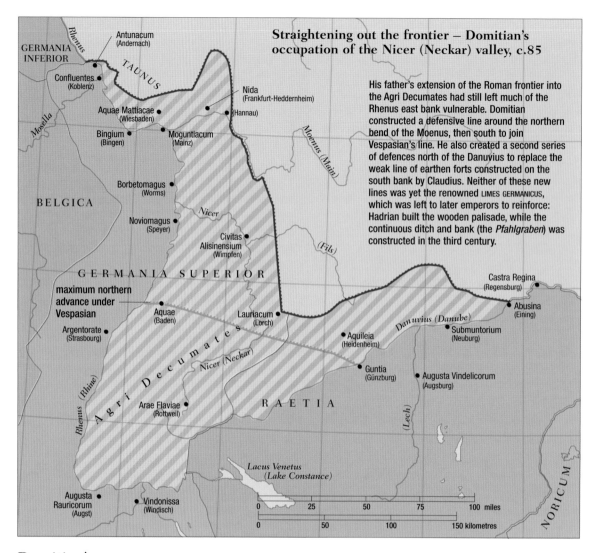

Straightening out the frontier – Domitian's occupation of the Nicer (Neckar) valley, c.85

His father's extension of the Roman frontier into the Agri Decumates had still left much of the Rhenus east bank vulnerable. Domitian constructed a defensive line around the northern bend of the Moenus, then south to join Vespasian's line. He also created a second series of defences north of the Danuvius to replace the weak line of earthen forts constructed on the south bank by Claudius. Neither of these new lines was yet the renowned LIMES GERMANICUS, which was left to later emperors to reinforce: Hadrian built the wooden palisade, while the continuous ditch and bank (the *Pfahlgraben*) was constructed in the third century.

Domitian's wars

While the military abilities of Vespasian and Titus were genuine, those of Domitian were not. And yet during his reign there were more wars and military campaigns against the empire's enemies than at any time since the late Republican period. This was clearly due to necessity – German and Dacian tribes were beginning to put pressure on the frontiers – but it may reflect Domitian's desire to emulate his father and brother's military victories. And, like his father, he courted the soldiers, giving each legionary a big pay rise of one-third, and taking a personal hand in as many campaigns as he could manage.

He claimed a triumph in 83 for subduing the Chatti, a warlike German tribe of the Taunus mountains that threatened Germania Superior in the region of Moguntiacum (Mainz). Even modern historians disagree on the outcome, many preferring the view of Tacitus that the conquest was illusory, even a joke. Those who disagree point to the archaeological evidence of the fortifications erected along a hundred and-twenty-mile line stretching from north of the Taunus around the western Moenus (Main) valley. This then incorporated the Nicer (Neckar) valley and joined Vespasian's northernmost line of the Agri Decumates. This was accomplished at the expense of the improbably huge ambitions of Agricola, the governor of Britannia (*see side panel right, above*). At Moguntiacum Domitian gathered detachments from nine legions: four taken from Britannia, the four in Germania Superior, and *XXI Rapax* from Germania Inferior. Under the command of Gaius Velius Rufus, the Chatti were ruthlessly driven out of the Moenus valley and away from the Rhenus to disappear in the wild German forests.

Domitian was also responsible for strengthening the north bank of the Danuvius, from his new German line, east to Abusina (Eining). The peace these new defences brought to the enlarged Germania Superior was to last until the third century. Civil administration was also given to the province as distinct from a mere

LEGATUS of the army. The first of these new governors was the well-known jurist Lucius Javolenus Priscus, appointed in 90. A further benefit soon became apparent, when Domitian was able to transfer two of its legions (*I Adiutrix* and *XXI Rapax*) to the lower Danuvius, where a far greater danger threatened.

The British detachments, who had expected to be returned home, were also sent; but it was not enough. The empire simply did not have enough experienced forces to deal with the encroaching threat on the lower Danuvius and, in 86, an entire legion (*II Adiutrix*) was moved from Britannia to Moesia to help counter what is known as the First Dacian War. In 85 Dacian tribes living north of the Danuvius crossed the river and invaded Moesia. They advanced to the south and slew the LEGATUS of the province, Oppius Sabinus. Domitian hurried to Moesia, and the initial success against the aggressors by his PRAEFECTUS PRAETORIO, Cornelius Fuscus, allowed the emperor to celebrate a triumph at Rome in 86... just before disaster struck.

Intending to counter-invade Dacia, Fuscus took one legion across the Danuvius, but was pushed back and finally caught just across the river. Since LEGIO *V Alaudae* disappears from the records at this point, it was presumably this legion that was wiped out with Fuscus. Domitian spent 87 planning a recovery campaign, and returned to Moesia in 88 with the army's new LEGATUS, Tettius Julianus. In the Second Dacian War, although Julianus secured a victory at the Pass of Tapae (the Iron Gate, near modern Bucova), the business was far from settled when, in the same year, the LEGATUS of the two legions stationed at Moguntiacum, Lucius Antonius Saturninus, raised his standard. The reasons for Saturninus's revolt are not clear, but perhaps he coveted the purple for himself and felt the time was ripe. In any event, Domitian's courting of his troops paid off. By the time he arrived in January 89, the other six legions in Germania had declared their loyalty and Saturninus had already been killed in a skirmish. This rebellion shook Domitian badly and it was at the root of the terror that he unleashed soon after.

Later that same year, Domitian attacked the Jazyges, Suebian Marcomanni and Quadi in the First Pannonian War. Domitian negotiated a settlement with the Dacian king Decebalus to avoid having to fight on two fronts. Compelled to return to the Danuvius three years later, Domitian fought the combined forces of the Suebi and the Sarmatae in the Second Pannonian War. Few details of this conflict exist, other than it lasted for eight months and in its course LEGIO *XXI Rapax* was lost.

TACITUS is largely responsible for the damning of Domitian's military reputation, but there is a clear reason for the contemporary historian's grumpiness towards the emperor. Domitian's need for British troops in Pannonia and Moesia helped to curtail the operations of the historian's admired father-in-law, the governor Gnaeus Julius Agricola. His predecessor, Julius Frontinus (g.74–76), had made some progress on the edges of Wales, but Agricola (g.76–84) cherished a far larger ambition. He wanted to conquer all of the British Isles, including Hibernia (Ireland). First, he completed the subjugation of Wales, then moved north, establishing a line of forts between the Itun Aestuarius (Solway Firth) and Tinea (Tyne). Next he advanced into Scotland and built a second fortified line between the Clota (Clyde) and Bodotria (Forth). From here he pressed on northeast in 84, aiming to bring the last Celtic army in Britain to battle. In this he was successful, meeting the Pictish force at Mons Graupius (probably the mountain of Bennachie, near Inverurie). For the Romans it was an overwhelming victory, but the advantage was never pressed home, because shortly after it Domitian wanted the reinforcements and recalled Agricola.

Back in Rome, Domitian's last years were a period of tyranny and cruelty. The DELATORES, already at work helping to fill the FISCUS, were kept busy uncovering supposed plots. Having been assiduous in the proper dispensation of justice in the early years of his reign, Domitian insisted on the formality of a trial for the victims, but it did not save them. The writers Pliny the Younger, Juvenal, Suetonius and Tacitus all write of the prevailing atmosphere of terror. Any charge, no matter how slight — failing to toast the emperor's health, for instance — resulted in confiscation of the man's estate and secured his execution. The Roman mob, not much affected, was treated to lavish shows in the arenas and circuses, but the senatorial order suffered heavily. The sensible ones, including the ex-British governors Frontinus and Agricola, retired from any form of public life and hid away on their country estates.

Dacian king Decebalus is depicted on Trajan's column, whose frieze celebrated that emperor's campaign which led to the Dacian's defeat in AD 106.

CHRISTIAN WRITERS later referred to Domitian as the 'second great persecutor' (the first being Nero). Given his devotion to Roman pagan religion, it is easy to see how such stories could have evolved, but hard evidence of his antipathy — other than considering Christians atheists from the Roman point of view — is lacking. Christians may have been among those banished or executed during the Terror, but no organised persecution is evident. Whereas there is clear evidence that the Jews were made to feel uneasy under Domitian, who scrupulously collected the Jewish tax and harassed Jewish tax dodgers during much of his reign.

The Roman empire at the death of Domitian, 96

The tribes of mountainous central Wales and those of Cornwall remained largely beyond effective Roman control during the 400-year occupation.

OCEANUS GERMANICUS

Hibernia

Deva (Chester)
Eburacum (York)
Lindum (Lincoln)

BRITANNIA

Londinium

Gesoriacum (Boulogne)

OCEANUS ATLANTICUS

GERMANIA INFERIOR
Colonia Agrippina (Cologne)

BELGICA

Augusta Treverorum (Trier)
Moguntiacum (Mainz)

GALLIA LUGDUNENSIS

GALLIA

Agri Decumates
GERMANIA SUPERIOR

Castra Regina (Regensberg)

Augusta Vindelicorum (Augsburg)

Carnuntum

AQUITANIA

RAETIA
NORICUM

Aquincum (Buda)

Lugdunum (Lyons)

Virunum

PANNONIA

NARBONENSIS

Mediolanum (Milan)
Julian Alps
Aquileia

Tolosa (Toulouse)

Genua

Sirmium (Mitrovica)

Danuvius

Dacia

Ariminum (Rimini)

DALMATIA

Viminacium (Kostolac)

Novae

Narbo (Narbonne)
Arelate (Arles)

Massilia

Salonae

Superior MOESIA Inferior

LUSITANIA

Caesaraugusta (Zaragoza)

Tarraco (Tarragona)

CORSICA

ITALIA

MARE ADRIATICUM

THRACIA

HISPANIA

TARRACONENSIS

Roma

Italica

Corduba

Neapolis

MACEDONIA

Nicom

Thessalonica

BAETICA

BALEARES

SARDINIA

Brundisium (Brindisi)

EPIRUS

MARE IONIUM

MARE AEGEUM

ASIA

Perga

Tingi

Carthago Nova

MARE TYRRHENUM

ACHAEA

Athenae (Athens)

Eph

MAURETANIA TINGITANA

Caesarea

SICILIA

Messana

Carthago

Syracusae

MAURETANIA CAESARIENSIS

Cirta

NUMIDIA

Hadrumetum (Sousse)

MARE INTERNUM

CRETA ET CYRENAICA

Byzacena

AFRICA PROCONSULARIS

Tripolitana

Leptis Magna

Cyrene

Domitian added no new territory to the empire beyond the occupation and fortification of the Agri Decumates. During the Flavian period several provincial boundaries were altered. Italia's from the central to Julian Alps was extended and straightened out; Dalmatia was enlarged to the northeast towards Sirmium, and Moesia was divided into two provinces; Epirus became recognised as a separate provincial entity (although it would be reunited with Macedonia from time to time). The provinces of Pannonia, Dalmatia and Moesia Superior were collectively referred to as Illyricum.

Roman empire at the death of Domitian, AD 96

Italia

client kingdom

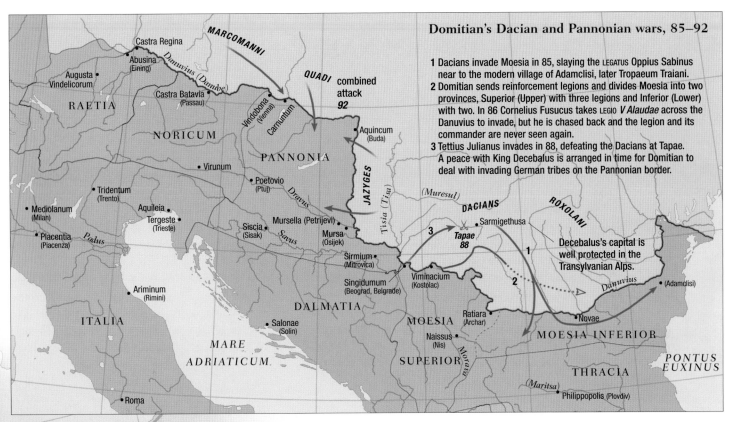

Domitian's Dacian and Pannonian wars, 85–92

1 Dacians invade Moesia in 85, slaying the LEGATUS Oppius Sabinus near to the modern village of Adamclisi, later Tropaeum Traiani.

2 Domitian sends reinforcement legions and divides Moesia into two provinces, Superior (Upper) with three legions and Inferior (Lower) with two. In 86 Cornelius Fuscus takes LEGIO *V Alaudae* across the Danuvius to invade, but he is chased back and the legion and its commander are never seen again.

3 Tettius Julianus invades in 88, defeating the Dacians at Tapae. A peace with King Decebalus is arranged in time for Domitian to deal with invading German tribes on the Pannonian border.

Decebalus's capital is well protected in the Transylvanian Alps.

When Domitian executed his harmless cousin Flavius Clemens in 95 on a charge of atheism (possibly a conversion to Christianity, more likely a failure to salute the emperor speedily), and exiled Clemens' wife Domitilla, the emperor's own niece, no one felt safe from his paranoia. A palace plot to assassinate Domitian was formulated between his wife Domitia, his chamberlain Parthenius and the PRAEFECTUS PRAETORIO Petronius Secundus. It was simple enough. Domitian was persuaded to give an interview to Domitilla's disgruntled steward, who came before his emperor with an injured arm on 18 September 96. Concealed in the bandages was a knife with which he fatally stabbed Domitian, who was just a month short of his forty-fifth birthday.

Domitian had no son to follow him, but he had not entirely ignored the question of his successor, having named the sons of his cousin Clemens. However, after having their father executed, they were dropped, and if he had other arrangements in mind, the assassin put an end to them. The conspirators, however, were prepared. They had secured a candidate for the principate, the old and respected senator Marcus Cocceius Nerva.

Inset, facing page: A coin shows a defeated German warrior kneeling before the triumphant Domitian.

CHAPTER FOUR   AD 96–138
THE NERVO-TRAJANIC DYNASTY

NERVA
Marcus Cocceius Nerva (r.18/9/96–27/1/98)

When Nerva uncovered the Piso conspiracy against Nero in 65, the grateful emperor rewarded his praetor-designate with triumphal insignia and placed his statue prominently in the palace. Nerva was on the early stages of the CURSUS HONORUM at the time, as would be expected of a young aristocrat.

Born on 8 November 30, Nerva could claim eminent ancestry. Before his first consulship, on his father's side there had been no less than five consuls starting with his great-grandfather, also Marcus Cocceius Nerva, in 36 BC; his grandfather, a distinguished jurist of the same name, accompanied Tiberius on his retirement to Capreae in AD 26. On his mother's side an aunt, Rubellia Bassa, was the great-granddaughter of Tiberius. In addition, his great-uncle Lucius Cocceius Nerva played a part in the negotiations that secured a treaty between Octavian and Antony at Brundisium in 40 BC. We know almost nothing about his early life before the Piso conspiracy, although the fact that his name does not appear on any legionary rolls suggests that he did not pursue the traditional aristocratic path of TRIBUNUS MILITUM; neither was he a public speaker nor legal advocate.

Following Nero's fall in 68, Nerva disappears from the histories again, but it is clear that he found favour with Vespasian because he shared the consulship with the emperor in 71, the only time that Vespasian ever held the office without his son Titus. He was also a consul with Domitian in 90 – Nerva, clearly an adept at foiling conspiracies, had alerted the emperor to the revolt of Antonius Saturninus in 89. This may not have saved him from imperial paranoia in the final years of Domitian's reign, and whether or not he was forced to withdraw from public life remains an open question.

On the face of it, Nerva seems an odd candidate for the principate. At sixty-six he was really too old for the job; his long-time support of the Flavians, with close ties to the unpopular Domitian, should have disqualified him in senatorial eyes; his distant relationship to the Julio-Claudians on his mother's side should have doubly damned him with the aristocracy. On the other hand, Nerva was a capable senator who had already demonstrated prudent and tactful behaviour, and was probably the best available person to become princeps. Despite his pro-Flavian stance of the past, for the senatorial order rejected by Domitian in preference to lowly EQUITES Nerva's accession was a triumph; and he was quick to take an oath not to execute any senator. But what pleased the senate did not necessarily appeal to the soldiers. Having been weaned from the Julian house, the troops liked the Flavians and resented Domitian's murder. There were rumblings the length of the frontier, but the legions acquiesced with bad grace to Nerva's accession, and in Rome the praetorians had no candidate to fuel their opposition. Their restraint, however, was short-lived.

It was politically expedient for Nerva to distance himself from Domitian, certainly in the eyes of the senatorial order – the Roman public was indifferent so long as the grain dole worked and there were plenty of gladiatorial diversions. But it was also useful to channel any popular resentment in the direction of the previous regime and away from the principate. An officially encouraged denigration of Domitian began almost immediately, although Nerva wisely retained much of his legislation simply because it worked. In a shrewd move he threw Domitian's Domus Augustana open to the public as a civic building, the Domus Populi, and lived in a modest house in the Horti Sallustiani, the garden district that Vespasian had preferred. Exiles were allowed to return, and property confiscated by Domitian was restored.

Nerva appointed men whom he knew and trusted to essential offices, men such as Sextus Julius Frontinus, who came out of retirement to become CURA AQUARUM, an office that had long been subject to mismanagement. Frontinus put an end to the many common abuses endemic in the delivery of water and published a work on Rome's water supply, *De aquis urbis Romae*. Despite the official line on Domitian, many of Nerva's AMICI were men with Flavian ties, who, by virtue of their links to the previous regime, were valuable to Nerva for what they knew. Unfortunately, some of this inner circle were DELATORES like the infamous A. Didius Gallus Fabricius Veiiento, one of Domitian's ill-reputed counsellors, who was to be found seated next to Nerva at imperial dinners. Nerva was also less willing to consult the senate than many senators would have liked,

Marcus Cocceius Nerva's adoption of Trajan to be his successor was a significant first for imperial Rome: his appointee was a native of Hispania, and thus the first non-Italian to rise to the purple.

generally preferring the opinions of his CONSILIUM. In general, however, Nerva managed to win over the senate without giving it any real power, retaining that for the principate, but he re-established the tradition of senatorial co-operation with the princeps, which would endure throughout most of the next century.

In a reign of only sixteen months, it is not surprising that Nerva undertook little public building. His name appears on numerous mileposts along provincial roads, but the programme was really Domitian's. He also appropriated Domitian's uncompleted forum that linked that of Augustus to the Templum Pax and dedicated it in 98, which is why we now know it as the Forum of Nerva. In addition, he built granaries and made repairs to the Amphitheatrum Flavium after the Tiberis broke its banks and flooded the low-lying district. For the benefit of the public, Nerva restored the more liberal theatre performances that Domitian had suppressed.

Nerva's greatest monument, however, was not a building but the institution of the ALIMENTA. Under this scheme small farmers pledged their land as security and were allowed to borrow up to a twelfth of its value from the FISCUS. The five per cent interest on the loan was repaid not to the FISCUS but to their MUNICIPIUM, which used the money to support the children of poor parents. The ALIMENTA was a great success, since it not only alleviated Italian poverty to some extent, but also caused a regeneration of Italian farming. Wealthy nobles followed the example and founded similar schemes of their own, so that soon several thousand children were being provided for in Italia, and more in the provinces as the concept spread. The ALIMENTA was to remain in place until the time of Diocletian. Additionally, for Italia's urban poor, Nerva granted allotments of land worth sixty million SESTERCES, and he exempted parents and their children from the five per cent inheritance tax.

These were popular measures, but they did not entirely succeed in winning everyone over to Nerva's principate. The conspiracy of Gaius Calpurnius Crassus, a descendant of the wealthy first triumvir, was uncovered and suppressed, and Crassus exiled, but the discontent of the praetorian guards was a greater worry. Dissatisfied that Nerva had not deified Domitian, they mutinied under the PRAEFECTUS PRAETORIO Casperius Aelianus – Domitian's appointee – in October 97. Taking the emperor hostage, it was demanded that Nerva hand over Domitian's murderers. Nerva had no option but to comply. Ignominiously, he was forced before the Roman mob to give a speech of thanks to the mutineers for their public-spirited action.

These two events coupled with growing unrest among the provincial troops convinced Nerva that he must appoint a successor who could not only keep order among the soldiers, but would also appeal to them. For this reason he passed over his male relatives and chose Marcus Ulpius Traianus (Trajan), announcing his appointment in late October 97 at the celebration of a victory in Pannonia over the Quadi and Marcomanni. Trajan was immediately acclaimed as Caesar and IMPERATOR, granted the TRIBUNICIA POTESTAS and named as Nerva's consular colleague for the following year.

The adoption of Trajan by Nerva is one of the most significant moments in the Roman empire's history, not because he was adopting a person outside his immediate family – that had been done by the Julio-Claudians – and not because he was pointing to a successor popular with the army. That, after all, was essential. What is extraordinary is that Trajan was not even an Italian. Now a man from the provinces could aspire to the purple. Trajan, who was based on the Rhenus at the time of his adoption, did not come to Rome but stayed with his troops; and he was there at Moguntiacum when Nerva died.

On 1 January 98, the start of his fourth consulship, Nerva suffered a stroke. Three weeks later he died at his villa in the Gardens of Sallust. From his headquarters on the Rhenus, Trajan insisted that Nerva's ashes be placed in the mausoleum of Augustus and asked the senate to vote on his deification.

TRAJAN
Marcus Ulpius Nerva Traianus
(nominated October 97; princeps 28/1/98–9/8/117)

'During a happy period of more than fourscore years, the public administration was conducted by the virtue and abilities of Nerva, Trajan, Hadrian and the two Antonines.' So said Gibbon in his massive work *The Decline and Fall of the Roman Empire* of the period he rightly considered to be ancient Rome's apogee. Of these five, Trajan – undoubtedly one of the greatest warrior-emperors of all time – was one of Roman history's most admirable figures, a man who by his actions deserved the renown that he enjoyed in his lifetime and in subsequent generations.

The home of the Ulpii was the Latin COLONIA of Italica in Baetica (close to modern Seville), and Trajan was born there on 18 September 53. His mother Marcia had given birth to a daughter, Ulpia Marciana, five years before her son's arrival. The Ulpii had settled in the

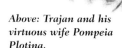

region late in the third century BC, but Trajan's father – also Marcus – was the first Ulpius to pursue a senatorial career. Born c.30, he is thought to have been an officer under Nero's famous general Domitius Corbulo in the early sixties. LEGATUS LEGIONIS of *X Fretensis* during the Jewish War, Vespasian rewarded him with a propraetorship and then a suffect consulship in 70. At the end of his term he was adlected by the emperor and returned to his native province of Baetica as its governor. There followed the governorships of Syria, Africa and Asia. He probably died before 100, having seen his son become emperor, and was deified in 113 as DIVUS TRAIANUS PATER.

The young Trajan, then, was supported by his father's sparkling career, and determined not to let him down. Maddeningly, the historical sources are scant on information about his early years, but we know that in the mid-seventies when he was about twenty-two he was an officer under his father in Syria. He married a woman much younger than himself, Pompeia Plotina, from Nemausus (Nîmes) in Gallia Narbonensis. He was a quaestor in c.78 and praetor in c.84. In 86, he was made a guardian to a child named Publius Aelius Hadrianus (Hadrian), a native of Trajan's home town of Italica, whose father had recently died. Domitian appointed Trajan to be LEGATUS LEGIONIS of *VII Gemina* in Hispania Tarraconensis, and he took the legion to the Rhenus in 89 to help crush the uprising of Antonius Saturninus. He next fought in the Dacian and Pannonian wars, and was rewarded with an ordinary consulship in 91. There followed the governorship of Moesia Inferior and then that of Germania Superior. And it was in his headquarters at Moguntiacum that the young Hadrianus, now a TRIBUNUS MILITUM, brought Trajan the news that he had been adopted by Nerva and nominated co-princeps and heir-designate.

Technically, because of all the imperial powers and prerogatives conferred on him, Trajan was already emperor before Nerva's death. Evidently, he felt no pressing need to go to Rome because after dispatching a solemn oath to never execute a senator, he proceeded to Pannonia. Being away from Rome at such a time would have been the undoing of any previous princeps, but at the properly mature age of forty-four conscientious, sober Trajan had the charisma to take

command of the empire simultaneously with finishing a distant military campaign. He spent the winter of 98 on the Danuvius, and did not reach Rome until the spring of 99. When he finally did arrive, his modest entry on foot indicated a common touch from the first. He embraced members of the senate, instantly bridging the chasm that Domitian and many predecessors had created. His wife Plotina was equally modest. On entering the palace she said, 'I enter here such a woman as I would hope to be when I depart.'

In sharp contrast to Nerva's treatment of Domitian (of whom Trajan seems to have cautiously approved), he saw to the honours and deification of Nerva, and then spent two years winning over all the classes of Rome. Yet Trajan's policies essentially continued those of Domitian; he was no less master of the state and had ultimate authority over all individuals, but his good nature and respect for those who had until recently been his superiors won him great acclaim. He was unofficially styled OPTIMUS PRINCEPS (the best first man) by the people.[†]

The Dacian wars

Trajan found military life more enjoyable than the comforts and trappings of the imperial palace – he had spent more than ten years as a TRIBUNUS – it was in his nature to want to push Rome's frontiers beyond those of Augustus, Claudius and the Flavians. And like Claudius, he might also have considered that a successful campaign of conquest would bolster his new reign. He had already signalled that the wily rogue King Decebalus of Dacia would be the first target in 98–9. Preparations for a great campaign began, with the transfer of legions and their attached auxiliaries from Germania, Britannia and other provinces, and the enrolment of two new legions: *II Traiana* and *XXX Ulpia*. This brought the empire's total strength to thirty legions, the highest number yet reached since the time of Augustus.

The political pretexts for an invasion of Dacia were several, not least the aggressive preparations of its king. But traders had informed Trajan that the land north of the Danuvius was rich in gold, silver and essential minerals. At the outset of his reign, a fat profit from conquest would be extremely useful. In 101 the emperor took the field with a large army estimated to have been about a hundred thousand men. The war required all the military technology, engineering and discipline for

Above: Trajan and his virtuous wife Pompeia Plotina.

Below: The reverse of Trajan's coin honours both his natural father on the right and his adoptive father Nerva.

---

† This title appeared on his coins from 105, but according to Dio Cassius he was not conferred the title officially until 114.

which the Roman army was renowned. The old road of Tiberius on the Roman bank of the Danuvius in the region known as Porta Ferea (the Iron Gates) was completely rebuilt. In his company was the brilliant civil engineer Apollodorus of Damascus, in whom Trajan was most fortunate. Apollodorus converted the old narrow path in the spectacular gorge into a breathtaking highway by cantilevering the road out from the sheer face of the rock so that the legionaries felt as though they were marching on water.

Trajan split his massive army in two. The first force crossed the river at Viminacium and advanced along the western flank of the Transylvanian Alps towards the Iron Gate Pass, while the second column crossed at Drobeta and made for the Vulcan Pass, to the southeast of Decebalus's stronghold at Sarmizegethusa. The first force won a victory at Tapae, where Domitian's general Tettius Julianus had defeated the Dacians in 89, but this failed to break the enemy's resistance by the time the winter set in. The forced break in hostilities was not wasted: the troops trained and engineers built more portable war engines. In the early spring Trajan moved with great speed, this time with a united force. The legions crossed into Dacia at Drobeta and then drove through the Carpathian passes into the heart of Transylvania. In 102 Decebalus was forced to a humiliating peace, and Roman garrisons were stationed in Banat and Transylvania. For its better protection, Pannonia was divided, as Domitian had done with Moesia, into Superior and Inferior provinces, jointly

receiving an increased garrison of five legions. Trajan then returned to Rome, celebrated a triumph, and added the title Dacicus to his nomenclature.

Decebalus, however, once left to his own devices, undertook to challenge Rome again. Having secretly rearmed, in 105 the Dacians overwhelmed the Roman garrisons north of the Danuvius and began raiding across the river in Moesia. Trajan responded immediately by gathering an even larger army. It is worth noting that Domitian's pacification of the Chatti, lampooned by Tacitus and Suetonius, had been so successful that Trajan felt confident in leaving only four legions in both provinces of Germania. One of the borrowed legions was *I Minerva*, commanded by Trajan's ward Hadrian. The army crossed the Danuvius early in 106 at Drobreta, using the massive bridge recently completed by Apollodorus – traces of its sixty stone piers still survive – and fought its way into Transylvania, and annexed the country to the empire. Decebalus, driven from his capital of Sarmizegethusa, chose to commit suicide rather than to be paraded in a Roman triumph and then be ritually strangled.

Over the next three years the new province was treated to a rapid process of romanisation, with road building and the planting of COLONIAE inhabited by citizens drawn mostly from the eastern provinces. The Dacians who escaped slavery were transported to the south bank of the Danuvius and resettled. Even as this was happening, Trajan ordered the annexation of Arabia Petraea on the death of Dabel, the Nabataean

Dacian king Decebalus decides to slit his own throat rather than fall captive of the Romans; from the frieze on Trajan's column in Rome.

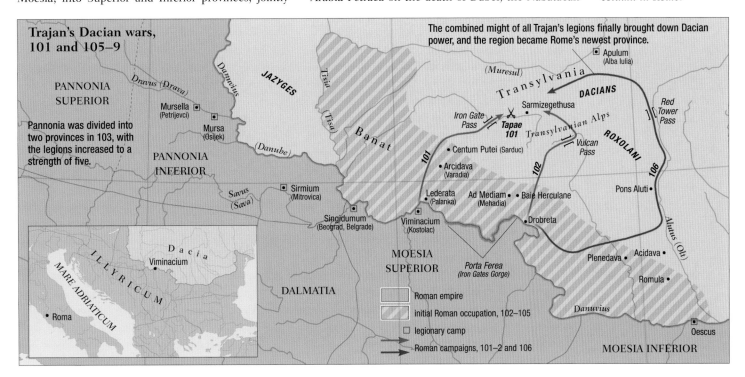

Trajan's Dacian wars, 101 and 105–9

The combined might of all Trajan's legions finally brought down Dacian power, and the region became Rome's newest province.

PANNONIA SUPERIOR

Pannonia was divided into two provinces in 103, with the legions increased to a strength of five.

PANNONIA INFERIOR

JAZYGES

Dravus (Drava)

Danuvius

Tisia

Tisa (Tisa)

Muresul

Transylvania

DACIANS

Apulum (Alba Iulia)

Iron Gate Pass

Sarmizegethusa

Tapae 101

Transylvanian Alps

Vulcan Pass

ROXOLANI

Red Tower Pass

Mursella (Petrijevci)

Mursa (Osijek)

Danube

Centum Putei (Sarduc)

Arcidava (Varadia)

Lederata (Palanka)

Ad Mediam (Mehadia)

Baie Herculane

Drobreta

Pons Aluti

Savus (Sava)

Sirmium (Mitrovica)

Singidunum (Beograd, Belgrade)

Viminacium (Kostolac)

MOESIA SUPERIOR

Porta Ferea (Iron Gates Gorge)

Plenedava

Acidava

Alutus (Olt)

Romula

Danuvius

Oescus

MOESIA INFERIOR

DALMATIA

Dacia

Viminacium

ILLYRICUM

MARE ADRIATICUM

Roma

Roman empire

initial Roman occupation, 102–105

legionary camp

Roman campaigns, 101–2 and 106

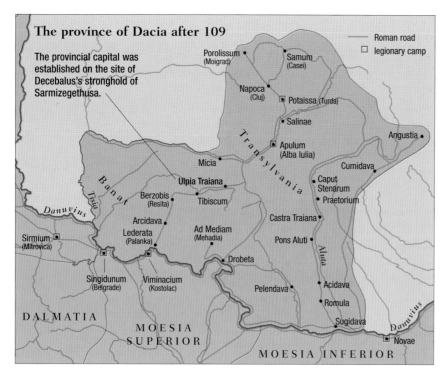

The province of Dacia after 109

The provincial capital was established on the site of Decebalus's stronghold of Sarmizegethusa.

history of both Dacian wars. Unusually, Trajan did not construct a temple in its precincts, a matter rectified later by Hadrian.

To the northeast of the Amphitheatrum Flavium, using a great part of Nero's Domus Aurea as the foundation, he built the largest baths complex in Rome, which would be exceeded in scale only by those of Caracalla and Diocletian. This required a new aqueduct, the Aqua Paola, which still supplies water to modern Rome. In Italia the Aqua Traiana was built in 109 to supply southern Etruria, and a new road linking Beneventum to Brundisium of the same year supplemented the southern section of the ancient Via Appia. He also involved himself in civil projects such as the harbours of and Centumcellae, the ports for Rome, and at Ancona and Brundisium on the Adriaticum. When old Ostia had silted up, Claudius had built a new harbour for Rome one and a half miles to the north (Portus). Later, Trajan enlarged the facilities and built a canal to bypass the lower Tiberis and link Portus to Rome for barge traffic.

Trajan was as passionate about games as anyone, and could be as extravagant. Now in his fifty-fourth year, he celebrated his return to Rome in 107 with LUDI that outdid those of Titus by running for a hundred and twenty-three consecutive days, and in which more than eleven thousand gladiators lost their lives. Augustus did not get through as many as this in his entire long reign. These were just the first of many such lavish spectacles. Not only the Amphitheatrum Flavium, but also the Circus Maximus was kept busy. It was Trajan who had the space improved from a string of wooden tiers into the massive stone monument that would find imitators all over the empire. In conjunction with Trajan's increase of the grain dole to the Roman mob, the contemporary satirist Juvenal wrote: 'NAM QUI DABAT OLIM / IMPERIUM, FASCES, LEGIONES, OMNIA, NUNC SE / CONTINET, ATQUE DUAS TANTUM RES ANXIUS OPTAT, / PANEM ET CIRCENSES.' (This loosely translates as: 'Long ago the people shed their anxieties, ever since we do not sell our votes to anyone. For the people – who once conferred imperium, symbols of office, legions, everything – now hold themselves in check and anxiously desire only two things, the grain dole and chariot races in the Circus.')

Juvenal's famous phrase, PANEM ET CIRCENSES (bread and circuses), pointed to the political importance of chariot races in diverting energies that might otherwise have gone into rioting, and it was chariot racing, not gladiatorial combat, that was the most popular spectator sport in Rome.

king. Since the days of Pompeius Magnus it had been a client kingdom, largely inhabited by nomadic Arabs, although cities such as Petra had grown wealthy on the lucrative trade routes to the east that passed through it. The smaller northern part was annexed to Syria, while the southern region became the new province of Arabia, with its capital at Bostra.

Trajan's building programme

The two Dacian wars had taxed Roman resources, but the vast wealth of the Dacian mines that now came to Rome as war booty enabled Trajan to support an extensive building programme almost everywhere, but above all in Italia and in Rome. Under the care of the tireless Apollodorus, Trajan set about transforming the capital. He had already commenced building a new forum behind that of Julius Caesar and beside that of Augustus, but the remaining room under the rising Quirinal was insufficient for his enlarged scheme. Accordingly, Apollodorus had a massive swathe cut into the hillside and completely removed the low col joining the Capitol to the Quirinal to make room. The rise of the Quirinal was then cleverly used to create a massive, tiered shopping centre, much of it still visible today. The Forum of Trajan – the largest of all the Roman imperial FORA – comprised the Basilica Ulpia, which served as a law-court, and two libraries, one Greek, one Latin. Between them rose Trajan's Column, sculpted with twenty-three spiral bands filled with two thousand five hundred figures, depicting the

Trajan's administration

To this point, the empire's politics could be chiefly characterised by the relationship between the princeps and the senate; whether it more – or less – conformed to Augustus's fiction of a determining senate with the guidance of the emperor. After him, with the occasional exceptions of Nero (thanks to Seneca and Burrus) and Claudius from time-to-time, the principate had been either aloof or downright autocratic. Trajan's was as autocratic as any, but his good relations with the senate allowed him to accomplish whatever he wished without much opposition. In his generally modest demeanour, it was his AUCTORITAS that was more important than his IMPERIUM. Writing in the biography of his father-in-law Agricola, Tacitus spoke glowingly of the newly won compatibility of autocratic rule and individual liberty established by Nerva and expanded by Trajan. Whether we should really believe that the principate and liberty had been made compatible, this was evidently held to be so by Rome's aristocracy.

It is easy to see why this belief should have been widespread. Claudius had perfected the Imperial Civil Service, but controlled its activities through his personal freedmen, rarely allowing any of the senatorial order to interfere. Trajan formed a professional elite from among senators to order and control the state's functions. He had no need to hog the office of consul to bolster his principate. During the twenty years of his reign, he held the consulship only six times, compared to Vespasian's nine and Domitian's seventeen. In the history of the empire to this point, only twelve PRIVATI had achieved the eminence of a third consulship; Agrippa had been the first. During Trajan's reign three served for their third time – Sextus Julius Frontinus (ordinary, 100), Titus Vestricius Spurinna (suffect, 100), Lucius Licinius Sura (ordinary, 107) – and ten served their second consulships. What these men had in common was their service as colleagues or juniors with Trajan from his days as a PRIVATUS, several were his prime LEGATI in the Dacian wars. He trusted them and, more importantly, they trusted the emperor. They were all of proven ability, energetic, used to strict organisation and decisive action, and happy to take orders. In this, they combined the best of Republican government's military nobility, but without the wastage of experience caused by the Republic's annual rotation of senior offices.

One taxing problem had arisen from the expansion and romanisation of the empire. Government service and the opportunities for quick wealth had taken many Italians abroad, draining Italia's MUNICIPIA of human resources. The provinces were also suffering in a reverse fashion as the local nobility increasingly gravitated towards Rome in search of greater political opportunities, draining their towns of experienced government. While this process had been gradual, and in Trajan's time was not yet far advanced, the signs were clear and he acted to prevent future increases in waste, at least in the field of finance. The emperor appointed CURATORES who, as representatives of the central government, assumed financial control of local authorities, both in Italia and in the provinces. The first recorded Italian MUNICIPIUM to receive a CURA is Caere in 113. In the case of the LIBERAE like Athens, whose finances were in need of regulation, Trajan had already sent a CURA in 109. The situation was little better in some of the senatorial provinces, and the one we know the most about is Bithynia, to which Trajan sent Pliny the Younger in 111.

The extensive correspondence between the two has been preserved and has given scholars a remarkable insight into Trajan's thinking; it certainly indicates that he wished to combine humanitarianism with discipline. It also points up Trajan's dislike of secret clubs that might centralise disaffection with the regime (*see panel below*).

ONE OF THE SECRET CLUBS Pliny encountered in Bithynia that gave him cause for concern was that of the Christians. He wrote to Trajan:

'I have never participated in trials of Christians. I therefore do not know what offences it is the practice to punish or investigate, and to what extent.... Meanwhile, in the case of those who were denounced to me as Christians, I have observed the following procedure: I interrogated these as to whether they were Christians; those who confessed I interrogated a second and a third time, threatening them with punishment; those who persisted I ordered executed. For I had no doubt that, whatever the nature of their creed, stubbornness and inflexible obstinacy surely deserve to be punished.... Soon accusations spread, as usually happens, because of the proceedings going on, and several incidents occurred. An anonymous document was published containing the names of many persons.'

Trajan responded:

'You observed proper procedure, my dear Pliny, in sifting the cases of those who had been denounced to you as Christians. For it is not possible to lay down any general rule to serve as a kind of fixed standard. They are not to be sought out; if they are denounced and proved guilty, they are to be punished, with this reservation, that whoever denies that he is a Christian and really proves it – that is, by worshipping our gods – even though he was under suspicion in the past, shall obtain pardon through repentance. But anonymously posted accusations ought to have no place in any prosecution. For this is both a dangerous kind of precedent and out of keeping with the spirit of our age.'

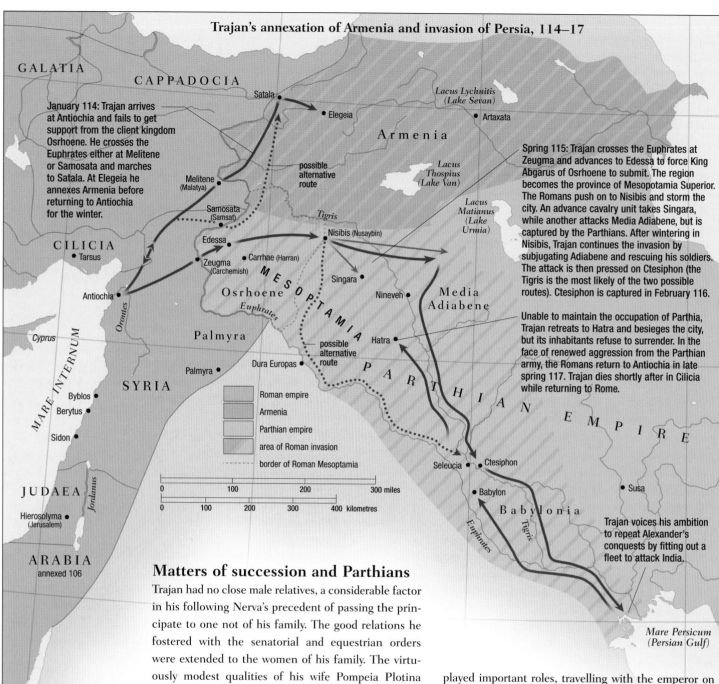

Trajan's annexation of Armenia and invasion of Persia, 114–17

January 114: Trajan arrives at Antiochia and fails to get support from the client kingdom Osrhoene. He crosses the Euphrates either at Melitene or Samosata and marches to Satala. At Elegeia he annexes Armenia before returning to Antiochia for the winter.

Spring 115: Trajan crosses the Euphrates at Zeugma and advances to Edessa to force King Abgarus of Osrhoene to submit. The region becomes the province of Mesopotamia Superior. The Romans push on to Nisibis and storm the city. An advance cavalry unit takes Singara, while another attacks Media Adiabene, but is captured by the Parthians. After wintering in Nisibis, Trajan continues the invasion by subjugating Adiabene and rescuing his soldiers. The attack is then pressed on Ctesiphon (the Tigris is the most likely of the two possible routes). Ctesiphon is captured in February 116.

Unable to maintain the occupation of Parthia, Trajan retreats to Hatra and besieges the city, but its inhabitants refuse to surrender. In the face of renewed aggression from the Parthian army, the Romans return to Antiochia in late spring 117. Trajan dies shortly after in Cilicia while returning to Rome.

Trajan voices his ambition to repeat Alexander's conquests by fitting out a fleet to attack India.

Roman empire
Armenia
Parthian empire
area of Roman invasion
border of Roman Mesoptamia

possible alternative route

0   100   200   300 miles
0   100   200   300   400 kilometres

Matters of succession and Parthians

Trajan had no close male relatives, a considerable factor in his following Nerva's precedent of passing the principate to one not of his family. The good relations he fostered with the senatorial and equestrian orders were extended to the women of his family. The virtuously modest qualities of his wife Pompeia Plotina have already been noted above and remained unchanged despite her elevation to Augusta in 105. She survived Trajan, dying probably in 121, and was honoured with a temple shared with her husband that Hadrian built in Trajan's Forum.

Trajan was close to his sister Marciana, five years his elder. She received the title Augusta, along with Plotina, in 105 and was deified on her death in 112. Her daughter Matidia became Augusta on her mother's death, and was in her turn deified in 119. Hadrian honoured their names with basilicas in the Campus Martius and the temple of DIVAE MATIDIAE. Trajan's women

played important roles, travelling with the emperor on public business and were frequently involved in making major decisions. They were respected throughout the empire, included on monuments as well as in inscriptions. Plotina, Marciana and Matidia, for example, all appear on the dedicatory arch at Ancona harbour along with Trajan. His grandniece Vibia Sabina, daughter of Matidia, married Hadrian in 100, and is the only indication we have that Trajan considered Hadrian a potential successor. The union survived almost to the end of Hadrian's subsequent principate, in spite of the couple's mutual loathing. It was to be the women who would play a pivotal role in the succession when Trajan died.

The annexation of Dacia had secured the Danuvian frontier, but Rome's eastern boundary was less certain. The great semi-circle of Roman lands stretching between Syria across Cappadocia to the Pontus Euxinus (Black Sea) was vulnerable to encroachment by the Parthian empire from Mesopotamia. Here, there were few natural obstacles to mark a secure frontier. An uneasy peace had existed between Rome and Parthia since the time of Nero, but the buffer state of Armenia in the north of the region posed a problem. By agreement with Nero, Rome had not annexed Armenia to the empire in return for maintaining a client king on the throne. In theory, at least, this king was supposed to rule in Rome's name, but with the approval of the Parthian king.

During Trajan's reign, the Caucasian tribe of Alani, beginning to feel pressure from migrating tribes of Huns, were threatening Armenia. Were they to be allowed to continue, it would turn into a flood and threaten imperial frontiers. Trajan decided that instead of keeping a Roman nominee on the Armenian throne he would annex the country. Since this was almost certain to result in an unstable province with a hostile enemy to the south, the seizure of Armenia necessitated the annexation of Mesopotamia, and war with Parthia. Given his later actions, it seems likely that Hadrian cautioned against such an enterprise, fearing that Rome's manpower would be insufficient. Trajan probably counted on the chronic internal struggles of the Parthians to hinder an effective response.

However, it was Parthia that made the first bellicose move in 113 when King Chosroes I (Khosrow) appointed Exedares, the son of his brother and predecessor, to the throne of Armenia, in breach of the Neronian agreement. For Trajan, the coronation of Exedares constituted a CASUS BELLI and he declared war. He sailed to Antiochia in October 113 and mobilised the Syrian army. As the preparations for an advance into Armenia progressed, Khosrow – who was indeed suffering dynastic problems at home – attempted a compromise. He offered to remove Exedares and replace him with his other nephew, Parthamisiris. It is not clear how this was intended to placate Trajan, who in any event refused to give a clear response, even though Exedares was deposed and replaced.

In the spring of 114 Trajan crossed the upper Euphrates, probably at Melitene, and advanced into Armenia. The local elite flocked to him and swore loyalty. At Elegeia near Erzerum, Parthamisiris laid down his crown before Trajan, who did not return it, and he pronounced Armenia a Roman province. He had won a bloodless victory without encountering the real enemy, and he had no intention of waiting for Parthia to react. After wintering in Antiochia, the Roman force struck into Parthian territory in the spring of 115. Trajan built forts along his lines of communication and pressed further to the east, eventually reaching the Parthian capital of Ctesiphon in February 116. Having advanced as far as the Persian Gulf, garrisoning wherever possible, Trajan returned to Babylon for the winter. There are indications that the emperor entertained an ambition to equal Alexander the Great's conquests. According to the historian Eutropius in his *Historiae Romanae Breviarium* (Abridgment of Roman History), written c.369 and dedicated to the emperor Valens: 'He also fitted out a fleet for the Mare Erythraeum [Red Sea], that he might use it to lay waste the coasts of India.'

If the anecdote is true, it was not to be Trajan's destiny. From this point on, events turned against him. The Parthians had traded land for time, and the territories so easily won were much more difficult to hold. The Roman communications were long and the forts spread dangerously thin on the ground. Uprisings all along the line threatened the precarious Roman hold. Trajan was forced to give up his newest province of Parthia by appointing a client king, Parthamaspates, and begin a gradual retreat to Mesopotamia. This arrangement proved to be short-lived. As soon as the Roman legions had left Ctesiphon, Khosrow returned and expelled Parthamaspates. The weary Roman army returned to Antiochia early in 117.

The invasion of Parthia sparked a terrible rebellion that overtook the eastern provinces. After the destruction of the Temple in Jerusalem by Titus, the Jews were dispersed from Judaea and a large number had settled in Mesopotamia. They hated the Romans with a fierce passion, and as early as 115 rose up, the insurrection rapidly spreading to those Jews settled in Aegyptus, Cyprus and North Africa. It is thought as many as a million people on both sides of the divide were slaughtered between 115 and 117. Trajan dispatched trusted LEGATI to the worst-hit regions and left for Rome, intending to direct operations from there; but he never completed the journey. Pausing briefly at Selinus in Cilicia, the emperor suffered a stroke and died within a few days on 9 August 117 – a little over a month short of his sixty-fourth birthday – with his wife Plotina and his PRAEFECTUS PRAETORIO Acilius Attianus at his bedside.

Trajan's wife Plotina (top) and his beloved older sister Marciana. All his women, including his sister's daughter Matidia (below), played influential roles in his life. All three were awarded the title Augusta.

Trajan's reign was one of the best periods in Roman history and is the moment when it reached its greatest extent, embracing the Mediterranean with openings on the Atlantic, the Black, Caspian, and Red seas, and – very briefly – the Persian Gulf. He richly deserved his title of OPTIMUS PRINCEPS, not only for his very real achievements, but also for the quality of his mercy (at least towards Roman citizens) and the modesty of his principate. Eschewing any notions of divinity, the soldier-emperor preferred to see himself portrayed as an ordinary man, a CIVILIS, a term that indicated comportment suitable for a Roman citizen. It is how he appears on the magnificent arch erected at Beneventum, surrounded by scenes of everyday life, ordinary citizens, businessmen, and the children he did so much to support through the expansion of Nerva's ALIMENTA. Time only increased Trajan's aura. In the late fourth century, when the empire had dramatically changed in character, each new emperor was hailed with the prayer, 'FELICIOR AUGUSTO, MELIOR TRAIANO!' (More fortunate than Augustus, better than Trajan).

HADRIAN

Publius Aelius Hadrianus /
Imperator Caesar Traianus Hadrianus Augustus
(r.11/8/117–10/7/138)

Hadrian was Trajan's second cousin, and the emperor became one of his guardians on his father's death. Hadrian later married Trajan's grandniece Vibia Sabina, daughter of Matidia.

Hadrian's Aelian ancestors had moved from Hadria, a small town in Picentine Italia to Italica in Hispania Baetica generations before his birth at the conclusion of the Second Punic War. The ancient histories are divided on whether he was actually born in Italica or in Rome, but it hardly mattered to a Roman, it was the PATRIA that counted. (Today it is believed that he was born in Rome, and only spent a brief period as a child in Italica before returning to the capital.) Hadrian was born on 24 January 76. His mother, Domitia Paulina, came from a distinguished family of Gades (Cadiz), which under the romanisation policy had grown into one of the empire's wealthiest cities. His father, Publius Aelius Afer, had climbed the CURSUS HONORUM to the point of praetor by the time of his death. Hadrian was a second cousin of Trajan (Hadrian's grandmother and Trajan's father were brother and sister). When Hadrian, aged only nine, lost his father in 85 Trajan became one his guardians; the other was Acilius Attianus, another eminent man of Italica, who was appointed PRAEFECTUS PRAETORIO by Trajan shortly before the emperor's death

As soon as he came of age, Hadrian began a rapid rise up the CURSUS HONORUM. He was only eighteen when he became a VINGTIVIRATE in 94 (history does not reveal which particular duty Hadrian was assigned) and for three consecutive years between 95 and 97 he was a TRIBUNUS MILITUM with LEGIO *II Adiutrix* in Pannonia, *V Macedonica* in Moesia Inferior, and *XXII Primigenia* in Germania Superior. In 101 he became a quaestor, a TRIBUNUS PLEBIS in 105, and praetor in 106. In the same year Trajan appointed him LEGATUS LEGIONIS *I Minerviae* in Germania Inferior. In the following year he was LEGATUS PRO PRAETORE of Pannonia Inferior, and in 108 suffect consul, ten years before the traditional age for the office. This meteoric career was clearly unusual, but at the point in 117 when he was LEGATUS SYRIAE and Trajan died, there was no indication from the princeps that Hadrian would succeed. Some other Augustan signs were there: he had been appointed commander of a legion before holding the praetorship and governor of a military province before becoming a consul. He was related to Trajan and had married his grandniece Vibia Sabina. More importantly, however, was the unavoidable fact that at that moment there was no better contender for the throne.

On the day after Trajan's death his wife Plotina and the PRAEFECTUS PRAETORIO Attianus, Hadrian's surviving guardian, announced that on his deathbed Trajan had adopted Hadrian. Plotina, Attianus and Hadrian's mother-in-law Matidia set off immediately for Rome to ensure the succession. Popular scandal held that Plotina had forged the adoption papers because she was secretly in love with Hadrian. Since they were almost the same age, there may be some truth to this, but Rome was ever a hotbed of gossip. On 11 August 117 the troops of Syria hailed forty-one-year-old Hadrian as their emperor, the day he considered his DIES IMPERII. Hadrian remained in Syria, but wrote to the senate to request divine honours for Trajan and to confirm his accession to the principate. He added the usual promise that he would never execute a senator. The senate's acquiescence was a mere formality in the face of the Syrian army's proclamation. Trajan was deified and permission given for the burial of his ashes within the POMERIUM†. They were eventually interred at the base of his column in his own forum.

There were immediate signs of disaffection among some in the senatorial class. Attianus informed Hadrian that the PRAEFECTUS URBI, Baebius Macer, and two exiles, Maximus Laberius and the Gaius Calpurnius Crassus who had rebelled against Nerva, were stirring up trouble. Crassus was killed while trying to leave his place of exile, but Hadrian took no action against the other two, a show of clemency he hoped would calm any other disaffected senators. From Antiochia he now proceeded with a policy in marked contrast to previous emperors who felt uneasy that their elevation might be disputed: that of expanding the empire's frontiers. Retrenchment and consolidation characterised Hadrian's reign, convinced as he was that the empire had reached the limits of its resources. He began immediately, recalling the troops from the lower Euphrates and abandoning Trajan's new provinces to client kings.

This abrupt reversal of Trajan's foreign policy was unpopular among the Roman elite, and further unrest broke out in Rome, even as Hadrian's mollifying policies were calming the Jews in the eastern provinces, and the stern actions of his trusted LEGATUS Quintus Marcius Turbo were restoring order in Mauretania. A plot against the emperor's life was uncovered and its implications were so serious that finally Hadrian hastened to Rome from Syria, arriving on 9 July 118. He was too late, however, to prevent the executions of the

conspiracy's four ringleaders: Lucius Publilius Celsus, Lucius Cornelius Palma, Lucius Quietus and Gaius Avidius Nigrinus. Senators and consulars, they were also close associates of Trajan's and probably resented Hadrian's adoption, as well as the dismemberment of the great emperor's expansionist policy.

Hadrian maintained that the executions took place without his consent. Whether true or not, their elimination made the new emperor's course easier and silenced opposition among the nobility to his frontier policy. The senators never forgave him, however, for breaking his solemn promise to them, and he was obliged to swear in person never again to mete out punishment to any senator unless the senatorial court decreed otherwise. But the odium the executions had raised caused him dismay until the end of his days. He made amends by holding lavish games to soothe the Roman plebs and by holding only his third – and last – consulship in 119, leaving the office free to the senate without hindrance. He was similarly sparing in his acceptance of other titles; and only became PATER PATRIAE in 128.

The obvious flaw in Hadrian's policy of staying within the frontiers and avoiding engagement in foreign wars was that a static army loses its edge, grows demoralised, and becomes a potential cause of trouble. Further, that the warlike tribes massing against the frontiers might interpret the Romans hiding behind their fortifications as a sign of weakness. In this, Hadrian was fortunate that the empire enjoyed peace throughout his reign, possibly because Trajan had convinced the tribal chieftains that attacking Rome was a dangerous task; at least for the time being.

In order to keep the frontier armies and garrisons up to scratch he made continual tours of inspection, organising constant exercises and reviews. As a result, only half of his reign was spent in Rome (*see side panel, next page*). A greater degree of equality was introduced to the army by increasing the men's comforts and levelling those of the officers. He was strict in ensuring that promotions were earned for merit, not favour, and earned the soldiers' devotion for his efforts. Hadrian also placed a greater reliance on the use of native auxiliary cavalry than had been the case previously, and reversed Vespasian's practice of only allowing them to serve under Roman officers. In fact, by this time it was

Hadrian and his wife Vibia Sabina. Their union was to be an unhappy one.

---

† A signal honour because burials within the city's sacred POMERIUM had been forbidden for centuries.

Hadrian the tourist

Derived from a series of inscriptions on various statue plinths, it is possible to outline most of Hadrian's travels (although there are discrepancies between the sources).

121 Gallia Lugdunensis, Germania Superior, Raetia, Noricum, Germania Superior

122 Germania Inferior, Britannia (where he began the construction of the wall that bears his name), Gallia Lugdunensis, Gallia Narbonensis, Hispania Tarraconensis

123 Mauretania (?), Africa (?), Libya, Cyrene, Creta, Syria, Mesopotamia (Melitene), Pontus, Bithynia, Asia

124 Thracia, Moesia (both), Dacia, Pannonia (both), Achaea, Athens

125 Achaea, Sicilia, Rome

127 Tours all over Italia

128 Africa, Rome, Athens

129 Asia, Pamphylia, Phrygia, Pisidia, Cilicia, Syria, Commagene (Samosata), Cappadocia, Pontus, Syria (Antiochia)

130 Aegyptus (Nilus trip; death of Antinoüs), Judaea, Arabia

131 Libyan desert, Syria, Asia, Athens

132 Rome

134 Syria, Judaea, Aegyptus (?), Syria (Antiochia)

135 Syria, and in 136 back toRome

The lengthy periods spent in the eastern provinces in the last years was necessitated by the Second Jewish War. His devotion to Greek culture explains the several visits to Achaea and Athens; the city elected him archon in 112 while he was still a PRIVATUS.

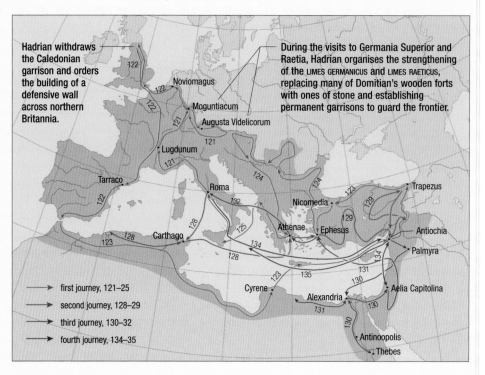

Hadrian withdraws the Caledonian garrison and orders the building of a defensive wall across northern Britannia.

During the visits to Germania Superior and Raetia, Hadrian organises the strengthening of the LIMES GERMANICUS and LIMES RAETICUS, replacing many of Domitian's wooden forts with ones of stone and establishing permanent garrisons to guard the frontier.

→ first journey, 121–25
→ second journey, 128–29
→ third journey, 130–32
→ fourth journey, 134–35

rare to find Italian officers, except at the highest level, most being enrolled from among the provincials. Throughout these reviews, Cassius Dio tells us, the emperor 'led a rigorous life and either walked or rode on horseback on all occasions, never once at this period setting foot in either a chariot or a four-wheeled vehicle.'

While Hadrian's travels were primarily motivated by matters military, he was probably Rome's most curious emperor, interested in a wide spectrum of his world: sport, science, architecture, literature, art, nature and especially Greek culture – he was sufficiently vain to curl his hair with tongs in the Greek manner. Writing in the third century, Tertullian refers to Hadrian as being 'OMNIUM CURIOSTATUM EXPLORATOR', which means he may be regarded as the first imperial sightseer. And his behaviour when travelling often resembled that of a modern tourist, visiting all the sites and monuments, climbing mountains to admire views of the sunset. His travels were also to visit the frontiers.

Hadrian's consolidation of frontiers

As a princeps with a care for the empire, Hadrian's main purpose was to avoid foreign wars and in pursuit of this policy he determined to return to the Flavian frontiers. However, this raised the concern that consolidation and lack of aggression across the borders would encourage barbarian ravages. To this point, the Roman frontiers had relied on traditional legionary camps and mobile garrisons, but now Hadrian erected many major and permanent structures. Having withdrawn from the short-lived Persian provinces, the emperor gave close attention to northern Europe. In Britannia the Roman garrisons were thinly dispersed in a line that stretched north from the Tinea (Tyne) valley to a small camp at modern Inchtuthil, near Perth. That the troops were vulnerable is attested to by the disappearance of LEGIO IX *Hispania*, which was wiped out during a serious tribal uprising at about the time of Hadrian's accession.

It was clear that the legionary resources there were overstretched, and Hadrian decided to pull back from lowland Caledonia to establish a firm frontier along the line of Agricola's original boundary between Luguvalium (Carlisle) and Segedunum (Wallsend, Gateshead). The best preserved of Hadrian's permanent frontier structures is the famous wall that bears his name in northern England. Stretching between the Ituna Aestuarius and the Tinea Aestuarius (Solway Firth and Tyne estuary), it was fully seventy-three miles long. Construction began in 122, the work being carried out by legionaries, and was completed by 128. The core was of lime concrete with a facing of dressed stone. It averaged fifteen feet

The Nervo-Trajanic House and the Adoptive Antonines

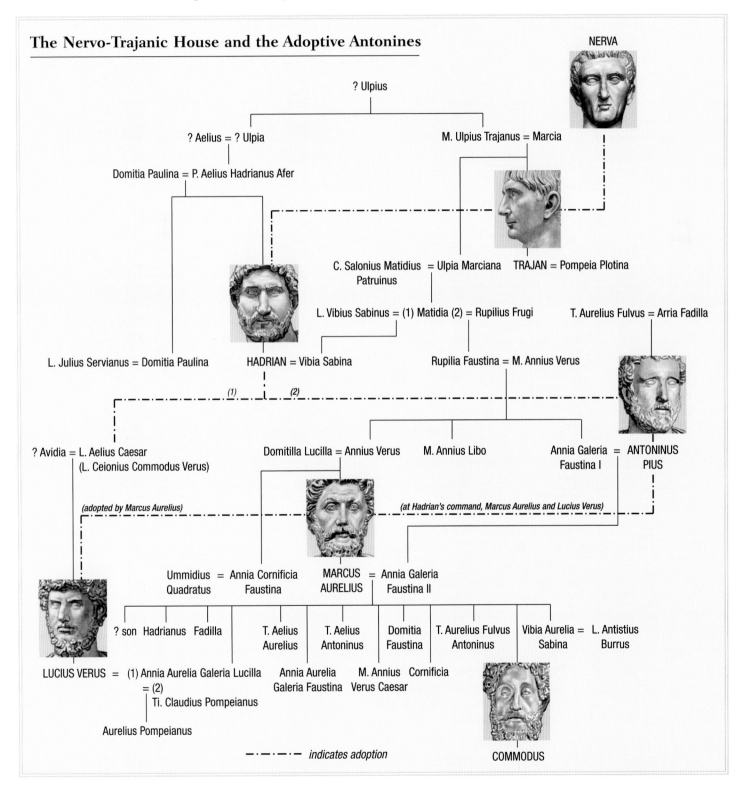

NERVA

? Ulpius

? Aelius = ? Ulpia   M. Ulpius Trajanus = Marcia

Domitia Paulina = P. Aelius Hadrianus Afer

C. Salonius Matidius = Ulpia Marciana   TRAJAN = Pompeia Plotina
Patruinus

L. Vibius Sabinus = (1) Matidia (2) = Rupilius Frugi   T. Aurelius Fulvus = Arria Fadilla

L. Julius Servianus = Domitia Paulina   HADRIAN = Vibia Sabina   Rupilia Faustina = M. Annius Verus

(1)   (2)

? Avidia = L. Aelius Caesar   Domitilla Lucilla = Annius Verus   M. Annius Libo   Annia Galeria = ANTONINUS
(L. Ceionius Commodus Verus)   Faustina I   PIUS

(adopted by Marcus Aurelius)   *(at Hadrian's command, Marcus Aurelius and Lucius Verus)*

Ummidius = Annia Cornificia   MARCUS = Annia Galeria
Quadratus   Faustina   AURELIUS   Faustina II

? son Hadrianus Fadilla   T. Aelius   T. Aelius   Domitia   T. Aurelius Fulvus   Vibia Aurelia = L. Antistius
Aurelius   Antoninus   Faustina   Antoninus   Sabina   Burrus

LUCIUS VERUS = (1) Annia Aurelia Galeria Lucilla   Annia Aurelia   M. Annius   Cornificia
= (2)   Galeria Faustina   Verus Caesar
Ti. Claudius Pompeianus

Aurelius Pompeianus

COMMODUS

— · — · — indicates adoption

(4.6m) in height and was intended to be ten feet (3m) thick, although modifications to the plan meant that it only reached this thickness at the base – and not always as much as that along its entire length. Small forts with sally-ports were built at a regular distance of one Roman mile, and in time sixteen main forts were attached to the wall; it is not known how many were erected during Hadrian's reign. The actual wall was only one part of the defences. Immediately to its north a V-shaped ditch was dug out to a depth of ten feet and with a width at ground level of twenty-seven feet (8m). Just to the south of the wall the so-called Vallum† was dug after the wall had been built. A flat-bottomed ditch with a raised bank on either side, its primary purpose was to keep civilians away from the military zone.

It proved to be a formidable obstacle to the Caledonian tribes, and yet it is hard to imagine that the ditch and wall alone would have kept out a determined attack – and indeed in future years there would be several serious incursions south of Hadrian's Wall. But the sheer scale of this undertaking was designed to prove Roman might and deter insurrection rather than act as an impregnable defensive barrier. It also served an economic purpose in defining Roman boundaries, allowing the tithing of goods passing in either direction, since the wall was porous to authorised north-south trade. The fifteen thousand auxiliaries who manned the wall, drawn from various parts of the empire, were a further bar to Caledonian marauders, and it is a testament to the project's success that it enabled the Romans to maintain a presence as far north as this for almost three centuries after its construction.

Hadrian's other great fortification can be found on the two hundred-mile section of the frontier stretching between the upper reaches of the Rhenus and Danuvius known as the LIMES GERMANICUS. Unlike the British wall, the LIMES were constructed of split-oak trunks embedded in a ditch and fastened on the inside by cross-planking. This explains why they have suffered far more over the centuries than the concrete and stone-faced Hadrian's Wall. Of similar construction, the hundred-mile-long palisade on the Raetian frontier followed the line established by Domitian between Lauriacum (Lorch) and the Danuvius near Abusina (Eining). No defences of this kind have been found along the lower Danuvius frontier; this is not really surprising since Dacia provided substantial protection and was well garrisoned.

---

† 'Vallum' is how it is known today, although the word means 'wall' and so is hardly appropriate for a ditch.

The Hadrianic administration

The provinces benefited from Hadrian's imperial perambulations, although in the first instance the cost of receiving the emperor and his 'burdensome' retinue fell on the cities and MUNICIPIA no matter how modestly Hadrian comported himself. In almost all cases, however, the provincials received far more than they had to give. Hadrian undertook public works wherever he went; new roads and bridges, aqueducts, modern harbours, lavish temples, public baths and games. Ephesus and Trapezus received new harbour installations, he built aqueducts at Athens and Corinthus, and new roads were laid and bridges raised as far apart as Hispania and easternmost Moesia Inferior. In addition Hadrian was Rome's greatest city-builder. New cities sprang up all over the empire, many in the Danuvian provinces. From Forum Hadriani in the extreme north (Voorburg-Arentsburg, Holland) to Colonia Julia Hadriana Avenio (Avignon) in Gallia, Hadrian's civic engineers were at work throughout his reign. The most famous is Hadrianopolis in Thracia, known better today as Adrianople (although it was renamed Edirne in the fifteenth century by the Ottoman Turks, which is how it is usually shown on modern atlases). Not every civil scheme was met with approval, however: the rebuilding of Jerusalem was to be the cause of a dangerous rebellion.

As a part of his consolidation of the frontiers Hadrian extended municipal rights to many of the settlements that had sprung up around the great frontier legionary camps. None of his predecessors had allowed any such towns charters as MUNICIPIA. In contrast he contemplated evacuating Dacia to conserve military resources, but was persuaded against a move that would have left so many recent settlers at the mercy of the local tribes. While the provinces gained much from Hadrian's construction activity and travels, adlection into the senate continued to deprive the provincial cities of wealthy and experienced administrators. As a consequence Hadrian was obliged to follow Trajan's precedent of sending in his own CURATORES to administer financially embarrassed localities.

Hadrian's attention to detail is also to be found in his famous codification of Roman law, also known as the Codification of the Praetor's Edict. In one respect, this can be seen as bringing within the principate's autocratic control an element of Roman life that had been allowed to escape it. On the other hand, it benefited citizens by providing a standard interpretation of the complex judicial processes that had grown up since the mid-Republican era. At that point in time the

urban praetors began to issue a statement of the programme of legal procedure and interpretation that
each proposed to follow during his term of office. In
theory this fixed how the laws would be interpreted
from that point on. However, his successor in office
was not bound by this EDICTUM PERPETUUM, in fact it
was only when the LEX CORNELIA of 67 BC was passed
that a praetor was even obliged to honour his own
edict, let alone that of his predecessors.

Nevertheless, situations would arise in which, to
suit the circumstances of the case being heard, the
praetor needed to add to the body of law or modify an
existing law to the extent that it might be considered a
new law; not a state of affairs that recommends itself
to autocratic rule. Therefore, Hadrian decided to codify all the accretions to the body of statute law in the
form of his own EDICTUM PERPETUUM, which would
have binding force thereafter. If any additions or further modifications were to be necessary, it would be
the emperor in future who would decide. For this
monumental task Hadrian appointed a famous jurist,
Salvius Julianus, who completed the work by 129,
bringing together in a straightforward and modern
document centuries of praetorian edicts. Hadrian's
Edict has been lost, but many excerpts made by commentators on it survived in Justinian's *Digest* of the
sixth century (*see chapter 17*).

Hadrian was not content to merely codify Roman
law, he intended to see it efficiently administered, and
to this end appointed four men of consular rank, each
of whom toured two to three given districts of Italia.
They were effectively circuit judges, known as the
QUATTUORVIRI CONSULARES. Augustus had organised
Italia into eleven regions, but none of these was allowed
to hold a judicial court, so Hadrian's innovation reduced
the often-crippling costs of bringing an appeal to Rome
and relieved pressure on the overcrowded courts of the
emperor and urban praetor. Not surprisingly, it was popular with the provincial citizenry, but the senate hated
it. In the Republican era the senate had treated Italia as
its private provincial fiefdom; now the peninsula was
the heartland of a great empire, and this novel function
seemed to reduce it to the status of a quasi-province.
Senatorial resistance to the QUATTUORVIRI CONSULARES
increased to the point that the office was abolished on
the emperor's death. But Hadrian's wisdom was not to
go unrecognised, and after two further reigns the office
was revived, with some modifications.

Hadrian also devoted much time to supervising the
public finances. His peaceful foreign policy, while disliked by the pro-Trajan faction of the aristocracy,

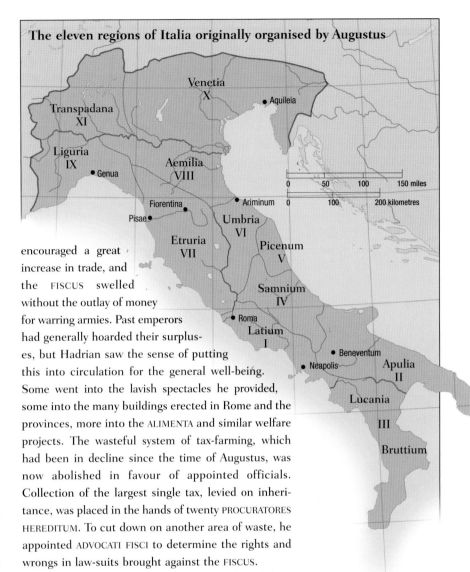

The eleven regions of Italia originally organised by Augustus

encouraged a great
increase in trade, and
the FISCUS swelled
without the outlay of money
for warring armies. Past emperors
had generally hoarded their surplus-
es, but Hadrian saw the sense of putting
this into circulation for the general well-being.
Some went into the lavish spectacles he provided,
some into the many buildings erected in Rome and the
provinces, more into the ALIMENTA and similar welfare
projects. The wasteful system of tax-farming, which
had been in decline since the time of Augustus, was
now abolished in favour of appointed officials.
Collection of the largest single tax, levied on inheritance, was placed in the hands of twenty PROCURATORES
HEREDITUM. To cut down on another area of waste, he
appointed ADVOCATI FISCI to determine the rights and
wrongs in law-suits brought against the FISCUS.

The men for these new offices were selected from
among the ORDO EQUESTER, and were only some of the
tasks with which Hadrian further enhanced the status
of equestrians. He continued the advancement of EQUI-
TES begun by Augustus, Claudius and the Flavians, but
went further in creating an Imperial Civil Service that
was finally removed from the household of the princeps, making its members public servants – although
under the emperor's absolute control – rather than his
personal agents. In doing so, he regularised the
Service's composition, throwing out the freedmen, and
making a civil career a proper CURSUS for EQUITES. In
doing so, he did away with the requirement of military
service that every EQUES had previously been obliged to
perform. As a logical consequence of this policy the
most radically changed office was that of the highest
equestrian, the PRAEFECTUS PRAETORIO. His ceased to
be a military function and he became a legal officer
presiding over the princeps' judicial CONSILIUM.

The emperor's wife, Vibia Sabina, could not compete with his predilection for boys, and the marriage remained barren.

Hadrian in Rome

Despite his prolonged absences from the capital, Rome was not ignored. Hadrian continued Trajan's energetic building programme; it was a period when Rome underwent as great a transformation as it had under Augustus. Hadrian was almost certainly the most artistically gifted emperor that Rome ever produced. He became a fine public speaker, he was a student of philosophy who could hold his own with luminaries in their fields, he wrote poetry and an autobiography, and he was a superb architect. He completed Trajan's Forum with a large temple dedicated to Trajan and Plotina, and then, when he was about forty-five began construction of a temple on the Velia unique in design and, with a length of more than three hundred feet (91m), larger than any other ever built by the Romans. Work began in about 121 and took approximately fourteen years, and when it was completed it dominated the eastern end of the Forum Romanum, facing out over the Amphitheatrum Flavium. Gigantic statues of the seated goddesses Venus and Roma were placed inside its two CELLAE. Trajan's architect Apollodorus is said to have sneered at the statues' pompous scale and said that they would bang their heads if they were to stand up. He was probably jealous that the emperor was at least as capable – if not more inspired – an architect as himself. The complex was dedicated in 135 on 21 April, traditionally Rome's DIES NATALIS (birthday).

On the Campus Martius, Hadrian began the Hadrianeum or 'Temple of Neptune', which is interesting for its sculpted representations of the provinces, indicating the blurring of the distinction between Italia and the provinces that was taking place during his reign. Nearby, on the right bank of the Tiberis above the Vatican, he commenced his mausoleum, larger than that of Augustus. Approached by a new bridge, the Pons Aelius, the mausoleum was still unfinished at the time of his death; both the mausoleum and Hadrianeum were completed by his successor, Antoninus Pius. Some twenty-five miles east of Rome, on the bank of the Anio at Tibur (Tivoli), Hadrian built his stupendously big palace. It was more a small city than a single complex, covering seven hundred acres and containing

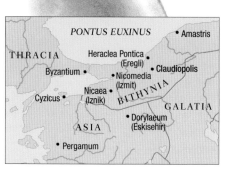

Above: The beautiful Bithynian youth Antinoüs, who captured Hadrian's heart and became his constant companion.

some hundred individual buildings in a multitude of architectural styles. Reflecting his life of travel, the adornment was superbly eclectic, although Greek styles predominated. Here Hadrian reconstructed many of the places he had visited, such as the Canopus of Alexandria and the Vale of Tempe.

But Hadrian's crowning glory is the Pantheon built between 118 and 125 on the site of Agrippa's original in the Campus Martius. This extraordinary feat of engineering provided a dome that has a height exactly equal to its diameter – a perfect half-sphere. The dome's span was not surpassed until modern times, and is greater than that of St. Peter's in Rome. As was his modest custom, Hadrian inscribed the architrave with the original dedication of Agrippa; he seldom put his own name on a monument. The Pantheon was dedicated to all the Roman gods, but its complete survival is down to the Byzantine emperor Phocas, who gave the building to Pope Boniface IV in 608 to convert it into the church of Santa Maria ad Martyres.

Hadrian and Antinoüs

One aspect of Hadrian's life that is most widely known is his relationship with the handsome youth Antinoüs. In a footnote to Gibbon's *The Decline and Fall of the Roman Empire*, the author wrote: *'The deification of Antinoüs, his medals, statues, city, oracles and constellation, are well known, and still dishonour the memory of Hadrian. Yet we may remark, that of the first fifteen emperors, Claudius was the only one whose taste in love was entirely correct.'* In the mid-fourth century the bigoted St. Anathasius commented: *'And such a one is the new God Antinoüs, that was the emperor Hadrian's minion and the slave of his unlawful pleasure... a sordid and loathsome instrument of his master's lust.'*

Antinoüs was born in the town of Claudiopolis in the province of Bithynia, probably on 27 November between 110 and 112. Very little is known about his parents, but his father was at least a freedman, since Hadrian would never have consorted with the son of a slave, and he may have been a provincial stone mason. Hadrian probably encountered Antinoüs during his trip to Bithynia in 123, when the boy would have been about twelve. The emperor's pederasty was widely known, his preference – in strict accordance with the Greek manner – being for boys above the age of thirteen. Accordingly, Hadrian concluded some kind of deal with the father, and had Antinoüs sent to Rome, to enter the imperial PAEDAGOGIUM. This institution, painted by some of the ancient histories as an infamous boy harem for the emperor, was a school for the education of future palace or civil service administrators. Its beginnings probably date from as early as the reign of Gaius, who would have housed his favourite charioteers there. Considering that most of its pupils would have been aged between ten and fourteen, there is perhaps an argument for its being in Hadrian's time a school for polishing handsome boys in courtly manners to be his companions.

By all accounts, Hadrian's infatuation with Antinoüs far exceeded his interest in any other youths. As the boy went to Rome, the emperor continued on his travels and so they did not meet again until 125, when Hadrian returned to the capital. From this point on until his untimely death Antinoüs remained constantly in Hadrian's company. The relationship was not likely to please Vibia Sabina. In a male-dominated Roman world, the barreness of their marriage was blamed on Hadrian's wife, but his sexual preferences can hardly be excluded from fault. Perhaps it was in compensation that he granted Sabina the title of Augusta in 128, and always had her accompany him on his provincial visits; perhaps too she was being used as a convenient cover to divert prurient provincial attention from her husband's true love.

Disaster struck in October 130. The imperial court was visiting Aegyptus at the time, and Antinoüs suffered an accident and drowned in the Nilus. Whether it was an accident, a suicide or something more sinister has been a fruitful source for speculation ever since. Whichever, Hadrian's extravagant mourning should dispel any argument that their relationship was not that of homosexual lovers. The vituperative St. Anathasius was certain of his facts: '...and forthwith his Imperial Majesty issued an edict strictly requiring and commanding his loving subjects to acknowledge his departed page a deity and to pay him his quota of divine reverences and honours as such: a resolution and act which did more effectually publish and testify to the world how entirely the emperor's unnatural passion survived the foul object of it.'

In his grief Hadrian raised a new city on the banks of the Nilus that he named Antinöopolis, and he peopled it with Graeco-Egyptian army veterans. The city became the centre of a new cult to worship Antinoüs the god, and he entered the pantheon first of Egyptian deities and soon after that of the Romans. In his beloved Greece Hadrian further encouraged the cult's growth, and traces survived in Achaea for another two hundred years. At his palace in Tibur and elsewhere, Hadrian erected numerous statues of the beautiful youth. Indeed, his obsession with three-dimensional representation was responsible for a vigorous revival of classical Greek sculpture and the temporary vanishing of Roman carved reliefs, normally so abundant.

Having seen to the rites for Antinoüs, Hadrian moved from Aegyptus to Judaea, where his normally benign care for his subjects was transformed into exceptional ineptness; perhaps his judgement was warped by his recent bereavement. Jerusalem still lay in ruins and he determined to rebuild the city as a COLONIA, which he named Aelia Capitolina. Aware of how troublesome the Jews could be, he decided to end its Jewish character by forbidding them to live in the refurbished city. Moreover, he proposed to build a temple to Jupiter on the site of the Temple of Solomon. These insults led to a general Jewish uprising that flared into open war by 132 under the leadership of the Jewish prince Simon Bar Kokhba. The Jews registered some initial successes but were eventually ground down by the size and strength of the Roman forces pitched against them. At least six legions became involved and Bar Kokhba shrewdly avoided open battles in favour of guerrilla tactics. But after three years of fighting, the flower of the Jewish forces was cornered at Bethar fortress, west of Jerusalem in 135, to be cut down by the Romans. Vengeance belonged to Hadrian, who killed or enslaved any Jews who had not already fled the region in the great diaspora. Jerusalem was entirely romanised, Judaism banned, and the name Judaea erased from the map†. The Jews were now entirely without a homeland, and would remain so until the mid-twentieth century.

A complex succession

At the conclusion of the Jewish rebellion Hadrian, now in his sixtieth year, was assailed by an illness (probably tuberculosis) that made him irritable and testy, especially with the senatorial class whom he suspected disapproved of his interest in Hellenistic culture, always an un-Roman taste. Moreover, although he was always polite towards them, the senators resented that he promulgated new laws by issuing CONSTITUTIONES PRINCIPIS instead of CONSULTA SENATUM. It was time to consider the succession seriously. Any aristocratic hopes that he would adopt his eighteen-year-old great-nephew Gnaeus Pedanius Fuscus Salinator were rudely dashed by the youth's sudden execution. There may have been some conspiring on the boy's behalf, but the

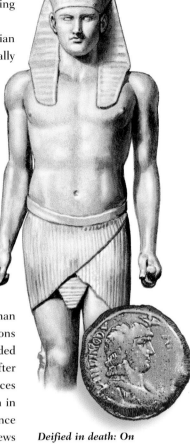

Deified in death: On Hadrian's orders Antinoüs entered the pantheon of Egyptian gods, and later that of the Romans too. Coins of him were minted, and his cult was to last for two centuries.

The image on this coin, issued on occasion of Hadrian's visit to Jerusalem, shows a Jewish mother with her children making a peace offering to the emperor. His actions there, however, led to a bloody uprising.

---

† Hadrian renamed the province, and from this time on it was known as Syria Palaestina, or simply Palaestina.

execution increased senatorial hatred for the emperor who had been responsible, so they held, for the consular deaths at the start of his reign, and for which he had not been forgiven. In 136 he adopted Lucius Aelius and elevated him to the rank of Caesar. The selection was not popular and odd anyway. Aelius had little to recommend him other than powerful political connections. His health was bad and he had no military experience. It has been suggested that he might have been Hadrian's bastard son, but there is no documentary evidence to support such a claim.

It turned out to be an unhappy choice because Aelius Caesar died of tuberculosis on 1 January 138. Hadrian turned to another and within six weeks adopted Titus Aurelius Fulvus Boionius Arrius Antoninus on 25 February. Antoninus was fifty-one and a senator of blameless reputation, who may have been related to Hadrian's adoptive mother Plotina. No time was wasted in bestowing on him not only the TRIBUNICIA POTESTAS and IMPERIUM PROCONSULARE but also the PRAENOMEN IMPERATORIS. Hadrian, with an eye to the future, wisely obliged Antoninus to adopt two sons to secure the succession beyond him: Antoninus's seventeen-year-old nephew Marcus Annius Verus and Lucius Ceionius Commodus, the seven-year-old son of the deceased Lucius Aelius Caesar. The former choice was a fortunate one, for he would become Marcus Aurelius, last of the great Roman emperors of the period; the latter was not so wise.

On 10 July 138, aged sixty-two, Hadrian died of his illness at Baiae, on the Bay of Naples. Having spent almost half of his reign away from Rome, and much time in Tibur when he was in Italia, and given his harsh treatment of senators and consulars, he had become a distant and unpopular character. Hadrian played a significant role both in developing the foreign policies of the empire and in its continuing centralisation of the administration. He remains an enigma, a man of so many disparate parts. Augustus was his proclaimed role model, but the real echoes are those of Claudius for his care of the empire, Nero for his interest in the arts, Vespasian for the supervision of the finances, and Trajan for his grasp of the empire itself. Few today would disagree that he was one of the most remarkable men Rome ever produced, and yet his passion for organisation meant that he introduced reforms into the principate that resulted in the growth of the bureaucratic machine that would soon restrict initiative and ultimately destroy the empire.

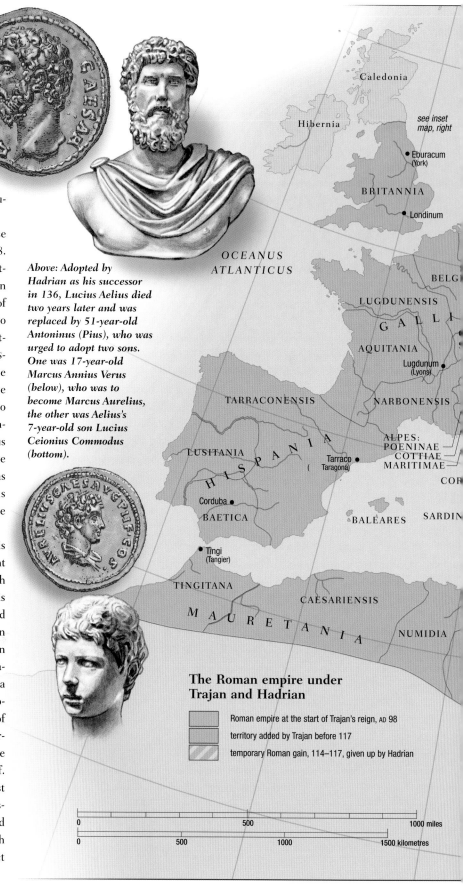

Above: Adopted by Hadrian as his successor in 136, Lucius Aelius died two years later and was replaced by 51-year-old Antoninus (Pius), who was urged to adopt two sons. One was 17-year-old Marcus Annius Verus (below), who was to become Marcus Aurelius, the other was Aelius's 7-year-old son Lucius Ceionius Commodus (bottom).

The Roman empire under Trajan and Hadrian

Roman empire at the start of Trajan's reign, AD 98

territory added by Trajan before 117

temporary Roman gain, 114–117, given up by Hadrian

VALLUM HADRIANI
Hadrian's Wall

- □ mile castle
- ▢ main fort
- ━ Roman road

C a l e d o n i a

OCEANUS
GERMANICUS
(NORTH SEA)

□ Habitancum
(Risingham)

(North Tyne)

□ (Lochmaben / Lockerbie)

Vercovicum
(Housesteads)

Vindovala
(Rudchester)

Camboglanna
(Birdoswald)

Brocolitia
(Carrawburgh)

Onnum
(Halton)

Condercum
(Benwell)

Blatobulgium
(Birrens)

Castra Exploratum
(Netherby)

Fanum Cocidi
(Bewcastle)

(Liddel)

Magnis
(Carvoran)

Segedunum
(Wallsend)

Uxelodunum
(Stanwix)

Arbeia
(South
Shields)

Tinea (Tyne)

Corstopitum
(Corbridge)

(Whickham)

(Houghton)

(Nether Denton)

Aesica
(Great
Chesters)

Vindolanda
(Chesterholm)

Cilurnum
(Chesters)

Pons Aelius
(Newcastle)

Ituna Aestuarius
(Solway Firth)

(Castlesteads)

Luguvalium
(Carlisle)

Luguvalium and Vindolanda
were the major civilian
settlements.

Corstopitum was the
main legionary camp
serving the wall.

Vindomara
(Ebchester)

(Silloth)

(Beckfoot)

Maia
(Bowness)

Concavata
(Drumburgh)

Abalava
(Burgh-by-Sands)

(Iluna)

(Eden)

B R I T A N N I A

| 0 | 10 | 20 miles |
| 0 | 10 | 20 | 30 kilometers |

Hadrian ordered the building of the great wall across northern England in 122, and it was completed in its original form by 128–29. Apart from its strategic value, this was a means of keeping the British troops busy, and so contrary to popular belief it was soldiers and not slaves that actually constructed the stone wall and forts, and dug the ditches than ran its length to its north and south. Later governors were obliged to rebuild and remodel the wall after several Caledonian invasions.

MARE CASPIUM

Danuvius

RAETIA

NORICUM

Carnuntum •

PANNONIA
SUP. INF.

DACIA

ILLYRICUM

DALMATIA

• Sirmium
(Mitrovica)

Danuvius

MOESIA
SUP.

MOESIA INF.

PONTUS EUXINUS
(BLACK SEA)

Armenia

MARE ADRIATICUM

ITALIA

THRACIA

BITHYNIA ET PONTUS

Tigris

Parthian empire

• Roma

Hadrianopolis
(Edirne)

MACEDONIA

GALATIA

CAPPADOCIA

Nisibis
(Nusaybin)

MARE
TYRRHENUM

EPIRUS

ASIA

MESOPOTAMIA

[PARTHIA
SUPERIOR]

ACHAEA

• Ephesus

LYCIA

CILICIA

SYRIA

Euphrates

• Ctesiphon

SICILIA

Antiochia •

[PARTHIA
INFERIOR]

CYPRUS

MARE INTERNUM

CRETA

PALAESTINA

Aelia Capitolina •
(Jerusalem)

RICA PROCONSULARIS

CYRENAICA

• Alexandria

ARABIA

Nilus

AEGYPTUS

MARE
ERYTHRAEUM

CHAPTER FIVE   AD 138–192

THE ANTONINE DYNASTY

Probably the most underrated emperor of the period, Antoninus Pius was to reign over the last period of complete peace the empire would enjoy.

ANTONINUS PIUS

Titus Aurelius Fulvus Boionius Arrius Hadrianus Antoninus Pius (r.10/7/138–7/3/161)

Antoninus was born on 19 September 86 at Lanuvium, an old Latin city some twenty miles to the southeast of Rome. His father's family had originally migrated to Rome from Nemausus (Nîmes) in Gallia Narbonensis and established itself firmly in the senatorial class. His paternal grandfather, Titus Aurelius Fulvus, had twice been a consul and also held office as PRAEFECTUS URBI; his father Aurelius Fulvus also held the consulship. On his mother Arria Fadilla's side his grandfather, Arrius Antoninus, had been consul twice. Most of Antoninus's youth was spent at Lorium, which was only twelve miles from Rome on the Via Aurelia. He later built a villa there, to which he would frequently retreat from the cares of the empire.

His early career appears to have been typical of that pursued by the sons of senatorial families. He entered public life while quite young, first as a quaestor in 112, then prætor in 117, and held his first consulship (ordinary) in 120 at the age of thirty-four. At some point between 110 and 115, Antoninus married

Annia Galeria Faustina, the daughter of Marcus Annius Verus (whose nephew of the same name he would later adopt). Shortly after the expiration of his term as consul Hadrian selected him as one of the QUATTUORVIRI CONSULARES, the magistrates of the four judicial districts into which the emperor had divided Italia. In 133–6 Antoninus served as proconsul of Asia – the only recorded time that he spent outside Italia – where his remarkable administrative qualities once again attracted Hadrian's attention. At the conclusion of his governorship Antoninus returned to Rome and was rewarded by being admitted to Hadrian's inner circle, a place on the CONSILIUM PRINCIPIS.

This exemplary career, then, was reason enough for Hadrian to adopt Antoninus after the death of his first-appointed successor, Lucius Aelius. Moreover, Antoninus had risen to be counted among the most respected of the senatorial order and a popular choice with the nobility. After the conferral of the imperial powers and prerogatives, Antoninus became joint-Augustus with Hadrian until the latter's death, on which day he became sole ruler of the Roman empire in his fifty-second year. The succession was already secured by Antoninus's adoption of Marcus Annius Verus, his nephew by marriage, who became Marcus Aurelius Antoninus, and the younger Lucius Verus, son of Hadrian's first choice for successor, Lucius Aelius.

The senate, which had become embittered by Hadrian's raising of the EQUITES to an almost equal level of nobility and by his perceived reduction of its powers, and especially at the hated institution of the QUATTUORVIRI CONSULARES, refused to deify the deceased princeps. Antoninus responded by refusing to undertake the government on any other basis and this, together with his compromise agreement to disband the QUATTUORVIRI CONSULARES, induced the senate to agree to ratify Hadrian's acts and deify him. Antoninus's devotion to Hadrian's memory is usually cited as the reason for his being officially styled Pius. But his twenty-three-year reign, one unequalled in Roman history for its peace and prosperity, showed such devotion to the wellbeing of his subjects that the title would have been deserved in any case. In everything Antoninus did, modesty was his watchword – which is why his reign is so easily overlooked.

Antoninus continued Hadrian's pacific policy and

no wars were undertaken, although there was some activity to prevent barbarian incursions along the lower Danuvius and against the Alani on the edges of Armenia. The only real war, if it could be called such, was fought against the Brigantes of northern Britannia. In this one theatre Antoninus did expand beyond Hadrian's frontiers, erecting a second wall well to the north of Hadrian's between the estuaries of the Clota and Bodotria (Clyde and Forth) along the line first fortified by Agricola in 84. There were conflicts with the Berbers in Africa and short-lived insurrections of Jews in Aegyptus, Armenia and Palaestina, but all were quickly suppressed.

The model ruler

A consequence of this peace was that trade and commerce flourished as never before. The high quality of municipal life, bolstered by continuing operation of the ALIMENTA, is revealed in the numerous inscriptions throughout the provinces that record the generosity of wealthy patrons or the charitable activities of a growing citizen-middle class. Antoninus had no intention of draining this prosperity by making imperial visits that would burden the provinces with the expenses of housing his court. In contrast to his two predecessors, Antoninus remained at or around Rome where he could receive messages from all parts of the empire equally quickly, and only left the capital to visit his nearby estate at Lorium in the Campania.

He was equally restrained in respect of lavish building programmes. He felt obliged to complete work begun by Hadrian, such as the mausoleum in which Hadrian's ashes were interred and the Hadrinaeum on the Campus Martius. He built the modest temple of Antoninus and Faustina (dedicated to his wife, who died in 141) and made repairs to Rome's ancient bridge, the Pons Sublicius, and to the Amphitheatrum Flavium. Outside Rome, Antoninus repaired several roads and renovated ports in Alexandria, Caieta and Terracina, built a bath complex at Ostia, an aqueduct at Antium, and small temples in his birthplace, Lanuvium.

Antoninus applied himself to the awakened interest in the law that Hadrian's Edict had promoted. He appointed to his CONSILIUM five expert jurists to advise him: Vinidius Verus, Salvius Valens, Volusius Mæcianus, Ulpius Marcellus, and Diavolenus. Under these men additions to the statute law introduced a new spirit of leniency and humanitarianism, which went so far as to legislate against abuse of slaves. In religion Antoninus lacked the skepticism of Hadrian,

and was devoted to the traditions of virtuous Roman worship. This meant that he was remarkably tolerant, and during his reign the adoption of new eastern deities increased, although he maintained Trajan's ambivalent policies towards the Christians.

During his third consulship, in 139–40 (he was to hold it for the last time in 145), Antoninus issued a series of unusual coins in preparation for Rome's nine-hundredth birthday in 147. Their significance lies in the imagery, which depicts entirely new religious-mythological images intended to emphasise Rome's historical roots to the Trojans, Latins and Sabines. The coins feature gods who had protected the city in the past and men such as Aeneas, Romulus, Numa Pompilius and Augustus. At the same time the issue indicated Antoninus as the logical successor to these great historical Roman figures.

In preparation for the succession, Antoninus's daughter Faustina the Younger married Marcus Aurelius in 145 and she soon became Augusta in place of her deceased mother. Marcus Aurelius was associated in the imperial powers, and he and Lucius Verus were both consuls on several occasions in preparation for their joint-accession. Antoninus Pius died at the age of seventy-four on 7 March 161 at his beloved Lorium. So the story goes, he passed away peacefully after giving his PRAEFECTUS PRAETORIO the password for the day, 'equanimity'. It summed up his reign. 'Probity' would have been equally appropriate; he left his adopted sons a reported surplus in the FISCUS of 675 million SESTERCES. In many histories Antoninus Pius merits only a small mention, perhaps because no great matters of import occurred in his long reign and because extravagance, cruelty and madness are more attractive in retrospect than modest but loving care of government. In his *Meditations*, Marcus Aurelius wrote of his adoptive father:

'Think of his constancy in every act rationally undertaken, his invariable equability, his piety, his serenity of countenance, his sweetness of disposition, his contempt for the bubble of fame, and his zeal for getting a true grasp of affairs.'

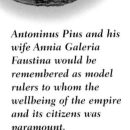

Below: One of a series of coins struck in 147 to celebrate Rome's 900th birthday. It shows Aeneas fleeing Troy with Ascanius and Anchyses.

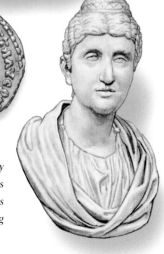

Antoninus Pius and his wife Annia Galeria Faustina would be remembered as model rulers to whom the wellbeing of the empire and its citizens was paramount.

MARCUS AURELIUS

Marcus Annius Verus / Imperator Caesar Marcus Aurelius Antoninus Augustus
(Caesar 139; r.7/3/161–17/3/180)

LUCIUS VERUS

Lucius Ceionius Commodus / Imperator Caesar Lucius Aurelius Verus Augustus
(r.7/3/161–January-February 169)

Marcus Annius Verus was born at Rome on 26 April 121 into a distinguished family originally from Ucubi, near Corduba, Baetica. His father was Annius Verus, his mother Domitia Lucilla. In the year of his birth, his grandfather, also Marcus Annius Verus, held his second consulship. He held a third in 126 and also served Hadrian as PRAEFECTUS URBI. Marcus was a serious youngster who enjoyed intellectual pursuits and embraced the teachings of rhetoric and philosophy. After his father's death, when Marcus was probably only three years old, the emperor Hadrian took an interest in him, and was said to have punned on his name Verus, calling the boy 'Verissimus' (most truthful). In 136 Hadrian betrothed him to Ceionia Fabia, daughter of Lucius Aelius, who was Hadrian's designated successor until his death on the first day of 138.

Like his older sister Fabia, Lucius Ceionius Commodus was also born at Rome, on 15 December 130. In making his succession plans, Hadrian betrothed the young boy to Annia Galeria Faustina (the Younger), daughter of the newly adopted Antoninus Pius, thus cementing a complex interdependent web of marriages to underpin the strength of the principate into the future. At the adoption ceremony held on 25 February 138 Marcus was one month off his seventeenth birthday and his adoptive brother Lucius was seven. Now a part of the family of Antoninus, Marcus took the names of Marcus Aelius Aurelius Verus, but was usually known as Marcus Aurelius Caesar. The younger heir-apparent became Lucius Aelius Aurelius Commodus, but on his final accession the Commodus was dropped and replaced by Verus to emphasise his relationship to his adoptive brother Marcus.

Marcus Aurelius and Lucius Verus enjoyed a similar education at different times, and sometimes shared the same teachers. Marcus continued studying philosophy and rhetoric with the orator Marcus Cornelius Fronto (c.95–c.160), who also instructed Lucius. Marcus counted among his acquaintances distinguished

Young Marcus Aurelius was a studious pupil, who immersed himself in the stoic philosophy of Epictetus; it imbued him with the ideals of a life led in virtue and reason.

thinkers, such as Herodes Atticus (c.95–177) and Aelius Aristides (117–c.181), but the major influence on his thinking was the stoic philosopher Epictetus, who had died shortly before Marcus's birth. The role of the stoic teacher was to encourage in his students a virtuous life of reason according to nature. Our knowledge of Epictetus's philosophy comes to us through two works composed by his student Arrian, the *Discourses* and the *Handbook*. And we know from his own writing in *Meditations* that Marcus read these books, which he borrowed from another teacher called Junius Rusticus.

Soon after his accession to the principate Antoninus Pius altered the provisions of Hadrian's succession plan by breaking off Marcus's earlier betrothal to Lucius's sister Ceionia Fabia, engaging him instead to his own daughter Faustina the Younger. This, of course, meant breaking off Lucius's earlier engagement to Faustina, and the implied greater favour shown Marcus would overshadow their relationship in the future. While Marcus Aurelius continued to live by and espouse stoicism, Lucius Verus was altogether a more lightweight figure. Marcus rose steadily through the CURSUS HONORUM, combining magistracies with priesthoods, and holding consulships in 140 when he was only nineteen and 145, the year he married Faustina. He received the TRIBUNICIA POTESTAS in 147, and perhaps also the IMPERIUM PROCONSULARE. Being the younger by nine years, Lucius was treated in an inferior manner. This was expressed through various signs, for instance when Marcus was

permitted to ride beside Antoninus, Lucius had to ride behind with the PRAEFECTUS PRAETORIO. However, he served as quaestor in 153, and became consul in 154 when he was aged twenty-four without ever having been a praetor. In 161 Marcus and Lucius were the consuls, the third time for forty-year-old Marcus. It was the year that Antoninus died.

Rome's first dyarchy

There was no opposition to Marcus's elevation – he had been ruling jointly with Antoninus for the last years of the reign. He immediately chose Lucius to be his co-princeps, as Hadrian had planned, and betrothed him to his daughter Annia Aurelia Galeria Lucilla. For the first time the empire was ruled jointly by two constitutionally elected emperors – a dyarchy. From the beginning of the year they were joint-consuls and held office for the entire year. Being the younger (adoptive) brother, younger partner, and son-in-law to Marcus Aurelius could not have been an easy position in life for Lucius. And there seems to have been an understanding that, while theoretically equal, Marcus was actually the senior partner. This was probably acceptable to Lucius, who seems to have been happier in the less responsible position. While Marcus was the sober, thoughtful philosopher, handsome Lucius was a vain man who highlighted his blond hair with gold dust. Early in 162 Lucius set out for Syria, where he became involved with a beautiful woman from Smyrna called Panthea. When tales of this affair reached Marcus, he advanced the wedding date, and

dispatched Lucilla from Brundisium to meet Lucius at Ephesus in the province of Asia, where the two were promptly married.

There was a very real reason for Lucius Verus being in the eastern provinces. The Parthian empire had recovered from Trajan's invasion of 115, and tension had returned to the region of the upper Euphrates and Tigris as bickering over who should control the king of Armenia had intensified during Antoninus's reign. The death of the emperor encouraged King Vologeses III to depose the Roman client king and place his own puppet on Armenia's throne. Roman forces sent to oppose him suffered severe setbacks. Marcus Aurelius argued that an imperial presence would underscore the seriousness of the empire's response and Lucius consented to go.

To this point, owing to the peacefulness of Antoninus's principate, neither Marcus nor Lucius had gained much military experience. As events transpired, this proved to be no drawback to the older co-Augustus, but it was a handicap for Lucius. On the advice of his CONSILIUM, Marcus made Lucius take the best LEGATI LEGIONIS available, including the notable strategist Gaius Avidius Cassius (c.130–175), and it was Cassius more than Lucius who prosecuted a successful campaign in 163–6. As Trajan had done, Cassius stormed and destroyed most of Parthia's major cities and strongholds, including Seleucia and the capital Ctesiphon. Within four years Parthia capitulated, Armenia was reoccupied, Mesopotomia annexed to the empire again, and a joint-triumph of the Augusti celebrated in October 166, during which the two young sons of Marcus, Commodus and Verus, aged five and three, were named as Caesars.

Every indication suggests that from this point on the joint-principate would have been as peaceful and ordered as that of Antoninus Pius, but storm clouds were gathering. Beyond the Danuvius and upper Rhenus, German tribes, increasingly compacted against the frontier by the pressure of other tribes in central and eastern Transrhenane Germany, were greedily eyeing Roman territory. Ironically, for the pacifist philosopher-emperor, the last fourteen years of Marcus Aurelius's reign were to be entirely devoted to deflecting a ruinous German invasion – the first of a long series of debilitating wars that would eventually bring the empire to its knees. But before these dire events transpired, rifts in the relationship of the two Augusti were becoming apparent.

Having enjoyed a time of self-indulgent pleasure while in the East, Lucius continued this lifestyle in

Left: The two joint-rulers were theoretically equals, but Marcus Aurelius (facing) dominated the easy-going Lucius Verus by both age and dedication to affairs of state. This seniority was initially accepted in good spirit by the younger man.

Faustina the Younger, Marcus Aurelius's wife for 30 years, was tainted by rumours of sexual promiscuity and political intrigue, but staunchly defended and trusted by her gentle-minded spouse.

Rome. He kept an entourage of actors and musicians about him and built a tavern in his house where guests gambled after dinner parties, drinking until they fell into stuporous sleep. He visited taverns and brothels dressed as a commoner, often partaking in drunken brawls, apparently unrecognised. Lucius was passionate about chariot racing, and buried Voluver, his favourite horse, on the Vatican hill. Marcus Aurelius disapproved of Lucius's spendthrift ways in what comes across as a brotherly indulgent manner. Marcus was once invited by Lucius to spend a two-week holiday in his ostentatious villa on the Via Clodia, north of Rome. While Marcus worked on affairs of state for the entire visit, Lucius and his companions spent the days and nights in revelry.

A familiar proviso has to be made here. The ancient histories recognise Marcus Aurelius as one the great Roman emperors; by contrast his 'sidekick' must be belittled. We should not doubt, though, that there were tensions in the dyarchy. After his return from Syria, Lucius showed far less deference to his adoptive brother, whose conscientiousness he found stuffy, and

serious strife between the Augusti probably lay in the near future. Fate, however, decided things differently.

The joint-triumph of 166 was overshadowed. With the return of the legions from the east came a devastating epidemic – possibly smallpox, perhaps typhus – which took a terrible toll. The plague wiped out whole regions of the empire, leaving some provinces, especially in Illyricum, so depopulated that future emperors would struggle to find methods of repopulation. The last years of the decade were dominated by efforts to overcome the plague and provide relief for the victims.

The great barbarian war

But there was to be no relief from the menace in the north that heralded the permanent transformation of the Roman world. The German tribes bordering the upper Rhenus and the length of the Danuvius had been rubbing shoulders with Roman civilisation for more than a century. In time, their semi-nomadic and primitive agrarian existence had, by Roman example, become more urbanised. Two tribes in particular, the Quadi and the Marcomanni, both ruthlessly suppressed

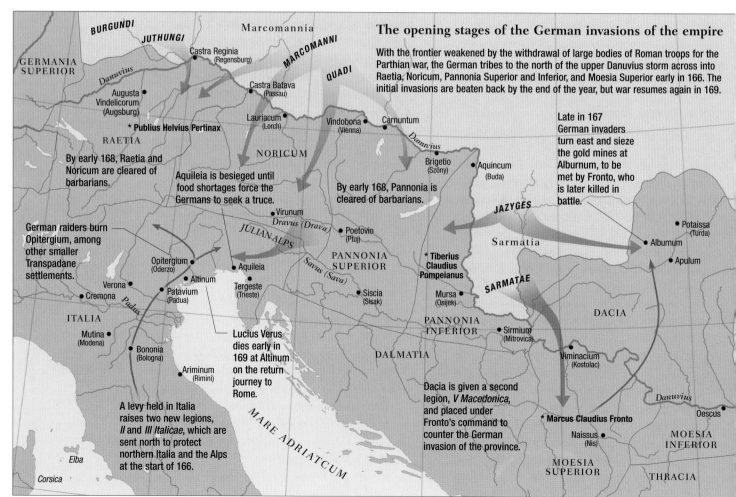

The opening stages of the German invasions of the empire

With the frontier weakened by the withdrawal of large bodies of Roman troops for the Parthian war, the German tribes to the north of the upper Danuvius storm across into Raetia, Noricum, Pannonia Superior and Inferior, and Moesia Superior early in 166. The initial invasions are beaten back by the end of the year, but war resumes again in 169.

Late in 167 German invaders turn east and sieze the gold mines at Alburnum, to be met by Fronto, who is later killed in battle.

By early 168, Raetia and Noricum are cleared of barbarians.

Aquileia is besieged until food shortages force the Germans to seek a truce.

By early 168, Pannonia is cleared of barbarians.

German raiders burn Opitergium, among other smaller Transpadane settlements.

Lucius Verus dies early in 169 at Altinum on the return journey to Rome.

A levy held in Italy raises two new legions, *II* and *III Italicae*, which are sent north to protect northern Italy and the Alps at the start of 166.

Dacia is given a second legion, *V Macedonica*, and placed under Fronto's command to counter the German invasion of the province.

first by Domitian and then Trajan, were determined to move into the richer territories that lay within the Roman borders. In 166–7, the barbarians began to pour across the Danuvius into Raetia, Noricum, Pannonia, and through Dacia into Moesia. This was nothing like the problems encountered in the earlier years of the principate: the fighting was more serious than anything the Roman army had ever experienced. One force of Germans even crossed the Julian Alps into Italy, laying waste MUNICIPIA and cities in the Padus valley and laying siege to Aquileia on the Adriaticum.

Incapacitated by rampant illness, it took the under-strength Roman army time to regain control of the military situation. But to a great extent it was achieved, thanks to the efforts of capable commanders: Tiberius Claudius Pompeianus in Pannonia Inferior, Publius Helvius Pertinax in Raetia, and Marcus Claudius Fronto in Moesia Superior. Having been delayed in Rome by the plague crisis, the two Augusti only departed for Aquileia at the start of 168. However, discouraged by the initial success of Pertinax to their north in Raetia, the barbarians surrounding Aquileia withdrew and asked for a truce as soon as the forces of Marcus and Lucius arrived in the region. With the situation apparently under control, Lucius pressed Marcus for a return to Rome, and it was as they were travelling south in the spring of 169 that Lucius suddenly became ill, near Altinum (Altino). Three days later, aged thirty-eight, Lucius Verus lay dead. Marcus brought his brother's body to Rome, oversaw the funeral, and provided support for the deceased emperor's family and freedmen. Imperator Lucius Verus was later deified as DIVUS VERUS.

Marcus remained in Rome until the autumn of 169, when a fresh invasion of Germans necessitated his presence at the frontier. The Jazyges, having been thwarted in Pannonia, turned their attention towards Dacia and seized the valuable gold mines at Alburnum. Marcus added Dacia to Fronto's command and reinforced the province with LEGIO V *Macedonica*, but the campaign was unsuccessful in evicting the barbarians, and Fronto was killed in battle. Marcus decided to take command himself. Before departing from Rome he married his daughter Lucilla, Lucius Verus's widow, to Tiberius Cladius Pompeianus and left him in charge of Rome. Unwilling to raise further taxes to finance the empire's defence, Marcus auctioned all the imperial valuables, even his wife's silk dresses, and then set out to confront the renewed German threat. However, fresh attacks by the Marcomanni diverted the emperor from immediately relieving Dacia.

His strategy centred on defeating each tribal incursion in detail to maximise the Roman army's superior tactics and discipline, while mitigating its weakness in numbers. In the initial counterattacks even slaves were drafted to bolster the manpower impaired by continuing plague losses. However, he also demonstrated political acumen in allowing large numbers of tribesmen into the empire as settlers and auxiliary soldiers. Augustus and Nero had done this before, but Marcus Aurelius was more systematic, and tied the settlers to their land by law (*see side panel*). In this way he hoped to alleviate some of the pressure on the borders as well as repopulating some parts of Illyricum. To a degree the strategy was successful. Based at Carnuntum, he won a victory over the Marcomanni in late 171 and over their neighbours the Quadi in 174, before transferring to Sirmium from where, in the following year, he inflicted a defeat on the Jazyges – a proper revenge for their killing of Fronto in 169.

Marcus soon emerged as a second Trajan; he had already raised two new legions, II *Italica* and III *Italica* for the defence of northern Italy and the Alps, now he constructed many new camps, and re-established the frontier fortifications. He even contemplated the annexation of Marcomannia (Bohemia) and Sarmatia, to eliminate the headwaters of the Albis (Elbe) and the Hungarian plain as staging areas for invasion. Such a plan would have undoubtedly stretched Roman resources beyond any reasonable limit, although it could be argued that the occupation of Sarmatia would have straightened

IN ORDER TO DEAL with the Syrian mutiny, Marcus Aurelius entered into a truce with the Germans. In return for the restitution of the many Roman citizens taken captive and in agreeing to a neutral zone five miles deep on the left bank of the Danuvius, the Marcomanni and Jazyges were given strictly defined rights of trading with the empire. Additionally, the Jazyges were granted a right of way through Dacia to their relations the Roxolani. Other tribes were allowed to settle in the plague-depopulated areas of Germania, Pannonia, Moesia and Dacia in return for service in the Roman frontier garrisons. Germans of fighting age were enlisted as Roman mercenaries; both of these precedents set a pattern subsequent emperors would follow, and so began the transformation of the empire's ethnic character that would one day leave control of the Roman empire in the hands of Transrhenane Teutonic warlords.

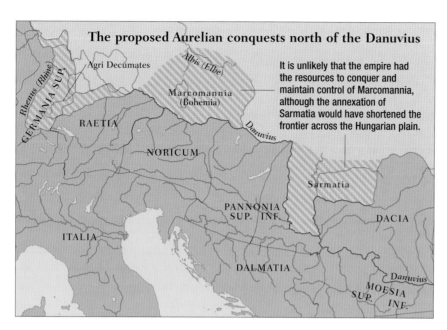

The proposed Aurelian conquests north of the Danuvius

It is unlikely that the empire had the resources to conquer and maintain control of Marcomannia, although the annexation of Sarmatia would have shortened the frontier across the Hungarian plain.

out and shortened the frontier there, as had the annexation of the Agri Decumates under Domitian. But Marcus never carried it out because his attention was suddenly diverted in 175 to Syria, where the redoubtable warrior Gaius Avidius Cassius, who was now proconsul of Syria, claimed the throne for himself. Gossip alleged he had conspired with Marcus's wife, but Cassius may have been reacting to inaccurate news of the emperor's death.

Marcus's response was quick and decisive. Leaving the northern wars in the hands of his LEGATI, he left for Syria. But before he arrived soldiers loyal to the emperor had already killed Cassius. Marcus then spent time settling eastern affairs and visiting several of the provinces. He even indulged himself with an extended stay in Athens, the home of stoicism, where he was initiated into the Eleusinian mysteries, as Hadrian and Lucius Verus had been. However, the northern frontier war was still raging, and he returned there in 177, taking with him his sixteen-year-old son Commodus, who had been elevated to co-Augustus and given the TRIBUNICIA POTESTAS and IMPERIUM PROCONSULARE. By appointing a hereditary successor, Marcus Aurelius was breaking with the tradition established by Nerva to adopt as princeps-designate a man of merit from outside the immediate family. And as events turned out, it was a poor decision for the empire.

The Aurelian administration

Marcus Aurelius continued the conscientious and careful administration of his four predecessors, and devoted much attention to judicial matters. He reinstated the QUATTUORVIRI CONSULARES abandoned by Antoninus Pius on his accession to appease senatorial

Coins of Marcus Aurelius and Faustina the Younger.

ire against Hadrian. For the most part his appointments to administrative positions were admirable. This is attested to by the fact that despite the ruinous war, Commodus was left with an adequately filled FISCUS (although a somewhat spartan palace since the war auction). Because he was unafraid of comparison with his subordinates, men of capability were allowed to control the Imperial Civil Service. The social mobility promoted by his predecessors continued, with provincial citizens advancing into the elite of the Roman aristocracy. Even those of plebeian birth could rise to eminence, as the case of Pertinax, defender of Raetia, indicates, a gifted general who would in turn get his chance at the principate.

Despite his adherence to stoic philosophy, Marcus Aurelius paid tribute to the ancient state cults, and showed great tolerance to all the new religions emanating from eastern mysteries. There was one significant exception to this universal toleration, the Christians. Although the sect was not persecuted through any official policy – indeed the Church's influence spread enormously during the second century – their usefulness as scapegoats for local crises made them subject to abuse. During the worst depredations of the plague in 167, sporadic acts of violence against Christians broke out in many parts of the empire. The worst took place at Lugdunum, where the atrocities amounted to a pogrom. Tertullian later called Marcus Aurelius a 'friend of Christianity', and indeed he was not the cause of the persecution, but neither did he nor his officials do anything to stop what is the worst stain on his principate.

Marcus Aurelius's marriage to Faustina the Younger was not a happy one, although it endured for thirty years, during which time she bore him thirteen children. Several died in childhood, but of those who survived, the two with the most bearing on history were the daughter Annia Aurelia Galeria Lucilla, who first married Lucius Verus and then Pompeianus, and the son Commodus. Despite his august name, Tiberius Claudius Pompeianus was a Syrian of lowly equestrian birth. Only fourteen when she married Lucius in 164, Lucilla was still only nineteen at her second marriage and Pompeianus may have been over fifty. Both she and her mother Faustina found him socially beneath their dignity. Marcus, however, had probably chosen Pompeianus, a loyal and valuable military officer, precisely because his social station foreclosed any ambitions of his own for the throne.

Faustina was accused of employing poison and of murdering people, as well as being free with her favours to gladiators, sailors and also men of rank, particularly

Gaius Avidius Cassius, with whom, as we have seen, she was suspected of conspiring to bring Marcus down. And yet, as he had gently treated Lucius Verus, Marcus trusted Faustina and defended her reputation. We know that she accompanied him on several campaigns because she was styled MATER CASTRORUM (mother of the camps). She was certainly with him in camp at Halala in southern Cappadocia in the winter of 175 when she died in an accident. Marcus dedicated a shrine in the Forum Romanum to her memory and had tiny Halala raised to the status of COLONIA and renamed Faustinopolis.

Because of the plague and the German wars, Rome and the provinces hardly benefited at all from any building programme under Marcus Aurelius. The best known monument stands in today's Piazza Colona in Rome and is a sculpted column similar to Trajan's. The spiral relief depicts Marcus's campaigns of 172–5 against the Marcomanni. However, there are important differences between the two columns. Whereas the imagery on Trajan's is an aggrandisement of conquest, Marcus's shows the defence of an empire under increasing pressure from across the frontiers, a pattern that would dominate the next century. The quality of the carving on Marcus's column is also regarded as being inferior to the superb realisation of Trajan's, but it points to a new development in Roman art, a move away from the Hellenistic style to something more recognisably 'gothic'. Many critics prefer the carvings on Marcus's column for their vigour. Begun in the last half of the decade, it was only completed in 193 by Septimius Severus. Another column, apparently undecorated, was raised in honour of Antoninus Pius on the Campus Martius. Three arches commemorating the joint-emperors' military achievements have been lost, although eight reliefs on the Arch of Constantine appear to have come from one of them, and three other reliefs displayed today in the Capitoline Museum came from another.

Given the extent of the frontier wars, it is hardly surprising that Marcus Aurelius figures little in monumental building, and we know him best from his writing. In his *Meditations* he used Greek to set down his innermost thoughts in a simple manner, as they occurred to him and without literary artifice, and they are in extraordinary contrast to the continual slaughter in the muddy northern forests. *'Everything harmonises with me which is harmonious with you, O Universe. Nothing is too early for me nor too late, which is in due time for you. Everything is fruit to me which your seasons bring, O Nature; for you are all things, in you are all things, to you all things return.'* On the nature of rule he wrote: *'Take*

care that you are not made into a Caesar, that you are not dyed with this dye[†]; for such things happen. Keep yourself simple, good, pure, serious, free from affectation, a friend of justice, a worshipper of the gods, kind, affectionate, strenuous in all proper acts...' words his son Commodus would have done well to heed.

The *Meditations* were written in breaks between the almost continual fighting on the frontier, probably at his alternate headquarters of Vindobona (Vienna) and Sirmium (Mitrovica), and it was at the latter where he died of natural causes on 17 March 180 at the age of fifty-nine – the last emperor of the period now known as *Pax Romana*.

COMMODUS

Lucius Aelius Aurelius Commodus / Marcus Aurelius Commodus Antoninus (Caesar 166; joint r. 177–17/3/180; sole to 31/12/192)

On his father's death Commodus succeeded to all power without opposition, and became the first princeps since Domitian to succeed his natural father. History has little bad to say about Marcus Aurelius, 'that philosophic monarch', as Gibbon called him, except that by elevating his son, he bequeathed Rome its worst emperor since Gaius Caligula, arguably one of the worst ever. And the end of his reign would lead inexorably through one unfortunate emperor to the most shameful episode in all of Rome's long history – an auction of the empire to the highest bidder.

Commodus, the first Roman princeps to be born to a ruling emperor, came into the world at Lanuvium, birthplace of Antoninus Pius, on 31 August 161. He was the tenth of Marcus Aurelius's thirteen children and a twin, although his twin brother died at the age of four. He was given the COGNOMEN Commodus after Marcus Aurelius's co-emperor, Lucius Ceionius Commodus Verus. In his childhood Commodus was groomed to succeed his father, and was styled Caesar at the age of five. After the revolt of Avidius Cassius, Marcus conferred on him the imperial powers in 177 when he was sixteen and made him co-Augustus.

Busts of the adolescent Commodus reveal a pretty

† A reference to the imperial purple, the most seductive trapping of imperial power.

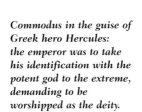

Commodus in the guise of Greek hero Hercules: the emperor was to take his identification with the potent god to the extreme, demanding to be worshipped as the deity.

and delightfully innocent-looking boy. As a young man, he was handsome, with curly blond hair. But he allowed himself to be easily influenced by others, especially if they possessed a poor character, which seemed to appeal to him. This is not an unusual trait in the child of a virtuous man and he might have been expected to grow out of it, but evidence of his cruel streak and tendency to excessive behaviour as he grew older worried many observers. It would not be unreasonable to suppose that the rebellion of Avidius Cassius in 175, when he mistakenly thought Marcus Aurelius had died, might well have been occasioned by a fear of the consequences if Commodus ever came to the throne. Indeed, his unfaithful mother Faustina, from whom Commodus took some of his bad character, was well versed in spotting a monster in the making, and may have inspired Cassius to act.

Although the eighteen-year-old emperor gave the army an immediate promise to continue prosecuting the war against the Germans, Commodus had no intention of keeping it. Had he been another Hadrian, his policy of appeasement might have been viewed as a sanguine understanding that Roman soldiers had suffered enough, and that the empire's resources were stretched almost to breaking point. But it seemed that his real reason was to get back to the luxuries of Rome and indulge himself in his favourite pastime of partaking in gladiatorial combat. Commodus rapidly concluded treaties with the Quadi and Marcomanni, which the soldiers ever after viewed as a betrayal of his father's name. However, the treaties proved successful in pacifying the barbarians, and it obliged them to accept various conditions in return for allowing some further German settlement in those areas Marcus Aurelius had offered in 169–70.

Leaving behind sufficient garrisons to man the Illyrian frontier, Commodus returned to Rome on 22 October 180 in a triumphal procession, after which Marcus Aurelius's ashes were interred in Hadrian's mausoleum. The new emperor received a hero's welcome, and if any in the joyous crowd recognised the many similarities

Commodus, the boy, and below, as the young Augustus.

Bruttia Crispina was married to Commodus in 178 when he was sixteen. Ten years later she was banished to Capreae for adultery and later executed. The couple had no children.

to this and the return of Gaius Caligula a hundred and forty years earlier, they were wise enough to keep their thoughts to themselves. Coins issued in 181 all display the youthful, triumphant warrior bringing the booty of victory to the citizens of Rome. As had many of his predecessors, Commodus distributed a CONGIARUM to the mob, often with coins bearing the legend MUNIFICENTIA AUGUSTA, which suggests that this was part of a conscious policy of winning popularity. He had few financial concerns at first, since Marcus Aurelius had left the FISCUS in a healthy state despite the war, but the tensions between the emperor and the senate probably date to his special taxation raised to fund the splendid games and the CONGIARUM.

There is little further to recommend the relatively long and completely inglorious reign of Commodus. He built nothing of consequence and did not concern himself with the administration of the empire, preferring to leave that in the hands of his PRAEFECTI PRAETORIO. The Antonines were traditionally associated with the cult of Hercules and, as statues of him attest, Commodus began to dress like the god, wearing lion skins and carrying the deity's famous club. This derangement was probably intended to strengthen his claim as the new founder of Rome, which he later renamed COLONIA COMMODIANA. And it was not long before he insisted on being worshipped as Hercules. He changed the names of the months to accord with all his titles: Lucius, Aelius, Aurelius, Commodus, Augustus, Herculeus, Romanus, Exsuperatorius, Amazonius, Invictus, Felix, Pius. If a further sign of his madness were required, his continual appearances in the arena dressed as a gladiator supplied it. We are told that not only would Commodus fight and defeat the most skilled gladiators, he would also test his talent by encountering the most ferocious of beasts. The sham must have been obvious; his human opponents were only supplied with wooden swords… and some limped, as did many of the drugged animals.

The first conspiracy against him was uncovered as early as 182, and those implicated included his older sister Lucilla and her cousin the ex-consul Marcus Ummidius Quadratus. Lucilla's second husband Tiberius Claudius Pompeianus may have been the plotter's choice for the throne, but if so, it is unlikely that the modest Pompeianus agreed with them. However, it was Pompeianus's nephew Quintianus who tried to stab Commodus, but was overpowered by praetorian guards before he could succeed. Quadratus and Quintianus were executed and Lucilla banished to Capreae, where shortly after she too was put to death.

One of the PRAEFECTI PRAETORIO, Tarrutenius Paternus, was also executed on suspicion of being involved in the plot. This left the remaining PRAEFECTUS, Tigidius Perennis, in sole charge of running the empire, the first man in possession of such power since Sejanus during the reign of Tiberius.

While Commodus concerned himself with the complexities of running his palace harem, comprised we are told of three hundred each of young girls and boys, and organising ever more bizarre gladiatorial games with himself as the Herculean star, Perennis attempted to handle the affairs of state. This he appears to have done with considerable ability, but without the protection of the indifferent princeps, his position was bound to cause envy. Perennis is known to have instigated the brutal crushing of an army mutiny in Britannia, and when a delegation of disgruntled soldiers arrived in Rome in 185 to complain of his conduct to Commodus, Perennis's enemies gathered. Beyond accusations of destablising the province, it was also pointed out to the emperor that his PRAEFECTUS had appointed one of his sons to govern militarily vital Pannonia, a move perceived as a threat to the divinity's all-too mortal life. Whether there really was a plot or not, Commodus had Perennis executed, along with his wife, sister and his sons.

Into his office stepped the man who had engineered the executions, Commodus's chamberlain, a freedman by the name of Marcus Aurelius Cleander. By comparison, Perennis had been a paragon of Roman virtue. Cleander filled his own coffers by the sale of public offices, especially that of consul. In 190 he managed to sell as many as twenty-five consulships, making a complete mockery of what was left of constitutional government.

In the same year a serious grain shortage – probably engineered by the PRAEFECTUS ANNONAE, Papyrius Dionysius, to discomfort Cleander – led to street rioting. Cleander let loose the praetorian guards and hundreds of people were slaughtered. In revenge the mob caught Cleander and tore his body to bits. A string of short-lived PRAEFECTI followed until Quintus Aemilius Laetus, PRAEFECTUS in 192, determined to put an end to the mad emperor, who had announced in November that he would celebrate the renaming of Rome and become consul in January 193.

Laetus, an EQUES from Hadrumetum in the province of Africa was careful in his choice of conspirators, but the senatorial order loathed Commodus, so it was not difficult to find support for the plan. Even within the palace precincts, courtiers terrified of the unhinged emperor were willing to join, among them the chamberlain Eclectus and the emperor's favourite concubine Marcia. Without fuss, supporters were placed into key positions around the empire. Septimius Severus and Clodius Albinus, fellow African provincials of Laetus, were given the governorships of Pannonia Superior and Britannia respectively. Another ally, Pescennius Niger, was sent to take charge of Syria. And after some debate the future emperor was selected: the defender of Raetia and now PRAEFECTUS URBI, Publius Helvius Pertinax.

The assassination called for Marcia to administer a fatal dose of poison on the evening of 31 December 192. This failed because Commodus, now thoroughly deranged at the age of thirty-one, became nauseous and vomited up his food and the toxic potion. But the conspirators had a reserve plan for such an eventuality. A courtier named Narcissus, who Commodus employed as a wrestling partner, overpowered and strangled the emperor in his bed on the same night. The body was later taken out, cremated and the ashes ignominiously buried in a civic cemetery.

It seems inconceivable that the madness of Commodus should have been allowed to bring the Roman empire almost to its knees, but it is a reflection on the one hand of the weakness of a debilitated senate and the abhorrent behaviour of the praetorian guards on the other. Pampered by the emperor, who invited gangs of the younger soldiers to his pansexual orgies and lavish feasts, and continually in receipt of extra donatives, the guard had descended into little better than enforcers for a regime of thuggery. The death of Commodus brought the Antonine dynasty to a close. It also spelled the end of the period of constitutional principates and heralded the long, weary fall of the Roman empire into despotic autocracy.

There is, however, a strange footnote to the end of Commodus. Pertinax, his successor, had his ashes exhumed and ceremoniously laid to rest in Hadrian's mausoleum alongside those of his father. Septimius Severus even went so far as to have Commodus deified in 197 – although this was purely an act of political petulance against the senate done for reasons of his own that will become clear later.

Commodus (top) and his sister Annia Aurelia Galeria Lucilla, whose first husband had been the co-Augustus Lucius Verus, had a stormy relationship that came to a bloody end when her plot of 182 to have him killed failed and she was executed.

CHAPTER SIX   AD 192–197

EMPERORS OF THE CIVIL WAR

PERTINAX
Publius Helvius Pertinax (1/1/193–28/3/193)

In many respects, the elevation of Pertinax resembles that of Nerva, who was also chosen by conspirators to replace an assassinated despot. Like Nerva, at sixty-six Pertinax was relatively old to become the emperor, and he too enjoyed a fine reputation among the senators for his commendable military service to the empire. He even revived the Republican title of PRINCEPS SENATUS (first man of the senate) with which to style himself, in deference to the aristocracy. These seemed to be good omens to inaugurate another reign like that of Nerva.

Pertinax was born on 1 August 126 into the humble household of his freedman father Helvius Successus, who had prospered in the clothing trade. The family lived in the Ligurian town of Alba Pompeia (Alba), some thirty-five miles southeast of Augusta Taurinorum (Turin), in the northwest of Italia. The young Pertinax was sent to Rome to study with the grammarian Sulpicius Apollinaris and in turn became a teacher of grammar. At some point in his mid-thirties, Pertinax looked for a more financially rewarding career in the army and became a TRIBUNUS MILITUM of a Gallic detachment in Syria. Promotion took him to Britannia, as a TRIBUNUS of LEGIO *VI Victrix* at Eburacum (York). He distinguished himself during the Parthian war of 163–6 and again against the German invasions of Raetia in 166–8, and rose quickly in the military, and then in government service.

During the German wars he enjoyed the patronage of Tiberius Claudius Pompeianus, who had married Marcus Aurelius's daughter Lucilla. Pertinax married into the aristocracy, gaining the daughter of the ex-consul Flavius Sulpicianus. In the early 170s Pertinax was adlected into the senate. In 175 he was named a suffect consul as colleague to the man who would succeed him as emperor, Didius Julianus. Pertinax was governor variously of Moesia Superior and Inferior, Dacia, Syria and Africa, before returning to Rome as PRAEFECTUS URBI in 189. The ancient histories disagree

slightly on this itinerary, because it seems that for a short period in 185 he may have been sent to Britannia to quell the army mutiny, the suppression of which was blamed on the PRAFECTUS PRAETORIO Tigidius Perennis, and which brought him down.

At dawn on the first of January 193 Laetus awakened Pertinax and informed him that Commodus was dead. He was then escorted to the CASTRA PRAETORIA, where Laetus persuaded the reluctant soldiers to recognise their new emperor with a promised donative of twelve thousand SESTERCES for each man. This done, Pertinax went to the Temple of Concord where the senate was sitting and, to a standing ovation – occasioned by the sheer relief that Commodus had gone – was bestowed with the imperial powers and prerogatives. Commodus was declared DAMNATIO MEMORIAE.

Pertinax immediately set about restoring the government shattered by Commodus. He reduced the exorbitant taxes that had funded Commodus's extravagant public games and reimplemented the ALIMENTA, as well as reviving a law that aided owners of uncultivated land to put it back into production. The senate was allowed to participate fully again in political life, and it began to seem as though the era of Nerva really had returned. But it was all an illusion.

An exacting disciplinarian and inflexible once he had decided on a course of action, Pertinax knew he had to deal firmly with the praetorian guard, which had become defiant of the senate and, under Commodus, almost unmanageable. There is also no denying that they were greedy, but Pertinax's refusal to pay them the substantial donative promised by Laetus on his accession was an unwise stand to take. His solid argument that stringent economies were necessary in order to return some liquidity to the FISCUS failed to impress the praetorians. Violence threatened to such a degree that the emperor was forced to back down and pay the donative, which he raised by selling off Commodus's property, including the concubines and youths Commodus had kept for his sexual pleasures. The gift silenced the rumblings, but only for a short time, for when the emperor pressed on with revisions of praetorian privileges, anger boiled over.

Pertinax was in Ostia overseeing the regulation of the interrupted grain supply when news reached him that a praetorian coup was planned to place the

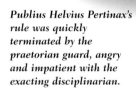

Publius Helvius Pertinax's rule was quickly terminated by the praetorian guard, angry and impatient with the exacting disciplinarian.

ITALIA

Mediolanum (Milan) •

Vercellae • (Vercelli)

• Augusta Taurinorum (Turin)

• Alba Pompeia (Alba)

Liguria   • Genua

Sinus Ligusticus

(Ligurian Sea)

consul Sosius Falco on the throne. Pertinax hurriedly rode back to the city to defuse the situation. By now even Laetus was unable to hold back the soldiers under his command, and a few days later on 28 March 193 a gang of praetorians entered the palace. With a bravado typical of him, Pertinax confronted the troops and was killed. His reign had lasted just eighty-seven days. In jubilation, the men decapitated the body and stuck the emperor's head on a lance to parade it through the city to the CASTRA PRAETORIA, while a sorrowing mob watched on, fearing for the future.

DIDIUS JULIANUS

Marcus Didius Severus Julianus
(r.29/3/193–1/6/193)

Considering his disgraceful actions shortly after the murder of Pertinax, it is sobering to note that Didius Julianus was the grandson on his mother's side of the celebrated jurist Salvius Julianus, who had undertaken the codification of the law for Hadrian. Nominally emperor for just over two months, the authority of his principate hardly extended beyond Rome, let alone to Italia or the empire. Didius Julianus would gain historical notoriety only for the means by which he became princeps: by placing the highest bid in an auction of the empire.

Dates given for his birth vary: Cassius Dio opts for 30 January 133, the *Historiae Augustae*† prefers the less likely 2 February 137. However, there is agreement that his birthplace was Mediolanum (Milan). Didius Julianus was typical of the provincial elite who had enjoyed greater social status during the reigns of Trajan, Hadrian and the Antonines. His parents' was a multicultural marriage: his father Quintus Petronius Didius Julianus was of a provincial Mediolanum family, while his mother, Aemilia Clara, originally came from Hadrumetum in Africa (Sousse, Tunisia). The maternal connection to his celebrated grandfather meant that Didius Julianus was educated in the household of Domitia Lucilla, mother of the emperor Marcus Aurelius, and enjoyed both her patronage and that of her son.

By the time of his accession, he could look back on a busy and varied military and political career. He was made an aedile in 160 and praetor in 163 and then held

secretarial positions to the governors of Asia and later Africa in c.168–9. In 170–1 he was LEGATUS LEGIONIS of *XXII Primigenia* stationed on the Rhenus at Moguntiacum (Mainz). His military highlight came in 173 in Belgica, where he had been appointed governor, when the Germanic Chauci tribe invaded. Inhabitants of the Waddenzee in modern Holland, they attacked south into the heart of what today is northern Flanders, causing widespread destruction. Didius Julianus recruited local troops and defeated the invaders. Since the construction of fortifications along the Fretum Gallicum (Dover Strait) that came to be known as the LITUS SAXONICUM (Saxon Coast) date from this period, it is likely that Didius Julianus was the man who advised Marcus Aurelius to construct them.

He became a suffect consul in 175 at the traditional minimum age of forty-two, which was quite late in life for this period, with Pertinax as his colleague. This was the mid-period of the war against the Marcomanni, so Pertinax was almost certainly active in Illyricum, but Didius Julianus's movements are unclear and he may have remained in Rome, taking care of affairs while Marcus Aurelius went to Syria as a result of Avidius Cassius's revolt. In 176 he was appointed to the governorship of Dalmatia, an important food-growing region vital to the provisioning of frontier armies. In 180 he moved back to the Rhenus as governor of Germania Inferior in command of *I Minervia* in Bonna (Bonn) and *XXX Ulpia Victrix* in Colonia Ulpia Traiana (Xanten).

So much for what appears to be an illustrious career, and yet a theme runs through it. In almost all cases Didius Julianus was placed in positions of control where nothing of vital military importance was occurring. The real wars were on the eastern frontier and along the Danuvius, not in Africa, Gallia or the Rhenus frontier. Was his military capability in doubt? And the prestige he acquired from his offices did not translate into respect from his fellow senators. He had the reputation of a sensualist and spendthrift. This was not the stuff of leadership; and events would reveal him an opportunist.

Under Commodus he was recalled to Rome, the new emperor suspicious of any well-known figure being near a provincial army. Some five years later he was sent to govern Bithynia and in 189 succeeded Pertinax as proconsul of Africa. It is not certain exactly when he returned to Rome, but Pertinax probably

Didius Julianus is chiefly remembered for being the first emperor to have won the purple in a bidding war for the affections of the praetorian guard.

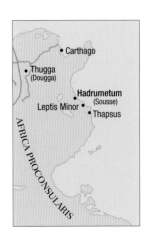

---

† It is believed that the *Scriptores Historiae Augustae* was probably written later in the fourth century AD. It purports to be a compilation made by six different historians, but stylistically appears to be the work of one hand and, while entertaining, is considered to be unreliable except where its claims coincide with other sources.

recalled him after the death of Commodus. He was certainly in the city in time to witness the effects of the stringent financial policy resulting in Pertinax's untimely death. With no clear succession the man theoretically in charge during an interregnum was the PRAEFECTUS URBI, Flavius Sulpicianus, who happened to be Pertinax's father-in-law. But knowing he was nothing without praetorian support, Sulpicianus hurried to the CASTRA PRAETORIA. There, he promised the soldiers – who had barricaded themselves in fear of mob revenge for the murder of Pertinax – a substantial donative if they would proclaim him emperor.

On hearing that the praetorians were unconvinced of Sulpicianus, Didius Julianus seized his opportunity. Almost tripping over his toga with indecent haste he rushed to the camp and claimed that, as close career colleagues, he was Pertinax's choice of successor – and the ignoble auction began with an improved offee over his rival's. Sulpicianus responded with a still-better donative. The praetorians almost certainly preferred Julianus over Sulpicianus, but were determined to see how much they could get, and egged on the two men. Each contender continued to up his bid until Sulpicianus reached the figure of twenty thousand SESTERCES per man, equivalent to about eight years' pay. Didius Julianus went for broke and offered twenty-five thousand. At this last bid, the praetorians agreed and the Roman empire was sold. Didius Julianus was then allowed through the gates into the camp, where the soldiers invested him with the purple For Julianus, the shameful deal sealed his bitter end.

At least Pertinax had attempted to restore order and good government to Rome, but his successor had no such opportunity. His only effective act was to put to death the praetorian's emperor-making PRAEFECTUS, Laetus. Cravenly, the senate confirmed his elevation, but mob violence erupted, with the crowd screaming for Pescennius Niger, governor of Syria, to return to Rome as their ruler. All classes of the city were fed up with the situation and each faction wanted its own strongman to come to the rescue.

Niger was not the only favourite. In Britannia there was Clodius Albinus, and also Septimius Severus in Pannonia Superior. Of the three, Severus was nearest to Rome and in command of two highly trained legions, I Adiutrix and X Gemina, with a call on the two stationed in Pannonia Inferior, XIV Gemina and

Manlia Scantilla, wife of Didius Julianus, and (bottom) their daughter Didia Clara. They survived his fall and death thanks to the clemency of his nemesis, Septimius Severus.

II Adiutrix. Only twelve days after Pertinax's death, the Pannonian troops proclaimed Septimius Severus at Carnuntum on 9 April 193. Didius Julianus attempted to negotiate as Severus marched unopposed into Italy, but his envoys kept defecting to Severus. At the end of May Severus reached Interamna (Terni), fifty miles north of Rome. On the last day of May the praetorian guard switched allegiance. The senate promptly revoked Didius Julianus's imperial powers and recognised Severus as emperor. Didius Julianus was put to death the following day. His reign had lasted for sixty-six days.

Severus entered Rome on 9 June 193. He considered his predecessor little more than a usurper who had taken advantage of the situation after the murder of Pertinax. Nevertheless, he refused to countenance any atrocities to the body of Didius Julianus, which was interred by his wife Manlia Scantilla and his daughter Didia Clara near the fifth milestone on the Via Labicana. The civil war, however, was not over. A few weeks prior to these events in Rome Clodius Albinus had assumed the imperial purple in Britannia, and so had Pescennius Niger in Syria. Neither made an immediate move and there was stasis as each waited to see whether Didius Julianus or Septimius Severus would be victorious.

PESCENNIUS NIGER
Gaius Pescennius Niger Justus
(r.April 193–autumn 194)

Pescennius Niger's early life and career are obscure. He was born into a central Italian equestrian family at some point between 135 and 140, but only held the rank of centurion in his early military career and became a PRIMUS PILUS in Aegyptus. Commodus adlected him into the rank of praetorian senators, and he campaigned successfully alongside Clodius Albinus against the Sarmatae in Dacia in 183. His reward for good service was a suffect consulship, probably in the late 180s, and again in 190. In the following year he was sent to govern Syria. While this might have been a further sign of favour from Commodus, all the evidence points to Niger having some involvement in the plot to assassinate the emperor. If so, then the appointment really came from the PRAEFECTUS PRAETORIO Laetus, who needed reliable and capable allies in key positions before putting Pertinax on the throne. Some sources claim that Niger owed his appointment to Narcissus, the athlete who strangled Commodus.

Pescennius Niger is described as being tall although quite fat, and we are told that if the wind was in the right direction his troops could hear his booming voice from a mile away. His military reputation and demands for stern discipline earned him the respect of his men. The only other personal details surviving in the ancient histories are that he was over-fond of wine and that he only ever had sex with children.

At about the same time in April the news of Pertinax's murder reached Pannonia, it came to Pescennius Niger in Antiochia. His faction in Rome was probably the largest of the three contenders, and he would have heard in the same dispatch that rioters in the Circus Maximus had shouted for him to seize the throne. Niger enjoyed several advantages: the equestrian governor of Aegyptus approved of his cause; Asellius Aemilianus the governor of Asia was a close ally; and crucially Byzantium offered him open gates, giving the Nigerians a toehold on the European coast. Within days all nine of the eastern legions proclaimed him emperor. On paper this gave him the strongest force of all: *XII Fulminata* and *XV Apollinaris* in Cappadocia; his own *III Gallica, IV Scythia,* and *XVI Flavia* in Syria; *VI Ferrata* and *X Fretensis* in Palaestina; *II Traiana* in Aegyptus, and *III Cyrenaica* in Arabia. Further, he was encouraged in his cause by a message from Vologeses V, king of Parthia, offering his (doubtless dubious) support; the Parthians, again, were seeking an advantage.

Septimius Severus, however, had geography on his side, and was in a position to reach Rome long before Niger could mobilise his forces. Unwilling to fight a war on two fronts, Severus offered the other rival, Albinus in Britannia, the title of Caesar, which effectively pronounced him heir to the throne. Having conciliated the potential western threat, Severus set out to deal with the more dangerous contender to his east. Niger's strategy was to occupy Byzantium and then advance to Perinthus, which straddled the two main roads from Europe to Asia. Severus, still in Italia preparing his army, appointed his brother, Publius Septimius Geta, governor of Dacia, and ordered his LEGATUS Lucius Fabius Cilo to proceed to Perinthus to counter Niger. Cilo drew detachments from the Moesian legions and reached Perinthus early in May 193. After a skirmish in the vicinity, Cilo was successful in denying Niger entry to Perinthus, who was obliged to fall back on Byzantium. A siege of the city began at the start of June, capably managed by Marius Maximus, LEGATUS LEGIONIS of *I Italica*.

Severus joined his advance units at Perinthus towards the end of the summer. With besieged Byzantium guarding the main crossing into Asia, Severus placed the bulk of his army in the hands of his general Claudius Candidus, with instructions to cross the Hellespontus at Callipolis and then advance to Cyzicus. The first battle took place there in December 193 or early January 194, where the Severan forces proved superior to those under the command of the Asian governor Aemilianus. With Cyzicus lost and Severan forces on the Asian coast, Byzantium was vulnerable and no longer a tenable stronghold. Niger began a retreat to Nicaea, while Severus slipped behind him to occupy Nicomedia, effectively blocking the way back to Byzantium. On the plain between Nicaea and Cius the Severan forces inflicted a severe defeat on Niger's army. Only the fall of night saved the Nigerian forces from utter destruction. In disarray, the remnant was routed across the Taurus mountains to Antiochia. Here, Niger learned that LEGIO *II Traiana* had defected to Severus and turned Aegyptus over to the Severan cause, and on 13 February 194 Severus's victory was celebrated in a festival held at Arsinoe. The other eastern provincial governors also switched their loyalty to Severus, and Niger faced revolts even in Syria.

As the Severans pushed through the mountain barrier to threaten Antiochia, Niger marched out with the Syrian army to meet them at Issus, where Alexander the Great had defeated the Persian army of Darius II in 333 BC. In that famous battle, it was the forces of the West that overcame those of the East, and so it was again in April 194. Abandoned by all but his most loyal troops, Niger hastened to Antiochia and ordered the city's evacuation before fleeing to Parthia. He never got there: short of reaching the Euphrates in mid-194 he was captured and killed. After hacking off his head, it was parcelled up and carried to Severus.

Pescennius Niger's remit ran wide with the Roman mob, but he lacked real support among the senatorial order. On paper he possessed the stronger

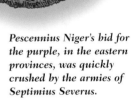

Pescennius Niger's bid for the purple, in the eastern provinces, was quickly crushed by the armies of Septimius Severus.

Vologeses V, king of Parthia, who promised to support Niger.

military force, but where Severus was able to concentrate his legions quickly, Niger's were scattered across a vast area and so he was unable to press home his advantage. In 69 Vespasian had been able to sever the Egyptian grain supply to Rome and so bring pressure to bear on Vitellius, but for Niger this tactic vanished with the defection of *II Traiana*. The towns that had supported Niger were punished with swingeing fines, and the centre of Antiochia was razed and the city reduced to the status of a village. Severus divided Syria into two provinces, Syria Coele (with the attachment of Comagene) and Phoenicia. His purpose was to prevent any future eastern governor gaining military power as great as Niger's. Having personally confiscated the estates of Niger's adherents, Septimius Severus made himself extremely wealthy, a useful adjunct to his victory.

It seems likely that at this point that the emperor would add to his glories by a conquest of the tottering Parthian empire of Vologeses, who after all had sided with Niger. Syria was crowded with legions, not only the vanquished eastern troops but also Severus's European army. That an invasion never took place is down to two obstacles in Severus's path: the siege of obstinate Byzantium still dragged on to his rear, but more importantly he had detected treasonable correspondence between his colleague Clodius Albinus and the senate in Rome. Parthia would have to wait. Septimius Severus had his troops declare Clodius Albinus a public enemy and prepared to evacuate the European legions from Syria to Viminacium on the Danuvius in preparation for a war in the west.

CLODIUS ALBINUS

Decimus Clodius (Septimius) Albinus
(r.April 193–19/2/197)

Geography played a part in Clodius Albinus surviving in his 'reign' longer than Pertinax, Didius Julianus and Pescennius Niger. Governor of Britannia at the time of Commodus's death, it would always take him a longer time to gather sufficient forces to back his claim to the principate. Politics, too, contributed to his relative longevity in the deal he struck with Septimius Severus to share power.

In many respects, of all the contenders of the period of civil war, Albinus had the most prestigious pedigree. He was an ancestor of a branch of one of Rome's most ancient families. By virtue of arriving in Rome a little earlier, the Claudians became patrician, while their tardier cousins the Clodians missed the opportunity to reach the noblest level of the ancient aristocracy and only achieved plebeian rank. They were, however, quick to seize aristocratic status when wealthy plebeians were permitted to become senatorial and consular in the mid-fourth century BC. Albinus was born into a wealthy family of Hadrumetum in the province of Africa. His birth date is unknown, but in accordance with his traditional progress up the CURSUS HONORUM, it has to have lain between 140 and 150. Herodian places the date at the end of this range on the grounds that his aristocratic blood lent him prestige among the senatorial order and so speeded his progress. Of his character, we also know little beyond snippets that suggest he enjoyed writing erotic stories, was a womaniser, a stern disciplinarian and ruthless commander. The Clodians had a long reputation for harshness, but if he was cruel he was far less so than his principal rival, Septimius Severus.

After a successful early military career, Clodius Albinus entered the senate during the reign of Marcus Aurelius. Later, while governing Bithynia in 175, Albinus remained loyal to the emperor when the revolt of Avidius Cassius took place in Syria. In common with his rivals for the throne, he distinguished himself in the Illyrian campaigns early in Commodus's reign and served as a suffect consul at some point in the mid-180s. In 189 he was made governor of Germania Inferior, and at the instigation of fellow-Hadrumetan, the PRAEFECTUS PRAETORIO Laetus – who was conspiring to assassinate Commodus – Albinus went to govern Britannia in mid-192. We must assume that he connived at the emperor's removal and was pleased at the plot's success and the accession of the chosen Pertinax, and therefore equally distressed at his murder in March 193. With his senatorial experience and assured of much support from Rome's nobility, Albinus began preparing his own claim on the throne.

His three legions, *II Augusta*, *VI Victrix*, and *XX Valeria Victrix*, proclaimed him emperor in April 193, and it appears that he received the support of *VII Gemima* in Hispania Tarraconensis and *III Augusta* in Africa. It is improbable that the death of Pertinax was the cause of this move, since his successor Didius Julianus was a fellow Hadrumetine on his mother's side and may have met with Albinus's cautious approval. The more likely motive is a refusal to allow Severus – another African, but from Leptis Magna – to seize the throne from Didius Julianus. But quicker off the mark, Severus entered Rome without a fight in June. However, even before leaving Pannonia for Italia, envoys from Severus arrived in Britannia with his offer to adopt Albinus by making him Caesar to Severus's Augustus, in preference to his own two young sons. We know that Albinus accepted the deal because coins portraying him as IMP.CÆSAR.D.CLODIVS.SEPTIMIVS.ALBINVS were issued in Rome in 194, and he shared the ordinary consulship (in absentia) with Severus in the same year.

Whether Albinus trusted this arrangement to last is not known, but given the general situation prevailing and the Roman propensity for favouring family, he must have thought that he would remain a very junior partner at the least; in this he was proved correct. The adoption was merely a ruse to keep Albinus out of the way until Pescennius Niger had been defeated in Syria, for returning to Rome early in 195, Severus named his seven-year-old son Caracalla as Caesar and his heir. While this was a sound means of securing the succession, it was also intended as a calculated insult designed to draw Albinus away from the safety of island Britannia and force a battle where Severus thought he could win it: in Gallia.

Albinus took the bait and in 196 crossed the Fretum Gallicum with some forty thousand troops, and marched to Lugdunum (Lyons) to set up a headquarters there. The governor of Hispania Tarraconensis, Lucius Novius Rufus, confirmed his support, which guaranteed Albinus the use of LEGIO *VII Gemina*. He was facing an opponent who could draw on the overwhelming forces of the Illyrian legions, and – critically – the four German legions also declared for Severus (the eastern army was already involved in a war against the Parthians). This meant that early in his campaign Albinus was obliged to strike a blow against those enemy forces closest to his lines of communication, *I Minervia* and *XXX Ulpia* commanded by the governor of Germania Inferior, Virius Lupus. Albinus achieved a victory with a section of his army near Augusta Treverorum, but was insufficiently strong to follow it up, and the province remained in the Severan camp.

Septimius Severus and his army left Viminacium late in October 196, but the emperor did not accompany his men all the way to Lugdunum. At Poetovio, having learned of the growing senatorial hostility to his cause, he diverted to Rome with a detachment under the command of Cilo. There he compelled the senators to do as his troops had done and declare Clodius Albinus a public enemy, and he appeased some tempers by showing clemency towards those senators who had supported Niger. He pleased the mob with a CONGIARIUM and games, and then left for

Clodius Albinus, while possessing the qualities required of a good emperor, was ultimately no match for Septimius Severus's cunning, daring and cold viciousness.

Gallia towards the end of the year.

The German delaying tactics had successfully robbed Albinus of the initiative in invading Italia before the Severans were ready because Severus had used the time to block the western Alpine passes. Like Julius Caesar before him, Severus refused to respect the constraints of winter campaigning and arrived in Gallia over the New Year of 196/7. If he had thought it would be an easy war, he had underestimated Albinus. Morale among the British and Spanish troops was good after their recent victory in the north, and although the Gallic provinces had few soldiers, many of the MUNICIPIA had backed Albinus and provided him with a large auxiliary force. The first battle took place at Tinurtium (Tournos) on the Arar (River Saône), sixty-five miles north of Lugdunum. At one point in the fighting Severus was unhorsed, although unharmed – an incident that was to have dreadful repercussions (*see the following chapter*). The battle earned Severus an indecisive victory, and Albinus retired to Lugdunum.

According the ancient sources the battle of Lugdunum, which was fought over two days from

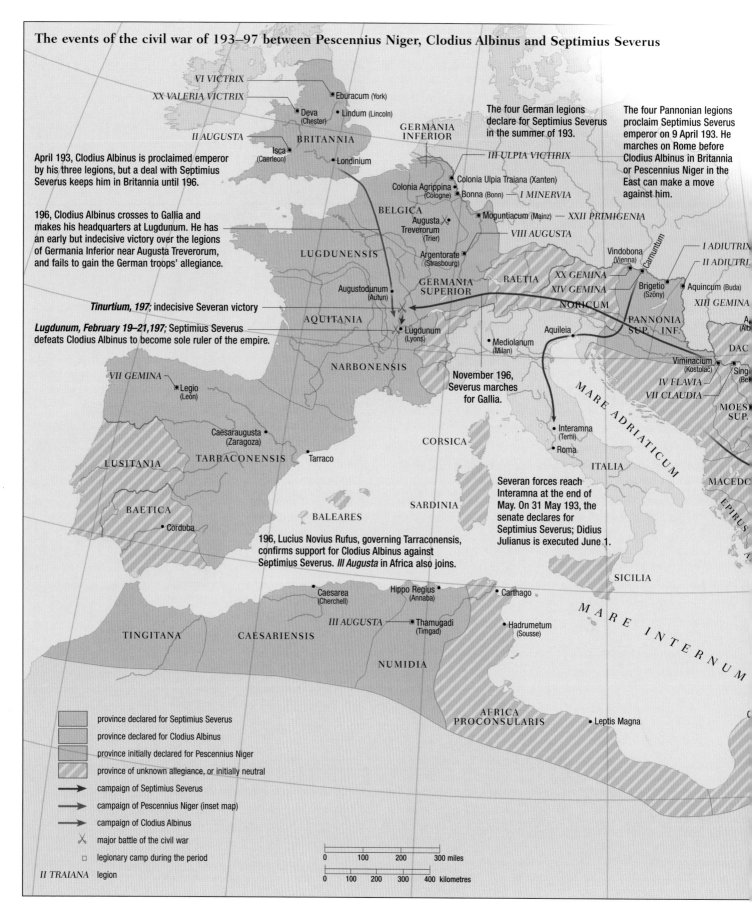

The events of the civil war of 193–97 between Pescennius Niger, Clodius Albinus and Septimius Severus

VI VICTRIX

XX VALERIA VICTRIX

• Eburacum (York)

• Lindum (Lincoln)

Deva (Chester)

GERMANIA INFERIOR

II AUGUSTA

BRITANNIA

The four German legions declare for Septimius Severus in the summer of 193.

The four Pannonian legions proclaim Septimius Severus emperor on 9 April 193. He marches on Rome before Clodius Albinus in Britannia or Pescennius Niger in the East can make a move against him.

Isca (Caerleon)

• Londinium

III ULPIA VICTIRIX

April 193, Clodius Albinus is proclaimed emperor by his three legions, but a deal with Septimius Severus keeps him in Britannia until 196.

Colonia Ulpia Traiana (Xanten)

Colonia Agrippina (Cologne)

Bonna (Bonn) — I MINERVIA

BELGICA

Moguntiacum (Mainz) — XXII PRIMIGENIA

196, Clodius Albinus crosses to Gallia and makes his headquarters at Lugdunum. He has an early but indecisive victory over the legions of Germania Inferior near Augusta Treverorum, and fails to gain the German troops' allegiance.

Augusta Treverorum (Trier)

VIII AUGUSTA

LUGDUNENSIS

Argentorate (Strasbourg)

GERMANIA SUPERIOR

RAETIA

Vindobona (Vienna)

I ADIUTRIX

II ADIUTRI

XX GEMINA

XIV GEMINA

Brigetio (Szöny)

Aquincum (Buda)

NORICUM

XIII GEMINA

Augustodunum (Autun)

Tinurtium, 197; indecisive Severan victory

AQUITANIA

PANNONIA SUP. INF.

A (Alb

• Lugdunum (Lyons)

Aquileia

Lugdunum, February 19–21,197; Septimius Severus defeats Clodius Albinus to become sole ruler of the empire.

NARBONENSIS

• Mediolanum (Milan)

November 196, Severus marches for Gallia.

Viminacium (Kostolac)

Sing (Be

DAC

VII GEMINA

• Legio (León)

IV FLAVIA

VII CLAUDIA

MOES SUP.

CORSICA

Caesaraugusta (Zaragoza)

• Tarraco

LUSITANIA

TARRACONENSIS

• Interamna (Terni)

• Roma

ITALIA

MACEDO

SARDINIA

BAETICA

BALEARES

Severan forces reach Interamna at the end of May. On 31 May 193, the senate declares for Septimius Severus; Didius Julianus is executed June 1.

EPIRUS

• Corduba

196, Lucius Novius Rufus, governing Tarraconensis, confirms support for Clodius Albinus against Septimius Severus. *III Augusta* in Africa also joins.

SICILIA

Caesarea (Cherchell)

Hippo Regius (Annaba)

• Carthago

MARE INTERNUM

III AUGUSTA — Thamugadi (Timgad)

• Hadrumetum (Sousse)

TINGITANA

CAESARIENSIS

NUMIDIA

AFRICA PROCONSULARIS

• Leptis Magna

province declared for Septimius Severus

province declared for Clodius Albinus

province initially declared for Pescennius Niger

province of unknown allegiance, or initially neutral

campaign of Septimius Severus

campaign of Pescennius Niger (inset map)

campaign of Clodius Albinus

major battle of the civil war

legionary camp during the period

II TRAIANA legion

0 100 200 300 miles

0 100 200 300 400 kilometres

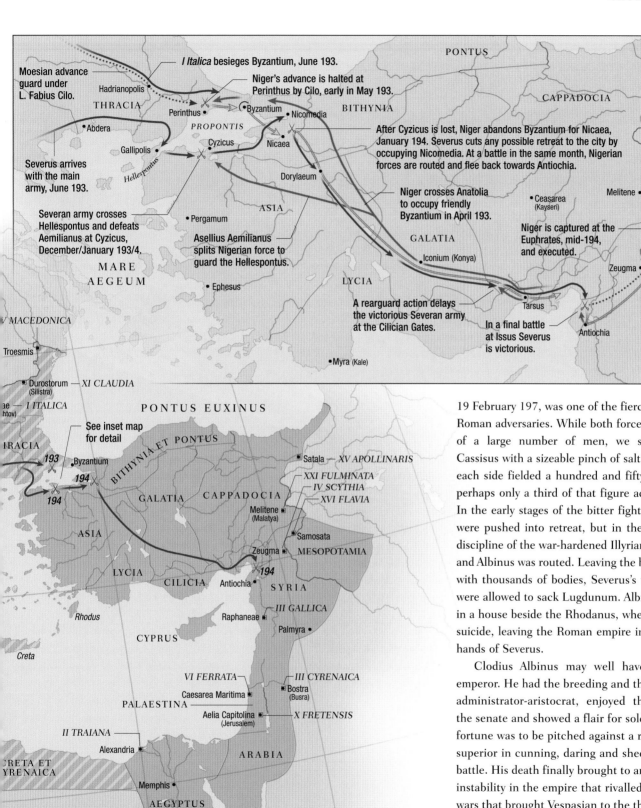

I Italica besieges Byzantium, June 193.

Moesian advance guard under L. Fabius Cilo.

Niger's advance is halted at Perinthus by Cilo, early in May 193.

Severus arrives with the main army, June 193.

Severan army crosses Hellespontus and defeats Aemilianus at Cyzicus, December/January 193/4.

After Cyzicus is lost, Niger abandons Byzantium for Nicaea, January 194. Severus cuts any possible retreat to the city by occupying Nicomedia. At a battle in the same month, Nigerian forces are routed and flee back towards Antiochia.

Asellius Aemilianus splits Nigerian force to guard the Hellespontus.

Niger crosses Anatolia to occupy friendly Byzantium in April 193.

Niger is captured at the Euphrates, mid-194, and executed.

A rearguard action delays the victorious Severan army at the Cilician Gates.

In a final battle at Issus Severus is victorious.

See inset map for detail

II Traiana is the first legion of the eastern provinces to abandon Pescennius Niger's cause and change allegiance to Septimius Severus after the defeats in Asia.

19 February 197, was one of the fiercest ever between Roman adversaries. While both forces were possessed of a large number of men, we should take Dio Cassius with a sizeable pinch of salt at his claim that each side fielded a hundred and fifty thousand men; perhaps only a third of that figure actually took part. In the early stages of the bitter fighting the Severans were pushed into retreat, but in the end the superb discipline of the war-hardened Illyrian legionaries told and Albinus was routed. Leaving the battlefield strewn with thousands of bodies, Severus's victorious troops were allowed to sack Lugdunum. Albinus was trapped in a house beside the Rhodanus, where he committed suicide, leaving the Roman empire in the undisputed hands of Severus.

Clodius Albinus may well have made a good emperor. He had the breeding and the qualities of an administrator-aristocrat, enjoyed the patronage of the senate and showed a flair for soldiering. His misfortune was to be pitched against a rival who was his superior in cunning, daring and sheer viciousness in battle. His death finally brought to an end a period of instability in the empire that rivalled that of the civil wars that brought Vespasian to the throne in 70. This one, however, had dragged on for several years and done immense damage to the fabric of Roman society and weakened the frontiers at a time when barbarian enemies surrounded it. The question on everyone's lips now was: would Severus be another saviour as had been Vespasian?

CHAPTER SEVEN   AD 193–235
THE SEVERAN DYNASTY

SEPTIMIUS SEVERUS
Lucius Septimius Severus (r.9/4/193–4/2/211)

Founder of a new dynasty, Septimius Severus introduced sweeping changes to the army that altered the course of Roman history and made a soldier's life better. A champion of legal reform, he was also greedy and calculatingly cruel when it suited the purposes of the state – as defined by the emperor. Sadly, his strict discipline did not extend to his two sons.

When he had entered Rome in June 193, Septimius Severus had shown some mercy to the memory of Didius Julianus in that his family had been left untouched and his ashes properly, if humbly, allowed burial. No such kindness was shown to Pescennius Niger and Clodius Albinus. After his decapitation, Niger's family, clients, supporters and even whole cities that had aided his cause were punished without mercy. Although surrounded, Byzantium refused to surrender, so Severus had Niger's head taken there and paraded before the walls as an example to its citizens of what they could expect if they persisted in their defiance. Nevertheless the well-fortified city held on for almost

eighteen months before capitulating in 196. Severus ordered the defenders put to the sword, the city sacked and its walls pulled down (*see side panel*). Albinus fared no better than Niger, although he had at least taken his own life in accordance with virtuous Roman tradition. Severus had his body laid out on the ground and rode his horse over it before having the corpse beheaded. The head went to Rome as a warning to any supporters and the corpse was tossed in the Rhodanus, along with the bodies of his executed wife and sons.

Who was this bloodthirsty man who had restored the empire to peace again, and who was to alter the course of its future? Severus was born 11 April 146[†] in the MUNICIPIUM of Leptis Magna, on the coast of Tripolitania, a region of the province of Africa. Wealthy since Punic times, Leptis Magna had been further endowed during the reign of Augustus and by the end of the second century it was an important commercial centre for the empire. His father Publius Septimius Geta was a member of the ORDO EQUESTER as a right gained by Severus's great-grandfather. Most likely of Punic origin, he had moved from Leptis to Italia and become an EQUES. His mother, Fulvia Pia, was descended from a family that had also moved from Africa to Italia. Little is known of Severus's father, other than that he had two cousins who became consuls. Depending on the sources, Severus was educated

---

BYZANTIUM was to remain in ruins for several years after Severus sacked it. But then his son Caracalla persuaded the emperor to pardon the Byzantines on the grounds that, due to its position, the city's strategic importance was too great for it to be abandoned. And so, early in the third century, Severus rebuilt Byzantium on a larger scale, surrounding it with a new circuit of defensive walls. The original fortifications had enclosed only a relatively small area, extending around the acropolis from the Golden Horn to the Propontis (Sea of Marmara). The new walls began about 550 yards (503m) further along the Golden Horn than those he had destroyed in 196, extending in a southerly direction to the new Hippodrome before curving back eastwards along the lower slopes of the hill above the Propontis.

The Hippodrome was one of the largest monuments erected by Septimius Severus. It occupied the area of what is now the park in front of the Blue Mosque. At the same time he erected a large baths beside the Hippodrome's northeastern corner known as the Baths of Xeuxippus. They were built to serve the crowds that thronged the Hippodrome to see the chariot races and other entertainments. It measured 1,312 feet in length and 386 feet in width (400 by 118m), and had an estimated capacity of a hundred thousand spectators. Constantine further enlarged it in the fourth century, after he made Byzantium his new capital of the empire.

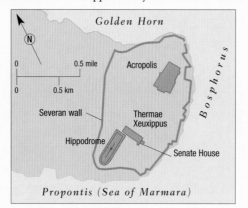

---

either well in Latin and Greek literature, or he was not very well educated at all. He certainly seemed unwilling to do very much public oratory, although in a credible but probably colourful story the *Historiae Augustae* tells us he spoke eloquently in his own defence against a charge of youthful adultery, and was acquitted by the proconsul Didius Julianus. The *Historiae* revels in irony. Accounts suggest that Septimius Severus was small of stature but powerfully built, although in old age he became very weak and ridden with gout.

Severus went to Rome after his eighteenth birthday and received the invaluable help of his consular cousins, who arranged his entry into the senate and gained him the attention of the emperor Marcus Aurelius. Surprisingly, for the warrior-emperor he would become, Severus was never a TRIBUNUS MILITUM – probably because his influential contacts made it unnecessary to take this normally useful step on the CURSUS HONORUM – and swiftly became a quaestor with a posting to Baetica. However, before taking up his post, he went to Africa to settle family affairs after his father's death, and while he was there he was reassigned to peaceful Sardinia because Moorish pirates were ravaging Baetica, and his inexperience counted against him. After completing his Sardinian quaestorship, he took the post of LEGATUS to the proconsul of Africa.

On his return to Rome Severus became a TRIBUNUS PLEBIS and in 175 married Paccia Marciana, who seems also to have been of African origin. The marriage, which remained childless, was to last a decade or so until her death. The *Historiae Augustae* is the only source to claim that Marciana, 'about whom he was silent in his own account of his life as a private citizen', bore him two daughters. The story is almost certainly a convenient fiction to explain a later claimed event, when Severus made a political alliance with the aristocracy by marrying the two supposed girls to the (real) senators Aetius and Probus (*see below*). However, several scholars, including in 1935 the usually estimable H.M.D. Parker (*The Roman World from AD 138 to 337*) have fallen into the trap of accepting this sole source.

In that same year, aged only twenty-nine, he was adlected into the senate by Marcus Aurelius. Severus's career continued to flourish as the empire passed from Marcus Aurelus to his son Commodus. He served as governor in Hispania Tarraconensis, was LEGATUS LEGIONIS of *IV Scythica* in Syria and held the governorships of Gallia Lugdunensis, Sicilia and Pannonia Superior. While at Lugdunum in 187, the now-widowed Severus married Julia Domna, a woman from a prominent family of the Syrian city of Emesa. The

story goes that when he wished to marry a second time, he investigated the horoscopes of potential brides, being very skilled in astrology himself. Since he had heard that there was a certain woman in Syria whose horoscope forecast that she would marry a king, he sought her hand through the mediation of friends. Almost at once Julia made him the father of two sons, eleven months apart: Bassianus (Caracalla) in April of 188, and Geta in May 189. In 190 he served as a consul for the first time, but since this was the year Cleander sold twenty-five consulships, the office's prestige was hardly significant.

As has been mentioned, Severus's appointment to Pannonia Superior in 192 was part of the PRAEFECTUS PRAETORIO Laetus's arrangements to place reliable (that is, largely fellow African) friends in key positions before the plot against Commodus could be brought to fruition. News of Pertinax's assassination on 28 March 193 quickly reached Severus, and only twelve days later on 9 April 193, Severus was proclaimed emperor by his legions. When Severus reached Rome in June, with the force of his army behind him, he ordered the praetorian guard to assemble outside the POMERIUM, unarmed and wearing only their tunics, as they would to attend a ceremony. And there he informed the cohorts that they were no longer needed, cashiered them, banished them from Rome and replaced them with men from his own legions. He also trebled the number of the COHORTES URBANAE and doubled the VIGILES in order to increase the city's security.

On his visit to the senate the following day, there was no pretense of the kind Augustus had employed; Severus simply delivered his reasons for assuming the principate and gave the familiar promise never to execute a senator unless so directed by the senate; a provision he had no intention of observing. He then held a state funeral for Pertinax, consecrating him as one of the deified emperors. This is the moment at which he is credited with marrying his fictional daughters and nominating his sons-in-law as consuls for the following year. He organised the grain supply, which had fallen into disrepair, gave the populace a CONGIARIUM and some lavish games, and departed from Rome thirty days after

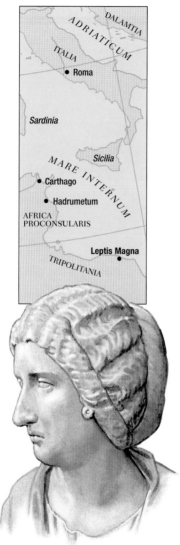

Julia Domna, second wife of Septimius Severus and mother of two emperors, would remain a power behind the throne for a quarter of a century. The coin below features Severus on the obverse, and Julia Domna with their two young sons, Caracalla and Geta, on the reverse.

arriving. The events that followed were detailed in the last chapter, although it bears adding that he broke his senatorial oath immediately by executing twenty-nine senators, as well as numerous EQUITES who had supported Albinus (*see side panel below*). Having dealt with his two rivals and made himself uncontested

Severus's premature death

During the battle of Tinurtium Severus was unhorsed and a rumour spread among his soldiers that he had been killed. In a panic they began choosing another emperor. But news of the emperor's death was premature and when he showed himself to his men, the battle continued to its indecisive conclusion. However, the speed with which he was almost deposed unnerved Severus, especially when he heard that supporters of Albinus in Rome had cheered the news of his supposed end. He therefore decreed the deification of Commodus, an act calculated to enrage the senators and EQUITES. On his return to Rome everyone feared his obvious rage. Countless members of Albinus's party were put to death, consulars, those of praetorian rank, nobles and many distinguished women; and their property confiscated to swell the FISCUS. One notable, Narcissus the athlete who had assassinated Commodus, was thrown to the lions in the arena. His unbridled cruelty earned Severus the quietly whispered nickname of the 'Punic Sulla', a reference to his African origin and the notorious dictator of the late Republic. But his vicious acts should not be likened to the opportunistic violence of a coward like Commodus. As Dio Cassius wrote: 'He ruled with vigour and, when he found it useful, a calculated cruelty.'

Above: An innocent victim – when her father, Plautianus, was appointed PRAEFECTUS PRAETORIO by Septimius Severus, Plautilla was married off to the emperor's eldest son, Caracalla, who soon came to loathe her, although history gives us no reason for his dislike. When her father fell from grace, so did she.

ruler of the Roman world, Severus next turned his attention to Rome's old foe, the Parthian empire. He needed no pretext – Vologeses' lukewarm support for Pescennius Niger more than provided the CASUS BELLI. In 197–9, in a swift repeat of Trajan's campaign of 115–7 and that of Lucius Verus in163–6, Severus captured the Parthian capital of Ctesiphon and reasserted Rome's claim to Mesopotamia. Of the estimated hundred thousand inhabitants of Ctesiphon, all the men were killed and the women and children sold into slavery. The already tottering state of Parthia was dealt a blow from which it would never recover – as Rome would later have reason to regret. On 28 January 198 – the centenary of Trajan's accession – Severus added the victorious title Parthicus Maximus to his nomenclature and elevated his sons: Caracalla to co-Augustus and Geta to the rank of Caesar.

Before leaving for the Parthian campaign Severus had appointed Gaius Fulvius Plautianus as one of the PRAEFECTI PRAETORIO. It is possible that Plautianus was a distant relative of Severus, since he also came from Leptis Magna. Plautianus accompanied the emperor on the campaign and then on an extensive tour of the eastern provinces that lasted for almost four years. By the time the imperial cortège returned to Rome in 202, Plautianus was the emperor's closest confidant and advisor, as well as being the sole PRAEFECTUS, having arranged from a distance the murder of his colleague.

The comparison made between him and Sejanus is telling, but Plautianus achieved a further status than Tiberius had allowed Sejanus, by marrying his daughter Plautilla to the heir-apparent Caracalla. In the following year lavish games celebrated Severus's DECENNALIA, after which the imperial family visited Leptis Magna. Severus intended to embellish his PATRIA and did so with a new forum and basilica standing parallel to a massive colonnade that joined the enlarged and modernised harbour to an imposing square beside the Hadrianic THERMAE.

It seems strange that such an extremely purposeful man as Severus should leave so much of the administration to Plautianus, who abused his position of power in many ways, but by 204 the PRAEFECTUS was finding his influence with the emperor on the wane. The emperor's Syrian wife Julia Domna, an intelligent woman who had surrounded herself with a retinue of scholars and writers, disliked and mistrusted him. And Caracalla, who was unhappily married to Plautilla, came to loathe his father-in-law. Severus, too, was tiring of Plautianus's ostentation, which at times seemed to surpass that of the emperor. Matters came to a head in January 205 when Caracalla informed Severus that Plautianus was plotting to have them both assassinated. Whether this was true or a fabrication of Caracalla's, Severus acted swiftly and Plautianus was taken and executed. His children were exiled, and Caracalla divorced Plautilla, who was banished to the Lipari Islands.

Two new PRAEFECTI PRAETORIO were appointed to replace Plautianus, and one of them points to an admirable aspect of Severus's interests, for he was the eminent jurist Aemilius Papinianus (Papinian). A conscientious judge, Severus appreciated legal reasoning and advanced the development of Hadrian's codification of the law. However, his position as ultimate appeals judge had brought an ever-increasing legal workload to his desk, and he came to rely heavily on his CONSILIUM, which was largely comprised of experienced jurists. His reign ushered in the golden age of Roman jurisprudence, and his court employed the talents of the three greatest Roman lawyers: Domitius Ulpianus (Ulpian), Papinian, and Julius Paulus (*see side panel on the facing page*).

Severan administration and building

The impression is given that Severus was one of the outstanding imperial builders. This is true of his hometown of Leptis Magna and the rebuilding of Byzantium, but apart from these monumental undertakings his reputation rests largely on the restoration of a very large number of ancient buildings – on which he had his own name inscribed, as though he had erected them. However, his military operations resulted in a large programme of road improvement. His most famous monument is his own arch in the Forum Romanum, which can still be seen today. This was dedicated in 203, the year of his DECENNALIA. Departing from the customary single arch, the Arch of Septimius Severus has three openings and, standing as it does on a high plinth above the Republican level of the Forum, it was never intended that triumphing troops should process through it. Coins show that it was originally crowned by statues of the emperor and his two sons standing in a chariot, flanked by further equestrian statues. The inscriptions and elaborate relief carvings celebrate the Severan victories over the Parthians in Mesopotamia and Assyria.

On the Palatine Severus made some massive additions to the imperial palace, so that the huge complex now covered virtually all of the hill that had once been the parkland preserve of the aristocracy. Beside Domitian's palace he enclosed the eastern end of the hill above the Circus Maximus, and constructed the massive cliff-like loggia that rationalised parts of Tiberius's palace and the additions made by Domitian above the Forum Romanum. His most curious building was known as the Septizonium (sometimes called Septizodium), which rose like a piece of stage scenery from the Imperial Way linking the Circus Maximus to the Colosseum. Only its footings – barely visible – exist today and they give no indication as to how curious it looked. If it had a practical purpose it is not clear, although a clue may be found in the *Historiae Augustae*, which claims that 'his building might present itself to those approaching from Africa', and 'he wanted to make an entrance into the Palatine House, that is into the royal entrance hall, from that side'.

Severus was responsible for substantial reforms of the financial administration. There were nominally still two treasuries: the AERARIUM of the people, theoretically under the senate's control, and the imperial FISCUS. In addition, there was the PATRIMONIUM PRINCIPIS, consisting of the great many domains throughout the empire administered by the emperor's procurators. Severus now reduced the AERARIUM to the

level of a municipal treasury for the city of Rome alone and diverted the revenues of the imperial and senatorial provinces as well as the PATRIMONIUM to the FISCUS. The initial funds received from the confiscated estates of Niger, Albinus and their supporters went into a new treasury called the RES PRIVATA PRINCIPIS. Since this was then to receive any new 'acquisitions' made by the emperor, it rapidly grew and outstripped the old PATRIMONIUM.

Severus also undertook a massive reorganisation of the army, one that was to alter the course of Roman society. On his return from the Parthian campaign, he stationed a new legion, *II Parthica*, just outside Rome at Albanum (Albano). He was the first ruler to station

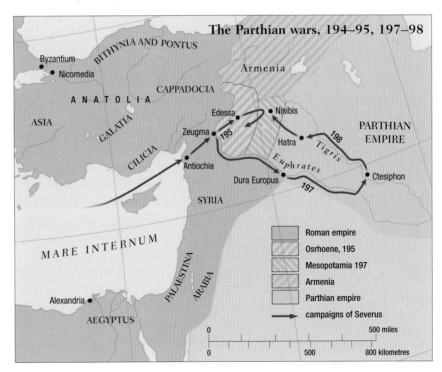

The Parthian wars, 194–95, 197–98

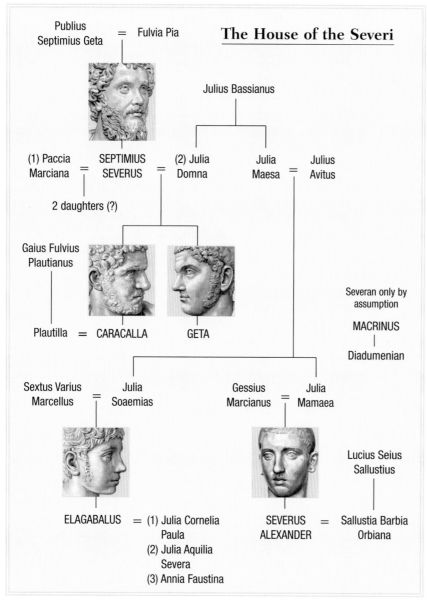

The House of the Severi

Publius Septimius Geta = Fulvia Pia

Julius Bassianus

(1) Paccia Marciana = SEPTIMIUS SEVERUS = (2) Julia Domna

Julia Maesa = Julius Avitus

2 daughters (?)

Gaius Fulvius Plautianus

Severan only by assumption

MACRINUS

Diadumenian

Plautilla = CARACALLA   GETA

Sextus Varius Marcellus = Julia Soaemias

Gessius Marcianus = Julia Mamaea

Lucius Seius Sallustius

ELAGABALUS = (1) Julia Cornelia Paula
(2) Julia Aquilia Severa
(3) Annia Faustina

SEVERUS ALEXANDER = Sallustia Barbia Orbiana

A denarius of Geta struck between 200 and 202 when he was about four. The inscription styles him as P.SEPT.GETA PONT. PRINC.IVVENTVTIS (pontifex, princeps iuventutis), the title created by Augustus for the junior princes.

a legion in Italia, a move sometimes interpreted as an African's indication that Italian supremacy in the empire was at an end. However, it was also part of a new strategy for guarding the empire's frontiers. This legion, together with the doubled number of cohorts that had replaced the previous praetorian guard, was a central reserve which could be sent quickly to wherever it was most needed. An additional two new legions, *I Parthica* and *III Parthica*, brought the Roman army's strength to thirty-three legions, compared with Augustus's twenty-eight and Trajan's thirty. The recruitment contained a much larger number of provincials than before, and a greater number of NUMERI (native soldiery) was enrolled, especially mounted archers from Mesopotamia and Palmyra.

Severus also took steps to ensure greater loyalty

from the troops and their officers. The soldiers' pay was increased by a half, and – in recognition of the extensions of the service periods made by previous emperors – they were allowed to marry (or cohabit under the common-law of CONTUBERNIUM). Where previously entry to the officer ranks was only allowed to the nobility or EQUITES, Severus provided greater promotion opportunities to non-commissioned officers and even rankers to join the elite and possibly enter the civil service. However, the burden of paying a much larger number of troops their better salaries fell on the taxpayers. It was a development that would lead to increased hardship, inflation, and in the end, throughout many areas of the empire, virtually wiped out the middle class of Roman society.

The order Severus was able to impose on the empire through the forces of arms and the law failed to extend to his family. His adolescent sons, Caracalla and Geta, displayed a sibling rivalry that sometimes resulted in physical injury. So close in age, it is hard to doubt that either had any intention of sharing the throne after their father's death. The antipathy between them was not lessened when Severus elevated Geta to co-Augustus with himself and Caracalla. Severus became convinced that the only way of restoring them to some sort of imperial responsibility lay in the discipline of military life. Despite his deteriorating health, the sixty-two-year-old warrior-emperor took his two squabbling sons to Britannia on campaign in 208.

Events in the province had taken a nasty turn. Back in 197, when Albinus made his bid for the purple, the province had been denuded of troops to support his claim. The new governor, Virius Lupus, was confronted by a serious situation. Taking advantage of the depleted Roman garrison, the Maiatae – a Caledonian tribe that had broken through the Antonine Wall during the reign of Commodus and been allowed to settle between it and Hadrian's Wall – overran a great part of northern Britannia. Hadrian's Wall was badly damaged, and military and urban centres as far south as Deva (Chester) and Eburacum (York) were overthrown. Lupus eventually restored some order by bribing the Maiatae to return home, and began rebuilding Hadrian's Wall, a task completed by his successor Alfenius Senecio.

Severus, together with Caracalla, Geta and the admirable PRAEFECTUS Papinian, arrived with enormous reinforcements and established his headquarters at Eburacum, from where he planned to take the war into Caledonia. Geta was charged with administering the province and the business of the empire, while Severus and Caracalla led the army. In 209 under

Severus's personal leadership and again in 210 under the command of Caracalla, the Romans penetrated deep into the north. But there was to be no repeat of Agricola's great victory of Mons Graupius. The tribesmen had learned their lesson on that occasion and refused to confront the Roman army in open battle. Adopting guerrilla tactics, they harassed the Romans at every opportunity. Roman losses were tremendous; Dio Cassius put the figure at no less than fifty thousand.

In the autumn of 210 Severus ceded a large tract of the country to the Caledonians in return for a peace treaty, before retiring to Eburacum. In the following year the Maiatae revolted again. This time Severus ordered the massacre of every tribe member, whether or not they were part of the fighting force. Anyone who was not Roman was to die. But he was unable to lead the expedition. Weak from illness and fearing his time was near, he remained at Eburacum, where he died on 4 February 211. His final words to Caracalla and Geta were reported as being: 'Agree with each other, give money to the soldiers, and scorn all other men.' They heeded the last two points, but not the first.

GETA

Lucius Publius Septimius Geta
(joint r.4/2/211–February 212)

This history will deal first with Geta, not because he was the principal of the two sons of Septimius Severus but simply because he did not last long. Geta was born on 27 May 189 at Mediolanum (Milan), where Severus was resident in between his governorships of Gallia Lugdunensis and Sicilia while Commodus was emperor. He was named after Severus's father and was only eleven months younger than his brother, Lucius Septimius Bassianus (Caracalla). History reveals little about his upbringing, but since his mother Julia Domna was a scholarly woman, it is likely that Geta received a well-rounded education. There is no indication, however, that he undertook any steps on the CURSUS HONORUM, indeed there was no need because of his early elevation to high state. He was made Caesar when he was only nine and co-Augustus with his father and brother late in 209 when he was twenty.

When Severus died in 211, the situation recalled that of half a century earlier when the empire was ruled jointly by two brothers, Marcus Aurelius and Lucius Verus. In that instance the authority of Verus was more official than real, and he was happy to defer to Marcus Aurelius in matters of state. Caracalla

might well have been satisfied had Geta behaved like Lucius, but Geta saw his IMPERIUM as being the equal of his brother's. The two were barely on speaking terms during the return journey to Rome from Britannia. Once in the capital, the situation worsened. Government soon ground to a halt as the brothers bickered on every appointment and over every policy decision. In the vast complex of the Palatine palace there was plenty of room for the brothers to avoid each other, and they went so far as to divide it between them. This may have been the source for some histories to claim that they intended do the same with the empire itself.

By the end of 211 hotheads among Caracalla's faction were advising him to have Geta murdered, and there was at least one unsuccessful attempt at the start of the festival of Saturnalia before the plotters finally succeeded in February 212. So the story goes, Geta was persuaded to attend a meeting of reconciliation on neutral ground – his mother's private quarters. In the spirit of friendship, Geta went unattended by bodyguards, but before he reached the appointed place he was set on by soldiers and stabbed. Wounded and bleeding, Geta ran to his mother and, clinging to her, died. One source suggests that Caracalla did the stabbing, another that he was present in the hallway, egging the soldiers on. The second experiment in joint rule had ended in fratricide; at least Lucius Verus had expired of natural causes.

Caracalla said the murder came in response to Geta's plotting, and the death started a wholesale slaughter of Geta's sympathisers. The looting and bloodshed lasted for many days, during which it is said as many as twenty thousand died. This is almost certainly an exaggeration promoted by those who hated Caracalla. However, we do know the extent to which Caracalla went to expunge his brother's hated memory through the often-clumsy erasures of Geta's name from the Severan monuments. There is an easily viewed example in the fourth line of the inscription on the Arch of Septimius Severus: Geta's name has been blotted out and replaced with additional honorifics for his murderer. Inevitably, popular feelings were strong for

Two busts of Geta show him as a boy of about nine and the young prince who found favour with the army. The sibling rivalry with his elder brother Caracalla led to Geta's murder about two months before his 23rd birthday.

Obverse of a coin featuring Geta as GETA PIUS AUGUSTUS BRITANNICUS, issued shortly after the conclusion of the British campaign in 211. It follows the convention of depicting younger men as though they were older.

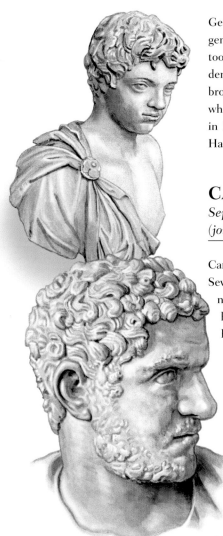

Geta and tradition soon idealised him as a kind and gentle prince, taken by treachery far too soon. This, too, is obviously an exaggeration, since there is no evidence that Geta was substantially better than his brother. His ashes were buried in the Septizonium, where they remained until the accession of Elagabalus in 219, who transferred them to the Mausoleum of Hadrian to join those of his father and brother.

CARACALLA

Septimius Bassianus / Marcus Aurelius Antoninus (joint r.4/2/211–February 212; sole r.to 8/4/217)

Caracalla was born in Lugdunum on 4 April 188, where Severus was serving as the provincial governor. The name Bassianus commemorated the Syrian family of his mother Julia Domna. The nickname by which history knows him, Caracallus (Caracalla), which derived from his favourite dress, the CARACALLUS or long, hooded Celtic cloak, was never used officially or in his presence. He was only ten when Severus elevated him to co-Augustus, and to establish the dynastic link Septimius Bassianus Caracalla became known as Marcus Aurelius Antoninus.

Caracalla is another of Roman history's enigmas. He may have been mentally unstable, but was clearly no Commodus, despite an obsession with becoming an oriental conqueror like Alexander the Great. Christian writers cited his cruelty, immorality, avarice and treachery, but this is probably attributable to his indifference to the continuing plight of the growing sect, and his attitude is in keeping with most of his predecessors. Few historians disagree that Caracalla was a brave soldier, successful administrator and did much to restore the security of the empire. As indicated by his adoption of barbarian dress, he had little sympathy with traditional Roman virtues or customs.

Caracalla was impatient to take control of the empire, so much so that Herodian claims he attempted to persuade his father's physicians 'to do him some mischief' as he lay on his sickbed in Eburacum. On his father's death, Caracalla immediately put into operation his plans to become the sole ruler. His first action was to make peace with the Caledonians. The Romans abandoned the Antonine Wall and withdrew behind the greatly strengthened Hadrianic wall, which was to provide security to northern Britannia for a further century. While it was a suitable arrangement, it was motivated by Caracalla's desire to return to Rome as

Busts of Caracalla as a young boy and the emperor who believed he was another Alexander the Great.

Coin portrait of Caracalla as the young Caesar.

quickly as possible to consolidate his position. His second act was the removal of any of his father's supporters who might be expected to enforce Severus's dictat that his two sons should rule jointly. Papinian was deposed from his position as PRAEFECTUS PRAETORIO and later executed, his old tutor and his father's counsellor were both put to death, as was his divorced wife Plautilla. Papinian was replaced by Marcus Opellius Macrinus, a native of Africa who had attracted the attention of Plautianus and risen to a high office in the imperial service. Geta might well have been a victim at this point but for the intervention of the army, who viewed the younger brother with greater affection, since he more resembled his father in character and appearance. Thus the Severans returned to Rome and the dreadful events related above.

When the terror of early 212 had subsided, Caracalla undertook a series of administrative reforms. In keeping with his father's military policies, the troops received further increases in pay and in legal rights. His most significant innovation, however, was the granting of citizenship to every single free man within the bounds of the empire, thus completing a process begun by Claudius 150 years earlier. This CONSTITUTIO ANTONINIANA was designed to achieve greater standardisation in the increasingly bureaucratic Roman state, but cynics point to the immense increase in taxable persons as the real reason. At the same time, he gave jurisdictional rights over citizens to the provincial governors. This was consistent with Hadrian's reform that reduced the necessity in Italia of bringing appeals to Rome for hearing, but extended it to the empire as a whole. Christian writers noted that this rather doubtful boon meant that while the martyrs henceforth could at least be executed as Romans, their right of appeal to the emperor was abrogated.

In the sphere of jurisdiction, Caracalla was quite unlike Severus, and was content to leave the hearing of cases to others. He also reintroduced the hated DELATORES, and his secret agents exercised a tyranny over all classes, including the senatorial order, to which he showed only disdain. For his administration, he drew on the EQUITES for his ministers, further humiliating the senate by giving his cousin by marriage, Sextus Varius Marcellus, the conjunctive offices of PRAEFECTUS PRAETORIO and PRAEFECTUS URBI. This made Marcellus the most powerful man in Rome after the emperor, and he acted as Caracalla's viceroy during the emperor's lengthy absences from the capital.

The reforms of the CONSTITUTIO ANTONINIANA failed to bring in sufficient revenue to cover the increased costs of Caracalla's lavish spending on the army. So he began following Nero's precedent of debasing the currency, a practice that was to continue and bring the empire to the brink of bankruptcy within forty years.

Caracalla began no concerted building programme, but he is remembered for starting the magnificent THERMAE ANTONINIANAE, which today bear his name as the Baths of Caracalla. Into this grandiose project went greater sums than many of his more illustrious predecessors had spent on several buildings. When completed after his death, it accommodated up to sixteen hundred bathers in utmost luxury. The baths complex measured 390 feet (119m) wide by 740 feet (226m) long. The largest room, the circular vaulted tepidarium, measured 82 by 170 feet (25 by 52m), with a dome height estimated at 125 feet (38m). The baths were sited amid huge gardens surrounded by two libraries and two temples, a stadium built on the vast cistern and ranges of shops. The water was supplied by a newly built extension of the Aqua Marcia known as the Aqua Antoniniana. Although the main building seems to have been completed just before Caracalla's death, the entire complex was not finished until the reign of Severus Alexander.

Caracalla's military campaigns

Caracalla did not spend long in Rome, and when he set out early in 213 for Gallia, and a military campaign in Germania Superior and Raetia, he was only to return to the city once for a brief duration. The reason for military activity in the north was a newly arrived tribe in the region called the Alamanni, which had migrated westward under pressure from more barbarians to the east of their original habitat. A great deal of money was spent on strengthening the frontier; many of the forts originally constructed of wood were remade of stone, and new ones built. On 11 August Caracalla crossed the Raetian LIMES and Suetrius Sabinus, governor of Germania Superior, set out from Moguntiacum (Mainz) in a pincer movement. The strategy was a success, and the Alamanni were soundly defeated near the Moenus (Main). Caracalla was hailed IMPERATOR and added the title Germanicus Maximus to his nomenclature.

Further to the north around the mouth of the Albis, however, the Roman campaign was less successful, and another German tribe had to be bribed to go away, a cost the empire could ill afford. After wintering in Rome, the emperor set out again early in 214 for a confrontation with Parthia, although his progress

was leisurely. He went by way of the Illyrian provinces of Pannonia and Dacia, and the Balkans, only crossing the Hellespontus – where he narrowly escaped drowning in a shipwreck – late in the year. Caracalla then visited Pergamum and Ilium (Troy) before wintering at Nicomedia.

Civil war between brothers and rival kings Vologeses VI and Artabanus V had brought instability to the weakened Parthian empire, and Caracalla wished to take advantage and consolidate Roman control in the region. However, the first move made against Armenia in 215 under the command of Theocritus, a freedman who had first won fame as an actor, was a failure, and the Romans retreated into northern Syria. Any plans Caracalla had for an immediate move against Parthia were forestalled by a

Below: After divorcing his wife Plautilla, Caracalla banished her to the Lipari Islands off Sicilia, where she was executed after his accession to the throne.

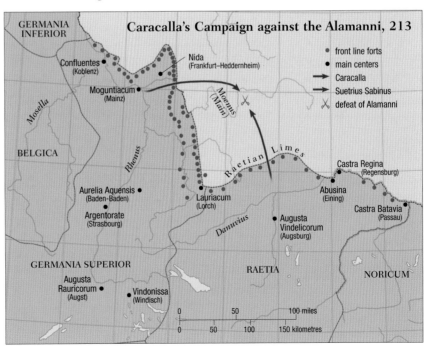

Caracalla's Campaign against the Alamanni, 213

GERMANIA INFERIOR

• front line forts
• main centers
→ Caracalla
→ Suetrius Sabinus
✕ defeat of Alamanni

Confluentes (Koblenz)
Nida (Frankfurt–Heddernheim)
Moguntiacum (Mainz)
Moenus (Main)
Mosella
Rhenus
Raetian Limes
BELGICA
Castra Regina (Regensburg)
Aurelia Aquensis (Baden-Baden)
Lauriacum (Lorch)
Abusina (Eining)
Argentorate (Strasbourg)
Castra Batavia (Passau)
Danuvius
Augusta Vindelicorum (Augsburg)
GERMANIA SUPERIOR
RAETIA
NORICUM
Augusta Rauricorum (Augst)
Vindonissa (Windisch)

0   50   100 miles
0   50   100   150 kilometres

A Parthian coin shows King Vologeses VI, who lost out to Artabanus V. No artefacts of Artabanus survived the destruction of the Arsacid dynasty in 227 by Ardashir, first of the Sassanian Persian kings.

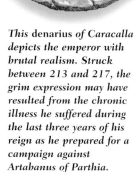

This denarius of Caracalla depicts the emperor with brutal realism. Struck between 213 and 217, the grim expression may have resulted from the chronic illness he suffered during the last three years of his reign as he prepared for a campaign against Artabanus of Parthia.

revolt in Aegyptus. The legion stationed in Alexandria had been withdrawn to join the war against the Alamanni in 213 and the garrison left behind was too small to handle rioters complaining about Caracalla's excessive taxation. With a considerable portion of his force, Caracalla went to Alexandria and dealt severely with the rebels. The governor was executed for his failure to contain the trouble and thousands of the city's young men were killed. Alexandria was cordoned off into zones to prevent the free movement of its residents, and games and other privileges were revoked.

There was another reason for the suspension of war with Parthia. The CASUS BELLI had been Rome's demand for the return of two deserters, but somewhat inconveniently Vologeses complied and handed them over. On his return from Alexandria to Antiochia at the end of 215, Caracalla asked for the hand of Artabanus's daughter in marriage. Artabanus had won the civil war with Vologeses, and was in no mood to do as Caracalla asked. There are clear indications that, in his incarnation of Alexander the Great, the emperor had dreams of uniting the two great civilisations, which puts his unlikely request in a more understandable light. In any event, the refusal became a new excuse for war. Caracalla proceeded to Edessa (Urfa) in 216 and annexed the buffer state of Osrhoene, and then advanced into Parthia, sacking several fortresses. But on hearing that the enemy had retired to consolidate for a more effective resistance, Caracalla did likewise, returning to Edessa for the winter.

Some modern observers have attributed an uncommon religiosity to Caracalla because the ancient sources mention the zeal with which he visited temples during his travels, but this does not fit comfortably with his secular character and there is a more prosaic explanation to hand. During the Alamanni campaign, Caracalla had become afflicted with a chronic illness that no physician seemed able to cure. Wherever he went, he attended temples famous for their connection to healing. After subduing the Alamanni, he went to the shrine of a Celtic god called Grannus – romanised as Apollo Grannus – at Aurelia Aquensis, which was renowned then, as it is today as Baden-Baden, for its healing waters. In Pergamum the emperor spent a whole night sleeping in the temple of Asclepius, the Greek god of healing. At Alexandria the exercise was repeated in the Serapeum, built by Ptolemy III in honour of the syncretic Graeco-Egyptian deity Isis-Serapis, who was associated with death and healing.

On 8 April 217 Caracalla set out from Edessa on a similar mission to make a sacrifice at the ancient temple of the Syrian deity Sin (Moon) at Carrhae (Harran). During a pause for the emperor to evacuate his bowels, he was attacked and killed by a common soldier called Julius Martialis. It seemed a fittingly ignoble end for a fratricide. After his divorce from Plautilla, Caracalla had been content to remain single, and there were no children. Whether Caracalla had made any plans for the succession is not known, but since he was only twenty-nine when he died and certainly lacked any Antonine prudence, it is unlikely to have yet occurred to him. The emperor's bodyguard took the murderer and killed him, while the troops hailed the PRAEFECTUS PRAETORIO Macrinus as the new emperor. The relief felt universally in Rome at the tyrant's death ensured that the senate immediately recognised the army's choice.

MACRINUS
Marcus Opellius Severus Macrinus
(r.11/4/217–8/6/218)

DIADUMENIAN
Marcus Opellius Diadumenianus Antoninus
(Caesar 11/4/217, co-Augustus in 218)

Macrinus was not remotely related to the Severi, although for historical convenience he is usually included in the dynasty. He also had the unique distinction of being the first Roman emperor who did not belong to the senatorial order and the only legitimate ruler of the undivided empire to never put foot in Rome during his reign. There is, however, little else to recommend him to history. Macrinus was born in the COLONIA of Caesarea in Mauretania Caesariensis in about 165. Before his appointment to imperial service by Plautianus nothing is known about his early life.

The subsequent course of his career points to Macrinus having received the well-rounded education of an EQUES with an emphasis on law, and when he went to Rome Plautianus employed his services as a legal adviser. He must have kept himself sufficiently aloof from Plautianus, however, because rather than suffer with him when the PRAEFECTUS PRAETORIO fell, Macrinus rose rapidly through the ranks of the imperial service to become controller of the RES PRIVATA PRINCIPIS, Severus's private estates. At some point he married and a son, Diadumenianus, was born. Caracalla appointed Macrinus PRAEFECTUS PRAETORIO to replace Papinian. He shared this command with Oclatinius Adventus, but the real power belonged to Macrinus since Adventus was an uneducated and ageing man who had risen from the ranks, a beneficiary of Severus's democratisation of the army.

Macrinus and Adventus accompanied Caracalla on the eastern journey in 213 and the subsequent campaign. Macrinus may already have entertained suspicions that Caracalla was concerned about his loyalty, and the motive for the emperor's murder seems to have been Macrinus's fear for his own safety. A story is told that bears the hallmarks of a dramatic device in a play. An astrologer advised the emperor's viceroy in Rome that Caracalla was in danger from Macrinus and his son. A letter of warning was dispatched to Caracalla, but when it arrived the emperor was watching a chariot race. Since it was known to be dangerous to interrupt Caracalla during a race, the courier gave it to the PRAEFECTUS. On reading its contents, Macrinus felt bound to make the astrologer's prediction come true.

Macrinus sought a possible assassin, someone sufficiently angered at Caracalla that he could be suborned to act in revenge, and found his man in Julius Martialis. Two motives are given. Cassius Dio says that Caracalla had refused to promote Martialis to the rank of centurion. Herodian's account provides a much stronger reason for revenge in that Caracalla had executed Martialis's brother on a trumped up charge. What is surely certain is that Macrinus had no intention of the assassin surviving to tell any tales and made sure of his death at the hands of the German bodyguard as soon as possible after the deed was accomplished.

Macrinus feigned great sorrow at Caracalla's murder, but canvassed support from among the troops, who proclaimed him on 11 April 217 after a delay of three days. Macrinus immediately identified himself with the Severi by taking the name Severus, and adding that of Antoninus to his son. He elevated Diadumenian to Caesar and named him as his heir. He also removed Adventus, sending him back to Rome to be PRAEFUCTUS URBI, a demanding task for which he was ill suited. Macrinus won some sympathy by the tried and tested policy of reversing the worst of his predecessor's taxes and announcing an amnesty for political exiles.

However, events prevented Macrinus from returning to Rome, a circumstance that quickly turned initial popularity into disaffection among the populace, especially after a particularly violent, late-August thunderstorm started a fire that damaged the Amphitheatrum

Flavium and caused widespread flooding, especially in the Forum Romanum. Blame for the dilatory response to the disaster was laid at the door of the PRAEFECTUS URBI, and Adventus was dismissed. The senators, while acquiescing to the eastern army's choice, were unhappy that Macrinus had assumed the imperial powers and titles before they had been conferred by the senate's customary decree. Recent history had shown that poor relations between ruler and senate need not be a serious handicap to an emperor, but losing the army's loyalty was inevitably fatal.

The Parthians, having retreated from Caracalla to regroup, now returned in strength and invaded Mesopotamia. Macrinus hoped to avoid a battle with Artabanus, but indecisive fighting took place in the vicinity of Nisibis. Neither side gained much advantage, but as soon as the campaigning season drew to a close, a peace was patched up that did not favour the Romans. Macrinus returned the Parthian prisoners taken during the fighting and paid a large indemnity to Artabanus. As a part of the settlement, Armenia passed out of Roman control, although retaining on paper a nominal recognition of Roman sovereignty. None of this was calculated to instil confidence within the army. Worse was to come. Along the lower Danuvius the Dacian tribes had invaded on hearing of Caracalla's death. Since the larger part of the European legions was tied up in the east, Macrinus was obliged to order his local commanders to reach a peace agreement with the Dacians.

Downfall of a 'usurper'

Unrest was further fostered when Macrinus, attempting some economies, announced a return to the Severan rates of pay for recruits, agreeing to give Caracalla's promised increases only to long-serving soldiers. With the recruits grumbling and the European legions clamouring for either a fight to the death with Parthia or an immediate return to their homelands, Macrinus's position was looking decidedly uncertain. And at this point the Severi struck back through the women – the indefatigable Julias (see panel on the following page).

Caracalla's mother Julia Domna and her immensely wealthy sister Julia Maesa had accompanied him to Antiochia. These two

A native of Caesarea in Mauretania, Macrinus failed to win the support of the senate and the people, so when the army lost faith in him, his fate was sealed. No date is given for the birth of his son Diadumenian, so we do not know how old he was when he shared his father's grim fate, but this denarius below, struck in 217–18, depicts him as little more than a late adolescent.

The Severan Julias

At frequent moments in Roman history, women as much as men became prominent in the administration of the empire, Livia Drusilla being the first. Few periods, however, were as dominated by the actions of women as that of the Severan dynasty, during which time four luminaries – all named Julia – worked with, behind, or against the emperors. They are the Julias: Domna, Maesa, Soaemias and Mamaea.

As the second wife of Septimius Severus, Julia Domna exercised influence in the empire for more than twenty years. She was born at the Syrian city of Emesa, younger daughter of Julius Bassianus, a member of the local aristocracy and hereditary high-priest of the sun-god El-Gabal, the office to which, despite his young age, her grandnephew Varius Avitus Bassianus was later elected. Her older sister Julia Maesa married the wealthy Emesene equestrian Julius Avitus and bore him two daughters, Julia Soaemias and Julia Mamaea. Maesa spent many years in Rome with her sister, during which time she accumulated an even greater fortune, which in error Macrinus allowed her to retain when he banished her from Antiochia.

Maesa's elder daughter, Julia Soaemias, was born in about 180. She married Sextus Varius Marcellus, a native of Apamea in Syria, who had a successful equestrian career before being adlected into the senate. They had numerous children, of whom Avitus became the emperor Elagabalus. Soaemias was a notorious adultress in Rome, and so the story that Elagabalus was the illegitimate son of her cousin-in-law Caracalla was likely to be believed. She plotted with her mother in the elevation of Elagabalus and later played a significant role in government and administration. She also established a SENACULUM MULIERUM on the Quirinal, which concerned itself with the behaviour of women. However, her own morals were always in question and she was accused of prostituting herself as part of the divine mysteries of El-Gabal. In consequence she was instrumental in allowing her son his extravagances.

Julia Maesa's younger daughter Julia Mamaea was quite different to her sister Soaemias. Not of the branch that drew benefit from the family's association with El-Gabal, Mamaea avoided contact with the oriental religion that characterised the reign of her nephew. She married an EQUES called Gessius Marcianus and in 208 bore him Alexianus, who later became the emperor Severus Alexander. Mamaea was said to have been converted to Christianity by Origen (185–c.253), one of the greatest of the early theologians of the eastern church, and was recognised as *religiosissima*.

A bust of Julia Mamaea shows the determined set of a ruler's face, for it was her guiding hand on the reins of government that made her son Severus Alexander's reign a generally wise and just one after the excesses of Elagabalus.

Right: coins of (left to right) Julia Domna, Julia Maesa, Julia Soaemias and Julia Mamaea

indomitable women now represented a threat to the new emperor and voiced aloud their suspicions that Macrinus was responsible for the death of their son and nephew. Macrinus ordered them to leave the city, but Julia Domna, seriously ill by now, chose to starve herself to death. Julia Maesa retired with her fortune to her native city of Emesa and the palatial family home, where her widowed daughters Julia Soaemias and Julia Mamaea lived with their sons. Soaemias's boy Varius Avitus Bassianus was the eldest, and although he was only fourteen he had just become the chief priest of El-Gabal, a Syrian form of the Phoenician god Ba'al.

When she overheard some soldiers on leave from LEGIO *III Gallicia*, which was stationed close to Emesa, remark on how like Caracalla Avitus looked, Julia Maesa conceived of a plot to place her grandson on the throne. She and Soaemias put about the story that Avitus was the illegitimate but only son of Caracalla, and that Macrinus had usurped his birthright.

When the garrison was promised a large donative, the soldiers accepted Avitus as Caracalla's rightful successor with the name Marcus Aurelius Antoninus and proclaimed the boy-priest emperor in May 218. Macrinus responded by sending a force of cavalry under the command of his PRAEFECTUS PRAETORIO Ulpius Julianus, but the troops deserted to Antoninus, killed Ulpius and sent his head back to Macrinus. The Antonine force at Emesa was now considerably enlarged, news of which, together with the 'discovery' of Caracalla's son, created further disaffection as it spread. Macrinus left Antiochia for Apamea where *II Parthica* was headquartered and attempted to restore confidence by rescinding the reduction in recruits' pay, offering a huge donative to all the men, and elevating his nine-year old son Diadumenian to co-Augustus.

These actions appeared to appease the legion temporarily, for Macrinus set out with *II Parthica* and cohorts of the praetorian guard to attack Antoninus, but in the ensuing skirmish the legion deserted. Macrinus was forced to retreat to Antiochia, with only the distant support of the governor of Aegyptus, Julius Basilianus, and that of Marius Secundus, governor of Phoenicia. This was small comfort, since Phoenicia had few troops and far-off Aegyptus had been drained to support the Alamanni campaign. With a severely reduced army, he met the Antonine force in battle outside Antiochia, where the outcome was never really in any doubt. Macrinus fled the battlefield and – disguised by having shaved his hair and beard – tried to reach Europe, but was recognised by a centurion at Chalcedon on the Bosphorus and arrested. He was taken back to Antiochia and put to death. Diadumenian shared his father's fate when he was caught attempting to flee to Parthia. The date of the final battle was 8 June 218, the day Antoninus counted as his DIES IMPERII, after which he became known as Elagabalus, in keeping with the oriental custom of identifying a priest with the god whom he served.

ELAGABALUS

Varius Avitus Bassianus / Marcus Aurelius Antoninus Elagabalus (r.8/6/218–6/3/222)

Good looking, effeminate and a moral pervert, Elagabalus brought to Rome a profligacy that outdid even the worst excesses of Commodus, drenching the city in a wave of despised orientalism. Varius Avitus Bassianus was born at some time between the fall of 203 and the spring of 204. His connection to the Severi was strong through his maternal grandmother Julia Maesa, widow of the consul Julius Avitus and sister of the Augusta Julia Domna. By the time of the events in 217–18, Elagabalus was consecrated to the honourable ministry of high priest of El-Gabal in his temple of Sol

Invictus (the Unconquered Sun). The boy was under his grandmother's thumb, for his flighty mother Julia Soaemias was more concerned with her latest lover, the camp commander of LEGIO *III Gallicia*, Publius Valerius Comazon. The wealthy family home in Emesa – which more resembled an eastern potentate's court than a virtuous Roman dwelling – was run by a team of eunuchs under the control of a certain Gannys[†]. And it was Gannys who, in consort with Julia Maesa, conceived the plan to place Elagabalus on the throne with the ruse that he was really Caracalla's son (in her far-advanced promiscuity Soaemias was clearly unconcerned at what this implied of her reputation). The plotters worked on Comazon, who agreed to smuggle Elagabalus into the legion's camp at nearby Raphaneae on the night of 15 May 218, and at dawn the next day presented the fourteen-year-old to the troops.

In the resulting battle with Macrinus, eunuchs and women played their parts. In a particularly dangerous moment, when it seemed that the emperor's forces might prevail, Julia Maesa and Julia Soaemias, who, according to the eastern custom, had attended the army, threw themselves from their covered wagon in front of the enemy and exhorted their troops to greater endeavours. As Gibbon wrote: '*Antoninus himself, who, in the rest of his life, never acted like a man, in this important crisis of his fate approved himself a hero, mounted his horse, and, at the head of his rallied troops, charged sword in hand among the thickest of the enemy; whilst the eunuch Gannys, whose occupations had been confined to female cares and the soft luxury of Asia, displayed the talents of an able and experienced general.*'

After the defeat of Macrinus, Elagabalus entered Antiochia and wrote to the senate claiming the TRIBUNICIA POTESTAS and IMPERIUM PROCONSULARE, an assumption that did nothing to endear the unknown boy-emperor to the Roman nobility. But as with Macrinus, there was little to be done but agree to an accession guaranteed by the army. According to his wishes, his grandmother and his mother were each proclaimed Augusta. The imperial court set out on the journey to Rome, but Elagabalus was in no hurry. Ignoring Julia Maesa's urgent pleas to reach the capital quickly, he spent the winter at Nicomedia indulging himself in the fanatical rites of his religion, which his mother eagerly encouraged. He also countered his grandmother's sensible suggestion that he should now

† History is unclear about Gannys, who is cited as a eunuch of Julia Maesa and also the well-endowed lover of Julia Soaemias. If the latter, his unwelcome influence over the young emperor offers a reason for his sudden execution by Elagabalus.

ASIA MINOR

• Antiochia

• **Emesa**
(Homs)

Cyprus

• Damascus

MEDITERRANEAN SEA

• Aelia
Capitolina
(Jerusalem)

put away the elaborate gowns of a Syrian priest and dress in a more appropriately Roman fashion by sending to Rome a painting of himself in full stately regalia. According to the now-contemporary Dio Cassius: *'He was drawn in his sacredotal robes of silk and gold, after the loose flowing fashion of the Medes and Phoenicians; his head was covered with a lofty tiara, his numerous collars and bracelets were adorned with gems of an inestimable value. His eyebrows were tinged with black, and his cheeks painted with an artificial red and white.'*

To the equestrian and senatorial orders this extravagant image was one of decadent barbarity. The influence of oriental cults had been on the rise since the days of Hadrian, but their outward expression was still one of suitable solemnity that avoided distressing traditional Roman virtues. However, it was simply a warning of what to expect. The display of superstitious gratitude to Sol Invictus was to be the only serious business of his reign. Elagabalus entered Rome in the spring of 219 in a great procession through the streets over which gold dust had been strewn. The god, a black conical stone believed to have fallen to earth from heaven and which Elagabalus had brought to Rome, rested on a bed of precious gems on a chariot drawn by six milk-white horses. Elagabalus did not ride with it, but holding the reins walked slowly backwards supported by his ministers, staring up in rapture at the divine presence. This procession was to be repeated on many occasions, eventually culminating in the magnificent new temple built on the Palatine, where the god was to dwell.

The temple, when it was completed, rivalled in size Hadrian's Venus et Roma (although the latter was an enclosed building, whereas the Temple of Elegabalus, as it is now known, was mostly comprised of an open court. It was the largest single structure on the Palatine, and completed the covering in imperial architecture of the hill that had once been the residential area of wealthy Roman families. Elegabalus wished his god to be married, and in accordance with his wishes the statue of Pallas was removed from the Vestal Virgins' custody. But on reflection the emperor rejected her as being too warlike and settled instead on the Carthaginian Urania. It was perfect symbolism – the Syrian Sun was joined in divine wedlock to the Phoenician Moon.

In the temple the richest wines, the most exotic sacrifices and the rarest aromatics were profusely consumed on the altar. All around troupes of Syrian girls performed lascivious dances to the sound of barbaric music. With carefully concealed disgust, leading members of the administration and army, clothed in long Phoenician tunics, officiated in the meanest functions. The emperor was officially styled Priest of the Unconquered Sun-God Elagabalus, and this title took precedence over all the other imperial titles. Among his imperial entourage came many low-born Syrians, who were now granted positions of high office. Foremost among them was Publius Valerius Comazon, who had proclaimed Elagabalus emperor at Raphaneae. He was appointed PRAEFECTUS PRAETORIO and shortly after PRAEFECTUS URBI, which made him the most powerful man in the administration.

Elagabalus was a cruel and treacherous youth. While some were raised, others were killed, and Comazon was a willing executioner. First to go was the eunuch Gannys, who had helped Elagabalus win his final battle against Macrinus. Several recalled provincial governors shared his fate, as well as men of consular rank and any who displayed probity. Moral depravity was a required characteristic for preferment. The care of the grain supply was given to a hairdresser and the PRAEFECTUS VIGILUM went to a favoured charioteer. Needless to say, none of these men was a capable administrator. The translation of this grotesque oriental cult into the heart of Rome filled the nobility with detestation. In 219 Julia Maesa married Elagabalus off to the nobly born Julia Cornelia Paula. But in the following year he divorced her to marry Julia Aquilia Severa. All of Rome was scandalised, for Severa was a Vestal Virgin. He threw Severa aside a year later and, having executed her husband only a short time before, married Annia Faustina, who counted Marcus Aurelius

Elagabalus: immoral or misguided?

While there is 'no smoke without a fire', we should consider much of the contemporary historians' invective as consequential to their detestation of a young oriental who was elevating his god above all others. To the stoics, neo-Platonists and neo-Pythagoreans who sought to establish a universal religion through the combination of all creeds, Elagabalus was creating a kind of pagan catholicism that ignored any god but his own. As to the sexual excesses, the practical Romans acknowledged homosexuality (although perhaps not transsexuality) as a given but did not accept its public exhibition. How much of what they claim Elagabalus got up to actually occurred in public, as against in the (crowded) privacy of the Palatine palace, is a matter of conjecture. However, modern commentators have questioned the authenticity of contemporary witnesses over the need of depilation to beautify a boy barely in his adolescence, which calls into question many of their other claims. Perhaps we should look less at the emperor's sexual antics as the cause of public hatred and more at the religious implications and the sheer incompetence of his civil administration.

among her ancestors. The histories insist that he married no less than five wives during his brief reign.

If this flurry of marital activity suggests the sexual antics of a youthful stud, it is misleading, for Elegabalus had little desire for any of his wives. He was not the first emperor to have shown a preference for sex with other young men, but none before him had flaunted their homosexuality so openly. (Hadrian's obsession with Antinöus had manifested itself to the public more as a cult than a public love affair). As Gibbon so neatly put it: *'The master of the Roman world affected to copy the dress and manners of the female sex [and] preferred the distaff to the sceptre.'* As he entered puberty Elagabalus had the hairs plucked from his body in order to appear more feminine, and delighted in appearing before his subjects wearing feminine clothes and cosmetics. A blond-haired Carian slave named Hierocles acted as the emperor's 'husband', and was sometimes employed to 'capture' Elagabalus when he offered himself to passers by as a prostitute and then administer a sound beating as a 'punishment'.

Elagabalus and Alexander

Elsewhere, there were continual signs of disturbance. The first came as early as the start of 219, and the rebels were the men of *III Gallica*, the very legion that had raised up Elagabalus. Having realised their mistake, they attempted to make their new LEGATUS LEGIONIS Verus emperor. He had been promoted through the ranks from centurion to adlection into the senate, but his pretence at imperial power was very short-lived. The praetorians still owed their allegiance to Elagabalus. Verus was executed and the legion cashiered. Shortly afterwards a lowly physician's son named Gellius Maximus, who had also been adlected into the senate and was a senior officer of *IV Scythica* in Syria, took advantage of *III Gallica*'s disturbance to declare himself emperor. Again, Elagabalus was able to rely on the praetorians to quell the revolt and Gellius Maximus was put to death. Other names crop up, including Uranius Antonius, Sallustius and a certain Seleucus, who may have been Julius Antonius Seleucus, governor of Moesia, or Marcus Flavius Vitellius Seleucus, a consul in 221. The fact is, there was a lot of unrest.

Julia Maesa became increasingly concerned that the emperor's conduct and growing unpopularity would threaten her own ascendancy and control of the government (she had even been given the unprecedented right of a seat in the senate). She determined that her other grandson Alexianus – a straight-laced

and likeable youngster of thirteen – should be given official standing. She tricked Elagabalus into adopting his cousin, on the grounds that he would be able to hand over the boring matters of government – that is the very few tasks Elagabalus bothered with – in order to devote more time to his priestly duties. Alexianus was adopted on 10 July 221 and became the heir to Elagabalus with the name of Marcus Aurelius Severus Alexander, and received a share in the imperial powers and prerogatives.

Alexander's friendly disposition soon endeared him to both the people and the soldiers. Elagabalus became jealous of his cousin's popularity and began to fear its consequences. By the beginning of 222, the processes of government were grinding to a halt as officials struggled to understand where the real authority lay. Elagabalus could still count on the unqualified support of his mother, Julia Soaemias, but he refused to speak to his grandmother, who clearly preferred Alexander. The tyrant sought first to corrupt his cousin by enticing him with all manner of perversions in a ridiculous attempt to damage his reputation, and when this failed, to kill him. But Alexander was well protected, thanks to his mother Julia Mamaea's prudence. Moreover, Alexander had become the firm favourite of the praetorians, who saw little of their emperor, since he had no interest in military matters.

Furious at failure, Elagabalus demoted Alexander from the rank and privileges of Caesar, but this roused the ire of a chilly senate and a furious CASTRA PRAETORIA. The guard swore to protect Alexander's life and keep a close watch on the emperor's conduct. The unstable situation could not last, and it may have been Maesa and Mamaea who conspired to leak a rumour to the praetorians that another attempt to assassinate Alexander had been barely foiled. The natural suspicion that they were too late and that their darling had already been murdered inflamed praetorian passions. The soldiers demanded that Elagabalus produce his cousin to prove that he was safe. The emperor responded by attempting to punish the ringleaders of what he considered to be a mutiny. The indignant praetorians rose up on 6 March 222 and massacred the minions of Elagabalus, his mother Julia Soaemias and the young emperor himself. They mutilated his corpse and then dragged it through the streets to the Tiberis and tossed it in. *'His memory was branded with eternal infamy by the senate; the justice of whose decree has been ratified by posterity,'* adds Gibbon.

The once-popular view of the failure of Elagabalus's reign as a clash of cultures between oriental and

A trail of wives: Elagabalus (above), a notorious bisexual, went through as many as five wives according to the contemporary histories. However, we only know of three (top to bottom): Julia Cornelia Paula, the Vestal Virgin Julia Aquillia Severa and Annia Fausta, who he put aside to remarry Julia Aquillia Severa.

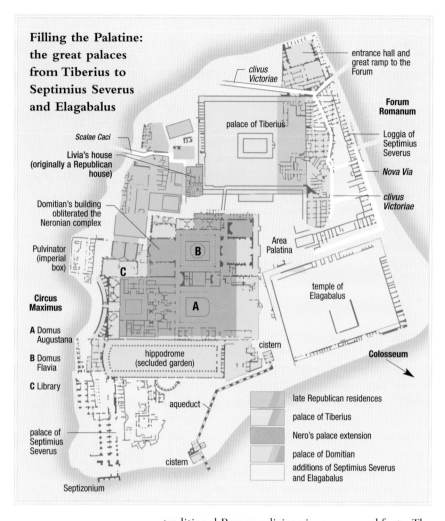

Filling the Palatine: the great palaces from Tiberius to Septimius Severus and Elagabalus

clivus Victoriae

entrance hall and great ramp to the Forum

palace of Tiberius

Forum Romanum

Scalae Caci

Livia's house (originally a Republican house)

Loggia of Septimius Severus

Nova Via

Domitian's building obliterated the Neronian complex

clivus Victoriae

Pulvinator (imperial box)

Area Palatina

B

temple of Elagabalus

C

A

Circus Maximus

A Domus Augustana

B Domus Flavia

C Library

cistern

hippodrome (secluded garden)

Colosseum

palace of Septimius Severus

aqueduct

cistern

Septizonium

late Republican residences

palace of Tiberius

Nero's palace extension

palace of Domitian

additions of Septimius Severus and Elagabalus

---

traditional Roman religions ignores several facts. The syncretisation of religions had always been a relatively smooth process due to the sheer number of cults present within the empire. And there seems to have been early acceptance of oriental cults such as that of Isis, to whom a temple had been dedicated in Rome before the accession of Augustus. The cult of Mithra, or Mithras, an ancient Indo-Iranian god of truth and light, reached Rome in the second half of the first century BC, and became widespread in the imperial period. The cult appealed to merchants, soldiers and charioteers. Even though Elagabalus's promotion of the Emesene sungod was certainly ridiculed by contemporary observers, this cult was popular among soldiers, who associated it with that of Mithras, and it would remain so. Indeed, many succeeding emperors – and not all of Syrian origin – would come to regard Sol Invictus as the primary – but not necessarily exclusive – deity of the Roman pantheon.

In most respects, the reign of Elagabalus recalls that of Caligula, a callow youth raised in luxury who then suffered dramatic changes of fortune;

Severus Alexander as a young adolescent.

the deaths of his father, grandfather, and his cousin, the emperor Caracalla, all within the space of one year must have been destabilising. Elevated beyond his abilities and lacking discipline, his reign tragically highlights the failure of despotic government without even the dubious safeguards that were implicit in the fabrication of the Augustan principate.

SEVERUS ALEXANDER
Marcus Julius Gessius Bassianus Alexianus /
Marcus Aurelius Severus Alexander
(Caesar from 10/7/221, r.6/3/222–March 235)

Alexianus was born in Arca Caesarea in Phoenicia on the first of October 208 (although some sources put the date three years earlier), the son of Gessius Marcianus, an EQUES, and of Julia Mamaea, niece of the then empress, Julia Domna, wife of Septimius Severus. Julia Mamaea was the antithesis of her flighty sister Soemias, and so was Alexianus in comparison to his cousin. At his mother's insistence he was raised quietly and educated well, and had little if anything to do with the worship of the Emesene sungod. When he was raised to the purple in March 222 he became Rome's youngest emperor, aged barely fourteen, and so the reins of government were in the hands of his mother and grandmother. However, Julia Maesa lived for only a short time after Alexander's elevation, after which Mamaea became the sole regent of her son and the empire. Her imperial title was MATER AUGUSTI NOSTRI ET CASTRORUM ET SENATUS ET PATRIAE. Her position in the government was confirmed by the title CONSORS IMPERII.

Herodian portrays the reign of Severus Alexander as a reaction not only against the profligate excesses of his cousin, but also as a rejection of the militaristic principles of Septimius Severus and Caracalla. In the Herodian picture, the ruler returns to something recognisable as an Augustan princeps, restoring to the senatorial order its ancient privileges, and favouring senators and the nobility over the EQUITES and army. However, Herodian was the emperor's biographer and his assessment is clearly flattering. Unfortunately, the work of his contempary, Dio Cassius, is largely missing for this period, so sensible comparison is not possible.

Maesa and Mamaea established a sixteen-man CONSILIUM of senators, which after the former's death may be regarded as Mamaea's government, until Alexander became old enough to take control. Since the CONSILIUM included the eminent jurists Ulpian and

Paulus, it marked a return to sane government after Elagabalus, but hardly indicates a restoration of government by consent of the senate. That Ulpian was appointed to the office of PRAEFECTUS PRAETORIO is used to argue a new precedence of senators over equestrians, the class that had usually filled the post. Under Alexander, the traditional incompatibility between the prefecture and membership of the senate was removed and henceforth the PRAEFECTUS could be VIR CLARISSIMUS or still VIR EMINENTISSIMUS (*see the side panel*). Nevertheless, equestrian PRAEFECTI did not automatically become adlected into the senate as a result of the reform and indeed for the next fifty years the majority of PRAEFECTI still belonged to the ORDO EQUESTER.

Alexander, under his mother's tutelage, restored prestige to the senate and respected its members. But despite his biographer's claims, he did not hand back any powers that had been gradually removed from the senate through the principate or break with the Severan principle of administration through a CONSILIUM and centrally controlled civil service. If anything, Alexander's regulation of some political offices tightened the autocratic power of the emperor. So vanished from the Roman political sphere the offices of TRIBUNUS PLEBIS and CURULE AEDILE from the senatorial CURSUS HONORUM. However, such offices had largely fallen into disuse as most of their functions were absorbed by the imperial bureaucracy, so this reform can be seen as more of an orderly tidying up of ancient Republican loose ends than an overt act of despotism.

For Rome and the empire, the first nine years of Alexander's reign were peaceful, as the realm recovered from the excesses of Elagabalus through Mamaea's careful government. In this she was aided by her son's complete devotion, which allowed for none of the discord that had marked earlier regencies. Two incidents marred the new order. Ulpian earned the displeasure of the praetorian guard for his unyieldingly strict command and, after an argument, some troops killed him in the emperor's palace. The other affected Alexander directly. In 225 Mamaea chose for him a bride named Sallustia Barbia Orbiana. She was from one of the few remaining genuinely patrician families, and her father Lucius Seius Sallustius was raised to the rank of Caesar. But Mamaea soon became jealous of the hold his new wife had over her son and forced him to divorce and banish her in 227. At the same time Sallustius was accused of an attempt on Alexander's life and executed. There is no record that Alexander resented this interference in his married life and thereafter he remained single, and

SINCE THE TIME of Marcus Aurelius the designation of officials had been changing through the increase in bureaucracy and the blurring of roles previously only held by a senator at the higher level and an EQUES at the lower. The titles were peculiar to the official's rank, so the senator is styled as VIR CLARISSIMUS (most distinguished gentleman) and the equestrian in the civil service as VIR EGREGIUS (honourable gentleman). The title VIR EMINENTISSIMUS (eminent gentleman) belongs only to the PRAEFECTUS PRAETORIO, always an EQUES who would have to give up the office if he were to be adlected into the senate. There had been notable exceptions, Sejanus in 31, Titus in the principate of Vespasian, and Plautianus in 203. Alexander's reform meant that the office could now be held either by an equestrian or by a senator.

Mamaea returned to her supreme position.

The return to a degree of economic stability allowed Alexander to undertake several building projects. The huge baths of Caracalla were finished and the Neronian Baths complex in the Campus Martius was enlarged and renamed the Baths of Alexander. The last of Rome's eleven great aqueducts, the Aqua Alexandrina, was put into service in 226 to bring water to the Campus Martius. Throughout Italia and the provinces further roads, bridges and baths were constructed through a generous alleviation of taxes to communities involved in works of public utility. Most especially, Alexander concentrated resources on road building along the Danuvius frontier.

Had his reign remained peaceful, Alexander Severus might have developed into a significant emperor, certainly in comparison with his immediate predecessors. But it was not to be, and in the following five years Alexander proved unequal to the major challenge of the time. With the constant pressure of barbarian tribes to the north and a reinvigorated Persia to the east, military skills more than domestic were the prime attribute of an emperor in the third century. Alexander's lack in this respect ultimately cost him his life.

The first great challenge appeared from Persia, where the Arsacid Parthian dynasty – Rome's most constant foe – was overthrown by the Sassanids. Even as he began mobilisation, Alexander attempted to negotiate with Ardashir, the triumphant Sassanian king, a process that had usually worked before. But the Sassanians were very different opponents than had been the

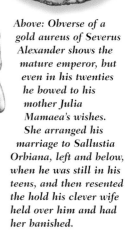

Above: Obverse of a gold aureus of Severus Alexander shows the mature emperor, but even in his twenties he bowed to his mother Julia Mamaea's wishes. She arranged his marriage to Sallustia Orbiana, left and below, when he was still in his teens, and then resented the hold his clever wife held over him and had her banished.

Parthians and all overtures were ignored (*see panel below*). A new legion was raised (possibly *IV Italica*) and detachments from the Illyrian legions were readied to march towards the eastern frontier.

Alexander and Mamaea left Rome for Antiochia early in 231 to be joined there by the European army units. A last attempt to negotiate resulted in a curt response that Rome should immediately evacuate the territories that rightfully belonged to the Persian empire. The events of the campaign that followed remain unclear, although the presence of the emperor leant additional weight to Roman policy, because early Sassanian successes were reversed. While the Romans met with severe losses, they also inflicted heavy casualties. The result was an acceptance of the *status quo* rather than any settlement. Mesopotamia was recovered, Ardashir made no further move for four years, and Alexander returned to Rome in 233 to celebrate a magnificent triumph.

The emperor's presence was now felt to be essential at the northern frontiers, where Germans had crossed the Rhenus and Danuvius to take advantage of the troop reductions made for the Persian campaign. Indeed, this serious incursion may well have been another reason for concluding the war against Ardashir.

SINCE THE DAYS of Alexander the Great the Parthians had been the dominant power in Persia. However, frequent debilitating wars with Rome weakened the ruling Arsacid dynasty, which under Artabanus V was finally toppled. Taking advantage, Ardashir (Artaxerxes), king of the neigbouring tribe of Fars, who had subdued an area from the Persian Gulf to Isfahan, rebelled and proclaimed himself the restorer of the ancient Achaemenid empire and true Zoroastrian faith. In 227 he invaded Parthia and overthrew Artabanus in battle on 28 April and assumed the title King of Kings, founding the Sassanian dynasty, named after his grandfather Sassan. The Sassanians were far more aggressive than the Parthians, who had only aspired to include Armenia within their boundaries. Ardashir's aims were to annex all of Asia Minor and eradicate Hellenistic culture from the region. It took three years for Ardashir to consolidate his position, so it was in 230 that news reached Rome that the Sassanians had overrun Mesopotamia, were threatening Syria and had laid claim to all the land that had belonged to Darius as far west as the Aegean.

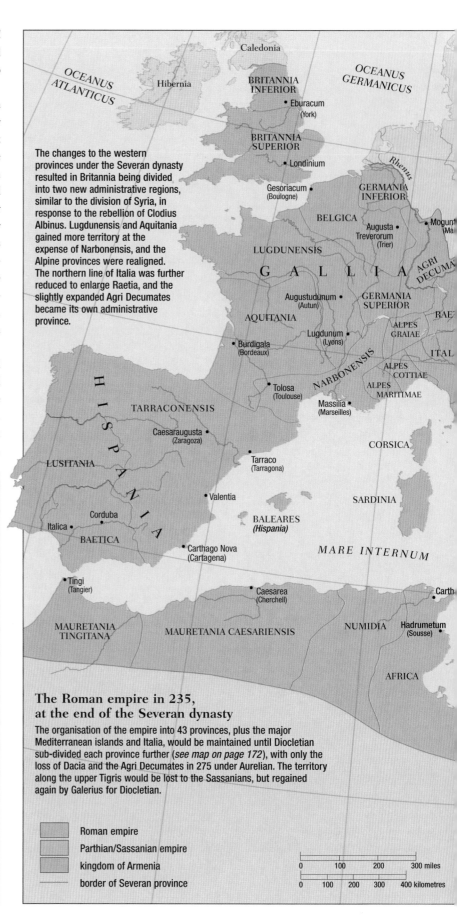

The changes to the western provinces under the Severan dynasty resulted in Britannia being divided into two new administrative regions, similar to the division of Syria, in response to the rebellion of Clodius Albinus. Lugdunensis and Aquitania gained more territory at the expense of Narbonensis, and the Alpine provinces were realigned. The northern line of Italia was further reduced to enlarge Raetia, and the slightly expanded Agri Decumates became its own administrative province.

The Roman empire in 235, at the end of the Severan dynasty

The organisation of the empire into 43 provinces, plus the major Mediterranean islands and Italia, would be maintained until Diocletian sub-divided each province further (*see map on page 172*), with only the loss of Dacia and the Agri Decumates in 275 under Aurelian. The territory along the upper Tigris would be lost to the Sassanians, but regained again by Galerius for Diocletian.

- Roman empire
- Parthian/Sassanian empire
- kingdom of Armenia
- border of Severan province

Accordingly, Alexander and Mamaea left Rome for Moguntiacum early in 234 to meet advance detachments of the Illyrian legions returning hurriedly from Syria. Their haste was understandable. Alexander had followed Marcus Aurelius's policy of granting the officers and soldiers on the frontier parcels of land, on condition that they and their sons continued to serve in the legions. The German invasion, therefore, was threatening more than the empire; it was a personal threat to the soldiers' families and homes. This also goes a long way to explaining the troops' fury with Alexander when, as was customary with him, he preferred to negotiate with the barbarian invaders. Viewing his pacific policy at best as cowardice and at worst as outright betrayal, the

troops began to seek a general who was not afraid to fight the invaders.

The common soldiery also despised the power that Mamaea exercised over her son, and her well-known favouritism towards the eastern legions. They wanted an emperor who was a western compatriot and chose Gaius Julius Verus Maximinus. A peasant of Thracian origin who had risen through the ranks because of his physical strength and soldierly abilities, he was in command of some Pannonian levies. In March 235, his soldiers invested him with the purple, and a few days later Alexander and Mamaea were murdered by their own soldiers at their camp near Moguntiacum. Thus came to an end the dynasty of the Severi.

The slight expansion of Pannonia Inferior was the most significant change along the upper Danuvius. The border with Pannonia Superior was straightened out in 212 by Caracalla so that Brigetio, the camp of LEGIO *I Adiutrix*, was assigned to the lower province. Moesia Superior was also expanded towards the east, as was Macedonia at its northeastern corner with Thracia.

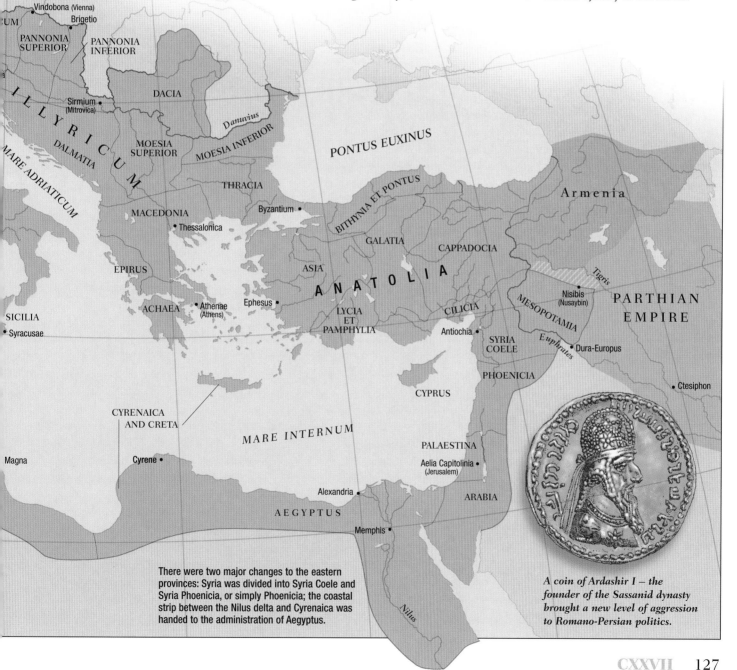

There were two major changes to the eastern provinces: Syria was divided into Syria Coele and Syria Phoenicia, or simply Phoenicia; the coastal strip between the Nilus delta and Cyrenaica was handed to the administration of Aegyptus.

A coin of Ardashir I – the founder of the Sassanid dynasty brought a new level of aggression to Romano-Persian politics.

CHAPTER EIGHT   AD 235–268
INTO MILITARY ANARCHY

MAXIMINUS THRAX
Gaius Julius Verus Maximinus
(r.March 235–c.April 238)

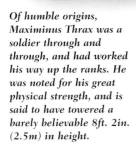

Of humble origins, Maximinus Thrax was a soldier through and through, and had worked his way up the ranks. He was noted for his great physical strength, and is said to have towered a barely believable 8ft. 2in. (2.5m) in height.

Coins of Maximinus, his wife Caecilia Diva Paulina and their son Gaius Julius Verus Maximus, who was elevated to Caesar in 236.

The accession of Maximinus marked the start of a fifty-year period of disorder in the Roman empire during which the militarisation of the government inaugurated by Septimius Severus continued apace and the debasement of the currency brought the empire to bankruptcy. It was also a prelude to a series of revolutions that would culminate in the division of the empire under Gallienus only eighteen years later, the period that this chapter deals with. It opens on the death of Severus Alexander with the intertwined rules of five emperors, the longest reigning of whom was Maximinus, the first barbarian to ascend the throne of the Caesars.

Maximinus was born in about 173 in a village in Thracia (hence the derisory COGNOMEN Thrax). It was said that his family were peasants and that as a boy he was a shepherd. His Roman naming may have originated from Gaius Julius Maximinus, the governor of Dacia, under whom he served as a ranker in 208 and who granted him Roman citizenship. His enormous physical strength attracted the attention of Septimius Severus, who promoted Maximinus to the rank of centurion. By the reign of Severus Alexander he had reached equestrian rank and was entrusted with greater responsibilities. As war against the Germans loomed, Maximinus was placed in charge of training recently recruited levies of Pannonian troops. These young soldiers were fiercely loyal to Maximinus, whose four decades of harsh military service placed him in stark contrast to the young and indecisive Alexander. His position was similar to that of Macrinus: he was a lowly equestrian, not a senator, and owed his elevation entirely to the vote of his soldiers. Unlike Macrinus, he had never held a civil post or been a LEGATUS LEGIONIS, let alone a PRAEFECTUS PRAETORIO, and his experience was entirely military.

We do not know how his elevation was reported to the senate, although some historical sources go so far as to suggest that Maximinus was the first to vindicate the *right* as opposed to the *power* of the soldiers to make an emperor without reference to the senate. It hardly matters; the senate had become powerless to intervene in any such choice, and therefore bowed to the inevitable and conferred the imperial prerogatives.

The immediate and pressing concern was to prosecute the war against the Germans that Alexander had delayed with his attempts to buy peace. Although Alexander's closest advisors were dismissed or killed, Maximinus seems to have left members of the previous regime in positions of authority. This might seem a sensible policy, given that his humble background would make relations with the EQUITES and senatorial order difficult. However, it meant that he faced retaliation from the Severan partisans. Almost immediately there were two mutinies. A number of centurions and officers of senatorial rank led the first. A pontoon bridge had been thrown across the Rhenus ready for the campaign, and they planned to destroy this after Maximinus had crossed with his forces. Thus isolated on the wrong shore of the river, they intended to replace Maximinus by a consular called Magnus. But the plot was leaked and anyone suspected of being involved was put to death without trial. Osrhoenian archers who had accompanied Alexander from Syria were the ringleaders of the second revolt. They championed another consular and friend of Alexander Severus called Quartinus, and invested him with the purple. But an officer and supposed friend of the archers named Macedo treacherously betrayed them in order to curry favour with Maximinus. Macedo murdered Quartinus but received only contempt from the emperor, who in turn had him executed.

Maximinus decided to remove all officers of senatorial rank from the army and replace them with his own promoted men. From this point on, his reign was effectively a war against the nobility, which accomplished little beyond fattening the purses of the DELATORES. Having quelled two rebellions, Maximinus now crossed the Rhenus and drove the German tribes back from the river to seek refuge in the dense forests. The Romans laid waste the farms and villages before retreating in safety for the winter. Maximinus intended a full-scale invasion in the following year, but was forestalled by unrest among the tribes across the Danuvius, and moved his headquarters from Moguntiacum to Sirmium. In 236 he named his son Maximus as Caesar and assumed the title of Germanicus Maximus. But by the spring of 238 he was still tied up at Sirmium when news of a serious rebellion in Africa reached him.

The spark that ignited trouble in Africa was largely the consequence of Maximinus's desperate need of money for the soldiers' pay and donatives. His procurator in Africa had begun confiscating wealthy landowners' property and some young nobles banded together and planned to assassinate the detested official. They armed their clients and the farmers who worked their properties, and then entered Thysdrus (El Djem, Tunisia), where they murdered the offending procurator and his bodyguard. The rebels then went to the aged proconsul of Africa, Gordianus (Gordian), and invited him to become emperor.

GORDIAN I

Marcus Antonius Gordianus Sempronianus
Romanus Africanus
(r.jointly January 238, in Africa)

GORDIAN II

Marcus Antonius Gordianus Sempronianus
Romanus Africanus
(r.jointly January 238, in Africa)

Gordian's background is cloudy. Since he was said to have been about eighty at the time of his accession, he was probably born in 159. On his father's side, he was descended from the powerful Gracchi who had dominated Roman affairs towards the end of the Republic, and on his mother's side from a relative of the emperor Trajan. His PRAENOMEN and NOMEN indicate that the family received Roman citizenship in the late Republic from Marcus Antonius, while the COGNOMEN suggests a link to Asia Minor. Gordian was the father of at least two children: a son of the same name and a daughter, whose own son was to become the emperor Gordian III.

At the beginning of January 238, after some consideration of his options, Gordian consented and was proclaimed emperor. He left his home in Thysdrus and moved to Carthago where, after elevating his son to be his colleague, he sent an embassy to Rome to explain his actions. Members of this embassy had an imperative to first remove the PRAEFECTUS PRAETORIO Vitallianus,

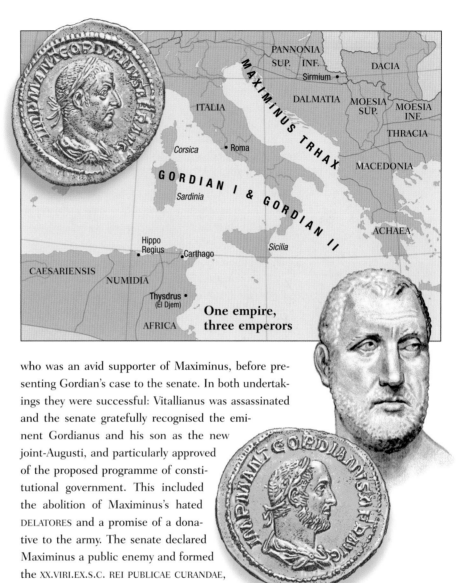

One empire, three emperors

who was an avid supporter of Maximinus, before presenting Gordian's case to the senate. In both undertakings they were successful: Vitallianus was assassinated and the senate gratefully recognised the eminent Gordianus and his son as the new joint-Augusti, and particularly approved of the proposed programme of constitutional government. This included the abolition of Maximinus's hated DELATORES and a promise of a donative to the army. The senate declared Maximinus a public enemy and formed the XX.VIRI.EX.S.C. REI PUBLICAE CURANDAE, or a commission of twenty, the members of which were assigned different parts of Italia, where they were to make preparations for the anticipated invasion of Maximinus.

Many of the provinces, with the exceptions of Dacia, Pannonia and those of Hispania, allied with the Gordiani, but a threat developed in Africa itself. At some earlier point, Gordian had attempted to remove from office the peculant Capellianus, governor of Numidia, and now he rebelled. His strength lay in his command of the only regular troops stationed in the African provinces, LEGIO *III Augusta*, whereas the Gordiani could only muster a local volunteer militia. When Capellianus began an advance towards Carthago, Gordian sent his son to oppose him. Gordian's hastily recruited levies were no match for Roman soldiers, and they were soon overwhelmed and Gordian II was killed in the battle. On hearing of his son's death, the father committed suicide after a reign of just twenty-two days.

Gordian I (top inset) and his son Gordian II. Made co-emperors in Africa by young land-owning nobles angry at Maximinus Thrax's confiscation of their property; their reign lasted twenty-two days.

PUPIENUS
Clodius Pupienus Maximus

BALBINUS
Decimus Caelius Calvinus Balbinus
(joint r.early February 238–early May 238, Italia)

Short-lived joint-Augusti at loggerheads: Pupienus (above) and Balbinus (below) allowed mutual suspicion to plague their government.

The reign of the two Gordiani may have been short, but its significance lies in the determination with which the senate set about immediately finding a replacement from among their own ranks to oppose the tyrant Maximinus. They chose two members of the commission of twenty to be the next Augusti. Pupienus was probably about sixty at the time of his elevation. Of humble origins, he had risen swiftly through the army ranks: PRIMUS PILUS (chief centurion), TRIBUNUS MILITUM, praetor, and proconsul of Bithynia, Achaea, Gallia Narbonensis and Germania Superior. He had secured victories over the Sarmatae and the Germans, and held two suffect consulships (the last possibly in 234), as well as the office of PRAEFECTUS URBI. Of Balbinus, we know less. Better-born than his colleague, Balbinus was probably about the same age as Pupienus and a distinguished administrator. For this reason he was to remain in Rome while Pupienus took command of the Italian defences.

Pupienus had earned a reputation for severity when he was PRAEFECTUS URBI, which may explain his unpopularity with the mob, in spite of his widely praised governorship in Germania Superior. In addition, the creation of two emperors by the senate did not please the military – especially the praetorian guard, which viewed any resurgence of senatorial prerogatives with deep mistrust. As news of the election spread throughout Rome, rioting broke out, in part a reaction against Pupienus, but also probably a sign of the disappointment felt by both soldiers and civilians at the loss of Gordian money. Eventually a compromise was made, and in March 238 the senate reacquired Gordian wealth by promoting Gordian's grandson Marcus Antonius Gordianus to the rank of Caesar.

Meanwhile, Maximinus had commenced his advance towards Italia with detachments from the Illyrian army gathered for the intended invasion across the Danuvius. Things did not go well for him. The haste of departure meant that his army was poorly pro-

visioned and already by the time it reached Emona (Ljubljana) the men were going hungry. But the deserted town had been stripped of any food, and the troops grew mutinous. Maximinus pushed on towards Aquileia, anticipating an easy victory and victuals to satisfy his men. However, this too was denied him. Due to the energetic activities of Tullius Menophilus and Crispinus, two members of the commission of twenty, the town was prepared, the fortifications strengthened, and the gates barred. Maximinus faced a long siege without engines and with starving soldiers. Pupienus, having successfully raised more troops in Ravenna, was in his line of advance, preventing Maximinus from simply going around Aquileia. His men were at the end of their tether, and finally soldiers of *II Parthica*, who wanted to get home to their wives and children at Albanum near Rome, went to Maximinus's tent and murdered him and his son while they slept.

Their heads were sent first to Ravenna and then on to Rome. And so it was that Pupienus entered Aquileia without a fight. Maximinus's starving Pannonian troops were even prepared to acclaim an emperor appointed by the senate, so desperate was their need for food. For their part, the German allies were happy to recognise Pupienus, remembering in gratitude his earlier administration of Germania Superior, and the men of *II Parthica* were happy to be sent to their homes. Retaining a sizeable detachment of the Germans for his personal bodyguard, Pupienus sent the various elements of Maximinus's army back to their respective provinces and returned to Rome.

The new experiment of joint-Augusti worked well for only a few days before mutual suspicion began to plague the government of Balbinus and Pupienus. Their problems were exacerbated by continual popular unrest, especially among the praetorians, who hated being ruled by two emperors appointed by the nobility, and were fearful that the German bodyguard of Pupienus was intended to replace them. Within days the praetorians had worked up a head of steam and marched on the Palatine. Each emperor believed the other was behind a plot to assassinate him, and was thus unprepared and easily taken. When the German bodyguard rushed to rescue Pupienus, the captors murdered both emperors and left their bodies in the roadway. They then took young Gordian and proclaimed him emperor. The experiment of senatorially elected emperors ended after only ninety-nine days, leaving the soldiers once again triumphantly in control of the election of a ruler – even though Gordian III was a boy of only thirteen years.

GORDIAN III

Marcus Antonius Gordianus
(r.May 238–25/2/244)

Gordian III was born in Rome on 20 January 225. His mother was a daughter of the senator Marcus Antonius Gordianus Sempronianus Romanus (Gordian I), but his father's name is not known and he probably died before the African uprising. History accords the early years of Gordian's five and a half-year reign little detail, probably because the thirteen-year-old's administration was in the hands of relatives or advisers. Pupienus and Balbinus were declared DAMNATIO MEMORIAE, otherwise it is likely that men who rose to prominence under the Severan and even late Antonine dynasties continued in office. LEGIO *III Augusta*, the African legion that had supported the rebellion of Capellianus, was disbanded in disgrace and its soldiers distributed among the German and Raetian armies. When the proconsul of Africa, Sabinianus, revolted in 240, the uprising was suppressed by the governor of Mauretania at the head of troops largely composed of auxiliaries. Meanwhile, on the northeastern frontier, a new threat had materialised when a large tribe of Goths entered Moesia Inferior. Early attempts to dislodge this warlike people appear to have been unsuccessful, and it took some three years before the situation improved.

In 241 a remarkable man was appointed to the office of PRAEFECTUS PRAETORIO. Another beneficiary of the Severan democratisation of the military, Gaius Furius Sabinus Aquila Timesitheus had risen through the ranks to the centuriate and then into the ORDO EQUESTER. He had held an astonishing number of senior posts from Asia to Germania and Arabia to Gallia, often as a propraetor or substitute for a senatorial governor. He had served on the staff of Severus Alexander during the Persian campaign and on the Rhenus before passing without incident to Maximinus as his procurator in Bithynia. He was procurator in Gallia Lugdunensis at the time of his recall to Rome to assist Gordian. Timesitheus's proven abilities quickly made him the central figure in Gordian's administration, and his authority was further enhanced by the marriage of his daughter, Furia Sabinia Tranquillina, to the young emperor in the summer of the same year. As to his character, the histories are silent; he was either possessed of extremely good fortune, or his career was the result of an unscrupulous nature. Whatever, for three years the Roman empire was under his rule.

Although the Gothic disturbances in Moesia Inferior remained a running sore, the Sassanid Persian empire was again the bigger challenge facing Gordian. Already during the last months of Maximinus's reign the ageing Ardashir I had captured Nisibis (Nusaybin) and Carrhae (Harran), and now his son Shapur I had invaded Syria and was threatening Antiochia. The summer of 242 was spent completing the removal of the Goths along the Danuvius and securing the frontier before Gordian and Timesitheus set out for Syria. The protection of Moesia was left in the capable hands of Tullius Menophilus, the defender of Aquileia against Maximinus, who proved successful enough in containing another tribe of the region, the Carpi, that by spring 243 large detachments of the Illyrian legions were freed to start marching eastwards to join Gordian.

The fighting commenced almost as soon as the reinforcements arrived, and the Roman army swept the Persians back. Antiochia was saved, Carrhae and Nisibis were retaken and the Romans won a decisive victory at Rhesaena. Plans to continue the push to Ctesiphon faltered, however, when Timesitheus suddenly died of an illness during the winter of 243–44. The surviving PRAEFECTUS, Gaius Julius Priscus, persuaded Gordian to appoint his brother Marcus Julius Verus Philippus (Philip) as Timesitheus's successor, a change that was to have

Left: A realistic likeness coupled with idealised physique and pose characterise this sculpture of Gordian III.

Shapur I, son of Ardashir I, ruled the Sassanian empire from 241 until his death in 272, and was a bellicose thorn in the side of a Rome shaken by Gothic incursions and internal strife. His greatest coup would come in 259–60, when he captured Valerian, the first Roman emperor to suffer this ignominy.

Young Gordian III and his wife Furia Sabinia Tranquillina, daughter of his PRAEFECTUS PRAETORIO *Timesitheus.*

Far right: Julius Marinus, father of Philip I the Arab.

grave consequences for the nineteen-year-old emperor. Timesitheus had been content to exercise his power as Gordian's adviser, but it was soon clear that Philip's ambition was no less than gaining the purple for himself. According to the Sassanian version of events, the Romans now proceeded to march down the Euphrates and early in 244 met the Sassanid army near Misikhe (Fallujah, to the west of Baghdad). Shapur's forces were triumphant and he commemorated the victory with a giant rock-carving at Naqsh-i-Rustam, which shows two Roman generals, one standing, one kneeling, bowing in submission before him. An inscription in three languages suggests that Gordian III was killed in the battle.

The Roman histories do not mention this battle, and it is accepted today that the two Romans represented are a defeated Philip (who almost certainly was not) and the later emperor Valerian, who would be captured by Shapur in 260. If the battle of Misikhe actually happened, it is not conceivable that the Romans were soundly defeated, because Philip was later able to negotiate terms with Shapur that left Rome hardly disadvantaged, which would not have been the case if Shapur's victory was as complete as his commemorative carving boasts. Indeed, Shapur was to remain quiet for another eight years. Roman sources paint a different picture. Using the failure of essential grain supplies to arrive on time, Philip fomented a rebellion among the troops by blaming Gordian for their misfortune. The emperor was said to have pleaded with Philip to save him, even offering to resign and serve as Philip's Caesar. It was hardly sensible to have a possible rival in his court, and after

the soldiers declared their desire to have a man and not 'a child' as ruler, Philip had Gordian murdered. This happened at Zaitha, near Circesium, where a cenotaph was built indicating that the emperor died of natural causes; which is what the senate was told. The official dispatch also informed the senate of Philip's own proclamation by his army, and requested that Gordian III be deified – a sure way of deflecting blame for the emperor's death from himself, although many Romans continued to believe that he was responsible.

PHILIP I THE ARAB
Marcus Julius Verus Philippus
(r. 25/2/244–September 249)

PHILIP II
Marcus Julius Severus Philippus
(co-Augustus 247–September 249)

Philip appears to spring into history fully formed; the only details of his early life are that he was born at some time early in the reign of Septimius Severus, possibly 204, in a village approximately fifty-five miles to the south-southeast of Damascus in the Roman province of Arabia. How much Arabic blood Philip had is uncertain, since Roman soldiers, immigrants and administrative staff had probably been inter-marrying in the region for many decades, but his origins were seized on by later historians for his nickname. We know where he was born (its modern name is Shahba') because he later endowed it as a COLONIA and named it Philippopolis (not to be confused with the ancient town of the same name in Thracia).

Philip's father seems to have been a certain Julius Marinus and the family held citizenship, perhaps only from as recently as Caracalla's CONSTITUTIO ANTONINIANA of 212–3. Philip married Marcia Otacilia Severa and a son was born in about 238 called Marcus Julius Severus Philippus. Philip's older brother Julius Priscus was Timesitheus's praetorian colleague, and after the latter's untimely death was influential in Philip's promotion to the vacant position. The fragmentary ancient sources tend to paint a dim picture of Philip as emperor, and may have glorified young Gordian by comparison. It is, therefore, predictable that they attribute Gordian's death to Philip as outlined in the previous section, and certainly it remained a popular

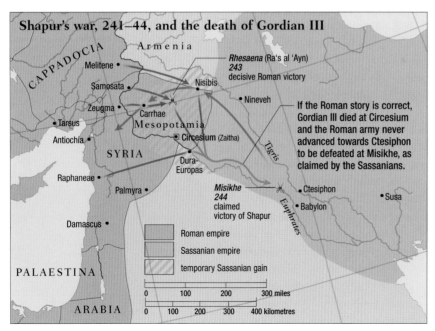

Shapur's war, 241–44, and the death of Gordian III

Armenia
CAPPADOCIA
Melitene •
Samosata •
Zeugma •
Nisibis
• Nineveh
Carrhae
Tarsus •
Mesopotamia
Antiochia •
☐ Circesium (Zaitha)
SYRIA
Dura-Europas
Raphaneae •
Palmyra •
Misikhe
244
claimed
victory of Shapur
• Ctesiphon
• Babylon
• Susa
Damascus •

Rhesaena (Ra's al 'Ayn)
243
decisive Roman victory

If the Roman story is correct, Gordian III died at Circesium and the Roman army never advanced towards Ctesiphon to be defeated at Misikhe, as claimed by the Sassanians.

Roman empire
Sassanian empire
temporary Sassanian gain

PALAESTINA

ARABIA

| 0 | 100 | 200 | 300 miles |
| 0 | 100 | 200 | 300 | 400 kilometres |

rumour among the nobility in Rome. But Philip's claim that Gordian died of natural causes – epidemics were rife among the troops in the east – may have been true; and certainly, he did not die of battle wounds as Shapur claimed.

It is equally predictable that the histories describe Philip's first act – a peace treaty with the Sassanians – as dishonourable to Rome. Yet examination of the terms reveals a different picture. Mesopotamia and Armenia Inferior remained under Roman control, a further indication that Shapur had won no great victory, since this settlement pushed him back from his earlier gains. Rome was disadvantaged in Armenia Superior simply in that its client king was only under nominal Roman control, but this situation had often prevailed before. Philip made his brother Priscus governor of Mesopotamia, and raised his own son – about seven at the time – to the rank of Caesar before setting out for Rome. He arrived in the capital no later than 23 July 244, the date given for the discharge of veterans of II Parthica. His attitude towards the senate was polite and deferential, and he established relations that remained generally cordial throughout his reign.

Details of Philip's care of government are scanty and the picture must be created from the archaeological evidence. His closest advisers were drawn from among his own family. The command of Moesia and Macedonia went to his brother-in-law Severianus, and Priscus was advanced beyond the governorship of

FOURTH-CENTURY TRADITION claimed that Philip became the first Christian emperor. The source for this gossip was a report by Eusebius, the bishop of Caesarea (c.260–c.340), the so-called Father of Church History, which stated that Philip was compelled to confess his sins before attending an Easter service. Eusebius also mentions as proof that Origen wrote to Philip and his wife. However, while Origen's epistle indicates the emperor's interest in the faith, it says nothing of his baptism. Neither contemporary Christian nor Roman literature mentions Philip's conversion, and it is unlikely that a man who had his father deified and elected his son to the office of PONTIFEX MAXIMUS would be admitted to the Christian Church. Perhaps it is sufficient for the rumour to have taken hold that Philip was a religiously tolerant emperor and his successor Decius was not.

Mesopotamia, by a promotion to PRAEFECTUS PRAETORIO RECTORQUE ORIENTIS (rector of the Orient), which effectively made him commander-in-chief of all the eastern legions – a position he was to abuse to his cost, and his brother's. In the provinces Philip's name appears on many milestones attesting to his maintenance of the roads and care for transportation, and evidently grateful provincials erected numerous dedications to him. In Rome the mob was kept happy with the distribution of three CONGIARIA, and the water shortage in Trans Tiberim (Trastevere), the western part of Rome, was alleviated by the construction of a new reservoir. On the other hand, the almost continual state of war on the northern frontiers meant an increasingly onerous tax burden fell on all classes of the population. A petition sent to Philip for tax relief from the tenants of an imperial estate in Phrygia indicates that even the rural peasantry suffered.

In 245–46 the Carpi, successfully contained by Tullius Menophilus two years previously, again crossed the Danuvius and neither the efforts of Moesia Inferior's governor, Prastina Messalinus, nor his LEGATUS Severianus were able to check the invaders. Accordingly, the emperor left Rome to take charge of the situation. Fighting was widespread in the region and Philip was occupied there for two years. There is evidence that the barbarians stormed towns and cities in Thracia and Macedonia, and there must have been incursions of Germans in Pannonia, because the emperor assumed the title of Germanicus Maximus. At the end of 247 the Carpi were decisively beaten in open battle and sued for peace.

Philip returned to Rome to celebrate a great triumph before entering his third consulship, with his ten-year-old son as colleague for his second time. On 21 April 248 Philip commemorated Rome's thousandth birthday with extravagant games and a CONGIARIUM to the people. It seemed as though peace and prosperity had returned, but it was an illusion.

Portrait busts and coins of Philip I the Arab, his wife Marcia Otacilia Severa and their son Marcus Julius Severus Philippus – Philip II, co-Augustus from 247, when still short of ten years old.

*Claudius Marinus
Pacatianus*

Iotapianus

*Lucius Aurelius Sulpicius
Uranius Antoninus*

Sponsianus

Silbannacus

News reached Rome in the early summer that the legions on the Danuvius had proclaimed one of their officers, Tiberius Claudius Marinus Pacatianus, as emperor. The tribes across the river profited from the confusion, and an alliance of Goths, Carpi, Peucini, and – recent arrivals – Asdingian Vandals swept into Moesia Inferior under the joint command of Argaithus and Gunthericus. The barbarians laid siege to the provincial capital of Marcianopolis, but due to the stout defences of Menophilus and the bravery of the local commander, the alliance warriors were beaten off with such severe casualties that they abandoned the invasion.

At the same time, three more revolts erupted in the east and a fourth in the west. The eastern disturbances were largely the fault of the emperor's brother Priscus, whose harsh administration and bludgeoning taxation led to the proclamation by the soldiers in Cappadocia of a certain Iotapianus, who claimed to be connected to Alexander. Whether this referred to Severus Alexander via the Severan dynasty of Emesa or to Alexander the Great is not known (the latter may sound far-fetched, but the Julian Caesars had claimed descent from the gods). In Syria the pretender was Lucius Aurelius Sulpicius Uranius Antoninus, who was a great deal more successful than the others, since he maintained his power base until 253. The third eastern revolt by a certain Sponsianus is only indicated by coin inscriptions, which is also true of that in the west. A coin found in the region of modern-day Lorraine, dated to Philip's reign, claims a Marcus Silbannacus as IMPERATOR AUGUSTUS. He may have been a commander of German auxiliaries in Germania Superior, and may be the defeated pretender in a civil war prosecuted by Philip's successor Decius, referred to by the historian Eutropius. Of Priscus, nothing more is heard after the outbreak of Iotapianus's revolt, leaving us to suppose that either he died naturally or was rightly a victim of the uprising he had caused.

Philip was so troubled by the rebellions of Pacatianus and Iotapianus that he offered to abdicate if the senate should desire it. None of the senators had an answer until Gaius Messius Quintus Decius, a suffect consul for 249, expressed the opinion that neither pretender was a fit man to rule Rome, and that in any case their own troops would solve the problem by killing them. In this Decius was quite correct, although why the rebelling soldiers turned on their choices is not known. Despite the removal of the chief usurpers, Philip remained uneasy at the level of disaffection among the Illyrian legions, so he proposed to demote his brother-in-law Severianus from the command and send the reluctant Decius to take over. Decius, a gifted diplomat, appeared to be a sensible appointment, but for Philip it was a dangerous blunder. Through vigorous but fair discipline Decius soon had the mutinous troops back in line, ensured their loyalty by arranging for the salary arrears to be paid up and led them successfully against the Goths on the lower Danuvius. What next occurred underlines how important it had become in this era for the legions to have their emperor in the field with them rather than in Rome. Impressed by their new commander, the soldiers proclaimed Decius emperor.

It seems that Decius had done nothing to create this situation and even wrote to Philip expressing his concern and offering to return to Rome to give up the insignia his troops had imposed on him. But Philip, distrusting his sincerity, left Rome under arms at the end of June, compelling Decius to detach a sufficiently large force and march towards Italia. The two armies met outside Verona at the end of September or the start of October 249 where a great battle was fought (*see side panel*). Although outnumbered, the Illyrian soldiers were confident in the tactical superiority of Decius, and Philip was defeated. The emperor either died in battle or was later assassinated by his own troops. When news of the defeat reached Rome, the praetorian guard murdered Philip's young son. Neither was deified.

THERE IS DISAGREEMENT between the ancient sources as to the final battle's location. Latin tradition is uniform in giving Verona, but a fragment from the seventh-century Byzantine historian John of Antioch places the battle at Beroea (Veroia) in Macedonia, and some modern historians now prefer this site. However, a glance at the geography would seem to preclude Beroea, which would have been a considerable detour for Decius marching directly towards Aquileia from the Danuvius. Timing also rules out Beroea. Decius's victorious arrival in Rome is documented as being early in October, and even if the battle had taken place at the end of September, he could not have reached Rome from Macedonia only a few days later. And no contemporary sources indicate that Philip moved his forces as far as Illyricum, let alone the lower Balkans, which makes Verona still the most likely site.

DECIUS
Gaius Messius Quintus Decius / Gaius Messius Quintus Traianus (r.September 249–1/7/251)

Philip's successor was born at the village of Budalia, near Sirmium in Pannonia Inferior to a provincial family, at some time between 190 and 201. His family may have been of Italian stock; his wife Herennia Cupressenia Etruscilla belonged to an ancient Italian family that had attained senatorial status. They had two sons, the elder called Herennius Etruscus and the younger known to history only as Hostilianus (Hostilian). His governorship of Moesia Inferior in 234–8 indicates that Decius achieved a senatorial rank early in his career. He was made PRAEFECTUS URBI during Philip's reign, and he was a suffect consul in 249 when the emperor charged him with the responsibility of restoring order among the legions of Moesia Inferior, *IV Flavia Felix*, and *XI Claudia Pia Fidelis*, after the rebellion of Pacatianus.

Two historical documents suggest that Decius arrived in Rome in early October of 249: an edict issued by him on 16 October and an Egyptian papyrus of 28 November mentions Decius as emperor. The senate confirmed his position and in turn Decius assumed the name of Trajan, showing that Philip's faith in his diplomatic skills was not misplaced. This was shrewd propaganda indeed. By this time Trajan's status as the greatest emperor since Augustus was

firmly established, and his adoption of the name was guaranteed to endear Decius to both the troops – especially those of the Illyrian provinces Trajan had commanded – and the senatorial order because of Trajan's reputation as a civil administrator. Decius formulated a traditionalist approach to government and during a peaceful first year undertook much restoration and reform. He instituted a vigorous programme of road-building, primarily along the Danuvius, but milestones in Hispania Tarraconensis, Britannia, Africa and Syria show his care for all the major provinces. Rome enjoyed the first burst of public building for almost twenty years. Extensive repairs were made to the Amphitheatrum Flavium, which had been left virtually unusable since a disastrous fire and the flooding in the reign of Macrinus, and new public baths were constructed along the Aventine hill.

However conservative Decius appeared, his rule was still autocratic, and he held the office of consul in every year of his reign. One of his more important administrative innovations was the creation of a special office that superficially resembled that of the censor. Reviving a defunct but revered institution was bound to appeal to the senatorial order, but it served another function in providing Decius with a powerful representative to take care of Rome whenever he was called to the frontier to repel barbarian invasions. His sons Herennius and Hostilian, whom he made Caesars respectively in September and December 250, were still too young to take responsibility in his absence. The man Decius appointed to the new office was a senator called Publius Licinius Valerianus (Valerian).

One of Valerian's functions was to help Decius revive veneration for the state-religion. For the first time the growing Christian communities throughout the empire, which had claimed converts at every level of society, became targets for persecution on the basis of religion rather than as a political expedient. During its centuries of expansion, the Roman State had remained tolerant of other creeds so long as their adherents were suitably reverent towards the state-religion, an adjunct of Roman politics. This was a condition that the monotheistic Christians were unable to accept. Decius's intention does not appear to have been to exterminate Christians so much as to have them return to the Roman fold through apostasy, for the state's part in the persecution was more passive than that of the people. In 248 popular fury against Christians had erupted into a pogrom in Alexandria, in which several hundred perished. Decius decreed that

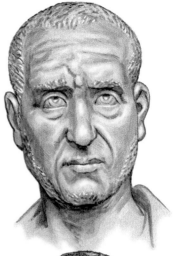

Above: Decius and his wife Herennia Cupressenia Etrusca had two sons: Herennius Etruscus and the younger Hostilianus (below), who would go on to become co-Augustus to Trebonianus Gallus for three months in 251 before being felled by the plague ravaging Rome.

Herennius Etruscus, Decius's elder son, who with his father fell foul of Trebonianus Gallus (below).

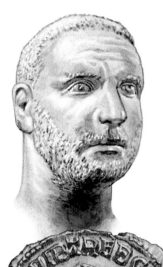

Below: Trebonianus's son Volusian, made first Caesar then co-Augustus with his father in 251.

Christians must make a public sacrifice to the Roman gods, after which each was given a LIBELLUS, a certificate from a commission set up specially for the purpose in every town. Those who refused were arrested and held without food or water in the hope that they would recant. Nevertheless, far more Christians died at the hands of citizens than by state execution.

Apostasies were numerous, but some Church leaders were ready for their martyrdom. The bishops of Jerusalem and Antiochia, Alexander and Babylas, died in prison, the great theologian Origen was spared but later died from the effects of his torture, and in Rome Pope Fabian (p.236–50), the twenty-first Christian pontif, was put to death on 20 January 250. The disorder in the sect that this caused is evidenced by the fact that the vacuum he left was only filled by his successor Cornelius midway through 251. Later Christian writers such as Eusebius, writing after the dreadful fourth-century persecutions of the emperor Diocletian, stigmatised Decius, but interestingly his edict does not seem to have been exclusively aimed at Christians. Surviving Egyptian LIBELLI show that the language was generalised and directed at the whole population and, therefore, the effect it had on Christians was not intended to be concerted.

In the summer of 250 there was barbarian activity on the Rhenus and Danuvius frontiers. Decius was successful in Raetia and Pannonia and so was his eldest son Herennius near Moguntiacum in the fall. But over the fierce winter the Goths crossed the frozen Danuvius and entered Moesia. Kniva, their chieftain, divided his force into two powerful armies, and one attempted to storm Novae (Svishtov, Bulgaria) but was driven off by Trebonianus Gallus, military commander of both provinces of Moesia. The two Gothic armies moved south, one to besiege Nicopolis, the other Philippopolis. Decius and Herennius were able to relieve Nicopolis, but Philippopolis fell to the barbarians, who sacked it and massacred the inhabitants. Events are confused, but it appears that the Macedonian governor, Julius Valens Priscus, had allowed his garrison to elevate him to the purple in collusion with the Goths, after which he treacherously surrendered the city to the enemy and was allowed to leave with his troops. He was declared a public enemy by the senate, and probably survived Decius to be executed by his successor.

Events now moved towards their tragic conclusion. The emperor, in company with his son Herennius and Trebonianus Gallus, pursued the Goths around the

region and finally engaged Kniva's forces on the first day of July 251 at Abrittus, some sixty miles north of Nicopolis. After initial successes in the battle, Decius was undone by the treachery of Gallus, who knowingly signalled the emperor forwards into marshy ground, where his soldiers became bogged down and were easily slaughtered by the enemy. The bodies of Decius and Herennius were never recovered, although another source places the death of Herennius earlier outside Philippopolis, where he was slain by an arrow. Of all the short-reigning emperors of the first half of the period of military anarchy, Decius had ruled best and most wisely; it was for later Christian writers to blacken his name. And Decius enjoyed the dubious distinction of being the first Roman emperor to be killed fighting a foreign enemy.

TREBONIANUS GALLUS

Gaius Vibius Trebonianus Gallus
(r.2/7/251–July 253)
Gaius Vibius Volusianus (Volusian)
(co-Augustus November 251–July 253)
Hostilianus (Hostilian)
(co-Augustus August 251–November 251)

After the battle in which Decius perished, the troops readily proclaimed Gallus emperor. Concerned with reaching Rome quickly to consolidate his rule, Gallus signed a shameful treaty with the Goths. In return for their withdrawal they were permitted to keep their booty but – far worse – they were also allowed to take their Roman prisoners with them, many of noble rank; in addition he promised the payment of an annual tribute. Gallus then went to Rome, where – to lend credence to his story that the Decii had died honourably – he raised Decius's younger son Hostilian to the rank of Augustus, and elevated his own son Volusian to that of Caesar. And so began a reign of barely two years, notable only for misfortune.

The city was suffering from another outbreak of the plague that had wracked the empire for the past fifteen years, and Hostilian succumbed to the disease and died in November 251. Gallus then elevated Volusian to the position of co-emperor. In matters relating to the epidemic, Gallus acted decisively and gained popular support by providing proper burials for all plague victims, even for the proletariat. In all other matters he failed to take any serious action, beyond reviving the persecution of Christians, probably as a diversion for Rome's restless mob. This was most likely a half-hearted pogrom, since the only recorded victim was Pope Cornelius, who was imprisoned and died in the summer of 253.

The Sassanians attacked in 252 and overran Mesopotamia, defeated the Romans at Barbalissus (Mesken, Syria) and advanced as far as Antiochia, which fell into Shapur's hands in the following year. Furious that the new governor of Moesia, Aemilius Aemilianus, had refused to pay the promised tribute, the Goths stormed back across the Danuvius, plundering the cities of the province and those of Thracia. A second band crossed from Europe into Asia and ravaged the country as far south as Ephesus. Gallus failed to react to any of these threats.

Aemilianus organised relief for the sacked cities, rallied his legions, renewed his men's confidence and went on the offensive. His sudden attack took the satiated Goths off their guard. Their scattered forces were herded back towards the Danuvius and, amid a great slaughter, hurled across the frontier. This unexpected success ensured a temporary peace, and the recovery of Roman prestige so impressed the soldiers that spontaneously they raised up Aemilianus and made the governor their emperor on the spot.

AEMILIANUS

Marcus Aemilius Aemilianus
(c.May–early August 253)

The fragmentary sources give conflicting information on Aemilianus, that he was born on a small island off the western coast of what is now Tunisia, that he was a 'Moor' or perhaps a 'Libyan'. We are told on one hand that at the time of his death he was in his fortieth year and on the other that he was forty-seven, which puts his birth date somewhere between 207–14. Eutropius reckoned he was from an insignificant family, while John of Antioch claimed that Aemilianus used his [distinguished] ancestry to justify his seizure of the purple. From coins he issued we know that his wife was C. Cornelia Supra.

His coins also help to pinpoint the approximate dates of his three-month reign, which is sometimes put as being between July and September. Due to the difference between the commencement dates for the New Year in neighbouring Dacia and Viminacium (Kostolac in Serbia), Aemilianus was able to issue coins for two Dacian years, but only one at Viminacium. Since the Dacian year began on 20 July and the Viminacian year ended 31 August, and that his successor Valerian also issued a coin at Viminacium in the same year as Aemilianus, it puts his reign at ending some time after the end of July but not extending beyond the middle of August.

There is also a conflicting tale relating to his refusal to pay the Goths their tribute, which states that it was not a change of policy or an initiative of Aemilianus's, but a false allegation of the Goths to prise more money out of Moesia and Thracia. In any event, having defeated the Goths and assumed the purple, Aemilianus raised as strong a force as he could and advanced into Italia, hoping to catch Gallus and Volusian before they had time to prepare. Gallus sent orders to Valerian, who at this point was commanding the armies of Raetia and Noricum, to take detachments of his legions and come to his assistance. But before Valerian could reach Italia, Aemilianus had advanced to Interamna, within fifty miles of Rome. It seems doubtful that Aemilianus would have stripped Moesia of soldiers or that the legions would have allowed him to leave their homes undefended against a possible counterattack from the Goths, which implies that his force was not very large. This may have encouraged Gallus to take the field without Valerian's support, and a battle was fought at Interamna. His troops, who were not hardened fighters and despised their emperor's apathy, soon realised the danger they were in and murdered Gallus and Volusian, then swore their allegiance to Aemilianus.

There is little more to say of the reign of Aemilius Aemilianus. On his defeat of Gallus it was already more than three-quarters through. It is not even certain that he had time to enter Rome, let alone make undertakings to the senate or receive the conferral of imperial powers. In Raetia, when Valerian's troops heard of the death of Gallus, they proclaimed their man emperor. News of the proclamation and the immediate arrival of Valerian at the head of a powerful and determined force prompted the Italian soldiers to rethink their position. According to the historian Zonaras, those who served with Aemilianus were weary of civil war and recognised that they would be no match for Valerian's troops. They also judged their emperor unworthy of the realm and – sure that Valerian was better suited for rule because he would assume affairs in a more authoritative fashion – they killed Aemilianus.

Aemilius Aemilianus and his wife C. Cornelia Supra. His short reign was ended by his own troops who were weary of civil war, and quickly disillusioned of his chances of success.

VALERIAN

Publius Licinius Valerianus
(r.c. July 253–June 260)

GALLIENUS

Publius Licinius Egnatius Gallienus
(co-Augustus c. September 253,
sole r. June 260–March 268)

The senate felt relief at the action of the Raetian troops in raising Valerian, because it avoided another civil war, and elevated one of their own number to the purple. In celebration, and to show goodwill towards the new emperor, the senate made his son Gallienus, who happened to be in the city, Caesar. On his arrival in the capital in the fall of 253, Valerian received the imperial powers from the senate and raised Gallienus to the rank of co-Augustus, making him a partner in the empire.

In contrast with so many of his short-lived predecessors, Valerian came from an old Roman senatorial family. His date of birth is uncertain, but would have been during the reign of Septimius Severus, probably before 200. This is likely because he is first mentioned in 238 as a consular negotiating with the embassy sent by Gordian I to Rome to secure senatorial approval of his rebellion against Maximinus Thrax, and to have held a consulship much before his mid-thirties is unlikely. Valerian married Egnatia Mariniana and they had two sons, Gallienus and another Publius Licinius Valerianus (*see family tree caption on page 141*). The marriage probably took place c.217, with the birth of Gallienus soon after in 218. Beyond his appointment by Decius to the reinstated role of censor in 251, Valerian's earlier career is unreported. In his turn, Gallienus married Julia Cornelia Salonina, and they had three sons: Publius Cornelius Licinius Valerianus (Valerian II), Publius Licinius Cornelius Saloninus Valerianus (Saloninus), and Licinius Egnatius Marinianus.

The two emperors enjoyed only a few months of peaceful administration in Rome before insurrections

Valerian and his wife Egnatia Mariniana.

along the Rhenus demanded their attention. The wisdom in making his mature son of 36 years a partner soon became clear. Valerian was able to remain in Rome while entrusting the defence of the frontier to Gallienus, who set off in the later months of 254. Commemorative coins point to his considerable success during the first three years of his command of the army, which was reinforced by detachments from Britannia – the first of a long series of military withdrawals from the island province that would eventually leave it at the mercy of Saxon invaders. Victories were secured on the right bank of the Rhenus, which prevented many German tribes from even reaching the river, while others were slaughtered as they attempted a crossing.

Gallienus also employed diplomacy and concluded a treaty with one German chieftain in a move to counteract the barbarians' numerical superiority, a tactic he would use in other parts of the empire. He is also credited with the massive strengthening of the Roman fortresses on the left bank of the Rhenus. Colonia Agrippina (Cologne) received a wall, repairs and extensions were made at Novaesium (Neuss), and a second line of defence was formed by making Antumnacum (Andernach) and Augusta Treverorum (Trier) into fortified garrison towns. However, some of these improvements may also have been the work of Marcus Cassianus Latinius Postumus (*see below and the following chapter*).

By 256 Valerian had concluded all the matters of state that had demanded his attention and determined to commence a campaign to regain Roman territory lost to the Sassanian empire by Trebonianus Gallus. Gallienus could look after western affairs, while Valerian concentrated on the eastern frontier. This is the moment when the historical sources first mention a real territorial division of the empire into West and East halves, with Gallienus initially ruler of the Western Roman empire. Gallienus may have envied his father's command of the East, for the pressures on him now mounted serially.

He made his eldest son, Valerian II, Caesar to share his burden. A ferocious German tribe from the northeast of central Europe, the Franks, broke through the northern LIMES, devastating Germania Inferior and Belgica before advancing as far south as Hispania Tarraconensis, where they destroyed Tarraco (Tarragona). The Franks then pushed further south to the narrow strait with North Africa and pillaged the coast of Mauretania Tingitana. Along the Raetian LIMES the Alamanni broke through in 258, overran the Agri Decumates, sacked the city of Aventicum (Avenches,

Switzerland), and began extending their ravaging to the interior of Gallia, already reeling from the passing of the Franks. Either a second wave of Alamanni or the first force doubling back from Gallia then raided eastwards through Raetia and attacked Italia itself by pouring through the Brenner Pass. This was the greatest horror of all. The militarised provinces of Germania Superior and Raetia had failed in protecting vulnerable Transpadane Italia, with its wealthy cities and light garrisons. Making a stupendous effort, Gallienus was able to mount a counterattack and won a victory over the Alamanni near Mediolanum (Milan). However, his triumph was marred by news of his son Valerian II's death somewhere along the Danuvius while he was campaigning there.

Gallienus then returned to the Rhenus, but in the next year alarming news of a revolt in Pannonia meant he had to leave the defence of Gallia and Germania Superior in the hands of his second-in-command, Marcus Cassianus Latinius Postumus. His second son Saloninus, who had accompanied him to Gallia, was left at Colonia Agrippina under the care of the PRAE-FECTUS PRAETORIO Silvanus. The situation on the Danuvian frontier was little better than in Gallia. Forces of Marcomanni, Sarmatae and Quadi were attacking Pannonia, while the Goths and Carpi were threatening Dacia and Moesia. In this maelstrom of confusion and uncertainty the Pannonian and Moesian legions had proclaimed their commander Ingenuus emperor. By prompt action and the aid of a large cavalry force commanded by the brilliant general Aureolus, Gallienus crushed Ingenuus at Mursa (Osijek) on the banks of the Dravus in 259, but the remnants of his army continued in revolt by investing another officer, Regalianus, with the purple. Regalianus proved to be a tougher proposition than Ingenuus and it was not until 260 that Gallienus subdued the rebellion and restored unity in Illyicum. He then secured stability in the region by concluding an alliance with Attalus, king of the Marcomanni, ceding parts of Pannonia, apparently in return for the king's daughter Pipa as his concubine (he was still married to Cornelia Salonina, who almost certainly was not present at this arrangement).

The first emperor captured

Valerian left Rome and reached Antiochia in 257, where advance detachments had wrested control of the city from the Sassanian garrison. However, Valerian was unable to immediately prosecute a war against Shapur because Anatolia was suffering its own series of barbarian assaults. These came from two fronts. In 257 a Scythian tribe called the Borani launched a seaborne raid across the Pontus Euxinus (Black Sea) on the small Roman outpost of Pityus. Their ships were supplied by the former Bosporan kingdom (modern Crimea), which had been a client and ally of Rome until the recent overthrow of its king, but was now compliant to the barbarians' demands. Although Pityus on the northeastern Euxine coast was beyond the bounds of the empire, the Romans had fortified the town years before and maintained a small garrison there. A first attack was driven back by its praetor, Successianus, for which he was rewarded with the office of PRAEFECTUS PRAETORIO by Valerian. But a second raid succeeded in capturing and sacking Pityus, following which the Borani sailed to Trapezus, stormed and burned it to the ground after plundering and murdering its citizens. Laden with booty, the Borani seemed content to sail back home. The Goths, too, raided in boats down the western coast before landing and marching west around Byzantium, crossing the Propontis and capturing Chalcedon. They then moved on to Nicomedia, whose inhabitants had already taken flight.

Valerian divided his forces, sending one part to the relief of Byzantium under the command of an officer called Felix, while he marched to the relief of Bithynia. The army never reached its destination: in the region of Carrhae the plague struck and killed many of Valerian's soldiers. At this point he heard that Shapur was attacking Syria again and threatening Antiochia. Valerian turned back, but faced the reality that, lacking resources, he could no longer overcome his enemy.

Late in 259 or early in 260 he sent an embassy to Shapur to request an interview to discuss a settlement. Persian assurances were given and, trusting in Shapur's good faith, Valerian set out with only a small retinue for Edessa where the Sassanian king was holding court. So the story goes, Shapur arrested Valerian the minute he appeared and inflicted on him the ultimate humiliation by using the emperor of Rome as a human stepping-stool to assist him in mounting his horse. Valerian was led off in triumph to die in captivity. The exact date of his death is not known, but he may have languished in

Regalianus's usurpation of the purple in 259 lasted long enough for him to have coins of himself and his wife Dryantilla minted.

Below: A vigorous intensity emanates from this naturalistic bust of Gallienus.

Gallienus, his wife Salonina, and two of their sons – Saloninus and Valerian II.

A bust thought to be of Gallienus's trusted cavalry commander Aureolus. His revolt in Italia in 268 set the scene for the emperor's end through treachery among his own command.

prison for as much as two years. After his death Valerian's body was skinned and the grisly trophy displayed to show how Rome's prestige had been eclipsed. Decius had been Rome's first emperor to be killed by foreigners; now Valerian was the first to be taken prisoner.

The shock waves of this disaster were felt in every quarter of the empire, and sparked rebellions on a massive scale to which ultimately Gallienus, now the sole ruler, had no effective answer, and which prevented any attempt to rescue or avenge his father. The main cause of unrest was the fear that, with the senior emperor's death, the far-flung provinces of East and West were on their own. The troops needed the assurance of a strong man at the helm right there with them. On the Rhenus Postumus was proclaimed emperor by the troops in 259, and in consequence Gallienus's son Saloninus and his PRAEFECTUS PRAETORIO Silvanus were murdered. Within a year, this Imperium Gallorum was recognised by Germania Superior and Inferior, Raetia, Gallia, Hispania and Britannia. For the next eighteen months Gallienus fought an indecisive war against his former second-in-command, but mounting pressures along the Danuvius became the more urgent problem. The eastern provinces were now at the Persians' mercy. In quick succession Antiochia was retaken, Tarsus captured and then Caesarea (Kayseri) in Cappadocia. Since no help could be expected from Gallienus, who at the time was occupied in fighting Postumus, one of Valerian's generals named Titus Fulvius

Macrianus proposed his two sons to the dispirited Anatolian garrisons and they were proclaimed joint-Augusti by the troops. This new Asian empire was acknowledged throughout Anatolia and in Aegyptus, but it remained Roman in character. Unlike the empire of Postumus, which was to last for fourteen years, the empire of the Macriani did not survive long, falling no later than 262 to the new power in the east, the Palmyrenes, with the full consent of Gallienus (*see the following chapter*).

It is, perhaps, a tribute to Gallienus's realism, as well as an indication of his limited resources, that he understood Postumus was in a better position to keep the barbarians at bay than a distant emperor, and so left him alone to get on with the job. In any event, a return of the plague in 262 kept Gallienus busy in Rome, followed by another incursion of Goths in the Balkans, which necessitated his presence in eastern Europe. The invaders raided Macedonia and Thracia, and pushed as far south into Achaea as Athens. It took until late July to evict them, and Gallienus returned to Rome in September 262 to celebrate his DECENNALIA. Although it included a spectacular procession involving all the classes, it was really a military pageant that underscored how much imperial power now depended on the goodwill of the soldiers.

Gallienus appears to have spent the years between 262–67 in Rome, leaving the defence of Italia and Illyricum in the hands of his senior officers. For the normally vigorous emperor, this uncharacteristic apathy points to a crisis of confidence, which is hardly surprising considering the palpable disintegration of the empire despite his every effort. However, he returned to his normal form when another invasion by the Goths ended the five-year holiday from war. The invaders – a branch of the Goths called the Heruli – had crossed the Pontus Euxinus and, towards the end of 267, laid waste Roman territory at the mouth of the Danuvius. There was an early naval victory under the Byzantine admiral Venerianus, but it did not prevent the Goths from plundering Cyzicus and then crossing into Achaea, ravaging every town and settlement in their path.

As Gallienus gathered his army, the Goths took a westward circuit across Achaea, Epirus, Macedonia and up into Moesia. Gallienus ordered the detachments of Byzantium and Thracia under the command of Marcianus to cut across the Gothic communications and prevent any retreat, while he laid his battle lines across their approach on the banks of the Nessus. In the resulting battle the Romans were supremely victorious and the Goths routed. However, the impending wholesale slaughter was abruptly halted by news of a revolt in Raetia and Italia.

This was a terrible blow for the emperor, for the pretender was his stalwart cavalry general Aureolus, who had been entrusted with Italia's protection. Gallienus returned and managed to drive Aureolus into Mediolanum, and then laid siege to the city. But he was robbed of victory in the first months of 268 by treachery among his own officers. These included the PRAE-FECTUS PRAETORIO Heraclianus, the general Marcianus, the commander of the Dacian cavalry Crecropius and two high-ranking career officers, Marcus Aurelius Claudius and Lucius Domitius Aurelianus (Aurelian). On the pretext of riding out with them to view some reported enemy movements, the conspirators fell on Gallienus and murdered him.

While ambition for power was an undoubted motive, it should be noted that the conspirators were all Illyrians, so in a sense this was not so much a dynastic change as a geopolitical one. In killing Gallienus, they were substituting an Italian emperor of Hellenistic sympathies for one who was first a soldier and second a native of the region from which Rome's best troops were now recruited. For reasons that will be stated later, the winner of the throne was Marcus Aurelius Claudius.

The reforms of Gallienus

The Hellenising influence that so disturbed the stern Illyrians seems contradictory to the war-like nature of Gallienus's reign. Yet he was different to the warrior-emperors of his era. Descended from ancient Roman aristocratic stock, he was of good education, well read, and interested in art and Hellenistic philosophy. Gallienus and his wife Salonina patronised a cultural movement conveniently referred to as the Gallienic Renaissance. The sculpture of this time indicates a revival of the classical Hellenistic form, with its echoes of other great artistic periods – Augustus and Hadrian, for instance. As Hadrian had done, Gallienus had himself appointed archon at Athens and was introduced to the Eleusinian Mysteries of the goddess Demeter.

Unlike his father Valerian, he showed tolerance towards Christians. Valerian had been persuaded by Macrianus that the ills besetting the empire in every quarter were aided by allowing Christians to turn people from the Roman gods, and in 257 he issued an edict to enforce recognition of Roman deities. However, this also allowed the higher clergy to worship Christ in the privacy of their own homes, extending the principle of syncretism to Christianity. A more severe ruling came in 258, promulgated in the eastern

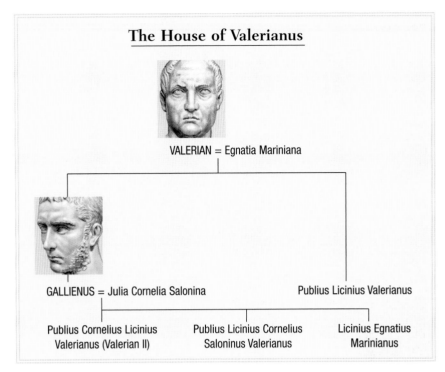

The House of Valerianus

VALERIAN = Egnatia Mariniana

GALLIENUS = Julia Cornelia Salonina

Publius Licinius Valerianus

Publius Cornelius Licinius Valerianus (Valerian II)

Publius Licinius Cornelius Saloninus Valerianus

Licinius Egnatius Marinianus

provinces. Under its provisions, recalcitrant clergy were executed, the property of senators and EQUITES became confiscate, and tenants were sent to the mines. Gallienus reversed his father's harsh policy, established peace with the Church, and even restored to it property lost under Decius and his own father.

Gallienus continued the military reforms begun under Septimius Severus and completed the democratisation of the army. Essentially opposed to the senatorial order, Severus had appointed equestrian PRAEFECTI to command the legions he raised instead of the senatorial LEGATI of the past, and preferred to use equestrian procurators instead of senatorial provincial governors. Gallienus went further and deprived senators of their ancient privilege of commanding legions. The senatorial rank of LEGATUS LEGIONIS disappears from the records at this point, to be replaced by the equestrian PRAEFECTUS LEGIONIS. Since this was the same title as the lesser rank of the camp commander, PRAEFECTUS [CASTRORUM] LEGIONIS, it was distinguished by the additional titles of VIR EGREGIUS, or AGENS VICES LEGATI. In all probability the qualification for this office was to have held the post of PRIMUS PILUS centurion twice. With the LEGATUS the other senatorial officers in the legion, the TRIBUNI LATICLAVII ('broad stripe' or senatorial military tribunes) also disappeared. Under Gallienus the final barriers separating lower from higher command were abolished, and any man who attained the centuriate could now rise to the very highest levels of command.

There is a degree of confusion about Valerian's family. Some authorities point out that the brother of Gallienus could in fact have been confused with his son, the Caesar Valerian II, and that they were one and the same. However, the consuls' list shows Licinus Valerianus holding the office of ordinary consul in 265, three years before his murder, and some seven years after Valerian II's death on campaign. This seems to indicate that he was brother to Gallienus and not his son. Further, some sources suggest that it was the elder son who was murdered by Postumus, but this simply does not fit the few facts that exist. There is reasonable doubt as to whether Valerian II was made co-Augustus with his father, but his coins only display CAES in his nomenclature. Saloninus was evidently made Caesar after his brother's death.

The barbarian invasions, 250–57, and the fragmentation of the Roman empire at the death of Gallienus, 268

OCEANUS GERMANICUS

OCEANUS ATLANTICUS

Britannia Inferior
• Eburacum (York)

Britannia Superior
• Londinium

• Gesoriacum (Boulogne)

Germania Inferior

Colonia Agrippina (Cologne)
FRANKS

Franks break through the LIMES GERMANICUS in 256, raiding into Germania, Belgica, Gallia and Hispania.

Alamanni occupy the Agri Decumates in 258, raiding into Germania Superior, burning Aventicum and invading Gallia. The Romans abandon the Agri Decumates.

Augusta Treverorum (Trier)
• Moguntiacum (Mainz)
ALAMANNI   MARCOMANNI

Belgica

Lutetia (Paris)

Rhenus   Agri Decumates   Danuvius   Vindobona   QUADI
Lugdunensis   Germania Superior   Carnuntum   SARMAT

Franks   Aventicum (Avenches)   RAETIA   NORICUM   PANNONIA SUP. INF.

Alamanni   (Brenner Pass)   Mursa (Osijek)

Aquitania   • Lugdunum (Lyons)   Aquileia   • Verona   Ulpia Tr

Mediolanum (Milan)   Mursa 259
Gallienus crushes the usurper Ingenuus.

• Burdigala (Bordeaux)   • Genua   DALMATIA

ITALIA   MARE ADRIATICUM

• Tolosa (Toulouse)   Narbonensis   258
Gallienus defeats the Alamanni.

Narbo (Narbonne)   CORSICA   • Roma   MARE

• Legio (León)   M SU

Caesaraugusta (Zaragoza)   Tarraco (Tarragona)   MARE TYRRHENUM

Tarraconensis   SARDINIA
Lusitania   • Toletum (Toledo)
Emerita Augusta (Mérida)   Baleares

• Olisipo (Lisbon)

• Corduba   Franks   SICILIA
Baetica

256–7 Franks raid the coast of Mauretania Tingitana.

• Hippo Regius (Annaba)   • Carthago

Tinigi (Tangier)   • Caesarea (Cherchell)   • Hadrumetum (Sousse)

MAURETANIA TINGITANA   MAURETANIA CAESARIENSIS   NUMIDIA   M A R E   I

AFRICA PROCONSULARIS   • Leptis Magna

Roman empire of Gallienus
allegiance to Gallienus or doubtful allegiance
Raetia seized by Aureolus for Imperium Gallorum
Imperium Gallorium (Gallic empire)
empire of the Macriani
Palmyrene empire
Sassanian empire

barbarian pressure point
major barbarian raid
Sassanian campaign
• city destroyed by barbarians
✕ major battle
FRANKS   barbarian tribe

0   100   200   300 miles
0   100   200   300   400 kilometres

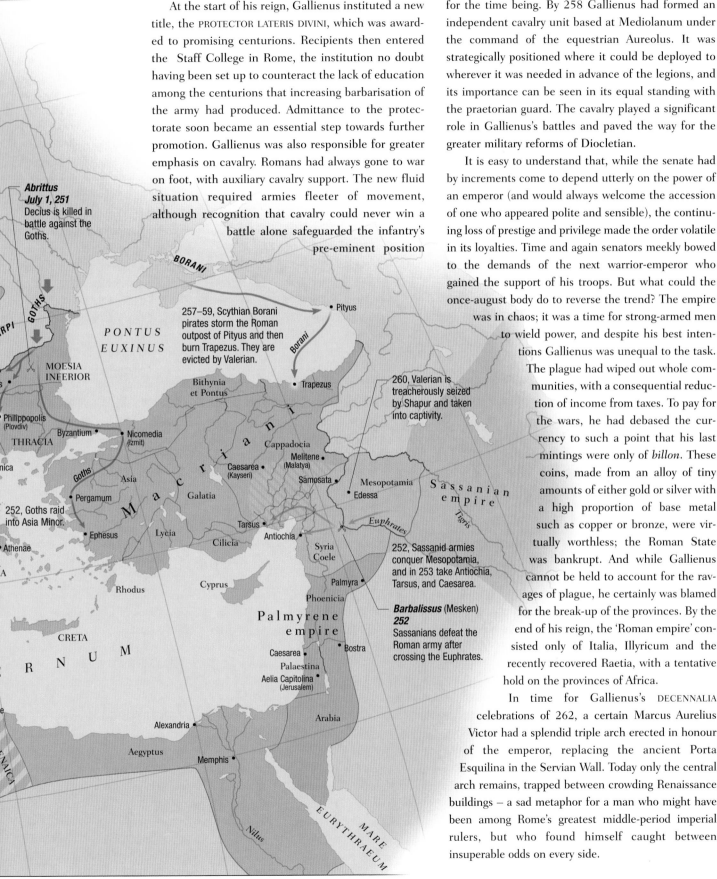

At the start of his reign, Gallienus instituted a new title, the PROTECTOR LATERIS DIVINI, which was awarded to promising centurions. Recipients then entered the Staff College in Rome, the institution no doubt having been set up to counteract the lack of education among the centurions that increasing barbarisation of the army had produced. Admittance to the protectorate soon became an essential step towards further promotion. Gallienus was also responsible for greater emphasis on cavalry. Romans had always gone to war on foot, with auxiliary cavalry support. The new fluid situation required armies fleeter of movement, although recognition that cavalry could never win a battle alone safeguarded the infantry's pre-eminent position

for the time being. By 258 Gallienus had formed an independent cavalry unit based at Mediolanum under the command of the equestrian Aureolus. It was strategically positioned where it could be deployed to wherever it was needed in advance of the legions, and its importance can be seen in its equal standing with the praetorian guard. The cavalry played a significant role in Gallienus's battles and paved the way for the greater military reforms of Diocletian.

It is easy to understand that, while the senate had by increments come to depend utterly on the power of an emperor (and would always welcome the accession of one who appeared polite and sensible), the continuing loss of prestige and privilege made the order volatile in its loyalties. Time and again senators meekly bowed to the demands of the next warrior-emperor who gained the support of his troops. But what could the once-august body do to reverse the trend? The empire was in chaos; it was a time for strong-armed men to wield power, and despite his best intentions Gallienus was unequal to the task. The plague had wiped out whole communities, with a consequential reduction of income from taxes. To pay for the wars, he had debased the currency to such a point that his last mintings were only of *billon*. These coins, made from an alloy of tiny amounts of either gold or silver with a high proportion of base metal such as copper or bronze, were virtually worthless; the Roman State was bankrupt. And while Gallienus cannot be held to account for the ravages of plague, he certainly was blamed for the break-up of the provinces. By the end of his reign, the 'Roman empire' consisted only of Italia, Illyricum and the recently recovered Raetia, with a tentative hold on the provinces of Africa.

In time for Gallienus's DECENNALIA celebrations of 262, a certain Marcus Aurelius Victor had a splendid triple arch erected in honour of the emperor, replacing the ancient Porta Esquilina in the Servian Wall. Today only the central arch remains, trapped between crowding Renaissance buildings – a sad metaphor for a man who might have been among Rome's greatest middle-period imperial rulers, but who found himself caught between insuperable odds on every side.

Abrittus
July 1, 251
Decius is killed in battle against the Goths.

257–59, Scythian Borani pirates storm the Roman outpost of Pityus and then burn Trapezus. They are evicted by Valerian.

260, Valerian is treacherously seized by Shapur and taken into captivity.

252, Goths raid into Asia Minor.

252, Sassanid armies conquer Mesopotamia, and in 253 take Antiochia, Tarsus, and Caesarea.

Barbalissus (Mesken)
252
Sassanians defeat the Roman army after crossing the Euphrates.

CHAPTER NINE   AD 259–271

IMPERIUM GALLORUM AND EMPIRES IN THE EAST

POSTUMUS

Marcus Cassianus Latinius Postumus
(r.late 259–January 269)

Even before the reigns of Valerian and Gallienus the prestige the German legions had enjoyed during the early imperial period had been eclipsed by that of the Illyrian army. Barbarian incursions along the Danuvius in the mid-third century appear to have had a greater impact on the empire, but the reduced legions on the Rhenus were facing no lesser threat in reality. The soldiers, almost all provincial Gauls, felt exposed to the enemy and neglected by Rome. The continued policy of favouring the eastern European frontier, they felt, impeded their defensive tasks. When Gallienus departed from Gallia to deal with the Pannonian revolt of Ingenuus in 259 at a time of terrible crisis, the Gallic legions turned to the best man on the spot and demanded he rule them.

Nothing is known of Postumus's life as a PRIVATUS beyond his appointment to the command of the German legions under Valerian. He was clearly a nationalistic Gallo-Roman of humble origins, whose distinguished military skills allowed him to rise through the ranks to become a PRAEFECTUS LEGIONIS. As usual, the political and military imperatives were driven by petty motives. A quarrel seems to have broken out over booty taken from barbarians near Moguntiacum by Postumus's soldiers. When Postumus distributed the spoils between his men, the PRAEFECTUS PRAETORIO Silvanus ordered him to surrender everything to himself and Gallienus's young son, the Caesar Saloninus, who was under the protection of Silvanus at Colonia Agrippina. The troops rebelled, proclaimed Postumus emperor, and marched on the city. At the threat of a siege, the town's garrison was obliged to hand over Saloninus and Silvanus, and both were put to death immediately.

The legions stationed in Germania Inferior and Superior were quick to endorse Postumus as emperor. And in the following year those western provinces most at threat from the barbarians acknowledged his rule: all of Gallia, Aquitania, the provinces of Hispania, Britannia and Raetia, the last being held until its seizure in 268 by Aureolus as part of his rebellion against Gallienus. Postumus reinvigorated the Roman will to drive out the various invaders, and a series of victories is commemorated by coins bearing legends such as VICTORIA GERMANICA and RESTITUTA ORBIS. By 263 the Franks and Alamanni were crushed, and although the northern LIMES were lost, some of the Agri Decumates was retaken. The speed with which Postumus recovered the initiative is indicated by a coin minted for 10 December 261 showing that he had assumed the title Germanicus Maximus.

As has been related, Gallienus tried to avenge his son's murder and crush the usurper, but twice failed to do so. On the first occasion the failure seems to have been caused by the unusual carelessness of his cavalry commander Aureolus, the second when Gallienus was wounded by an arrow and had to break off the assault. Added to which, the revolt of the legions under the Macriani in Anatolia required his urgent attention. Thereafter, while never recognising Postumus's IMPERIUM, Gallienus accepted the reality of the separate empire to his west. This position was undoubtedly made more acceptable because Postumus made no threatening moves to expand his territory, a reasonable policy that ironically may well have brought about his ultimate downfall. His avoidance of a confrontation with Rome even extended later to refusing an invitation by Aureolus to join his revolt against Gallienus. This may have been in pique at losing Raetia to Aureolus, but it seems more likely that Postumus's Gallic nationalism was a greater preoccupation than the loss of a small, mountainous and difficult province, and he was happy to abandon Aureolus to his inevitable fate.

The administrative policies that Postumus pursued indicate that his intention was not to found a separate Gallic state completely independent of Rome but to create a form of collegiate structure that would eventually join forces with the other 'empires' of Rome to counter the external threat on all borders. The concept was a forerunner of Diocletian's Tetrarchy of the fourth century. Far from being overtly Gallic in the old Celtic sense, Postumus assumed all the imperial powers and prerogatives of a Roman emperor, including

Postumus's separate Gallic empire in the West would remain unchallenged by Gallienus for nearly a decade as he contended with troubles on the eastern frontiers.

Ulpius Cornelius Laelanius headed a short-lived rebellion against Postumus in 268.

the titles of PONTIFEX MAXIMUS and PATER PATRIAE, and he set up independent consuls and a senate at Augusta Treverorum. Postumus held the consulship five times during his ten-year reign (259, 260, 261, 266 or 267, and 268) and – in the constitutional tradition of Augustus – renewed his TRIBUNICIA POTESTAS annually from his accession.

Repairs to the ravages wrought by the barbarian raids were made, and commerce revived. Rome's western provinces had suffered less than the rest of the empire in the internecine dynastic battles of recent years, and Spanish, British and Gallic trading had remained for the most part undamaged. Recovery from the Frankish attacks was, therefore, readily accomplished, and commerce gave Postumus a currency far less debased than that of Gallienus. However, after 265 the joyous coinage suffered from a sudden deterioration of its silver content. The answer may lie in Postumus's refusal to march on Rome. His soldiers felt that only his recognition as the sole ruler of the Roman empire would legitimise their rebellion as well as provide them with the rewards they deserved. Paying increased donatives inevitably meant reducing the quality of the coins – and it was not enough to satisfy rapacious military pockets.

LAELANIUS

Ulpius Cornelius Laelianus (r.c.December 268)

Preparations to celebrate Postumus's DECENNALIA at the end of the year were abruptly cut short by the rebellion of Ulpius Cornelius Laelianus at Moguntiacum. No written or epigraphic evidence exists to inform of the office held by Laelianus, but many coins bearing his name and style (IMP.) have been found. Since his proclamation took place at Moguntiacum and presumably with the approval of the local troops, he was either the PRAEFECTUS LEGIONIS of *XXII Primigenia* stationed there or governor of Germania Superior. There clearly was disaffection for Postumus among the soldiers throughout the Gallic empire, as evidenced by the subsequent actions of his own men. However, Postumus led a force against the usurper and Laelianus was either killed in action or by the troops of Postumus afterwards. Eager for fresh booty – there is a suggestion that Laelianus may have led a successful Transrhenane expedition against some barbarians – Postumus's troops prepared to sack Moguntiacum. When Postumus attempted to hold them back, his men's patience snapped and they killed him.

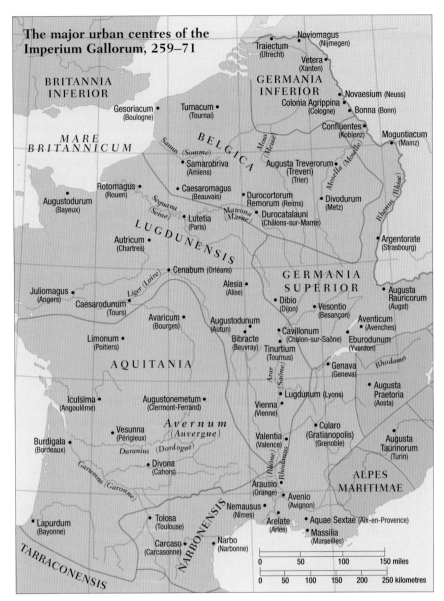

The major urban centres of the Imperium Gallorum, 259–71

MARIUS

Marcus Aurelius Marius (r.c.December 268)

In place of Postumus the troops raised a simple soldier, Marius, to the purple. Almost nothing is known about him, beyond the legend that he was a blacksmith by trade, and was killed by a sword of his own manufacture. There is no possibility that the Treveran senate accorded him any honour because his reign lasted little longer than three days before he was in turn murdered. There is every possibility that this was not an attempt on the part of Marius to seize power, but rather the outcome of a confused attempt by one faction of soldiers to protect their own interests over those of another faction, probably that of the wealthy military commander Victorinus.

The central importance of the coin to Roman political spin is never more clearly underlined than with Marcus Aurelius Marius. Even though he lasted only three days before being murdered, he managed in this time to mint some coins to legitimise his 'reign'.

VICTORINUS
Marcus Piavonius Victorinus (r.269–271)

Victorinus had been one of the military architects of Postumus's victories over the barbarian invaders, and had shared the consulship with the him in either 266–67 or 268. Having remained behind in Augusta Treverorum while Postumus marched against Laelianus, when news reached the city of the Gallic emperor's death the garrison had little hesitation in electing Victorinus emperor in his place. Whether the troops of Marius thought twice about their choice and killed him or whether partisans of Victorinus in Moguntiacum did the deed remains a mystery. However, while the IMPERIUM of Victorinus was recognised throughout Gallia and in Britannia, the provinces of Hispania were swaying in their affections and refused to do so. He ignored the rebuttal since he had his mind set on the recovery of Raetia from Aureolus, but a campaign was never mounted because of problems further to the south. The successes of the new emperor of Rome, Claudius II Gothicus, had undermined faith in the Gallic empire to the point where the city of Augustodunum (Autun) revolted and asked Rome for help.

Marcus Piavonius Victorinus

Domitianus

Victorinus was obliged to take his forces and besiege the city before any Roman aid could arrive. Augustodunum shut its gates and held out for seven months, praying for Roman help. But when it did finally arrive, it was a largely symbolic gesture. Claudius sent the PRAEFECTUS VIGILUM of Rome, Julius Placidianus, with what was effectively a police force. However, perhaps fearing that his resources were insufficient to relieve Augustodunum, he did not cross the Rhodanus, but made camp near Cularo (later Gratianopolis, Grenoble) where he could protect Gallia Narbonensis and Italia. In 270 Augustodunum fell to Victorinus's forces and was plundered. Victorinus returned in triumph to the north and took up residence in Colonia Agrippina where, in early 271, his quartermaster Attitianus murdered him in what appears to have been a matter of private revenge. However, Victorinus's wealthy mother Victoria held sufficient authority among the troops to secure the succession for her nominee, the senatorial governor of Aquitania, Tetricus. But before outlining his imperial career it is necessary to backtrack slightly, and examine the scant evidence for another 'emperor' of the period.

Tetricus and his son Tetricus II. Their defeat and deposition by Aurelian ended the Imperium Gallorum of Postumus.

DOMITIANUS
(r. a few weeks c.270–71)

One historical source identifies Domitianus as the general under Gallienus who defeated the Macriani in the Balkans, but this is to be doubted because of the better evidence of that man being Aureolus. Indeed, the very existence of Domitianus has been doubted, related only to the find of a single coin in France and long regarded as a modern forgery. However, the discovery of a second coin towards the end of 2003 in a field in Oxfordshire and authenticated by British Museum experts in February 2004, proves his historical reality.

That he aspired fully to the purple is evidenced by the two coins' common inscription: IMP[ERATOR] C[AESAR] DOMITIANUS P[IUS] FELIX AUG[USTUS]. However, there is confusion about where this short-lived emperor actually reigned. Recent suggestions that his domain was Britannia (because one of the coins was found there) should be discounted. Trade between Gallia and Britannia remained largely unaffected by the upheavals of the Imperium Gallorum, and coinage would have travelled freely, no matter who had minted it. The Danuvius frontier and eastern Gallia have been suggested as more likely venues. Of these, the former seems less plausible, for the formidable Aurelian, on behalf of Claudius, was active throughout the whole region. It seems realistic, therefore, to attribute Domitianus to Gallia, and his rebellion one against Tetricus, to whom he probably fell some weeks after proclaiming himself.

TETRICUS
Gaius Pius Esuvius Tetricus (r.271–March 274)

Tetricus might have faced a serious threat from Aurelian, who had recently succeeded Claudius, but the new Roman emperor had his hands full with a Gothic invasion along the Danuvius (*see chapter 10*). Besides, with Raetia secure, the region of Narbonensis bounded by the Rhodanus and the Alps back in his hands thanks to Julius Placidianus, and with the defection of Hispania from the Gallo-Roman empire, Aurelian was content for the time being to leave well alone in the west. Although Tetricus was acclaimed in the north, he took the purple at Burdigala (Bordeaux) in spring of the same year and set out for Augusta Treverorum. On the way, his forces encountered a band of Franks who had broken through the frontier to profit from the murder of Victorinus, and Tetricus's small force overwhelmed and slaughtered the invaders. After a further campaign along the Rhenus, Tetricus returned in late 272 and established Augusta Treverorum as his capital, where he entered his second consulship in 273 and elevated his son Tetricus II to the rank of Caesar.

Tetricus followed the example of Postumus and made no threatening moves against Rome. While Aurelian was engaged with the Gothic wars, this pacific policy may have made sense, but having dealt with the Goths and defeated the short-lived empire of Palmyra, Aurelian returned to Rome from the eastern provinces in 273 and determined to reunite the empire under one ruler. The task that had so completely defeated Gallienus no longer looked so daunting. Tetricus had only maintained his position with difficulty. For one thing, Gallia and Britannia were again prey to barbarian raids across the frontier rivers and pirate attacks from the sea; for another the governor of one province, a certain Faustinus, had raised the banner of rebellion with the support of soldiers who were opposed to Tetricus's passive policy. And the common people were disillusioned with an emperor who could no longer guarantee their security. As Aurelian marched across the Alps, a reluctant Tetricus took the field together with his son. The two armies faced off against each other in the early spring of 274 near Cavillonum (Châlons-sur-Marne).

The story given in the histories is that, worn out by the pressures of government, Faustinus's insurrection and the insubordinate attitude of his own troops, Tetricus had made arrangements to betray his army to Aurelian in return for the Roman emperor's protection. This account reflects the propaganda of the Aurelianic authors and is probably a classic example of the victor writing the history. Other fragments suggest that Tetricus – who had hardly been an unsuccessful ruler – remained resolute to the last and did not betray his soldiers. He did, however, lose the battle and he would thus have owed his life not to his suggested treachery, but rather to Aurelian's need to stabilise a new administration in the western part of the empire without fuss from the senate, who hailed Tetricus as one of their own. The two Tetrici were displayed in Rome during Aurelian's triumph, but whether for political or humanitarian reasons, or because he was simply keeping his side of the bargain, the emperor pardoned them. Like Zenobia (*see pages 149–150*) Tetricus was to end his life quietly in Italia, where he died at an advanced age at an unknown date. With him ended the Imperium Gallorum of Postumus.

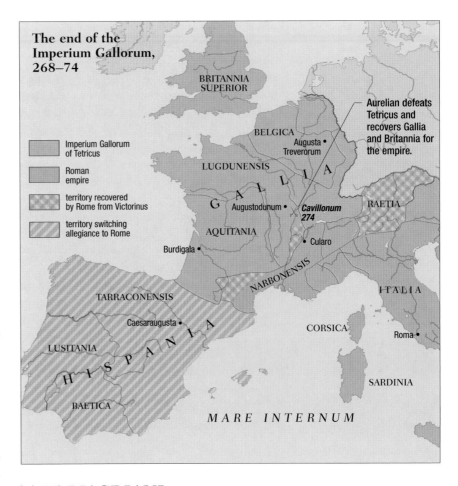

The end of the Imperium Gallorum, 268–74

Imperium Gallorum of Tetricus

Roman empire

territory recovered by Rome from Victorinus

territory switching allegiance to Rome

BRITANNIA SUPERIOR

BELGICA
Augusta Treverorum •

LUGDUNENSIS

G A L L I A

Augustodunum •   *Cavillonum 274*

AQUITANIA

• Cularo

Burdigala •

NARBONENSIS

RAETIA

ITALIA

TARRACONENSIS

Caesaraugusta •

H I S P A N I A

CORSICA

Roma •

LUSITANIA

SARDINIA

BAETICA

MARE   INTERNUM

Aurelian defeats Tetricus and recovers Gallia and Britannia for the empire.

THE MACRIANI

Titus Fulvius Macrianus
Titus Fulvius Iunius Macrianus
Titus Fulvius Iunius Quietus (r.260–c.262)

When the capture and subsequent death of Valerian left the eastern provinces at the mercy of the Sassanian empire, one of Valerian's generals, Macrianus, and Ballista, the PRAEFECTUS PRAETORIO, gathered the remnants of the divided Roman forces at Samosata and deliberated on what to do next. With his hands full in Gallia attempting to wrest the region from Postumus, it was clear that the eastern legions could expect no immediate help from Gallienus. Since Macrianus was elderly and frail, and Ballista – an unusual paragon of virtue for the time – rejected the notion of power, at some point before 17 September 260 they decided to proclaim the two sons of Macrianus, Quietus and another Macrianus, co-emperors. The origins of the Macriani are unknown, but the father had risen to a high rank under Valerian. As his procurator, he would have had

Titus Fulvius Macrianus

control over the war chest, which certainly helped the elevation of his sons. The regime's other claim on the hearts of the beleaguered soldiers was a tremendous victory over Shapur's forces at Corycus in Cilicia engineered by Ballista that compelled the Sassanians to retire to the Euphrates.

In common with the Imperium Gallorum, this new Syrian state was entirely Roman in character, as numerous coins attest. However, unlike Postumus, Macrianus the father was not content with their position in Syria and Asia and determined to commence a westward expansion with the aim of securing the Balkans. Leaving Quietus and Ballista in Syria, he took detachments of troops and set out in company with his eldest son to cross over into Europe. It is possible to see this strategy as a genuinely helpful move to protect the Balkans against barbarian incursions from the north, but it might equally have been a cynical land-grab from the dominions of Gallienus, and this is certainly how the beleagured emperor viewed it. By this time Gallienus had abandoned his futile war against Postumus and, unwilling to cede any part of his grip on the Illyrian and Balkan provinces to another usurper, sent Aureolus to meet them (a sound reason for rejecting the unknown Domitianus as the man in command). The Syrian army met Aureolus and his powerful squadrons of cavalry in Illyricum or on the borders of Thracia, and in the battle both Macriani were killed. This success was empty while Quietus and Ballista still held Asia Minor, however, and it was out of the question to dispatch a Roman army to return the Macriani empire to the fold. In this crisis the eastern power of Palmyra became a valuable ally.

Titus Fulvius Iunius Macrianus (top) and his younger brother Titus Fulvius Iunius Quietus.

ODENATH OF PALMYRA
Septimius Odaenathus (r.c.260–c.267)

The state of Palmyra lay between Roman Syria and the Euphrates, and in Roman times it had grown wealthy on the lucrative trade route between Persia and the Mediterranean. It lay beyond the region effectively annexed to the Roman empire by Pompey in 63 BC. Indeed, the Palmyrenes were more closely bound to Parthia when Marcus Antonius tried to raid the city in 41 BC, and the Arsacid dynasty encouraged friendly relations between Ctesiphon and Palmyra. Yet thereafter, political ties with Rome grew increasingly strong. There is epigraphic evidence that during his trip to the eastern provinces in AD 18 that preceded his murder in Syria, Germanicus visited Palmyra in an administrative capacity. Trajan extended the road system to Palmyra and Hadrian gave it the privileges of a LIBERA (a state free from taxation). Under Septimius Severus, Palmyra was raised to the status of a COLONIA. In all this, then, Palmyra had retained a degree of autonomy while nevertheless gravitating inexorably into the Roman orbit.

The advent of the Sassanid dynasty of Persians changed the balance of power in the region. The Palmyrenes, who supplied auxiliaries to the Roman army, came to see the impossibility of the Romans maintaining their eastern frontier. Not only were the more frequent wars generally unfavourable to Rome, but Sassanid ambitions for Palmyra meant the development of a Palmyrene defensive policy that was self-reliant. Odenath's father had attempted independence some years previously, but had been arrested by the governor of Syria and executed. Epigraphic evidence at Palmyra establishes Odenath's immediate ancestors to a time when the family must have received its citizenship from Septimius Severus. By 258 Odenath is recorded as a prince of Palmyra, with Roman titles such as CLARISSIMUS and CONSULARIS. These do not mean that he was a member of the Roman senate, less so a consul, but the honorifics reflect Roman recognition of his pre-eminent position in the Palmyrene administration. However, his devotion to Rome appears to have been qualified. One story relates how he sent a caravan laden with rich gifts to Shapur, seeking an alliance, but Shapur scorned the offerings and demanded complete subjection. Since Odenath claimed in his embassy that he had injured no Persian interests, the proposition was evidently made before his attack in retaliation for the capture of Valerian in 260. Clearly, Odenath was weighing Rome against Persia and seeking independent advantage for Palmyra, not as a client of either empire.

In the crisis of 260, having been rejected by Shapur, Odenath threw in his lot with Rome. Proclaiming himself REX, he gathered an army from Syria and Arabia, and attacked the Persians after their capture of Valerian at Edessa with such severity that

Shapur was driven back across the Euphrates, leaving booty and prisoners in Odenath's hands. To this point the Palmyrene king had acted on his own initiative, but far from earning the displeasure of Gallienus, the emperor decided to legitimise Odenath's position. With true Roman disdain for the title REX, Gallienus entrusted Odenath with the supreme command of all Roman forces in the East under the title DUX ROMANO-RUM. This politically astute move provided Gallienus with a proxy force to maintain Roman arms in the face of Shapur; but the first mission was the recovery of the empire of Macrianus. Odenath did not wait. By a mix of force and diplomacy, he detached most of the Syrian cities from Ballista, and then at the end of 261 or the start of 262 attacked the Macriani capital of Emesa. Ballista was killed in the fighting, and the townspeople assassinated Quietus shortly after.

By the gift of Gallienus and the force of his arms over Macrianus, Odenath had effectively made himself the undisputed ruler of the eastern part of the Roman empire, but in his political wisdom he refrained from making such an overt declaration. Furthermore, the emergence of a Palmyrene empire was likely to be opposed by the Sassanians, and without the force of full-scale, trained Roman legions, a convincing conquest of Persia was beyond him. Nevertheless, he could inflict some damage on the enemy, and proceeded to do so in 262 with an army composed of Roman legionaries from Anatolia, and cavalry and archers from his own kingdom. The campaign was attended by great success. Mesopotamia and much of Armenia were recovered, and the triumphant army took Nisibis and advanced unstoppably on Ctesiphon. However, Shapur's scattered armies recovered from the shocks and gathered to defend the capital. Unable to meet a concerted Persian attack, Odenath contented himself with looting the city's outskirts and retiring safely behind the re-established frontier. For his efforts in Rome's name Gallienus rewarded Odenath with the title IMPERATOR.

Despite enlarging Palmyrene interests beyond recognition, Odenath and his elder son by a previous marriage fell to the assassin's knife in 266–7, possibly at Emesa. Since the government fell into the hands of his second wife Zenobia, whose very young son Vabalathus had been only second in line to the throne, it was inevitable that she should be accused of plotting to kill her husband and stepson. Whether she was behind the conspiracy or not, Zenobia was certainly the beneficiary of their deaths, and she did not possess her deceased husband's political caution when it came to dealing with Rome.

ZENOBIA & VABALATHUS
(r.267–272, Romano-Palmyrene empire)

After his death, Odenath's Palmyrene title King of Kings and his Roman office CORRECTOR TOTIUS ORIEN-TIS passed nominally to his young son Vabalathus, a child of between four to six years in age at the time, judging by portraits on the first issue of coins. But the real power lay with his formidable mother and regent, Zenobia. Gallienus may now have regretted his support for a regime that showed every indication of growing into a separate and dangerous new power in the East, for he refused to confirm Vabalathus in the titles he had granted Odenath. It was, of course, an empty gesture, since Gallienus had no practical means of enforcing any form of Roman sovereignty over Palmyra; and within a year he was dead. His successor, Claudius, continued the policy of refusing what Zenobia considered her son's right, but was too preoccupied with the Alamanni and Goths to intervene in Palmyrene affairs.

Anatolia, nominally regained by Gallienus after the defeat of the Macriani, had returned its allegiance to Rome, and with it Aegyptus. Zenobia took advantage of the wars in Europe to begin the expansion of Palmyra to incorporate the provinces of Asia Minor. In the winter of 268–69 she occupied Antiochia. The evidence for this is that the city's mint, which had been producing coins in the name of the new emperor Claudius, issued coinage in the joint-names of Vabalathus and Claudius (*see the following page*).

After Odenath's assassination, his second wife Zenobia ruled in Palmyra on behalf of her young son Vabalathus.

With Antiochia secured, it was time for Aegyptus. The route lay due south through Arabia, and the Palmyrene army pushed forward to Bostra and then Philadelphia (Amman), as milestones commemorating Vabalathus testify. Command of the seventy thousand-strong army, which was comprised of Palmyrenes, Syrians and barbarian contingents, was given to a certain Zabdas, and a pro-Palmyrene Egyptian called Timagenes contributed an allied force. Aegyptus was particularly vulnerable because the governor Probus was absent, commanding the Roman navy operating against a Gothic fleet in the Aegeum (*see the following chapter*). After a hard battle, the Nilus delta came under Zenobia's control.

However, the victory was not secure. Probus returned to his province, ejected the Palmyrene garrison, and attempted to cut Zenobia's lines of communication. This move proved disastrous. Timagenes, with his intimate knowledge of the country, was able to flank the Roman army and take it by surprise. To avoid his capture, Probus committed suicide, and the Romans capitulated, allowing Zenobia to reoccupy Alexandria. Now the Alexandrian mint began issuing coins in common with those of Antiochia. However, there is an interesting aspect to both these issues. One face of the Antiochene coins (it is hard to determine obverse from reverse) features the beardless young face of Vabalathus with the inscription VABALATHVS.V.C.R. IM.D.R — VIR CLARISSIMUS REX IMPERATOR DUX ROMANUM, while the head of Claudius appears on the other. This feature suggests that Zenobia was still anxious to avoid an open breach with Rome, perhaps until she had consolidated her gains. The later Alexandrian coins are similar, except because of the date the Roman emperor's head has changed to Aurelian's. The reason for the latter is explained by the fact that, yet unready to tackle the Palmyrene problem, and perhaps wanting to put Zenobia off her guard, Aurelian made a concord with her and granted all the titles to her son that Gallienus had conferred on Odenath.

Zenobia returned to Antiochia to prepare for the occupation of Anatolia. This undertaking had begun even before the Egyptian campaign, and by the beginning of 270 Cappadocia and Galatia were in her

Zenobia had aspirations of empire, and in the name of Vabalathus (below) took on the might of Rome. Eventually, in 271, she would assume the title Augusta, with her son as Augustus — a move that incurred the wrath of the then emperor, Aurelian, with dire consequences for Palmyra.

The Sassanian, Macriani and Palmyrene empires, 252–72

MACEDONIA   THRACIA   260–61

Late 260–early 261
The elder Macriani are killed in battle by Gallienus's forces under the command of Aureolus.

Lampsacus (Lapseki)

ASIA

Pergamu

Smyrna (Izmir)

MARE AEGEUM

Ephesus

Halicarnassus (Bodrum)

hands. The queen, however, was determined to expand the boundaries to the Aegeum and Euxinus. But she was thwarted from taking much of Bithynia by the sterling efforts of its praetor, Vellius Macrinus, who fortified Nicaea, withstood the Palmyrene assault, and then retorted with a powerful counterattack that repelled Zenobia's army. Undeterred by this — as she thought — temporary setback, in the summer of 271 she assumed the title of Augusta and Vabalathus that of Augustus. This flagrantly advertised breach of the convention agreed with Aurelian was publicly flaunted on the coinage, and he would ignore it at peril to his reign. Aurelian's steady hand on the Italian government had returned stability, so the emperor prepared for war. At this point, it is time to return to the events of 268 outside Mediolanum, immediately after the murder of Gallienus by his own senior officers.

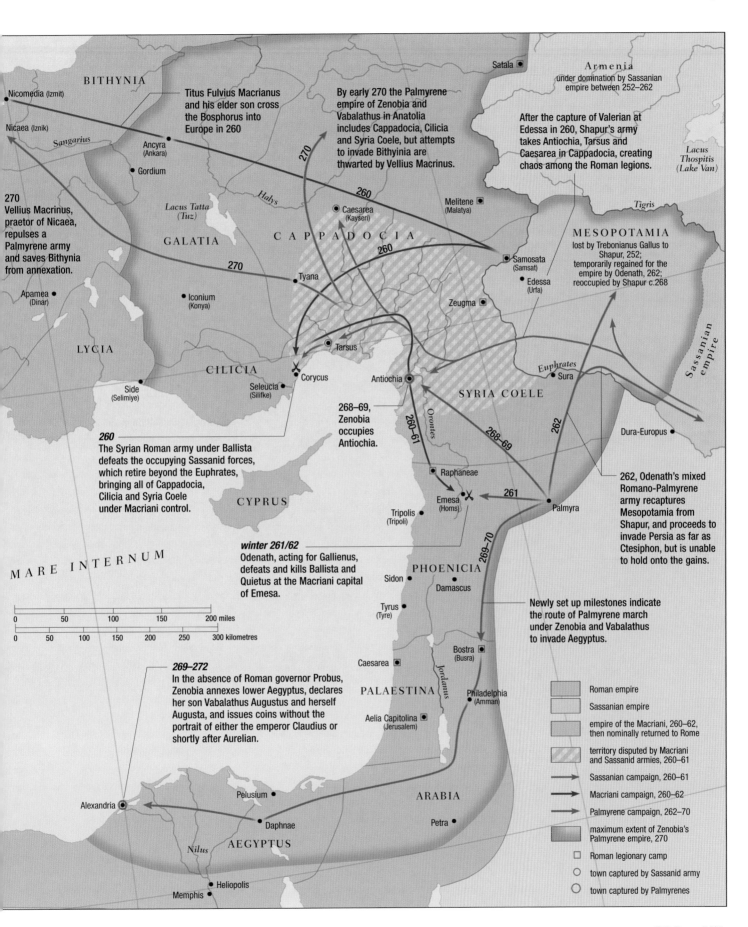

BITHYNIA

Nicomedia (Izmit)

Nicaea (Iznik)

Sangarius

Ancyra (Ankara)

Gordium

Satala

A r m e n i a
under domination by Sassanian
empire between 252–262

Titus Fulvius Macrianus
and his elder son cross
the Bosphorus into
Europe in 260

By early 270 the Palmyrene
empire of Zenobia and
Vabalathus in Anatolia
includes Cappadocia, Cilicia
and Syria Coele, but attempts
to invade Bithyinia are
thwarted by Vellius Macrinus.

After the capture of Valerian at
Edessa in 260, Shapur's army
takes Antiochia, Tarsus and
Caesarea in Cappadocia, creating
chaos among the Roman legions.

*Lacus
Thospitis
(Lake Van)*

270
Vellius Macrinus,
praetor of Nicaea,
repulses a
Palmyrene army
and saves Bithynia
from annexation.

*Lacus Tatta
(Tuz)*

Halys

Caesarea
(Kayseri)

Melitene
(Malatya)

Tigris

GALATIA

CAPPADOCIA

260

MESOPOTAMIA
lost by Trebonianus Gallus to
Shapur, 252;
temporarily regained for the
empire by Odenath, 262;
reoccupied by Shapur c.268

Apamea
(Dinar)

Iconium
(Konya)

270

Tyana

Samosata
(Samsat)

Edessa
(Urfa)

Zeugma

LYCIA

Tarsus

Side
(Selimiye)

CILICIA

Seleucia
(Silifke)

Corycus

Antiochia

Euphrates
Sura

SYRIA COELE

268–69,
Zenobia
occupies
Antiochia.

Orontes

260–61

268–69

262

Dura-Europus

*Sassanian
empire*

260
The Syrian Roman army under Ballista
defeats the occupying Sassanid forces,
which retire beyond the Euphrates,
bringing all of Cappadocia,
Cilicia and Syria Coele
under Macriani control.

CYPRUS

Raphaneae

261

Palmyra

262, Odenath's mixed
Romano-Palmyrene
army recaptures
Mesopotamia from
Shapur, and proceeds to
invade Persia as far as
Ctesiphon, but is unable
to hold onto the gains.

Tripolis
(Tripoli)

Emesa
(Homs)

M A R E   I N T E R N U M

winter 261/62
Odenath, acting for Gallienus,
defeats and kills Ballista and
Quietus at the Macriani capital
of Emesa.

PHOENICIA

Sidon

Damascus

269–70

Newly set up milestones indicate
the route of Palmyrene march
under Zenobia and Vabalathus
to invade Aegyptus.

0	50	100	150	200 miles

| 0 | 50 | 100 | 150 | 200 | 250 | 300 kilometres |

Tyrus
(Tyre)

Caesarea

Bostra
(Busra)

269–272
In the absence of Roman governor Probus,
Zenobia annexes lower Aegyptus, declares
her son Vabalathus Augustus and herself
Augusta, and issues coins without the
portrait of either the emperor Claudius or
shortly after Aurelian.

PALAESTINA

Jordanus

Philadelphia
(Amman)

Aelia Capitolina
(Jerusalem)

ARABIA

Pelusium

Alexandria

Daphnae

Petra

Nilus

AEGYPTUS

Heliopolis

Memphis

Roman empire

Sassanian empire

empire of the Macriani, 260–62,
then nominally returned to Rome

territory disputed by Macriani
and Sassanid armies, 260–61

Sassanian campaign, 260–61

Macriani campaign, 260–62

Palmyrene campaign, 262–70

maximum extent of Zenobia's
Palmyrene empire, 270

Roman legionary camp

town captured by Sassanid army

town captured by Palmyrenes

CHAPTER TEN   AD 268–285
RESTORATION OF IMPERIAL UNITY

CLAUDIUS II GOTHICUS
Marcus Aurelius Claudius
(r.March 268–January 270)

By the end of Gallienus's reign, the Roman empire that his father Valerian had divided between them was riven. Powerful rival empires had sprung up: under Postumus in the West, under first the Macriani and then Palmyra in the East. In Italia, Illyricum and the Balkans, Rome faced onslaughts from the Alamanni and Goths along the northeastern frontier and the Euxinus coast. And yet, within the space of seven years, the reassertion of Roman military ascendancy would be achieved. This extraordinary turn-around was due to three warrior-emperors, all natives of Illyricum, who drove the barbarians from the northern provinces and returned the independent empires of Gallia and Palmyra to Roman sovereignty. As a natural consequence of renewed stability and an improved confidence among the legions in their rulers, the number of local rebellions that had plagued Gallienus also declined in importance.

The officers who had connived at the death of Gallienus had already made their choice of successor, which had lain between the fifty-five-year-old Marcus Aurelius Claudius and, his junior by only two years, Lucius Domitius Aurelianus (Aurelian). The new emperor would need to calm the troops' uncertain temper, and because Aurelian was a noted disciplinarian, the decision went in favour of Claudius, a courteous man of milder disposition. However, the sudden news of Gallienus's death led to some mutinous muttering, and the soldiers were only placated by a donative of twenty AUREI each. Claudius was then adopted without further opposition.

The first of the great Illyrians was born in Dalmatia on 10 May probably in 213 or 214. In keeping with many emperors of the later third century, the early life and career of Claudius is obscure. The *Historiae Augustae* further complicates the issue by offering legendary attributes to ennoble the emperor

Claudius II Gothicus's two-year tenure as emperor was spent waging war against the Goths.

the author spuriously regarded as an ancestor of the first Christian ruler, Constantine the Great. Claudius is described as having fiery eyes, being tall in height, and strong enough to knock out the teeth of man or beast with a single punch. The emperor Decius rewarded him after Claudius demonstrated his strength while wrestling another soldier in the Campus Martius. His ancestors were said to include the Trojan king Ilus and even Dardanus, son of the Greek father-of-gods Zeus and ancestor of the Trojan royal family. We can happily discard these delightful fabrications; the truth was assuredly more prosaic. He was most likely of modest circumstances, and the Illyrian background suggests a military career, with slight evidence to indicate service in the cavalry under Aureolus.

Claudius faced a perilous situation, and it is to his credit that he put aside restitution of the empire and concentrated on ridding Italia of the Alamanni and the Balkans of the Goths. He turned first, however, to the two most immediate requirements: Aureolus, the rebellious MAGISTER EQUITUM, and the senate in Rome. The fate of Aureolus was speedily settled. Having heard of the emperor's death, he surrendered on terms, but was executed shortly after, probably to appease the resentment of Gallienus's soldiers. The senate welcomed the removal of Gallienus to such an extent that only a firm dispatch from Claudius prevented the persecution of his relatives and supporters. Unfortunately, the third son of Gallienus, Licinius Egnatius Marinianus, who was one of the ordinary consuls in 268, may have been murdered together with Gallienus's brother Publius Licinius Valerianus before Claudius's edict reached Rome. The senate recognised Claudius and acceded to his directive to deify Gallienus.

The Alamanni, having already invaded Raetia in the confusion that followed Aureolus's rebellion, had penetrated unopposed into Italia through the Brenner Pass earlier in the year, because Gallienus had denuded the region of troops to fight the Goths at Nessus. Through a series of rash decisions by their commanders, the Roman cavalry sent forward to oppose the barbarian advance was defeated. Claudius deposed the unsuccessful DUCES and appointed Aurelian as DUX EQUITUM. Claudius advanced with his legions to meet the Alamanni host on the shore of Lacus Benacus

(Garda) in November. With approximately thirty-five thousand soldiers, he faced upwards of a hundred thousand enemies. No details of this great battle have survived, but the reinvigorated Romans were the supreme victors. More than half of the Alamanni army was captured or slain, and the remnant fled back into the wilds of a Raetia largely abandoned by Rome.

Claudius entered Rome a hero with his assumed title of Germanicus Maximus, and a grateful senate conferred on him the constitutional imperial powers. He announced his intention to become one of the consuls for 269, and then turned to matters of state. Following their defeat at the hands of Gallienus, the Goths had renewed their attacks on the Balkans, and in larger numbers than before. This represented a far greater threat than that of the Imperium Gallorum of Postumus. It is probable that, after Postumus's death, Hispania broke off its allegiance and, with open rebellion in Gallia at Augustodunum, Claudius felt he could safely leave the rival state to self-destruct. As we have seen, he contented himself with sending a small police force to guard eastern Narbonensis under Julius Placidianus, commander of the VIGILES, and prepared to oppose the Goths, setting out for Illyricum in the spring of 269.

The Goths had set out from Palus Maeotis (Sea of Azov) in the summer of 268 in a fleet of ships said to have numbered two thousand, which had been built with the assistance of their neighbouring tribe, the Heruli, transporting a host of three hundred and twenty thousand men. The first targets were the cities of the Moesian Euxinus coast, but these proved to be difficult to capture. After failing at Tomi, Odessus and Marcianopolis, then Byzantium and Cyzicus, and losing many ships in a bad storm, the Goths sailed through the Hellespontus into the Mare Aegeum. After making repairs, the fleet sailed around Chalcidice and laid siege to Potidaea and Cassandria. On hearing that the Roman army was marching towards them, the Goths then raised the two sieges and changed their campaign plan by dividing into two armies.

The larger group abandoned the fleet to march overland, intent on reaching the Danuvius and eventual safety in their own lands. The smaller group was to sail around the Aegeum, ravaging the island and coastal cities before returning to the Euxinus and sailing home. This naval contingent was thwarted by poor intelligence of the region, and met with little success against the cities' strong fortifications. Claudius ordered the governor of Aegyptus, Tenagino Probus, to command the Roman fleet, and he eventually drove off the Gothic

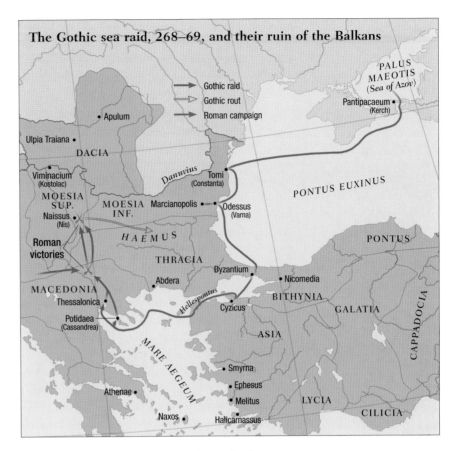

The Gothic sea raid, 268–69, and their ruin of the Balkans

ships. It was at this time that Zenobia took advantage of his absence from Alexandria to launch the Palmyrene attack on Aegyptus, related in the previous chapter.

To meet the challenge on land, Claudius devised a strategy intended to surround the Goths. He posted Aurelian and the cavalry on the border of Macedonia to prevent the Goths from plundering Illyricum, while he commanded the infantry blocking the road to the Danuvius. The strategy succeeded, and in a preliminary battle near Doberus in Pelagonia (northern Macedonia), Aurelian's Dalmatian horsemen killed three thousand Goths. The main engagement was decided at Naissus (Nis) in Moesia. The superior numbers of Goths at first pressed the Roman foot back, but they were ill-disciplined and unprepared for a wholly typical Roman flanking tactic. The Romans inflicted such heavy losses – a reported fifty thousand dead – that the barbarians began a retreat in the direction from which they had come. Claudius had no intention of letting the enemy escape and they were harassed every foot of the way. Eventually, forced into the hilly region of Haemus (Balkan Mountains), the Goths were surrounded. Some were captured, others surrendered, and of these some were pressed into Roman service in the AUXILIA, while more were settled on farms as COLONI. In doing this, Claudius was following in the precedent of Marcus Aurelius and also anticipating later Roman policy; a practical solution in the face of the depopulation of the land caused by the plague. For the success of this campaign, Claudius added Gothicus to his nomenclature.

The short reign of Claudius and his lack of economic resources meant he was unable to accomplish much in his civil administration. Gallienus had so debased the coinage that even had he the time away from his military duties, Claudius could not have undertaken any immediate fiscal reconstruction. He made no significant alterations to the reforms of Gallienus, and granted no extra privileges to the senate. Nevertheless, he was courteous towards senators and maintained good relations with them throughout the barely twenty-two months of his reign. As he was concluding the war against the Goths, Claudius was informed that Vandals were massing on the Danuvius opposite Pannonia and former allies of Rome the Juthungi were threatening Raetia. So, leaving Aurelian in command at Haemus, he went to Sirmium to take charge of the defences, and it was there in January 270 that he succumbed to the plague that had broken out among the defeated Goths and spread to the Roman troops. Genuinely mourned by soldiers and senate, he was deified, and the senate had his golden statue erected in front of the temple of Jupiter Optimus Maximus and a silver statue set on a column on the Rostra in the Forum Romanum. His reign was also commemorated on a gold portrait-shield in the senate house.

QUINTILLUS

Marcus Aurelius Claudius Quintillus
(r.c.February–c.May 270)

On leaving Italia, Claudius had left his brother Quintillus in command of the troops concentrated at Aquileia. When news of the emperor's death reached them there the troops proclaimed Quintillus emperor. Eutropius describes Quintillus as 'a man of singular moderation and grace, and comparable or even preferable to his brother…chosen emperor by the soldiers, and, with the agreement of the senate, named Augustus'. It is probable that the senate preferred Quintillus above Aurelian, the natural warrior-successor to Claudius, whose uncertain temper they feared. However, Quintillus was not an improvement over his brother in military matters. Aurelian swiftly finished the war against the remaining Goths attempting to

Quintillus, brother of Claudius II Gothicus was soon deserted by his army when Aurelian was proclaimed emperor by his own troops.

escape Haemus to return to their homes across the Danuvius, and then moved to Sirmium, where he was proclaimed emperor by the legions of Claudius.

Clearly bewildered by this turn of events, Quintillus made no move to counter the usurpation of his imperial powers and consequently his soldiers deserted him. According to one source, having learned of Aurelian's ascendancy and having failed in an attempt to turn his troops against Aurelian, he found himself abandoned and committed suicide by opening his veins on the twentieth day of his reign. The various historical sources give conflicting times for the length of Quintillus's reign, from seventeen to seventy-seven days. It is hard to credit that he received the conferral of imperial powers from the senate in Rome and had time to order the issue of coins in his name in Claudius's mints as far apart as Rome, Mediolanum and Cyzicus all within the space of seventeen days. Nor is it possible to credit Aurelian with concluding the war against the Goths and transferring to Sirmium in the same space of time. Therefore, the longest time given for the reign of Quintillus seems most probable. In any event, he contributed nothing, and by far the better man was now sole ruler of the still-fragmented Roman empire.

AURELIAN

Lucius Domitius Aurelianus
(r.c.May 270–c.October 275)

According to only two historic sources, the *Epitome de Caesaribus* and Zosimus, Aurelian faced two rebellions at the outset of his reign. A third, that of Domitianus, has been dealt with earlier, and almost certainly did not concern Aurelian. Septimius (or Septiminius) declared himself emperor, probably in Dalmatia, and a certain Urbanus did the same, probably also in Dalmatia. These revolts were another example of local commanders taking matters into their own hands in response to real or imagined threats from the Gothic invasion that Aurelian had largely quelled. In both cases, the usurpers were soon killed by their own troops, and some modern historians have identified Urbanus as a fiction. In any event, neither rebellion had any significant effect on Aurelian's accession in his fifty-sixth year.

Aurelian was born on 9 September 214 or 215 in Sirmium (Mitrovica). His father was a COLONUS (tenant) of a senator named Aurelius, from who he took his COGNOMEN, although whether he was adopted or simply attached the name himself at a later date is not known. Like his fellow Illyrian and colleague Claudius, Aurelian's was a military career; and he may also have served under Aureolus as a DUX EQUITUM (commander of cavalry). Aurelian married Ulpia Severina and she bore him a daughter. In the fall of 274, Ulpia was granted the title Augusta and the Severan styles MATER CASTRORUM ET SENATUS ET PATRIAE.

Dates generally given for Aurelian's accession are confused by events of the time. At a later date, Aurelian himself placed his DIES IMPERII on the day of Claudius's death, but this was a ploy to dismiss Quintillus as a mere usurper. The month of May is most likely, which would allow time for the campaign against the Juthungi during the summer, and accord with his arrival at Rome in the winter in time to take up his first consulship in January 271. This also agrees with his first piece of administrative business, the concord with Zenobia, which led to the issue of the double-headed Alexandrian coins of Vabalathus. Aurelian's first task was the subjugation of the Juthungi that his sudden death had denied Claudius. The barbarians had already crossed the Alps into Italia and enriched themselves with booty from several sacked towns. As Aurelian approached they retreated from Italia but were intercepted in Raetia, where the Romans defeated them in battle and pursued them across the Danuvius. The Juthungi sued for peace and a renewal of their status as friends and allies of Rome, but Aurelian refused them, granting only the right to return in safety to their own territories.

He then hastened to Rome where the senate conferred on him the imperial powers without delay. The question of Zenobia and Palmyra was paramount, but Aurelian knew that the army was weary of continual warfare, and reorganisation would be required before he could take to the field in the breakaway eastern provinces. He therefore concluded the agreement with Zenobia related in the previous chapter, and granted Vabalathus the titles Gallienus had given to his father Odenath. It was an expedient that in appearance maintained Rome's sovereignty in the East, but there was no doubt that it also enhanced the real power of Zenobia and Vabalathus, who held Aegyptus and most of Asia Minor. Over the Imperium Gallorum Aurelian followed Claudius's example, since signs of a worsening internal situation there were evident, and left it to its own disruption. This left him free to attend to urgent civil administrative tasks, among them the closure of the Roman mint because of the peculation of its officials. This was probably intended as the first step in a total reorganisation of the financial administration, but any further work was halted by a Vandal invasion of Pannonia.

Aurelian ordered the governors of the two provinces to gather all food supplies and deny the barbarians provisions, which had the desired effect of slowing down their advance. As soon as Aurelian arrived in Pannonia, he attacked the Vandal force, inflicting a severe defeat. When the Vandal chieftains asked for peace terms, Aurelian deferred the decision to the troops, realising the soundness of a policy that would ensure the army's full support for his rule. The vote was for peace, and terms were arranged that allowed for the Vandals to return home, with a supply of food while they were on Roman soil. In return, Aurelian took hostage the two chieftains' sons and gained a unit of two thousand horsemen as auxiliaries. These men soon proved their new loyalty and usefulness when an isolated band of some five hundred broke away from the main body of retiring Vandals and made raids on nearby settlements. The Romano-Vandal cavalry was sent in pursuit, rounded up the outlaws and killed them to the last man.

Aurelian was prevented from celebrating the Vandal peace in Rome because a far more dangerous situation had developed in Italia. The rebuffed Juthungi had made an alliance with the Marcomanni and Alamanni and swept down through the Brenner Pass as far south as Placentia (Piacenza) on the Padus. Aurelian advanced to a position between Mediolanum and the river to the north of the barbarians, intending to cut off their line of retreat. Instead, the Roman army fell into an ambush set up by detachments of the allied Germans, and the emperor suffered his first defeat. The Roman forces were scattered, leading to rumours that the empire was lost. In Rome labourers thrown out of work by the closure of the mint rebelled under the leadership of the procurator Felicissimus. They were also encouraged by elements in the senate, who saw Aurelian's defeat at Placentia as evidence that his authority was at an end.

This was far from being the case. The ill-disciplined barbarians failed to follow up on their victory and, instead of pursuing the disordered detachments

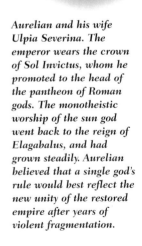

Aurelian and his wife Ulpia Severina. The emperor wears the crown of Sol Invictus, whom he promoted to the head of the pantheon of Roman gods. The monotheistic worship of the sun god went back to the reign of Elagabalus, and had grown steadily. Aurelian believed that a single god's rule would best reflect the new unity of the restored empire after years of violent fragmentation.

of the Roman army, they split into separate bands to plunder the rich countryside. Aurelian reformed his legions and began dealing with each band in detail. Two battles were fought near Ticinum (Pavia) at Fanum Fortunae in which the Germans were completely defeated and most of the host lost their lives. The few that succeeded in escaping north were allowed to flee; Aurelian had more vital matters to settle in Rome. He returned to the capital in anger, rapidly rounded up those senators who had suggested opposing his authority, and either confiscated their estates or had them executed. The rebellious mint-workers retreated to the Caelian hill and blockaded themselves inside the imperial mint, prepared to resist. But it was a hopeless cause against the skill of Aurelian's soldiers. In the resulting skirmish, thousands were wounded or killed, and their leader Felicissimus was executed on the spot. The surviving engravers were exiled to Serdica (Sofia), which no doubt accounts for the improved quality of minting there.

With peace restored in Rome, Aurelian began work on the massive monument for which history best knows his name, the Aurelian Wall. After consultation with the senate, work began in 271 to enclose the fourteen districts of the city first laid out by Augustus, including the previously unfortified district of Transtiberim (Trastevere) across the Tiberis (*see side panel*). The city had long outgrown the ancient Servian Wall, which had been allowed to fall largely into ruin by the mid-third century, much of its fabric looted for other buildings. The construction of this new wall was tantamount to admitting the future inability of Roman forces to prevent barbarians raiding into Italia and being capable of reaching as far south as the capital. In consequence several other cities also received new fortifications or had older ones refurbished.

The reduction of Palmyra

When, in the summer of 271, Zenobia assumed the title of Augusta and her son Vabalathus that of Augustus, Aurelian determined to return the eastern provinces to central Roman sovereignty. He anticipated little opposition in Asia Minor and Aegyptus, but expected that oriental Syria and Zenobia's heartland would be a tougher nut to crack. He decided on a double-campaign of encirclement, and designated a senior member of his staff, Marcus Aurelius Probus (not a relative of the defeated governor), with the conquest of Aegyptus, while the emperor commanded the second army, whose objectives were first to retake Asia Minor and then northern Syria. Probus sailed first and

encountered little resistance in the fall of 271 because Zenobia had decided to concentrate her army in Syria, and the Egyptian population was mostly pro-Roman. Aurelian left Rome at about the same time to concentrate the expeditionary force in Illyricum. This was formed from detachments of the legions of Raetia, Noricum, Pannonia and Moesia, supported by Dalmatian cavalry and other auxiliary contingents. His progress was delayed by an incursion of Goths into Moesia, but these were quickly overcome, and the army marched to Byzantium and then into Asia.

Since Zenobia had failed to secure Bithynia and her hold on Galatia had been at best tentative, Roman progress across Anatolia was swift and unopposed. The first opposition came at Tyana, a town guarding the passes through the Taurus Mountains. Infuriated its inhabitants' resistance, Aurelian promised his troops that when it was taken, they could sack the town and take all the booty that could be gathered. With the treacherous help of a local, some of Aurelian's men were able to work their way up and occupy a hill overlooking the walls, from which position the artillery soon persuaded Tyana to capitulate. Aurelian now reconsidered his promise and restrained his soldiers from plundering, and the town was spared. If the army was disgruntled at this change of heart, the victors were soon pleased to find city after city surrendering without resistance as news of Aurelian's clement policy spread.

With the willing submission of Cilicia, the way lay open to press on towards Antiochia, where the main body of the Palmyrene force under Zabdas was stationed. This was protected by heavy cavalry and infantry units posted along the banks of the Orontes to the north of the city. Aurelian now showed his flair for shrewd tactics by using his lightly armed Dalmatian horsemen to engage their heavily armoured opponents, but then to retire when attacked and wait for the heat of the sun to wear down the Palmyrenes. The repeated tactic worked, and the exhausted Palmyrene advance guard was completely defeated.

It was really only a skirmish, but Antiochia was cut off from Palmyra and Zenobia decided to abandon the city and withdraw to Apamea. Zabdas considered that their position was still dangerous, so the Palmyrenes fell farther back on Emesa. They were only allowed a short breathing space while Aurelian settled matters in Antiochia before the Roman army went in pursuit. After a short and decisive skirmish with a Palmyrene rearguard left at Daphne on the outskirts of Antiochia, Aurelian passed through Apamea, Larissa and Arethusa,

The Aurelian Wall

Construction of the Aurelian Wall continued throughout the life of the emperor and was not completed until the reign of Probus, c.278. It was built according to standard Roman army fortifications with an average width of 12 feet (3.7m) and a height of 20 feet (6m). At regular intervals of 98 feet (30m), rectangular towers of uniform shape were erected to accommodate heavy artillery to keep assailants from the wall, which had a circuit of some 12 miles. Since no soldiers could be spared for the project due to the impending Palmyrene campaign, Aurelian entrusted the work to the civilian building corporations under military engineers. The original wall's simple construction was necessitated by the civilian workforce's unfamiliarity with military fortifications.

The wall was not designed to withstand a concerted siege because the barbarians had no siege equipment; its primary purpose was to deter barbarian raids without hindering normal commerce. Accordingly, all major roads entering the city were given access through eighteen gates with a wide arch, protected by projecting semi-circular towers. The four principal gates spanning the Via Flaminia to the north, the Via Appia, Via Ardeatina, and Via Ostiensis to the south were double-arched to accommodate the extra traffic.

Aurelian's foresight proved to be faulty. Within only twenty-five years the emperor Maxentius was obliged to undertake a considerable reinforcement (although this was not to protect against barbarians but to resist the rival Roman army of Constantine). And at the beginning of the fifth century, the massive Visigothic invasion of central Italia induced the emperor Honorius to double the height of the walls and towers, reduce the width of the gateway arches, and make the principal gates single-arched. The original semi-circular towers were also reinforced with the addition of projecting square bastions.

Large sections of the wall can be seen today, especially in the south between the Porta Latina and Porta Ostiensis (San Paolo), enclosing the Baths of Caracalla. Close observation of the Porta Latina

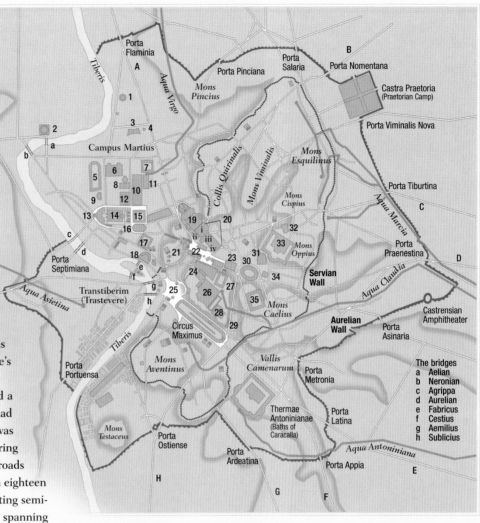

over the Appian Way reveals its history. Originally it had two arches and was faced with travertine. In the time of Honorius it was reduced to a single arch faced in marble and the crenelated wall above more than doubled in height. Aurelian's two semicircular towers were first enlarged and then raised before being reinforced by the square basements faced with marble that can be seen today.

1	Mausoleum of Augustus
2	Mausoleum of Hadrian
3	Solar clock of Augustus
4	Ara Pacis (now moved)
5	Domitian's Circus (Piazza Navona)
6	Baths of Nero
7	Hadrineum (Temple of Neptune)
8	Pantheon
9	Odeion of Domitian
10	Saepta Julia
11	Temple of Isis
12	Baths of Agrippa
13	Theatre of Pompeius
14	Porticoes of Pompeius (site of Julius Caesar's murder)
15	Largo Agrentina
16	Theatre of Balbus
17	Portico of Ocatavia
18	Theatre of Marcellus
19	Trajan's Forum
20	Imperial Fora: i) Augustus; ii) Julius Caesar; iii) Nerva; iv) Templum Pax
21	Capitol and Temple of Jupiter Optimus Maximus
22	Forum Romanum
23	Temple of Venus et Roma
24	Palace of Tiberius and Logia of Septimius Severus
25	Forum Boarium
26	Palace of Domitian
27	Temple of Elegabalus
28	Palace of Septimius Severus
29	Septizodium
30	Amphitheatrum Flavium (Colosseum)
31	Baths of Titus
32	Portico of Livia
33	Baths of Trajan
34	Ludus Magnus
35	Temple of Claudius

The main roads
A Via Flaminia
B Via Nomentana
C Via Tiburtina
D Via Praenestina
E Via Latina
F Via Appia
G Via Ardeatina
H Via Ostiense

which opened their gates to him, and came face to face with the Palmyrene army of some seventy thousand outside Emesa. Here, the tactics that had worked so well at Antiochia almost brought disaster on the Romans, but seeing that his light cavalry was being overwhelmed, Aurelian sent in the heavy Roman legions against the Palmyrene light infantry. The power-shock of massed Roman foot had rarely been bested in open battle, and it was no different at Emesa. The Palmyrene army was routed and the legions wheeled around to attack the enemy's heavy cavalry in its rear. Caught between the legions behind them and the reinvigorated Dalmatian horsemen to the front, the Palmyrene casualties were enormous. Zenobia and Zabdas retreated across the Syrian desert to Palmyra and prepared for a siege while they anticipated reinforcements from the Sassanians, with whom she had made a deal.

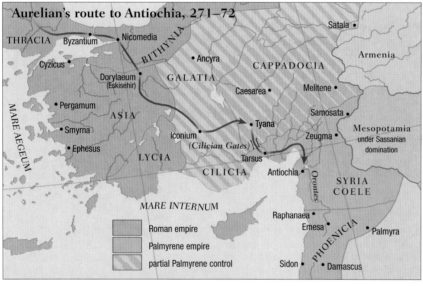

Aurelian's route to Antiochia, 271–72

Roman empire
Palmyrene empire
partial Palmyrene control

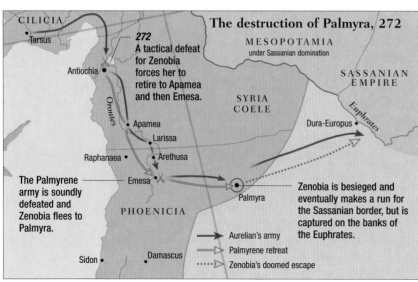

The destruction of Palmyra, 272

272
A tactical defeat for Zenobia forces her to retire to Apamea and then Emesa.

The Palmyrene army is soundly defeated and Zenobia flees to Palmyra.

Zenobia is besieged and eventually makes a run for the Sassanian border, but is captured on the banks of the Euphrates.

Aurelian's army
Palmyrene retreat
Zenobia's doomed escape

This was a nervous time for the besieging Romans. With Palmyra lying eighty miles from Emesa and surrounded by desert tribes fiercely loyal to Zenobia, Aurelian was concerned about his thin and vulnerable line of communication to the coast. In addition, he was worried about the possibility of Sassanian intervention. In the course of the siege Aurelian was wounded, and his men began to suffer from the summer heat and poor food. However, a flurry of diplomatic activity and the promise of financial reward eventually persuaded the nomadic tribesmen to switch allegiance. With the tables turned, the Romans had secure lines of communication and Palmyra was cut off. Starvation in the city was soon apparent and capitulation seemed inevitable, when Zenobia made a breakout and fled for Persia in mid-272. She was captured on the banks of the Euphrates by a cavalry detachment sent in pursuit and brought before the emperor. He received the queen politely, and waited for Palmyra to open its gates, which it soon did. Again, Aurelian forbade any plundering by the victorious troops, content with the capture of Zenobia, Vabalathus and the leaders of her independence faction.

A court was convened at Emesa to try the Palmyrene rebels, and in a shameful act of cowardice Zenobia blamed her ministers for her actions. The ringleaders were executed and the remaining prisoners, together with Zenobia and Vabalathus, were placed on ships to be sent to Rome for Aurelian's triumph. While crossing the Propontis, however, the vessel carrying the prisoners was shipwrekced in a storm, and only Zenobia and her son on their own ship survived to be paraded in Rome before the cheering crowds.

A swift conclusion of the Palmyrene business was called for because news of an invasion by the Carpi on the Danuvius had reached Aurelian. Leaving an EQUES called Marcellinus to govern Mesopotamia (in absentia, since the province was yet to be regained from the Sassanians, who had retaken it after Odenath's death), and a cavalry officer called Sandarianus as military governor of Palmyra, Aurelian set out for Moesia Inferior, which he reached in the fall of 272. A fierce campaign soon restored order and some of the invaders were settled in plague-depopulated areas of Moesia and Thracia. Palmyra, however, was not finished with Aurelian; he was about to go to Rome when he was handed a disturbing dispatch from Marcellinus. A certain Apsaeus had involved many leading Palmyrenes in a revolt and, despite its nationalistic character, had approached Marcellinus with a proposal of making him emperor. Loyal Marcellinus informed the conspirators that he would need some time to consider the proposal, and promptly sent a post-horse to the emperor with news of the alarming developments. Aurelian reacted with astonishing speed, and leaving Moesia crossed Anatolia by forced marches to reach Palmyra at the start of 273. However, the duration was long enough for Apsaeus to become distrustful of Marcellinus's intentions and proclaim another, Antiochus, king of Palmyra. He raised the standard of rebellion by attacking Sandarianus, who was killed together with his garrison of six hundred archers.

Luckily, the time had been insufficient for the Palmyrenes to reconstruct the city's fortifications, and it was taken without a fight. This time Aurelian did not hold back his troops and Palmyra was thoroughly sacked. Because of his insignificance Antiochus was spared, but the other rebel leaders were executed. Next, the army hastened south to Aegyptus, where a merchant called Firmus, probably a member of Zenobia's party, had organised a rebellion in concert with Apsaeus. However, this had not spread widely through the province, and Aurelian's speed in reaching Palmyra deterred further malcontents from joining Firmus. Shut up with his confederates in a suburb of Alexandria, Firmus's stronghold was quickly invested, and he committed suicide rather than fall into the emperor's hands. Aurelian had the walls of Alexandria razed as a preventative to further rebellion.

Reunification and state control

With peace secured along the Danuvius and – with the exception of Mesopotamia – the eastern provinces returned to Roman sovereignty, Aurelian was free at last to deal with the Imperium Gallorum. As has been recounted, Aurelian met Tetricus in the early spring of 274 near Cavillonum and was victorious. After settling the most urgent administrative matters in Gallia, he appointed Probus to the command of the Rhenus troops and returned to Rome before the spring was out to celebrate his victories, justifiably satisfied with his work. In less than four years he had established peace along the frontiers and restored the eastern and western provinces lost under Gallienus; for his efforts the populace hailed Aurelian as RESTITUTOR ORBIS (restorer of the world). According to the ancient sources, Aurelian's triumph in Rome surpassed any previous celebration. Zenobia and Tetricus were present as captives in the procession, but mindful of arousing ire among the senatorial order at the sight of one of their members so humiliated, Aurelian restored Tetricus to his rank and estates, and awarded him with high

office. Zenobia too was given her freedom and settled with a pension in a villa near Tibur (Tivoli). Of her son Vabalathus, would-be Augustus of the East, nothing more is heard.

An urgent reform of the monetary system became the first of Aurelian's priorities, without which internal stability could not be guaranteed. The rampant inflation caused by Gallienus's depreciation of the coinage had led to a collapse of faith in the currency. However, faced with a shortage of precious metals for minting, Aurelian's reforms were makeshift at best. Instead of recalling the mass of worthless *billon* introduced by Gallienus, he attempted to restore confidence in its face value through better workmanship and a slightly improved ratio of silver and gold to base metal. With a proper coating, the new money had the appearance of true silver or gold coins, although its intrinsic value was hardly improved. This solved only a part of the problem, but through other enforced reforms to the food supply and its pricing, the emperor lessened the gap between the value of the currency and the inflated cost of goods.

Aurelian's reforms were aided by the overthrow of Palmyra and the recovery of the eastern provinces, which resulted in a gradual increase of wealth from official confiscations and re-established revenues to the FISCUS. As a result he was able to relieve the populace from the food shortages, which in turn helped to reduce the prices of goods. The middle class of less wealthy equestrians also benefited when he cancelled all arrears to the FISCUS, and his popularity soared in consequence of his publicly burning the debt records in the Forum of Trajan. For the mass of citizens Aurelian's reign marked a return to the kind of state-controlled care that had obtained in the days of the Antonines and Severi. He regulated the cost of bread by fixing the price the COLLEGIUM PISTORUM (millers' and bakers' guild) could sell a loaf, but in return increased the supply of corn coming from Aegyptus so that the bakers should not lose out. In addition, he replaced the badly managed and almost defunct system of the corn dole with a daily distribution of two pounds of bread free of charge to all registered citizens; a right that became hereditary.

In this respect Aurelian went further than any emperor before him by extending the dole to provisions such as pork, oil and salt. However, these benefits came at the price of freedom among the COLLEGIA of butchers, oil processors and bakers, whose previously voluntary associations were transformed into compulsory ones, and may even have been subject to military control. There is evidence for this in the new barracks constructed in the vicinity of the FORUM SUARIORUM intended for the COLLEGIA SUARIORUM, or pork wholesalers. That they were to work in a barracks and that their activities were strictly controlled by the PRAEFECTUS URBI indicates the degree to which military discipline was applied to the food traders. There is no visible indication that similar barracks were built for the two other meat COLLEGIA: BOARII (beef dealers) and PECUARII (mutton dealers), but it seems likely. Aurelian had done the same with the builder's craft guilds involved in constructing Rome's new defensive wall. In this, we see that Aurelian's reforms were designed to extend the supremacy of the state over the lives of all citizens, a hegemony that would be increased greatly by Diocletian and Constantine in the fourth century.

Religious and military reforms

Aurelian's most visible innovation was the establishment of Sol Invictus at the head of the Roman pantheon of gods. He had a temple to Sol built and invested members of the senate to be its priests. As we have seen, the worship of Sol in this particular form had been established by Elagabalus and affronted stern Romans, but unlike Elagabalus Aurelian made no attempt to identify himself with the god he revered. Nor was the worship of Sol Invictus accompanied by any of the oriental excesses of Elagabalus. The institution of the religion has political significance. Throughout the third century the empire had been increasingly drawn towards a form of monotheism, which was often at odds with the political aspirations of its rulers. There was, therefore, a need to find a universal deity whose manifestation incorporated the huge variety of cults, while at the same time centralising individual worship in the state religion. Aurelian felt that, having restored unity to the empire, all its citizens should join in common recognition of its majesty. In earlier times this had been achieved through the imperial cult, but the period of anarchy had debased the cult's prestige, and now Aurelian focused the emotional needs of the empire through the widely spread worship of the sun. During this period, and for some time thereafter, the traditional imperial headwear of oak leaves mutated into the 'rays' of the characteristically spiked gold diadem of Sol Invictus, which a few previous emperors had worn; forerunner of the crowns of medieval kings of Europe.

The improved fortification of Italian cities was not echoed along the northern frontiers, probably because of the shortness of Aurelian's reign. On the Rhenus,

Probus reoccupied part of the LIMES GERMANICUS abandoned to the Alamanni in 258 but not to lasting effect, and the Alamanni returned to the Agri Decumates in 275, after which the region was lost to the empire. Aurelian himself repelled a renewed invasion of the upper Danuvius in late 274, and made repairs to the LIMES RAETICUS, but further downriver he was forced to accept the vulnerability of Dacia to repeated Gothic invasions. Reluctantly, he decided to abandon the province and save the ruinous cost of garrisoning it. On the credit side, moving the romanised population to the river's southern shore went a long way towards repopulating the provinces of Moesia, Pannonia and Thracia that had been ravaged by barbarian invasions and the recurrent plague. Accordingly, Aurelian created a new province of Dacia and another called Dardania out of parts of the two Moesias and Thracia, and established the Dacian legions, *V Macedonica* and *XIII Gemina*, at Ratiara (Arar) and Oescus, making Serdica (Sofia) the capital.

He raised two new legions, *I Illyricum* and *IV Martia*, drawn from among the population of Illyricum but stationed in Phoenicia and Arabia. The creation of these Illyrian legions underlines Aurelian's intention of stationing troops of European loyalty in the eastern provinces. However, establishing the frontier with Persia meant retaking Mesopotamia, and this was to be the programme for 275. In preparation Probus was reassigned to Aegyptus, there to strengthen the frontier made uncertain by the revolt of Firmus.

Before setting out for Antiochia the sixty-year-old emperor was obliged to suppress a revolt at Lugdunum (his ruthlessness was to leave a bitter taste for years) and repel a German invasion near Vindelicia, the region of Raetia in the vicinity of Augusta Vindelicorum (Augsburg). Then he gathered his Illyrian legions and headed for Byzantium — but never reached the city. While encamped at Caenophrurium, situated between Perinthus and Byzantium, the emperor's confidential secretary, Eros, fearing for his life after being caught out in a lie, circulated a forged document among several of the senior staff. It purported to be a list of officers Aurelian had condemned to execution for one reason or another. Eros had shrewdly used his knowledge of military politics to ensure that each man would have some misdemeanour on his conscience and had wisely added his own name to the list to convince them of his trustworthiness. Knowing Aurelian's notoriety as a disciplinarian, the group did not hesitate to march to his tent and murder him. Thus, in such utter silliness, died one of Rome's greatest emperors.

TACITUS

*Marcus Claudius Tacitus Pius Felix Invictus
Augustus (r.c.November 275–April 276)*

There was an INTEREGNUM of about a month, during which Aurelian's wife Ulpia Severina may have reigned, since some of her coins were issued after her husband's death. If this was so, it was with the senate's tacit approval in the hope that it would avoid public unrest. The emperor's murder created a unique situation, in which the Illyrian soldiers refrained from naming his successor. This was partly because they liked Aurelian and did not want to appear part of the officers' conspiracy by profiting from naming their own choice, and partly because of Marcus Aurelius Probus. As Aurelian's most devoted supporter, the Illyrians wanted to discover Probus's wishes in the matter of succession, And, in abstaining from any precipitate decision, they hoped to avoid giving the eastern troops the opportunity to proclaim their own emperor. As a result, a situation developed that had no precedent: the soldiers referred the decision to the senate. During the INTEREGNUM the senate accorded Aurelian divine honours in appeasement of his troops, and deliberated on his successor. In such a novel situation, their debate might have become protracted were it not for news of renewed unrest on the northern frontier that urged speed. Their choice was Tacitus, a consular and already seventy-five years old.

No reliable information exists on Tacitus prior to his consulship with the PRAEFECTUS VIGILUM Julius Placidianus in 273. The attempt of the *Historiae Augustae* to link his ancestry to the Trajanic historian Gaius Cornelius Tacitus should be completely discarded. At the time of his elevation he was in Interamna (Terni), from where he made his way to Rome to accept the instruments of power. It would be simple to interpret his accession as a revival of senatorial authority over the soldiers, but nothing in Tacitus's six months on the throne indicates any such thing. Indeed, the reigns of Tacitus and his successor Florian were little more than an extension of the INTEREGNUM that followed Aurelian's death before the proclamation of Probus, his obvious successor. Were it not for the conspiracy that ended Aurelian's life and inter-army jealousy, neither would have become emperors.

Tacitus made his first business the seizure and execution of Aurelian's murderers, and his second the appointment of his half-brother Marcus Annius Florianus (Florian) as his PRAEFECTUS PRAETORIO.

Despite his advanced years, Tacitus proved to be extraordinarily energetic. A horde of Heruli Goths – apparently recruited by Aurelian for the Persian campaign – had overrun Asia Minor after the expedition had been cancelled by the emperor's murder. Cheated of their opportunity for plunder, the barbarians ravaged through Pontus, Galatia, Cappadocia and as far south as Cilicia. Tacitus and Florian rounded up the barbarians and, by a mix of arms and persuasion, drove them back home. Tacitus had appointed another family member to be governor of Syria, but this Maximinus exercised such a harsh administration that a plot was formed to assassinate him. Having killed Maximinus, the angry conspirators, blaming Tacitus for their oppression, followed him as he made his way back to Europe and killed him.

Tacitus was 75 years old when he was chosen for the purple.

FLORIAN

*Marcus Annius Florianus Pius Felix Invictus
(r.c.April 276–c.July 276)*

Tacitus's death led to renewed civil war. Florian assumed the purple as a hereditary right without waiting for the soldiers' proclamation or the senate's recognition. However, within three weeks the eastern legions proclaimed Probus emperor. Believing he had the numerical advantage, Florian reversed his army's direction and marched south to engage Probus, but he had underestimated his opponent.

Probus had not risen to his position under Aurelian without demonstrating an astute military ability. Aware of his disadvantage in numbers, he employed Fabian tactics and avoided a pitched battle at Tarsus, where the two sides met. Using the rugged terrain, Probus's experienced Egyptian troops kept drawing out Florian's Europeans, who became demoralised and then, when disease broke out among them, mutinous. Unwilling to face a prolonged campaign in adverse conditions, Florian's men chose the easy option and murdered him.

Florian, half-brother of Tacitus, quickly became the victim of renewed civil war.

PROBUS

Marcus Aurelius Probus
(r.c.May 276–c.September 282)

Marcus Aurelius Probus had already enjoyed a long, distinguished military career by the time he was proclaimed emperor.

Probus, a native of Illyricum, like the other two great warrior-emperors of the third century, was born in August 232 at Sirmium. During his reign he continued Aurelian's consolidation of the frontiers and the reconstruction of Gallia, which, as he had discovered during his tenure on the Rhenus in 274, was still vulnerable to barbarian attack. He returned from Cilicia in order for the senate to ratify his imperial powers, and then immediately left Rome for Gallia, where separate bands of Longiones backed by Alamanni had crossed Germania Superior by way of the Nicer (Neckar) valley and Franks in the north had crossed the Rhenus. Probus split his force and sent his DUCES to oppose the Franks while he tackled the Longiones. Both armies were victorious, and Probus captured the Longiones' chieftain, Semnon, together with his son. A treaty was agreed, and Probus set Semnon and his son free.

Another German tribe, the Burgundi, had come to the Franks' aid, and Probus moved north to confront them across the Rhenus. The enemy was by far the stronger numerically, and Probus again demonstrated his military shrewdness. He arranged for his troops to line the Roman bank and shout obscenities at the Germans. In short order the easily insulted barbarians took the bait and began to cross the river to reach their sneering tormentors, but their disorderly advance placed them in a perilous position. Roman archers began to pick off the advancing warriors wading waist-deep in the strong current and those that made it to the left bank were not allowed to organise themselves before the legions fell on them. Terms were offered to the defeated Burgundi, but when they refused to hand over all their prisoners of war, Probus attacked again and captured their leader, Igillus. The prisoners were enlisted and distributed among the provincial garrisons, including one contingent that was sent to serve in Britannia. There, they were to demonstrate their loyalty to the emperor by refusing to support the province's governor when he attempted to rebel against Probus.

A concerted programme of new fortifications was begun, as well as repairs to forts that had become dilapidated during the period of the Imperium Gallorum. Many new forts were constructed on the eastern bank of the Rhenus to command all the major river crossings and provide protection for Roman towns in Germania Inferior and Superior, and Gallia. One of Probus's peculiarities was a passionate belief in viticulture as a means of stabilising the economy. He had many vineyards planted throughout the western provinces, including Britannia, where the climate was more clement than it is today and where the grapes flourished reasonably, particularly in the south.

In 278 Probus was in Illyricum, repelling an invasion of Vandals, and restoring security in the provinces (as well as planting more vineyards). And in 279 he was in Lycia, which was being plagued by Isaurian brigands. These warriors took refuge in the mountain fortress of Cremne, from which they were eventually ousted through a betrayal by a disgruntled bandit who felt he had suffered unfairly at the hands of their leader, Lydius. The region had never been properly romanised, so Probus established colonies of army veterans on their own land in return for the service of their sons when they reached the age of eighteen. In time these men would become the backbone of the Eastern Byzantine empire, albeit their history of brigandage would always present their masters with problems.

In Aegyptus a desert tribe called the Blemmyes broke through the southern border and advanced northwards along the Nilus in 280, capturing the cities of Ptolemais Hermiou (El Manshah) and Coptos (Qift, now a small village). This did not occupy Probus himself, and he was content to allow some of his DUCES to eject them, which was swiftly done, while he organised the large-scale reconstruction of the dykes, canals and bridges along the Nilus. It was the first time since the reigns of Trajan and Hadrian that this had been done properly, and the increase in productive land led to a dramatic improvement in Rome's grain supply. During the time he spent in Aegyptus, Probus had been planning a campaign against the Sassanians to recover Mesopotamia, but this was cancelled when news of a revolt in Gallia and unrest on the frontiers demanded his attention in Europe. It is possible that a treaty was agreed with the new king, Vahram II, which suited the Sassanid ruler because he was still consolidating his reign after the death of Shapur I in 272. It also suited Probus, since he could leave the eastern provinces, reasonably sure that there would be no immediate Persian activity against Roman interests.

On the way across the Balkans, he prevented the worst effects of a barbarian invasion of a Scythian tribe, the Bastarnae, from afflicting the Illyrian provinces by allowing their settlement on lands in Thracia. This was part of the continuing policy of the later third century of repopulating the devastated region after the plague epidemics, but it was also a factor in the degeneration of the empire. Taken in combination with their enrolment as levies in the army, whole swathes of the frontier regions were being barbarianised. Eventually, there would come a time when almost all the legions were comprised of men who had more sympathy with the tribes it was their duty to repel than with the Roman state they had sworn to serve.

The rebellion in Gallia centred on Lugdunum, whose inhabitants were still smarting from the harsh treatment meted out to them by Aurelian. A native of nearby Albingaunum, who had accumulated his wealth through banditry and was connected with the Franks, had raised the standard of revolt. How he intended to succeed is not known, unless he hoped for military aid from his Frankish allies, but faced with the sudden appearance of the emperor at the head of his legions, the fight went out of the rebels. At the same time Bonosus, one of Probus's DUCES, revolted. Commander of the Rhenus fleet, Bonosus had somehow let a band of Germans capture and burn a squadron of ships. Fearful of Probus's retribution, he took shelter in having himself proclaimed emperor. Despite his carelessness with the fleet, Bonosus appears to have been a good soldier because the rebellion required considerable force in its suppression. The fighting was only stopped when Bonosus, despairing of his position, hanged himself. Probus spared the lives of his sons and wife. This affair may have had repercussions elsewhere in Hispania and Britannia. The slight evidence at Valentia is the erasure of Probus's name from official inscriptions. The unnamed governor's revolt in Britannia – in which the recently arrived Burgundi refused to take part – was put down by Victorinus, who was consul with Probus in 282.

Indirectly, the emperor's devotion to growing grapes at every opportunity and the state of relative peace along the Danuvius contributed to his downfall. Mindful of the danger caused by under-employed soldiers, as part of his agrarian reforms Probus put the legions stationed at Sirmium to reclaiming the marshy land around the city. After celebrating a triumph in Rome, Probus set out for Illyricum in the summer of 282, intending to mobilise the army for a renewed attempt to recover Mesopotamia. While he was at Sirmium news arrived that the army in Raetia had proclaimed Probus's PRAEFECTUS PRAETORIO Carus, who was in command there, as emperor. Angered by the labourers' work they had been subjected to in recovering the swamps for the planting of vineyards, the soldiers at Sirmium sided with their fellows in Raetia, rose up in mutiny and murdered Probus.

CARUS
Marcus Numerius Carus / Marcus Aurelius Carus (r.c. September 282–c. August 283)

As soon as Carus heard of Probus's murder, he sent a dispatch to the senate to announce his elevation by his troops. He nominated first his elder son, Marcus Aurelius Carinus, and soon after his younger son, Marcus Aurelius Numerianus (Numerian), as joint rulers with himself, and gave them each the rank of Caesar.

Carus was a break with the run of Illyrian emperors, since he appears to have been born in Narbo (Narbonne). He was probably in his early fifties at his accession in 282, which can only be inferred from the knowledge that he possessed two sons and an adolescent grandson. Disdaining any senatorial approval, Carus did not bother to visit Rome, but leaving Carinus as Caesar of the European provinces, made for Syria with Numerian to complete Probus's plans for the reconquest of Mesopotamia. To further strengthen his dynastic ties he arranged the marriage of Numerian to the daughter of Arrius Aper, his appointed PRAEFECTUS PRAETORIO.

In a short reign, Carus accomplished much. Marching through Pannonia, his army defeated forces of Quadi and Sarmatae that had broken into the province. The Romans encountered little resistance from Sassanian border guards on the Euphrates, and once again Mesopotamia was returned to Roman sovereignty. Carus now invaded Persia by way of Armenia and marched down the Tigris. King Vahram II – still distracted by domestic challenges to his authority – was unable to mount a concerted opposition. The Romans reached the capital, Ctesiphon, and Carus added the title Parthicus

Sassanian king Vahram II, successor to Shapur I.

Carus's reign was short, but he achieved much.

Bonosus, Probus's commander of the Rhenus fleet, had himself made emperor to avoid his master's retribution for having lost a squadron of ships to marauding Germans.

Maximus to his titles. He was pressing further south when he suddenly died in late July or early August 283. The circumstances of his death are mysterious. Illness is the most plausible explanation, but several reports suggested that lightning struck him down. Of course, he may have been the victim of an assassination, but the smooth succession of Numerian points to death by natural causes.

Right: The brothers Carinus and Numerian as co-Augusti. Numerian (below) had no stomach for war and abandoned his father's Persian campaign.

Right: Carinus and coins of his wife Magnia Urbica and their son Nigrinianus. Carinus was made of sterner stuff than his younger brother, had campaigned under his father, and continued to do so against the Quadi when he became emperor. His character would be denigrated after his death, and he became known as 'the evil emperor Carinus' for his supposed brutality and sexual voraciousness.

NUMERIAN
Marcus Aurelius Numerianus
(r.c.August 283-c.November 284)

CARINUS
Marcus Aurelius Carinus
(r.c.August 283–July 285)

Unlike his father, Numerian shuddered at a soldiers' life. The rigours of military campaigning held no attraction for him, and he much preferred studying literature and writing his own prose. It is not known whether he concluded any treaty with Vahram, although subsequent events point to the fact that he just left Persia without making any diplomatic contact at all. By March 284 he was in Emesa and apparently in good health; some Christian traditions also place him in Antiochia at some point, where he is said to have ordered the martyrdom of the bishop (later St. Babylas). So the story goes, at some point after leaving Emesa, his vision became impaired, and he took to riding in a litter to protect his eyes from the sunlight. This seclusion provided his father-in-law Arrius Aper[†] with the opportunity to kill his weakling emperor. For some days the PRAEFECTUS kept the crime secret, until the imperial bodyguard noticed the odour of decay issuing from the litter. A more likely explanation is that Numerian expired from an illness and his staff officers colluded in concealing his death from the troops until a suitable successor could be found.

The discovery of the body led to an assembly in Nicomedia on 20 November 284, at which Valerius Diocles, COMES DOMESTICORUM (commander of the cavalry arm of the imperial bodyguard), accused Aper of assassinating Numerian. Diocles personally executed the PRAEFECTUS PRAETORIO for the crime and the troops proclaimed Diocles emperor. Once again, the soldiers had followed the precedent of making and unmaking emperors in quick succession, but in the elevation of Diocles they had made an emperor whose like Rome had not seen since Trajan.

The death of his father Carus in Persia left Carinus, as the elder of the two Augusti, responsible for maintaining a semblance of order among the soldiers. There is evidence that he continued his father's campaigns against the Quadi, before spending the winter of 283–84 in Rome, where he also commenced his second consulship, with Numerian

---

† The preferred name is Arrius, but some historians call him Flavius Lucius (or even Lucius Flavius) Aper. Since several PRAEFECTI PRAETORIO were named Aper, the confusion is understandable.

as his colleague. A poetic source claims that Carinus visited Britannia in 284 to conduct a campaign of some sort, and assumed the title Britannicus Maximus, also shared with Numerian. However, the date contradicts his inscription found at a villa situated between Sorviodunum (old Salisbury) and Vindocladia (Badbury), dated to 282–83. His title on the stone is CAES. This suggests his presence in the province as Caesar under his father, and the timing of the events that followed makes the later (poetic) date extremely unlikely.

Soon after receiving news of Numerian's death, Carinus had to mobilise an army to deal with a usurper called Marcus Aurelius Julianus, who had risen in revolt in Illyricum (possibly on the borders of northern Italia). Carinus drew soldiers from the German legions and left the Rhenus frontier dangerously under-protected, and then met Julianus near Verona. Carinus was the victor, and encouraged by success, proceeded into Illyricum to meet Diocles. The rival emperors met in Moesia in the valley of the Margus in July 285.

According to historical tradition, the army of Carinus was on the point of victory when the emperor was treacherously slain by a trusted officer (but whose wife he had allegedly seduced). The story of Carinus's murder is consistent with the negative literary tradition that referred to him as 'the evil emperor Carinus'. He is depicted as a bloodthirsty tyrant, executioner of senators, rapist of their wives and murderer of those who had teased him when they were together in school. The *Historiae Augustae* records that he had nine wives and ignored his real wife, Magnia Urbica. It is doubtful that Carinus had either the time or the energy for such excessive sexuality, and if he was – as the more warlike of the brothers – brutal, he was surely no better nor worse than any run-of-the-mill third-century emperor. The literary damnation of Carinus was almost certainly orchestrated by his successor in what was, by now, a time-honoured tradition of rewriting history; and the man who followed Carinus was certainly able to do that.

Marcus Aurelius Julianus: he usurped the purple in Illyricum, but was defeated by Carinus, who in turn fell foul of an assassin during the battle on the Margus against the usurper Diocles – now known as Diocletian.

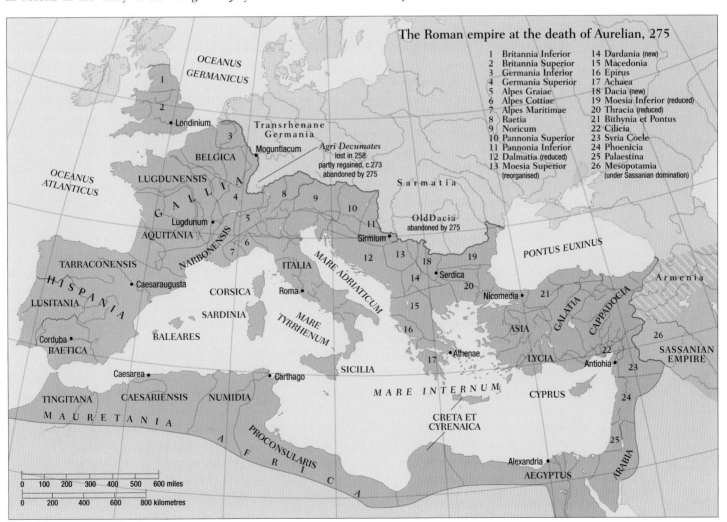

The Roman empire at the death of Aurelian, 275

1	Britannia Inferior	14	Dardania (new)
2	Britannia Superior	15	Macedonia
3	Germania Inferior	16	Epirus
4	Germania Superior	17	Achaea
5	Alpes Graiae	18	Dacia (new)
6	Alpes Cottiae	19	Moesia Inferior (reduced)
7	Alpes Maritimae	20	Thracia (reduced)
8	Raetia	21	Bithynia et Pontus
9	Noricum	22	Cilicia
10	Pannonia Superior	23	Syria Coele
11	Pannonia Inferior	24	Phoenicia
12	Dalmatia (reduced)	25	Palaestina
13	Moesia Superior	26	Mesopotamia
	(reorganised)		(under Sassanian domination)

CHAPTER ELEVEN AD 284–313
THE TETRARCHY

DIOCLETIAN

Valerius Diocles / Gaius Aurelius Valerius Diocletianus
(r.20/11/284–1/5/305 abdicated; d.3/12/311)

MAXIMIAN

Marcus Aurelius Valerius Maximianus
(Caesar summer 285, co-Augustus
1/4/286–1/5/305 abdicated; reinstated
November 306–November 308; d.July 310)

In a reign spanning more than twenty-one years, Diocletian altered the course of the Roman empire beyond recognition. Not only did he convincingly end the phase known as the Military Anarchy, his reforms also laid the foundations for the way the empire would be governed from this time on, and ultimately secured its continuity in the East for more than a thousand years. This state of affairs did not come about through harbouring any sentiment towards past tradition or custom. Indeed, Diocletian completed the process begun over three hundred years earlier by Augustus, of consolidating absolute power in the hands of one man and then delegating portions of responsibility to a few hand-picked subordinates who reported only to the emperor. From this point in history, the role of the senate was reduced to that of a (sometimes) useful body of consultants; to be treated courteously, listened to when the advice made sense, but otherwise ignored.

Valerius Diocles was born in about 245 on the coast of Dalmatia, possibly at Salonae (Solin) or nearby Spalatum (Split)[†]. Of low birth, in childhood he would have received little formal education, which makes his later achievements all the more astonishing. He had a wife Prisca and a daughter Valeria. As a native of Illyricum he had easy access to a military life and, in the newly democratised army, a path to the higher echelons of command. Although he owed his promotion to his undoubted military abilities, he seems to have had misgivings about his merit as a strategist, and frequently left the tougher planning decisions to his generals. As Diocletian rose through the ranks, his prudent decisions as an officer appear to have been concerned with victory rather than personal

Above right: Diocletian, creator of the tetrarchy, in his later years.

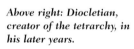

[†] Modern histories sometimes use Salonae and Spalatum interchangeably, but the two were distinct in Roman times.

glory. Under Carus he found favour with the emperor and was appointed to the rank of COMES DOMESTICO-RUM. In 283 he served as a consul.

The forty-year-old who won the battle on the Margus in July 285 would now emerge as a complex mix of attributes: clever politician, cunning manipulator, able administrator, passionate architect, by turns clement and harsh – a set of characteristics best summed up as 'fair but cruel'. He adopted an unexpected kindness towards the officials who had held posts under Carinus, and reconfirmed their appointments. He even went so far as to step into the consulship left vacant by Carinus and share it with Aristobulus, who had been Carinus's colleague of choice.

Diocletian was faced with many problems. The reunified empire was far from secure, internally or externally. The chief obstacle to the maintenance of imperial unity was the ever-present possibility of military revolts. While these threatened, no real progress was possible in securing the frontiers from barbarian invasion, let alone attending to an urgently required reform of the government, which was his long-term goal. If military revolts were to be avoided, it meant that the emperor would have to assume command in all major campaigns, thus denying generals victories that might induce their troops to proclaim them.

This policy of imperial mobility, which lay at the heart of everything Diocletian did, predicated two innovations. Rome was too far removed from the regions of military activity, and so could no longer feature as the administrative centre, and if the emperor was forever on the move, the court must be mobile too. The place of the resident court officials, the PALATIUM, situated in the Palatine palace, was taken by a 'travelling staff' of the emperor's companions (the COMITATUS). Diocletian was a practical statesman and he understood that an omnipresent emperor could not deliver the level of action required to achieve his aims. He had no son to whom he could depute some of the duties while maintaining overall command, and so he followed the precedent set by Nerva of appointing a worthy colleague as his partner.

His choice fell on Maximianus, an Illyrian officer born in about 249–50 at Sirmium and a close friend some five years his junior. In character Maximianus was the opposite of Diocletian; while the latter was a shrewd statesman, the former was typical of his countrymen, uncultured and often brutal, but a superb strategist. The emperor was therefore able to entrust command of the frontiers into the hands of an expert, while taking comfort that their deep-rooted friendship would prove a safeguard against a possible usurpation. Diocletian appointed Maximianus Caesar in the summer of 285, and he adopted the names of Marcus Aurelius Valerius Maximianus (Maximian). To further emphasise the nature of their relationship, Diocletian assumed the title of JOVIUS and gave the title of HERCULIUS to Maximian, for Jove was the father of the gods, the supreme controller, while Hercules was the god of the earth. Diocletian now moved his peripatetic court to Nicomedia, from which he issued forth on military assignments when his presence was required, while Maximian took command of the western provinces, making Mediolanum his capital.

Maximian's first priority was Gallia, which had fallen prey to barbarian raids across the Rhenus as a consequence of Carinus's severe depletion of troops in 284. The reduced garrisons had also allowed the Bagaudae, a roving band of brigands under the leadership of chiefs Aelianus and Amandus, to cause widespread damage throughout the province. The revolt had closed the roads connecting to the frontier and so needed to be subdued with urgency. Maximian found these rebels a difficult challenge because they adopted guerrilla tactics to which his soldiers were unaccustomed. However, the rebels were suppressed by the spring of 286 and his troops proclaimed him Augustus on the first day of April. This was exactly the kind of situation Diocletian had hoped to avoid, but he wisely acceded to the mens' claim and, by recognising Maximian as co-emperor, he prevented any discord. Edicts were now issued in their joint names, but

Maximian's reverence of his friend's intellect meant that Diocletian retained supreme power over the legislation. There was no division of the empire between the two Augusti, and although Diocletian normally resided at Nicomedia and Maximian at Mediolanum, both campaigned far from their headquarters as the occasion demanded.

In the two years from 286 Maximian restored order along the upper Rhenus, which was not a simple task. An alliance of Alamanni and Burgundi had crossed the river at numerous points between its source and Moguntiacum. Although the incursions appeared too vast to encompass, the Romans were aided by the devastated, barren countryside. Famine decimated the barbarians' numbers and plague reduced them further. The outcome was a number of skirmishes during which Maximian acquired prisoners for his eventual triumph in Treveri (as Augusta Treverorum was now known), after which the remnant fled across the Rhenus and fell into a civil war. Along the lower Rhenus the Franks had found new allies among the Heruli Goths and Chaibones, a warrior-people from the distant parts of eastern Transrhenane Germania. Maximian was able to split the allies and defeated the Chaibones near Colonia Agrippina, before crossing the Rhenus to fight the Franks. In a great battle on the river's east shore his PRAEFECTUS PRAETORIO, a vigorous man in his thirties called Gaius Flavius Valerius Constantius, won Maximian a great victory. At this point Gennobaudes, one of the Frankish chieftains, proposed a treaty. In return for being named king of the Franks and protected by Rome in his authority, he and his warriors would swear allegiance to the empire. Thus, in 288, the first ever barbarian client kingdom was set up as a buffer state on the northern frontier.

The Gallic coast had become a haven for Saxon and Frankish sea-pirates in the latter years of the Imperium Gallorum. To deal with the problem, Maximian established a base at Gesoriacum† (Boulogne) and put its operations under the command of an experienced sailor called Carausius, a native of Menapia (the region that lies between the modern Rhine and Scheldt estuaries). This appointment was based on an uncharacteristically

This coin of Maximian bears the image of the fighting god Hercules on the reverse to attest to the co-Augustus's adopted title of HERCULIUS, god of the earth. His partner Diocletian, as senior, had the title JOVIUS, father of the gods.

---

† Modern Boulogne in France and Bologna in Italy both derive their names from the same Latin word 'Bononia', Bononia Felsina in Italia and Bononia Gesoriacum in Gallia. The location is usually referred to simply as Gesoriacum to avoid confusion.

The usurper Carausius first made Britannia his base, then extended his power along the Gallic coast.

Having forced Diocletian and Maximian to accept his power, Carausius struck this coin, showing him with his 'co-Augusti'.

poor judgement of character. Carausius's efforts met with immediate success, but instead of turning over the booty to the provincial authorities, he used it to enlarge his fleet and power base. Instead of destroying the pirates' ships, he claimed them for himself and enlisted the sea-raiders to man them. On hearing of Carausius's disobedience, Maximian ordered his execution, but the proscription was leaked. To protect his own interests Carausius proclaimed himself Augustus and slipped across to Britannia with all his ships in 287. Maximian ordered the fitting out of a punitive fleet, but bad weather and poor seamanship brought it to disaster. Having established his authority in Britannia, Carausius was able to return to Gallia and recover Gesoriacum. He extended his hold along the coast and made an alliance with the Franks of the Low Country. For the time being Maximian and Diocletian were obliged to acknowledge Carausius's power, which – either as a snub or a peace offering – he proudly proclaimed on his coins that showed him as the third Augustus alongside his 'colleagues'.

In 289–90 Maximian faced another uprising of the Alamanni, who had crossed the upper Danuvius into Raetia. This time, encumbered by other disruptions, Maximian required Diocletian to assist in their ejection. In the two years following, Maximian led punitive expeditions into Alamanni territory, which quietened them for several years.

Meanwhile, Diocletian spent much of his time sandwiched between the lower Danuvius and the eastern provinces. While he was in Syria in 288, he took advantage of Vahram II's continuing internal strife and tidied up the situation left by Numerian's abrupt evacuation of Persia. An Arsacid, Tiridates III, was placed on Armenia's throne, returning the country to the Roman sphere of influence. Further, Diocletian compelled Vahram to give up his claims on Mesopotamia. On the lower Danuvius, Diocletian prosecuted two successful wars against the Sarmatae in 289 and 292, and subjugated an invasion of Saracens in Syria in 290. In 291 he was needed in Aegyptus on the upper Nilus to put down another rebellion of the Blemmyes.

Creation of the Tetrarchy

After about eight years' experience of rule, much of it spent warring in widely spaced theatres, Diocletian was becoming convinced that the constitutional arrangements he had made in 285 were inadequate to govern the modern Roman empire. It was clear that two rulers could not be expected to meet all the demands made of them, and the failure to dislodge Carausius was a direct consequence of their lack of administrative resources. Accordingly he decided to apply mitosis to the imperial cell by appointing two Caesars to help the Augusti. Since Diocletian had no sons and Maximian's son Maxentius, aged about ten, was far too young, the adoption of non-family members was repeated in dual ceremonies held simultaneously in Mediolanum and Nicomedia on 1 March 293. Diocletian nominated one of his staff officers, Gaius Galerius Valerius, who adopted the name Maximianus, thereby further strengthening the ties between the two Augusti, and Maximian nominated his PRAEFECTUS PRAETORIO Constantius.

Diocletian wished to enforce the unity of what became known as the tetrarchy (rule by four) through inter-marriage as well as adoption. It is not clear whether Constantius had already married Theodora, Maximian's stepdaughter, or whether he put aside his mistress Helena in order to marry Theodora at this time. By Helena he had a twenty-year-old son called Constantinus (Constantine). Galerius was compelled to divorce his wife in order to marry Diocletian's daughter, Valeria. Because of his slightly greater age (about forty-three at the time), the Augusti made Constantius the senior of the two Caesars, and each respectively had conferred on them the titles of JOVIUS and HERCULIUS. With this collegiate board of rulers, Diocletian had dissolved the problem of constitutional succession that had so plagued the principate. In theory, each Augustus would abdicate as he reached the appropriate age for retirement, and his adoptive-nominate Caesar would take his place as Augustus, in turn immediately nominating his own Caesar. In theory it was a stable political system and it had the advantage that each new Augustus would first gain experience of government as a Caesar. Nor were the two new Caesars limited in their IMPERIUM, as Maximian had been in 285. They were given an equal share in the TRIBUNICIA POTESTAS, were allowed to issue coinage in all their names, and shared in the honorific titles and any victory won by any of the tetrarchs.

Finally, each tetrarch was entrusted with approximately one quarter of the empire to rule. Diocletian assumed responsibility for the eastern provinces including Aegyptus, Maximian received Italia, Germania Inferior and Superior, and the provinces of Africa and Hispania. To the Caesars, Galerius was assigned the Balkans as far as the Oenus (River Inn) in the west, and Constantius received Gallia and

Britannia. There was no legal definition of these assignments, which were largely based on expediency, and the two Augusti were free to enter either of the two Caesars' territories when required.

With Gallia and Britannia in his realm, it fell to Constantius to subjugate Carausius; in preparation, he promptly left Mediolanum and established his capital at Treveri. The first phase was designed to drive Carausius out of Gesoriacum and away from the Gallic coast, and for this purpose Constantius had flotillas built on all the rivers of the region, which issued from the estuaries and attacked the outlying enemy ships. The tactic succeeded in its principal aim, but failed to draw out Carausius's main fleet, which went into hiding behind the bulk of Vectis (Isle of Wight). Wisely, Constantius refrained from undertaking a seaborne invasion until he was better prepared, and turned instead on Gesoriacum. In 293 the city was besieged and finally fell after the Romans constructed a barrage across the harbour mouth to prevent any relief reaching it from Britannia. Constantius then attacked northwards across the low-lying coastal plain of Belgica, driving Carausius's Frankish allies back into their forest domains. For this failure, Carausius lost his authority in Britannia and fell victim to an assassination plot orchestrated by his chief minister Allectus, who assumed the usurped title of Augustus in his place.

The restoration of Britannia to the Roman empire was delayed for another three years while Constantius made his preparations for an invasion. When it came in 296, retribution against Allectus was swift. Two fleets were used, one under Constantius sailed from Gesoriacum, the other under his PRAEFECTUS PRAETORIO Asclepiodotus from the Sequana (Seine) estuary. The British fleet stationed in the sound between Vectis and the mainland was rendered ineffective because of thick fog, in which Asclepiodotus slipped past to land at Clausentium (Bitterne). Allectus, who did not know that the fleet of Constantius was approaching his capital of Londinium along the Tamesis (Thames), marched south to meet Asclepiodotus, but was defeated and killed. Constantius arrived in time to prevent the destruction of Londinium by renegade detachments of Allectus's army and, with the taking of the city, the province of Britannia was fully restored to Rome.

In previously driving back the Franks from their alliance with Carausius, Constantius had captured many prisoners. He treated them in a similar manner to the way Maximian had Gennobaudes, and by granting them land on the island of the Batavians (the region of south Holland), he established a Frankish tribe, the Salii, who would have a profound impact on the events of the sixth century. As Allies, the Salian Franks served Rome under the command of the governor of Germania Inferior. Thus, through the diplomatic efforts of Maximian and Constantius, the Franks were bound – for the time being – to the empire through settlement and treaties, and Roman authority was firmly re-established in Gallia. The Alamanni, on the other hand, were not so easily placated. In 298 a band raiding some forty miles from the Rhenus in Germania Superior attacked Constantius and his bodyguard. He was only saved by reaching a fortified town in the nick of time, and then in a counterattack was lightly wounded. Infuriated, the Caesar drove the Alamanni back across the river.

Between 293–96, Galerius was successful in his provinces along the Danuvius, developing the region's economic and agricultural life while engaging in several frontier wars with the Marcomanni and Sarmatae. And then in 297 Diocletian appointed him commander-in-chief of the army detailed for war with Persia, and Maximian took over from Galerius in Illyricum. Among the Augustus's achievements was a defeat of that ancient foe the Carpi that was so complete the tribe was erased from the list of barbarian invaders. In the following year Maximian campaigned in North Africa against a Berber confederation the Romans called the Quinquegetani (five peoples) that had broken through the Numidian frontier. The war was swift and successful, and Maximian returned to Italia to visit Rome for the first time in his reign.

The causes of the looming war against the Sassanid Persians had its roots in 293, when the unhappy reign of Vahram II ended with his death and the coronation of his son Vahram III. The son found it even harder to secure united support for his rule, and he was overthrown after only four months by Narses, a man more in Shapur's mold. Diocletian had already spoken of the 'hostile Persian nation' in 296, the year that a Sassanian army entered Armenia and threw out the Roman client king Tiridates III installed by Diocletian eight years earlier. Narses declared war on

The tetrarchs show their unity in this sculpture, now to be found in Venice.

Former chief minister, then murderer, of Carausius, Allectus declared himself Augustus in Britannia. He held on to the title for three years.

Rome and began an advance on Syria. Galerius moved to oppose him, but the war opened disastrously for the Romans. Either through poor intelligence or because he underestimated the enemy, Galerius took insufficient forces with him as he crossed the Euphrates at Niceophorium (also Callinicum, now Raqqa). Between there and Carrhae (Harran) the two armies met, and the Sassanians won a great victory. Mesopotamia fell again into Sassanid hands. Ancient sources say that Diocletian was so angry at this defeat that he publicly humiliated Galerius by making him run beside his chariot for a mile.

His own sense of failure was probably punishment enough for Galerius, who hastened to make good his reputation. In the following year (298), reinforced with detachments taken from Illyricum, he routed the Sassanians from Armenia, taking a huge booty that included the royal harem. Narses was so anxious to recover his possessions that he sued for peace. Galerius demurred, but Diocletian overrode the Caesar's wishes and made a treaty favourable to Rome. Not only was the province of Mesopotamia returned, it was extended north to the Tigris, and the client kingdom of Armenia was also extended to include the Caucasian Iberia. Further, merchants trading between the two empires were obliged to use the road that passed through the Roman garrison town of Nisibis, where they had to pay customs duties. The peace thus established was to last for forty years.

One other event of importance occurred in Diocletian's sphere of influence, one that was to have sweeping consequences for both the army and provincial government. It was probably in the summer of the same year that Narses overran Armenia – perhaps even taken as an example – that a certain Lucius Domitius Domitianus had himself proclaimed Augustus at Alexandria. However, the historical sources refer to the usurper as Aurelius Achilleus, yet the coins he issued from the Alexandrian mint are the physical evidence for Domitianus, inscribed IMP. C. LVCIVS DOMITIVS DOMITIANVS AUG. This suggests that there were in fact two different usurpers. The coinage extends over two years corresponding to Diocletian's twelfth and thirteenth years of reign, 296 and 297. But Diocletian only arrived in Aegyptus early in 298 and suppressed the rebellion by putting the usurper Achilleus to death. We must, therefore, suppose that Domitianus either died of natural causes or was killed by his successor in the summer of 297. Whatever the motive for this revolt, Diocletian viewed it as a nationalist rising that proved any weakening of central government

could have fatal consequences. He determined on a radical series of changes to the way the empire would in future be organised and governed. As Septimius Severus had once done with Britannia and Syria, the emperor planned on further dividing provinces into smaller units, the better to avoid large states within the empire falling into the hands of ambitious governors. He was to go much further than Severus.

Reforms of the army and provinces

At the beginning of his reign Diocletian had stated his aims of returning good, sound government to the empire, and twenty years of (almost) uncontested rule provided the conditions to allow reforms that laid the basis for late Roman government and social organisation. Under his direction undisguised absolutism came to the Roman empire, which made implementing the many changes a far simpler task than any of his predecessors had faced. Two of the most important reforms affected provincial organisation: the division of the old provinces into smaller administrative units, and the total separation of military and civil power.

The basic structure of the Roman provinces had remained largely unchanged since the time of Septimius Severus, who completed the reorganisation of Augustus. Diocletian began a process of further dividing the provinces into more compact units. Only the smallest, such as Sicilia, were left untouched; others were either halved or further divided into fractions†.

Some of the provincial governors were still selected from the among the senators, but all the appointments were in Diocletian's hands, and what had been a nominal control by the senate now almost disappeared entirely, with only two small provinces left in its preserve to govern. The new administrators were responsible to a PRAEFECTUS PRAETORIO, except for Africa and Asiana, whose governors reported directly to the emperor and were still called proconsuls. Of the remainder the two consular governors were styled CONSULARES, the praetorian CORRECTORES, and a governor of equestrian rank was given the generic title of PRAESES, who had the rank of PERFECTISSIMI.

This division had a twofold benefit in further reducing the power of individual governors, and making local administration more effective and efficient, particularly in view of his taxation reforms (*see side panel on page 174*). Control of the PRAESIDES was organised by grouping the provinces into twelve

Domitius Domitianus's short-lived usurpation of the purple in Alexandria in 296 led Diocletian to institute wide-ranging reforms within the provinces to strenghten central government.

---

† This process continued under later emperors until by the fifth century there was in excess of 120 provinces.

dioceses: Oriens, Pontica, Asiana, Thraciae, Moesiae, Pannoniae, Italia, Viennensis, Galliae (frequently also called Septem Provinciae), Britanniae, Hispaniae and Africa. Each dicoese was placed under a new equestrian official, the VICARIUS, who acted as a representative of the PRAEFECTUS PRAETORIO of each tetrarch. The PRAEFECTI, who had not held a military command over the praetorian guard since the reforms of Hadrian, retained judicial powers and had supreme command of the armies of the empire. However, this praetorian power was regulated by giving the VICARI direct access to the tetrarch; it was the Augusti and Caesars, not the PRAEFECTI, who heard any appeals from the VICARI. Thus Diocletian reduced the danger associated with the monopolisation of power by chief ministers. Italia and the praetorian guard were the great losers in this restructuring. The proud Latin heartland of Italia was broken up into fourteen provinces of its own diocese and treated like any other region of the empire; eventually, even its traditional tax-exempt status would be removed. As for the praetorians, Diocletian reduced them to no more than the garrison of Rome.

The process of correcting the weaknesses inherent in the Augusto-Severan military reforms had begun under Gallienus, but Diocletian went much further. In the Augustan system provincial governors and army LEGATI were usually appointed because of their social or political status and not for their military skills, so they frequently had little army experience. Gallienus had already removed from senators the command of troops in provinces where legions were stationed, giving it instead to officers of equestrian rank. But in smaller provinces under equestrian control, civilian and military functions were still combined. Diocletian made the separation absolute, except in Mauretania and Isauria (the new province of western Cilicia in the dicoese Oriens), where unsettled conditions demanded the sole command of military and civilian administration. From this point on, command of the frontier armies was in the hands of professional career soldiers styled DUX (DUCES in the plural). The term had already gained common currency, but under the tetrarchy it became an official ranking.

Under Augustus the legions and corresponding AUXILIA, raised from among provincials who had not yet received citizenship, were stationed in the imperial frontier provinces, with no provision made for reserves. To conduct a war meant denuding other sections of the frontier, leaving them open to barbarian attack – a situation continuously repeated throughout the chaos of the third century. The Roman army had also been deficient in cavalry, its relatively few units provided by the AUXILIA. Gallienus had been the first to recognise the necessity of a larger cavalry force with independence from the infantry, and Aurelian had expanded the notion. Further development now created a fully mobile field army to complement the increasingly stagnant LIMITANEI (frontier garrisons), with an ever greater emphasis on cavalry.

On his accession Diocletian had some forty legions at his disposal and, in accordance with his greater division of the provinces, it is possible that he increased this number to as many as sixty, although many of these may have been below the strength of the old standard. The objective was to spread the available resources more efficiently throughout the frontier provinces, and ensure their support from the increased AUXILIA so that draining manpower from adjacent provinces should no longer be necessary. Additionally, the independent cavalry gained in importance as the mobile arm of the field army. This is highlighted by the name used to describe the cavalry, VEXILLATIONES – the term that had once described infantry detachments of the Republican legions. Diocletian and Maximian also detached mobile units from their legions to act as reserves, encamped at way-station towns such as Aquileia. Others formed an elite cavalry corps called the SCHOLAE PALATINAE, which effectively replaced the praetorians as the imperial bodyguard and travelled wherever any of the tetrarchs went, providing a highly motivated stiffening to the garrison troops. Contemporary critics claimed Diocletian quadrupled the army's size, but doubling it seems more likely.

Taxes and the division of labour

Of course, the increase in the size of the army and the added burden of expanded provincial administration meant more and new taxes to pay for them, and highlighted the problem of spiralling inflation that had resulted from the period of anarchy. Diocletian had new gold coins struck at a greater rate of metal purity and created a new silver standard. While these measures restored confidence in the face value of the currency and helped to stabilise the economy, they did not go far enough. The problem was that copper did not hold its value anything like as well as gold and silver. The result was a continuing inflation as expressed in copper coin, the basis for everyday commerce among the empire's populations. To offset this, in 301 Diocletian issued his EDICTUM DE PRETIIS (Edict on Prices) for the protection of the poor. Maximum legal

The reorganisation of the empire by Diocletian, showing the new dioceses and provincial boundaries

prices were imposed on a wide range of products and services, although critics like the contemporary writer Lactantius claimed that the measure was a complete failure because it served only to drive goods off the market and into a black economy. Perhaps the very fact that for the first time in fifty years a government was seen to be enacting legislation in such meticulous detail had a psychologically beneficial effect. Certainly many sites have produced fragments of the massive, inscribed edict.

One effect of the new taxation system was a grading of the population into classes, each with an obligation to the state. While this process had been ongoing since

Republican times, Aurelian had introduced a greater degree of state involvement in the system and now Diocletian brought rigid control to what had been a voluntary service among the nobility and, among the lower classes, a natural inclination for son to follow father in trade. He benefited from Aurelian's militarisation of the various COLLEGIA, which more easily allowed him to effectively regulate the workforce. Diocletian decreed that no worker might leave his COLLEGIUM or change his trade, and sons were legally bound to follow their father's vocation. The compulsory occupations included soldiers, builders, bakers, members of town councils, and COLONI (tenant farmers), to name but a few.

Below: Diocletian in his earlier years sported a beard.

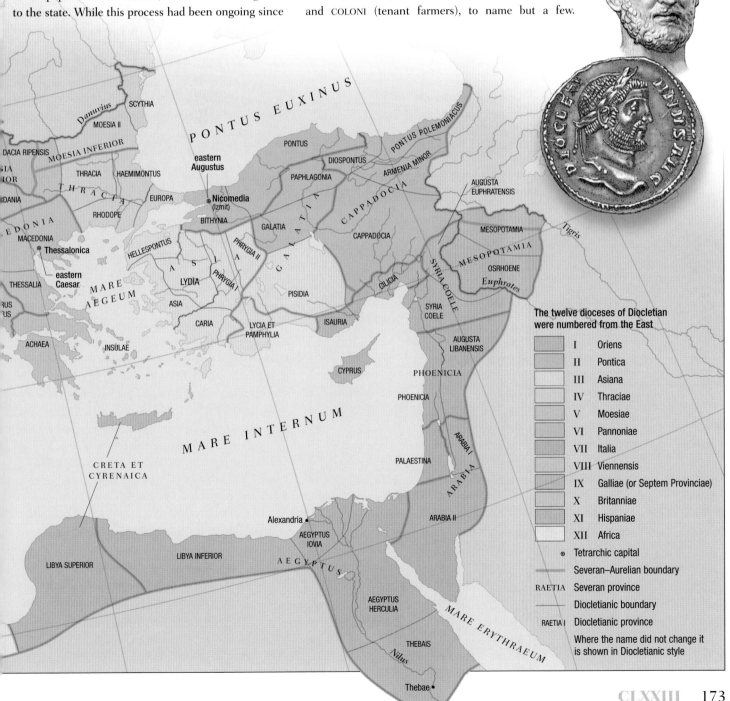

The twelve dioceses of Diocletian were numbered from the East

I	Oriens
II	Pontica
III	Asiana
IV	Thraciae
V	Moesiae
VI	Pannoniae
VII	Italia
VIII	Viennensis
IX	Galliae (or Septem Provinciae)
X	Britanniae
XI	Hispaniae
XII	Africa

⊙   Tetrarchic capital

Severan–Aurelian boundary

RAETIA   Severan province

Diocletianic boundary

RAETIA I   Diocletianic province

Where the name did not change it is shown in Diocletianic style

Although promotion was not made impossible, the privilege was jealously guarded. The policy created a caste system throughout the empire that stifled initiative, dampened ambition, reduced land workers to virtual slavery and proved ultimately detrimental.

Fourth-century writers credit Diocletian with the adoption of many forms associated with an oriental monarchy. Layers of court officials, eunuchs and chamberlains restricted access to his presence, and he was rarely seen in public. He introduced the ceremony and etiquette of the Persian court, which included ADORATIO – the prostration of those granted an audience and the kissing of his garment's purple hem. Diocletian was no longer addressed as princeps or by

the soldierly IMPERATOR but as DOMINUS NOSTER (Our Lord). It would be easy to see these developments as the self-aggrandisement of a power-crazed tyrant, but his abdication after twenty years of rule negates this view. In the same way that he had identified himself with JOVIUS – although not with the godhead – the attributes of a glorified potentate were the essential means of establishing the emperor's abiding and supreme authority.

Diocletian's oriental courtly manifestations echoed those of Aurelian, but Diocletian did not elevate Sol Invictus to the head of the Roman pantheon, returning that honour to Jupiter Optimus Maximus, who is also JOVIUS. In fact, unlike Aurelian, Diocletian was very conservative in his religious beliefs and practices, and he made offerings to numerous Roman and oriental gods. His devotion to the old religion meant that he was averse to any new creeds that might undermine the empire's unity. His distrust first manifested itself against the Manichaeans, adherents of a Persian creed that blended Zoroastrianism, Christianity and Neo-Platonism. But it was from the Christians that he met with the strongest opposition. There was no official persecution of Christians during the early years of his reign, which may be attributed to his wife and daughter's profession of the faith, or perhaps his underestimation of a Church suffering from schism.

This situation changed abruptly in 302. The blame is usually laid at the feet of Galerius, an uncompromising opponent of Christianity who after his Persian victories had gained considerable influence with Diocletian. Christians were expelled from the court and any soldiers who persisted openly in their faith were cashiered. On 23 February 303 Diocletian issued an edict to compel Christians to worship the state's gods in the face of fierce penalties. Two further edicts aimed at the clergy led to mass arrests and even executions, and in 304 extended the provisions of the third edict to cover all Christians. For the first time, an anti-Christian edict included the closure of churches, their destruction and the burning of sacred books.

Diocletianic tax reforms

The many tax reforms were progressively introduced and added up to the establishment of a standard unit of taxation, based on the labour and animal stock employed on agricultural land, and on the area of land owned. This resulted in a calculated unit of liability, which was subjected to a rate of taxation applied

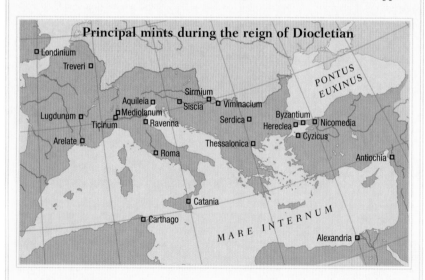

Principal mints during the reign of Diocletian

uniformly throughout the empire, the rate altering depending on the annually predicted needs of the FISCUS. However, with his attention to detail Diocletian refused to accept such a simplistic method of assessing a unit of liability. It needed to be an equitable system to be both practical and fair (and so avoid localised unrest). Therefore, allowances were made to take into account the fertility of the land, available modes of cultivation and the cash-value of the resulting type of crops that could be grown. For the first time, the Roman government was able to budget. After estimating the annual outlay and dividing the figure by the number of tax-payer units in the empire, or any part of it, the rate of taxation could be calculated. These measures and the increased complexity of tax legislation led to an enlarged bureaucracy, which became typical of the late Roman period. Lactantius moaned that Diocletian's tax reforms resulted in an empire that contained more tax-collectors than tax-payers.

Diocletian, constitutional architect

According to Lactantius, Diocletian was a mad builder. '*He had a limitless passion for building, which led to an equally limitless scouring of the provinces to raise workers, craftsmen, wagons and whatever was necessary for building operations. Here he built basilicas, there a circus, a mint, an arms-factory, here he built a house for his wife, there one for his daughter.*' Diocletian only visited Rome once, yet he did not stint on its monuments. He made extensive repairs on a lavish scale to many buildings in the centre that had been damaged by a fire that broke out in the Theatre of Pompeius in 284. The theatre's colonnade was restored, as were the Basilica Julia and a range of temples surrounding the Forum Romanum. The fire also destroyed the senate house, and despite having little use for its members, Diocletian had a new CURIA built, which still stands today. Most extensive were his glorious baths, the largest in Rome, capable of holding three thousand bathers.

However, most of his public works were undertaken in the provinces, especially at Nicomedia. Here, ascerbic Lactantius tells us, the spate of building was such that: 'Suddenly a great part of the city was destroyed, and all the inhabitants started to migrate with their wives and children, as if the city had been captured by the enemy. And when these buildings had been completed and the provinces ruined in the process, he would say: "They have not been built rightly; they must be done in another way".' For himself, Diocletian built a massive palace at Salonae on the Dalmatian coast overlooking the Mare Adriaticum. It was modelled on a Roman army camp and more resembles a medieval king's castle than the familiar open Roman palace. To these undertakings should be added the extensive attempt to create a LIMES along the border regions of Arabia, Syria and Palmyra. New roads and a series of forts and fortified towns linked Bosra in the south to Nicephorium on the Euphrates in the north. Similar work was done along the Danuvius, completing the task of restoring to the empire a new security.

Diocletian made his only visit to Rome as an emperor towards the end of 303, together with Maximian, to celebrate Diocletian's twenty years of rule in a month-long series of festivities commencing on 17 November. Diocletian was about fifty-eight and suffering from some chronic complaint – a reason given for his acceding to Galerius so easily over the Christian persecution – and wanted to order the moment of his abdication. If he alone stood down, it would leave Maximian, a soldier not an administrator, as senior Augustus, with Constantius as his colleague, thus condemning Galerius to serve as Caesar to Maximian, whom he despised. The solution was for both Augusti to abdicate simultaneously, and each to promote their Caesar. This was not what Maximian wanted, and it took Diocletian all his persuasive powers to obtain his consent, finally extracted as an oath in the temple of Jupiter Optimus Maximus. The timing set for joint abdication was in the spring of 305,

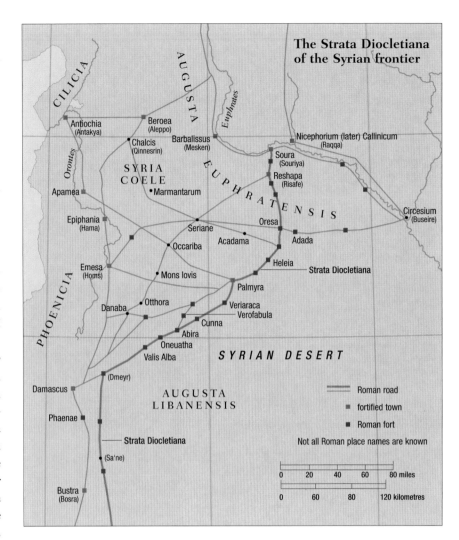

The Strata Diocletiana of the Syrian frontier

after Maximian had also celebrated his VICENNALIA.

The obvious choices to succeed Constantius and Galerius as their Caesars were hereditary: Maximian's twenty-year-old son Maxentius and, his elder by some nine years, Constantine the bastard son of Constantius. Maxentius had married Galerius's daughter Valeria Maximilla, and in 298 Constantine had been betrothed to Maximian's infant daughter Fausta. Constantine had already distinguished himself in service to Galerius against the Persians in 298 and under Diocletian against the Sarmatae in 299, but Maxentius seems to have been passed over for military commands, probably reflecting Diocletian's doubts over his qualities as a future Caesar. The detestation Galerius felt for Maximian extended to his son (despite his being Galerius's son-in-law), which also counted against his promotion. Diocletian was, therefore, faced with a dilemma: could he afford to pass over the legitimate son of an emperor, in favour of the bastard of a Caesar? Maximian's abdication promise would not withstand such a slight, and so neither was chosen.

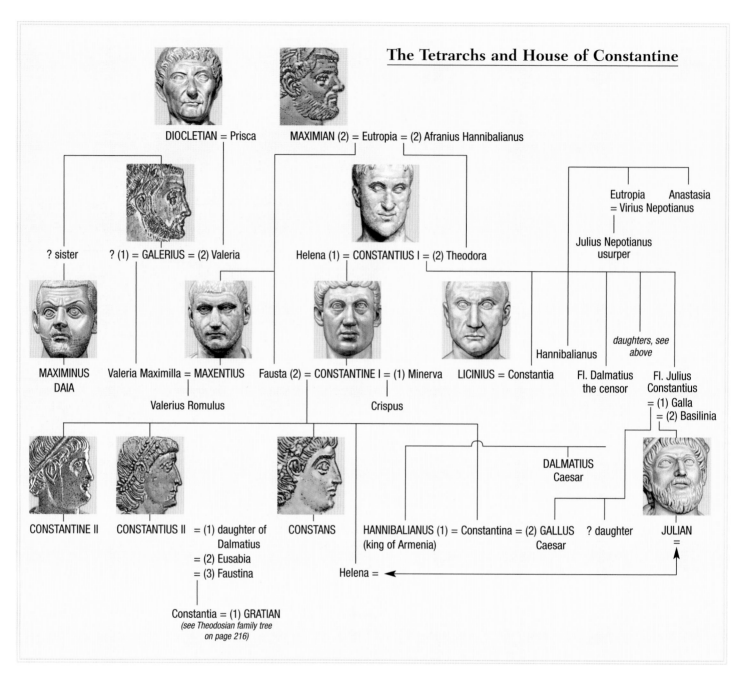

The Tetrarchs and House of Constantine

DIOCLETIAN = Prisca   MAXIMIAN (2) = Eutropia = (2) Afranius Hannibalianus

Eutropia   Anastasia
= Virius Nepotianus

Julius Nepotianus
usurper

? sister   ? (1) = GALERIUS = (2) Valeria   Helena (1) = CONSTANTIUS I = (2) Theodora

Hannibalianus   *daughters, see above*

MAXIMINUS DAIA   Valeria Maximilla = MAXENTIUS   Fausta (2) = CONSTANTINE I = (1) Minerva   LICINIUS = Constantia   Fl. Dalmatius the censor   Fl. Julius Constantius = (1) Galla = (2) Basilinia

Valerius Romulus   Crispus

DALMATIUS Caesar

CONSTANTINE II   CONSTANTIUS II = (1) daughter of Dalmatius = (2) Eusabia = (3) Faustina   CONSTANS   HANNIBALIANUS (1) = Constantina = (2) GALLUS (king of Armenia)   Caesar   ? daughter   JULIAN =

Helena = ←

Constantia = (1) GRATIAN
(see Theodosian family tree on page 216)

On the first day of May 305 at Nicomedia and at Mediolanum, Diocletian and Maximian formally abdicated in the presence of their soldiers, becoming SENIORES AUGUSTI and PATRES IMPERATORUM ET CEASARUM. Diocletian announced the elevation of his choice of Caesars to serve the new Augusti Constantius and Galerius. Lactantius tells us of the troops' bafflement at Constantine being passed over and their bewilderment at hearing the names Flavius Valerius Severus (a friend of Galerius, but less popular with the troops) and Galerius's nephew Maximinus Daia read out. Shortly after these ceremonies, Diocletian retired to his palace at Salonae, there to raise vegetables on the

extensive roof-gardens, and Maximian retired to Lucania in the south of Italia. While unwell and worn-out, Diocletian was content to watch the outcome of his dynastic scheme from his cabbage patch, but Maximian was restless in his retirement. As a result of these arrangements, the next eight years would be a time of civil war, although quite different in character from any of the previous upheavals. While some protagonists would strive for sole IMPERIUM, others would seek to secure a position as Caesar or Augustus within the tetrarchic structure. The events of 305–13 reveal a complex pattern of intrigue and treachery, open war and quickly made alliances, as quickly broken.

CONSTANTIUS I CHLORUS

Gaius Flavius Valerius Constantius (Caesar 1/3/293, co-Augustus 1/5/305–25/7/306)

GALERIUS

Gaius Galerius Valerius Maximianus (Caesar 1/3/293, co-Augustus 1/5/305–early May 311)

Born into a noble Dardanian family on 31 March c.250, Constantius Chlorus ('the pale') entered into military service early and due to his abilities found swift promotion through the ranks to become governor of Dalmatia before serving as PRAEFECTUS PRAETORIO to Maximian. He was about twenty-two when, while serving in Pannonia in 272/3, his mistress Flavia Julia Helena bore him a son called Constantinus (Constantine). History remains hazy about Helena's actual relationship with Constantius at the time; due to the influence she would have on the spread of Christianity many legends were later fostered. One of the more important of these was the absolute assumption that she was the legal wife of Constantius, thus making Constantine, the first Christian emperor, a legitimate son. Helena was born at Drepanum (later renamed Helenopolis) on the Gulf of Nicomedia. If they *were* married, Constantius

divorced her in about 292 in order to marry Flavia Maximiana Theodora, stepdaughter of Maximian. Of this union there were six children – all boys, according to Eutropius – including Flavius Dalmatius and Flavius Julius Constantius. Eutropius, however, was wrong because there were at least two daughters, Constantia and Anastasia. Constantius's career as Caesar to Maximian is covered above.

Some five years younger than his colleague, Galerius was born in Dacia Ripensis near Serdica (Sofia) at a small settlement later renamed Romulianum after his mother Romula – a woman from beyond the Danuvius; nothing of his father is known. His family were peasants, and Galerius was a herdsman as a youth. Uneducated and tough, Galerius also found fortune by entering military service, rising to the rank of PRAEFECTUS PRAETORIO to Diocletian, after which, his career as Caesar is also detailed above. The name of his first wife, who bore him a daughter, Valeria Maximilla, remains unknown, but he divorced her in 293 to marry Galeria Valeria, Diocletian's daughter; and he also had a son, Candidianus, by an unknown mistress.

An accurate historical assessment of the characters of the two new Augusti is inevitably difficult due to the prejudices of the later Christian writers. Galerius, of low birth and held responsible for the terrible Christian persecution, is portrayed as a monster, while Constantius of noble birth, father of Constantine the Great, and known to have largely disregarded the Diocletianic religious edicts, is a wise and kindly ruler. However, if the acts of their reigns are used as the measure, these prejudicial portraits are shown to be reasonably fair to the facts. Constantius gained tremendous respect and even affection among the provincials of Gallia and Britannia, whereas Galerius was direct and vigorous, a man of action, but also an unimaginative

Left: Constantius I Chlorus, father of Constantine the Great, was much loved but died a year into his reign.

CONSTANTIUS HAD little opportunity for monumental building, but Galerius lavished money on his capital of Thessalonica in the eighteen years of his reign as Caesar and Augustus. An unusual four-way arch was erected to celebrate his triumph over the Sassanid Persians in 298, its piers decorated with busy reliefs depicting religious and military scenes. This stood astride the Via Egnatia, linking the massive palace complex on one side of the road to his mausoleum on the other. The palace contained a large circus (or hippodrome in the Greek-speaking eastern provinces) as well as private apartments and civic audience halls. Despite the imperial splendour of his mausoleum, which survives today as the church of Agios Giorgios, Galerius was interred at his home town of Romulianum.

administrator, and frequently cruel. Had Constantius survived longer than a year as Augustus, he might have grown into a worthy successor to Diocletian.

Soon after the inauguration in August 305 the members of the second tetrarchy made a new distribution of the empire between them. Hispania was added to Constantius's holdings of Britannia and Gallia. His Caesar, Severus, took over the African diocese and Italia, and Pannonia was removed from Galerius and given to him. In compensation Galerius was given command over the whole of Asia Minor west of the Taurus mountains as well as the remaining Illyrian and Balkan provinces. His Caesar, Maximinus Daia, received the remainder of the eastern provinces and Aegyptus. Because of their respective rankings as Caesars Constantius became the senior tetrarch. However, Galerius's subordination meant little, for both the new Caesars were his men – Maximinus the son of his sister, Severus a long-time close friend – and neither seemed to possess the strength of character to counter his will. Thus, through Severus, he exercised considerable influence in Constantius's dominions, and effectively ruled three-quarters of the Roman empire. In addition, Constantius's son Constantine, residing with Helena at Byzantium, within Galerius's dominion, besides being a useful tribune represented a convenient hostage in any potential confrontation with Constantius.

This unhappy situation was altered at the end of year when news of a massive invasion of Pictish tribes in northern Britannia arrived at Treveri. Constantius appealed to Galerius to release his son to help in repelling the barbarians from his diocese. Probably much against his better judgement, Galerius complied, and Constantine left Byzantium immediately to cross Europe. Relieved at this news, Constantius went to Gesoriacum to begin preparations for the British campaign and his son – now a mature man of thirty-three – joined him there. In the early spring of 306 the expeditionary force crossed the narrow Fretum Gallicum. During his twelve years of rule, Constantius had managed to restore order, discipline and confidence in the British garrison since the chaos years of the Imperium Gallorum and the depredations of Carausius and Allectus. With a stiffening of detachments from Gallia, the campaign to evict the Picts was swift and completely victorious. Constantius assumed the title of Britannicus Maximus for the second time and retired

Galerius and his second wife Galeria Valeria, daughter of Diocletian; he was to have a fraught political relationship with the rising Constantine.

to Eburacum (York), where suddenly he died on 25 July 306. His COGNOMEN Chlorus refers to his pale skin, which may have been due to a wasting disease such as leukaemia. His untimely death in his fifty-sixth year almost wrecked Diocletian's tetrarchic system.

Constantine had ever been a popular figure with the eastern army, and in a short space of time achieved a similar level of affection among the western troops. The British and Gallic armies had no hesitation in proclaiming him Augustus in his father's place and – wisely or not – he accepted. There can be little doubt that he wished to avoid a return to the uncertainties of being a hostage to Galerius, and making his own claim for recognition was the best way to prevent such a situation arising. However, wishing to avoid civil war, he wrote to Galerius requesting confirmation of his elevation. While waiting for the reply, Constantine took the mobile units of his army back to Gallia to deal with a minor revolt of Franks, and then went south in force to Narbonensis, a move that – in its proximity to Italia – might be interpreted as passively threatening.

If Galerius had thought to raise Severus to Augustus and nominate another of his own creatures to the rank of Caesar, the acclaim of the western army for Constantine thwarted him. Mindful also of his own troops' affection for Constantine, he offered a compromise that recognised Constantine at the lower rank of Caesar to serve under Severus as Augustus. Partly because Constantine did not feel strong enough yet to dispute Galerius, and partly out of respect for Diocletian's constitutional arrangements, he accepted this inferior status, and so the tetrarchy survived in its original structure.

SEVERUS II
Flavius Valerius Severus
(r.Caesar 1/5/305;
co-Augustus August 306–March/April 307,
abdicated, d.16/9/307)

MAXENTIUS
Marcus Aurelius Valerius Maxentius
(r.28/10/306–28/10/312)

As has been related, Maxentius had been passed over by Diocletian in 305, along with Constantine, but while the latter was now a Caesar, Maxentius was no more than a young PRIVATUS dwelling in Rome, married to Valeria Maximilla, the daughter of Galerius, who had borne him a son named Valerius Romulus.

Given Diocletian's estimate of Maxentius's abilities, it is less likely that ambition drove him to a *coup d'état* than that he was raised to the purple by the praetorian guard. Having reduced the number of cohorts, Diocletian had also affronted the guards' dignity by downgrading them to lowly garrison status for the city of Rome. Galerius now took the further step of abolishing the CASTRA PRAETORIA. In Maxentius, the remaining praetorians in concert with the COHORTES URBANAE, who had shared the camp, saw a means of avenging themselves on Galerius. The common people also gave their full support to Maxentius because Galerius had decided to tax them as part of the Diocletianic Italian provinces – something that had never happened in imperial Rome's history. With a loathed census for taxation purposes in the offing, and the tacit support of the PRAEFECTUS URBI Annius Anullinus, Maxentius assumed the purple on 28 October 306 without opposition except that of Abellinus, the VICARIUS and a supporter of Galerius, who was put to death for his resistance.

Amid the universal rejoicing for a legitimate son of an Augustus 'justly' succeeding his father Maximian, Maxentius must, nonetheless, have been worried. The depleted praetorian guards represented little in the way of an army, and while he could take comfort from his recognition by Africa, the Tyrrhenian island provinces, and southern and central Italy, he still had to proceed cautiously. Northern Italy remained loyal to Severus in Mediolanum, and it was to isolate him politically that Maxentius determined on a complex course of action. In an attempt to placate Galerius he assumed the old title of princeps instead of Augustus, and struck coins in honour of the Augusti and Caesars, by which move he hoped to ingratiate himself with them, particularly with Constantine.

More importantly, he made overtures to his father in Lucania. Many of Maximian's soldiers were now serving with Severus, and if they could be induced to return to their old allegiance, the maintenance of his position would be assured. Maximian had expressed his disapproval of an elevation made by the praetorian guard, but Maxentius seduced his father with an offer of the imperial insignia and told him it was his responsibility to resume his position as senior Augustus, which he hoped would legitimise his usurpation. Maximian consented, but before he set out for Rome he tested the water by writing to Diocletian, inviting him to re-enter public life in the interests of peace for the empire. The response was almost two years in coming.

Galerius appeared to be more alarmed that the praetorians had seized the old privilege of making an emperor than he was at the actuality of Maxentius's usurpation, for he had no high opinion of the pretender. His first act was to order Severus as the western Augustus into action. Severus left Mediolanum early in 307, but Maxentius's trust in old loyalties proved well placed. Unwilling to fight against the son of their old commander, the majority of men deserted Severus, forcing him to flee back north with only a few remaining troops. Maximian, who had now reached Rome and, for the second time, assumed his position as Augustus, chased Severus to Ravenna, where peace terms were arranged. In return for his life being spared, Severus abdicated and was imprisoned as a hostage against Galerius at a small village to the south of Rome called Tres Tabernae.

Father and son now had control of the whole of the African and Italian dioceses with the exception of Raetia I and II, and the obvious next course of action was to make an alliance with Constantine to protect their position from Galerius. This was achieved in the spring of 307, when Maximian completed the betrothal agreement and took his daughter Fausta – now aged about fourteen – to Treveri and married her to Constantine. He also raised his new son-in-law to the rank of co-Augustus. In return Constantine acknowledged Maxentius as the senior emperor. Constantine later issued coins as a further gesture of goodwill that styled Maxentius as Augustus, and he had the name of Severus erased from all the monuments that had been set up to him. Maximian continued to remain at Constantine's court, while Maxentius looked after affairs in Rome. This division was to have serious consequences.

Meanwhile Galerius had mobilised his own forces, and in the summer of 307 he advanced without opposition through Italia until he reached Interamna, to the north of Rome. Here, he encountered problems. Although his army was larger than that now available to Severus, it was insufficient to the task of storming Rome's mighty Aurelian Wall, and his forced march had prevented bringing any siege engines with him. Worse, his troops had ravaged the surrounding countryside in their progress, while Rome was well provisioned with supplies from Africa and Sicilia. Privation sapped the mens' will to continue the siege, and several even deserted to return home.

Severus II – an unloved and unlucky Augustus.

Maxentius, son of Maximian, and his own son Valerius Romulus (below).

Galerius had no alternative but to beat a hasty and disorderly retreat to the north. In this condition the army should have made easy pickings, but for some reason Maxentius remained firmly behind the city walls. There can have been no lingering sympathy for his wife's father, so he must have relied on Constantine to pursue the enemy, but whatever the reason for his dilatory attitude it was a political and military blunder.

At Constantine's court, Maximian was losing faith in his son. Knowing that there would never be peace between Maxentius and Galerius and that a bloody civil war would result, he asked Constantine to join him in crushing Galerius's retreating army before marching on Rome to demote Maxentius. Several factors held Constantine back, among which should be counted his disapproval of undoing Diocletian's system, which at the same time, with the removal of Galerius, would leave Maximinus Daia free to consolidate his power in the eastern dioceses. Relations between the three Augusti deteriorated sharply when news of Galerius's debacle in Italia resulted in Hispania declaring for Maxentius. This effectively robbed Constantine of six provinces, and he broke off friendly relations with Maxentius. When Maximian, now fifty-seven, heard that his wayward son had disobeyed orders and had Severus put to death on 16 September 307, he set out for Rome determined to depose him. However, he had underestimated the hold that apparent success had given Maxentius over the troops, and when Maximian went up to his son and dramatically ripped the purple robe off his shoulders, they refused to support their former commander. Maximian was forced to flee from Rome back to Gallia and Constantine's court early in 308.

Congress at Carnuntum

Galerius – thanks to Maxentius having let him get out of Italia so easily – could sit and lick his military and political wounds. In his bewilderment at the empire's confusion he turned to Diocletian for his experience. Galerius nominated the retired Augustus for the consulship of 308, and then made the unprecedented move of convening a conference at Carnuntum in an attempt to settle differences between the multiplying rulers. To this Diocletian was coaxed into attending, along with Maximian. In the midst of their mutual hatred, Galerius and Maximian shared one thought in common, that Diocletian should re-enter public life and resume his old office. In this they were both disappointed, for Diocletian

refused the offer. Moreover, at the conference's conclusion in November 308 he dashed Maximian's hopes for a favourable outcome and allowed Galerius to triumph. Maximian was forced to resign again and Diocletian insisted that all his imperial acts since his formal abdication in 305 be annulled. This, of course, included his legitimisation of Maxentius – who was declared a usurper and public enemy – and his grant of the title Augustus to Constantine. Diocletian now appointed another old friend of Galerius, Licinianus Licinius as Augustus to replace Severus, and gave him the administration of Italia, Africa and Hispaniae, although these were actually under the control of Maxentius the usurper. Constantine was demoted to the rank of Caesar, and the position of Maximinus Daia was left untouched.

Although Diocletian had, in theory, re-established a tetrarchy, it was done in a manner inconsistent with his system because Licinius had achieved the rank of Augustus without ever having been a Caesar. The promotion was also bound to cause resentment in the two junior members at having Licinius promoted over their heads. In an attempt at consolation, Galerius bestowed on them both the title of FILII AUGUSTORUM (sons of the Augusti). To Constantine this only added insult to injury. Not only did he throw the empty honour back in Galerius's face, he also refused to accept his demotion at Diocletian's order. His defiance was marked by tumultuous cries of approval from the Gallic provincials and his troops. Alarmed at his growing power, the other Caesar, Maximinus Daia, had himself proclaimed Augustus by his Syrian army on the first day of May 310, and Galerius was obliged to acknowledge the *fait accompli*.

The unhappily divisive outcome of the congress at Carnuntum had little immediate effect on Maxentius, who retained the loyalty of his main army in Italia. But in Africa – so essential for Rome's food supply – Maxentius had reason to suspect the loyalty of the civilian and military administration and demanded of the VICARIUS, Lucius Domitius Alexander, that he send his son to Rome as a hostage. Incensed, Alexander refused and a rebellion erupted during which he was proclaimed Augustus by his African troops at the end of 308. The loss of the African grain supply was a serious blow to Maxentius, but while he still held Hispaniae, famine was not a dire threat, and no immediate action was taken against Alexander. And then in the following year Maxentius suffered a great personal loss with the death of his son Romulus, in whom he had placed all his hopes for the future of the Herculian dynasty.

Constantine is depicted on this coin struck in 308/9 as FILIUS AUGUSTORUM, *an 'honour' he loathed.*

Meanwhile, Maximian had returned to the shelter of Constantine's court at Treveri. There Constantine accorded him all the courtesies due to a father-in-law and ex-Augustus, while carefully ensuring he remained in honourable inactivity. For a year all was peaceful, but in 310 Maximian's restlessness got the better of him again, and while Constantine was away campaigning against the Franks near Colonia Agrippina, Maximian took advantage of his absence to win over some of the garrison. He removed himself south to Arelate (Arles) and had himself proclaimed Augustus for a third time. The adventure was doomed to failure. Constantine speedily concluded his affairs on the Rhenus and hastened to the chastisement of his father-in-law. Maximian fled to Massilia, where he was besieged and his own men eventually persuaded him to capitulate.

Constantine spared his life, but soon afterwards, in July, he was found dead. The official verdict was suicide, but it would not be hard to forgive Constantine if, exasperated by the sixty-year-old reprobate's continual scheming, he had ordered his execution.

Constantine faced a constitutional dilemma caused by the nullifying of Maximian's acts, since his position of Augustus had rested on Maximian's recognition of his status. He now turned to another basis for his authority and allowed the rumour to spread that his father Constantius Chlorus was the natural son of Claudius Gothicus. With this fiction, he claimed descent from an earlier emperor and so legitimised his imperial position on the principle of hereditary succession. At the same time he also invented a foundation on which he might ultimately establish title to a sole constitutional IMPERIUM within the empire. He now disassociated himself from the Herculian dynasty of Maxentius, founded by Maximian, by replacing Hercules as his protecting deity with Sol Invictus, worshipped as Apollo in Gallia. He was ready to move. On the pretext of coastal attacks on Hispaniae by Frankish pirates, Constantine entered the diocese and annexed the provinces to his own administration. He could, of course, argue that he was only getting back what should rightfully have been his in the first place.

The loss of Hispaniae on top of Africa was a disaster for Maxentius. Famine spread quickly in Rome, and street violence became endemic between the pampered praetorians and the starving mob. As many as six thousand may have perished. Maxentius had to snatch back Africa. In the spring of 311 he sent his PRAEFECTUS PRAETORIO Gaius Rufius Volusianus to Africa. Alexander – elderly and no military genius – proved no match for Volusianus, who quickly defeated the usurper and had him executed. With Africa restored, the food supply was secured, and with wealth confiscated from Alexander's supporters, Maxentius celebrated a triumph. He then had his father deified and struck coins in his memory as well as that of Constantius. Neither were maudlin gestures – deification of his father improved his own position as Augustus, and honouring Constantine's father was not only a political snub, it was also an indication of his claim to the whole of the western half of the empire. War with Constantine was now inevitable.

The rise of Constantine

Galerius, who was in his mid-fifties, was in ill health by the spring of 311, suffering from a cancer that the Christians gleefully attributed to divine retribution for his hatred of their faith. In his *Ecclesiastical History* Eusebius tells of his suffering with a somewhat un-Christian relish: *'From them [his suppurating cancer wounds] came a teeming indescribable mass of worms, and a sickening smell was given off; for the whole of his hulking body, thanks to over-eating, had been transformed even before his illness into a huge lump of flabby fat, which then decomposed and presented those who came near with a revolting sight.'* The doctors, who could not bear to be near their smelly patient, Eusebius tells us, were instantly put to death. Perhaps he also believed that his sickness was a judgement of the angry Christian god because he issued an Edict of Tolerance on 30 April granting freedom of worship under certain conditions. But it did nothing to save him, and he died a few days later.

In one sense Galerius's death simplified the political situation. The empire was now in the hands of four Augusti: Constantine held the western provinces, Maxentius Africa, the Tyrrhenian islands and Italia, Licinius the Balkans and much of Asia Minor, and Maximinus Daia – technically now the senior Augustus – Aegyptus up to eastern Cappadocia. But the complex interweaving of mutual mistrust between them all precluded any peaceful outcome. Immediately on hearing of Galerius's death, Maximinus Daia increased his grip on the eastern provinces. He overran Pontica and Asiana, and forced Licinius to a settlement that left him only the Illyrian dioceses, with the Bosphorus and Hellespontus the boundary between them. Constantine needed an alliance with one or the other in order to prosecute his war on Maxentius without interference, and selected Licinius simply because he

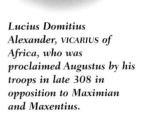

Lucius Domitius Alexander, VICARIUS *of Africa, who was proclaimed Augustus by his troops in late 308 in opposition to Maximian and Maxentius.*

was the nearer. They quickly concluded a treaty and sealed the pact with the betrothal to Licinius of Constantine' half-sister Constantia.

In December 311 Diocletian died at Salonae in his massive palace (*see side panel below*). Lactantius claims he committed suicide from the disappointment at seeing the fruits of his constitutional labours ruined. In whatever circumstance he met his end, Diocletian was to remain one of the most extraordinary of Roman emperors. Eutropius wrote the best epithet. '*...he alone of all men, since the foundation of the Roman empire, voluntarily returned from so high a dignity to the condition of private life, and to an equality with the other citizens. That happened to him, therefore, which had happened to no one since men were created, that, though he died in a private condition, he was enrolled among the gods.*'

THERE IS CONSIDERABLE disparity in the histories about the year of Diocletian's death, although the day – 3 December – more readily finds agreement. Years ranging from 311 to 316 are given. However, considering the poor and deteriorating state of the emperor's health, the earliest date makes the most sense. It also complies with the actions of Constantine, who must have felt the greatest reluctance to begin the dismemberment of the Diocletianic constitutional system while the great man still lived.

With the death of the one man to whom Constantine owed his allegiance – more to his philosophy than to his substance – he was finally free to begin the remarkable series of campaigns that were to make him the sole ruler of the Roman empire. In the early spring of 312 the war began. His prospects, however, looked unpromising. Because he had no intention of repeating the errors of previous emperors by depleting his garrison in the face of renewed barbarian activity across the Rhenus, he set out from Gallia with only a quarter of his available force, an expeditionary army of about forty thousand men. To his front, Maxentius could call on at least four times that number, if not as much as the recorded hundred and eighty-eight thousand. The hard core of this army was the praetorian guard and his father's veteran soldiers, plus a novel cavalry force called CLIBANARII, whose riders and mounts were protected by iron armour. Constantine, however, was much the better general and his troops were more than a match for Maxentius's slovenly soldiers, most of whom he planned to keep under his own command in Rome, where stores were being stockpiled in anticipation of a siege. The Aurelian Wall, satisfactory against

Helena, mother of Constantine, was a professed Christian and had much influence over her son's views on religion.

barbarians, was deemed insufficiently strong to defy a trained Roman army, and Maxentius began strengthening and transforming it in the uncompromisingly tough manner of his buildings (*see side panel facing, top*). The rest of his army was scattered between outposts in northern Italy, with a sizeable detachment stationed at Verona under the command of Ruricius Pompeianus to defend the Brenner Pass in case Licinius should attempt an advance from Raetia or Noricum

Constantine crossed the Alps and dropped into Italia due west of Augusta Taurinorum (Turin), where he took the outpost garrison of Segusio (Susa) entirely by surprise. The main body of the enemy was gathered before Augusta Taurinorum, but through use of clever tactics Constantine managed to lure the CLIBANARII into an enclosure. The weight of their armour frustrated their efforts, and Augusta Taurinorum was captured. The victory caused all the Transpadene cities and towns except Verona to open their gates. In order to secure his lines of communication with Licinius, Verona had to fall, but Ruricius Pompeianus proved to be no pushover. From his temporary headquarters at Mediolanum, Constantine tried negotiating, but when this failed he marched on Verona, and there outside the city a great battle was fought that lasted well into the night before Ruricius was killed and the opposition melted away. Verona capitulated, soon followed by Mutina (Modena) after a short siege.

At this point, Constantine's victories had come at a high price. Injury and death had reduced his original expeditionary force to about twenty-five thousand men, nowhere near enough to face up to Maxentius. Constantine's history to this time had shown no signs of recklessness, and it was perfectly obvious that he would have to retire, or beg reinforcements from Licinius. And yet this highly cautious man did neither: against all expectation he advanced towards Rome and what looked like certain defeat. His confidence in ultimate victory certainly did not lie in the scale or discipline of his army – it was the righteousness of his cause that gave him strength. For by this time Constantine was to all intents and purposes a Christian. This is not to say he was a convert, but his mother Helena was a professed Christian and this, in combination with his natural tolerance, had reduced his Roman immunity to the mysteries of the religion. Eusebius tells of how, in later life, Constantine himself told the chronicler of how he had received a vision while worshipping Apollo, in which a cross stood above the sun, accompanied by the words 'Conquer with this', followed by XXX, the years of the reign due to him.

MAXENTIUS WAS an energetic builder during his six-year reign. In addition to the massive strengthening of the Aurelian Wall, he contributed the largest vaulted building ever attempted by Roman civil engineers. The Basilica Nova of Maxentius was actually completed by Constantine, and is sometimes confusingly known by the latter's name as a result. Described by many modern critics as the most magnificent monument in the whole of the Forum Romanum and by others as the climax of Roman architecture, it stands on the northern side of the eastern end of the Forum, and actually crossed the Via Sacra. The gigantic rectangle measured 350 feet by nearly 250 feet (107 by 76m), and the monumental weight of the coffered ceiling was carried by only four huge piers (the much earlier Basilica Julia, one-third the size, required 74 columns to carry its much lighter roof). Originally decorated with marble veneers to the lower courses and moulded stucco to the upper walls and ceilings that was overlaid with paint and gilding, what remains today is only brick-faced. The Basilica Nova used innovative architecture that threw out most of the previous classical forms, and with its mix of groin- and barrel-vaults, is the forerunner of the great Romanesque religious basilicas of the medieval era.

South of the city beside the Via Appia Maxentius laid out a palace complex, the ruins of which can be seen today. It included a large circus capable of holding fifteen thousand spectators, and a massive, domed mausoleum set in a rectangular colonnaded enclosure. As Maxentius was never to rest in his mausoleum, neither was his statue to grace his beautiful basilica. After completing the building, Constantine set up the colossal statue of himself that can be seen today in pieces in the courtyard of the Palazzo dei Conservatori in Rome.

This is the later Christian view. And yet it is difficult to believe that Constantine should have received such religious certainty as to risk everything on his small army defeating Maxentius, who was on his own ground. There is more to the story. Constantine must have weighed the risks very carefully. On his side he had the affection not only of his own troops, but those of the eastern dioceses; and undoubtedly many in the Maxentian camp admired his reputation. Maxentius's soldiers were rightly doubtful of their own leader's military abilities – he had let Galerius escape from Italia without a fight and now preferred to hide behind Rome's walls instead of confronting Constantine in open battle despite an overwhelming superiority in numbers. The Christian histories tell us nothing of Constantine's military intelligence. Like any sensible general, he must have had agents within the city, who would have informed him of the extreme disaffection in which Maxentius was held after the famine, the sloppy discipline of his army, and the inevitable divisions between praetorians and regular soldiers.

Everything pointed to the fact that a determined march by a fiercely loyal army of highly trained and battle-hardened troops would – at the least – lead to a stream of desertions from the enemy's ranks and the alienation of Maxentius. Nevertheless, he sought extra insurance and had his men paint the Christian symbol on their shields. Close to Constantine as the tutor of his eldest son Crispus, Lactantius says that during the night before the final battle Constantine was commanded in a dream to do this. Under his new standard,

the so-called LABARUM (*see side panel below*) the army marched on Rome. Given that hardly any of his soldiers were Christians – more likely adherents of Mithras – this was an extraordinary exhibition of Constantine's new-found belief in the Christian god. Receiving divine instruction by way of dreams or visions was a commonplace to the superstitious Romans, so perhaps in addition to his confidence in military strategy he determined to have every advantage on his side; and so his men advanced as the first Christian army in history.

Constantine's aggressive tactics bore fruit. Maxentius now decided to alter his strategy of staying

The Labarum (Chi-Rho) of Constantine

The term LABARUM is of uncertain derivation, although it may have been familiar as a form of Roman army standard from the reign of Hadrian. Eusebius described that of Constantine as a long spear, overlaid with gold, and a transverse bar that formed the figure of a cross. 'On the top of the whole was fixed a wreath of gold and precious stones, and within this the symbol of the Saviour's name, two letters indicating the name of Christ by means of the initial letters, the letter X [chi] intersection P [rho] at the centre.' The monogram was not Constantine's invention, for it was familiar to many Christians, but his adoption of it boosted its popularity enormously. A purple banner was suspended from the crossbar bearing the Greek inscription *touto nika*, rendered in Latin as IN HOC SIGNO VINCES (in this sign you shall conquer). Eusebius tells us that it 'being also richly interlaced with gold, presented an indescribable degree of beauty to the beholder'. Standards of a similar design were supplied to all the legions, replacing the traditional eagles, and the monogram was also engraved on the troops' shields. The Roman legions had become a Christian army.

put behind his massive fortifications. The change of plan may well have been forced on him because of the uncertain temper of the mob, restless since the recent food riots caused by Constantine's annexation of Hispania. After crossing the Tiberis by way of a specially constructed pontoon bridge and the Pons Mulvius (Milvian Bridge) next to it, Maxentius's vanguard went upstream until it reached the pass of the Saxa Rubra. Here, advance units of Constantine's small army blocked the way, and the whole column, many still fording the river, was brought to a standstill. Constantine seized the initiative. Leaving a sufficiently large force to hold the defile, he took his army across the ridges behind which the enemy was massed in the river valley. When he reached the Via Cassia, which joins the Via Flaminia at the Pons Mulvius, there was enough room to deploy his men into attack formations. The bridge was the objective, and the rocky ridges on either side protected his flank. Maxentius, hemmed in between the hills and the river, had no alternative but to convert the left flank of the strung out column into his centre. In one swift tactic, Constantine had reduced the fighting capacity of Maxentius into a numerical inferiority.

Below: A triumphant Constantine is depicted gazing up to heaven.

Constantine's first assault broke the resistance of the enemy's front ranks and drove their supporting troops back in confusion towards the river, which was swollen with winter run off from the Appenines. Thousands of Maxentius's panicking men were drowned in the raging waters and many more, including Maxentius, were swept to their deaths when the pontoon bridge beside the Pons Mulvius collapsed under their weight. It was 28 October 312, the very same day when, six years earlier, Maxentius had unilaterally assumed the purple. He was not yet thirty.

Constantine entered Rome on the following day, carrying the head of Maxentius, whose body had been recovered some way down river. There was much rejoicing of the people and senate, who gratefully erected a statue of Constantine holding a cross in his right hand. Work was immediately begun on the magnificent arch by the Amphitheatrum Flavium that to this day bears witness to his victory over the 'usurper' Maxentius. And by virtue of Constantine's shields, the battle of the Pons Mulvius became the first official Christian victory.

MAXIMINUS DAIA
Gaius Galerius Valerius Maximinus Daia (r.Caesar 1/5/305; Augustus 1/5/310–July 313)

LICINIUS
Gaius Valerius Licinianus Licinius (r.11/11/308–19/12/324, abdicated, d.early 325)

Constantine wasted no time in beginning the second part of fulfilling his destiny. The day after entering Rome on 29 October 312 he formally recognised the nominal powers of the senate. Then he had the senators confer on himself the status of senior Augustus, which since the death of Galerius had been that of Maximinus Daia. In theory, his invested him with the constitutional right to nominate consuls, and he immediately sent a dispatch to Maximinus naming him his colleague for 313, together with an order to stop the continuing persecution of Christians. To this, Maximinus paid temporary lip service, presumably to

eastern provinces was a useful weapon in the armoury against Maximinus Daia. The provisions of this new tolerance were compiled into what became known as the Edict of Milan, and were sent to all PRAESIDES in the western dioceses. Licinius was less happy to accept Constantine's assumed seniority, but eventually agreed to recognise it in return for the right to legislate within his own dominions, and for the legitimisation of his bastard son to become his successor. They had yet to agree on how to divide up Maxentius's army and no settlement on the future administration of Italia and its adjoining provinces had been reached when the conference was interrupted by Constantine's urgent recall to the Rhenus. There, a Frankish rebellion in Germania Inferior was terrorising the populace. He successfuly crushed the uprising during the following months, but his absence provided Maximinus Daia with his best opportunity to press home the attack on Licinius.

Beyond a birth date in the mid-260s in Dacia Ripensis, a peasant upbringing and an army career that brought him into contact with Galerius as a comrade-in-arms, nothing further is known about Licinius before his elevation to the purple on 11 November, 308. The tetrarchic enemy he now faced was of equally lowly origins. Maximinus Daia, son of a sister of Galerius, was born in Illyricum on 20 November 270. He married, but his wife and daughter's names remain unknown. Despite his lowly birth and lack of education, Maximinus encouraged the promotion of learning in his part of the empire, and seems to have had a statesman's grasp of politics and propaganda.

Like Galerius, he was an ardent Christian persecutor, and when Galerius ended the persecution in 311 with his Edict of Tolerance, Maximinus had acquiesced. However, after only six months he revised his policy and reintroduced a suppression of the Christians throughout his dominions. Although recusants were frequently sent to the mines, there were relatively few executions; but the propaganda was extreme. And it is clear that Maximinus understood the organisation of the Christian Church better than his colleagues, because he set up a pagan priesthood that was graded in a similar way to the Christian hierarchy. Naturally enough, the Christian writers excoriated him, and Lactantius claims that he could not keep his hands off Valeria, daughter of Diocletian and widow of Galerius, even while she was still in mourning. However, it should be noted that the dispossessed relatives of Galerius and Severus seem to

Facing: Maximinus Daia, Augustus of the territories of Aegyptus and north to eastern Cappadocia when Constantine ousted Maxentius in 312, aimed to increase his dominions, which brought him into conflict with Licinius (left, with his wife Constantia, half-sister of Constantine), who was Augustus of the Balkans and much of Asia Minor. The struggle between the tetrarchs for ultimate power was about to reach its final phase.

prevent Constantine from interfering in his sphere of influence – and countering his plans to conquer the dominions of Licinius.

During his stay in Rome Constantine ordered the complete disbandment of the praetorian guard because of its support for Maxentius, and began the process of returning to the Christian Church all the property that had belonged to it before the Diocletianic edicts. In the New Year he left Rome for Mediolanum to celebrate the marriage of his half-sister Constantia to Licinius, after which a second of those phenomena of the tetrarchic system occurred – the two Augusti held a conference.

The recent wedding might have pointed to there being common ground between the two Augusti, but this was far from the case, and the negotiations were protracted, tough and uncompleted when they parted company. However, there was little disagreement from Licinius to Constantine's proposal of complete religious tolerance; the message of freedom to Christians in the

The struggle for supreme power between the tetrarchs, 308–13

OCEANUS GERMANICUS

BRITANNIAE

Augusta (Londinium)

MARE BRITANNICUM

Germania II

Belgica II

Treveri (Trier)

Rhenus

Germania I

Lugdunensis II

Lutetia (Paris)

Belgica I

313, Constantine and Licinius make an accord, dividing the empire between them. The Edict of Milan is proclaimed.

308, conference appoints Licinius Augustus of Italia, Africa and Hispaniae, all of which are in the hands of Maxentius, and Hispaniae should belong to Constantine.

Juliomagus (Angers)

GALLIAE

Lugdunensis I

Danuvius

Carnuntum

310, using the pretext of Frankish pirate attacks, Constantine annexes Hispaniae. The loss of the diocese creates famine in Rome and forces Maxentius to retake Africa, temporarily lost to the usurper Alexander.

Aquatanica I

Augustodunum (Autun)

Sequania

Raetia II

Norricum Ripense

Pannonia I

Valeria

Augustonemetum (Clermont-Ferrand)

Ludgunum (Lyons)

Norricum Mediterraneum

Venetia

Savia

PANNONIAE

Pannonia II

Brigantium (La Coruña)

Novem Populi

Aquatanica II

Alpes Graiae

Raetia I

Mediolanum (Milan)

Segusio (Susa)

Augusta Taurinorum (Turin)

Verona

Aquileia

Mutina (Modena)

Flaminia

Sirmium

Dalmatia

Legio (León)

Gallaecia

Tolosa (Toulouse)

Massilia

Tuscia et Umbria

ITALIA

311, Diocletian dies in December.

Salonae

Caesaraugusta (Zaragoza)

Tarraconensis

Tarraco (Tarragona)

Corsica

Pons Mulvius October 28, 312 Constantine is victorious over Maxentius.

Roma

Campania

Praevali

312, in the spring Constantine attacks Italia, overwhelming the Segusio garrison, defeating Maxentius's forces at Taurinorum, Verona and Mutina before advancing on Rome.

Lusitania

Augusta Emerita (Mérida)

Valentia (Valencia)

Sardinia

Apulia et Calabria

Olisipo (Lisbon)

Carthaginiensis

Lucania et Bruttii

Corduba

Baetica

Carthago Nova (Cartagena)

308, at the end of the year the VICARIUS Alexander's troops proclaim him Augustus in rebellion against Maxentius.

Lilybaeum (Marsala)

Sicilia

HISPANIAE

Tingi (Tangier)

Caesarea

Hippo Regius

Numidia Cirtensis

Carthago

Thamugadi (Timgad)

Proconsularis

Hadrumetum

Mauretania Tingitana

Mauretania Caesariensis

Mauretania Tabia

AFRICA

Numidia Militana

Byzacena

311, Maxentius dispatches Volusianus to reconquer Africa, who is successful in deposing Alexander and regaining desperately needed grain supplies for Rome.

Leptis Magna

Tripolitania

Division of the empire between the contenders

Constantine

Maxentius

Gallerius / Licinius

Maximinus Daia

held by Maxentius, annexed by Constantine

retained by Gallerius, disputed by Constantine and Licinius

territory of Licinius overrun by Maximinus Daia

Campaigns

Constantine

Maxentius

Licinius

Maximinus Daia

0   100   200   300   400   500 miles

0   100   200   300   400   500   600   700 kilometres

have preferred to live under his protection rather than that of Licinius.

Early in 313, while the winter snow still lay thick on the ground, Maximinus left Syria and crossed Anatolia with an army of some seventy thousand to besiege Byzantium. The city capitulated after eleven days, leaving the way open into Thracia and the dominions of Licinius, and a few days later his army was encamped around Heraclea. Concluding the conference in Mediolanum with Constantine, Licinius hurried back to the Balkans and mobilised what army he could, probably only thirty thousand men. He then marched to Hadrianopolis (Edirne), before turning towards the relief of Heraclea. Maximinus raised the siege to meet the threat, and battle was joined at

Campus Serenus (the plain of the River Ergenus) near Hadrianopolis, on 30 April. By superior tactics and through the exhaustion of Maximinus Daia's men, Licinius was victorious. At Constantine's request, and no doubt because Licinius would not have turned his back on such a successful talisman, his men went into battle with the Christian symbol painted on their shields, so once again the army of the Christian god had prevailed over the forces of paganism.

Maximinus fled the battlefield disguised as a slave. He paused only briefly at Nicomedia to gather up his family. While there, he issued an edict granting religious freedom along the same lines as the Edict of Milan. If the purpose of this was to rally support from the increasingly large Christian minorities, it failed to work. It might also have been a politically motivated move aimed at gaining support from a more important quarter – Constantine; if so, it also failed. With his family, he escaped across Anatolia to Cilicia to raise another army, hoping to close the Taurus passes to the pursuing Licinius behind him. The hastily constructed hill forts, however, did not stop Licinius, and by mid-summer Maximinus was surrounded by land and sea in the vicinity of Tarsus. There he died of his own hand by taking poison. Suitably for the great persecutor, it was a lingering death because the poison was slow-acting, and gave him four days of agony before killing him.

Thus, the whole eastern half of the empire fell into the hands of Licinius. It is very doubtful that Constantine's Christian persuasion had swayed him greatly, and his actions following Maximinus's death were certainly not those of a charitable conqueror. With inhuman cruelty he ordered the deaths of all Maximinus's leading ministers and government officials. Then he turned on the family. Maximinus Daia's eight-year-old son and seven-year-old daughter were put to the sword, and their mother drowned by being thrown into the Orontes. As if to prove their wisdom in preferring the protection of Maximinus, Licinius executed Candidianus, the illegitimate son of Galerius, and Severianus, son of the former emperor Severus. When she was later found hiding in Thessalonica, Galerius's wife Valeria too was put to death. Constantine had caused the end of the dynasty of HERACLIUS by peaceful methods, his colleague ended that of JUVIUS with a bloodbath.

**Campus Serenus
April 30, 313**
Licinius defeats Maximinus Daia, who flees via Nicomedia to Cilicia.

311, Galerius dies in the spring. Licinius takes over his dominions.

311, Maximinus Daia overruns Anatolia and seizes the province of Europa from Licinius.

CHAPTER TWELVE   AD 313–364
CONSTANTINE AND BYZANTIUM SUPREME

CONSTANTINE I THE GREAT
Flavius Valerius Constantinus
(r.Caesar August 306; Augustus spring 307;
sole emperor 19/12/324–22/5/337)

Right: The purposeful, honest and clean-cut Constantine would take until 324 to achieve sole rule over the empire.

Above: Helena, the emperor's mother, and (below) his second wife, Maximian's daughter Fausta.

Constantine changed the course of first-millennium history. Because of his policies Christianity was spread throughout the Roman empire, and thus became the faith that fired the Western world. The political expediencies that persuaded the ambitious emperor to embrace Christianity are largely forgotten. Nor did his conduct in later life always appear appropriate for a humble servant of Christ. But Constantine, by playing the religious card, united a fractured empire under one standard – the Chi-Rho.

The emperor who, as much as Diocletian, influenced the future course of the Roman empire, was born at Naissus (Nis) on 27 February in either 272–73 (although dates as late as 288 are also given†). When his father Constantius was appointed Caesar by Diocletian in 293 and made to marry Maximian's stepdaughter Theodora, Constantine and his divorced mother Helena were sent away to Byzantium. Constantine was a TRIBUNUS MILITUM at Diocletian's court at Nicomedia and fought alongside Galerius against the Sassanid Persians in 298 and the Sarmatae on the Danuvius in 299. His first wife, Minervina, bore him a son, Flavius Julius Crispus, and his second, Fausta, the daughter of Maximian, gave him three more sons: Flavius Claudius Constantinus (Constantine II), Flavius Julius Constantius (Constantius II), Flavius Julius Constans; and two daughters, Constantina and Helena the Younger.

With the death of Maximinus Daia in the late summer of 313, the empire was in the hands of Licinius, holding the Illyrian and eastern provinces, and Constantine, who held the rest – except for the still unresolved question of Maxentius's Italia. The following ten years of joint rule were destined to be stormy, and the fate of Italia was the first in contention. Christian writers put the blame on Licinius, but the first breach was most certainly engineered by

† The earliest date must be more accurate, since he is recorded as fighting the Persians with Galerius in 298 – unlikely if he was only ten or eleven years old at the time.

Constantine. It was his intention to create a buffer state between the two Augusti under the control of a Caesar, which would comprise the diocese of Italia and that of Pannonia, which Licinius had received on the death of Severus. Constantine installed his brother-in-law Bassianus, who had married his other half-sister Anastasia, with authority over Italia-Pannonia. Apart from the fact that this was a tacit seizure of Pannonia, territory Licinius considered his own to administer in accord with their agreement at Mediolanum, he correctly considered Bassianus to be nothing more than his rival's creature. Constantine's inclusion of Pannonia was probably designed to provoke a response, and it did. Licinius, via an intermediary called Senecio, instigated Bassianus to a military revolt against his imperial brother-in-law. But the plot was uncovered, and Bassianus arrested and executed. Constantine now demanded Licinius hand over the culpable Senecio, but he would not – a refusal that pointed to his complicity in the conspiracy.

Constantine determined on an invasion of the Balkans before Licinius could concentrate all his

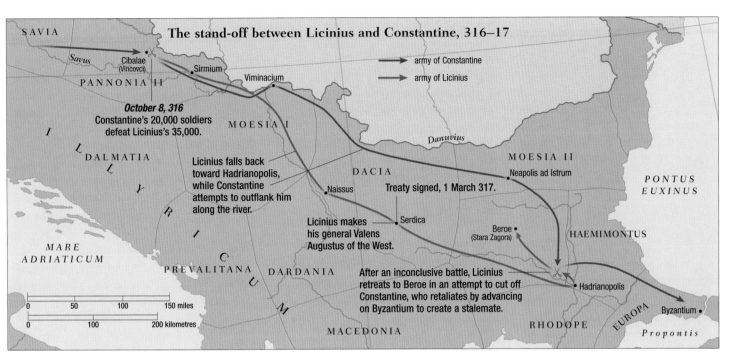

The stand-off between Licinius and Constantine, 316–17

→ army of Constantine
→ army of Licinius

October 8, 316
Constantine's 20,000 soldiers defeat Licinius's 35,000.

Licinius falls back toward Hadrianopolis, while Constantine attempts to outflank him along the river.

Treaty signed, 1 March 317.

Licinius makes his general Valens Augustus of the West.

After an inconclusive battle, Licinius retreats to Beroe in an attempt to cut off Constantine, who retaliates by advancing on Byzantium to create a stalemate.

forces – several of his legions were still ensuring the security of the eastern provinces after the defeat of Maximinus Daia – and marched in the summer of 316 seeking to secure Pannonia at least. Licinius, however, managed to muster thirty-five thousand troops to face Constantine's force of twenty thousand, but despite his numerical superiority he was defeated at Cibalae on 8 October, losing more than half his men. Licinius fell back through Sirmium to Serdica, where he proclaimed Aurelius Valerius Valens, commander of the Danuvian army, his imperial colleague and named him Augustus of the West. Valens concentrated all the remaining forces before Hadrianopolis and a second battle was fought at Campus Mardiensis in Thracia, but its outcome was indecisive. Licinius then retreated northwest to Beroe (Stara Zagora), which placed his forces between the Danuvius and his rival, cutting Constantine's line of communication to Gallia. Licinius planned to pin Constantine in the Balkans until detachments from Anatolia could arrive and catch his enemy in a pincer manoeuvre. However, Constantine began an advance on Byzantium, threatening to occupy the city and block the Bosphorus with his fleet. It was a stand-off.

At Serdica on 1 March 317 Licinius agreed to a treaty, the terms of which were better for Constantine, at least in territorial gains. Except for Thracia all of Illyricum was ceded to Constantine and Licinius agreed to put Valens to death. In return, Constantine retreated from the legislative powers of the senior Augustus and recognised the right of each Augustus to issue edicts within his own realm. Further, they agreed that neither emperor should enter his colleague's provinces except in the event of barbarian invasion. Although the coinage of both remained universal legal tender, in effect the Augusti had divided the empire into a Latin half in the West and a Greek half in the East. In a sign of outward unity, three new Caesars were elevated. Two were Constantine's sons, Crispus and Claudius Constantinus, the other was the illegitimate son of Licinius, whom Constantine had recognised at Mediolanum, named Valerius Licinianus Licinius after his father. None was old enough to have any real share in the power, Crispus was fourteen or fifteen the other two were mere infants.

A full-scale civil war had been averted, and for the next six years an uneasy truce remained in place. The cause for estrangement and final warfare would be Christianity. Previous emperors had regarded the faith as divisive to national unity; Constantine was determined to use its power as a unifying movement, which could only be done by making Christianity, if not the whole of, at least a vital part of the state-religion. Since most of the army and the upper classes were convinced pagans, it was not practical to unite the Christian Church to the state, but he wanted to utilise its moral and economic advantages for the state's benefit. In 318 he issued an edict that added up to a constitution. It recognised the jurisdiction of the episcopal courts and, where by mutual agreement the litigants brought a case before the bishops, accorded

Licinius made his general Valens (above) his imperial colleague and Augustus of the West in opposition to Constantine – a short-lived promotion.

their decision the same validity as that of the civil MAGISTRI. The further steps towards a union of Church and state were not always smooth, as the Donatist schism indicates (*see side panel below*).

Constantine began a massive programme of religious building, including a basilica for the pope on the site of what had been the camp of the mounted praetorian guard, and many other churches, among them the

first St. Peter's. To the people he presented himself as the champion of Christians everywhere. Licinius by comparison, while bowing to the Christian ethic, remained essentially pagan in his personal pursuits and beliefs. Nevertheless, at first the unity of the Church was important to him, if only to keep the peace with Constantine. What changed his mind was a schism that promised to be more divisive than that of the Donatists to Constantine. A deacon and presbyter of Alexandria called Arius (c.250–336) had professed a heresy that had split the eastern arm of the Church in two. Under Bishop Alexander, the orthodox held that Christ was God, whereas Arius maintained that Christ was only 'His Creature'. The Arians held sway at the imperial court because Arius – after his expulsion by Alexander in 318 – had become a confidant of the empress Constantia. Further, his follower the writer Eusebius of Nicomedia, probably a relative of the PRAEFECTUS PRAETORIO Julianus, was favoured by Licinius. At two synods convened at Licinius's order, one in Bithynia the other in Palaestina, the orthodox view was denied and the teachings of Arius held to be in accordance with the Christian faith, and the reinstatement of Arius was demanded. Bishop Alexander's answer was to summon another synod at which Arius and his followers were excommunicated from the Catholic Church.

This open defiance of the emperor's wishes infuriated Licinius, who decided unification of Church and state was impossible to achieve. At the same time he could hardly be expected to tolerate the existence of such a powerful organisation operating outside the

SCHISMATIC ACTIVITY within the Church was bound to annoy Constantine, who required a unified clergy whose authority was recognised by all, otherwise the partnership between Church and state would be undermined. As early as 313 the emperor had to arbitrate in Africa in what is known as the Donatist schism. Donatists argued that those Christians who had recanted or had given up sacred books to the Diocletianic inquisition were sinners or TRADITORES (surrenderers), and that their readmittance to the communion should be qualified. They argued with the more tolerant over how far the Church should be a mixed body of sinners and the righteous.

The quarrel that resulted in Constantine's involvement occurred when Carthaginian Christians elected the arch-deacon Caecilian to the position of bishop vacated by the death of his predecessor. The rigorists alleged that Caelian had co-operated with the inquisition. Constantine hoped that the episcopal courts would settle the issue, but when the Donatists refused to accept the verdict in favour of Caecilian, he decided to retry the case himself. In 316 he rendered a verdict that concurred with the bishops' and ordered the expulsion of the Donatists from the Church. The disturbances that rocked Africa over the next four years forced Constantine to admit defeat, since he did not want to earn himself the reputation of a persecutor. Reluctantly, he extended tolerance to the heretics and so failed in his aim of unity within the Church.

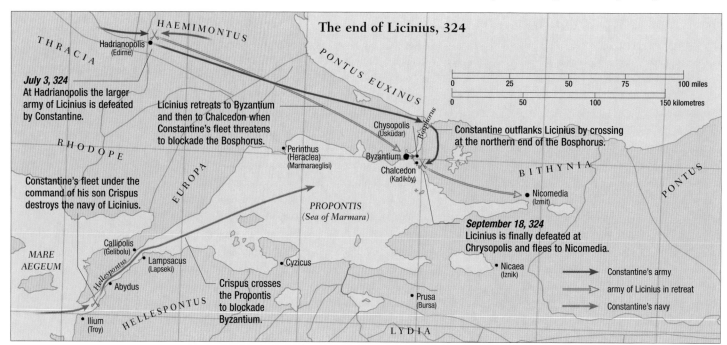

The end of Licinius, 324

July 3, 324
At Hadrianopolis the larger army of Licinius is defeated by Constantine.

Licinius retreats to Byzantium and then to Chalcedon when Constantine's fleet threatens to blockade the Bosphorus.

Constantine outflanks Licinius by crossing at the northern end of the Bosphorus.

Constantine's fleet under the command of his son Crispus destroys the navy of Licinius.

September 18, 324
Licinius is finally defeated at Chrysopolis and flees to Nicomedia.

Crispus crosses the Propontis to blockade Byzantium.

THRACIA — HAEMIMONTUS — Hadrianopolis (Edirne) — RHODOPE — EUROPA — PONTUS EUXINUS — Chysopolis (Usküdar) — Bosphorus — Perinthus (Heraclea) (Marmaraeglisi) — Byzantium — Chalcedon (Kadiköy) — BITHYNIA — PONTUS — Nicomedia (Izmit) — PROPONTIS (Sea of Marmara) — Nicaea (Iznik) — Callipolis (Gelibolu) — Lampsacus (Lapseki) — Cyzicus — MARE AEGEUM — Hellespontus — Abydus — Prusa (Bursa) — Ilium (Troy) — HELLESPONTUS — LYDIA

| 0 | 25 | 50 | 75 | 100 miles |
| 0 | 50 | 100 | 150 kilometres |

→ Constantine's army
⇨ army of Licinius in retreat
→ Constantine's navy

state's control. In 320 he struck at the Church's power by forbidding the holding of any further synods, restricting the philanthropic activities of the clergy and banning women from attending services with men. At the same time he began expelling Christians from the palace, army and the bureaucracy. Several men were even condemned to death for failing to comply with his edict. There was a secondary advantage to the expulsions of officials from their offices: Licinius was becoming increasingly convinced that the Christians in his service were spies for Constantine.

The recantation of Licinius brought about the final confrontation between the two halves of the empire. Since 317 Constantine and Licinius had held joint-consulships to symbolise their unity. In 321, as a calculated snub, Constantine nominated his two sons Crispus and Constantinus, and in 322 held the consulship himself with his younger son. Licinius responded by assuming the consulship himself with his son. It was a breach of friendly relations, and both sides began martial preparations. In the same year Constantine was occupied by an invasion of Sarmatae in Pannonia, which he successfully repelled. And then, in 323, Goths entered Thraciae. Constantine used the invasion as an excuse to enter his colleague's domain, as by agreement under such circumstances he was entitled to do. Licinius, however, viewed it as an act of aggression and declared war in the spring of 324.

Constantine's army consisted of one hundred and twenty thousand infantry, ten thousand cavalry, and a fleet under the command of Crispus of some two hundred war-galleys and as many as two thousand transports. Licinius was able to muster an even larger army drawn from all the eastern provinces: one hundred and fifty thousand infantry and fifteen thousand cavalry, together with a powerful fleet stationed in the Hellespontus. The numbers, however, did not benefit him, and he suffered a defeat at Hadrianopolis on 3 July 324 and fell back on Byzantium. Meanwhile, Crispus engaged the enemy fleet at the narrows of the Hellespontus to force a way through towards the Bosphorus, and destroyed most of Licinius's ships. With Byzantium cut off, Licinius crossed the Bosphorus to Chalcedon, and there repeated his exercise of a decade earlier by conferring the purple on his general Martius Martinianus, and ordered him to prevent Constantine from entering Bithynia. However Constantine outwitted Martianus by landing where he was not expected, at the northern tip of the Bosphorus. On 18 September Licinius was brought

again to battle at Chrysopolis and defeated. He escaped to Nicomedia with thirty thousand men and sued for peace. Through the good offices of his wife and Constantine's sister, Constantia, his life and that of Martinianus were spared. Licinius was allowed to retire to Thessalonica as a PRIVATUS, but caught engaging in intrigue shortly after, Constantine had him executed. The same fate befell Martinianus, but young Licinius was spared – for the time being. For the first time in thirty-nine years, the Roman empire was in the hands of a single ruler.

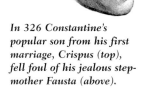

Licinius (above) and his son Licinius II (below)

Establishing the Holy Land

A domestic tragedy occurred in 326 that involved Constantine's first son and his wife, and was to leave the emperor wracked by guilt. The imperial family had gone to Rome to commemorate Constantine's VICENNALIA, and the DECENNALIA of the elevation to the rank of Caesar of his sons Crispus and Constantius. Crispus was a popular figure since his victory over the fleet of Licinius, and high in his father's esteem. But Crispus was also the son of Constantine's first wife, Minervia, and aroused the jealousy of Fausta on behalf of her own sons. After the celebrations, Crispus, who had been given command of the western provinces, left for Treveri, and – according to the histories – Fausta prepared her plot to bring him down.

Constantine had just issued a severe edict against sexual misconduct, and in this she saw her opportunity. One or two months later, when the family was reunited at Pola on the Histrian peninsula, Fausta accused Crispus of an adulterous attempt on her, and Constantine had his son executed. But Fausta's victory was short-lived. On the information of Constantine's mother Helena, Fausta was found guilty of a sexual affair with a slave, and condemned to death in accordance with the edict's suitable punishment by being thrust into a vat of boiling water. These are the bare facts offered by the histories – the matter was so sensitive that no record was made in the emperor's vast bureau, or none has survived. This burst of un-Christian cruelty seems so out of keeping with Constantine's character that it hints at far deeper motives than a simple case of inter-family jealousy, but if so, these are lost to time.

Some Christian writers claimed that it was the guilt he felt over these events that made Constantine turn to Christianity, but this is inconsistent with the facts; he was already a Christian in thought and

In 326 Constantine's popular son from his first marriage, Crispus (top), fell foul of his jealous stepmother Fausta (above).

Helena's pilgrimage to Judaea, where she visited known sacred sites like Christ's birthplace, and identified places where key events of Jesus's life occurred, established the Holy Land as the essential destination of pilgrimage; her 'discovery' of fragments of the True Cross began the long obsession with holy relics.

This coin celebrates the status of Constantinopolis as Roma Nova.

actions (those immediately above excepted) if not yet by baptism. Over the vexatious question of the Donatists Constantine convoked a council of bishops from Galliae at Arelate in 314, which included Pope Silvester I (p.314–35), after which the Donatists asked for the emperor's own court to judge the matter. In thanking the clergy for attending, Constantine referred to the blessing God had conferred on him in showing him the errors of his past life and guiding him into the way of truth. This is written evidence of his conversion to Christianity at a time well before the tragic domestic events of 326. The privileges extended to the episcopal courts in 318 are further evidence that Constantine regarded himself as Christian, even though he avoided interfering with pagan cults until much later. In the year before the execution of Crispus, Constantine called a council of Church leaders at Nicaea to settle the division between orthodoxy and Arianism. The outcome of the Council of Nicaea was satisfactory in that Constantine managed to get the dissident parties to agree to a compromise, which should have guaranteed the unity of the Church – always the emperor's primary consideration. This was the *homo-ousion* or consubstantiality of the Son and the Father, and it was inserted into the Creed. Constantine could take satisfaction from a job well done. Unfortunately, it was not to remove the basic disagreement, despite Arius's willingness to accept the compromise.

It was, perhaps, an act of expiation for his hand in the executions of his son and Fausta that he donated all Fausta's property to the Church, and in penitence that Helena undertook her pilgrimage to the Holy Land shortly after. Her journey was remarkable in so far as few Christians to this point had taken much notice of Judaea as Christ's birthplace and the land of his mission. Local tradition held that Helena visited some sites because she knew them to be holy shrines, but having the mother of the empire's Christian ruler endorse their validity established the Holy Land as the essential place of pilgrimage. During her journey Helena proclaimed the Via Dolorosa and identified all fourteen Stations of the Cross. She also discovered the spot where Jesus fed the five thousand, preached his Sermon on the Mount, the place of the Annunciation and Joseph's carpentry workshop. She is also said to have acquired several pieces of the True Cross, and thus founded the passion for hunting down relics. Helena did not merely visit as a tourist, she caused the building of the Church of the Nativity in Bethlehem and the Eleona Church on the Mount of Olives, which

was the Mount of the Ascension. According to Eusebius of Caesarea, at the place of Jesus' crucifixion she started building the Church of the Holy Sepulchre, although this is usually credited to Constantine. Eusebius said: *'She came, fired by... fervour, in order to know this land [and] explored it with remarkable discernment...and by her endless admiration for the footsteps of the Saviour she granted those who came after her the fruits of her piety.'*

The great city that bore Constantine's name for more than a thousand years until its fall to the Ottoman Turks in 1453 was begun in 324, shortly after his victory over Licinius. It should be doubted that Constantine actually dedicated Constantinopolis to his own name, or that he was building a city to supersede Rome in scope. He had spent many of his years in his western tetrarchic capital of Treveri, but all his impressionable youth at Byzantium. And he was aware that the West was now eclipsed in the imperial partnership. Trade and culture buzzed in the East, as Asia grew in importance. Making his new 'tetrarchic' capital in the East was a logical step, and where better than the city that had nurtured his youth? More to the point, in contrast to Rome, this was to be the Christian capital of the world.

The new city was styled Roma Nova and probably only became known as Constantinopolis after the emperor's death. However, it is convenient to refer to Byzantium as Constantinople from this point on. A massive building programme began, greater even than Diocletian's at Nicomedia, the effects of which Lactantius had compared to a barbarian raid. The principal construction took over six years and Constantinople was dedicated on 11 May 330. But even then the city lacked a proper water supply, which was only provided by the emperor Valens in about 373 in the form of aqueducts and conduits. The new city, at least four times larger than old Byzantium, surrounded a new forum and senate house. Constantine had the hippodrome of Septimius Severus remodelled and a magnificent palace built for his court, although Constantinople did not become a regular imperial residence until the end of the century.

Certainly Rome was to be snubbed and its prestige diminished, and as if to emphasise the point, the fragments of the True Cross brought back from Judaea by Helena were installed above the cupola of the triumphal arch known as the MILLON – the First Milestone. From here all distances in the empire were now to be measured; no longer did all roads lead to Rome, Constantinople was literally the centre of the world.

Constantine's later administration

In his administration Constantine followed many of Diocletian's reforms, extending and refining rather than innovating. He adopted Diocletian's elaborate, oriental court ceremony and took to wearing a bejeweled diadem as the symbol of his exalted position. The separation of civilian and military commands was completed, and the division of the army between infantry and cavalry was formalised under two new senior commanders, the MAGISTER PEDITUM (infantry) and the MAGISTER EQUITUM (cavalry) who reported to the emperor through the MAGISTER MILITUM.

Constantine also confirmed the lateral division of the army between the RIPENSES (the LIMITANEI of former years, who manned the LIMES) and COMITATENSES, or frontier and mobile field troops. There is a perceptible ranking apparent between the prestige of these two types of soldiers because the COMITATENSES received a higher pay than the RIPENSES, a factor that would contribute to a steady decline in frontier morale in the years to come. The praetorian guards, demoted by Diocletian but reinstated by Maxentius, were abolished altogether as Rome's garrison, and replaced by units of the SCHOLAE cavalry. The military functions of the PRAEFECTI PRAETORIO were removed and they joined the VICARI as purely civilian administrators.

Constantine reorganised the structure of government under the MAGISTER OFFICIORUM, who controlled the SCRINIA (imperial bureau), which also included the SCHOLA AGENTIUM IN REBUS. This intelligence-gathering corps replaced the numerous free-lance agents of previous regimes, such as the DELATORES, SPECULATORES, and FRUMENTARII. From this time on spies, or AGENTES, were under military discipline. The COMITATUS of Diocletian formed an important part of Constantine's council, in addition to the PRAEFECTI, which he named the SACRUM CONSISTORIUM. In the past members of the emperor's CONSILIUM had sat with him, now as the Augustus seated himself the councillors stood in his presence. The title COMES (count) became attached to certain high offices, including the command of small regional armies of COMITATENSES. Although at first a COMES was a member of the court, Constantine later freely bestowed the title as an honour to the deserving.

Religious toleration had been promised at Mediolanum: 'Let no one molest another,' Constantine had written. But the edict contained a warning for pagans that the wise would do well 'to be persuaded that purity and holiness can only be obtained by submission to the Holy Laws of God'. In 325 the solar image disappeared from coins to be replaced by the LABARUM, the Chi-Rho Christian monogram. At first there was no suppression of pagan temples, although the erection of statues of idols was forbidden and pagan festivals were banned. Later, imperial AGENTES began a programme of confiscating the treasures of pagan temples and several, including the temple of Asclepius at Aegae and the shrine of Aphrodite at Aphaca in Phoenicia, were closed. Nevertheless, Constantine continued to let pagan officials serve in the administration, even as Christian bishops began to predominate, and he styled himself PONTIFEX MAXIMUS until his death. Finally, he issued an empire-wide edict banning the holding of gladiatorial games, although the city of Rome continued to defy the command for the better part of a century.

Under Constantine, the regulation of the workforce begun by Aurelian and continued by Diocletian was made absolute; workers became virtual prisoners of their trade and their workplace. The lavish spending on new buildings and the increased army made heavy demands on the FISCUS, and the emperor drew bitter criticism when he introduced a new tax called the *chrysargyron* that fell on the senatorial class and town-dwellers. This was levied every four years and had to be paid – onerously – in gold or silver. The sixth-century Greek historian Zosimus noted that Constantine's taxes were so excessive that fathers were forced to hire out their daughters as prostitutes to pay their debts. If this had really been the case, the worthies would have been breaking Constantine's morality laws and faced severe penalties, so it is improbable that such extreme tactics were actually resorted to. But that the burden of taxation made all the classes groan certainly was the case.

He also established the base unit of gold currency, the SOLIDUS, at a lighter weight than the old AUREUS with a ratio of 72 coins to the pound, a value it retained for centuries. To achieve what had eluded previous emperors Constantine required large amounts of the precious metal. This was acquired by calling in and restriking coins that were already in circulation, but in addition the melting down of gold ornaments, largely seized from pagan temples, and access to the Armenian mines that Diocletian's eastern campaigns had made accessible, helped enormously.

The oriental splendour of his court exceeded that of Diocletian, the emperor appearing with piled up false hair, often multi-hued, skillfully arranged by a team of stylists, above which he wore a diadem

Despite his role as a Christian emperor, Constantine still accepted the pagan office of PONTIFEX MAXIMUS, as this coin proves.

encrusted with pearls and valuable gemstones. He wore flowing robes of pure silk embroidered with flowers of gold, and where Diocletian's presumptions were to adorn the majesty of his position, Constantine's seemed more like an effeminacy so in contrast to his down-to-earth warrior youth. Gibbon summed up his last years by making the most invidious comparison in his lexicon: *'In such apparel, scarcely to be excused by the youth and folly of Elagabalus, we are at a loss to discover the wisdom of an aged monarch and the simplicity of a Roman veteran.'* Later writers even suggested that Constantine dallied with Elagabaline homosexuality, but this is to be doubted and more likely should be credited to early Christian historians qualifying their admiration for the emperor in suspecting that it was not really Constantine but his mother Helena who was was the real power behind the emergence of the Christian state.

Despite the apparent effeminacy of his court and his advancing years – he was about fifty-five – Constantine was still vigorous, and undertook several military campaigns on the frontiers. In 328 he moved the imperial court to Treveri, from which, with young Constantine, he supervised operations against the Alamanni. Late in 332 the Sarmatae appealed for help against a threatening invasion of the Goths, and young Constantine was sent to take command, while his brother Constantius, who had been raised to the rank of Caesar in 324, followed him. The Roman army crossed the Danuvius and inflicted a crushing defeat on the Goths, forcing them to accept Roman suzerainty. Two years later the Argaragantes, the major tribe of the Sarmatae broke faith with Rome, but a full-scale war was averted when the dependent tribe of Limogantes, who had been armed by Rome against another invasion of Goths, rose up against their masters. In panic as many as three hundred thousand Argaragantes surrendered to Constantine. Some of the men were enlisted in the

Constantine II as Caesar.

Constantius II as Caesar.

Constans as Caesar.

army, and others were given land in the Balkans and northern Italia. This further barbarisation of the empire nevertheless helped to secure peace along the Danuvius for more than a generation.

In 333 Constantine's youngest son Constans was raised to the rank of Caesar at the age of ten, and in 335 the emperor made a fourth Caesar of the MAGISTER MILITUM, his nephew Flavius Dalmatius, a reward for putting down a usurper. This revolt took place in Cyprus, when an officer called Calocaerus had himself proclaimed Augustus. The circumstances that led to the rebellion are unknown, but Dalmatius swiftly repressed it, and put the usurper to death. Its significance to history is that it seems to have awoken a fear in Constantine over a smooth succession, and brought to his mind that young Licinius was residing quietly in Africa. Determined to remove any dynastic threat, Constantine resorted to a particularly vindictive – not to mention un-Christian – method. As the son of a slave-woman, Licinius was reduced to his mother's status and then arrested as a technical runaway. He was taken to Carthago and put to death there in the following year.

In the East the Persians were once again on the offensive. After a period of internal struggles a new king, Shapur II, had ascended the Sassanid throne in 310. For a space of twenty years he consolidated his position and then prepared to recover the territories ceded to Galerius. Alarmed at the possible threat to Syria, young Constantine was sent to assume control of the eastern legions. In 334 the Sassanians kidnapped Tiran, the Arsacid king of Armenia, and carried him off to the Persian court, where he was brutally blinded. The Armenian nobles appealed to Constantine for help and, in response at their temerity in defying him, Shapur attacked in 335 and annexed Armenia. Recognising the pointlessness of placing another Arsacid on the throne, Constantine appointed his nephew Hannibalianus, who was married to his eldest daughter Constantia, king of Armenia. Hannibalianus immediately force-marched his army into Armenia, where he surprised and routed the Persians in 336.

At this point the Roman empire was effectively divided into five military regions under the control of Constantine's three sons and two nephews: young Constantine ruled Galliae, Hispaniae and Britanniae; Constantius Asiana and Oriens; Constans Italia, Africa and the dioceses of Pannoniae and northern Moesiae; Dalmatius received the remainder of the Balkans; and Hannibalianus ruled Armenia and Pontica. Of course,

Below: Constantine's nephews.

the supreme administration remained in the hands of the emperor. Early in 337, Constantine established himself at Nicomedia in preparation to co-ordinate the follow up to Hannibalianus's success in Armenia. It was there in May that he fell ill. Knowing that his death was near, the 'Servant of God' took the final step in his religious conversion and at the age of about sixty-four received the sacrament of baptism. Constantine died on 22 May, the Feast of the Pentecost, and he was laid to rest in the Church of the Holy Apostles in his city of Constantinople as the thirteenth of that illustrious number. However, the Roman senate – probably to appease the fury of the Roman mob that the emperor should be buried in the East – granted him divine honours, and so the first Christian emperor joined his pagan predecessors in the pantheon of Roman divinities.

His body was treated less kindly. Like any aspiring empire-builder Constantine had raised too many buildings too quickly with far too few skilled workers or decent materials. In consequence the jerry-built church began to suffer, and within only twenty-five years had fallen so far into disrepair that the dome was in danger of collapse, and the unpopular Patriarch Macedonius removed the emperor's body to the safety of St. Acacius the Martyr. To many, this was sacrilege, others seized the opportunity to attack Macedonius. In the ensuing riot several were

killed and so many wounded that 'the courtyard was covered with gore'. Despite its sad state, the Church of the Holy Apostles continued to stand until 550, when Justinian had it completely rebuilt; but by that time no trace could be found of the twelve sarcophagi or the great tomb of Constantine.

During his reign Constantine had unified the empire, secured the frontiers and safeguarded the provinces from civil war. He had enhanced the prestige of Roman arms and completed the complex series of administrative and military reforms of Diocletian. On the debit side of the balance sheet, most inhabitants of the empire were neither happy nor prosperous. Ground down by taxes and condemned to the unremitting drudgery of compulsory service, most were no better than slaves of the state. The massive weight of imperial bureaucracy that would characterise the late Roman empire and that of the succeeding Byzantine empire in the East had now come into being, together with the evils of corruption through the choice of imperial favourites for the many offices established. Rome had lost its pre-eminence and the old gods were almost gone. The theocratic state left by Constantine was still the Roman empire, but one that Augustus could not possibly have recognised.

Dalmatius

Hannibalianus

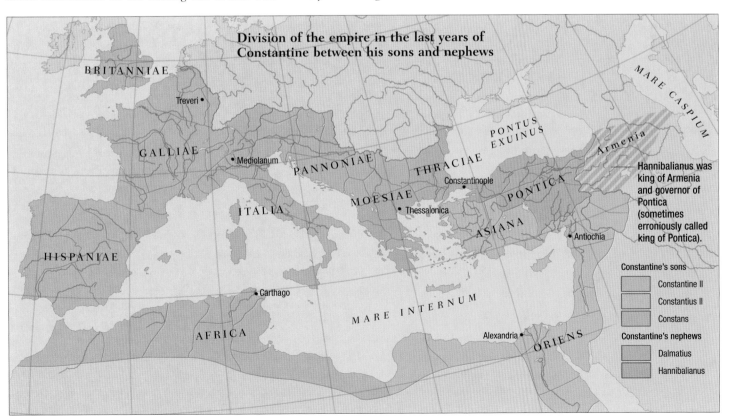

Division of the empire in the last years of Constantine between his sons and nephews

BRITANNIAE

Treveri

GALLIAE

Mediolanum

PANNONIAE

THRACIAE

PONTUS EXUINUS

MARE CASPIUM

Armenia

Constantinople

PONTICA

ITALIA

MOESIAE

Thessalonica

ASIANA

Antiochia

HISPANIAE

Carthago

MARE INTERNUM

Alexandria

ORIENS

AFRICA

Hannibalianus was king of Armenia and governor of Pontica (sometimes erroneously called king of Pontica).

Constantine's sons
Constantine II
Constantius II
Constans

Constantine's nephews
Dalmatius
Hannibalianus

Fulfilling his gubernatorial duties in Asiana when news of his father's death reached him, Constantius was the closest to Constantinople and so the son who went to preside over the funeral. Here, the emperor's body lay in state inside the palace. Eusebius said it was 'a marvellous spectacle such as no mortal had exhibited on earth since the world began'. The problem for the COMITATUS was that Constantine may have created a pool from which to pick a successor, but he does not appear to have actually named which Caesar should have IMPERIUM over the others. In this uncertainty, the court ceremony continued in Constantine's name as if his death had not happened. The INTERREGNUM lasted for almost three months before the army made the decision. The soldiers everywhere proclaimed that they would only accept Constantine's sons, reigning jointly. Accordingly, on 9 September 337, Constantine II, Constantius II and Constans became co-Augusti.

In the weeks before his father's funeral, the grace and comportment of Constantius had greatly impressed Constantinople's aristocracy and citizens, but as soon as his father had finally been laid to rest he discarded the polite mask and instigated a bloody sequel. The flimsy pretext was a written message allegedly found clenched in the deceased Constantine's fist accusing his two half-brothers, Dalmatius and Julius Constantius, of having poisoned him, and begging his sons to revenge him. However improbable this must have seemed, the people of Constantinople accepted it. Julius Constantius and his eldest son were cornered and both butchered a few feet from the palace steps, while Dalmatius was killed shortly after, together with his two sons, the Caesars Dalmatius and Hannibalianus king of Armenia. Constantine's two brothers-in-law, many of his closest friends, senators and the PRAEFECTUS PRAETORIO Ablavius met similar fates, even though the latter's daughter was betrothed to Constans.

Although this massacre was co-ordinated by Constantius, it seems obvious enough that the other brothers, at the very least, supported the dynastic cull, except perhaps Constans, who was only fifteen or sixteen. And by its effects, when all three brothers met at Viminacium in the summer of 338 to divide the empire between them, they were the only living adult males of the immediate imperial family. The territorial distribution altered little and, with a few adjustments, they each retained the provinces they had held as Caesars: Constantine II held sway over Britanniae, Galliae and Hispaniae; Constantius kept the eastern provinces and Aegyptus; while young Constans

CONSTANTINE II
Flavius Claudius Constantinus
(r.Caesar 1/3/317; Augustus 9/9/337–spring 340)

CONSTANTIUS II
Flavius Julius Constantius (r.Caesar 13/11/324;
Augustus 9/9/337–3/11/361

CONSTANS
Flavius Julius Constans (r.Caesar 25/12/333;
Augustus 9/9/337–January 350)

MAGNENTIUS
Flavius Magnus Magnentius
(usurper, r.January 350–353)

Constantine the Great's inheritors and would-be heirs, clockwise from left: coins of Constantine II, Constantius II, the usurper Magnentius and Constans.

All sons of the empress Fausta, Constantine II was born at Arelate in the summer of 316, Constantius II in Illyricum on 7 August 317, and Constans at some point between 320–23, either at Treveri or in Illyricum. Although he was the eldest of the brothers, Constantine II was to lead the shortest life, dying as a result of the sibling rivalry that was to dog the next fifteen years.

received the largest patrimony: Africa, Italia, the Illyrian dioceses, Macedonia and Thraciae. This gave him the control of Constantinople, although in the event this was to be of little significance.

Unfortunately for the empire, none was the man his father had been. As the eldest, Constantine II attempted to exert his authority over the others, especially Constans, his closest neighbour and still little more than a child. Constans refused to submit to his will and late in 339 asked Constantius for his help in return for giving him authority over Constantinople. Constantine II then invaded Italia in 340, but Constans – proving that neither did he require the aid of Constantius, nor was he a less shrewd commander than his eldest brother – ambushed Constantine near Aquileia. Constantine II was slain during the battle and his body thrown into a river, and Constans assumed command of the western and central empire. However good a soldier he may have been, administrative responsibility was a quality the young man did not possess. Had he a spark of his father's imperial abilities, he might have made much of his huge realm, but brought up in an autocratic court, the spoiled baby of the family, swamped by pomp and ceremony, he preferred to ally himself to the memories of Caligula, Nero, Commodus and Elagabalus. The few duties he performed – including a visit to Britanniae in 343, the last legitimate Roman emperor to do so – were of little effect. It is true that his campaign of 341–2 against the Franks *was* successful, but with its conclusion he gave himself over to a life of depravity.

In the Pannonian governor Sextus Aurelius Victor's *History of the Caesars* Constans is described as 'a leader in avarice' and as having 'contempt for his soldiers'. This refers to his neglect of the frontier legions in preference to indulging himself with homosexual orgies that involved selected numbers of his blond German captives. For some seven years the army put up with its ruler's antics, but the evident discontent began to alarm Constans' chief ministers. By the end of 349 the army was on the brink of revolt. Matters came to a head at a dinner given on 18 January 350 at Augustodunum (Autun), when Constans was absent on a game hunt. In the course of the meal an officer of British extraction called Magnentius suddenly stood up wearing a purple cloak, and was proclaimed Augustus by his fellow officer-guests. Warned of the revolt, Constans fled, but was soon captured and killed on the spot where he was discovered.

The chaos this murder caused spread rapidly throughout the western dioceses. The Illyrian troops caught in the middle were uncertain whether to follow Magnentius or Constantius. Alarmed at the situation, the emperor's sister Constantia persuaded their venerable general, a man of humble Moesian origin who had served under Constantine the Great named Vetranio, to assume the title of Caesar and lead his men against the usurper. She wrote to Constantius, imploring him to back her choice, which it seems he did. He accepted Vetranio as a fellow ruler, although with what level of IMPERIUM is unclear, since he refused to send him any money or reinforcements.

Magnentius's brother Decentius.

Meanwhile, in the vicinity of Rome, Julius Nepotianus, the son of Constantine the Great's half-sister Eutropia, proclaimed himself emperor on 3 June 350 and attacked the city with a band of gladiators. Magnentius – cutting diamond with diamond – quickly moved against him, dispatching a force sufficient to overwhelm Nepotianus within twenty-seven days. The young man suffered the punishment for usurping a usurper by being beheaded and having his head paraded around Rome on the sharp end of a spear.

Constantius's faithful old general Vetranio, whom he, for a short while, raised to the purple.

Although Constantius had his hands full battling the Sassanians, he could not ignore the threat that Magnentius posed and, detaching enough troops to make up a large army, he marched for the West. On his way he met with Vetranio at Serdica, and the two men moved on to Naissus. There, on 25 December 350, Constantius persuaded the Illyrian troops to reaffirm their oath to him, after which he stripped Vetranio of his temporary purple and allowed the old soldier to retire on a state pension for the remaining six years of his life. However, the unfolding events made it clear that he could not reclaim the West, let alone rule both halves of the empire on his own; he needed someone to look after the eastern dioceses and guard against Persia, and while encamped at Sirmium he ordered his young cousin Gallus from Constantinople to join him on the Danuvius, and there elevated him to the rank of Caesar.

Julius Nepotianus, who tried to usurp the usurper Magnentius in 350.

GALLUS

Claudius Constantius Gallus
(r.[East] Caesar 3/15/351–354)

Gallus, youngest of the three children of Julius Constantius (half-brother of Constantine I through Constantius Chlorus) and Galla was born in 325–26 at Massa Veternensis in Etruria, northern Italy. He is described as blond-haired and handsome, but of an intemperate character. His mother died at some point before 331, by which time Julius Constantius's second wife, Basilina, had also died giving birth to his half-brother Flavius Claudius Julianus (Julian). His sister had become the first wife of Constantius II in about 335 and her passing may have facilitated her father's fall. Gallus escaped the massacre of 337 that took both his father and elder brother Julian because he was thought to be suffering from a terminal illness.

It is possible that Gallus was entrusted to the care of Eusebius the bishop of Nicomedia in company with his younger half-brother Claudius Julian. Here, and later at Macellum in Cappadocia, the two boys were given a spiritual and classical education as befitted their status, and the six-year sojourn is described as pleasant. Macellum had originally been the palace of the kings of Cappadocia, and by Roman standards it was probably not luxurious, but the estate's proximity to the bustling entrepôt of Caesarea (Kayseri) meant that it was hardly isolated. Julian, however, later noted that Gallus possessed a violent streak, which he attributed to their 'forced stay' at Macellum.

Gallus was aged about twenty-five when he was called to Sirmium in March 351 to receive the rank of Caesar from Constantius and the hand of the emperor's

sister Constantina, to whom Constantine I had given the title Augusta when she married Hannibalianus. The marriage was meant to ensure the loyalty of Gallus, but it was also an effective snub to Magnentius, who himself had sought to wed Constantina in order to legitimise his usurpation and make an alliance with Constantius. It might even have been a way of removing his meddlesome sister from the volatile West and allowing her to vent her political aspirations by controlling the young and inexperienced Caesar. In any event, the arrangement between the rulers was not to be a successful one, and this was more the fault of Constantius than Gallus. According to Julian, the emperor's jealousy of Gallus began the moment he proclaimed him Caesar. Constantius made the choice of his ministers for him, and appointed his PRAEFECTUS PRAETORIO, Thalassius, and QUAESTOR SACRI PALATII, Montius Magnus.

After the ceremonies, as Constantius left Sirmium to face Magnentius, Gallus went to Antiochia, visiting his young half-brother in Nicomedia on the way. The meeting of Gallus and Julian, when it reached the ears of Constantius aroused his suspicions, but he was a man who naturally suspected everything and every person. However, the emperor had no time to dwell on domestic matters because Magnentius had used the time well and crossed from Gallia into the Balkans. The armies met on 28 September 351 at Mursa (Osijek), where Gallienus had crushed the usurper Ingenuus, and where Magnentius suffered a similar fate. However, he managed to escape with a part of his force and return to Galliae to begin gathering another army.

Magnentius then conspired to assassinate Gallus. He sent one of his servants to Antiochia with money enough to bribe some of Gallus's guard. But the plot leaked because the woman in whose home Magnentius's envoy lodged overheard the conspirators' unguarded discussions. She went to the palace and informed Constantina, and Gallus had the messenger and soldiers arrested, tortured and executed. If the plot was intended to throw Constantius into confusion it failed in its purpose. The emperor pursued Magnentius, and after several inconclusive skirmishes, finally defeated him at Lugdunum in 353, after which Magnentius fell on his own sword.

Gallus had been more than usually vulnerable to assassination because his MAGISTER PEDITUM Ursicinus had been sent to crush a rebellion of Jews in Palaestina that had started in the space of time between Constantius's removal of himself to defeat Magnentius and Gallus's arrival in Antiochia. As one

Claudius Gallus Caesar was married to Constantius's ambitious sister Constantina. Their irresponsible behaviour in Asia was to rouse the emperor's ire and lead to Gallus's doom.

history recorded: 'Through the murders of many thousands of men – even those too young to pose a threat – Gallus [that is Ursicinus in his name] suppressed the Jews, who, having murdered soldiers at night, had seized arms for the purpose of rebellion. And he put to the torch their cities Diocaesarea, Tiberias and Diospolis, and many towns.' In addition, Gallus is credited by some sources with many successes against the Sassanians, but this is improbable for one very good reason. Shapur II had concluded a treaty with Constantius in 350 and had withdrawn from Nisibis in order to check a series of nomadic incursions on his eastern borders. Dealing with this threat meant that there was an uneasy peace on the Romano-Sassanid border during Gallus's reign as Caesar, so it is unlikely he had need to undertake any military campaigns.

Gallus fell foul of the senatorial class of Antiochia when – after Theophilus, the CORRECTOR of Syria, opposed his move to lower the price of grain – he aroused the anger of the mob against the nobility. Theophilus was taken out and butchered, and street rioters put many houses of the wealthy to the torch. There then followed a series of trials engineered through AGENTES against innocent victims of Gallus and Constantina's jealousy. Several senators were executed and their estates confiscated, while Gallus roamed the streets at night in disguise soliciting passersby for their opinion of their Caesar. His actions against the nobility pleased the mob and Gallus furthered his popularity with many games and races at the hippodrome.

The PRAEFECTUS PRAETORIO Thalassius did nothing to restrain Gallus's violence, but he kept suspicious Constantius informed of the Caesar's every move. When Thalassius died of natural causes in 353, Constantius hastened to appoint a certain Domitianus as the successor before Gallus should take the matter into his own hands, and sent him to Antiochia to ensure a continued watch on his cousin. Constantius feared that the excesses of Gallus might precipitate open rebellion in Syria at a time when he was still facing a serious situation along the Rhenus as a result of Constans' neglect and Magnentius's depletion of frontier troops. But Gallus, enraged by the haughty Domitianus, ordered Montius Magnus to see to his death. Montius pointed out that in executing the PRAEFECTUS PRAETORIO Gallus would be exceeding his authority. As the story goes, Constantina strode up to the quaestor and 'dragged down Montius from his judgement-seat with her own hands', and with the consent of Gallus the soldiers killed both men.

However, there may have been a more cogent reason for the two deaths. Soon after his arrival in Antiochia Domitianus had dispatched his son-in-law Apollinaris, who had been in charge of the management of the palace at Antiochia, to Mesopotamia, where there was a large concentration of troops in winter quarters. The later discovery of an imperial robe at Tyrus (Tyre) was connected to Apollinaris's father. And Montius was associated with two TRIBUNI FABRICARUM, officers of the armoury, named Epigonus and Eusebius, who had promised arms in the event of a revolution, and whose names Montius offered up under torture. Putting these disparate pieces together suggests a palace conspiracy that Gallus had no alternative but to defuse. The MAGISTER EQUITUM Ursicinus was recalled from Nisibis to preside over the treason trials of Epigonus, Eusebius and Apollinaris. Gallus then appointed the half-brother of his mother, Vulcacius Rufinus, as his PRAEFECTUS PRAETORIO. At the time, the spring of 354, Constantius was engaged in a campaign against the Alamanni when he heard of the treason trials and the execution of his appointee. Furious at being thwarted, he ordered the replacement of Rufinus by another of his men, Volusianus Lampadius, and determined on the removal of Gallus. After concluding a peace with the barbarians, he retired to Mediolanum and requested the presence of Gallus and Constantina there.

It appears that from Athens, where he was residing, Claudius Julian tried to warn his half-brother of the emperor's real intentions, but Gallus was finally lured into journeying to meet Constantius for what he believed to be his elevation to co-Augustus. He may still have been saved had not Constantina died of a fever as they travelled through Bithynia, thus severing his legal connection to Constantius and losing in his wife his best supporter. As a precaution, Constantius removed all the troops along the route Gallus was taking, and so when he reached Poetovio near the border of Pannonia with Noricum, he had only a few guards available to him, and was easily arrested by a corps of troops under the command of an officer called Barbatio, accompanied by the AGENS IN REBUS Apodemius.

Gallus was stripped of his imperial robes by Barbatio and dragged to Pola in Histria where he was interrogated about the treason trials and deaths of the officials. Unwisely, he laid all the blame for these events on the ambitions of his dead wife, which news so enraged Constantius that he condemned Gallus to summary execution; he was only twenty-nine. The emperor then turned to Gallus's half-brother.

JULIAN THE APOSTATE

Flavius Claudius Julianus (r.Caesar 6/11/355; Augustus spring 360–26/6/363)

Claudius Julian's father, Julius Constantius, was the younger of the two sons born to Constantius Chlorus by his second wife Theodora. The family had been obliged to live in exile, albeit a comfortable one, due to Theodora's arch enemy, the Augusta Helena, Constantine's mother. However, after Helena's death, Constantine invited Julius Constantius to return to Constantinople and reinstated him in his affections. It was here in May or June 332 that his third son Julian was born to his second wife, Basilina. As has been related, when Constantius II caused the murders of Gallus's father Julius Constantius and his older brother Julian in 337, Gallus and his young half-brother Claudius Julian were spared.

Julian was sent to Nicomedia to be tutored by Bishop Eusebius and brought up as a good Christian. It is generally assumed that Gallus accompanied him, but if it was so it may not have been for the whole period, since the historian Socrates claims that Gallus was studying at Ephesus, where he had inherited

Flavius Claudius Julianus: the austere face of the man who decided to reinstate the pagan gods of old.

property, when Constantius had him exiled to Macellum. So when Eusebius was translated to the see of Constantinople in 339, it was probably only Julian who went with him to the capital. Eusebius died in 341 and in 342 Constantius sent the ten-year-old Julian and seventeen-year-old Gallus to Macellum, where they remained in effective isolation for six years before Gallus was recalled to become Caesar in 349. Julian, however, was ignored, for which fact he was very happy. Free to do as he pleased, he spent the next six years wandering the Greek world in search of every philosophical school he could find.

When he returned to Nicomedia he enrolled at the school of Libanius, a philosopher who had rejected Christianity and proclaimed himself a proud pagan. From Nicomedia Julian travelled first to Pergamum, then Ephesus, and finally to Athens in the early summer of 355. During these journeys he gradually became convinced that he must reject Christianity and return to the ways of the old Roman gods. Nevertheless, he was too astute to avow his faith openly, especially with the uncertain temper of his cousin Constantius II all too evident. Having voiced his fears to Gallus that Constantius was his enemy, he must have watched from afar with some horror as the events in late summer of 354 unfolded in Illyricum and his half-brother was executed. Julian now lived in dread, burying himself in his scholastic studies and hoping to remain ignored. But the removal of Gallus had not solved any problems of government for Constantius. The empire was still too large for one man to rule, and Julian was the only surviving relative of Constantine. So it was, in the summer of 355, when he was just into his twenty-fourth year, that Julian received the imperial summons to attend Constantius in Mediolanum.

Constantius did not hold his young cousin in any affection. The Christian bias of St. Gregory of Nazienzen, a fellow-student of Julian's in Athens, paints an exaggerated but essentially correct picture in describing him: '...that oddly disjointed neck, those hunched and twitching shoulders, that wild, darting eye, that swaying walk, that haughty way of breathing down that prominent nose....' Julian, deprived of any company of his own age and bookish, was a shy and socially dysfunctional young man whose speech was halting and whose laughter when provoked was described as being 'nervous and uncontrolled'. Disdainful of his scholarship, Constantius had his student beard shaved, his long hair cut in short trooper style, his out-of-condition body stuffed into a military uniform and, on 6 November, paraded him before the troops to acclaim him as Caesar.

A few days later Julian married Constantius's second sister, Helena the Younger, in order to cement the alliance between the two men. For his part, Julian had no reason to love his cousin and emperor. Aged just five at the time of his father's death, he had only later discovered the part Constantius had played in that murder, and he feared that unless he trod very warily, he would soon suffer the same fate as Gallus. By contrast, Constantius felt he had little to fear from Julian, who had absolutely no military experience and would therefore behave perfectly as was intended, a figurehead of the emperor. He was dispatched rapidly to Galliae with, as Libanius later put it, 'the authority to do nothing save wear the uniform.' As he had done with Gallus, Constantius appointed all Julian's ministers and generals on his behalf, confident that they would win the war against the Alamanni.

But Constantius had seriously underestimated the wandering scholar. When Julian discovered that his PRAEFECTUS PRAETORIO and MAGISTER EQUITUM were reporting directly to Constantius and not to him, he quickly perceived that this was a deliberate attempt to diminish his authority rather than a perfectly sensible arrangement in view of his lack of civilian administration and military experience. Julian was a conscientious student in all he undertook, and made it his business to learn soldiering fast.

So it was that the successful lightning campaign of 356 resulted as much from his efforts as those of his cautious generals. On 1 December 355, Julian, who was in Augusta Taurinorum (Turin), learned that the Franks had captured Colonia Agrippina. However, his first priority was the Alamanni, who had occupied large parts of Galliae. He moved to Vienna (Vienne in France) for the winter. From there in the spring, the army swept through Augustodunum (Autun), Tricasini (Troyes), Durocortorum (Reims) and Mediomatrici (Metz), clearing the Alamanni before it. Julian then pushed the enemy through the Vosges. From here he turned north and retook Colonia Agrippina. In the following year he won a great victory over the Alamanni near Argentorate (Strasbourg). In this battle thirteen thousand Romans faced more than thirty thousand Alamanni, and left over six thousand dead on the field for a loss of only two hundred and forty-seven legionaries. By 359 Julian had recovered the length of the Rhenus frontier and spent time supervising the repair and extension of the fortifications. While this was being done, he made his new capital on the Sequana (Seine) at Lutetia Parisiorum.

Julian did more in this period than command his army. He proved to be an able administrator and became widely liked for correcting the injustices of Constantius's appointees. Two instances point to his popularity with the provincials. The first is a commendation from Hilary, the bishop of Limonum Pictonum (Poitiers), that praises Julian as an able representative of the emperor to the Gallic provincials. The second is the epigraphic evidence of an inscription found near Beneventum in Apulia, which reads: 'To Flavius Claudius Julianus, most noble and sanctified Caesar, from the caring Tocius Maximus, VIR CLARISSIMUS, for the care of the RES PUBLICA from Beneventum.'

Meanwhile, on the eastern front Constantius was having a much less happy time. Fractious border skirmishes had escalated to the point that in 359 Shapur II sent an embassy to the emperor demanding the return of Mesopotamia and Armenia which had been 'fraudulently extorted from my grandfather'. If the ambassadors were to return empty-handed, he threatened, he would take to the field as soon as the winter was past. He was as good as his word, and towards the end of the year captured the key fortress of Amida (Diyarbakir), which controlled the headwaters of the Tigris and the approaches to Cappadocia. Before the year was out, Sassanian forces had built a strong position in Mesopotamia and were threatening fortified Nisibis and the province of Osrhoene.

Constantius reviewed his situation and decided that he needed reinforcements, and so in January 360 Julian in Lutetia received the demand that he strip his army of three hundred men for every unit under his command, plus four AUXILIA of Gallic and Frankish allies. Apart from the obvious fact that to comply would reduce his strength by a half, he had promised his Gallic detachments that they would never have to serve in the East. This situation had obtained before along the Danuvius, when the settled soldiers were asked to abandon their homes, wives and families to the mercy of barbarians across a weakly defended frontier. And the outcome was the same: the troops refused.

For his part, Julian later claimed in a letter to the Athenians that he had no desire to disobey the emperor's command, and even went so far as to encourage the men with the riches that awaited their victory in the East. He promised that their families would be transported with them at public expense. But these

Constantius underestimated the military abilities of scholarly young Julian (below).

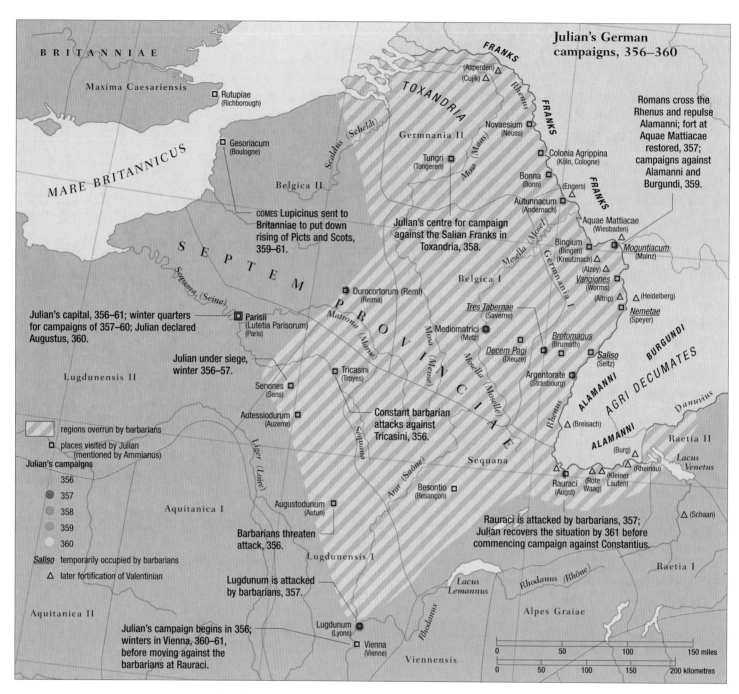

Julian's German campaigns, 356–360

Romans cross the Rhenus and repulse Alamanni; fort at Aquae Mattiacae restored, 357; campaigns against Alamanni and Burgundi, 359.

COMES Lupicinus sent to Britanniae to put down rising of Picts and Scots, 359–61.

Julian's centre for campaign against the Salian Franks in Toxandria, 358.

Julian's capital, 356–61; winter quarters for campaigns of 357–60; Julian declared Augustus, 360.

Julian under siege, winter 356–57.

Constant barbarian attacks against Tricasini, 356.

Barbarians threaten attack, 356.

Lugdunum is attacked by barbarians, 357.

Julian's campaign begins in 356; winters in Vienna, 360–61, before moving against the barbarians at Rauraci.

Rauraci is attacked by barbarians, 357; Julian recovers the situation by 361 before commencing campaign against Constantius.

regions overrun by barbarians

places visited by Julian (mentioned by Ammianus)

Julian's campaigns
356
357
358
359
360

Saliso temporarily occupied by barbarians

△ later fortification of Valentinian

0   50   100   150 miles
0   50   100   150   200 kilometres

entreaties failed to calm the aroused spirit of the troops, who vilified Constantius as unfit to rule them. Julian apparently retired to his chambers, but was disturbed in the night to be told the army was marching on the palace. According to his own words, he prayed to Jupiter and was told by the god to accept the diadem. By this time Julian had enjoyed five years of growing experience and become not merely a good general, but one of Rome's finest. His years of secretive worship had also convinced him that it was his destiny to restore the empire to the old Roman gods, and he was at the head of an army whose soldiers were still mostly pagans.

There was no alternative. According to Ammianus Marcellinus – an officer in one of the SCHOLAE and one of the best sources for the period (*see side panel opposite*) – since no suitable object to act as a crown could be found, the standard-bearer of a legion removed the great gold chain that was the insignia of his office from his shoulders and placed it on Julian's head. It was late February or early March of 360 and he was not yet twenty-eight.

For a year little happened. Julian was uncertain about how to proceed – and to an extent his hands were tied by the promises he had made to so many of his Gallic troops – and Constantius was unable to. Negotiations between the two emperors became acrimonious. Constantius did manage to stir up trouble among the Alamanni, but this only ensured that Julian was even more tied to his frontier, so it was not a particularly effective tactic. His concern over what Constantius might do also held him back when news of an invasion of northern Britanniae by Scots and Picts arrived during 360. Fearing in the face of the Alamanni to leave Galliae himself, he sent his MAGISTER EQUITUM Lupicinus to handle the barbarian raiders. Peace in the diocese was essential, for by this time, Ammianus informs us, British grain was as essential to Galliae as Egyptian and African was to Italia. Lupicinus took a force made up from Heruli and 'Bataviani' (Salian Franks), together with two units detached from Moesian legions. Ammianus fails to report the outcome, but evidently the marauders were repulsed and peace re-established.

And then in 361 the stalemate broke. Some success in the East against the Sassanians had led to a lull in the war and Constantius took advantage to detach units and head for the West. Because of his promise, and because of his unwillingness to denude the frontier garrisons, the army Julian could call on was pitifully small, only some twenty-three thousand troops. Since he was also uncertain how loyalties lay in northern Italia and along the Danuvius, he decided to split his army into three separate forces to make his strength appear greater than it really was. Ten thousand would cross the Alps into Italia and, via Aquileia, enter Illyricum. A similar number was to march through Raetia and Noricum, while Julian took three thousand to the upper Danuvius and then sailed downriver to meet the two other contingents at Sirmium. Julian was the first to arrive and, impatient to push on, took his small force to Naissus (Nis), where he decided to pass the winter. He had been there for approximately four weeks when astonishing news arrived from Constantinople. Constantius was dead, and Julian had been proclaimed by the armies of the East.

Julian had won his bloodless victory by the hand of fate. Constantius had moved from the Syrian frontier to Antiochia and was setting out to cross Anatolia when he was stricken by a fever and died at the small village of Mopuscrenae on 3 November 361. He was just forty-four years old. On Julian's orders Constantius's body was taken to Constantinople in state, and the emperor himself attended to the obsequies on 11 December and led the mourning for his enemy, we are told, with every sign of genuine sadness. Constantius was laid to rest

beside his father Constantine the Great in the Church of the Holy Apostles; it was the last time that Julian was to set foot in a Christian church.

The inauguration of Julian's reign was not, however, entirely without incident. During the last weeks of December 361, the emperor convened a military tribunal at Chalcedon – on which he did not himself serve – to try several of Constantius's former ministers. Ammianus was gloomy about the fate of those tried because the judges '...oversaw the cases more vehemently than was right or fair, with the exception of a few...'. Some were acquitted, many were banished, and a few were executed, including the two chief AGENTES of Constantius's intelligence network, who were sentenced to be buried alive. Ammianus was particularly distressed at the treatment meted out to Ursulus, Constantius's COMES SACRUM LARGITIONUM, who had previously served with distinction as Julian's finance minister in Gallia before being transferred to the East. Ursulus had passed a remark disparaging the eastern army's inefficiency during the siege of Amida in Mesopotamia Superior. The soldiers had not forgotten it and now demanded Ursulus's head. Although he was not a member of the tribunal, the emperor could have intervened to save his old friend, and that he did not do so disappointed Ammianus and many other of Julian's admirers.

Once Julian was emperor, he instituted radical reforms at court. The thousands of flunkeys were reduced to a skeleton staff, and frugal simplicity ruled daily life. His political and religious reforms were just as drastic.

'The language of truth is unadorned and always simple'

Ammianus Marcellinus, his motto above, is the effective chronicler of his age. Most knowledge of his background is obtained from autobiographical references in his *Res Gestae*. However, it does not offer us a place or date of birth. It is variously assumed that he came from Antiochia, Alexandria, or Thessalonica, and he calls himself a 'Greek'. He tells us that he was an ADOLESCENS in 357, and so must have been born sometime before 338. In his twenties, he joined the army as PROTECTOR DOMESTICUS on the staff of Ursicinus, MAGISTER EQUITUM in the East. This appointment suggests that Ammianus was of a family enjoying high rank, since he was too young to have built a distinguished military career that the position usually required. Although he did not always agree with Julian's actions, their bookish interests cemented a mutual empathy. And it is clear that Ammianus preferred literary pursuits to those of soldiering when he tells us that 'I was now overcome with excessive walking, to which as a gentleman [INGENUUS] I was not accustomed.'

Restoration of the old gods

Julian was a very different emperor to those of the Diocletianic courts and the family of Constantine. After the recent death of his wife Helena the Younger he remained celibate, austere in his wishes for comfort, and had showed little interest in food or wine. His purge of the imperial court was swift and extraordinarily thorough. Libanius describes how the imperial cortège had grown exponentially since the time of Diocletian: *'There were a thousand cooks, as many barbers, and even more butlers. There were swarms of lackeys, the eunuchs were more in number than flies around the flocks in spring...'* Of the thousands of chamberlains, major-domos, and drones, none remained when Julian was finished, and he furnished himself with little more than a skeleton staff.

Julian's reforms of religion and government were equally ambitious, and seemed to be oriented towards an older Republican tradition. He gave greater powers to the senate, which he studiously attended, walking on foot as a sign of respect. He was assiduous in hearing judicial matters, and made steps to reform the bureaucracy where he detected a decline in administrative or moral standards. In one instance he noted that in Illyicum, at least, the VICARI had been rendered ineffective because CORRECTORES and PRAEDSIDES were reporting directly to the PRAEFECTUS PRAETORIO, and on June 6, 362, he issued an edict banning governors from bypassing their VICARIUS. He also imposed penalties on governors who purposefully delayed appeals in court cases they had heard. With a non-existent imperial COMITATUS, Julian relied heavily on the senate and consulars to act as intermediaries between emperor and his subjects, which again gave more power and prestige to the old upper classes of Constantinople.

There is some question that Julian's apostasy was rapid, any more than Constantine's conversion had been. However, there is no doubt that by the time he had become sole ruler of the empire the process was complete. Consequently, the people who suffered the most were the Christians. But Julian had no intention of reverting to the days of persecution, perhaps because at heart he was a merciful man, mostly because he had learned that martyrs seemed to have an opposite effect on the Christian Church to that intended. He repealed the decrees by which the pagan temples had been closed down and their sacrifices declared illegal, and issued an edict of religious tolerance, exactly as Constantine had done, but of course with the opposite effect. And then in a masterstroke, he offered an amnesty to all the orthodox churchmen who had been exiled under Constantius's pro-Arian government. Ammianus noted that Julian had found by experience 'that no wild beasts are so hostile to men as are Christian sects in general to one another'. He hoped that after the opposing leaders had shown their viciousness to one another, the mass of Christians would see the error of their ways and return to the old religion.

There was far more to his dislike of Christianity than that it had made adherents among honest Romans. From his own writings it is clear that he held Christianity to be the single culprit for the ills of the empire. Instead of Constantine's unity of Church and state binding emperor and people, Julian saw only an effete creed that insidiously robbed Romans of their solid virtues by preaching the feminine qualities of meekness, gentleness and charity. No wonder the army was barely capable any longer of manning the frontiers if Christian fifth-columnists were telling the soldiers to turn the other cheek. It was, of course, a simplistic view – as late as the fifth century Mithras remained the preferred deity of the frontier troops. However, the lessons of Maximinus Daia were not lost on Julian, and he made plans to organise the soon-to-be-revived pagan cults along Christian lines: charitable and social institutions like those offered by the Christian churches would be founded for the support of widows, orphans and the sick. But none of this came to pass, for paganism seemed in no hurry to revive.

The invasion of Persia

In the summer of 362 Julian moved his austere court to Antiochia in preparation for war against Persia. In the six weeks he travelled across Anatolia he discovered to his dismay that the Christians were not tearing each other apart. Indeed, relaxing again after the initial fear of persecution had faded, the many Christian communities he passed appeared to be flourishing, while those of the pagans seemed to be no stronger than in Constantine's day.

Julian had already aroused the irritation of the populace of Constantinople with his continual impassioned speeches on the subject of Neo-Platonism in the marketplaces and the forum. Now, as he progressed at a leisurely pace, he stopped at every temple on the route, detouring when necessary, to officiate at one sacrifice after another until he earned the nickname 'the butcher'. Desperate to compete, Julian demanded of the pagan priesthood that it must adopt a Christian lifestyle: no priest was to go to a tavern, frequent the theatre or engage in a base profession.

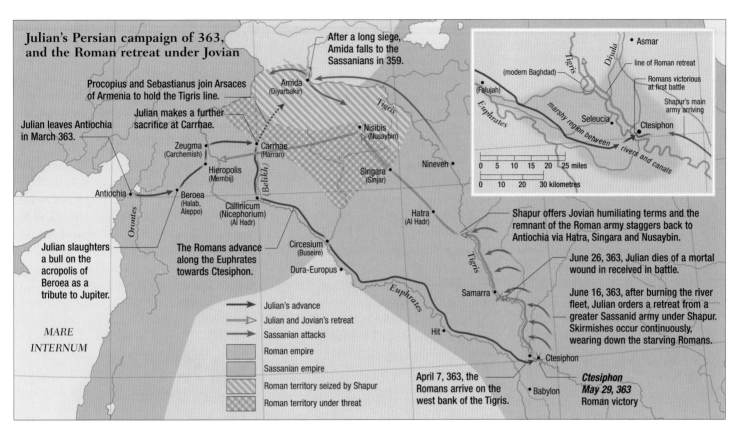

Julian's Persian campaign of 363, and the Roman retreat under Jovian

After a long siege, Amida falls to the Sassanians in 359.

Procopius and Sebastianus join Arsaces of Armenia to hold the Tigris line.

Julian makes a further sacrifice at Carrhae.

Julian leaves Antiochia in March 363.

Amida (Diyarbakir)

Tigris

Nisibis (Nusaybin)

Zeugma (Carchemish)

Carrhae (Harran)

Singara (Sinjar)

Nineveh

Hieropolis (Membij)

Antiochia

Beroea (Halab, Aleppo)

Callinicum (Nicephorium) (Al Hadr)

Hatra (Al Hadr)

Julian slaughters a bull on the acropolis of Beroea as a tribute to Jupiter.

The Romans advance along the Euphrates towards Ctesiphon.

Circesium (Buseire)

Dura-Europus

Tigris

Euphrates

Samarra

MARE INTERNUM

Hit

Ctesiphon

April 7, 363, the Romans arrive on the west bank of the Tigris.

Babylon

Shapur offers Jovian humiliating terms and the remnant of the Roman army staggers back to Antiochia via Hatra, Singara and Nusaybin.

June 26, 363, Julian dies of a mortal wound in received in battle.

June 16, 363, after burning the river fleet, Julian orders a retreat from a greater Sassanid army under Shapur. Skirmishes occur continuously, wearing down the starving Romans.

Ctesiphon May 29, 363 Roman victory

Asmar

line of Roman retreat

Romans victorious at first battle

Shapur's main army arriving

(modern Baghdad)

(Falujah)

Euphrates

Tigris

Diyala

marshy region between

Seleucia

Ctesiphon

rivers and canals

0 5 10 15 20 25 miles
0 10 20 30 kilometres

Julian's advance
Julian and Jovian's retreat
Sassanian attacks
Roman empire
Sassanian empire
Roman territory seized by Shapur
Roman territory under threat

Still nothing worked, and so on 17 June 362 he promulgated an edict with far-ranging consequences. It banned any Christian from acting as a teacher of rhetoric or literature. His reasoning was that no Christian who professed to teach the classics – in those days, virtually the whole of the school curriculum – could be of the required moral standard, since he was teaching something he did not himself believe in. With the future of the empire's education in doubt, and with hot-headed young Christians willing to flirt with martyrdom, tensions ran high. Then the emperor reached Antiochia and became immediately immersed in planning for the imminent Persian campaign, and any further tightening of the screw was postponed until his return from the war. Fortunately for the Christians he did not.

Between 350–58 Shapur had been occupied with nomadic raids and incursions on his eastern borders, and so an uneasy peace had existed between Sassanid Persia and Constantinople. But in 359, after the prolonged siege of Amida (Diyarbakir) that had prompted Ursulus's unfortunate remarks, the fortress fell into Shapur's hands. Since then there had been a dangerous build up of Persian troops in Mesopotamia Superior, and Julian was conscious that he would have to act if the situation was not to become worse. The army set out from Antiochia on 5 March 363. Using his trademark whirlwind strategy, Julian force-marched to Beroea (Aleppo) and on to Hieropolis (Membij), then slightly north to cross the Euphrates into Mesopotamia at Zeugma. By 27 March the army was all on the eastern side of the river, following its course southward, and Julian had constructed a flotilla to guard his supply line. His generals Procopius and Sebastianus were sent to help Arsaces, the client king of Armenia, to guard the northern Tigris line. By 7 April, after a few minor skirmishes and some sieges but without any serious trouble, the Roman army was on the west bank of the Tigris a short way north of Ctesiphon. Here, Sassanian resistance began to tell, and drawn up between the river and the city walls a Persian army stood ready for battle.

The Romans crossed the Tigris on 29 May and, despite having to fight their way across and form up on the opposite bank, were victorious. But it availed Julian nothing. His engineers advised that the siege would be drawn out and time was not on their side. The retreating Persians had scorched the earth to deny the Romans supplies, and the marshy ground, criss-crossed with canals and irrigation ditches between the two rivers, was badly flooded. The soldiers, close to starving, were further demoralised by squelching from one quagmire to another, while being tormented by swarms of flies so thick that, according to Ammianus, they blocked out the sky. Worse, scouts reported that a far larger army under Shapur's command was approaching. Julian's ambitions for glory were frustrated and we are told that in his anger he had his fleet burnt. However, this act was less one of petulance than of common sense, for it would have struggled to sail upstream, and leaving it behind would only benefit the Sassanians. Julian ordered the retreat on 16 June. As the Romans trudged along the east bank of the Tigris they were constantly harassed by Persian horsemen. During a particularly heavy attack on 26 June the emperor dashed out without his armour to rally his men and was struck in the abdomen by a Persian spear. His officers carried him back to his tent, but he was too severely wounded to survive and died shortly after.

At his death Julian was only just thirty-one and had been on the throne for a little over three years. In that time he achieved no legislation of any significance and wasted much of it attempting to revive a dying religion of confused parameters. It was, though, another case of an untimely death robbing the empire of a man who might well have become one of its finest rulers. His outstanding qualities – education, energy, an ability to inspire his soldiers, integrity and incorruptibility – were let down by his faults. His religious fanaticism blinded Julian to the priorities needed for good government, and his hesitancy – seen in continually asking the gods for

guidance instead of making his own decisions – turned into inflexibility once the divine course had been laid out for him. And with his passing, the line of Constantius Chlorus came to an end. Where would the empire go from here? The immediate answer was something of a joke, more of a comma in history than a full-stop.

JOVIAN
Flavius Jovianus (r.27/6/363–16/2/364)

Ammianus Marcellinus, who had so ably commented on the reign of Julian, gives a graphic explanation for the proclamation of Jovian as the next emperor. He was born at some point in 331 at Singidunum (Belgrade). His father Varronianus had a distinguished career under Constantius II and his father-in-law Lucillianus had commanded the army against the

British coastal garrisons are hard put to keep the sea-raiding Saxons at bay.

The renewed barbarian pressure on the frontiers, 363, after Julian removed troops for the Persian campaign

Despite Julian's best efforts to maintain frontier strength along the Rhenus during his battle with Constantius, continued draining of the troops leaves the region vulnerable to renewed attacks by Saxons in Germania II and Franks in Germania I.

The Sarmatae, squeezed between the Danuvius and the Visigoths, are being annihilated by their barbarian foe.

SAXONS

FRANKS

Treveri (Trier)

BURGUNDI

ALAMANNI

SUEVI

MARCOMANNI

Vindobona (Vienna)

Aquincum (Buda)

GEPIDAE

SARMATAE

VISIGOTHS

OSTROGOTHS

PANNONIAE

Poetovio (Ptuj)

Lugdunum (Lyons)

Mediolanum (Milan)

Aquileia

Marcianopolis

Ravenna

THRACIAE

DACIAE

VIENNENSIS

ITALIA

MARE ADRIATICUM

Thessalonica

ASIA

Roma

MARE   INTERNUM

Sassanians in 350. These factors more than his own abilities seem to have given him preferment, and Jovian had risen to become PRIMICERIUS DOMESTICORUM of the imperial guard. He was a well-liked, genial soldier of bluff temperament, and a Christian. He had, however, no particular qualities to recommend him as a ruler. The beleaguered Roman army commanders had little time for discussion, surrounded as they were by Sassanid forces the morning after Julian's death. Their first choice was the PRAEFECTUS PRAETORIO of the eastern provinces, Sallustius Secundus, but he declined the purple on the grounds of his advanced age and a growing infirmity. At that point, a small group of the SCHOLAE began to shout for their commander. Ammianus claims that the assembled army took up the acclamation, but by a dreadful mistake the men mistook the cry 'Jovianus!' to be 'Julianus!' because they thought their former emperor had recovered from his injury. The error became evident when the tall figure of Jovian was paraded before them, by which time it was too late to back down.

Under Jovian's uninspired leadership, the weary army continued its dreary northwards retreat along the east bank of the Tigris under renewed Sassanian harassment. Eventually the Romans made a forced crossing of the Tigris and, while he was still in a position of strength, Shapur offered terms to the new emperor. These were extremely unfavourable to Jovian, but he felt there was no option but to accept them. In return for being allowed an orderly retreat, Rome ceded territories in northern Mesopotamia, including five satrapies along the upper Tigris, five Roman frontier forts, including the two key strongholds Nisibis (Nusaybin) and Singara (Sinjar), and all the land to the east of them. Jovian also bound the Romans to a promise not to assist Armenia against Persian attack, effectively renouncing any claims over the client kingdom. The army was furious at these degrading terms and blamed Jovian for what had really been Julian's fault. But the troops still faced a hundred-mile march to safety across the desert, and without much in the way of supplies, since Shapur refused to offer any provisions as a part of the treaty. The only benefit Jovian gained was a promise of peace for thirty years.

During the trek from the Tigris to Hatra and Nisibis, the desert almost finished Shapur's abandoned task. Only by killing all their camels did the troops survive to limp on to Nisibis, where Jovian refused to enter a city he had promised to Shapur. The exhausted remnant of the army was given a few days to recover before continuing to Antiochia. During the rest, Julian's embalmed body was given into the hands of Procopius who, operating along the northern Tigris line, had avoided the debacle following Julian's withdrawal from Ctesiphon. He was a kinsman and old friend of the deceased emperor, and some said Julian had secretly appointed Procopius to succeed him. Procopius took the body for burial at Tarsus, where Julian had intended to establish his court. At Antiochia Jovian issued an edict of religious tolerance, which was received by the Christians in great relief – they, at least, were happy with the pagan tyrant's removal.

Jovian left Antiochia in mid-October, taking the army in easy stages through Anatolia, greeted at every stop by cheering Christian communities. On the first day of January 364 he assumed the consulship with his infant son Varronianus at Ancyra (Ankara) before moving on to the small town of Dadastana, half way to Nicaea. There, on the morning of 16 February, Jovian was found dead in his bedroom. The emperor was fond of his food and wine, and the mushrooms he had eaten the night before were suspected by some, while others blamed the fumes of an untended charcoal brazier in his bedchamber, from which he had suffocated. No one, however, suspected foul play. Jovian had been emperor for only eight months.

Facing: Raised to the purple by embattled troops after Julian's death, Jovian, a bluff soldier, was ill-equipped for the role of imperial leader.

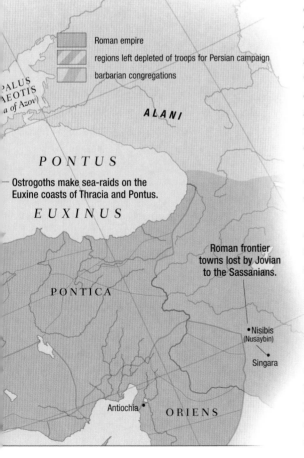

Roman empire

regions left depleted of troops for Persian campaign

barbarian congregations

PALUS
MAEOTIS
(Sea of Azov)

ALANI

PONTUS

Ostrogoths make sea-raids on the Euxine coasts of Thracia and Pontus.

EUXINUS

Roman frontier towns lost by Jovian to the Sassanians.

PONTICA

Nisibis
(Nusaybin)

Singara

Antiochia

ORIENS

CHAPTER THIRTEEN   AD 364–455
VALENTINIAN AND THE THEODOSIAN DYNASTY

VALENTINIAN I
Flavius Valentinianus (r.26/2/364–375)

Pondering on a choice of new emperor, the CONSISTO-RIUM and army leaders held a conclave at Nicaea. After much deliberation over a suitable candidate they agreed on an obscure officer called Flavius Valentinianus, who was still at Ancyra with his unit, and sent a dispatch to inform him of their decision. Valentinian arrived in Nicaea on 24 February 364, which being the BISEXTILIS meant that Valentinian's elevation was postponed for two days (*see side panel*). For once the soldiers had not had a hand in selecting the emperor, but Valentinian reassured them that the army's welfare was his greatest priority. Further, to appease the civilian administration of the East he promised to appoint a colleague as co-Augustus. However, he appeared to be in no hurry to do so and it was a month later that he astonished everyone by nominating his even more obscure brother Valens, who assumed the title on 28 March.

Valentinian seems like a strange choice for the conclave to have made. He was the uncouth and illiterate son of a Pannonian rope-maker, who refused to conceal his peasant origins and flew into uncontrollable

Valentinian: a good soldier, and a vigorous and thorough, if often brutal, administrator.

rages when opposed. However, at forty-two he was still a commanding, even forbidding presence, not at all like his brother. Valens, seven years the younger, was pot-bellied, grotesque in appearance and possessed of neither courage nor ability. What the brothers had in common was a notorious brutality, and perhaps it was this quality that had been mistaken for stern discipline. One example of this cruelty of *realpolitik* was the fate of poor little Varronianus, Jovian's infant son. According to John Chrysostom, the later bishop of Constantinople (398–404), the child had his eyes put out 'from fear of what might happen in the future, though he had done no wrong'. However, for Valentinian the appointment of Valens gave him a faithful lieutenant who acknowledged his older brother's superiority and would cause no trouble.

Valentinian was born in 321 at Cibalae (Vincovci) in southern Pannonia – five years after Constantine had defeated Licinius there – the eldest son of Gratianus, a peasant-soldier renowned for his strength and wrestling skills. In a distinguished military career, Gratianus rose through the ranks first to TRIBUNUS MILITUM, then to COMES AFRICAE and finally COMES BRITANNIAE. Suspected of having supported Magnentius, Constantius II confiscated his estates when Gratianus retired to set up his rope-making business. This did not apparently prevent his sons Valentinian or Valens entering into military careers, but Constantius's suspicions of them remained active. When Julian was acting as Caesar in the West in 357, Valentinian in command of a cavalry unit was accused of acting against the emperor's best interests, and Constantius dismissed him from service. Returned to civilian life, Valentinian married his first wife, Marina Severa, who died some time after giving birth to a son Gratianus (Gratian) in 359. He married again to a woman called Justina – of whom we shall shortly hear more – by whom he had a second son, Valentinianus (Valentinian II), and two daughters, Galla and Justa. Valens married Albia Domnica, but if there were any offspring, history does not record them. Both Valentinian and Valens were fiercely pro-Christian, with Valens preferring the teachings of the Arians.

Valentinian had been recalled to service by Jovian to assist the new emperor's father-in-law Lucillianus in visiting the various governors of the Gallic

THE BISEXTILIS occurred every four years, and was the equivalent of the modern leap year. Before the time of Julius Caesar the Romans had a civic year of 366¼ days. The pontiffs were responsible for making adjustments by adding or subtracting days from the civic year to match to the solar year, but when Caesar reformed the calendar the civic year was about three months ahead of the solar year. Caesar extended the year 46 BC to 445 days to correct this, and from 45 BC he made the civic year consist of 365 days. This required a further adjustment by adding an extra day every four years – called the BISEXTILIS – as we have it today. The extra day was added between 23 and 24 February, which is why the 24th and 25th days in February of a leap year were ill-omened (did they really exist?) and no business could be conducted.

provinces. Their task was twofold: to put a gloss on the conclusion of the Persian campaign and to elicit support for Jovian's succession. For his good offices Valentinian was promoted to command of a detachment of the Scutari legion in Galatia, which is where he was when Jovian suddenly died. After Valentinian's election, the court removed to Constantinople, where Valens was elevated to co-Augustus. The rest of the year and the winter months of 365 were spent at a villa three miles outside Naissus in a series of conferences that resulted in the division of the empire into two spheres, as had Valerian and Gallienus a hundred years earlier. Although history generally accords the official division of the empire into East and West spheres to Theodosius in 395, to all intents and purposes Valentinian's dispositions had sundered it into two separate entities. To popular surprise, Valens was given control of the Eastern dioceses and the eastern Balkans, while Valentinian took Galliae, Italia, Africa and Illyricum. Valentinian then went to the Rhenus to confront the renewed barbarian threat that had followed the departure of Julian in 361, and left his brother to meet the usurpation of Procopius (*see the following section*).

Valentinian had his hands full with a large-scale invasion of the Septem Provinciae by the Alamanni confederation, angered by his refusal to pay them the level of tribute to which previous emperors had accustomed them. Valentinian advanced to Durocortorum (Reims) and sent two DUCES, Charietto and Severianus, against the invaders, both of whom were defeated and died in the action. Their armies, under the new command of the MAGISTER EQUITUM Dagalaifus, were equally ineffective against the widely scattered Alamanni in 366, and Valentinian replaced him with another MAGISTER called Jovinus, who managed, after several battles, to push the Germans out of Galliae.

In 367 Valentinian was distracted from a punitive expedition against the Alamanni by problems in Britanniae and the province of Germania II. A combined force of Picts, Attacotti and Scots had overcome the DUX Fullofaudes and the British provinces were in a state of anarchy. At the same time, Frankish and Saxon forces were harrying the northern continental coast. Valentinian was unable to visit Britanniae because he fell ill – seriously enough to consider the matter of succession, and he elevated his eight-year-old son Gratian to be co-Augustus with him. Accordingly, Valentinian sent his COMES DOMESTICORUM Severus to Britanniae on an investigative tour. The answer came back that only a full-scale counterattack would relieve

the diocese. Accordingly, in the following year, Valentinian sent the COMES Theodosius to recover Britanniae, while Severus and Jovinus remained with the emperor to campaign against the Alamanni.

Theodosius landed in Britanniae in 368 with four legions, many recruited from those tribes who had remained allies of Rome, including the Salian Franks (Batavi) and Heruli, and proceeded to Londinium. After restoring order to the south, he began a brilliant campaign of guerrilla tactics against the Caledonian invaders that pushed them back north and beyond Hadrian's Wall. There were other benefits, since he also restored the confidence and organisation of the provinces' garrison, which had become demoralised by the defeat of Fullofaudes. Theodosius installed a new VICARIUS and military commander, and returned to Valentinian in 369 to be appointed MAGISTER EQUITUM in place of Jovinus.

Meanwhile, through a combination of diplomacy and intrigue Valentinian had carried the war across the Rhenus and deep into Alamanni territory. After an attack on Moguntiacum (Mainz) in early 368, the emperor connived with friendly Alamanni agents to have a chieftain called Vithicabius assassinated by his own bodyguard. In the confusion, Moguntiacum was retaken, and then the Roman army marched along the north bank of the Moenus (Main) before turning south, crossing it, and coming down the east bank of the Rhenus, burning dwellings and food stores along the way. The first serious resistance was encountered at Solicinium (Schwetzingen), where a great battle was fought, in which Valentinian was almost killed. Valentinian and ten-year-old Gratian, who had accompanied his father, returned to Treveri for the winter. From 369 to the end of his reign, Valentinian began a systematic programme of defensive construction. Many of the forts that Caracalla had built or refurbished in stone, were enlarged and new ones erected, from the mouth of the Rhenus in the north to Lacus Venetus (Lake Constance) in the south.

The northern forts were erected in reaction to renewed Saxon attacks in 370, which were brutally suppressed through treachery. Aided by detachments under the command of Severus, the COMES of Germania Inferior Nannienus fought several battles until the Saxons sued for peace. A treaty was agreed under which the Saxons exchanged a force of young warriors to serve in the legions in return for a safe passage to their homeland. But once the retiring barbarians were strung out, the Roman army fell on them and killed every one of them. Valentinian attempted further diplomacy to gain his ends against the Alamanni chieftain Macrianus, which failed in theory but worked in practice. He decided to make allies of the Burgundi, bitter enemies of their neighbours the Alamanni, and use them to attack Macrianus and, if unable to defeat his army, drive it into the waiting arms of the Romans. However, when Valentinian refused to meet the Burgundian envoys personally, his high-handedness angered them, and they returned home unwilling to support any Roman offensive. Nevertheless, the proposed alliance of their hated enemies with the Romans alarmed the Alamanni so much that they scattered, fearing an imminent attack. Theodosius was able to take advantage of their flight by crossing the Raetian LIMES and hitting the tribesmen on their flank. Many prisoners were captured, but they received a kind fate in being settled along the Padus valley where, according to Ammianus, they flourished.

Valentinian's administration

The civil administration under Valentinian was generally rigorous and thorough, if not even sometimes brutal, and away from the Rhenus frontier, peaceful. The one exception was Africa, where maladministration and corruption in the Tripolitanian cities hampered attempts to prevent incursions from nomadic desert tribes, and Mauretania suffered a tribal rebellion in 372. This occurred because of the corruption of the COMES Romanus, who took sides to fill his own pockets in a dispute between the legitimate and illegitimate children of a Moorish prince and client of Rome called Nubel. In 374 Provincials led by a certain Firmus revolted against these peculations, and Valentinian sent Theodosius to restore order. Firmus was defeated, but Theodosius also pursued the evidence against Romanus and had him arrested. From this point until his untimely death in 376 (*see under the section on Gratian*) Theodosius governed the diocese wisely and restored its profitable contribution to the empire.

Valentinian is credited with keeping the Roman empire from crumbling away by restoring confidence in the army and the frontier defensive system. However,

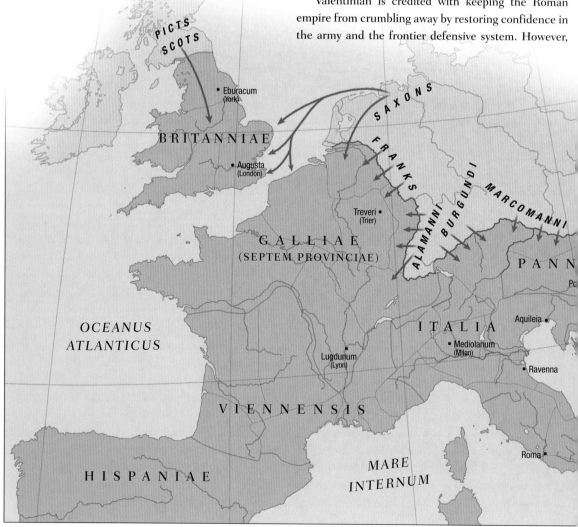

he did so at the expense of the civilian population and the traditional nobility, and it was the army commanders that were now the new aristocracy. The army's requirements took precedence over the needs of the public, and in this subordination of the civilian population, we can see the recognisable beginnings of the medieval feudal state that the Franks would later perfect. In Valentinian's world, the role of the senatorial class – whether in Rome, Mediolanum (his capital) or Constantinople – was utterly diminished. In Rome, the once august senate was little more than another municipal council with a parochial outlook. Deprived of the glory of imperial administration, the capabilities of its members had atrophied and its ability to give good counsel dwindled. This was now a world where military men made the important decisions, and the emperor delegated his authority to an ever longer chain of bureaucrats. These officials did not always perform their duties well, further alienating the populace from the imperial government. The increasing burden of taxation to pay for the army and the bureaucracy crushed the people, and it is understandable that they resented paying for a security that they did not always receive.

Unlike his Arian brother Valens, Valentinian was an orthodox Nicene, but he wisely refused to become embroiled in the religious controversies of the time.

He even dismissed a deputation of eastern Nicene bishops who appealed to him to control Valens' Arian excesses. He was, however, more partisan when it came to heretics, particularly the Manichaeans – who were banned from assemblies in Rome in 372 on the pain of death – and the Donatists in Africa. In 373 he completed the work Diocletian had given up, banned the heresy and condemned the Donatist bishops. However, some Christians received extraordinary privileges, such as a law passed in 371 that exempted from onerous municipal services any clerics who could prove they were ecclesiastics before his accession. Towards the pagans he exercised remarkable tolerance, permitting the retention of the title PONTIFEX MAXIMUS and passing legislation that confirmed the rights of pagan divination. However, he is blamed for later appearing to rescind this with a series of trials exclusively aimed at the senatorial order, whose members were accused of using magic (which may have meant divination) and being adulterers. However, the real purpose behind these sham trials was the extraction of property for the FISCUS, and the downgrading of the senatorial order – a process that would continue after his death.

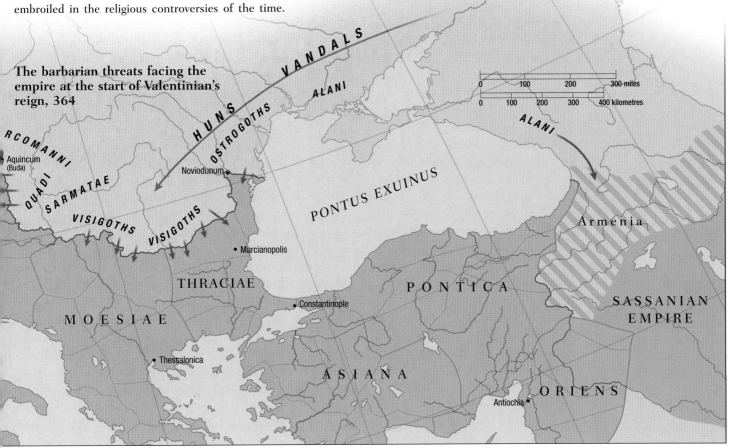

The barbarian threats facing the empire at the start of Valentinian's reign, 364

In 373 trouble erupted with the Quadi, a tribe that had been mostly peaceful for several generations. The problem arose from resentment at the way Roman forts were being built on what they considered their side of the Danuvius. A low-level amount of resistance had led to the construction programme falling behind schedule, but as the man in charge, Marcellianus, increased the pressure the unrest turned to open acts of sabotage. In an attempt to restore peace King Gabinius of the Quadi arranged a meeting with the Romans, but in a fit of frustration during the negotiations, Marcellianus slew the king. Allying with their neighbours, the more warlike Sarmatae, the Quadi crossed the Danuvius along its north-south reaches and began ravaging the undefended Pannonian countryside of Valeria. Two legions were dispatched to counter the invaders, but were routed by Sarmatian forces. Meanwhile, further to the east, another Sarmatian army invaded Moesia, but was driven back by legions under the command of an extraordinary young man, DUX MOESIAE Theodosius, son of Valentinian's MAGISTER EQUITUM Theodosius, who was now governing Africa.

Valentinian only heard of the disaster in Pannonia in the later months of 374. In spring 375 he set out from Treveri and went to Carnuntum, which he found deserted. Ignoring an embassy from the Quadi that tried to present their righteous case (and disassociating themselves from the actions of the Sarmatae), Valentinian determined to punish them. His army crossed the Danuvius at Aquincum (Buda[pest]) and pillaged the lands of the Quadi without mercy. As winter approached, the Romans retired to Brigetio (Szöny) in Valeria, intending to continue the campaign in the spring. On 17 November another deputation of Quadi arrived in an attempt to persuade Valentinian to desist. The emperor granted the envoys an audience, but the Quadi, while being placatory, would not budge from demanding an apology for the murder of their king. As he listened, Valentinian grew angrier and angrier. Becoming ever redder in the face, he suddenly stood up in an apoplectic fit, paused, and collapsed to the floor in a faint. Realising his death was near and that Gratian was far away at Treveri and his brother Valens even further in Antiochia, he called for his second son, Valentinian, and made him co-Augustus with Gratian; after which, at the age of fifty-four, Valentinian expired. The empire was, therefore, in the hands of three rulers, a child of four years, a boy of sixteen, and a middle-aged sadist without any merit. And on these three the Romans depended at one of the most critical times — they were about to face a new and more terrifying barbarian foe: the Huns.

VALENS
Flavius Valens (r.28/2/364–9/8/378)

Ammianus informs us that Valens was *'dilatory and sluggish; of a swarthy complexion; had a cast in one eye; his limbs were well set; his figure was neither tall nor short; he was knock-kneed, and rather pot-bellied.'* He was also illiterate. Although there was little to recommend Valens as a ruler, the empire did benefit from his unswerving loyalty to Valentinian. Ammianus says: 'He attended to his wishes as if he had been his orderly.' Thus was the empire spared the exhausting sibling wars of Constantine's children, and the brothers were free to concentrate their energies — to a better and lesser extent — on the enemies of Rome. After the division of the empire between them, Valens returned to his capital and, after a brief sojourn, left Constantinople for Syria where, despite the treaty with Jovian, trouble was again brewing with the Sassanians. He had been gone only a few days when news from the capital reached him that Procopius, that distant cousin of Julian, who had been responsible for his burial arrangements, had rebelled.

Having attended to Julian's funeral, Procopius had deemed it wise to disappear from the vengeful Valens' sight, since the rumours that Julian had nominated him as his successor were flying around. He had retired to his extensive estates in Cappadocia, but when a warrant for his arrest arrived, contrived to escape across the Pontus Euxinus and hid among barbarians in the Crimea. A few months of this misery drove him back to Constantinople determined that if his life was already forfeit he should go out in a blaze of glory and seize the purple. In this scheme Procopius was aided by the wretchedness of the populace, ground under increased taxation and the peculation of

Valens, brother of Valentinian, was illiterate and thuggish. His reign ended with Rome's most disastrous defeat in battle since Cannae in 216 BC.

212   CCXII

Valens' greedy ministers. More importantly to his aims, he encountered two Gallic legions, the *Divitenses* and *Tungricani Juniores*, on furlough before moving to the Danuvius. Disgruntled at being forced from their homes and in return for his lavish promises the men were eager to proclaim Procopius emperor on 28 September 365. Although the elite of Constantinople disassociated themselves from Procopius, they neither opposed his cause nor the wishes of the ecstatic mob, which believed his claims of descent from Constantine. Along the lower Danuvius the Goths, who counted their long peace made with Constantine ended now that no person of his imperial bloodline sat on the throne, had begun to invade. The troops in Bithynia and Thraciae gathering to counter the invasion offered their support to Procopius; and so did three thousand of the Goths, who were willing to serve a kinsman of Constantine – even if they frankly disbelieved his fictitious claim, it gave them an excuse to strike at the empire.

Valens was panicked by the speed with which Procopius had usurped his throne and, stuck in Anatolia without the immediate support of his legions, appealed to Valentinian for help. But, as we have seen, Valentinian was preoccupied in the West and sent back a characteristically curt reply: 'Procopius is only enemy to ourselves, the Alamanni are the foes of the whole Roman world.' It was only the persuasion of some tough officers that prevented Valens from abdicating on the spot when he realised he was on his own. But he was not. Under the command of his Syrian MAGIS-TER EQUITUM Lupicinus the eastern legions rallied, and marched into Galatia ready for battle. Ammianus makes no direct link between this Lupicinus and the man Julian sent to recover Britanniae from the Picts and Scots in 360, but there is every reason to suppose they are the same. Ammianus describes him as being: '…a stout and experienced soldier, who was apt, however, to set up his horn on high and to talk in the style of a tragic hero. It was long a matter of debate whether his greed predominated over his cruelty or the reverse.' And this perfectly characterises the actions of Lupicinus in handling the imminent Gothic migration.

The loyalty of Valentinian's Illyrian legions ensured that the war between his brother and Procopius was quarantined in Anatolia, and during the fall and winter of 365–66 the latter was the more successful. His forces captured Cyzicus and successfully defended against a siege of Nicaea. But he was holding onto the purple by means of sham embassies from Aegyptus, Africa and even Persia that purported to support his cause, and by demoralising Valens' troops with fake messages of Valentinian's death. The falsehood of the latter soon became manifest, and the failure of the corn supply from Aegyptus put paid to the lie of the embassies. The populace began to lose faith when Procopius collected two year's taxes in a single month, and any weak senatorial support faded as he seized their estates to raise finance.

Valens appealed to veteran officers among the mutineers who knew in their hearts that Procopius was an imposter, no kinsman of Constantine. And then in the spring of 366, he marched his main force from Pisidia to the plains of Thyatira in Lydia, where the two armies met, and he defeated Procopius's general Gomoarius. A second battle soon followed where Valens met Procopius himself at Nacolea. Initial successes for Procopius turned sour when many of his troops – lacking their promised rewards and encouraged by the cries of their opponents that they were fighting for a foul usurper – turned their weapons and joined Lupicinus and Valens. Procopius fled the field with two officers, Barchalba and Florentius, to hide in the surrounding hills. But despairing of their fate, his companions bound him during the night and took him at daybreak to Valens' camp. His head was at once severed from his neck, packed up and sent to Valentinian as proof of the usurper's death. And for their treachery, Barchalba and Florentius were also put to to the sword.

Procopius, having fled persecution by Valens after rumours that his distant cousin Julian the Apostate had appointed him his successor, returned from a miserable exile among barbarians in a desperate gambit to seize the purple.

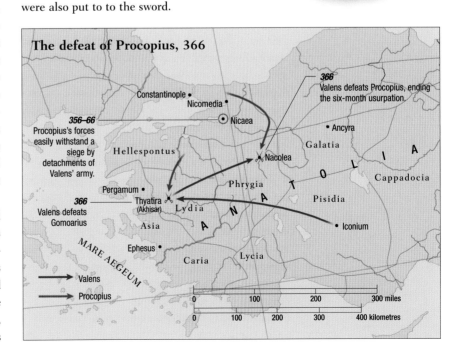

The defeat of Procopius, 366

366 Valens defeats Procopius, ending the six-month usurpation.

Constantinople
Nicomedia
Nicaea
356–66 Procopius's forces easily withstand a siege by detachments of Valens' army.
Ancyra
Galatia
Hellespontus
Nacolea
Pergamum
Phrygia
Cappadocia
366 Valens defeats Gomoarius
Thyatira (Akhisar)
Lydia
Pisidia
Asia
Iconium
Ephesus
Caria
Lycia
MARE AEGEUM

Valens
Procopius

0   100   200   300 miles
0   100   200   300   400 kilometres

The Gothic war

The Visigoths – or Tervingi branch of the Goths – who had offered their services to Procopius, now posed a problem. They had arrived too late to help the usurper, but they were still unwilling to return home empty-handed; Valens had them bound into captivity and dispersed among the cities south of the Danuvius. This aroused the ire of Athanaric, chief IUDEX (judge) of the Tervingi, who wanted to know why some of his people, who had entered Roman territory at the wish of the emperor Procopius, were being detained. Valens' intemperate response was to dispatch an army in the spring of 367 under the joint commands of Victor and Arintheus, the MAGISTRI EQUITUM and PEDITUM respectively of Thraciae. In the face of this force, the Visigoths fled into the fastness of the Carpathians, and apart from a few skirmishes and some pillaging, little was accomplished. In the following year adverse weather caused the Danuvius to flood, which hampered the campaign; instead the emperor spent the time reconstructing the ruined fortifications of Trajan and Hadrian. In 369, the Romans moved further east to cross from Noviodunum in the most northerly corner of the province of Scythia. This campaign was so successful that the Romans fought their way right through Athanaric's Tervingi and into the lands of their kinsmen, the Greuthungi, or Ostrogoths, defeating them as well.

Athanaric sued for peace terms and a treaty was arranged that was ruinous for the Visigoths, a semi-civilised nation emerging from barbarism which relied greatly on cross-border trade with the empire. The customary tribute was withheld, and only two market-towns along the entire length of the Danuvius were allowed to carry on the operations of trade. Since he was a stern man of old Gothic tradition, Anatharic would not set foot on Roman soil, and since it was beneath the dignity of the emperor to cross the river to meet the loser, a compromise was reached; the two leaders signed the treaty on a raft moored in the middle of the Danuvius. If the terms of the treaty were unfavourable to the Tervingi, so, it would turn out, were they unfortunate for Rome.

For Valens the apparently satisfactory outcome of the Gothic war was well timed, because his presence was now needed again in Anatolia. Under the terms of Jovian's treaty of 363 with Persia, Rome had rescinded control over Armenia, and Shapur had grasped the opportunity of the Procopius usurpation to extend Sassanian power in the region. After bribing the Armenian lords to defect from their king, Arsaces (Arshak), Shapur had him arrested and flung into the grimly named Prison of Oblivion. In 367 Shapur invaded Armenian Iberia and besieged Pap, the young son of Arsaces, in his fortress of Artogerassa. In the following spring Pap escaped and fled to Valens, who was at Marcianopolis in Thraciae campaigning against the Goths. As soon as the treaty with Anatharic was signed, Valens sent Arintheus with Pap to install him on the Armenian throne, which transgression led Shapur to lay waste whole regions of Armenia. A larger Roman force counterattacked in 370, and in 371 Valens' MAGISTRI defeated Shapur's army. The result was a truce, probably necessary in Shapur's case because he was obliged to deal with a Kushan invasion on his eastern frontier. However, Armenia remained a problem for Valens when the boy-king Pap demanded control over several cities in Mesopotamia and Osrhoene, including Edessa. Fearing Pap's defection to Persia if he was denied, Valens sent an expedition against him, and he was captured and executed. In his place another Arsacid, Varazdat, was placed on the puppet throne. Shapur argued that this was transgressing the treaty of 363, and war again loomed.

The second Gothic war

The year 375 was to be ill-omened for the Roman empire. Even as Valentinian died as a result of his uncontrolled temper, a new terror was rising up from the vastness of the central Asian steppe to fall without mercy on the Gothic nations. The vast horde of Huns, originating in Mongolia and impelled westward by some unknown force, had subjugated the Scythian tribes of Alani, dwelling between the Don and Rha (Volga) rivers, before encountering the Ostrogoths in the year mentioned above. With terrifying speed, the pony-mounted Huns swept around and down on the Visigoths, who withdrew in panic to the very edges of the Danuvius and sent embassies to Valens pleading for asylum within Roman borders. According to contemporary historian Eunapius, the sight along the river bank was an extraordinary one: *'The multitude of [Goths] escaping from the murderous savagery of the Huns...amounted to not less than two hundred thousand men of fighting age. These...stretched out their hands from afar with loud lamentations, and earnestly supplicated that they might be allowed to cross over the river...and promising that they would faithfully adhere to the imperial alliance if this boon were granted them.'* The figure mentioned here referred only to the warriors, and the request was, therefore, being made on behalf of a host probably numbering double that.

Preparing his Persian war in Antiochia, Valens was thus faced with a dilemma. A refusal would undoubtedly lead to a Gothic invasion, forcing him to fight on two fronts. A transfer of troops in 374 to his brother's army in Pannonia had weakened Valens' mobile forces, and he needed an aggressive and costly recruitment campaign to replenish it. His advisers – among them Lupicinus – were quick to point out the advantages to be gained in granting the Visigoths their request. Not only would they strengthen the Roman army, in doing so they would also relieve local landowners of a duty to provide manpower (they could pay a tithe in much-needed gold instead), and the Visigoths would provide a bulwark on the borders against the Huns. Several groupings of Goths were seeking asylum, but when he made up his mind, Valens dealt with only one, that under the leadership of two chieftains named Fritigern and Alavivus. Valens already knew Fritigern from when he had supported him in a struggle against Athanaric that had stemmed from Athanaric's persecution of Gothic Christians. The clinching point of the deal was Fritigern's promise to promote the cause of Arianism over orthodox Christianity, and Valens granted admission to his group. This did not, however, prevent other Goths from slipping across the Danuvius in the confusion that followed.

Because of the pressing matters in the East, Valens left the supervision of the crossing and resettlement in the hands of Lupicinus, now COMES THRACIAE and Maximus, DUX MOESIAE (and probably the later usurper of Gratian's throne). The emperor's conditions stated that the Goths were to deliver up their weapons to Roman officials on their arrival on the river's southern shore. In return they were to be fed before their wide dispersal to allotted farmlands and the eventual enrolment of the men in the army. Alas, Lupicinus cared little for efficiency – his principal aim was to make a fast profit out of the crisis. He and Maximus also seriously underestimated the numbers of refugees and the operation's logistics. With insufficient forces available, they were unable to prevent another crossing lower down the Danuvius of equally terrified Ostrogoths and surviving Alani. Instead of an orderly dispersal, Lupicinus kept the refugees in appalling conditions close to the Danuvius. Their valuables were taken as payment for inadequate supplies of food and, as hunger increased, so the exploitation worsened. Ammianus, again a witness, writes: *'Slaves, money and furniture all being exhausted, they began – even the nobles – to sell their own children. Deep must have been the misery endured by those free German hearts before they yielded to the cruel logic of the situation.'*

However, in Thraciae Lupicinus proved as incompetent as he was corrupt. Having failed to disarm the Visigothic warriors, his forces were almost annihilated by the rioting barbarians outside Marcianopolis in 377. The Tervingi joined up with the Greuthungi, and the combined Gothic nation then rampaged through Thraciae and Moesiae; after which, we hear nothing more of Lupicinus. For Valens, it was the worst possible outcome. He was forced to abandon Antiochia, leaving behind but a skeleton force – ironically containing many Goths whose fathers had remained in Anatolia in Roman service after earlier incursions – and return to Constantinople on 30 May 378. It was during a brief pause in the capital that he received news that should have been pleasing to the fifty-year-old emperor: his nephew Gratian had secured a string of great victories against barbarian enemies in the West. However, this only conceived in his heart an envy for Gratian and a determination to win a victory in which his brilliant nephew should have no hand. Valens set out for Hadrianopolis, near where the barbarian host had gathered. While encamped close by the city Valens received a letter from the hand of Gratian's COMES DOMESTICORUM, Richomeres, to inform him that his victorious co-Augustus – still only nineteen – was on the way with his army.

Valens was torn between the common-sense advice of both his MAGISTER EQUITUM Victor and Richomeres to wait the few days necessary to make conjunction with Gratian and his own bitter jealousy of his nephew, which predicated an immediate attack. Two other factors pressed him into rash action. The MAGISTER PEDITUM Sebastianus, who had served under Julian in Mesopotamia, fresh from a minor victory over an isolated band of Goths, was enthusiastic for instant battle. And then there were the reports of his scouts, who erroneously put the enemy numbers at ten thousand. On 9 August 378 a last-minute attempt was made to negotiate with the Goths, but the talks broke down when an over-eager Roman unit sallied forth and carried both sides into battle. For Valens, it was a disaster. His scouts had grossly underestimated the forces of the enemy, and the Visigoths fell on the legions in fury. According to Ammianus: *'In the great tumult the infantry, exhausted by the efforts and the perils of the fighting, no longer able to think or plan, their spears broken, rushed recklessly with drawn swords into the dense masses of the enemy, careless of their lives now that all escape was impossible.'*

The Romans held their own early on but were crushed by the surprise arrival of Greuthungi cavalry, which split their ranks. Valens was either killed by an arrow or, according to a different version, wounded in the battle but escaped to a nearby farmstead only to be burned to death by Gothic marauders. Two-thirds of

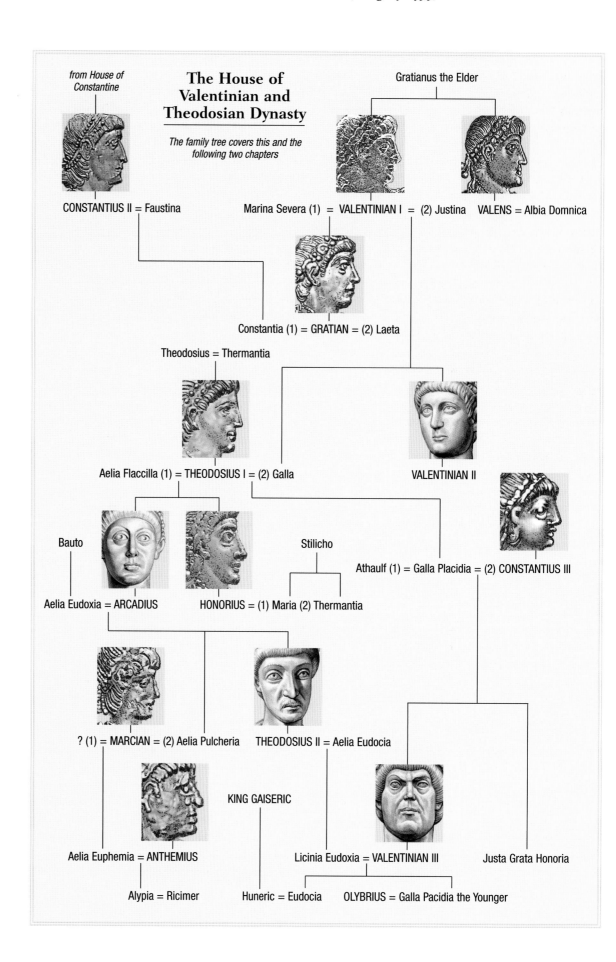

from House of
Constantine

The House of
Valentinian and
Theodosian Dynasty

*The family tree covers this and the
following two chapters*

Gratianus the Elder

CONSTANTIUS II = Faustina

Marina Severa (1) = VALENTINIAN I = (2) Justina   VALENS = Albia Domnica

Constantia (1) = GRATIAN = (2) Laeta

Theodosius = Thermantia

Aelia Flaccilla (1) = THEODOSIUS I = (2) Galla

VALENTINIAN II

Bauto

Stilicho

Athaulf (1) = Galla Placidia = (2) CONSTANTIUS III

Aelia Eudoxia = ARCADIUS

HONORIUS = (1) Maria (2) Thermantia

? (1) = MARCIAN = (2) Aelia Pulcheria   THEODOSIUS II = Aelia Eudocia

KING GAISERIC

Aelia Euphemia = ANTHEMIUS   Licinia Eudoxia = VALENTINIAN III   Justa Grata Honoria

Alypia = Ricimer   Huneric = Eudocia   OLYBRIUS = Galla Pacidia the Younger

the Eastern army perished at Hadrianopolis, in what Ammianus called 'the most destructive defeat since the battle of Cannae', and the ecclesiastical writer Tyrannus Rufinus (c.340–410) 'the beginning of evils for the Roman empire then and thereafter'.

GRATIAN

Flavius Gratianus (r.co-Augustus 367–25/8/383)

Gratian was born on 18 April 359 at Sirmium, the eldest son of Valentinian I and his first wife, Marina Severa. In 367, he was with his father on campaign against the Alamanni, when Valentinian was stricken with an illness. Fearing that the emperor was dying, the court immediately scrambled to find his successor. The MAGISTER MEMORIAE Rusticus Julianus was popular with the ministers, while the army supported the MAGISTER EQUITUM Severus. However, Valentinian recovered and designated Gratian as his successor by proclaiming him co-Augustus in an attempt to forestall any further friction between the imperial court and his senior officers. The general concern over Gratian's elevation is understandable. Not only was he just eight but he showed little interest in military matters, being a studious boy. According to Ammianus, Valentinian assuaged the officers' fears by telling them that Gratian's ability to rule would be based on his sense of justice and the nobility of his character, and that the boy would in time grow to be a military commander.

In pursuing his son's military education, Valentinian took him on the campaign of 368, but after it became clear that Gratian was not up to the rigours of military life, the emperor kept him behind the front lines. The leading rhetorician of the time, Ausonius, was appointed to be the young prince's tutor, and he proudly described his student as possessing a golden mind. By all accounts, he was a passable poet, but also enjoyed athletics, at which he excelled, and his skill at hunting Ausonius called 'almost supernatural'. At the age of fifteen he was married to Constantia, daughter of the late emperor Constantius II. (Constantia narrowly escaped capture by the Quadi in Pannonia while on her way to the wedding.) After her death in 383 he married Laeta, about whom nothing else is known.

Gratian was resident at Treveri in Gallia when Valentinian died at Brigetio in November 375, and heard that his half-brother, Valentinian II, had also been nominated as co-Augustus. One version of the account suggests that it was the MAGISTER PEDITUM in Pannonia who arranged to have Valentinian II proclaimed emperor, in order to quell a threatened rebellion by the army, which wanted to install its own candidate. However, it may have been that the emperor, fearing that sixteen-year-old Gratian was still no warrior, would not be acceptable to the soldiers, whereas the infant Valentinian II could be vested with the imperial title, which would allow his mother Justina and the generals who supported her a continued free hand in the infant's name. Gratian, upset that he was not consulted, nevertheless acquiesced to the army's demands and accepted Valentinian II's elevation in a graceful manner. Thus Gratian controlled Galliae, Britanniae and Hispaniae, while the regents of Valentinian II ordered the affairs of Illyricum, Africa and Italia.

When his uncle Valens requested his help against the Goths who had revolted in Thraciae after their crossing of the Danuvius in 376, Gratian ordered the dispatch of some Pannonian legions under the command of DUX Frigeridus, and several Gallic legions under his COMES DOMESTICORUM Richomeres. However, the most senior of his generals, a Frankish noble called Merobaudes who had taken service under the empire and risen to high rank, disobeyed by leaving a greater strength of troops along the Rhenus frontier to guard against a possible Alamanni attack. Merobaudes' defiance of the emperor's orders suggests that his officers did not hold Gratian in high esteem. As the situation in Thraciae deteriorated, it became clear that Gratian himself would have to take to the field, and was preparing to do so when the Alamanni invaded across the Rhenus at the beginning of 378. He now had reason to thank Merobaudes for his foresight, for with a small mobile force, the garrisons along the river were sufficient to mount a campaign against the barbarians and defeat them. Gratian then turned on the southernmost tribe of the Alamanni nation, the Lentienses, and won a great victory in Argentaria† in February, killing some thirty thousand of the enemy. With the western provinces temporarily secured, he set out for the East again, but before he could arrive, Valens made the fateful decision to attack the massed Goths at Hadrianopolis on 9 August 378.

With the empire of the East in chaos, Gratian

Gratian, a studious young man with limited military skills, nevertheless presided over some lucky victories. But his preferment of barbarian generals left his standing with the troops shaky.

---

† Argentaria was the district surrounding Argentorate (Strasbourg). The battle took place near the site of modern Colmar, about 30 miles south of Strasbourg.

wisely decided that his limited military skills were insufficient to the task of restoring order against so large a host. Besides, he was uncertain that his recent victories had restored the frontier's security. He recalled the superb skills of his father's DUX MOESIAE, Theodosius, who had distinguished himself in 373 in the campaign against the Sarmatae. Although he was only about thirty-two, Theodosius had retired to the family estates in Hispania Callaecia (Galicia) after his father – the MAGISTER Theodosius who had done so well for Valentinian in Britanniae and Africa – had fallen foul of palace intrigues and been executed two years earlier (*see side panel*). When the call to duty arrived, Theodosius welcomed it, and on 19 January 379, Gratian raised him to be his co-Augustus.

A STRANGE STORY attaches to the possible reason for the execution at Carthago of the elder Theodosius after a long, loyal and glorious career. This event happened in 367, a few months after Valentinian I's death at Brigetio, and is oddly unaccounted by Ammianus. Some years before Valentinian's demise, Valens came to hear that certain aristocrats in Antiochia had consulted a spiritualist in an attempt to discover the name of the cruel Eastern emperor's successor. The seer established the answer by suspending a ring on a cord above a disc marked with the letters of the Greek alphabet and shaking it up and down. As the ring bounced around the perimeter of the disc it spelled out words. The answer given was ØEOΔ (THEO). The questioners immediately assumed a high-born and accomplished young Antiochene called Theodorus would be the next Augustus in Constantinople. Valens promptly had the unfortunate Theodorus executed along with many of his philosopher (and therefore presumably pagan) friends. Doubtless, four years later, the fame of the elder Theodosius reminded jealous Valens that the four fatal letters spelled Theodosius every bit as well as Theodorus. His counsels, therefore, to Justina – as avowed an Arian as her brother-in-law – to have the orthodox elder Theodosius executed may well have been influential.

Gratian's religious persecutions

In 381 Gratian moved his court from Treveri to Mediolanum and, unusually for the time, visited Rome. He had proved himself an inspiring leader in the field, but now in his early twenties, he was growing lazy. According to Ammianus, like Commodus, he was more concerned with participating in displays of personal prowess in the arena than with supervising military affairs. And life in the cities provided him with a greater opportunity to indulge in the predilection he felt for the more handsome of his tall blond Alani bodyguards. However, he reconciled this un-Christian affection with a great piety, and his adherence to the orthodox creed led to conflict with provincial bishops, and between himself and the still-pagan senatorial aristocracy. When the case of Priscillian, a Hispanic noble who was preaching a new ascetic form of Christianity in the south of Galliae, reached Gratian, the emperor intervened. Priscillian had gained many followers, including several provincial bishops. Some of the clergy, including the influential Hyginus, bishop of Corduba, wanted the new sect branded as heretic and its followers condemned, and Gratian agreed with them. Priscillian was saved – at least for a while – by the intrigue of his bishop-followers, who bribed the local governor to rescind the imperial order for his arrest; and it would not be Gratian who would settle Priscillian's place in the Church.

The emperor's orthodoxy was felt with a particularly heavy hand in Rome when, in 382, at the instigation of Ambrosius (Ambrose), the formidable bishop of Mediolanum, Gratian had the altar and statue of Nike (Victory), that Julian had restored to the senate house, swept away. He expropriated the wealth of the temple of Vesta and its Vestal Virgins for the FISCUS, and withdrew the state subsidies that funded many pagan activities. When the senate protested, Gratian rejected the title of PONTIFEX MAXIMUS and the ceremonial robes that went with that ancient and most Roman of offices. It was, therefore, with no great regret that the Roman senate would hear of his death shortly after.

Early in 383 Gratian went north to counter another incursion of the Alamanni. This coincided with news of the proclamation by his troops of the COMES BRITANNICAE Magnus Clemens Maximus as Augustus, and in fact the barbarian incursion and the proclamation may have been connected. In any event, a few days later Maximus landed in Galliae and confronted Gratian near Lutetia Parisiorum. Gratian may have won the day, but his preferment of barbarians in his household and guard had destroyed the soldier's affection for their young emperor, and when his Moorish cavalry unexpectedly defected, most of his troops followed suit. Gratian fled towards the Alps, but was caught at Lugdunum by Maximus's MAGISTER EQUITUM, Andragathius, who killed him on 25 August 383.

The events of Gratian's reign highlight the continuing trend of assimilating barbarians and making many of them – notably the Frank Merobaudes – a part of the imperial court. Indeed, before many more years have passed, there will be no recognisable Roman in a position of power, not even an Italian. We are approaching the time in Roman history when it might be compared to the old adage about the lunatics taking over the asylum. His elevation and his death show that once again it was the power of the army that made and broke emperors, and with few exceptions this would remain the case until the fall of the Western empire. Ammianus wryly observed that despite his 'golden mind', Gratian's talents lay in the opposite direction for what the empire needed. However, he had conferred on the empire one lasting benefit – the elevation of Theodosius to supreme power.

MAGNUS MAXIMUS

Magnus Clemens Maximus
(u.spring 383–28/8/388)

Magnus Maximus was a fellow Galician of the elder Theodosius and may even have been a distant relative, but if not, certainly one of his clients. It is thought that he served under Theodosius during the campaign of 367–69 in Britanniae as a junior officer with either the Heruli or Batavian legions, and again in Raetia against the Alamanni chieftain Macrianus in 370–72. History is quite clear that he went to Africa in 373, when Theodosius was sent by Valentinian I to suppress the Moorish rebellion of Firmus. A part of his task was to work with Gildo, one of Firmus's brothers who had remained loyal to Rome, and arrest the VICARIUS Vincentius, who was suspected of being an accomplice of the peculant COMES Romanus. The relationship with Gildo almost certainly has a bearing on the treacherous behaviour of Gratian's Moorish cavalry at the battle outside Lutetia. In about 375, Maximus may have been promoted to the position of DUX MOESIAE, and in the following year have been the grasping assistant to Lupicinus in the resettlement of the Goths in Thraciae; but this could also have been an entirely different Maximus.

Certainty returns in 380, when Maximus became COMES BRITANNICAE, and in the following year led the British legions to victory over invading Picts and Scots. The reasons for his rebellion against Gratian are not made clear, but several possibilities, or a combination of them, exist. The most fanciful is to be found in the Welsh *Mabinogion*, which contains a story called *The Dream of Macsen Wedig* (MAXIMUS IMPERATOR). In this Welsh legend, Maximus is married to Elen, the only daughter of the ageing high-king of the Celts called Eudaf Hen, to rule over the British kingdom after the king's death. The old king's disgruntled nephew, enraged at his displacement, goes to Caledonia to raise an army of Picts and Scots to overthrow the Roman usurper. In the course of battle, despite a defeat at the hands of Maximus, the two rivals become close friends.

Now king of Celtic Britannia, Maximus is incensed to hear of his relative Theodosius's elevation by Gratian, and sets out to take control of the Western empire. A more prosaic reason may be found in the last sentence: Maximus had undoubtedly hoped that his relationship with Theodosius the father would lead to a promotion as the son's colleague. But Theodosius named his infant son Arcadius as his successor in January 383, thus shattering any hopes that Maximus may have had of sharing the imperial power legally. Finally, it is worth noting that the British troops were thoroughly fed up with Gratian and his hated guard of Alani, and all too willing to make Maximus their choice for the purple.

Maximus himself, however, was only too happy to employ barbarians, such as his Gothic MAGISTER EQUITUM Andragathius. The Alamanni invasion of Galliae prior to Maximus's crossing may have been engineered on his behalf by a chieftain named Fraomar to divert Gratian. Fraomar had been sent to Britanniae by Valentinian I to strengthen the defences there after 369, and Maximus had forged a friendship with the Aleman. Following Gratian's defeat, Maximus established his court at Treveri and sent ambassadors to Theodosius and Valentinian II. Theodosius received the news of Gratian's death with horror, but he was powerless to do anything because political upheavals in Persia were occupying his attention and Huns were beginning to worry at the Danuvian frontier. With reluctance, Theodosius accepted the situation – Maximus was in control of the western provinces, and it would have to stay that way until he was in a position to change it.

He did, however, reach an accord with him: that he would leave the pretender alone as long as Maximus recognised Valentinian II's sovereignty over Italia and Illyricum. This accord of 383–84 was helped by the embassy to Treveri of Ambrose (b.374–97), the bishop of Mediolanum. As a fellow Nicene Christian Ambrose pleaded with Maximus to leave the young Valentinian – of Arian persuasion – alone. He also purchased time for Valentinian's Frankish MAGISTER MILITUM, COMES Bauto, to fortify the Alpine passes against Maximus. However, almost immediately after Ambrose had departed, Maximus named his infant son Flavius Victor as co-Augustus and refused to recognise the rights of Valentinian II.

The usurper Magnus Clemens Maximus made his infant son Flavius Victor (below) his co-Augustus.

His illegitimate claim to the imperial powers did not make Maximus a poor ruler. While he would not allow any transgressions from the Alamanni, his friendly relations with several of their number eased the pressures on the frontier, and the Gallic economy prospered. He struck good coinage, and issued new legislation to ease some of the previous tax burden on the populace and the provincial nobility. He reorganised the diocese by making new sub-divisions, creating Lugdunensis III and Lugdunensis Senonia, while Gildo governed those African provinces not under Valentinian's control. In religious matters, his adherence to a strictly Nicene creed brought about Priscillian's demise. Priscillian had resumed his see of Avila after the rescinding of Gratian's order, but was now brought before a council at Burdigala (Bordeaux) and condemned as a heretic. He appealed to Maximus at Treveri, but his enemy, the orthodox bishop Hydatius, accused Priscillian's followers of sorcery. On this pretext, Maximus's PRAEFECTUS PRAETORIO, Evodius, had several seized and tortured to extract confessions. On the basis of these, Priscillian was executed. Heresy was also to be the excuse for invading Italy, to save the empire from the Arianism of young Valentinian and Justina, his domineering mother.

In 387 Maximus crossed the Alps in force. Valentinian and Justina fled to Aquileia and then to Thessalonica, where Theodosius met them and took the imperial fugitives under his protection. The emperor of the East began preparations for a war against Maximus, and in his careful way he did not hurry them. This was not to be a campaign to drive the pretender from Italia, it was to be a war of eradication. So it was only in June 388 that he was ready and marched with great rapidity into Illyricum, meeting Maximus's army under the command of Andragathius in battle at Siscia (Sisak) on the Savus, and put the rebels to flight. Two more skirmishes at Emona (Ljubljana), against Maximus's brother Marcellinus, and Poetovio (Ptuj) followed until Maximus was captured at Aquileia and brought before Theodosius. Maximus argued that he thought he had Theodosius's approval when he usurped the throne from Gratian, and for a moment it looked as though the emperor would spare him. Knowing Theodosius's reputation for clemency, his soldiers took no chances and whisked Maximus away to execute him instantly. His infant son Flavius Victor was captured by Arbogastes (Arbogast), the MAGISTER EQUITUM, and also put to death.

Maximus was just another usurper in Rome's long

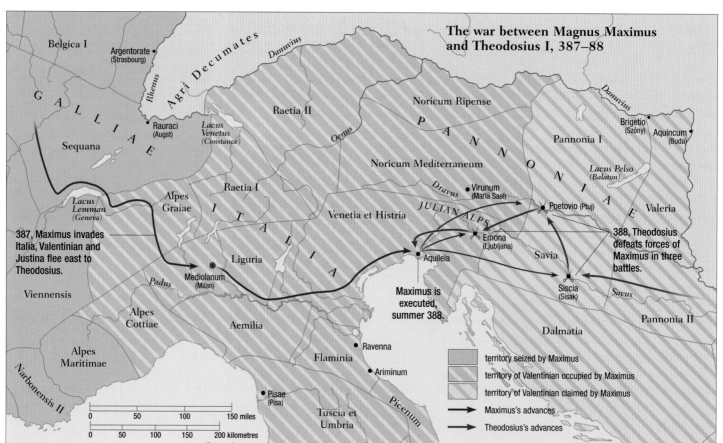

The war between Magnus Maximus and Theodosius I, 387–88

387, Maximus invades Italia, Valentinian and Justina flee east to Theodosius.

388, Theodosius defeats forces of Maximus in three battles.

Maximus is executed, summer 388.

	territory seized by Maximus
	territory of Valentinian occupied by Maximus
	territory of Valentinian claimed by Maximus
→	Maximus's advances
→	Theodosius's advances

history, but his five-year reign marks a turning point. His cause, if misguided, was an earnest one; he intended to provide good government. Maximus was also the first of a series of what we might call the 'modern' Roman generals of the West to hold power, and he could have claimed the legitimacy of his usurpation through that most medieval of beliefs – that might is right. His religious policies began the long battle between Church and state, as to whether a secular ruler had the right of control over episcopal matters. And as for the common soldier's hatred of Gratian's policy of preferring barbarians over Romans, Maximus went even further in promoting non-Romans to high office, surely a recognition that hardly any of the soldiers were actually Romans any longer. Finally, Maximus was the last really powerful emperor of the West, and his defeat made Constantinople the *de facto* centre of the Roman empire.

VALENTINIAN II
Flavius Valentinianus
(r.co-Augustus 22/11/375–15/5/392)

The reign of Valentinian II was unremarkable other than it emphasised the subordination of the Roman West to that of the Roman East. He was only four when he became co-Augustus with his half-brother Gratian and his uncle Valens, and for the greater part of his reign he was a minor under the thumb of his ministers and his mother Justina. And even when he achieved his majority he was expressly the junior partner to Theodosius. Valentinian II was a victim of fourth-century Roman politics, in short, the puppet of formidable people who exercised his government in his name.

Valentinian II was born in 371, the second son of Valentinian I by the emperor's second wife, the Sicilian Justina. The historian Zosimus claims that Justina had been married previously to the usurper Magnentius, Constans' murderer. This is certainly colourful, but he offers no proof of such an unlikely match. When Valentinian I died at Brigetio in November 375, the younger Valentinian was proclaimed on 22 November at Sirmium. Shortly after, the imperial family moved to Italia and Valentinian II's court was established at Mediolanum. Justina had prudently concealed her adherence to the Arian creed from her orthodox husband, but now – abetted by a powerful Gothic (and therefore Arian) faction at court – revealed her faith and determined to rear her infant

son in the heresy. This brought her into direct conflict with the redoubtable bishop of Mediolanum, Ambrose, who had extinguished the last embers of Arianism in his diocese and was determined to 'save' the young emperor (*see side panel below*).

In fact, the first clash happened while Justina and Valentinian were still at Sirmium, where Justina championed the election of an Arian bishop to the see, but was defeated by the efforts and persuasive oratory of Ambrose. At the Council of Aquileia in 381, over which he presided, Ambrose secured the ejection of the two remaining Arian prelates in the West, the Illyrians Secundianus and Palladius. In the following years the struggle intensified, and Ambrose was frequently in danger of his life. Yet, despite a level of popularity among the people that bordered on devotion and would have made it possible for the bishop to depose Justina with one word, he never spoke it. Eventually, Justina abandoned her campaign against Ambrose, and indeed had to call on him to save the imperilled throne from Maximus in 383–84. The course of this history has not finished with Ambrose, who famously later clashed with Theodosius. Both Theodosius and Maximus used Valentinian's Arianism against him. Theodosius is supposed to have said in a letter that he deserved Maximus's enmity because he had deserted the true faith. Maximus argued that his claim to the purple was more legitimate than Valentinian's because the latter had deserted the true faith of his father.

When Justina and Valentinian were forced to flee to Thessalonica in 387, Theodosius was at first reluctant to take up arms against Maximus. According to Zosimus he was only persuaded to do so after Justina sent to him her daughter Galla to plead their cause because she knew that Theodosius was susceptible to the charms of attractive women. His wife, the Augusta Aelia Flavia Flacilla, had died recently, and apparently Theodosius

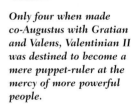

Only four when made co-Augustus with Gratian and Valens, Valentinian II was destined to become a mere puppet-ruler at the mercy of more powerful people.

ALTHOUGH HE WAS unable to wean the young Valentinian from the Arian heresy until after Justina's death, Ambrose was successful in enacting legislation in the emperor's name that benefited Christianity in general. In 384 the Roman senate made an attempt to restore the altar of Nike (Victory) to the senate house and the pagan rites connected with it. Ambrose carried the day, and the senators' petition was rejected, and would be again by Theodosius in 389.

became besotted with Galla and married her. After the defeat of Maximus, Theodosius stayed in Mediolanum for three years. At the beginning of this period Justina died, and Theodosius and Ambrose were finally able to disengage Valentinian from his heretical Arianism to the Nicene creed, albeit only as a catechumen†.

Valentinian was not allowed to enter into the administration, however, and Theodosius undertook all governmental matters, and appointed Valentinian's ministers and military officers. The most important of these was the MAGISTER MILITUM Arbogast, who Theodosius promoted to the rank of COMES GALLIAE and charged with the protection of the western provinces in place of the recently deceased COMES Bauto. Before leaving for Constantinople on 16 June 391, Theodosius obliged Valentinian to accompany Arbogast to Galliae, and the unwilling junior Augustus removed his court from Mediolanum to Vienna (Vienne), all too aware that the real ruler of the West was the COMES GALLIAE. Arbogast was a Frank, who had served with Gratian in the Pannonian campaign of 380 and under Theodosius against Maximus. He could count among his relatives the COMES Bauto, possibly his father, and his uncle the COMES Richomeres. There is little doubt that he was widely regarded as one of the finest soldiers of his time, and adored by his men for his 'flame-like' qualities of leadership and all-conquering energy. They especially saw in this gruff Frank an incorruptibility uncommon in officers of Roman extraction because he cared nothing for gold or the finer trappings of life. It goes without saying that Arbogast and Valentinian had nothing in common beyond a sneering contempt for the latter by the former and a resentful dread of too-powerful Arbogast by the young emperor.

Arbogast never shrank from laying hands on Valentinian's counsellors if he suspected them of any corruption – and several must have given him reason – and one intimate, a certain Harmonius, he ran through with his sword in front of the terrified emperor. Valentinian frequently complained about this state of affairs to Theodosius, but his protestations fell on deaf ears. Matters came to a head when, determined to exert his IMPERIUM, Valentinian issued a written order to Arbogast demanding his immediate resignation from all his offices. Arbogast stared at the note for a few moments, and then slowly ripped it into pieces before walking away. A few days later, on 15 May 392,

Eugenius, a professor of rhetoric, was appointed emperor by Arbogast who, while virtual ruler of the West, felt it unwise as a pagan barbarian to assume the purple himself.

Valentinian, now barely twenty-one, was found dead in his apartments. The official verdict was suicide, for which the only possible motive was despair that if he did not take his own life, someone else soon would. Since a suicide's soul was supposed to reside in purgatory, perhaps Ambrose's assurances to Valentinian's grieving sisters that he had been carried up to heaven indicated that the bishop suspected foul play. If so, once again he said nothing.

EUGENIUS
(u.22/8/392–6/9/394)

The reign of Eugenius was wholly the creation of Arbogast the 'king-maker'. Although he was virtual ruler of the West, and the death of Valentinian had no effect on the army's affection for him and the civil functionaries obeyed his every word, Arbogast could not assume the purple. He was no fool and knew that, being a barbarian, it was unwise to assume the semblance as well as the substance of imperial power. Historical records still kept fresh the reign of Maximinus Thrax, the murderer of young Severus Alexander a century and a half before, since which time no full-blooded barbarian had been hailed by the troops. Perhaps more to the point, Arbogast was not even an Arian, he was a pagan.

His choice fell on Eugenius, a middle-aged professor of rhetoric who had formerly served as head of the FISCUS, and whom COMES Richomeres had recommended to Arbogast as a clever and obedient subordinate. For his part, Eugenius was not anxious to receive this dangerous honour, but on reflection he realised that he had no alternative but to accept. His reception

---

† One receiving Christian instruction before baptism or confirmation.

by the troops was a foregone conclusion – he was the nomination of their magnificent commander. According to the poet Claudian, this translation in his fortunes 'made the barbarian's lackey lord of all'.

Well and good, but what was Theodosius to make of all this? When the embassy from the West arrived in Constantinople to inform the emperor of Valentinian's death and the elevation of Eugenius Theodosius was furious – it was his right alone to designate a fellow-Augustus. Nevertheless, none was better acquainted with Arbogast's military skills, so Theodosius returned a diplomatic reply and began preparing for a difficult war. All through 393 those preparations continued, while Arbogast extended his power into Italia. His antagonist was Ambrose, who was vehemently opposed to Arbogast's protégé acclaimed in Galliae.

However, Arbogast's very paganism now came to his aid. The ancient cities of Italia were the last refuges of heathen worship in the empire, and while Eugenius was a Christian, he was also a rhetorician and willing to extend tolerance to the gods whose classical names, as a matter of tradition, featured in many of his orations. The aristocrats of the Italian cities, especially those in Rome, were happy to acclaim one who might allow them a greater freedom of worship than they had enjoyed for decades, and the petitions were immediate. By the middle of 393 the temples of Rome were reopened, the smoke of sacrifices clouded the air, and conservatives were once again celebrating the ancient Roman festivals of Lupercalia and Saturnalia. The altar of Nike was restored to the CURIA, and Eugenius went so far as to grant petitioners revenues to bestow on many temples.

Reports of the pagan revival in Galliae and Italia soon reached the ears of Theodosius. In November 293 he issued an edict against idolatry and made the practice of augury over steaming entrails an act of treason against the emperor. As Eugenius approached Mediolanum, Ambrose withdrew to a self-imposed exile in Bononia (Bologna), from where he continued to excoriate the horrors being perpetrated in his see. He wrote to Eugenius exhorting him to return to his Christian ways, and telling him that no matter how mighty he, the emperor, might think himself, God could see into his heart. There can be little doubt that whatever he thought privately, Eugenius would not go against the wishes of Arbogast.

As he led the army out of Mediolanum in 394 to meet Theodosius, Arbogast threw back the taunt that on their victorious return he would stable the cavalry's horses in the basilica and press-gang clerics into the

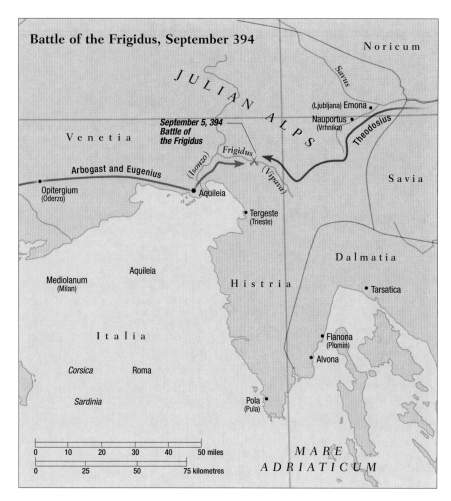

Battle of the Frigidus, September 394

army. Thus it was in late spring 394, that when Theodosius marched again for the West, he knew he was not only facing a usurper but also fighting for the faith. The two great armies met on 5 September slightly to the north of Tergeste (Trieste), on a small tributary of the Isonzo called the Frigidus (Vipava). To the east, the host of Theodosius advanced under the holy LABARUM of the Christian emperor; to the west the army of Eugenius and Arbogast stood under banners bearing the symbol of Sol Invictus. The following battle lasted for two days, and losses on both sides were horrendous. But on the second day a hurricane wind blew in from the east, benefiting Theodosius. The pagan army could barely see in front of them for the dust blasting into their faces. Later, Christian historians naturally attributed this good fortune to the blessing of God. The western army soon capitulated and Eugenius was beheaded at the emperor's feet. Arbogast escaped into the hills, but after a few days' wandering decided not to test the famous Theodosian clemency again, and took his own life. Once more the empire was united under one ruler. In Rome the temples were hurriedly closed up and the idols were packed away, nevermore to be seen.

THEODOSIUS I THE GREAT

Flavius Theodosius (r.19/1/379–17/1/395)

Theodosius, the last emperor to rule the whole of the empire, would be called 'the Great' for his establishment of the Roman Catholic Church.

The reign of Theodosius has already interwoven its way into many of the previous pages, but the repetition of some events provides an opportunity to present them in a different light. The story of the Roman empire's last great ruler of West and East begins in approximately 346 when Theodosius was born at Cauca (Coca), a small town in the northwest of Carthaginensis, adjacent to the provincial borders of Gallaecia, Lusitania and Tarraconensis, on a tributary of the upper Durius (Douro), some thirty miles from modern Segovia†. He was of illustrious birth because his father, the elder Theodosius, and mother Thermantia, were both from powerful provincial families, the real aristocracy of the mid-fourth-century Roman empire. His father's glorious military career has been outlined in an earlier section, and according to the laws of Diocletian and Constantine the son was forced to follow his father into the army at an early age. We are told that he was affable but

---

† Both historians Zosimus and Idiatus say that Theodosius was born in Cauca in the province of Gallaecia, but – while close to the border – Cauca is not in Gallaecia. As a Spaniard, Idiatus should have known, so perhaps he was referring to another Cauca unknown to us, but still not the one where Theodosius was born.

with a noble, commanding presence, and a man of slender education – not surprising in one who spent all his youth in the military.

Campaigning with his father in Britanniae, Africa and Illyricum, he had plenty of time to learn the military arts from an expert, and his own abilities propelled him rapidly up the ranks until by 373 he was DUX MOESIAE, when he was about twenty-seven. On the execution of his father in 376, he retired to the family estates. At some point, probably during this period, Theodosius married Aelia Flavia Flacilla (*see side panel opposite*), who was of a noble Galician family, She was to give him three children, two sons, Arcadius and Honorius, and a daughter, Pulcheria. Arcadius was born either in 377 or 378, on the brink of his father's recall to duty, Honorius on 9 September 384, and Pulcheria, who died in childhood, in 385.

The reason for this absence from military duty is not known. Recent suggestions which have been made that a furious Valentinian dismissed him after the loss of a Pannonian and a Moesian legion to the Sarmatae in Valeria in 374, when he was DUX MOESIAE, and therefore responsible for the defeat, do not fit the facts as known. As Thomas Hodgkin points out in *The Barbarian Invasions of the Roman Empire*, Theodosius covered himself in glory at this time; and reliable Ammianus is silent on the matter. Besides, Theodosius was apparently still on active military duty when Valentinian died, and his retirement seems to coincide with his father's execution in the following year. It would not be stretching the point too far to suggest that Theodosius did not want to aggravate the jealousy of Valens any more than his victories in Illyricum might already have done, and so prudently made himself as invisible as possible in a part of the empire as far away as he could get from the senior Augustus. In any event, the sabbatical lasted only three years before Gratian recalled Theodosius and gave him command of the East to clear up the unholy mess Valens had made of the Gothic inundation.

It was fortunate for the empire in the days and months following the disaster at Hadrianopolis in August 378 that while barbarians might exact a severe victory over civilised Roman arms, they had ever proved incapable of a cohesive policy afterwards or of improving on their tactical advantage. The Goths tried repeatedly to break into the shuttered city, but were driven back by the terrifying Roman catapults and ballistas. Disorganised bands of warriors fell in heaps to the arrows, bolts and huge stones hurled from the walls. It was a picture to be repeated all over the Balkans. While the Goths held the countryside, they could not break down the cities' defences, and were incapable of consolidating their position. In not too many days, Constantinople found itself under siege. A stout defence was mounted, much at the exhortation of Valens' widow, Dominica, and a detachment of Saracen cavalry sent by the nomadic queen Mavia all the way from the edges of the provinces of Arabia. Unable to take the capital, the Goths retired and contented themselves with ravaging in every direction, through Thraciae, Daciae, Moesiae and even into Pannoniae at the very edges of Italia.

Receiving the summons from Gratian, Theodosius immediately set off to meet the young emperor at Sirmium. Whether Theodosius had been warned in advance of Gratian's intentions is not clear, but he appears to have had no hesitation in accepting the honour conferred him on 19 January 379. Gratian raised him to be his colleague in the imperial powers, and granted him all the territories of Valens with the addition of eastern Illyricum, the dioceses of Daciae, Thraciae and Macedoniae (the designation Moesiae disappears at some point during this period). From Sirmium, Theodosius moved south, skirting the largest concentrations of Gothic marauders, and came to Thessalonica. The city had recently withstood a prolonged siege, but a plague had inflicted great losses among the Goths, who had retreated from the locale; a miracle attributed to the prayers of the saintly Thessalonican Bishop Acholius.

With its access to the Aegeum for distant communications and the shortest line to Gratian's Illyrian capital of Sirmium, Theodosius judged Thessalonica to be the place from which to organise the task ahead. He vowed that until he had cleared the Balkans of the barbarians he would not put foot in his capital. Within weeks, the military officers, senators of Constantinople and imperial administrators had convened to pay court to the new Augustus and be directed in their roles in the battles to come. If a few of these worthies held any suspicion towards the new emperor they only had to compare him to Valens, his timid, indecisive, but vengeful predecessor, to know that in Theodosius they had a man in whom they could put their faith.

The problem he faced, however, was a severe lack of manpower occasioned by the terrible losses at Hadrianopolis. Theodosius overcame the disadvantage through a series of rapid promotions and surrounded himself with a large number of dashing, active officers whom he directed in tactics learned in Britanniae – guerrilla warfare. As long as a continual stream of short, sharp attacks – hit and run if necessary – could

be maintained, the Romans had a chance of shaking the Goths' confidence and at the same time repairing the fallen morale of the Roman soldiers. His critics – and there were a few – were made uneasy by the increase in the numbers of higher ranks: while before it was customary to have two commanders-in-chief of the COMITATENSES, the MAGISTER EQUITUM and MAGISTER PEDITUM, now there were five, probably the majority with the horse. In keeping, Theodosius doubled the lower ranks of DUCES, TRIBUNI and centurions. This apparently happened without an increase in the total manpower of the army, but in the war being waged good leadership counted for more than sheer manpower. There was another very good reason for filling his CONSISTORIUM with a large number of brave and experienced officers. To bulk out the depleted ranks Theodosius engaged the services of captured Goths, and for them to become a properly organised fighting machine in the Roman style these fierce but ill-disciplined warriors needed an officer they would obey because of his terrifying record on the battlefield.

THE CHRISTIAN WRITERS of the time portray Aelia Flavia Flacilla as another great Roman woman in the mould of Livia and the Severan Julias. Theodosius was concerned to avoid the disruptions that always shook the empire whenever there was no clear successor, and determined to establish a dynasty to ensure a peaceful succession within his family. He was fortunate in Flaccilla and rewarded her for providing him with two sons by conferring on her the title of Augusta, the first so named since Constantine made his mother Helena an empress. Although the title was hardly a new one, in the elevation of Flacilla there are some striking precedents that may be noted in the way she is represented on the coins struck in her honour. Flacilla is not shown as a mere Roman matron, but dressed in the PALUDAMENTUM (the imperial purple robe) with the jewelled fibula at her shoulder. This is the clothing of an emperor and military leader. And on her head sits the identical diadem that Theodosius wears. The implication is clear, the Augusta is the equal of Augustus, and his partner not only in the family, but also in the government and the military command of the empire. However, we have to question this portrait of the great Christian matron-warrior. She was undoubtedly charitable, but evidence points to her being weak-willed, terrified of her husband's rages and molly-coddling of her children when she was with them. Neither of her sons showed even the faintest spark of their determined and intelligent father; perhaps they inherited the spinelessness from the mother. Flacilla's legacy to the women of the dynasty was that they, too, could aspire to the highest offices in the land and, as we shall see, two in particular seized the opportunity: Aelia Eudoxia and Galla Placidia.

Recovery of the East

In contrast to the ruined misery of the countryside around Thessalonica, Theodosius lavished magnificence on his senior commanders and the civic dignitaries. While this was a reflection of his princely state and no less than he had been accustomed to, it was also another means of raising the court's morale. The policy did, as a consequence of its cost, put more strain on the region's already ruined finances, and led some doubters to wonder whether there might not come a time when they would crave again the parsimony of a Valens.

The ancient histories give no coherent account of Theodosius's tactics, but there is no doubt that his strategy was a triumph. One example that has survived shows Theodosius's wisdom in selecting Goths who had demonstrated their loyalty and then promoting them. Modares, a Visigoth of royal lineage, was made a MAGISTER and given command of a detachment of troops. With his knowledge of the local terrain and the moral weakness of his countrymen, his warriors fell on a large band of revelling Goths that had been looting. In their drunkenness, the enemy was unable to rally, and were soon all killed. As many as four thousand wagons and all their women and children were taken. It is the Goth Jordanes, writing a century and a half later, who tells us: *'For the emperor, keen in intelligence, strong in courage, and wise in counsel, tempering the severity of his orders by liberality and an affable demeanour, was ever rousing the demoralised army to brave deeds.'*

On 17 November 379 Theodosius was able to send messengers to all the great cities of the empire announcing a victory over the Goths, the Alani and the Huns, large groups of the latter having followed the Goths across the Danuvius. It was not, however, entirely the end of the war. The provinces south of the Balkans, Epirus, Thessalia and Achaea, were still overrun by Fritigern's Visigoths, and Ostrogoths were attacking across the Danuvius into Pannoniae. At the beginning of 380, Theodosius fell seriously ill, and was forced to call on his colleague for help in evicting the barbarians. Gratian advanced to Aquileia, from where he supervised the defence of Pannoniae, while giving to two Franks the command of the attack on the Goths. These men we have already met: the COMITES Bauto and Arbogast. The campaign was successful in clearing Macedonia and Thessalia and finally containing the remaining horde along the southern bank of the Danuvius in the region of Moesia Secundus where, four years previously, Valens had intended to settle them. In the course of a battle against either Bauto or Arbogast, Fritigern was slain.

Gratian, aware that it would be almost impossible to entirely expel the Goths from Roman territory, and in any case wishing to honour the bargain made with them by his Uncle Valens, proposed a treaty. Its terms granted the Goths land on which to settle, provided that it was comingled with restored Roman property, that they should become romanised, and that the men should serve in the army and pledge their sons to the same. In short, the Gothic nation should become FOEDERATI, or confederates of Rome. On his sickbed, and fearing imminent death, the catechumen Theodosius had called on Acholius to baptise him. Restored to good health later in 380, Theodosius rose from his bed a convinced adherent of the orthodox faith. He also returned to active duty to find that Gratian had already concluded the very contract with the Goths that he had wished for, and he accepted it gratefully. And finally, on 24 November 380, he could make his way to Constantinople and enter his capital in all the state and glory due an IMPERATOR.

On 24 January 381 he welcomed old Anatharic to the capital. The IUDEX, who had remained to the north of the Danuvius in keeping with his vow never to set foot on Roman soil, had been forced to break it and flee from those returning Ostrogoths who had been bested by Bauto and Arbogast. Theodosius personally escorted the venerable old man through the city gate and to the imperial palace, and there received his former enemy with great courtesy. A fortnight later Anatharic died, overcome perhaps by the lavishness of his reception and the incredible glory of the capital, or perhaps of a broken heart for the loss of his nation. Theodosius granted him a sumptuous state funeral, which consideration for their old leader further disposed the Goths towards reconciliation.

In Republican days the Roman army was clearly divided into the legionaries, Roman- or Latin-born citizens, and the AUXILIA, drawn from allied nations that had no rights of citizenship but through their efforts might hope to win the right one day. In the intervening centuries, this distinction had all but disappeared, and after Caracalla's CONSTITUTIO ANTONINIANA became meaningless, since every free-born man in the empire was automatically a citizen. The term remained only to describe units of a lesser standing to the COMITATENSES, such as the native levies that garrisoned many of the frontier forts. However, with the FOEDERATI, the empire had again created a Republican-style AUXILIA, a large military resource to be called on when required, none of whose members were Roman citizens but retained their own system of government and administration. There was an important difference to the ancient system in that FOEDERATI were not required to pay any taxes, which did not endear them to the hard-pressed provincial Romans struggling to recover from the very devastation the Goths had caused. And in this contract between FOEDERATI and emperor – the grant of land in return for military service – it is possible to see the beginnings of medieval feudalism, and the inexorable shaping of the Europe to come.

Theodosius in Italia

One of the great boons of Theodosius's reign was peace with the Sassanian empire. His inability to immediately take the field against Maximus in the events that transpired after Gratian's death in 383, and which led to the uneasy accord that left Maximus alone in 384, have already been noted. However, to signal that he had no intention of sharing power with Maximus on any legal basis, at the end of 383 he raised his five-year-old son Arcadius to be his colleague in the imperial powers. Skirmishes with Huns were occupying him on the northern frontier, and in Persia Ardashir II had just been deposed by his nephew, Shapur III.

The new Persian king was an unknown quantity, and Theodosius was unwilling to campaign against Maximus until he knew better what the oriental brew might throw up. At the same time, the Saracens – who had repudiated their previous treaty of 377 – resumed raiding the frontier from Arabia to Syria in 383. However, this uprising appears to have been crushed by the MAGISTER PEDITUM Richomeres in a campaign of the same year. As for the Sassanians, Theodosius sent on an embassy to them another extraordinary man he had raised up, a full-blooded Vandal called Stilicho. Given the title MAGISTER MILITUM PER ORIENTEM, Stilicho travelled to Shapur's court and, after protracted negotiations, reached an accord in 387 that ensured peace between Rome and Ctesiphon for the duration of Theodosius's reign. Since Armenia had always been the rose between the two thorns, Stilicho's winning proposition was to divide it between the two empires. The Roman client king Arsaces (Arsak) retained possession of the western part of the country, while the Persians nominated a Sassanid called Khosro to rule over eastern Armenia. Thus, in the same year, Theodosius was prepared to deal with Maximus when the usurper crossed the Alps to invade Italia.

The events of the battle with Maximus in 388 are related above, and it is the period that Theodosius spent in Italia that concerns us now. Having appointed Arbogast as COMES GALLIAE, Theodosius, his new wife Galla, daughter of Valentinian I, and his infant son Honorius (Arcadius had been left behind in Constantinople) spent the winter with Valentinian II in Mediolanum. In the following year, Theodosius journeyed with Valentinian to Rome. It should have been a joyous occasion for the Roman aristocracy on that day – 13 June 389 – to receive after so long a great emperor, but this one was bearing the banner of Christ with which to berate the recusant Romans. It came, then, as a great relief to find that the senior Augustus intended to wield carrots instead of sticks in his efforts to rid Rome of paganism. A CONGARIUM to the cheering citizens was tendered with stately affability and good-humoured bantering with the crowd. He visited the homes of nobles and commoners alike, and a few days later the assembled senate received him in the CURIA (from which no doubt the altar of Nike had been prudently removed to its final and lasting obscurity). The two Augusti then returned to Mediolanum and remained there throughout the rest of that and the following year – the year of the great clash between the emperor and Ambrose, the bishop of Mediolanum.

Neither was present at the events in Thessalonica that sparked Ambrose's righteous fury and led to the first excommunication by a great Church leader of a powerful secular ruler. At Thessalonica, which had suffered so ruinously during the Gothic war, there had been much unrest among the populace. Their resentment was over the quartering of troops in their homes. Roman soldiers had been bad enough in the past, but the barbarian ones were much worse. The situation spiralled out of control when the MAGISTER PEDITUM, himself a Goth called Botheric, imprisoned the city's most popular charioteer on charges of 'abominable immorality', more than likely homosexual acts, of which the Graeco-Roman charioteers were frequently accused, although not usually imprisoned for.

Botheric ignored the popular protest at his actions, and the mob attacked the garrison headquarters and cut him down. When Theodosius heard of the insult he flew into a rage. Ambrose attempted to dissuade the emperor from taking vengeance on many for the crimes of only a few, but without undertaking any judicial enquiry, Theodosius ordered COMITATENSES to show the city no mercy. It seems that Theodosius, usually regretfully clement once a rage had subsided, sent another dispatch to countermand his original order, but it arrived too late for Thessalonica. The soldiers chose to wait until a day of races and, when most of

A great advocate of the Church in Italy, the bishop of Mediolanum, Ambrose, clashed with Theodosius over matters of religion and his interference in episcopal affairs, but a senseless massacre in Thessalonica caused him to resort to the ultimate sanction – the emperor's excommunication.

Thessalonica's citizens were gathered in the hippodrome, fell on them in a fury. Seven thousand souls lay amid the gore and shambles of their deaths by the evening; some sources double the figure.

A crime on such a scale, a mass murder undertaken without even the semblance of Roman justice could not be overlooked, and Ambrose, who had already had a few clashes with Theodosius over points of religion and the rights of the emperor to dispense justice in episcopal matters, would not. The bishop refused to meet his emperor face to face but wrote a strong letter, which confirmed his continuing regard for Theodosius but at the same time insisted on a public repentance. Until such was forthcoming, said the bishop, he would withhold communion from Theodosius. If the COMITATUS expected to witness a towering rage, they were to be surprised. On the following Sunday, as the emperor was attempting to enter the basilica, Ambrose stood in the doorway and forbade him passage into the church. Astonishingly, Theodosius appears to have accepted this rebuff meekly, and returned to the palace a saddened man.

However, he would not yet back down, and sent his PRAEFECTUS PRAETORIO, a low-born Gaul called Rufinus – of whom we shall hear more later – to negotiate. On seeing Rufinus, Ambrose commanded him to go away, berating him for being the real criminal who had bent the emperor's mind to commit the crime. On hearing of the failure of his embassy, Theodosius went himself to Ambrose and repented. But Ambrose was unbending: the emperor must express his repentance publicly and pass an edict forbidding the execution of any citizen until after a period of thirty days, in which time either justice or natural mercy should prevail. Theodosius agreed both to this wise law and to his public humiliation.

It was a relief to his troubled spirit to present himself at the basilica, dressed only in sackcloth and unadorned by his imperial diadem, to prostrate himself before the high altar and do penance. But when he was finished, it turned out that Ambrose was not. He pointed out sternly that before Theodosius could receive the communion he must remove himself beyond the altar railing and leave the sacred enclosure, which was reserved for priests. Although Theodosius was only following the procedure of Constantinople, where the emperor as the right of his august person celebrated communion at the altar apart from the mass of citizens, he quietly obeyed Ambrose and accepted his words: 'The purple only makes emperors, not priests.' It was a turning point for Christendom. A cleric had asserted the rights of the spiritual over the temporal power of the ruler, and in accepting the condemnation and punishment of a priest, the emperor had for the first time recognised an authority greater than his own.

Succession of the dynasty

After leaving Mediolanum on 16 June 391, Theodosius arrived at Constantinople on 22 November, and in the intervening years before the battle of the Frigidus in the latter part of 394, concerned himself with administration. He worked tirelessly to improve the lot of the common man in a way rare among emperors of the fourth century. To the law Ambrose had obliged him to pass, he added that a certain part of any condemned man's estate must go to his children, and that the father's crime must not be held against them. He set standards by which farmers were no longer forced to sell their produce to the state at less than the market rate. But much of his legislation dealt with religious matters. As early as 380, when he was recovering from the illness that had prompted his baptism by Acholius, he had issued an edict that defined the Roman Catholic Church forever. This proclaimed that only those who professed the Nicene creed, the consubstantiality of the Holy Trinity, could be considered *Catholic* Christians, and all others were pronounced 'mad' and 'heretic'. This edict effectively ended the Arian controversy by outlawing the creed of Arius, and in the following year at the Council of Constantinople it was decreed that Arian churches be handed back to orthodoxy, and that the see of Constantinople should become second only after that of Rome.

The emperor's early tolerance of pagan practices that did not include blood sacrifice, magical auguries or anything that smelled of treason against the Augustus began to give way to a growing intemperance. He strengthened the existing legislation against sacrifices in 385; in 391 he banned all non-Christian rituals in Rome and Alexandria; and in 392 came the most swingeing edict that outlawed every form of pagan worship throughout the empire, whether in public or in private. The edict of 391 did not, however, lead to the widespread destruction of the old temples, for Theodosius supported the preservation of temples and monuments as useful buildings or as works of art. But in Alexandria the ancient and famous Serapeum, at which Caracalla had fruitlessly sought a cure for his illness, was torn down by official sanction. The blame for this wanton act of destruction is not, perhaps, to be laid entirely at the emperor's feet. His tacit approval was almost certainly obtained by the manipulation of local officials who had already exceeded their authority in pulling down pagan buildings and encouraging the persecution of pagan worshippers. Had he known all the facts, Theodosius would almost certainly have disapproved, for he never sought to force his subjects into recantation, and he never caused persecution. The epithetical 'Great' had previously been awarded to Constantine as the establisher of frontier security and the expander of Roman territory. Theodosius had accomplished the former but added nothing to the empire, even halved Armenia's client status. So it is for his establishment of the Roman Catholic Church that he is known today as Theodosius the Great.

Neither proscriptions nor confiscations marked the fall of Eugenius in 394. Triumphant, Theodosius entered Mediolanum and pardoned all the usurper's supporters. The children of Eugenius and Arbogast, although not professing Christians, had taken sanctuary in the basilica, and Ambrose requested the emperor to show them mercy, which he did by handing them into the care of an imperial NOTARIUS.

Since he was now approaching his fiftieth year, Theodosius turned his attention to the succession. Valentinian II had died childless, so there was no other male heir to complicate matters, and he decided to divide the empire between Arcadius in the East to rule at Constantinople and Honorius in the West at Mediolanum. Whether this was actually intended to be such a formal division as later history has made it is doubtful; as we have seen, such partitions had been made before. But it is not really relevant, since the division was made permanent by the weakness of his sons and the mutual hatred that existed between their chief ministers, Stilicho and Rufinus.

Honorius, who was only ten, was at the time resident with Arcadius in Constantinople, his older brother not yet seventeen. Having made his decision and appointed Stilicho regent, Theodosius immediately sent for his younger son to attend him. The timing for a journey was poor. The winter snows had set in, and so it was only in mid-January that Honorius arrived at Mediolanum, in the company of his cousin Serena, Stilicho's wife, to discover that his father had fallen dangerously ill. Theodosius recovered at the sight of his young son sufficiently to attend the games held to celebrate the boy's safe arrival, but collapsed during the racing and was taken to his bedchamber. On the following night of 17 January 395 Rome's last great emperor passed away, and his death was the 'beginning of the end of all things'.

Young Arcadius was slothful, and weak both of intellect and character.

ARCADIUS
Flavius Arcadius (co-Augustus [East] January 383; Augustus 18/1/395–1/5/408)

HONORIUS
Flavius Honorius (co-Augustus [West] 393, Augustus 18/1/395–26/8/423)

For forty days Theodosius's embalmed body lay in state in the palace before it was transferred to the basilica on 25 February for a High Mass presided over by Ambrose, whose funeral oration still survives. In it, Ambrose reminded the mourners of the deceased emperor's Christian humility after the Thessalonica massacre: '*Stripping himself of every emblem of royalty he publicly in church bewailed his sin. That public penance, which private individuals shrink from, an emperor was not ashamed to perform; nor was there afterwards a day on which he did not grieve for his mistake.*'

After the mass the imperial cortège began the journey to Constantinople and Arcadius, leaving Honorius at Mediolanum in the care of Stilicho. Both boys had spent their lives to this point under the shadow of the purple, for Theodosius was elevated only shortly after the birth of Arcadius in 377 or 378. Arcadius was made co-Augustus in

Arcadius's brother Honorius: a moral destitute, whose one passion was rearing chickens.

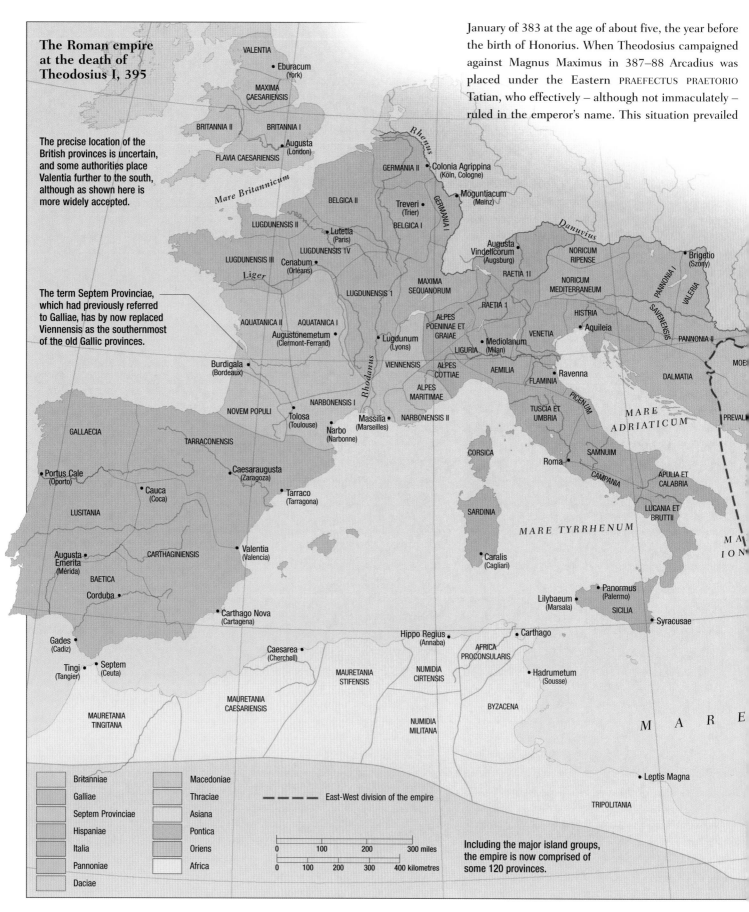

The Roman empire at the death of Theodosius I, 395

The precise location of the British provinces is uncertain, and some authorities place Valentia further to the south, although as shown here is more widely accepted.

The term Septem Provinciae, which had previously referred to Galliae, has by now replaced Viennensis as the southernmost of the old Gallic provinces.

January of 383 at the age of about five, the year before the birth of Honorius. When Theodosius campaigned against Magnus Maximus in 387–88 Arcadius was placed under the Eastern PRAEFECTUS PRAETORIO Tatian, who effectively – although not immaculately – ruled in the emperor's name. This situation prevailed

VALENTIA
Eburacum (York)
MAXIMA CAESARIENSIS
BRITANNIA II
BRITANNIA I
FLAVIA CAESARIENSIS
Augusta (London)
Mare Britannicum
Rhenus
GERMANIA II
Colonia Agrippina (Köln, Cologne)
Moguntiacum (Mainz)
GERMANIA I
BELGICA II
Treveri (Trier)
BELGICA I
Danuvius
LUGDUNENSIS II
Lutetia (Paris)
LUGDUNENSIS IV
Augusta Vindelicorum (Augsburg)
NORICUM RIPENSE
Brigetio (Szöny)
LUGDUNENSIS III
Cenabum (Orléans)
MAXIMA SEQUANORUM
RAETIA II
NORICUM MEDITERRANEUM
PANNONIA I
VALERIA
Liger
LUGDUNENSIS I
RAETIA I
SAVENENSIS
AQUATANICA II
AQUATANICA I
ALPES POENINAE ET GRAIAE
HISTRIA
PANNONIA II
Augustonemetum (Clermont-Ferrand)
Lugdunum (Lyons)
VENETIA
Aquileia
MOE
Burdigala (Bordeaux)
VIENNENSIS
ALPES COTTIAE
Mediolanum (Milan)
LIGURIA
AEMILIA
Ravenna
DALMATIA
ALPES MARITIMAE
FLAMINIA
PICENUM
MARE ADRIATICUM
PREVAL
NOVEM POPULI
NARBONENSIS I
Tolosa (Toulouse)
Massilia (Marseilles)
NARBONENSIS II
TUSCIA ET UMBRIA
GALLAECIA
Narbo (Narbonne)
CORSICA
SAMNUIM
Roma
APULIA ET CALABRIA
TARRACONENSIS
CAMPANIA
Caesaraugusta (Zaragoza)
Tarraco (Tarragona)
LUCANIA ET BRUTTII
Portus Cale (Oporto)
Cauca (Coca)
LUSITANIA
SARDINIA
MARE TYRRHENUM
MA
ION
Augusta Emerita (Mérida)
CARTHAGINIENSIS
Valentia (Valencia)
Caralis (Cagliari)
BAETICA
Corduba
Panormus (Palermo)
Lilybaeum (Marsala)
SICILIA
Carthago Nova (Cartagena)
Syracusae
Gades (Cadiz)
Caesarea (Cherchell)
Hippo Regius (Annaba)
Carthago
Tingi (Tangier)
Septem (Ceuta)
AFRICA PROCONSULARIS
Hadrumetum (Sousse)
MAURETANIA STIFENSIS
NUMIDIA CIRTENSIS
MAURETANIA CAESARIENSIS
BYZACENA
MARE
MAURETANIA TINGITANA
NUMIDIA MILITANA
Leptis Magna
TRIPOLITANIA

Britanniae
Galliae
Septem Provinciae
Hispaniae
Italia
Pannoniae
Daciae
Macedoniae
Thraciae
Asiana
Pontica
Oriens
Africa

– – – – East-West division of the empire

| 0 | 100 | 200 | 300 miles |
| 0 | 100 | 200 | 300 | 400 kilometres |

Including the major island groups, the empire is now comprised of some 120 provinces.

until Theodosius returned from Mediolanum after his sojourn in Italia in 391, bringing with him his PRAE-FECTUS, Rufinus, who now aspired to add to his own title that of Tatian's. Through various subterfuges, Rufinus secured Tatian's deposal and took his place in 392. Thus it was under the regency of the ruthless and ambitious Rufinus that Arcadius had been left in 394 when Theodosius again went West to confront Eugenius and Arbogast.

The Vandal Stilicho's star had risen rapidly after his successful embassy to Persia in 387. In the following year, he had been allowed to marry Serena – the emperor's favourite niece and his adopted daughter.

Stilicho maintained that Theodosius had given the care of both his sons to him, and in this he claimed technical seniority over Rufinus. However, his geographical location meant that his principal care was for Honorius. Stilicho was no less ambitious than his Eastern rival, but knowing he was a full-blooded barbarian, he contented himself as had Arbogast with ruling through his ward; not so Rufinus. Throughout Constantinople and the East he was notorious for his avarice and corruption, and used the high office to accumulate great wealth in preparation for his ultimate ambition: the purple. If the eighteen-year-old Arcadius had been even the half of his father, Rufinus would have been put in his place, but the boy was slothful and stupid, possibly because of his closeted upbringing. Small of stature and swarthy of complexion, Arcadius's character was as weak as his intellect. When a man of feeble temperament is ruler of half the known world, he is bound to attract men of ambition like a lamp attracts insects, and so it was that Rufinus was not alone in his scheming.

His opponent was a eunuch of far lower station but in much better proximity to the light, Eutropius the PRAEPOSI-TUS SACRI CUBICULI (superintendent of the sacred bedchamber). Elderly, bald-headed, and wrinkled, he had formerly enjoyed much success as a catamite and a pimp before working his way up through the imperial household. But he shared Rufinus's lack of scruples and his overweening ambition – and he detested the PRAEFECTUS. The next step in Rufinus's plan was the marriage of his daughter to the emperor. This Eutropius intended to prevent at any cost, but of course he had no daughters of his own to put forward, so he settled on a girl of Frankish descent – some sources claim she was the daughter of COMES Bauto. A good-looking young woman, her Greek name was Eudoxia and she had acquired a good education and a deal of cosmopolitan sophistication. Taking advantage of an absence from the capital of Rufinus, who had urgent business to attend to in Antiochia, Eutropius aroused Arcadius's interest in Eudoxia, and by the time the PRAEFECTUS returned to the capital, the pair was formally betrothed. The wedding took place on 27 April 395, just over two months since the death of Theodosius the Great.

Rebellion of Alaric and the Goths

At about the time of the wedding the Goths living in the empire rose in revolt. Their leader was a twenty-five-year-old called Alaric. Born probably in about 370 at Peucé, an island in the Danuvian delta, Alaric was of the noble Visigothic family of the Balthi. He had accompanied the army of Theodosius and taken part with thousands of his countrymen in the battle of the Frigidus. But the great emperor's death broke the spirit of the Romano-Gothic contract in the minds of many battle-hardened Goths. And the penurious policies of Rufinus – and probably also of Stilicho – towards the FOEDERATI who were still sitting in Italia contributed to a searing anger at their treatment. There is a suggestion that Alaric, a commander of an auxiliary unit, expected to receive a senior position from Theodosius if the war against Eugenius were to be successful, and that either Stilicho or Rufinus denied him in this.

Alaric could clearly see an opportunity, for almost all the army was still in the West and the East lay undefended. The Visigoths saluted him as their leader and made him their king. These troops were no longer the disordered barbarians who had entered the empire in 376. Some twenty years of Roman discipline had instilled in them a fighting character that rivalled any Roman legion. In a matter of weeks, the Visigoths spread havoc throughout Daciae and and Thraciae, and advanced to within a short distance of Constantinople. The city was saved by the intervention of Rufinus, who bribed Alaric to go away, and the Visigoths turned their attentions to the ravaging of Macedoniae.

Alarmed at the close call, using Arcadius as his mouthpiece, Rufinus ordered Stilicho to return the legions of the Eastern army to him. The fragments of contemporary history are maddeningly unclear about Stilicho's intentions during this confused period, and his actions often appear to be contradictory. He complied with Arcadius's demand, but on his own terms. Strengthening the Eastern legions with detachments of his own soldiers, Stilicho led the whole army into Illyricum. This was obviously intended to be interpreted as a threat to Rufinus, but instead of heading for Constantinople Stilicho turned south to pursue Alaric and cornered the Visigoths, who had taken shelter behind strong fortifications. Perhaps he wanted to subdue the barbarians before continuing to advance on Constantinople to depose Rufinus and take up his regency of Arcadius. If so, his next actions seem to disprove both arguments. Instead of besieging Alaric, Stilicho gave way to a further demand from Arcadius

Primitive likeness of Alaric from a coin. The Visigothic king sought to form an autonomous nation within the embrace of the Roman empire, but in the process wreaked more than a decade of military and political havoc.

for the return at once of his army – but without Stilicho, who was to return to Mediolanum.

Stilicho dispatched the Eastern troops towards Constantinople under the command of a Gothic officer called Gainas and, having detached his own units, returned to Italia. Free to recommence pillaging, Alaric's Visigoths swarmed through Thessalia, and advancing through the famous pass of Thermopylae, razed towns and villages in Boetia and Attica. Events at Athens are not clear, but in some way the local dignitaries managed to come to terms with Alaric, and he left the city unharmed. The Visigoths next turned south into the Peleponnesus. City after city fell, including Sparta. That most ancient enemy of Athens and once glory of the Greek fighting spirit was razed to the ground.

Stilicho waited only long enough to recruit from along the Rhenus to return to the Peleponnesus and confront the Visigoths at Pholoe, not far from Olympia. Alaric's men could not believe that the Romans had returned so swiftly and, taken by surprise, they were completely surrounded. And then what happened? Nothing. This confrontation of the brave Stilicho and the wily Alaric remains one of Roman history's great mysteries. Stilicho deliberately let the Visigoths escape. The sources are patchy, and where they exist, downright improbable as to the reasons for what happened. Was Rufinus playing a game by bribing Alaric to go and ravage in Illyricum to disconcert Stilicho? Was Stilicho returning the ball by sending Alaric back towards the East to upset Rufinus? The suggestion that has been made that Stilicho did not want to war on Alaric because he viewed the Visigoths as a potentially useful FOEDERATI army – in fact he did employ them shortly after – does not stand close examination. After all, had he wanted Alaric for an ally he would surely have sent an embassy to make a deal, not gathered an army and taken it all the way to Achaea. We are, therefore, left with the mystery. Stilicho returned to Italia, and Alaric concluded a treaty with Arcadius whereby he was awarded the title MAGISTER MILITUM PER ILLYRICUM, effectively confirming him in a prefecture he had already taken by force. It was a move designed to create a buffer state that would keep Stilicho out of Eastern affairs.

Rufinus, however, never lived to see this treaty. Under the influence of the eunuch Eutropius, Arcadius's beautiful barbarian empress Eudoxia had used her charms to mould her husband into hostility towards the PRAEFECTUS. Rufinus had persuaded himself that Arcadius would make him his colleague and was pressing the emperor as hard as he dared. At this point the Eastern army under the Goth Gainas arrived and halted outside the Golden Gate, where traditionally emperors came out to greet their returning troops. On 27 November 395 Arcadius appeared, accompanied by Rufinus, who expected his elevation that same day. Imperious and arrogant, the PRAEFEC-TUS PRAETORIO walked among the soldiers not noticing that they were closing in around him. A moment later a sword flashed, followed by others, and he fell dead. According to the historian Claudian, the man who struck the first blow cried out: 'With this sword, Stilicho strikes you!' What is true is that Gainas was an ally of Stilicho and probably planned the assassination partly as a tribute to friendship and almost certainly to place himself in an advantageous position at Arcadius's court. With Rufinus dead, feeble Arcadius was ruled by three persons: his Frankish empress Eudoxia, Eutropius the eunuch and now PRAEFECTUS PRAETORIO, and Gainas the Goth, friend of Stilicho and now MAGISTER MILITUM PER ORIENTEM.

Under Eutropius the government became more corrupt than ever, with the open selling of offices throughout the Eastern empire. In 399 he was nominated for a consulship – a purely meaningless title by this time, it was still one to which the nobility aspired and which the emperors frequently held. It filled the senatorial class of Constantinople with disgust that a former slave, prostitute and a eunuch should so debase the value of the office; but it was to be his last. Since he had gained full control of Arcadius, Eutropius had pursued a vigorous policy of excluding military men from the emperor, particularly the German officers, and it was Gainas who decided that he must be terminated.

In the spring a revolt broke out among the Gothic settlers in Phrygia under their COMES Tribigild, and Gainas went to handle the situation. But he colluded with Tribigild, and sent back a message to the emperor that the Goths were offering to return to peace for a reasonable settlement – the head of Eutropius. Arcadius was not happy with this suggestion, but Eudoxia urged him to agree. Eutropius's continual reminders that she owed her position to his good offices had become irksome, and she was jealous of the eunuch's hold over her husband; she wanted him dead too. Arcadius agreed, and Eutropius fled to find sanctuary in the church of St. Sophia. Although he was safe there, he was also trapped, and eventually gave himself up in return for his life. Arcadius exiled

Eutropius to Cyprus, but he was soon recalled, tried at Chalcedon, and executed in the autumn of 399.

Gainas fared little better on his return to the capital in 400. For some six months he tried to initiate his own primacy, including a failed attempt to seize the imperial palace, after which he was forced to withdraw from the city. Before all of his forces had left, hostile elements shut the gates, trapping about seven thousand of his Gothic troops inside, whereon the mob, now thoroughly fed up with barbarian soldiers, slaughtered them; many were burned alive in a church in which they had taken refuge. Gainas and his remnant force wandered in a westerly direction through Thraciae, but they suffered a rebuff while trying to cross the Hellespontus into Asia, and turned north. Somewhere on the northern border Gainas fell into the hands of King Uldin of the Huns, who took off his head and sent it to Arcadius as a grisly goodwill present.

Eudoxia, Arcadius's Frankish wife, who moulded her feeble husband to her will.

Stilicho and Alaric

In the West, Italia and especially Rome had suffered at the hands of the Moor Gildo, who had once befriended the usurper Magnus Maximus. After the revolt of Firmus in 374, which Theodosius the elder had suppressed, his brother Gildo had acquired some of the original powers of Firmus. During the reign of Valentinian II, Gildo managed to assume the title of COMES AFRICAE and came to control the provinces of Mauretania, Numidia and Africa Proconsularis. Then in 397 Gildo cut off the grain supply to Rome. Stilicho organised an army to cross the Mare Internum to retake the provinces. He entrusted its command to another of Gildo's brothers, Mascezel, who had good cause for his sibling hatred. Opposed to Gildo's ambitions, Mascezel had deserted to Italia, and to punish the defection Gildo had Mascezel's two sons slain. He sailed in 398 with some thirty-six thousand troops to confront seventy thousand under Gildo on the border of Proconsularis and Numidia. Here, apparently he was visited in a dream by the recently deceased Bishop Ambrose, who informed him of the place of victory, 'Here', and the time,

Below: Ivory relief of Stilicho, the barbarian general who wielded great power under Rome's two weak emperors.

'Three days hence'. The Roman army waited and prayed, and then attacked the superior force of Gildo. Due to one of those fateful events that often do more to determine the outcome of a battle than tactics or the power of arms, this conflict was over in moments. An impetuous standard-bearer of the enemy dashed forwards and received a wound. As he fell, so did the standard, and the African army thought Gildo had given the signal to surrender. Gildo was put to flight and either committed suicide, or was taken and executed.

Not much has been said about Honorius because – despite his relatively lengthy reign – in truth there is little to reveal. Morally destitute and otherwise incapable of any real emotion, he remained a remote figure securely wrapped up by Stilicho in the palace at Mediolanum and later at Ravenna. In his later years, he became engaged in the only activity – apart from a little sport in his youth – that interested him: raising chickens. Shortly before the African expedition, he married Stilicho's daughter Maria, which clearly placed Stilicho at the peak of his influence and power. However, the beginning of the fifth century – the year 1153 by Roman reckoning – also marks the beginning of the end that Theodosius's death foretold. In the early summer of 401 Alaric attacked Italia from Illyricum in concert with an invasion through Raetia by the pagan Ostrogoth Radagaisius. Stilicho seems to have countered Radagaisius with comparative ease – although it would not be the last Rome would see of this particular barbarian. Alaric was another matter.

Had the senate and Honorius known the secret of this vibrant thirty-year-old's heart, disaster might have been avoided. Alaric, like so many invaders who came after him, did not seek the destruction of the Roman empire. He wanted to be adopted by it, to form his own nation within its boundaries and thereby become like one of the old Latin states, offering civic obligations and military service in return for his own IMPERIUM within the state. But to the Romans, the Visigoths were rapine savages. A huge army with thousands of women and children – an entire nation in fact – poured through the passes of the Julian Alps into northern Italia. Bypassing Aquileia and Ravenna, they turned west towards Mediolanum and short of the Western capital, at the small village of Pollentia (Pollenzo), met Stilicho's army on Easter Sunday, 402. The battle was bloody and indecisive, but Stilicho turned the Visigoths and they retreated eastwards.

Stilicho was technically the victor, but he allowed Alaric to retire over the passes and into Illyricum without pursuit; the third occasion on which he had let the Visigothic king escape. The reason for this clemency would seem to be an agreement the two leaders reached intended to further Stilicho's desire to extend his control over Arcadius and the Eastern empire. In order to reach Constantinople Stilicho would have to fight his way through territory held by the Visigoths; better to make Alaric his ally.

There were two consequences of the invasion worth noting. First, Mediolanum had proven too vulnerable to attack by roving barbarians, so to better protect the emperor's person Stilicho selected Ravenna for the new imperial court. Ravenna was geographically less accessible to marauders and it was surrounded on the landward side by lakes and marshy ground, making it difficult to invest. Even if the city should come under attack its proximity to the Mare Adriaticum and the great Roman naval base made provisioning – as well as a quick escape – possible. From this point on Ravenna became the capital of the Western empire. Second, Alaric's avowed intention, as divined by the pattern of his movements, had been to reach Rome. Knowledge of this panicked the citizens, who clamoured for better protection. Stilicho ordered a further reinforcement of the city gates and the raising of the Aurelian Wall where needed, but ironically the strength of Rome's fortifications would ultimately count for less than its citizens' weak fortitude.

In 404 Honorius and Stilicho paid Rome a visit. It was only the fifth time in a century that the ancient capital had seen an emperor within the POMERIUM. Young Honorius seems to have made a good impression on the Romans, noble and common alike, as he stood beside his father-in-law and his wife Maria. Her younger brother Eucherius followed behind them, wearing only the garb of a wealthy PRIVATUS, because Stilicho was wary of giving his son any imperial insignia. The visit was also memorable because it marked the last ever games of gladiatorial combat. Although banned since the edict of Constantine, their allure still tempted the Roman mob. To this celebration the emperor was invited and, much as a modern tourist might be driven to watch a cock-fight while shuddering at the outcome, Honorius accepted. At some point during the height of the bloodshed, a monk walked firmly into the ring and began to separate the gladiators. The crowd, furious at his temerity, shouted and booed, and the monk soon became a martyr. But he did not give his life in vain. Honorius was so moved by the scene that he recognised the monk as a saint, and decreed that even in the eternal city there should be no more blood spilled in the arena.

Religious discord in the empire

In the following year Radagaisius appeared again at the head of an army said to number two hundred thousand, intent on gorging itself on the spoils of the empire. Stilicho raised his army of thirty legions, supported by King Uldin and his Huns and detachments of Visigoths, probably on loan from Alaric as a part of the concordat. Radagaisius made the error of advancing towards Rome across the Appenines, where the Roman legions hemmed the invaders in the valleys and forced them to starvation. Eventually the Ostrogoths melted away and Radagaisus was captured and put to death.

If Stilicho needed a pretext for invading Arcadius's sphere of influence, a developing religious dispute between the Churches of East and West provided one. The cause was the outspoken John Chrysostom, the bishop of Constantinople (b.398–404). Like Ambrose, he was forthright in his views, especially when it came to the lascivious behaviour of the Augusta Eudoxia. With good reason she loathed Chrysostom, whose name is the Greek for 'golden mouth', since he openly referred to her from the pulpit as a 'Jezebel'. Nor was the bishop always popular with some of the capital's aristocrats and wealthy citizens, at whose foppery and extravagance he continually railed. In 403 he fell foul of ecclesiastical politics when the jealous Bishop Theophilus of Alexandria (b.385–412) persuaded the synod at the Council of Chalcedon to depose him from his see. Chrysostom appealed to Arcadius, but Eudoxia bent her submissive husband to ratify the decision, and the bishop was exiled to Bithynia.

However, the common people loved their godly prelate and riots broke out that became so threatening Arcadius hastily recalled Chrysostom. Unfortunately exile had not silvered his pious but insufferable tongue. Fearing further riots if he again banished the troublesome bishop, the emperor compromised by having Chrysostom barred from his churches. At Easter 404, when some two thousand catechumens, unable to take their baptism from the bishop in a church, gathered instead at the Baths of Constantine and became unruly, soldiers were called in to restore order. This was done so harshly that it turned into a slaughter, for which Chrysostom was blamed and banished again on 24 June. His supporters saw the hand of divine retribution when Eudoxia died of a miscarriage on 6 October.

Chrysostom appealed to Pope Innocent I (p.401–17) in Rome, who convoked a Latin synod that unanimously agreed to overturn the banishment.

Innocent and Honorius insisted that Arcadius restore Chrysostom to his see, and reproved the Eastern emperor for his incompetent mishandling of the business. Arcadius deigned his brother no reply. But he responded by imprisoning a delegation of Latin bishops dispatched to attempt a settlement and subjecting them to humiliation before sending them back empty-handed. The rift was complete and condemned the Eastern Church to an inferior status (see side panel). Chrysostom was never recalled and died in his place of exile in September 407.

Arcadius's appalling treatment of the ecclesiastic delegation was sufficient for Stilicho to justify declaring war in 406. Alaric had been preparing for some time, awaiting the order to attack Constantinople. In the event, the only hostile action to take place was the blockading of the Eastern empire's shipping from Italian ports, because Stilicho received alarming news that changed everything. Increasing pressure from Huns on their own eastern borders forced the massed tribes of Vandals, Alani, Suevi and Burgundi to take advantage of the particularly harsh winter of 406–07 to cross the frozen Rhenus to the west bank on a wide front. At Moguntiacum the severely weakened Roman garrison was overwhelmed and all Galliae lay open for the taking. A few weeks later Constantine, COMES BRITANNICAE, crossed to Galliae, ostensibly to deal with the barbarian invasion. Instead, he proclaimed himself Augustus Constantine III, set up court at Arelate (Arles) and soon extended his power to Hispaniae.

The situation was desperate. Stilicho simply did not have the forces to deal with either threat, although he did send a close friend and one of his best generals, a Goth named Sarus, in command of a unit of his fellow countrymen to attack Constantine, an expedition that enjoyed some small success (see the next section). But then events at Constantinople and in Italia overtook Stilicho. On the first of May 408 Arcadius died of unknown causes at the age of thirty-one, leaving the Eastern empire in the hands of his seven-year-old son Theodosius II. Shortly after this event, Alaric's army

IN THE WEST, the Church triumphed over the state when the indomitable Ambrose had humbled mighty Theodosius. However, in Constantinople the similar clash of wills between the weakling emperor Arcadius and his bishop had a very different outcome. The humbling of John Chrysostom before the emperor came to characterise the place of the Church in the Eastern orthodoxy as being subservient to the earthly power of the divinely empowered emperor. In turn, this led to the Byzantine emperor being head of both the Church and the state.

marched and encamped itself on the Italian border. The Visigothic king sent an embassy to the senate at Rome (he always considered the now-parochial city as the centre of the empire) demanding recompense for his costs in fitting out the expedition against Arcadius. At first the senators refused to make any payment, but Stilicho's counsel prevailed and gold sufficient for Alaric's immediate needs was handed over. And in further compensation for the campaign's cancellation Stilicho dispatched the Visigoths to deal with Constantine in Galliae. He no longer needed Alaric for his ambitions in the East and, reminding the court of his pledge to Theodosius the Great, planned to go to Constantinople to take up the regency of Theodosius II.

But Stilicho had overstepped the mark. The Christians at court had been righteously appalled by the haste with which he had married his second daughter, Thermantia, to Honorius earlier in the year after her sister, the empress Maria, had died. Among the Italians there was a growing resentment that a barbarian Vandal should know his place and not set himself up above both emperors. And the troops had become restless at Stilicho's preferment of barbarians, and all at his increasingly harsh discipline. The discontent festered and eventually resulted in a mutiny at Ticinum (Pavia), which Stilicho put down, but his threat – not carried out – to enact a decimation, convinced Honorius that his MAGISTER MILITUM had lost the affection of the soldiers. Too, the signal lack of success against the usurper Constantine and the apparent abandonment of Galliae to the barbarians had lost him the faith of the people. When the hostile minister Olympius began whispering in the emperor's ear, Stilicho's days were numbered.

Rumours were put about that Stilicho's real intention was to place his son Eucherius on the Eastern throne in place of Theodosius II. While this hardly fits the character of the man, there is no denying that as the descendant of Theodosius the Great by Stilicho's marriage to Serena, Eucherius had an imperial pedigree that his Vandal father did not. At this point even Stilicho's best officers abandoned his doomed cause, including his friend Sarus, whose betrayal was the most bitter, since he made a night raid on Stilicho's tent intending to kill his commander, only to find that he had fled to Ravenna. And it was in Ravenna that Stilicho was arrested by an officer called Heraclianus, tried, found guilty and executed on 23 August 408.

At this point it is expedient to go back to the situation in Galliae at the beginning of 407 and follow the campaigns of the usurping Constantine III.

CONSTANTINE III
Flavius Claudius Constantinus (u.early spring 407; co-Augustus [West] 408–18/9/411)

When Magnus Maximus crossed from Britanniae to attack Gratian in 383, his removal of Roman troops weakened the diocese, and put a greater strain on the garrisons along Hadrian's Wall and those defending the LITUS SAXONICUM of the southeast from Saxon sea-raiders. The almost continual sense of dread led to conflict between the remaining military units, their commanders and the civilian administration. There seemed to be an increasing isolation from the centre of Roman power and a feeling that Roman Britanniae might well have to soon fend for itself. It is understandable, then, that Britanniae had become a 'province fertile in usurpers'[†].

More worryingly, the military officers and their largely Gallic troops knew full well how concerns in matters further to the east were weakening the Rhenus defences and the Raetian LIMES. If the barbarians were to breach the frontier, Britanniae would become cut off, and their homes in Galliae would be ravaged. So it was, in the reign of weak Honorius and the Vandal Stilicho, that a series of upheavals shook the island. In 406 the troops hailed their commander – known only as Marcus – emperor, but he was assassinated shortly after. Stilicho's pressing demands for further troop reductions in Britanniae to replace those he was taking from the Rhenus may have sparked this revolt. Not long after another officer called Gratianus was acclaimed. His reign lasted a bare four months, before he too was murdered at the start of 407. By this stage there were few senior officers of any ability left, and news of the breach at Moguntiacum spread panic among the island's bureaucrats. They chose a 'common soldier' of ability – he was probably a centurion – by the name of Constantinus and raised him to the purple with the appellation Constantine III in the spring of 407. If the civilians hoped he would now provide some security for the diocese, they were to be sorely mistaken. Constantine moved quickly, crossing the Mare Britannicum to Gesoriacum, and taking virtually all the mobile army of Britanniae with him, leaving the island near-undefended.

The disaster at Moguntiacum spelled the end of the Roman hegemony in Galliae. The great host that crossed the frozen river on the last day of 406 consisted of Vandals, Suevi and Alani, with the Burgundi

---

† Jerome, epistle to Ctesiphon

soon following the initial crossings. The German tribes fanned out across Galliae, took Aquitania by 409 and crossed the Pyrenees into urbanised Hispaniae, homeland of the Theodosian dynasty, where they soon set up competing kingdoms.

It is to be doubted that Constantine III had much effect on the barbarian invasion, or even that he could have done much to oppose them had he wished. Over the next few years we have to imagine that the old Gallo-Hispanic provinces brought to heel by Julius Caesar were awash with different competing tribes whose long envy of Rome made them want the mantle of Roman civilisation more than plunder. Plunder, however, they also took as they dodged between the ambitions of competing Roman usurpers and the occasional armies sent against them from Italia, including Alaric's Visigoths, who had been dispatched by Stilicho to confront the double threat of barbarians and Constantine. (These, however, soon returned to the easier pickings in Italia.) The confusion must have been incomprehensible.

Into this violently bubbling human broth came Constantine, bent on taking the throne from Honorius. His Gallic troops, having discovered their towns and homes destroyed, were reduced to virtually destitute wandering nomads, merely another 'tribe' on the move. Constantine probably came to an agreement with the barbarians that left them free to ravage the west and central regions of Galliae, while he sent his two generals Justinianus and the Frank Nebiogastes to lead the vanguard down the Rhodanus valley. Here, he was able to garner the as yet unharmed and prosperous cities into his empire and take over their administration.

It was at this point that Stilicho sent the Gothic officer Sarus to check Constantine's further progress. At first he enjoyed a great success and defeated Justinianus in battle, while Nebiogastes was lured into a trap and murdered under the flag of truce outside Valentia (Valence). Sarus then attempted to besiege Constantine in Valentia, but the usurper's centre and rearguard under the admirable command of Edobich the Frank and a Briton named Gerontius forced Sarus to raise the siege and then beat a retreat back over the Alps. Further humiliation was heaped on him when he was forced to hand over all the collected booty to the brigands who held the high passes in order to buy a safe passage into Italia.

In May 408 Constantine reached Arelate and made it his capital. During the summer he determined to prevent the development of a war on two fronts by making a pre-emptive strike on Hispaniae, where cousins of Honorius were gathering a rag-tag army against him. Meanwhile forces in Italia were assembling to mount a counterattack. Constantine now called for his monastic son Constans to leave his seclusion and join him in Arelate. When Constans complied, he was made Caesar and given the command of detachments under Gerontius to take Hispaniae from the Theodosians. Constans' force was by far the superior and the cousins were defeated without difficulty. Two, Didymus and Theodosiolus, were captured, while two others, Lagodius and Verianus, escaped by ship and fled to Constantinople.

Constans left his wife and household at Caesaraugusta (Zaragoza) under the care of Gerontius and returned to Arelate to discover that the threatened Roman counterattack had not materialised. This was due to the mutiny at Ticinum that shortly led to Stilicho's execution, and to the events in Italia that transpired as a consequence. The Italian troops' hatred of their German colleagues spilled over and in Rome they began slaughtering the families of the FOEDERATI, including recruits from Radagaisius's

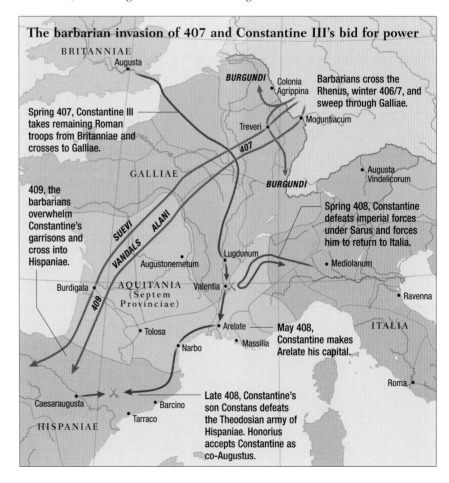

Raised to the purple by Britanniae's administrators panicked at having been abandoned by a weak Rome, Constantine III promptly took the remaining imperial troops from the island. He contested the throne with Honorius in Western provinces fallen into chaos in the wake of barbarian invasion from across the Rhenus.

The barbarian invasion of 407 and Constantine III's bid for power

BRITANNIAE
Augusta

BURGUNDI
Colonia Agrippina

Barbarians cross the Rhenus, winter 406/7, and sweep through Galliae.

Spring 407, Constantine III takes remaining Roman troops from Britanniae and crosses to Galliae.

Treveri

Moguntiacum

407

GALLIAE

Augusta Vindelicorum

BURGUNDI

409, the barbarians overwhelm Constantine's garrisons and cross into Hispaniae.

SUEVI VANDALS ALANI

Augustonemetum

Lugdunum

Spring 408, Constantine defeats imperial forces under Sarus and forces him to return to Italia.

Mediolanum

Burdigala

AQUITANIA (Septem Provinciae)

Valentia

Ravenna

409

Tolosa

Arelate

Massilia

Narbo

May 408, Constantine makes Arelate his capital.

ITALIA

Roma

Caesaraugusta

Barcino

Tarraco

Late 408, Constantine's son Constans defeats the Theodosian army of Hispaniae. Honorius accepts Constantine as co-Augustus.

HISPANIAE

defeated force. In desperation, those that escaped fled to the eastern Italian coast, where Alaric was roaming unchecked through Etruria. As their only hope of refuge, an estimated thirty thousand Germans flocked to his standard, leaving Honorius in Ravenna without any significant military power beyond the small force of Sarus and his Gothic troops, who had escaped the fate of their countrymen in Rome. Constantine seized this opportunity to send envoys to Ravenna offering his support to the feeble emperor. Honorius eagerly recognised Constantine as his distant colleague and co-Augustus, and the two were joint consuls for 409. Little good it did Honorius.

With Stilicho gone and Honorius's army in disarray or absent without leave, Alaric returned, spurning the attractions of Aquileia, Mediolanum and Ravenna, intent on reaching that goal he had always desired – Rome. Unopposed, the Visigoths ravaged the countryside and, in September 408, stood before Rome's mighty walls. Of course, Alaric had none of the Romans' clever siege engines, but he was content to blockade the city and wait. Inside, the citizens prayed for relief from Ravenna, but none came because Honorius had no intention of committing his few and uncertain forces to rescue the old capital from its fate. As winter approached the food ran out, and shortly before Christmas Alaric accepted a bribe to go away: five thousand pounds of gold, thirty thousand pounds of silver, three thousand pounds of pepper and thousands more of hides and silk clothing. Alaric raised the siege and marched his army north, but only as far as Ariminum (Rimini), where the Visigoths encamped while their king negotiated with the emperor for the territories of Venetia and Histria, Dalmatia and Noricum. For once in his life Honorius showed some spirit and, despite the contrary counsel of his ministers, refused any such deal. Strangely, Alaric considered his options and lowered his demands to the

territory of Noricum. Still Honorius refused to budge. This firm stand was supported by his general Sarus, whose real reason for defiance was a deadly blood-feud with Alaric and especially with Alaric's brother-in-law Ataulfus (Athaulf), for some slight he had suffered at their hands in the past.

Baffled by the emperor's obduracy, Alaric turned again to the south and marched on Rome, but this time he informed its citizens that he had no intention of putting them to the sword and burning the city, he only wanted to overthrow Honorius. Faced with a second siege and the ingratitude of an emperor who had offered no help, the senate – with Alaric's approval – elevated the PRAEFECTUS URBI, an intelligent, art-loving Greek named Priscus Attalus, as Augustus. Attalus had the pagan vote because of his tolerant attitude, and his Arian baptism commended him to the Goths, who had remained faithful to the promise made to Valens to adhere to Arianism. Everything was now in place, with Alaric as Attalus's MAGISTER MILITUM, to proceed to Ravenna and depose Honorius, but for two unexpected events. The emperor's young nephew, Theodosius II, responded generously to his uncle's appeal for help, and out of the blue ships arrived at Ravenna carrying six Byzantine legions – forty thousand men. Buoyed up by this new, loyal army, Honorius withdrew the offer he had been forced to make of sharing power with Attalus. And in Africa, on which Rome entirely depended for its grain, the governor Heraclianus (the officer who had executed Stilicho) refused to supply any further provisions to the rebellious city. Alaric demanded that detachments be sent immediately to Carthago to depose Heraclianus, but Attalus honourably though unwisely refused to send barbarians against a Roman province.

With his patience exhausted, in the early summer of 410, having publicly stripped Attalus of his purple, Alaric again enclosed the city in a siege. This time, there was little delay, and towards the end of August the Goths burst in through the Salarian Gate at the foot of the Pincian hill, and for three days Rome was sacked: the first time for nearly eight hundred years a foreign foe had taken the city, although the disaster hardly impinged on the emperor (see side panel). Surprisingly, the damage was restricted because Alaric had issued instructions that no church was to be harmed and no citizen who freely surrendered was to be harmed. Nevertheless, the Visigoths were not angels, and doubtless many suffered at their hands. When the three days were over, taking Honorius's half-sister Galla Placidia with him, Alaric moved towards the south of Italia and prepared to sail his army to Sicilia and then Carthago,

Sad pawn in a struggle for power: Priscus Attalus, cultured PRAEFECTUS URBI of Rome, was elevated to Augustus in 409 by the senate, stripped of his purple by Alaric one year later; he then endured years of nomadic life with the roaming Visigoths, before being made Augustus again in 414, only to be quickly deposed, removed to Hispaniae by the Visigoths, captured by Honorius's troops, paraded in triumph at Rome, and finally sent to die on the Lipari Islands.

The imperial chicken farmer

Rearing chickens is said to be the only occupation of Honorius that gripped his torpid imagination – a fact that appears to have been well known even as far away as Britanniae. There is a story told of how he received the news of Rome's sacking by Alaric that, while undoubtedly apocryphal, indicates the low esteem in which his contemporaries held him. A chamberlain rushed into his presence crying out, 'Roma has perished!' The distraught emperor looked up and replied, 'Roma perished? It is not an hour since she was feeding out of my hand.' When it was explained that it was only the city that had been destroyed, the relieved Honorius said, 'I thought you meant that I had lost my *bird* Roma.'

deal with Heraclianus, and relieve Rome of the impending famine. But he got no further than Cosentius (Cosenza) when he was stricken with a fever, and the great Visigothic king died a few days later.

The year 409, when he shared the consulship with Honorius, was the high-water mark of Constantine III's success. By September, the barbarians who had crashed across the Rhenus and had spent the intervening two years ravaging Galliae, had reached the Pyrenees, where they came up against Constantine's garrisons in the passes. In short order, they overwhelmed the Romans and poured into Hispaniae. Constantine was about to send his son Constans to handle the crisis when word arrived that his MAGISTER MILITUM Gerontius had rebelled and proclaimed his own creature called (another) Maximus, who may also have been his son, as co-Augustus. He then made a compact with some of the barbarians who had encountered Constantine's garrisons and enrolled them in his army with promises of the booty to be gained in Arelate. And in the year of Rome's sacking, Gerontius advanced into Narbonensis, with Constans taking a detachment to go and meet him. This was not the only disaster facing Constantine. Left to its own devices the diocese of Britanniae, facing increasing Saxon raids along the southern coasts and incursions of Scots and Picts in the north, revolted against Constantine's nominal control, and the Britons expelled his tax collectors and officials. At this point the island passed entirely from any form of Roman control and became, in the words of one contemporary, 'an island ruled by tyrants'.

In a final, desperate gamble, Constantine gathered his remaining forces and crossed the Alps in the summer of 410, encouraged by the entreaties of Honorius's MAGISTER EQUITUM Allobich, who wanted Honorius replaced by a more capable ruler. However, Allobich was suspected of the connivance and executed, leaving Constantine to turn around and retreat to Arelate. Constans fared no better, being driven back from the Pyrenees by Gerontius, who besieged him at Vienna. The city capitulated early in 411, and Constans was put to death. Gerontius now pressed on and besieged Arelate. Constantine was left without any capable officers since the defection of his PRAEFECTUS PRAETORIO Decimius Rusticus to the cause of another usurper, Jovinus (*see the next section*). But now another man entered the picture, a general worthy of Stilicho, who had placed his services at the command of Honorius, Flavius Constantius. In command of a reorganised Roman army, Constantius

descended from the Alps and fell on the besieging troops of Gerontius, putting them to flight. Constantine still held on in newly besieged Arelate, hoping for reinforcements under his Frankish MAGISTER EQUITUM Edobich, who was raising recruits among his countrymen in northwestern Galliae. Sadly for Constantine, Constantius got wind of the stratagem, and defeated Edobich, after which Constantine's scattered Rhenus garrisons defected to Jovinus.

Before his surrender, Constantine III took holy orders and became a priest, and then on receiving promises of safe conduct for himself and his youngest son Julianus, opened the gates. Constantius honoured his pledge to spare Arelate and its inhabitants, but Constantine and Julianus were sent under escort to Ravenna. However, before reaching the city, soldiers from Ravenna met the party, bearing orders to execute the 'usurper', and the late Augustus was beheaded on the spot, together with his son, on 18 September 411. It seems strange to relate, but their heads were sent all the way to Carthago, there to be prominently displayed as a warning to all anti-emperors. This signal, however, did not dissuade Heraclianus, who had held loyally to Honorius in the arrest and execution of Stilicho and against Alaric, from raising the standard of rebellion himself in 413. He sailed with a vast fleet for Italia, but perhaps his heart was not in revolt, for when he was met by the COMES Marinus, he faltered and abandoned his fleet to return to Carthago in one ship, where he was immediately arrested and put to death – an appropriate revenge for his murder of Stilicho.

Maximus, declared co-Augustus by the rebelling MAGISTER MILITUM Gerontius.

CONSTANTIUS III
Flavius Constantius
(r.co-Augustus [West] 8/2/421– 2/9/421)

Despite all the setbacks Honorius survived on the Western throne longer than an emperor of his meagre talents at that time had any right. But the last years of his reign did not really belong to him, but to his general Constantius, and the amazing woman who Constantius finally married, the emperor's half-sister Galla Placidia. It has been noted that the two sons of Theodosius the Great, Honorius and Arcadius, inherited none of their father's abilities in any respect. This benefit fell to their half-sister born in about 390, daughter of Theodosius and his second wife Galla, neither of whom she would have had much recollection, since her mother died when she was

Constantius III died of pleurisy months after becoming co-Augustus.

about four, and Theodosius departed soon after for his final campaign in the West. As a consequence, she was placed in the care of Stilicho's household and raised by his wife Serena, her cousin. She was, therefore, with Serena in Rome at the time of Alaric's first siege rather than at court in Ravenna. For some unexplained reason, Serena became a victim of politics with the senate, who decreed her death, with which it appears Placidia concurred. There is a suggestion that Serena was pressing Placidia to marry her son Eucherius, but if so it seems an unreasonable excuse for condemning her foster-mother to death.

Thus it was that she was still at Rome during the third siege and the sack, and became a royal hostage of Alaric, treated with all due respect but a prisoner for ransom nonetheless. After the Visigothic king's death his brother-in-law Athaulf was proclaimed king in his place. Athaulf was a curious figure; at first, unlike Alaric, determined to destroy everything Rome stood for, but by turns coming to the exact opposite view and declaring that he wanted to be known to posterity as the man who restored the empire to its former splendour. This transformation was evidently taking place at this point in time because the restitution of Placidia was less willingly offered, and for the very good reason that captor and hostage were falling in love. Meanwhile, there was another suitor for her hand.

Constantius was a native of Illyricum, born at Naissus (Nis). He had served in many campaigns under Theodosius the Great and had come into his own when Honorius most needed a strong arm to rest on. He is described as having a sulky look, with a broad head set on a thick neck, with large, full eyes that darted about as he scowled – the complete tyrant in appearance, perhaps not unlike Marcus Antonius. Appearances apart, he was a polite man, and good company at suppertime. And for the decade after Stilicho's death Constantius was the dominant Roman military leader. As we have seen, he rapidly saw off Gerontius and defeated Constantine III in 411. After these victories Honorius allowed him to keep the spoils, which provided sufficient funds for him to celebrate an ovation and, more importantly, secure the release from Athaulf of Placidia, with whom he was madly in love. However, this was not a simple matter because the Visigoths had decided to leave Italia, and Placidia went with them into Galliae. Athaulf's destination seems to have been suggested to him by the pitiable ex-Augustus Attalus, who was still making his nomadic home with the Visigoths, and that was Moguntiacum, where Jovinus, yet another usurper, had claimed the purple.

Of noble Gallic birth, Jovinus seized power at Moguntiacum, with the help of an Alani chieftain called Goar and a Burgundian called Guntiar (Guntiarius). Additionally, he enjoyed the substantial support of the somewhat bewildered provincial aristocracy, as his fine-quality coinage struck at Lugdunum, Treveri and Arelate indicates. Early in 412 Athaulf began negotiations with Jovinus, but these were broken off when the Goth Sarus rode into camp with a handful of compatriots to offer his services to Jovinus, unaware that he was falling right into the hands of his arch-enemy. Sarus had defected from Honorius in disgust that one of his faithful servants had been murdered at the imperial court and the emperor had refused to make restitution. But in offering his support to Jovinus, he had ridden to his death. Athaulf's troops surrounded Sarus's small force, and all were overwhelmed and slain. Claiming that he had rid Jovinus of a nuisance, Athaulf wanted a share of power, but Jovinus insulted him by elevating his own brother Sebastianus to co-Augustus. At the start of 413 Athaulf offered Honorius the heads of the usurpers in return for an honourable peace with the Visigoths, and the offer was accepted. Athaulf did not delay, and shortly after Jovinus arrived bound and in company with the head of his brother. That of Jovinus was also struck off and – puzzlingly – the heads were sent to Carthago to be displayed outside the gate alongside those of Constantine III, his son Julianus and Heraclianus.

As a footnote, we should remember Maximus, whom Gerontius had set up in Hispaniae in opposition to Constantine III. He was deposed in 411 and allowed to retire, but suffered execution in 422, after being accused of fomenting another rebellion. As for Guntiarius and his Burgundi, Constantius granted them land on the west bank of the Rhenus in 413 and gave them the status of FOEDERATI. In this capacity, they later migrated into the Rhodanus valley and, by the 450s, held Lugdunum as their capital.

Galla Placidia's marriages

Unfortunately for Constantius, negotiations with Athaulf had not resulted in Placidia's return. He pressed for her restitution, and Athaulf demanded concessions of land, money and corn in ever-greater amounts. As the Visigoths moved to the south they made a surprise attack on Massilia, but were repulsed by the garrison commanded by a certain Bonifacius, after which they went to Narbo. And there, in January 414, Athaulf and Galla Placidia were wed. Honorius had dismissed Athaulf's many requests to marry his

The Gallic noble Jovinus (top) seized power in Moguntiacum in 411, and made his brother Sebastianus (above) co-Augustus. Two years later their severed heads lay at Honorius's feet.

sister, and the Visigoth's sense of Teutonic honour may explain why, after a love affair of four years, he had delayed. But towards the end of 413, Honorius relented, we are told, because he conceded the good advice of a general called Candidianus. Placidia took her Christian vows as a Roman matron befitting her imperial status; Athaulf was garbed not as a German chieftain but in the raiment of a Roman senator. Amid the splendour of the nuptials, presided over by the Arian bishop Sigesarius, something unique had taken place – the union of barbarous Gothia with civilised Rome, another of the signal events that beckoned the dawning medieval era.

Shortly after the wedding of his beloved to another, Constantius received in Arelate an embassy seeking tax concessions headed by a young Gallic noble called Avitus, who will be of some consequence in future affairs. But the distractions of administration did not deter Constantius from his hatred of Athaulf. Despite the marriage alliance to the imperial family, he refused to stop his attacks on the Visigoths, and he used every method to drive them from Narbonensis and into Hispaniae, now much despoiled by the Vandals and Suevi. They settled for a while at Barcino (Barcelona), where a servant who bore him some ancient grudge assassinated Athaulf in 415. His brother Walia honoured the dying Athaulf's last wish and restored Placidia to the Romans in return for the right to settle on land spanning southern Aquitania and the western half of Narbonensis Primus. A treaty was finally concluded in 418, and Tolosa (Toulouse) became the Visigothic capital under nominal imperial authority. Once again, the Visigoths were FOEDERATI, and combined armies of Goths and Romans protected Galliae and northeastern Hispaniae from Vandal raids.

There was one major setback to the alliance in 420, when the Vandal king Gunderic defeated a Romano-Gothic army and became ruler of a unified Vandal-Alani kingdom centred on Baetica. This allowed him to take control of key ports and, more importantly, the Roman galleys moored there. A vast pirate fleet that assiduously raided the Baleares, Corsica, Sardinia and coastal cities now replaced Roman naval power, which for so many centuries had dominated the Mare Internum. Their booty helped shore up the fledgling Vandal kingdom and fuelled a desire for further conquest. In 428 Gunderic's successor and half-brother, the shrewd and militarily outstanding Gaiseric (or Genseric), led all eighty thousand of his people across the narrow strait to begin an assault on Mauretania.

Constantius met his bride-to-be – the betrothal

was commanded by Honorius – at the foot of the Alps to escort her to Ravenna. However, a modest period of mourning was allowed her, during which time Constantius paid his suit and she rejected it. But Placidia really had no choice, and finally agreed to be married in 417. Not surprisingly, Constantius ensured that the celebrations were even more sumptuous than those of Athaulf; the fame of their spectacle had radiated from Narbo to every part of the empire. Within two years Placidia bore Constantius a daughter, Justa Grata Honoria, followed by a son, Valentinian. The years following the wedding were uneventful with King Walia guarding the Gallic frontier against the Vandals, and the high point was a triumph celebrated by Honorius, in accordance with tradition, at Rome. The occasion was less than glorious, however. Poor itinerant ex-Augustus Attalus, having witnessed Placidia's first marriage, had somehow wandered up into Galliae, and been proclaimed emperor again in 414, but was soon deposed and removed by the Visigoths to Hispaniae. From there he had taken ship and been captured by one of Honorius's quinqueremes and taken to Rome. A poor excuse, but the only triumph Honorius was likely to enjoy. In the course of the procession, Attalus was forced to kneel before the emperor, who ordered the thumb and forefinger from his right hand to be amputated, and his exile to the Lipari Islands, where he was left to die.

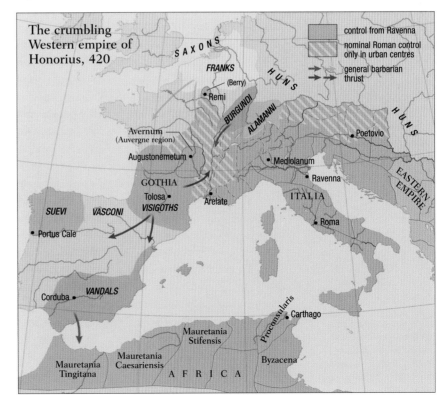

The crumbling Western empire of Honorius, 420

control from Ravenna
nominal Roman control only in urban centres
general barbarian thrust

SAXONS
FRANKS
(Berry)
Remi
BURGUNDI
ALAMANNI
HUNS
HUNS
Avernum (Auvergne region)
Augustonemetum
Poetovio
Mediolanum
Ravenna
EASTERN EMPIRE
GOTHIA
Tolosa
VISIGOTHS
Arelate
ITALIA
SUEVI
VASCONI
Roma
Portus Cale
Corduba
VANDALS
Proconsularis
Carthago
Mauretania Stifensis
Byzacena
Mauretania Tingitana
Mauretania Caesariensis
AFRICA

Galla Placidia was discontented with her position at court and kept badgering Honorius to elevate her husband, and reluctantly the emperor gave in. On 8 February 421, Constantius became Constantius III, co-Augustus with Honorius, and Placidia became styled Augusta. In keeping with the custom, statues of Constantius were sent to Constantinople for erection in the Eastern capital. However, news of the unilateral addition to the Augusti did not sit well with Theodosius II – or rather with his sister Pulcheria, who effectively ruled in his name. The statues were returned and Theodosius refused to recognise Constantius, who in consequence began somewhat petulant preparations for a war against the Eastern empire. However, conflict was avoided because Constantius developed pleurisy and, depressed by the curtailment of his freedom through the tedious court ceremonial he was obliged to observe, he continued to sicken and died on the second day of September 421.

Widowed for a second time, Placidia now found herself in a difficult position, because her half-brother Honorius, who had always held her in an affection that bordered on the incestuous, finally gave vent to his repressed feelings. He started to kiss her at public functions in a manner that was obviously more than brotherly. Honorius wavered between fondness and mistrust, was jealous of her ministers and close associates, and his moods affected the court adversely. Fights between his servants and those of the Augusta became commonplace, even spilling out into the streets. Placidia quarrelled with Honorius, and the conflict became so bitter that in the spring of 423, she withdrew to the court of her nephew Theodosius in Constantinople, taking her two children with her. Had she been able to command her brother's behaviour and so stayed in Ravenna, Placidia would have been able to avoid what happened when Honorius, aged thirty-nine suddenly died of 'dropsy' (probably a disease of the lungs) on 26 August 423. Into the imperial vacuum stepped the PRIMICERIUS NOTARIORUM (chief of the notaries), a man called Joannes – another usurper.

Galla Placidia, half-sister of Honorius, wife of Constantius III, and through him mother of Valentinian III, who became co-Augustus to Theodosius II in 425 at the age of six.

The usurper Joannes, a clerk and probably the puppet of Honorius's MAGISTER MILITUM, was put to death at Ravenna after 18 months.

JOANNES

Also Johannes
(u.September [West] 423–c.March 425)

How an obscure clerk became the emperor in Ravenna is hard to understand, and the ancient histories have little to offer in the way of explanation. The office of PRIMICERIUS NOTARIORUM – a chief clerk and diarist – was a useful one, but hardly at the forefront of the imperial bureaucratic hierarchy. The only explanation that fits the politics of the period is that Honorius's MAGISTER MILITUM Castinus supported the pretension of Joannes, predictably because he expected to enjoy the real power without the pain that any experienced general knew attended imperial failure; much as had Arbogast supported Eugenius.

As befitted his position while a PRIVATUS, Joannes was an intelligent man, and the historian Procopius praised his mild manner and also his general abilities as an administrator. However, his eighteen-month reign was beset by all the ills that a pretender to the throne might be expected to attract. Theodosius II refused him any sort of recognition, a revolt against him in Narbonensis resulted in the PRAEFECTUS PRAETORIO being slain in Arelate, and COMES Bonifacius (he who had defended Massilia so bravely against Alaric), now governing Africa, typically cut off the grain supply.

It might have been hoped that Theodosius would not welcome Galla Placidia and the infant Valentinian, son of Constantius III from whom the Eastern emperor had also withheld recognition, but this turned out not to be the case. When at Constantinople Theodosius elevated Valentinian to the rank of Caesar, it was clear that war could not be far away. And in pursuance of an offensive policy, Joannes bequeathed one great benefit to the Western empire, the promotion of a young man called Aëtius. The son of a mixed marriage of an Italian mother and Gaudentius, a Visigoth in the service of the empire who had risen to become COMES AFRICAE, Aëtius had been given in his youth first as a hostage to Alaric, who taught him the military arts, and then to the Hunnish king Rugila. It was from this last acquaintance that Joannes hoped to benefit, and sent Aëtius on an embassy to the Huns to seek military help in the coming war with Constantinople. In this he was successful, receiving a detachment of some sixty thousand Huns to come to Joannes' aid. However, the Eastern empire reacted too quickly for Aëtius to save his master.

Theodosius accompanied the army sent to dethrone the usurper as far as Thessalonica, where he was detained by an illness. Galla Placidia and the five-year-old Valentinian continued on under the overall protection of the MAGISTER MILITUM, the Alan Ardaburius and his son Flavius Aspar (of whom in time much more will be related), and the specific guardianship of Candidianus, the general who had ten years before persuaded Honorius to let Placidia marry Athaulf. Candidianus scored some useful victories in the northeast of Italia, which offset the disaster that befell Ardaburius. He, too, had had successful skirmishes in Dalmatia, but while sailing to Aquileia his ship was blown off course and landed on the marshy coast among the enemy, close to Ravenna. Taken in chains before Joannes, he contrived to convince the usurper of his treachery to Placidia's cause, and his life was spared. The Byzantine force, now under Aspar's command, hastened to the marshes and dykes surrounding Ravenna and managed to ford the lagoon and take the city's defences by surprise early in 425.

With hardly any casualties, Ravenna was taken, Joannes captured and wily Ardaburius freed. The later historian Socrates recounts how the Byzantines were guided through the watery maze by an angel, but the contemporary Philostorgius attributes the defeat of Joannes to the treachery of his supporters, who had been suborned by Ardaburius. We are also told that Joannes had weakened his forces by sending detachments to Africa to oust Bonifacius. Joannes was taken to Aquileia, where Placidia and her children were waiting. He was then dragged into the circus, where his right hand was cut off, after which in a mockery of a triumph, he was led around the city riding on an ass to the jeers of the mob before being executed. To punish Ravenna for supporting a pretender, the city was sacked for three days, which loss proved Rome's gift as it regained the status of capital. Valentinian III – now six – was taken there to be crowned with the diadem and become co-Augustus with Theodosius.

Only three days after Joannes' death, Aëtius belatedly returned at the head of his army of Huns. This sudden and frightening influx of Rome's occasional ally but usually deadliest foe forced Aspar to rally his troops, fresh from their pillaging of Ravenna, and take the field. But the initial skirmishes were hollow – neither side was keen to spill blood. The Huns were rattling their swords in order to raise the price of their quietly going home, and this was agreed between the Augusta Placidia and Aëtius. In receipt of a handsome sum of gold, the Huns retired peacefully, and Placidia gave Aëtius the title of COMES PER ITALIA, from which position he became her chief adviser.

THEODOSIUS II

Flavius Theodosius (co-Augustus [East] 402; Augustus [East] May 408–28/7/450)

Theodosius, son of Arcadius and Aelia Eudoxia, was born in April 401. He was the fourth child but the first boy, so his arrival was received with great joy, both by his family and by the populace of Constantinople. He was baptised and crowned Augustus in January of the following year. When his father died in 408, the seven-year-old was fortunate in his PRAEFECTUS PRAETORIO, Anthemius. This able and high-principled man had dominated the last years of Arcadius's reign, in stark and welcome contrast to the feckless emperor's previous counsellors. Now he became regent to young Theodosius, and was instrumental in the reconciliation between East and West (even to sharing a consulship with Stilicho in 405).

Despite this apparent accord, the death of Stilicho made it more readily possible for Anthemius to cement relations between Constantinople and Ravenna, which remained cordial until the elevation of Constantius III in February 421. Anthemius put to good use the continual influx of Germanic tribes by using them to counter the barely civilised Isaurian tribes that had been plaguing southern Anatolia since 403. And he was the real architect in 413 of the great new land walls to protect Constantinople, known as the Theodosian Walls, that still stand today. For unknown reasons, Anthemius did not last beyond 414, at which point Theodosius became dominated by his sister, Aelia Pulcheria, only two years his senior but already named Augusta, and the real power behind the throne.

Weak and easily led, Theodosius was developing in a manner that suggested he would not be much of an improvement on his father. However, he possessed the charm Arcadius had lacked, was an earnest student in Latin and Greek classics, mathematics, natural sciences and in art. In fact he became such an adept at illuminating manuscripts that he was given the Greek nickname *Kalligraphos*. While as a boy he was surrounded by the paraphernalia of religion, it is doubtful that he became as involved as Pulcheria, who was exactingly devout and pious, and demanding in the same way with her two other sisters, Arcadia and Marina. In the days of their mother Eudoxia, the palace had resembled the bordello that John Chrysostom had railed against, now it rang to the chants of monks and felt more like a cloister. Quietly secluded amid this

Theodosius II was studious and weak. Secluded in a court dominated by the pursuit of religion, he was content to leave the running of affairs of state to his strong-willed sister Aelia Pulcheria (below).

ecclesiastical threnody, Theodosius was content to pursue his studies and leave matters of state to Pulcheria. In 420 he decided to take a wife, and asked her to help him find one. She settled on a beautiful young Greek girl named Athenaïs; a pagan. This problem was overcome by having her baptised, with a change of name to Aelia Eudocia, and the couple were married on 7 June 421.

In the following year she gave Theodosius a daughter, who he named Licinia Eudoxia; so to avoid confusion we shall continue to refer to her mother by her Greek name, Athenaïs. In his delight at her birth, Theodosius awarded his wife the title of Augusta in 423. This was a move not calculated to put Pulcheria in a good mood, and she soon conceived a jealousy of her sister-in-law similar to that Julia Mamaea had for her daughter-in-law in 227, when Sallustia began to dominate Severus Alexander. In the same summer, the empire's third Augusta arrived at court, Galla Placidia with her children Justa Grata Honoria and Valentinian, seeking refuge from her half-brother Honorius's unwelcome advances. The events resulting from the death of Honorius in August of the same year demanded Pulcheria's full attention, and her feelings against her sister-in-law Athenaïs were put on hold as she organised the mobilisation of the Byzantine army that would defeat the usurper Joannes.

It was fortunate for Theodosius that the empire's relations with the Sassanians remained cordial, for it relieved him of fighting with enemies on two fronts. He had received the recognition of King Isdigerdes at his accession and the Persian court's moderate attitudes towards Christianity assured peace between the empires until the king's death in 421. On the accession of his son, Vararanes V, hostilities broke out anew. The new king allegedly began a persecution of Christians, and some Roman citizens were harassed. Vararanes launched a campaign against Rome's eastern frontier, but was very quickly defeated by several able generals, including the redoubtable Ardaburius of Ravenna fame. The outcome was a treaty called the One-Hundred-Year Peace. Each empire's borders were to be respected, and kept largely demilitarised. There were several infractions, including one in 440–41 when Isdigerdes II came to the Sassanian throne, but otherwise the treaty held for the rest of the fifth century.

At home, the peace was not so well kept between Pulcheria and Athenaïs, each trying to outdo the other in the religious sphere. The marriage of Licinia Eudoxia to Valentinian III in 437 only reinforced the struggle. Years before, Athenaïs had made a vow that if

Aelia Eudocia, pagan Athenaïs before her baptism into the Church, was chosen for Theodosius as his wife by his sister Pulcheria.

her daughter did marry Valentinian she would make a pilgrimage to Jerusalem in thanksgiving. When she returned in 439 the important relics she brought to the capital – including the original chains with which Herod had bound St. Peter – gained her enormous prestige, putting in the shade Pulcheria's return of the saintly John Chrysostom's relics to Constantinople. Athenaïs' fall from favour with Theodosius was engineered by eunuchs in Pulcheria's camp, who fabricated a charge of adultery with the MAGISTER OFFICIORUM Paulinus, himself a confidant of the emperor. Protesting her innocence, Athenaïs took herself away from the court and, after a pause of three years, returned to Jerusalem in 443, where she remained until her death in 460. Paulinus was exiled to Caesarea in Cappadocia, and executed in 440.

The Theodosian Law

Theodosius's greatest legacy was the result of a commission set up in March 429. With the emperor's participation, it was to publish the first great pandect of Roman law. In the age since Diocletian, when the last comprehensive law code had been issued, both Eastern and Western emperors had published a large number of general constitutions. Many were no longer relevant to modern-day concerns, and many more were unworkable or contradictory. There was the additional problem of harmonising the codes of the East and the West, and creating a process by which each half of the empire could recognise one another's laws.

A commission of nine scholars compiled all the legislation enacted in both the East and the West since the time of Constantine the Great. Theodosius seemed less interested in ridding the legal system of contradictions – although many were reconciled – than he was in providing a truly comprehensive set of laws. After six years, a first edition was completed in 435, but not published. A second commission improved the language and created a system by which the code could be further emended and enlarged as necessary in the future. The CODEX THEODOSIANUS was finally promulgated on 15 February 438 jointly in the senates of Rome and Constantinople (Rome still the centre of Western jurisprudence). The code had enormous influence, both in itself and in future legal history. Together with the work of those great third-century jurists Ulpian, Papinian and Julius Paulus, it became the basis for Justinian's much more ambitious judicial reforms in the following century. It is also possible to trace considerable portions of King Alaric II's LEX ROMANA VISIGOTHORUM of 507 to the CODEX THEODOSIANUS.

Attila and the Huns

By the turn of the fifth century, the Huns had settled east of the Danuvius, particularly along the plains of what is now Hungary. From here, they had caused the empire only occasional problems and, as we have seen, even consented to serve under Roman arms when it suited them. What misery the Huns inflicted on the other barbarians along the empire's edge was of little consequence, other than being the principal cause of the massed barbarian migrations of 407. On the borders of the Eastern empire, the Huns were appeased by tribute payments, as the Goths had been before them. Their king Roua received an annual payment of some three hundred and fifty pounds of gold, and this helped to maintain an uneasy peace. However, the situation changed dramatically in 434, when Roua died and was succeeded by the two sons of his brother Mundzuk, named Bleda and Attila. After the older brother's death some years later, Attila was for nineteen years to become the terror of all the Christian world.

Almost sixty years earlier, Ammianus had described the Huns as: *'a race savage beyond all parallel...They are certainly in the shape of men, however uncouth, and are so hardy that they neither require fire nor well flavoured food, but live on the roots of such herbs as they get in the fields, or on the half-raw flesh of any animal, which they merely warm rapidly by placing it between their own thighs and the backs of their horses.'*

Attila was clearly a man of the same mould, for he is described in contemporary sources – no proven images of him exist – as being short, with small, beady eyes, a snub-nose, swarthy like his race, and with a head too large for his body, his chin adorned with a straggly beard. Surprisingly for the destruction he caused, Attila was no great general – the only pitched battle he fought against disciplined troops, he lost. His tactics were those of a bully, and given a bloody nose, he ran off. However, that day was some time in the future. Attacks against the Eastern empire began in 441, and for six years skirmishes along the Danuvius and in Pannoniae were an irritant, but gave Constantinople little cause for immediate alarm as long as the Huns continued to receive the agreed annual tribute. But in 447 the situation changed dramatically. By this time Bleda had died (no contemporary sources suggest that he was murdered by his brother, a popularly held belief) and Attila was in sole command of the Hunnish army. When he demanded double the tribute, seven hundred pounds of gold each year, Theodosius either flatly refused, or at least dithered on the decision.

In the eight years since his crowning, Attila had raided far across northern Europe to the shores of the Oceanus Germanicus (North Sea). But in the year of refusal he was back on the Danuvius, and his forces stormed across the river. Many cities were razed, including Philippopolis, Sirmium, Naissus and Serdica. The cruelties Attila inflicted in this campaign earned him the title 'Scourge of God' by the Christian communities so afflicted. He then split his army in two. One arm swept southwards into Thessalia, the other advanced on Constantinople. Between them they destroyed everything between the Mare Adriaticum and the Aegeum, as far south as Thermopylae, and as far east as the Hellespontus, where the Huns inflicted a defeat on Roman forces at Callipolis (Galilipoli). Only the capital's massive new walls completed by Theodosius in the nick of time saved the empire from total disaster. That and the old enemy of the barbarian ravager – the land laid so much to waste could no longer support the horde, and Attila's Huns drifted back towards the Danuvius, and negotiations for peace commenced. The slaughter in Naissus had been so terrible that the Roman ambassadors were unable to enter its ruins for the mass of human bones and an all-pervading stink of death. Attila's peace terms trebled the annual tribute and demanded full payment of arrears, and the Romans had no choice but to comply, at a dreadful cost to the people in Theodosius's dominions.

With Athenaïs far away in Jerusalem and Pulcheria no longer the emperor's confidante, there was no one close to Theodosius who might have raised in him some spirit to resist. Under the obviously astute 'diplomacy' of Attila, the empire's wealth was being drained away, and only Theodosius's death brought a halt to this state of affairs. Theodosius had one great love other than scholarly pursuits and illumination, and that was hunting. And it was while he was out on 28 July 450 that a fall from his horse killed him; he was in his forty-ninth year. He and Athenaïs had produced no male heir, so it was down to Pulcheria to direct the succession, which she did by contracting a marriage with a Thracian ex-soldier and senator called Marcianus (Marcian), and placing him on the throne beside her.

Attila, king of the Huns, whose horde swept the European mainland in an orgy of destruction that would test the empire to its limits.

Marcian's story is told at the start of chapter 14, but he undertook one important task that bears on events in the West – he refused to pay Attila any further tribute. Was this bravery, or a calculated gamble? Marcian's spies had informed him that Attila's plans for a vast operation against the Western empire were so far advanced that he would be unwilling to delay them for a punitive attack on Constantinople, which in any case would only have the unsatisfactory outcome of the raid of 447. Rejoicing broke out some days later when news arrived that the Huns were on the march...towards the Western empire.

VALENTINIAN III

Placidius Valentinianus (r.Caesar c.October 423; co-Augustus [West] 424–3/15/455)

Born in 419, Valentinian was granted the title NOBILISSIMUS by his uncle Honorius, an indication that he might be considered the emperor's heir. As we have seen, Theodosius in the East recognised neither his father Constantius's elevation nor initially Valentinian's legitimacy in the purple. This changed when Galla Placidia exiled herself to Constantinople with Valentinian and his sister Justa Grata Honoria. Theodosius, then in his twenty-fourth year, went so far as to betroth his baby daughter, Licinia Eudoxia, to his young nephew in 424, before the Byzantine army moved to unseat the usurper Joannes. Twelve years after his betrothal, Valentinian returned to Constantinople in 437 to marry Eudoxia. Barely aged seven when he was crowned in Rome, his mother Placidia utterly dominated his reign, and she was to precede him to the grave by only five years. The other figure who held the reins of power was Aëtius. Ineffectual, spoiled, devoted to religion and astrology in equal measure, Valentinian III was not fitted to rule, and showed neither the aptitude nor inclination to do so. The only effective measure he seems to have taken was to grant greater ecclesiastical power to the bishop of Rome, especially Pope Leo I the Great (p.440–61). The story of his reign, then, is really that of the Augusta Galla Placidia.

The two great calamities of Placidia's reign were the loss of Africa to the Vandals, and the invasion of the Huns under the terrible Attila. The first disaster may well be blamed on certain steps taken by Placidia that led to the mutual enmity of her two great

Intellectually destitute, weak-willed Valentinian III was utterly dominated by his redoubtable mother, Galla Placidia.

counsellors, Bonifacius and Aëtius. Bonifacius had driven Alaric from the walls of Massilia in 412, wounding the Visigothic king by his own spear, it is said. His next appearance in history is in 422 quarrelling with Castinus, Honorius's MAGISTER MILITUM, who refused him a high position in a planned campaign against the Vandals in Hispaniae. Irritated, Bonifacius evidently left and made his way to Africa, which by this time was almost a no-man's land. Here, he managed to stamp his authority on the provinces, in spite of only holding the rank of TRIBUNUS MILITUM. However, his services to the Theodosian house in withholding grain from Joannes earned him Placidia's affection, and she appears to have confirmed his position and made him COMES AFRICAE during a visit he made to pay her court in Ravenna.

As the master of Italia, Aëtius had wanted this office as well, for his father had once been COMES AFRICAE, but he hid his dissatisfaction behind a mask of friendliness towards his rival. Then he intrigued. Placidia listened to his counsel, that Bonifacius would develop into another Gildo, and seize the African provinces as his own kingdom. To prove Bonifacius's treachery, she should write and, without specifying a reason, summon him to Ravenna. Aëtius argued that Bonifacius would refuse her order, which would prove his malign intent. Aëtius then wrote to his 'good friend' Bonifacius to warn him that the Augusta was plotting against him, and he would know this to be true when he received a letter from her summoning him to Ravenna for no stated reason. Like Placidia, Bonifacius accepted this advice, and when the letter arrived, made no move, confirming the Augusta's worst fears. She had him declared a public enemy in 427.

Africa was no longer well supplied with troops, and in desperation Bonifacius made a compact with Gaiseric, king of the Vandals still battling the Visigoths and Suevi for mastery of Hispaniae. Late in 428, Gaiseric brought eighty thousand Vandals across the narrow strait and began advancing through the Mauretanian provinces towards Numidia and Africa Proconsularis. Meanwhile, friends of Bonifacius in Rome had uncovered the treachery of Aëtius and went to him at Carthago to lay the facts before him. When Placidia was also informed, she relented and forgave Bonifacius, but felt unable to break with Aëtius, who was warring against the Franks. Now Bonifacius had to persuade the Vandals to quit Mauretania, but Gaiseric scorned him, and continued his advance along the North African coast. In early skirmishes, Bonifacius won some victories, but it was clear he could not hold on for long, and Placidia had no reinforcements to send. At this desperate point Theodosius II in Constantinople showed himself to be a friend of the West again by dispatching a Byzantine naval force under Aspar, son of Ardaburius and the young general who had triumphed over Joannes at Ravenna. Sadly, it was not enough, and Bonifacius was defeated in a great battle in 431, and compelled to flee with his forces to Italia, leaving Mauretania and Numidia in Vandal hands.

On his victorious return from the Frankish campaign, Aëtius dashed to confront his rival, and in the ensuing battle, Aëtius was technically defeated, but challenged Bonifacius to single combat to determine the outcome. In this somewhat Teutonic conflict, Bonifacius received a mortal wound of which he died three months later, in 433. Still furious with him over his conniving, Placidia did not immediately restore Aëtius to his full powers, but the Augusta could hardly keep her most skilled general on the shelf, and he was soon back in the field battling in Galliae against Visigoths, Burgundi and Franks. There were many successes, but none sufficient to more than maintain a semblance of imperial control over the eastern region of the former Gallic provinces. Across the Mare Internum, Gaiseric had remained out of Africa Proconsularis in return for FOEDERATI status, and so grain for bread in Rome – albeit in reduced quantities – still came, and some nominal imperial presence was maintained at Carthago. But at his capital in Hippo Regius (Annaba), Gaiseric had no intention of abiding by this agreement, and in 439 he attacked Proconsularis. The loss of Carthago was a shock to the Romans, but their hands were full elsewhere.

Attila in the West

By now Attila's eye was turning to the dominions of Valentinian III, with whom he had previously remained on reasonable, if somewhat lordly terms. If he needed a pretext for invasion – which is hardly believable – it came in the form of a particularly Roman scandal. In 449 Valentinian's sister Honoria was caught in an affair with her steward, who was promptly executed. She was kept in solitary confinement, but in her anger she smuggled out a ring to Attila suggesting he intervene as her champion. Attila described this as an imperial marriage proposal and demanded half the Western empire as her dowry. The preposterous claim was firmly denied by Placidia and Aëtius, and they prepared for the inevitable war. Aëtius needed the Visigoths as allies, but after the peace of 419–29, there had been ten years of war, the Visigothic king Theodoric I trying to take

Narbonensis and Aëtius retaliating by attacking what had been Aquitania Secunda, now Gothia. After 439 there had been peace but little friendship between the courts of Ravenna and Tolosa. Nevertheless, Aëtius was able to persuade Theodoric of their common cause, and to this alliance he added the Salian Franks, descendants of those Salii that Constantius I had settled on the island of the Batavians at the end of the third century. Their neighbours, the Ripurarian Franks, however, joined Attila.

Attila counted among his warriors countless of the German tribes, including the Saxons, who were already raiding defenceless Britanniae. In the spring of 451 this vast host, numbered by historical sources – undoubtedly exaggerating – as between five hundred thousand and seven hundred thousand, crossed the Rhenus in an armada of rough-hewn boats and swept south, sacking first Colonia Agrippina, then in succession Moguntiacum, Argentorate, Remi (formerly Durocortorum), and were on the verge of taking Cenabum Aureliani (Orléans) when Aëtius met them in June, in what was perhaps the greatest single engagement western Europe was to witness before 1914. The battle of the Catalaunian Plain near Durocatalauni (Châlons-sur-Marne) resulted in Attila suffering his first and only reversal and, according to contemporary accounts, left more than two hundred thousand dead, among them King Theodoric, who had been unhorsed and trampled to death. Military strategists have since criticised Aëtius for allowing Attila to retreat across the Rhenus, but the Romans had also taken massive losses and were in no position to pursue the enemy. Perhaps, also, Aëtius felt a continued threat from the Huns would hold his Gallic alliance together.

The architect of the Western empire's security, fraught and doubtful as it had been, and in reality a crumbling away of provinces, did not witness the success of her general Aëtius, for Galla Placidia, approaching her sixtieth year, died in Rome on 27 November 450. The imperial court had been in Rome for twenty-five years, but her body was returned in state to her beloved Ravenna. She was, therefore, also spared the horrors to come. When he returned in 452, Attila wreaked a terrible revenge on Italia. Descending the Frigidus, he besieged Aquileia, which held out for three months before falling and being put to the torch. With dreadful rapidity other major cities followed suit– Concordia, Altinum (Altino), Patavium (Padua) – while others opened their gates and were saved from burning but not from pillage, and the citizens were taken into slavery. At Mediolanum, the Hunnish king set up his

Bonifacius, COMES AFRICAE, was an able warrior who fell foul of power politics and intrigue at court in Italia, and was ultimately forced to relinquish the Roman holdings in Africa to the Vandals.

Attila's pretext for war on the West: Justa Grata Honoria, Valentinian III's sister, placed into solitary confinement after having been caught in delicto flagrante with a servant, smuggled a ring to the Hun and asked him to be her champion.

court, and prepared to take the war south to Rome. Aëtius, no longer able to call on Gallic and Gothic allies, was no match for the Huns. But Rome and Italia were saved by the intervention of Pope Leo I, already raised high by Valentinian, who went to meet Attila where the River Mincio meets the Padus. Here, by means we can only guess at, Leo convinced the Hun to turn back. The Huns migrated into the reaches of the Danuvius and fell into squabbles between themselves and concentrations of Ostrogoths. Attila was contemplating a further attack against Constantinople, when he died in his sleep in 453, and Christian Europe gave a great collective sigh of relief. In the following year the Ostrogoths won a great victory over the demoralised Huns, after which the most of the nation drifted away to regions around the Mare Caspium (Caspian Sea), having in its time brought Europe to its knees. Those that remained took service in the Eastern Roman army as mercenary auxiliaries and were to have a part to play in later events (see chapter 17, Belisarius in Africa).

In all these events, the emperor had played little part, but Valentinian had a sting in his tail. His position relative to powerful Aëtius is reminiscent to that of his uncle Honorius to Stilicho forty-six years before. In the palace in Rome, where Valentinian had mostly resided during the Hunnish invasion, wily eunuchs began to poison his vacant mind against Aëtius, who was promised in marriage to the emperor's youngest daughter, Galla Placidia the Younger. Since Valentinian had no son, the marriage would have placed Aëtius in line for the succession. The whisperings of chamberlains had their effect, so much so in fact that Valentinian was driven himself to strike the killing blow with his own

dagger. Asking a palace official after the murder whether he had performed a good deed or not, the courtier replied: 'I am scarcely able to say. One thing, however, I do know, that you have chopped off your right hand with your left.' And so it was. In the middle of March 455, while watching some athletes training in the small part of the Campus Martius left unbuilt, two henchmen of Aëtius sprang out from behind a bush and stabbed the emperor to death. It is a reflection of how low Valentinian had fallen in people's esteem that his murder was not avenged. With Theodosius II in his grave five years, his sister Pulcheria for three and now Valentinian III gone, the dynasty of Theodosius the Great had ended, although not quite the house, for Galla Placidia the Younger would marry another emperor, Olybrius.

THERE IS AN interesting footnote to the story of Attila's retreat from Italia in 452. Tradition asserts that the thousands who fled from the wrath of the Huns hid out among the reeds, marshes and lagoons of the northwestern coast of the Adriaticum above Ravenna, and there built a village on stilts. The settlement grew and became named after the region, Venetia, and developed into the city we know today as Venice. Unlike the rest of Italia, Venice retained its independence under a form of republican government. Over the centuries it prospered and grew into the great trading city-nation that, in 1204, brought the Byzantine empire and Constantinople in particular to its knees.

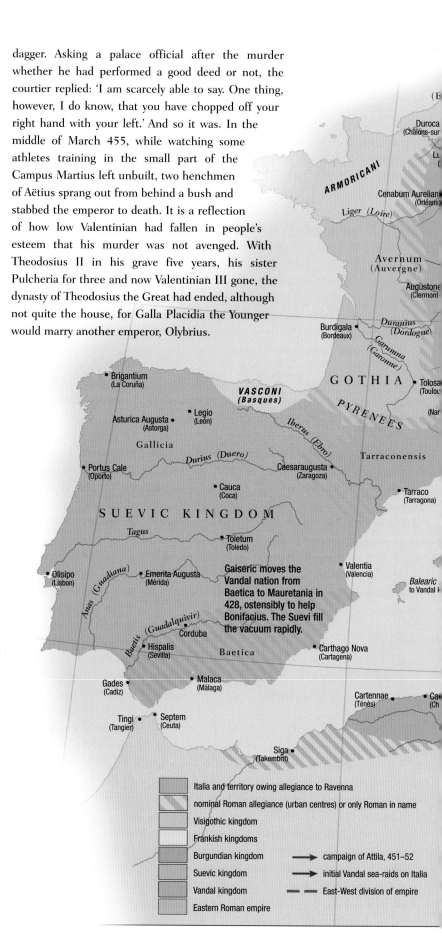

Gaiseric moves the Vandal nation from Baetica to Mauretania in 428, ostensibly to help Bonifacius. The Suevi fill the vacuum rapidly.

Italia and territory owing allegiance to Ravenna

nominal Roman allegiance (urban centres) or only Roman in name

Visigothic kingdom

Frankish kingdoms

Burgundian kingdom

Suevic kingdom

Vandal kingdom

Eastern Roman empire

campaign of Attila, 451–52

initial Vandal sea-raids on Italia

East-West division of empire

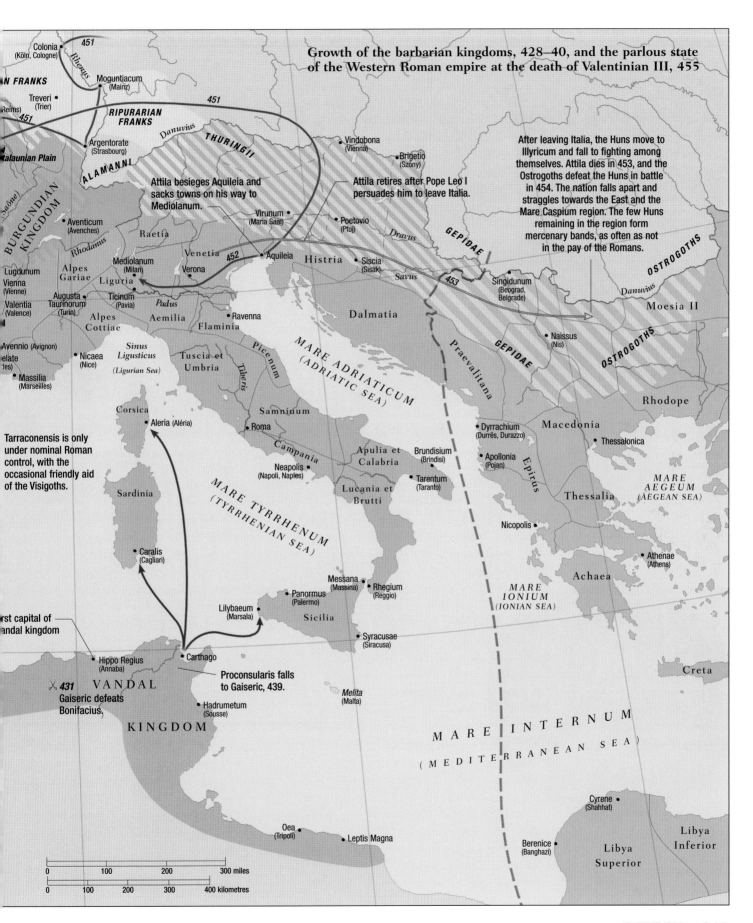

Growth of the barbarian kingdoms, 428–40, and the parlous state
of the Western Roman empire at the death of Valentinian III, 455

After leaving Italia, the Huns move to Illyricum and fall to fighting among themselves. Attila dies in 453, and the Ostrogoths defeat the Huns in battle in 454. The nation falls apart and straggles towards the East and the Mare Caspium region. The few Huns remaining in the region form mercenary bands, as often as not in the pay of the Romans.

Attila besieges Aquileia and sacks towns on his way to Mediolanum.

Attila retires after Pope Leo I persuades him to leave Italia.

Colonia (Köln, Cologne)
451
Rhenus
Moguntiacum (Mainz)
N FRANKS
Treveri (Trier)
Reims
RIPURARIAN FRANKS
451
Danuvius
THURINGII
Argentorate (Strasbourg)
alaunian Plain
451
ALAMANNI
Saône
BURGUNDIAN KINGDOM
Aventicum (Avenches)
Raetia
Rhodanus
Vindobona (Vienna)
Brigetio (Szöny)
Virunum (Maria Saal)
Poetovio (Ptuj)
Dravus
GEPIDAE
Lugdunum
Vienna (Vienne)
Valentia (Valence)
Alpes Gariae
Mediolanum (Milan)
Verona
Liguria
Venetia
452
Aquileia
Histria
Siscia (Sisak)
Savus
453
Singidunum (Beograd, Belgrade)
Danuvius
Moesia II
OSTROGOTHS
Augusta Taurinorum (Turin)
Ticinum (Pavia)
Padus
Alpes Cottiae
Aemilia
Flaminia
Ravenna
Dalmatia
GEPIDAE
Naissus (Nis)
OSTROGOTHS
Avennio (Avignon)
les
Nicaea (Nice)
Sinus Ligusticus (Ligurian Sea)
Tuscia et Umbria
Picenum
Tiberis
MARE ADRIATICUM (ADRIATIC SEA)
Praevalitana
Rhodope
Massilia (Marseilles)
Corsica
Aleria (Aléria)
Roma
Samnium
Campania
Dyrrachium (Durrës, Durazzo)
Apollonia (Pojan)
Macedonia
Thessalonica
Tarraconensis is only under nominal Roman control, with the occasional friendly aid of the Visigoths.
Sardinia
MARE TYRRHENUM (TYRRHENIAN SEA)
Neapolis (Napoli, Naples)
Apulia et Calabria
Brundisium (Brindisi)
Tarentum (Taranto)
Epirus
MARE AEGEUM (AEGEAN SEA)
Thessalia
Lucania et Brutti
Caralis (Cagliari)
Nicopolis
Achaea
Athenae (Athens)
rst capital of andal kingdom
Messana (Massina)
Rhegium (Reggio)
Panormus (Palermo)
Lilybaeum (Marsala)
Sicilia
Syracusae (Siracusa)
MARE IONIUM (IONIAN SEA)
Creta
Hippo Regius (Annaba)
Carthago
Proconsularis falls to Gaiseric, 439.
431
VANDAL
Gaiseric defeats Bonifacius,
Hadrumetum (Sousse)
Melita (Malta)
KINGDOM
Cyrene (Shahhat)
MARE INTERNUM (MEDITERRANEAN SEA)
Libya Inferior
Oea (Tripoli)
Leptis Magna
Berenice (Banghazi)
Libya Superior

0   100   200   300 miles
0   100   200   300   400 kilometres

CHAPTER FOURTEEN
FALL OF THE WEST

PETRONIUS MAXIMUS
Flavius Anicius Petronius Maximus
(r.17/3/455–31/5/455)

After Valentinian III's murder, the choice of the army and the people fell on Petronius Maximus, quite simply because he was the highest-ranking senator in Rome and promised to make a good emperor. Apart – possibly – from that it was said he was the grandson of the usurping emperor Magnus Maximus, his CURRICULUM VITAE was exemplary. He was born in about 397 and seems to have embarked on a senatorial career by about 411 as a praetor, a purely honourary office by this time that entailed paying for races in the Circus. At the age of eighteen he was admitted to the imperial council in the junior post of TRIBUNUS ET NOTARIUS. This was followed by a series of high-level imperial appointments: COMES SACRARUM LARGITIORIUM; PRAEFECTUS URBI (held twice); PRAEFECTUS PRAETORIO ITALIAE (also held twice). In 433 he became a consul for the first of two times. At the age of about fifty he attained the rank of Patrician (*see side panel, right*). With a statue raised in his his name in the Forum of Trajan by none less than Honorius himself, Petronius Maximus was clearly the man for the job. And yet his reign lasted for only two and a half months and as a consequence of his demands on Valentinian's widow (as some later accounts claimed) was responsible for yet another sack of poor war-torn Rome.

His downfall can be attributed to two primary causes: the first his own surprising ineptitude that lost him the affection of the senate and people, and his attempts to ally himself by marriage to Valentinian's widow to the Theodosian house. His first mistake was not to prosecute Valentinian's two murderers, Optila and Traustila, and worse, to receive them into the circle of his

When sexagenarian Petronius Maximus demanded that Valentinian III's young widow Licinia Eudoxia marry him, it was said that she called on the Vandal king Gaiseric to help her.

Gaiseric, established in Africa since 428, was to be the bane of the Roman empire for another 22 years.

friends. Whatever his reasons were for this, his subjects suspiciously detected his hand in the assassination – and it would be hard to blame them. Further execration resulted from the emperor's muddle of harshness mixed with feebleness. But Rome was even more appalled by Maximus's demands that Valentinian's widow, the beautiful Licinia Eudoxia, marry him. That she was still in widows' weeds and would be for many months, and that at thirty-three she did not want to marry a sexagenarian, counted for nothing. With her aunt Pulcheria dead, there was no one of her family left to save her, so she adopted the tactic that her sister-in-law Justa Grata Honoria had employed, and called on barbarians to save her; not the Huns, however, this time the appeal was to Gaiseric.

The Vandal king may well have been pleased to be given a plausible excuse to raid Rome, but neither Alaric nor Attila had ever bothered with pretexts for their aggression and nothing Gaiseric had done to date indicated that he was any different. Only two chronicles mention the traditional story of Eudoxia's plight, and one – John of Antioch – cites it as little more than a popular legend. While it is a great deal less romantic, it is far more probable that Eudoxia needed no barbarian rescue from the new emperor, and that Gaiseric had been planning on the final subjugation of Rome from the moment he captured Carthago. Whether or not he ever received Eudoxia's cry, his fleet set sail from Carthago in May and sailed to Ostia. Maximus might at this dire moment have saved his reputation through

BY THE FIFTH CENTURY, the term 'patrician' meant something very different to its Republican usage, when it referred to the first families of Rome. The patriciate had largely vanished by the time of Augustus, and any remaining members fell to the intrigues of Nero's DELATORES. Constantine the Great revived the title in the fourth century, but only as a personal honorific and not a hereditary dignity. In this way, Aëtius wore this rare distinction for the last twenty years of his life, and to the common folk the title Patrician came to be associated wth the head of government and real power in the state, the first minister.

the organisation of a vigorous defence of the city, but he did the opposite. Cowering in the palace and preparing to flee north, he issued a proclamation that anyone who wished was free to leave Rome.

He need not have bothered. The senators and wealthy had already packed up and fled. But the common people had nowhere else to go, and in their fear and fury, rose up with the garrison soldiers on 31 May – only two days before Gaiseric's sails hove to and three days before the Vandals were at the city gates – and tore Petronius Maximus limb from limb, throwing the dismembered parts of his body into the Tiberis.

Rome was, to a degree, once again saved by the good offices of the venerable Pope Leo I, who went out to meet Gaiseric to see if he could repeat the charms that had turned Attila. The Vandal king was persuaded to the extent that he promised there would be no damage to buildings and no deaths. What he wanted was booty, and for fourteen days the city was subjected to 'a leisurely and unhindered' extraction of its wealth. Although its fabric was untouched, the roof covering of the temple of Jupiter Optimus Maximus was half stripped. The Vandals probably desisted when they realised that what appeared to be a sheath of solid gold was in fact copper with a thin gold coating. Trinkets, adornments, statues, bullion, jewels and everything that could be moved was taken.

If Eudoxia really had appealed to Gaiseric, she perhaps received more than she had wished for. As the Vandals left, they took the empress with them, together with her daughters, the princesses Eudocia and Galla Placidia the Younger, who in the previous year had been married to a senator of Constantinople named Olybrius (although his location at this time is not clear). Despite several imperial embassies, Eudoxia and Placidia were to suffer seven years of courteous detention before being sent to Constantinople at the entreaty of the emperor Leo I in 462. Eudocia was to remain, for she married Gaiseric's son Huneric – she a Catholic, he an Arian – a union that would form the basis of Vandal claims to the Roman throne.

With the death of Aëtius, the chronicler Marcellinus wrote, 'With him died the Western empire, nor since then has it been able to recover.' But the historian Priscus did not even mention the name of Maximus; he summed up the remaining inheritors of the Western purple disdainfully: '...although I know their names, I shall not mention them. For it so fell out that they lived only a short time after attaining the office, and as a result of this accomplished nothing worthy of mention....'

AVITUS

Marcus Maecilius Flavius Eparchius Avitus
(r.10/7/455–17/10/456)

For two months after the Vandals' departure a silence reigned in Rome, its senators and garrison too depressed even to find another to raise to the purple. And then in mid-August the senate met with dismay news that the Gallic provinces had taken matters into their own hands and elevated a nobleman of Avernum (the Auvergne region of southern-central France) to the vacant throne. This had happened at Arelate on 10 July 455. Hands tied, the senate accepted Eparchius Avitus without a murmur. Avitus was born of a Gallic senatorial family probably in 395, making him about sixty at his accession. He was well educated and eloquent, and had at least three children, Agricola, Ecdicius, who later became MAGISTER MILITUM under Julius Nepos in 475, and Papianilla, who married Sidonius (*see side panel*).

Elderly Eparchius Avitus was elevated by the Gallic provinces when the Roman senate failed to replace Petronius Maximus. He would be declared unfit to rule by his own MAGISTER UTRIUSQUE MILITAE, the powerful Ricimer.

IN A PERIOD of poor historical record, one man stands out: Gaius Sollius Apollinaris Sidonius (c.430–c.489). He was an aristocrat of Lugdunum (Lyons), son and grandson of the PRAEFECTUS PRAETORIO GALLIAE, and later the bishop of Augustonemetum (Clermont). He received a classical education, undertook some military service, and married Papianilla, the daughter of Avitus; and he accompanied her father to the imperial court in Rome. Surviving the deposition of Avitus, he served as a senator and PRAEFECTUS URBI in 468–69, before retiring to Avernum. As a bishop (b.472–c.489) he became an expert on ecclesiastical matters, but also vigorously defended his see against the depredations of King Euric of the Goths in 474. His position close to the centre of power gave him a valuable insight into the politics of this difficult period, during which secular offices were closed to men of ability and an ecclesiactical life was an honourable alternative. He was later canonised as St. Apollinaris Sidonius (not to be confused with St. Apollinaris, a possible apostle of St. Peter in the second century).

As a boy, Avitus had formed a friendship with the Visigothic king, which extended into his early adulthood and would be the most important factor in his rise to power. The name of Avitus was first bruited in 415 when he was only twenty and chosen to head a deputation to the MAGISTER MILITUM and future co-Augustus Constantius III, who was governing from Arelate and mooning over Placidia. Avitus pleaded so eloquently for some tax concessions that Constantius willingly granted his request. In his military career he served under Aëtius and eventually rose to the rank of MAGISTER PEDITUM PER GALLIAE. At some point a younger brother

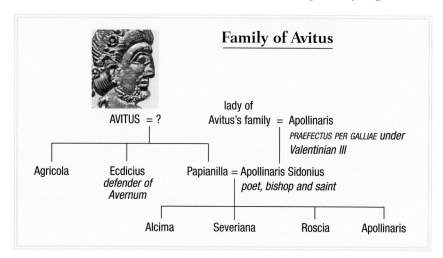

Family of Avitus

AVITUS = ?

lady of Avitus's family = Apollinaris
PRAEFECTUS PER GALLIAE under Valentinian III

Agricola

Ecdicius
defender of Avernum

Papianilla = Apollinaris Sidonius
poet, bishop and saint

Alcima   Severiana   Roscia   Apollinaris

named Theodorus was sent as a hostage to the Visigothic court of Theodoric I at Tolosa. Paying his brother a visit, Avitus so impressed the king that he was asked to renounce his Gallo-Roman nationality and live permanently at Tolosa. Sidonius tells us that this offer was rejected scornfully, but it seems that Avitus did remain for some time with Theodoric, and was instrumental in saving Narbo from a barbarian siege in 436.

Between 439–45 he served as the PRAEFECTUS PRAETORIO for Galliae before retiring to his estate, Avitacum near Augustonemetum, in the heart of Avernum. But the threat of invasion by Attila the Hun in 451 brought Avitus at the request of Aëtius back to public service to use his influence with Theodoric. He, more than any other, was the conduit by which the Visigoths made alliance with Rome against the common enemy. In 455 the short-reigning Petronius Maximus appointed Avitus MAGISTER UTRIUSQUE MILITAE and sent him on an embassy to Theodoric II[†] to reconfirm the Visigoths' status as FOEDERATI.

When the news arrived of Petronius Maximus's

† After his death in battle against the Huns in 451, Theodoric I was briefly succeeded by his son Thorismund, who died in 453 to be succeeded by his brother Theodoric II.

death and the Vandal sack of Rome, Theodoric urged Avitus to assume the purple for himself. 'We do not force this on you, but we say to you: with you as leader, I am a friend of Rome; with you as emperor, I am her soldier,' said Theodoric according to Sidonius. The Visigothic king had his own agenda: protection for the emperor against any other claimant and protection from the hated Vandals; in return he wanted Rome's recognition of his planned attack across the Pyrenees to wrest Hispaniae from the Suevi. This tribe had occupied almost all of the land since the Vandals crossed to Africa, apart from the beleaguered Roman enclave of Tarraconensis, now only centred on the hinterland of its capital Tarraco.

Avitus, having accepted his destiny, spent three months in Galliae raising a sufficient force of arms to establish his IMPERIUM in Rome, among them Gallic troops and contingents of barbarian allies. When the Augustus entered Rome on 21 September, it was not to universal cheering. One commentator, Prosperi, noted that Avitus 'entered Italia with his comrades in this *appropriated* honour.' We are told by Sidonius that before his arrival in Rome, Avitus went and recovered the lost provinces of Pannoniae. This unlikely expedition might possibly have recovered some part of Noricum, where the emperor had campaigned in his youth, but Pannoniae – largely freed of Huns after the nation's break up in the previous year – was now a virtual no-man's land overrun by Ostrogoths in the east and Geppidae in the west. If Pannoniae was under any nominal Roman control it was Constantinople that had the means to order it.

Ricimer the shadow puppet master

The business of Avitus's sixteen-month reign was mostly preoccupied with establishing his authority with various parties; most immediately over his leading military commanders, a COMES of the Suevi nation named Ricimer – who barely concealed his barbarian contempt for the emperor – and Majorian. To Marcian, the emperor in Constantinople since August 450, he sent an embassy asking for recognition and a sharing of the rule, but during his reign this was not forthcoming. The Vandals were the most pressing problem, since Gaiseric's fleet was still blockading Roman ports. Marcian had already asked Gaiseric to leave Italia alone, but the Vandal king did not deign him a response. Avitus also sent envoys to Gaiseric, boldly threatening that if the Vandals did not abide by the treaty of 442 he would 'make preparations, trusting to the domestic forces and the support of his

allies'. The latter presumably referred to the Visigoths and the assorted FOEDERATI he had brought with him to Rome. The 'domestic forces' were those of the Italian field army under the joint-commands of the COMITES Majorian and Ricimer – in reality the biggest threat facing Avitus. Fortunately for Avitus the ending of the sailing season in November prevented any immediate Vandal response to his bluff.

Two major events took place during 456. The first began with embassies between the courts of Theodoric II and Rechiarius, king of the Suevi. Theodoric complained of Suevi raids across the Pyrenees, but these were only an excuse to make war. In his support, the Visigothic king had COMES Fronto, sent as the Gallo-Roman ambassador on behalf of Avitus to insist that the Suevi stop attacking what little was left of Tarraconensis. This allowed Theodoric to pretend that his invasion was in Roman interests and under the emperor's authority. Early in the year, a massive army descended into what had been the Roman province of Gallaecia and over the summer months destroyed the Suevi kingdom. Rechiarius was defeated in a great battle at the River Urbicus (Orbigo) near Asturica Augusta (Astorga), the Suevic capital, on 5 October. The king fled the field but was later captured at Portus Cale (Oporto), where he was imprisoned and then put to death. The second event was a triumph for Ricimer. As the sailing weather improved in the spring, Gaiseric recommenced raiding along the southern coast of Tyrrhenian Italia, and gathered a large fleet off Corsica. Ricimer met this threat with a smaller Roman fleet that outmanoeuvred Gaiseric's and destroyed all his ships. Next he landed near Agrigentum (Agrigento) in Sicilia, and defeated a Vandal army, recovering all of the island province apart from a small enclave centred on Lilybaeum (Marsala).

Ricimer's victories should have reflected well on Avitus, but any joy was soured by a famine in Rome. Starved by now for over a year by the Vandal occupation of Africa, the people, led by a senate suspicious of the Avernian emperor, laid the blame at the feet of Avitus. It is easy to see why the senate should have hated him. During his brief reign Avitus only appointed Gauls to office at both junior and senior levels, denying noble Roman youths the opportunity for advancement. With such a sweeping policy of Gallicisation, the senators wanted him gone, and they soon had their way. Avitus was forced to dismiss his 'COMITATUS', the hungry barbarian contingents that were placing a greater strain on the scanty supplies than the mob could stand. And at this moment, fresh from his victory, idol of the army and

the most powerful man in the empire, Ricimer publicly declared Avitus unfit to rule.

He had personal reasons for reaching this decision. Although his mother was a Visigoth, he counted himself after his father a member of the Suevi, who, through the machinations of Avitus, had been brought to destruction at the hands of Theodoric. The revolt spread to Ravenna, and on 17 September the MAGISTER PEDITUM, a Visigoth Avitus had installed there named Remistus, was killed. Avitus fled from Rome towards the safety of Avernum, but was taken prisoner on 17 October at Placentia (Piacenza) by Ricimer, who now held the title of MAGISTER UTRIUSQUE MILITAE. Ricimer felt unable to execute Avitus, other than his assumption of the purple an innocent old man, but he stripped him of his insignia and consecrated him as bishop at Placentia, where he died about a year later.

MAJORIAN
Julius Valerius Maiorianus
(r. 1/4/457–2/8/461)

For the next sixteen years, Ricimer was virtually head of the Roman commonwealth – for this is the term that best describes the last years of the Western Roman empire. Born in about 405, he was an Arian Christian and the son of a prince of the Suevi and the daughter of Walia, king of the Visigoths and successor of Athaulf. His sister was married to Gundiok, king of the Burgundi. Such connections concentrated in his hands the kind of power denied to those earlier Teutonic knights who had come to the failing empire's rescue, men like Stilicho, Merobaudes, Gainas or Aëtius. Ricimer spent his youth at the court of

Majorian, the first of Ricimer's many appointees to the purple, was the first military man to head the West in 70 years. His sound military and administrative qualities worked against him, and Ricimer was soon casting about for a more amenable puppet ruler.

Valentinian III, where he won distinction fighting under Aëtius. Ricimer was more in the mould of Stilicho and Aëtius, but he had learned how fragile the position of power behind the throne could be – Honorius had conspired against Stilicho, and Valentinian against Aëtius. Weak emperors had still managed to outmanoeuvre their powerful protectors. As a German, he knew there would only be unrest if he assumed the title of Augustus, so there appeared to be two options open if he were to maintain power. He could either dissolve the Western court and govern legitimately as a DUX of the Eastern emperor, or set up his own puppet emperors and rule through them. The latter, of course, was the more attractive proposition, and he even went so far as to have his name inscribed on the coinage along with his emperors'. History deals harshly with his memory for the way in which he raised puppets one after another, and one by one broke them when he tired of their subservience or was angered by any show of independent spirit.

The first of Ricimer's shadow-Augusti, Majorian, held the post of COMES DOMESTICORUM, commander of the elite unit of the imperial guard. He was not raised to the purple immediately after the deposition of Avitus, probably to allow time for Ricimer to enter into correspondence with Constantinople. During the four-month INTERREGNUM the MAGISTER UTRIUSQUE MILITIAE held all the powers of the state, until on 28 February 457 he abandoned the office, nominated Majorian in his place, and assumed the title of Patrician. By declaring himself *the* Patrician, Ricimer was clear that from this time on, he would be the only member of the patriciate. Majorian's elevation to the purple on 1 April 457 took place at the army camp at Columellae, six miles from Ravenna. In Constantinople the new emperor Leo approved Ricimer's choice – only two months previously he had succeeded Marcian under circumstances similar to Majorian's elevation and so was hardly in any position to cavil (*see page 262*). As a result the two courts were in more harmony than had been the case for some years.

Majorian came of warrior stock. His maternal grandfather of the same name had held high military office in 379 when Theodosius the Great came to the throne. His father had been a faithful companion to Aëtius, and Majorian had distinguished himself as a general against Franks and Alamanni under Aëtius. Valentinian III had called Majorian from an early retirement to give him joint-command of the Italian army with Ricimer, in which role he was probably co-responsible for the overthrow of Avitus. For the first

time in seventy years, Rome again had a soldier-emperor at the helm – and the last had been the usurper Magnus Maximus. In short order Majorian sent troops north to eject a small Alamanni force that had broken through the Raetian Alps and himself led an army to the rescue of the Campania, whose rich soil was being ravaged by Vandals. The enemy was driven off with some loss on their side and little to the Romans. On 1 January 458 Majorian served his consulship in conjunction with his Byzantine colleague Leo, and the rest of the year and that following were spent at war with the Visigothic king, who was aroused by the deposition of 'his' emperor Avitus. The details of this war are lost, but the outcome evidently favoured Majorian, for he concluded a treaty with Theodoric II that included rights for the Romans to use Gothic bases in Hispania for a reconquest of Africa.

Majorian's judicial additions

In his administration, Majorian was able to demonstrate the flexibility of the CODEX THEODOSIANUS, to which he made a number of remarkable NOVELLAE (additions). Their nature tells a tale of Italia at the time, of a desperate misery in the main. The population was falling due to a decline in the birth rate, so Majorian forbade women to become nuns until their fortieth year, and made widows remarry a second husband five years after the death of the first – these laws despite the force of the Church against them. It had become a customary practice among impoverished families burdened with too many children to force younger sons into the clergy to keep down the cost of raising them. More often than not, this was done against the son's will. Under Majorian's NOVELLA, where this was proven, the family was forced to remit one-third of their property to the forcibly consecrated son, who was permitted to return to secular life. Any archdeacon found guilty of co-operating in the offence was fined. Majorian remitted all arrears of taxes and revived the institution of the DEFENSOR CIVITATIS that had originally come into being in the first half of the fourth century. This civil servant's duty was to protect the poor and inform the emperor of abuses committed by rapacious imperial officers in his name – a form of local ombudsman.

The wording of one NOVELLA in particular points to the destruction of Rome's greatest monuments that was already taking place at this time, the material being used for new constructions. *'We...are determined to remedy the detestable process which has long been going on, whereby the face of the venerable city is disfigured. For it is too plain that the public edifices...*

are being pulled to pieces at the suggestion of the city officials, on the pretence that the stones are wanted for public works....We therefore decree that no buildings or ancient monuments raised by our forefathers for use of beauty, shall be destroyed by any man.'

Returning to his war with the Vandals, Majorian had conceived of a strategy for the recovery of Africa: not with a frontal assault on Carthago, but by an invasion of Mauretania from Hispania. To that end – with the aid of Theodoric – a fleet of three hundred triremes was gathered in the harbour of Carthago Nova (Cartagena). However, Gaiseric got wind of the plan, and laid waste the provinces of Mauretania that Majorian intended as his beach-head. And then in May 460, by some means not recorded, the Vandal king managed to sneak into the harbour where the Roman fleet was in preparation and carry off the ships. Writing a century later, Procopius tells a delightfully silly tale of how, in order to ascertain his enemy's strength, Majorian dyed his tell-tale golden hair a bluish-black and in this disguise took himself as an ambassador to Carthago and Gaiseric's court. The Vandal king, apparently, fell into a great fear when he later discovered how he had been tricked, and prepared for war, but was saved because before the Roman fleet could sail, Majorian fell ill with dysentery and died. So, perhaps, should an Augustus who looked to be a promise of recovery have unfortunately but honestly expired, but the truth was otherwise.

No doubt Majorian's failure to retake Africa detracted from his reputation, but his real downfall came about because of the very qualities the empire so desperately needed: a zealous military nature and the hands of sound administration. These were proving far too spirited for the great Patrician, and Ricimer dethroned him on 2 August 461 and had him put to death near Dertona (Tortona).

SEVERUS III
Libius Severus (r.19/11/461–15/8/465)

To say that Libius Severus was a Lucanian from the south of Italy, that he 'lived religiously', and to give the dates of his reign is the sum of knowledge about Ricimer's second puppet. His death in Rome may have been the result of natural causes or it may have been because he drank from a cup poisoned by the Patrician's hand. The events of his four-year reign, therefore, barely concern Libius Severus, rather more those outside the sphere of his ineffective influence.

The second of Ricimer's shadow-emperors, little more than his Lucanian provenance and 'religious' character are known of Severus III.

In the East Leo refused to recognise the 'usurper' of his colleague Majorian's throne, throwing out phrases like: 'Severus, who snatched the sovereignty of the West.' To the south Gaiseric also had reason to be displeased by the turn of events, for he had nominated his own candidate. As has been related, six years earlier in 455 Gaiseric had carried off from Rome the Augusta Eudoxia and her two daughters to Carthago. According to the contemporary historian Priscus: *'Gaiseric, although many embassies had been sent to him at different times, did not dismiss the women until he had betrothed the elder daughter of Valentinian (Eudocia was her name) to his son Huneric. Then he sent back Eudoxia, the daughter of Theodosius II, with Placidia, her other daughter, whom Olybrius had married. Gaiseric did not cease from ravaging Italia and Sicilia, but pillaged them the more, desiring that, after Majorian, Olybrius would be emperor of the Romans of the West by reason of his kinship by marriage.'*

Olybrius was, of course, Huneric's brother-in-law, and by this loose connection, Gaiseric demanded his right to determine the Roman ruler. To the northwest Aëgidius, a comrade of Majorian, raised the standard of revolt in Belgica and made a dangerous alliance with Gaiseric. Aëgidius was the last MAGISTER MILITUM PER GALLIAE and he had exiled himself from Ricimer's long arm to Noviodunum (Soissons), which was in the hands of the Salian Franks. There, he had been chosen by the Franks to be their king, with the title REX ROMANORUM, and was now bent on revenging Majorian's death. He sent to Gaiseric to become his partner in a joint invasion of Italia. The plan was foiled, however, when Aëgidius was attacked by the Visigoths over a border dispute, and slain some time after the start of 464. The Visigoths annexed a large part of his territory, but, Aëgidius's son Syagrius held onto Noviodunum and adopted his father's title, thereafter enlarging his small kingdom again at the expense of the Visigoths (*see side panel on the following page*).

SYAGRIUS WAS THE LAST of the independent Roman administrators of Gallia, and from 464–86 he governed a large territory lying between the Mosa, the Scaldus and the Sequana (Meuse, Scheldt and Seine rivers). In 486 Syagrius found himself in the path of the territorial expansion of the Salian Frankish king Hlodwig or Chlodovech (Clovis) and was defeated at the battle of Soissons in the same year. Syagrius fled to seek refuge at Tolosa with Alaric II, but the Visigothic king faced his own problems with the emergent Frankish nation, and had no wish to give Clovis an excuse to make war. Instead of granting Syagrius sanctuary he imprisoned him and then extradited him to Clovis, who had him secretly executed in 487. Within a short space of time the Franks expanded to occupy all of the ancient provinces of Roman Galliae (except for Amorica), pushing the Visigoths south of the Pyrenees. For a while, only the Burgundi retained any national sovereignty, but by the sixth century, they too were absorbed, and all the Frankish subjects – Celtic Gauls, Romano-Gauls, Alani, Burgundi – became known simply as 'Franks'.

When, almost unnoticed, Libius Severus slipped away on 15 August 465, Ricimer nominated no successor, and for the next twenty months the Patrician was the sole source of government in the West. During this period, he must have pondered on whether there was any point in expending the commonwealth's dwindling income on the figure-head of an emperor when it was he that did the actual work. However, there was pressure from Leo in the East, who had his own candidate to be his imperial colleague, and a failure to respond might lead to a costly war. And that raised the consideration of whether a better benefit was to be obtained by an alliance with Constantinople or Carthago, for Gaiseric was insistently championing his candidate Olybrius. Eventually, to the Vandal's towering rage, the decision went to Constantinople, and Ricimer agreed to Leo's choice of Anthemius to be the next wearer of the Western purple.

ANTHEMIUS
Procopius Anthemius (r.12/4/467–11/7/472)

In the spring of 467 the population of Rome came out to Portus Augusti et Traiani at Ostia to greet their new emperor, colleague of Leo I in Constantinople. Accompanying Anthemius was his wife Euphemia, daughter of an emperor, his sons Marcian (*whose rebellion in 479 is discussed in chapter 15*), Romulus and Procopius, and his daughter Alypia. It should be imagined that among the throng of senators, soldiers and the mob, Ricimer was also there to welcome – and assess – this somewhat less than known quantity: spirited or subservient? At some point along the Via Ostiensis towards Rome, on 12 April, Anthemius received the imperial powers of the Western Roman empire – in reality only Italia and a precarious toehold down the Rhodanus valley and in Avernum.

Anthemius was the son-in-law of Marcian, the previous emperor of the East, and a Byzantine noble of standing. On his father's side he was descended from Procopius, the kinsman of Julian Apostate who revolted against Valens and briefly seized the throne of Constantinople. On his mother's side his grandfather Anthemius had been the PRAEFECTUS PRAETORIO and regent to Theodosius II, the real architect of the great land wall of Constantinople. He himself had risen to become COMES ILLYRIAE, MAGISTER PEDITUM and a consul. Spurned as Marcian's successor, he had served Leo loyally and won him a decisive victory over marauding Huns and Ostrogoths near Serdica (Sofia) in 455. This, then, was the man Ricimer had to judge, so it is questionable as to whether it was the Patrician cementing his hold over the emperor when he married Anthemius's daughter Alypia at the end of the same year, or vice versa. No one asked what Alypia thought.

One important part of the compact between Ricimer and Leo that had led to the elevation of Anthemius was to take war to Africa in concert and rid the world of Gaiseric and his Vandal kingdom. The description of this vast and doomed undertaking more properly belongs to the Eastern sphere, and is detailed in the following chapter. Anthemius, however, also faced a war in the West against the Visigoths and their able king, Euric (r.466–84), who had recently succeeded Theodoric II. Euric decided that the continual changes of emperor meant that Rome was so divided that he could take over all of Galliae without opposition. Anthemius called on the Armorican Bretons for help, but in 469 Euric defeated their king, Riothamus, who fled to the Burgundi – still Rome's allies – for

Anthemius (right) and his wife Euphemia, daughter of the emperor Marcian.

sanctuary. Two years later, Anthemius undertook yet another offensive against the Visigoths, but again it was a disaster, and marked the end of any Roman influence in the Gallic provinces. Now everything except Italia was lost in the West beyond small, short-lived pockets around Arelate, Massilia and in Avernum, heartland of that valorous Gallic tribe the Averni, whose most famous son Prince Vercingetorix bravely resisted Julius Caesar before the dawn of empire. Here Ecdicius, son of the late emperor Avitus, now led Roman resistance against new barbarians.

The honeymoon period – if there had ever really been one – for Anthemius and Ricimer was over. The great enterprise against Carthago that might have united Patrician and Augustus failed, and failure only emphasised that Rome and Ricimer had humbled themselves before the East to no avail. The almost complete loss of everything beyond the Alps contributed to a sense of despair, and hot-headed Anthemius was increasingly fretting at his puppet status. When his health began to fail, Anthemius accused various persons of working magic on him, and several were put to death, including the MAGISTER MILITUM Romanus, an adherent of Ricimer. The Patrician left Rome in anger and took himself to Mediolanum, where he called to his standard the troops who had served under him in the Vandal war. He also enjoyed the support of his brother-in-law, the king of the Burgundi. However, Ricimer was persuaded by the Ligurian nobles to attempt reconciliation, and the task fell to Epiphanius, bishop of Mediolanum. Anthemius was not easy to please, he is said to have retorted: '*I have not even spared my own flesh and blood [to please him], but have given my daughter to this skin-clothed Goth [sic], an alliance I cannot think on without shame for myself....*' But the words of Epiphanius swayed him, and a truce was effected.

The peace was of short duration. In a little over a year hostilities broke out in early 472. Having learned what was happening, the Eastern emperor Leo dispatched the senator Olybrius to Mediolanum to arbitrate between Ricimer and Anthemius, or perhaps (as some accounts claim) to wrest the crown from Anthemius. In any event, at this point – about April – Ricimer proclaimed Olybrius emperor, thereby conciliating Gaiseric and possibly neutralising the opposition of friends of Anthemius at the Byzantine court, since Olybrius was also a Byzantine. Ricimer then marched on Rome, besieged the city for five months, and reduced its inhabitants to a piteous state of starvation. At the end of this period, there was a last

desperate battle 'near the bridge of Hadrian', and Ricimer entered Rome, found the emperor and slew him. One source (Joannes Antiochenus) claims that Anthemius himself threw open the gates and was slain by Ricimer's young nephew Gundobad. Anthemius perished on 11 July 472, leaving Olybrius, Gaiseric's unexpected prize candidate, on the throne. He might have worried that his fate would be similar to his immediate predecessor's, another puppet in Ricimer's stable of shadow emperors, but the great Patrician suffered a haemorrhage a few days later and died on 18 August.

One footnote to this final battle is of interest. Among the combatants was a certain barbarian called Odoacer, who would soon make himself Rome's first king in almost a thousand years.

OLYBRIUS
Ancius Olybrius (r.April 472–23/10/472)

Such was the state of the time that history can supply some detail about Olybrius the PRIVATUS, but little or nothing of Olybrius Augustus. He was a scion of the powerful Anician family of Italia. In about 454 he had married Galla Placidia the Younger, daughter of Valentinian III and Licinia Eudoxia, and the sister of Eudocia who was married to Gaiseric's son Huneric. When Gaiseric captured Rome the Vandals took Eudoxia and her two daughters with them, it is presumed that Olybrius was in Constantinople and so avoided the sack but suffered the distress of knowing that his wife was held at Carthago. By virtue of his sister-in-law's marriage to Huneric, he became a vassal kinsman to the Vandal king.

In duration his reign lasted for barely eight months, and of the first five nothing is known except for his coinage struck in Mediolanum. It was a time of upheaval, and it is reasonable to imagine that he accompanied Ricimer's attack on Anthemius and took part in the siege. As to his fitness to rule, abilities in legislation, or fiscal policies, Olybrius's own death of

Brother-in-law to the Vandal king's son Huneric, Olybrius had always been Gaiseric's choice for the Western throne, but the long wait to get him there was wasted when the emperor died of illness after only six months.

'dropsy' little more than three months after his predecessor's precludes any conjecture. From a political perspective, Ricimer's choice had been wise. Not only would Olybrius's Italian aristocratic heritage have recommended him to the senate, but he would have been a more palatable candidate than the Greek Anthemius.

Only one item of his administration is clear: after Ricimer's death he conferred the title of Patrician on the young Burgundian prince Gundobad, whose mother was sister to Ricimer. Gundobad had come to Italia to seek his fortune with his powerful uncle and found his desires fulfilled somewhat sooner than he could have hoped for. With the title came the loyalty of the majority barbarian element of the Roman army and so, when Olybrius dropped dead on 23 October 472, into young Gundobad's hands fell the remnants of the Western Roman empire.

GLYCERIUS
(5/3/473–24/6/474)

There was another INTERREGNUM, this time of five months, doubtless a necessary pause while Gundobad consolidated his power and learned a little more about what was what and who was who. Then, on 5 March 473, he raised the COMES DOMESTICORUM Glycerius to the throne at Ravenna, and it seems as though the new emperor reigned only in the north because none of his coinage was struck in Rome, only in Mediolanum and Ravenna. Not surprisingly, the Byzantine court of ageing Leo refused to accept Gundobad's puppet, viewing Glycerius as an Augustus made 'more by presumption than by constitutional selection'. Leo appointed Julius Nepos, MAGISTER PEDITUM of Dalmatia, to command an army and go to Italia to reclaim it from the usurper. But Leo died in January of 474 to be succeeded by his grandson, the infant Leo II, with his father Zeno as regent and co-Augustus. Incongruously, these events meant that Glycerius was the most senior of the three reigning emperors.

Immediately, Glycerius was faced with a new barbarian threat. Theudemir and Widemir were the brother-kings of the Ostrogoths who had settled in Pannoniae. For twenty years they had engaged in warfare with their barbarian neighbours, Suevi, Huns and Sarmatae, and their settlements had become impoverished. Eventually they heeded the cries of their people for the conquest of richer lands and split the tasks between them. With his more powerful force Theudemir intended to attack the stronger Eastern Roman empire, while Widemir took his weaker force into Italia. It seems, however, that he died in this enterprise, and it was his son, also Widemir, who was the recipient of an embassy from Glycerius. With blandishments and flattery, the emperor shamelessly suggested the Ostrogoths bypass Italia and go to raid in Galliae, theoretically still a part of the empire and only in a tiny part actually so. The smooth-talking worked, and Widemir led his Ostrogoths across the Alps and down into the valleys of the Rhodanus and Liger (Loire), where they soon made cause with their kinsmen the Visigoths, and removed from Rome those few remaining outposts of imperial resistance in the south: Arelate and Massilia; Avernum and a tiny enclave north of Remi alone held out.

The ignominy of Glycerius's foreign policy did nothing to endear him to his subjects, and he seems to have spent much of his time in northwestern Italia, hovering close by his patron's Burgundian territory. One instance underlines his unpopularity. Unable to excoriate the emperor in person, the populace of Ticinum (Pavia) treated his mother, who dwelt there, so insultingly that he threatened severe reprisals for their behaviour and was only dissuaded from carrying out his threat by Epiphanius, the city's saintly bishop. No one, therefore, was greatly perturbed to hear that Julius Nepos was coming to the rescue, and Glycerius was on his own. Even the puppet-master Gundobad deserted in the hour of his emperor's need, for his father Gundiok had died shortly after Ricimer, and the Patrician decided that his future was better served by taking up the Burgundian mantle there rather than face hostilities with a powerful Byzantine army.

Glycerius must have perceived the outcome. Without the support of senate, people or army, his cause was lost, and he made his way to Rome to throw himself on the mercy of the Eastern invader. So it was that on 24 June 474, Julius Nepos was raised to the purple where he had landed, at the Portus Augusti et Traiani opposite old Ostia, and granted the deposed Glycerius his life and retirement to obscurity as a consecrated bishop in Dalmatia. His kindly fate recalls that of Avitus, but unlike the former bishop of Placentia, Glycerius survived for a considerable time. And, in the following year, he enjoyed sweet revenge of a kind, when Nepos was forced out of Italia and returned to Dalmatia whence he had come, to discover that Glycerius was to be his personal bishop.

JULIUS NEPOS
(24/6/474–28/8/475 abdicated)

Julius Nepos, son of Nepotianus, MAGISTER PEDITUM in Thracia between 458–61, and nephew of the Patrician Marcellinus, MAGISTER PEDITUM in Dalmatia between 461–68, was married to a niece of the emperor Leo. The major events of his fourteen-month reign took place in what was left of the Gallic provinces, as the Visigoths attempted to wrest Avernum from imperial control. Unlike that friend of Rome, Theodoric II, his brother King Euric was a bitter Arian and strongly anti-Roman. Sidonius, who had been elected bishop of Augustonemetum in 472 described Euric's sentiments. 'I fear that this Gothic king is plotting not so much against the walls of Roman cities as against the laws of Christian churches.' But it was against the walls of Augustonemetum that Euric's fury fell in 474, stoutly defended by Ecdicius, son of the emperor Avitus. Nepos bestowed on Ecdicius the title of Patrician and made him MAGISTER MILITUM of the Roman army, although this was an empty position because the emperor had no resources to send him. At the end of the campaigning season, Euric withdrew, leaving the city untaken but with half its walls in lying in ruins; a return of the Goths next season would write its end.

However, in the following year Euric changed his strategy and threatened an invasion of Italia by way of the Alpes Maritimae, along the coastal route once made fit for troop movements by Marius in the days of the late Republic, and regularly used by Julius Caesar in his conquest of Gallia. To counter this alarming

development, a council of Ligurian bishops turned to Epiphanius, the peacemaker of his age. The bishop set out across the Alps to seek an embassy with Euric and persuade him to desist from his planned invasion. In this mission Epiphanius was successful, but at the cost of Nepos having to agree to abandon Avernum to the Visigoths. The fate of brave Ecdicius is unclear, and conflicting sources of the time do little to throw any light on the matter, but in effect he disappears from the story with the fall of Avernum to the Visigoths through treacherous Roman diplomacy.

Nepos now needed a replacement for the offices of Patrician and MAGISTER MILITUM and appointed a certain Orestes, who promptly took his army from Rome to Ravenna, and there proclaimed his son Romulus emperor. Like his predecessor, Nepos had little alternative but flight, and left Italia for Salonae in Dalmatia on 28 August 475. Romulus came to the throne on 31 October. Nepos outlived the Western empire by four years, dying on 15 May 480 at the hands of assassins, the COMES Ovida and Viator, whose motives for his murder are unknown.

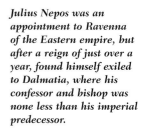

Julius Nepos was an appointment to Ravenna of the Eastern empire, but after a reign of just over a year, found himself exiled to Dalmatia, where his confessor and bishop was none less than his imperial predecessor.

ROMULUS AUGUSTULUS
(31/10/475–4/9/476, abdicated)

Orestes had had a curious career. An Illyrian provincial born in Pannonia, he had made his way to the court of Attila as a young man, where he had been employed by the king of the Huns as his personal NOTARIUS. After Attila's death he had entered imperial service, and commanded the household troops under the short-lived emperor Anthemius. At the time of his revolt against Nepos, his son Romulus was aged about fourteen, so it remains a mystery as to why Orestes did not seize the purple himself. For he was as full-blooded a Roman as Trajan or Diocletian, and therefore did not suffer the drawback of barbarian prospects like

Bearing the name of Rome's founder and that of its first princeps, Romulus Augustulus was a child when he came to the throne, and still one when he left it less than a year later. His only claim on history lies in being the last Augustus of the Western Roman empire.

Arbogast, Stilicho or Ricimer. Perhaps it is an indication of how low the prestige of the title Augustus had fallen in mens' minds that real power should be more identified with the title Patrician.

Nevertheless, it was his young son he placed on Ravenna's throne, and at his accession the boy became Romulus Augustus, but everyone knew him as Augustulus, the 'little emperor'. The short reign of this, the last Roman emperor in the West, so poignantly bearing the name of the nation's founder and wearing the title bestowed on its first great princeps, was marked only by one significant event, a peace treaty with Gaiseric. Orestes concluded this, probably in return for Rome confirming the Vandals' toehold on Sicilia at Lilybaeum. However, it was not the barbarians abroad that would bring down the Western Roman empire, but those within Italia.

By this time the Roman army contained no man of genuine Roman extraction, let alone even any Italians or at the very least Gallic troops. It was composed of the many Teutonic tribesmen that had taken service with the eagles of the ancient legions more and more over the past hundred years. These troops now asked Orestes for what Rome had granted the Visigoths, a land of their own. However, unlike the settlement given to Walia, the barbarian legionaries wanted one-third of Italia for themselves, and this was an outrageous demand a Roman like Orestes could never accede to. He probably believed that it would be open to negotiation, but he misjudged the temper of his own soldiers. Under the leadership of Orestes' own standard-bearer – the Herulian Goth Odoacer, who was first heard of outside the walls of Rome at the deposition of Anthemius – the soldiers mutinied.

Orestes retreated with his loyal retainers and Romulus to the dubious sanctuary of Ticinum, pursued by the mutineers, hoping that their discipline would dissolve without his leadership and their resolve fail. But Odoacer proved a resilient general, and the town was surrounded and quickly taken. For two terrible days Ticinum was sacked, as the enraged plunderers tried to find Orestes and the boy-emperor. Peace only settled when it was revealed that their quarry had fled again, this time to Placentia (Piacenza). And it was there, only five days after the elevation of Odoacer, that Orestes was taken and at once beheaded.

Young Romulus did not share his father's end because he had continued his flight to Ravenna in the company of his uncle Paulus, who was probably hoping to take ship to Constantinople. Sadly, Odoacer's men found him, and Paulus was slain. However, when

Romulus was dragged before the victorious Odoacer at Ravenna, the Goth was moved to mercy by the boy's innocent beauty and his pitiful state. Instead of having him executed, Odoacer granted the little Augustus a palace and a generous pension for life. And so on 4 September 476 Romulus Augustulus retired to the splendid villa near Neapolis that had originally been built by Lucius Lucullus, the great Republican general who had defeated Mithridates. Not even a fragment of history exists to tell us anything more of the fate of the last Roman emperor of the West.

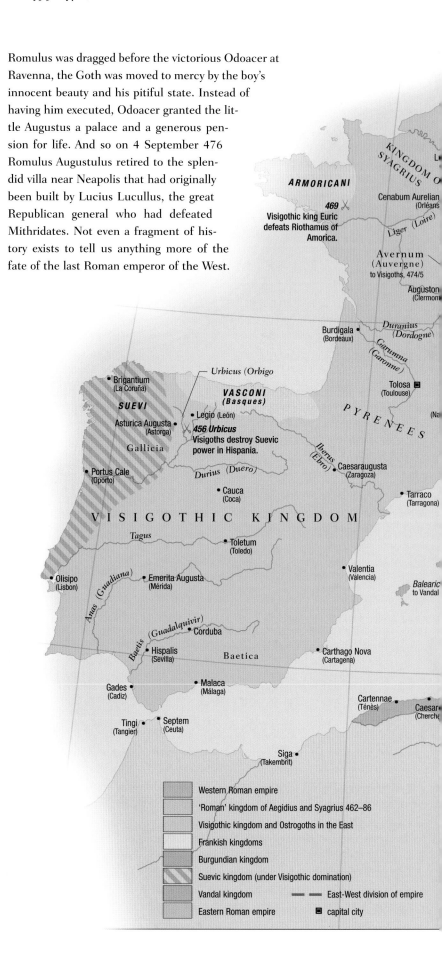

The Western Roman empire at the accession of Romulus Augustulus, 475

Colonia
(Köln, Cologne)

Moguntiacum
(Mainz)

☐ Treveri
(Trier)

num (Soissons)

RIPURARIAN
FRANKS

ni (Reims)

Durocatalauni
(Châlons-sur-Marne)

Argentorate
(Strabourg)

Danuvius

THURINGII

LANGOBARDI
(Lombards)

ALAMANNI

Vindobona
(Vienna)

Brigetio
(Szöny)

ALAMANNI

Only nominal
Roman control

OSTROGOTHIC
KINGDOM

GEPIDAE

OSTROGOTHS

BURGUNDIAN
KINGDOM

(Saône)

Aventicum
(Avenches)

Raetia

Virinum
(Maria Saal)

Poetovio
(Ptuj)

Dravus

Virinum

Rhodanus

Histria

P a n n o n i a

Singidunum
(Beograd,
Belgrade)

Danuvius

☐ Lugdunum

Vienna
(Vienne)

Venetia

Aquileia

Siscia
(Sisak)

OSTROGOTHS

Moesia II

Augusta
Taurinorum
(Turin)

Valentia
(Valence)

Liguria

Mediolanum
(Milan)

Ticinum
(Pavia)

Verona

Padus (Po)

Placentia
(Piacenza)

D a l m a t i a

Savus

GEPIDAE

Naissus
(Nis)

Only nominal
Roman control

Alpes
Cottiae

Aemilia

☐ Ravenna

effective control to
Eastern empire

Praevalitana

Dacia

Thracia

Avennio (Avignon)

Nicaea
(Nice)

*Sinus
Ligusticus*
(Ligurian Sea)

Flaminia

Tuscia et
Umbria

Picenum

Tiberis

MARE ADRIATICUM
(ADRIATIC SEA)

Salonae
(Solin)

Rhodope

Arelate
(Arles)

Massilia
(Marseilles)

Corsica
to Vandal
kingdom

Aleria (Aléria)

Samnium

Roma

✕ 456
Ricimer's fleet destroys
the Vandal navy.

Campania

Apulia et
Calabria

Brundisium
(Brindisi)

Dyrrachium
(Durrës, Durazzo)

Macedonia

Thessalonica

Neapolis
(Napoli, Naples)

Apollonia
(Pojan)

Epirus

Sardinia
to Vandal
kingdom

MARE TYRRHENUM
(TYRRHENIAN SEA)

Tarentum
(Taranto)

Lucania et
Brutti

MARE
AEGEUM
(AEGEAN SEA)

Caralis
(Cagliari)

Nicopolis

Thessalia

to Vandal
kingdom

Messana
(Massina)

Rhegium
(Reggio)

Athenae
(Athens)

Panormus
(Palermo)

MARE
IONIUM
(IONIAN SEA)

Achaea

Lilybaeum
(Marsala)

Sicilia

Agrigentum
(Agrigento)

✕

Syracusae
(Siracusa)

Creta

☐ Carthago

456
Ricimer regains most of Sicilia after
defeating the occupying Vandal army.

Hippo Regius
(Annaba)

Melita
(Malta)

V A N D A L   K I N G D O M

Hadrumetum
(Sousse)

M A R E   I N T E R N U M
(M E D I T E R R A N E A N   S E A)

Cyrene
(Shahhat)

Oea
(Tripoli)

Leptis Magna

Berenice
(Banghazi)

Libya
Superior

Libya
Inferior

| 0 | 100 | 200 | 300 miles |
| 0 | 100 | 200 | 300 | 400 kilometres |

CHAPTER FIFTEEN   AD 450–518
POWER IN THE EAST

MARCIAN
Flavius Valerius Marcianus
(r.[East] 25/8/450–January 457)

Marcian's bold policy of denying Attila paid off, and the Huns left Constantinople alone as they went to ravage the Western empire. But his freedom was largely illusory, since he was as much the creature of his Teutonic patrician Aspar as was Majorian of Ricimer in Ravenna.

The death of Theodosius II left the question of the succession open for the first time in over sixty years, since his only surviving child, Licinia Eudoxia, had married Valentinian III. As the Augusta, Theodosius's sister Pulcheria was the logical choice for the throne, although not the normal one – no woman before her had succeeded to the Roman empire. However, it was where Pulcheria desired to be and she was aided in this by Flavius Aspar, the son of Ardaburius and hero of Ravenna in 425 in the battle that deposed the usurper Joannes and placed young Valentinian III on the Western throne. He selected an officer on his staff named Marcian and engineered his candidacy as her husband. Pulcheria pragmatically consented in return for a pledge that her new husband would honour her vow of virginity. With the support of Aspar and the last representative of the Theodosian house in the East, Marcian received the acclamation of the senate and the army. On 25 August 450, Pulcheria sat beside her husband while the bishop of Constantinople placed the imperial diadem on his head. It symbolised that Marcian shared in the imperial powers and it was also the first instance of a religious coronation, soon to be much imitated in the West. Supporting Marcian's claim, Pulcheria gave out (truthfully or not) that Theodosius on his deathbed had nominated him as her groom. That this was a political union is

underlined by the fact that Marcian kept his promise and respected his wife's virginity and swore to be a staunch champion of religious orthodoxy. Soon after, he had his only daughter, Aelia Marcia Euphemia, marry the future Western emperor, Anthemius.

Later Byzantine writers looked back at Marcian's seven-year reign as something of a golden age. He secured the political and financial security of the East, established the orthodox line to which with few exceptions future Byzantine emperors would adhere and achieved a remarkable degree of political stability. Nevertheless, despite his undoubted abilities, much of his success must also be accorded to luck.

Relatively little is known about Marcian before his accession to the throne. The chronicles variously ascribe his birthplace as being Illyricum and Thracia, but generally consent to 392 as his natal year. Like many other public men from that region, he made his career in the military. His father had been a soldier and Marcian served under Ardaburius and Aspar, first at Philippopolis in Thracia. In 421–22 he went as a TRIBUNUS with his unit to fight the Persians, but apparently fell ill in Lycia and never saw action in the campaign. From this relatively inauspicious beginning, he served as DOMESTICUS to Aspar, by then the MAGISTER UTRIUSQUE MILITIAE. While this placed Marcian in the military elite, it did not provide him with any singular distinction. In 432, he served with Aspar in the failed North African campaign, where he was captured by the Vandals. Later fanciful stories claim that Marcian met Gaiseric, who predicted he would one day become emperor (*see the following section*). From this point to his accession in 450, nothing is known other than his eventual return at some point to Constantinople with borrowed funds and his elevation to the senatorial rank, most certainly thanks to Aspar.

As was related at the end of chapter 13, Marcian's reign began with an immediate change in policy towards the Huns. In Theodosius's last years the eunuch chamberlain Chrysaphius had been the architect of a futile plot to assassinate Attila in an attempt to staunch the flow of tribute payments. In 448 Chrysaphius had managed to suborn one of Attila's envoys by the name of Edecon and involve him in the murder plot. Perhaps Edecon was an *agent provocateur* on a mission to uncover the eunuch's duplicity, because when the Byzantine mission arrived at Attila's camp, he confessed the whole plot. Attila demanded that Theodosius deliver up his chamberlain for execution, but when those courtiers who supported Pulcheria – a natural enemy of anyone with her brother's ear – clamoured for Chrysaphius's death, Theodosius showed some backbone, and refused. Spirit went only so far, however. The embarrassed emperor agreed to pay Attila his blood money but ensured that Chrysaphius contributed generously. As a result, Attila dropped his demands for the eunuch's killing. It benefited him little in the long run. With Pulcheria back in power Chrysaphius's days could be counted on the fingers of one hand. Marcian had him executed and then refused to pay any further tribute to Attila.

Marcian's obduracy may have been ill-founded, but as it turned out, he was enormously successful. As we have seen, Attila had already become too absorbed in Western imperial politics to deal with the recalcitrant Marcian, and before he could refocus his attention on

the East the Hun died in 453 and his empire disintegrated. Marcian quickly formed alliances with those peoples previously under Hunnish domination, especially the Ostrogoths, to thwart their re-emergence. Indeed, he even granted them FOEDERATI status and permitted their settlement in Pannoniae. At one stroke, the new emperor had established peace in his European dominions, and consequently benefited from his gamble. The senatorial aristocracy, which had been strongly opposed to Theodosius treating with barbarians, heartily supported Marcian's decision to refuse Attila, and the policy also resulted in saving the FISCUS enormous sums. By the end of his reign, Marcian was able to leave his successor one hundred thousand pounds of gold.

Marcian's financial policies were designed to further his standing with the aristocracy, already predisposed toward him. The COLLATIO GLEBALIS, the property tax so obnoxious to the senatorial class, was easily repealed, since the emperor no longer had to

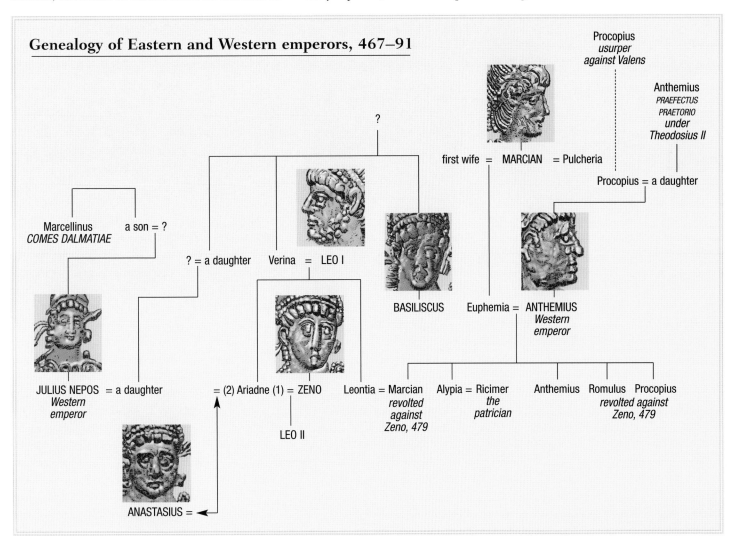

Genealogy of Eastern and Western emperors, 467–91

subsidise the Huns. Marcian also ended many of the financial obligations owed by praetors, who were expected to put on lavish public games and distribute a CONGIARIUM to the populace of Constantinople. This was particularly hard on provincial senators, who had to move to ruinously expensive Constantinople for the months of their office. Now only the highest-ranking senators, the ILLUSTRES, were eligible to serve and even they were relieved of spending the huge sums that had been traditionally associated with holding the office. Marcian attempted to address other financial issues. On his accession he proclaimed a remission of all aged debts owed to the state. While this most benefited the wealthier classes, it did to some extent improve life for a broader spectrum of society. He also campaigned against the sale of government offices, a corrupt practice whose endemic nature continually led to bureaucratic instability.

A few of Marcian's legal enactments survive. In the second NOVELLA of his legal code he defined the business of an emperor as being 'to provide for the care of the human race'. The first NOVELLA deals with complaints about the government from 'endless crowds of petitioners...because of the want of integrity and severity' in the judges. Perhaps his most significant NOVELLA rescinded a law of Constantine, which had in turn been an extension of an Augustan law, which made it unlawful for a member of the senatorial class to marry a HUMILIS (freeborn poor woman), Marcian's

edict allowed such a match on the presumption that the lady in question was of good moral character. The change in the law later benefited the emperor Justin in the 520s, when, with a little further modification, he was able to permit his son Justinian to marry Theodora.

Little military action happened during Marcian's tenure apart from some minor campaigns against Saracens in Syria and the Blemmyes in Aegyptus. In these two provinces there was also domestic revolt as a result of the Council of Chalcedon (*see below*). The absence of large-scale conflict also meant that the emperor was able to amass more funds than might otherwise have been the case. But it seems, too, that Marcian actively avoided confrontation: the assassination of Valentinian III and the subsequent Vandal sack of Rome in 455 were met with silence from the East. The emperor contented himself with sending embassies to Gaiseric requesting the surrender of the empress Eudoxia, and her daughters, Placidia and Eudocia. These were unsuccessful and so, according to Priscus, in about 456 Marcian resorted to sending a bishop 'of Gaiseric's own [Arian] sect' named Bledas. But again the embassy was met with refusal, and it was to be Marcian's successor Leo who secured the women's release.

The decline of papal influence

The chief event of Marcian's reign was the beginning of the great monophysite quarrel (*see side panel*) and the Council of Chalcedon. Shortly after his accession the conspicuously pious and orthodox emperor had written in friendly and respectful tones to Pope Leo the Great. He called him the 'guardian of the Faith' and asked for his prayers, declaring himself anxious to support the council the pope had proposed in order to settle the question raised by the monophysites Eutyches and Dioscurus. Leo had already asked Theodosius II to summon a council, and Marcian clearly only meant to carry out this commission as Theodosius's successor; however, his involvement was to have lasting repercussions. Marcian was no friend to Dioscurus, the archbishop of Alexandria, since he had tried and failed to prevent the emperor's recognition in Aegyptus. The aged Eutyches had been for thirty years archimandrite of a monastery outside the walls of Constantinople, and although not a learned man, carried the banner of the Monophysite cause. His teaching had disturbed the Eastern Church since immediately after the Council of Ephesus in 431, and he had been accused of heresy in 448 and dismissed.

The Council of Chalcedon

The monophysite controversy that was the main issue at the Council of Chalcedon concerned the political and religious tensions between the Christians at Alexandria and those at Antiochia. The argument revolved around Christ's nature(s). Antiochene theologians stressed Christ's human nature because he needed to be truly human if he were to be considered the saviour of man, while the monophysite Alexandrians stressed Christ's divinity and his role as teacher of divine truth. These differences were intensified by the rivalry between the two ancient sees – the Antiochenes had been better at getting their candidates appointed at Constantinople, by this time the most powerful bishopric in the East.

In essence, the outcome of the council was to define Christ's nature as combining both the Antiochene and Alexandrian concepts, but in so doing it refuted the Alexandrian monophysite definition and declared it a heresy. The same fate befell Antiochene Nestorians, adherents of the teachings of Nestorius, who had become bishop of Constantinople in 428. He argued that Mary should be called the 'bearer of Christ', not the 'bearer of God', thus stressing that Mary was the mother of his human nature, that Christ's divine nature was separate and eternal and did not come through his human mother.

Pope Leo hoped for a time to restore peace without another general council, and wrote to Marcian saying so. However, it is clear that in summoning a council on 17 May 451 Marcian was acting on a misunderstanding and that he had not yet received the pope's letter. Leo accepted the *fait accompli* and appointed the bishop of Lilybaeum, Paschasius, and a priest named Bonifacius as his LEGATI. The council, which was to have met at Nicaea, where many bishops had already gathered, was delayed because Marcian was too involved in the business of government to leave the capital. Instead he ordered the bishops to Chalcedon, on the other side of the Bosphorus from Constantinople, so that he could attend without leaving the capital. Eventually, the council opened in the church of St. Euphemia on 8 October and lasted until 1 November. Given that between five and six hundred clerics attended, and the council's remarkably brief duration, it is nothing short of astonishing that any decisions should have been reached at all. And yet the council achieved everything it set out to do. Eutyches, who had been reinstated in 449, was again condemned; and a new statement of faith was drawn up, known as the Chalcedonian Definition, according to which Christ was established as the possessor of one person with two natures – human and divine.

An interesting aside to the events of the council is that when he attended the sixth session on 25 October the emperor opened proceedings with a speech in Latin, emphasising that it was still the Eastern empire's official language on solemn occasions.

On 27 February 452, Marcian in conjunction with Valentinian III proclaimed that the decrees of the council were the law of the empire. But there was another, less satisfactory outcome for the Western Church. When the main business of the council was completed, the delegates decreed that the see of Constantinople should rank second only to that of Rome, that its bishop be given the title 'patriarch', and its control be extended to cover the whole Eastern empire. While the papal LEGATI were obliged to accept this ruling, they were unable to swallow its clear implication: from that point on the pope's supremacy would be only titular, and that the two sees would in reality be equal. From this famous decree, known as Canon Twenty-Eight, derived the ecclesiastical rivalry between the Latin and Orthodox Churches that would grow increasingly bitter over the centuries.

Marcian's proclamation of the Chalcedonian Definition produced uniformity at Constantinople and in the European provinces, but he was unable to enforce them so successfully in Syria and Aegyptus. The rest of his reign was troubled by revolution in these provinces, unrest only quelled after his death when the party of Aspar began to compromise with the heretics. Marcian remained largely beholden to his former patron, and his trust was repaid. Aspar was appointed MAGISTER MILITUM PER ORIENTEM and given the title first patrician, while his eldest son Ardabur (named for his grandfather) was made MAGISTER UTRIUSQUE MILITIAE. This preference of the Teutonic element of the court was unpopular and, despite the Aspar's power, a strong anti-Germanic sentiment sprang up among the aristocracy. Nonetheless, when Marcian died aged 65 in January 457 – reportedly of gangrene in his feet caused by too much pious penitence – it was to Aspar that everyone turned. Marcian, without a son as a consequence of respecting the wishes of his imperial wife (and having none illegitimate), had nominated no one as his successor; and Pulcheria had preceded him to the grave in 453. Thus the throne of Rome looked emptier than it had done since the death of Julian.

It was expected that Aspar would adorn himself with the purple. He had earned great recognition as long ago as 424 at Ravenna. In 432 he commanded the army Theodosius II sent to North Africa against Gaiseric, and although this failed in its objective Aspar's reputation had remained undiminished. In fact there had been no reason why Aspar should not have succeeded Theodosius, rather than place his domestic Marcian on the throne; but for two things. He was an Alan and, like nearly all Christian barbarians, an Arian. There could be no question, therefore, of Aspar's own elevation to the purple. However, like Arbogast sixty-four years before, and like his colleague in the West, Ricimer, he was content to be a king-maker. The First Patrician's choice fell on another of his staff, an orthodox Christian named Leo.

This ivory disk celebrates the patrician Flavius Aspar's pre-eminent position in the Byzantine government with the inscription:
FL ARDABUR ASPAR VIRINIUSTRIS COM.ET.MAG.MILITUM ET CONSUL ORDINARIUS.

LEO I

Flavius Valerius Leo (r.[East] 7/2/457−3/2/474)

When it came to managing his choice of emperor, Aspar was to have less success than Ricimer, his colleague in the West. In part, this was due to the character of the man he chose, but the process of coronation also had an effect. However the elevation of the emperor, whether through inheritance or − like Marcian and Leo − by the means of domestic service, once he was hailed Augustus, the elaborate Byzantine court ceremonial wrapped him in divinity in the eyes of the adoring crowd. Only the most ascetic of men could avoid being enveloped in the trappings of power this gave. In being made Augustus, Leo became the part and took on the dignity of his purple mantle. He still enjoyed the traditional honour of being raised on the soldiers' shields, but then, as Marcian had done, he attended a mass in the Church of Holy Wisdom to be formally crowned by Patriarch Anatolius. The significant difference between this and Marcian's coronation is that Leo received the imperial diadem from a prelate who, after the Council of Chalcedon, was the recognised head of the Church in the East. In this there is a clear indication of the increased importance of the patriarchate's recognition of the Augustus, and a clear reflection of how the order of accession was changing − away from the traditional soldier-proclaimed emperor to a new, religious, more mystical concept of kingship, in which the Church's tacit approval was at least as important, if not more so, than that of the soldiers.

Bust and coin of Leo I, another man raised to supreme power by Aspar, but one who proved to be no puppet in the patrician's hands.

Leo hailed from Dacia, and was born there in about 401. His upbringing was probably little different to that of Marcian, and his eventual position on Aspar's staff hints at a respectable early military career. Before his elevation to the purple he had married Aelia Verina, and they had three children: Ariadne was born before his accession, a second daughter Leontia was born in 457, and an unnamed son died aged five months in 463. (The timing of the

two daughters' births in relation to Leo's accession was to have a bearing on the events of a rebellion against Leo's successor, Zeno, in 479.) Of Verina's origins, little is known, but the name Aelia was probably assumed when she became empress, since it had been commonly retained as an Augusta's name from the time of Theodosius I's first wife, Aelia Flacilla. She had a brother named Basiliscus, who also benefited from this sudden proximity to the throne.

Within two months of his accession Leo made moves to improve relations with the Western empire, by recognising Ricimer's choice of Majorian as emperor, and agreeing to serve with his imperial colleague in the consulship in 458. This accord with Ricimer was ultimately to lead to the ill-fated joint-expedition against Gaiseric, but more importantly it increased Leo's influence in the West (although the two fell out for four years over Ricimer's replacement for Majorian, Libius Severus, in 461). These actions point up an important aspect of Leo's character. He had little formal education, but he was possessed of sound common sense and − as it turned out − an independent mind. The servility of the Byzantine court was useful to the new emperor. He learned rapidly how to play the various factions off against each other, and from his success in this drew the confidence to resist the too imperious edicts of his erstwhile patron Aspar. If Leo was supposed to be a puppet in the mould of Ricimer's, Aspar soon found himself mistaken. Within weeks of his accession, a furious row broke out between them when Aspar asked Leo to appoint one of his fellow Arians to the post of PRAEFECTUS URBI. According to the contemporary historian Candidus, this was a certain Vivianus. Due to his long history of deference Leo gave in at first, but immediately regretted his cravenness. That night he called for the orthodox senator Tatian and secretly installed him. Candidus tells us that in the morning when he discovered what had taken place, Aspar was so angry that he marched into Leo's apartments and grasped the emperor by his robes and told him it was not fit for their wearer to tell lies. Leo is alleged to have responded: 'It is not fitting that an emperor should be bound to do the bidding of any of his subjects, especially when by his compliance he injures the state.'

This last comment undoubtedly referred to the concerns of many courtiers at the dominance of the German faction, of which Aspar was the most distinguished figure. Leo, determined to curb this dangerous Teutonic element in the court, resolved on a policy of purging the army of Germans and reconstructing it around a core of Isaurians. These were the hardy mountain people who lived in the wild region of the Taurus, south of Iconium in Anatolia. Although because of where they lived they were Roman citizens, the Isaurians were generally regarded as half-savage, more barbarian even than the Germans, and their antecedents had often formed the core of pirates who plagued the eastern Mare Internum at the time of Pompeius Magnus in the first century BC. Leo also organised a new elite corps of three hundred romanised Thracians for his imperial guard. These he called the EXCUBITORII (sentinels), and they were additional to the SCHOLAE, who had by this time become a largely decorative guard.

Aspar fought to preserve the *status quo* and inevitably attitudes between the two factions hardened. Yet despite this thirteen-year-long breach between the emperor and his first patrician, Aspar remained a great power. To the hopes of his supporters and the fear of his enemies, it seemed likely that sonless Leo's successor would be found among Aspar's sons: Ardabur, Patricius or Hermenric. On the emperor's side the leading influence was that of an Isaurian chieftain, whose barbarous name was Tarasicodissa Rusumbladeotus, but which became conveniently changed to Zeno when he married Leo's daughter Ariadne. This honour indicated that Zeno was the head of the anti-Aspar party and that – after Ariadne gave birth to the younger Leo – he would secure the succession either for himself or his son.

A bungled invasion of Africa

Aspar also had powerful adherents, chief among them was Basiliscus, the brother of the emperor's wife Verina. Some orthodox sources claim he was of barbarous birth, but contemporary – and orthodox – Priscus is surely a better observer in describing Basiliscus as a hellenised, well-educated Roman. The contrast between Aspar and Basiliscus was extreme: one the greatest general of his time, an ill-educated barbarian who enjoyed the company of 'actors and jugglers', a convinced Arian; the other a fanatical monophysite and a man unfitted for leadership of any kind. But these two religiously opposed men found common cause against the Isaurians, and it was evident that in their desperate battle to have the edicts of the Council of Chalcedon overturned, the monophysite faction in Constantinople was even prepared to recruit Arians to their cause. However, even his friends laughed behind Basiliscus's back at his passionate and ill-concealed craving to wear his brother-in-law's imperial diadem. So when these points are considered, it seems astonishing that Leo –

that man of common sense – should allow himself to be persuaded by his wife to put Basiliscus in command of the long-overdue war against Gaiseric and the Vandal kingdom; but that is precisely what he did.

Thirteen years had passed since Gaiseric's sack of Rome, during which time – apart from Majorian's ill-starred invasion attempt in 461 – the empire had not raised a hand against him. The West, almost on the point of collapse, was in no position to accomplish anything, but the East's tardiness seems harder to defend. Apologists of Marcian, among them the historian Procopius in his *De Bello Vandalico*, excused his inertia by claiming he had made a pact with the Vandal king after the Roman defeat under Aspar in the campaign of 432. Gathered in a courtyard awaiting news of their fate, the captured soldiers sat down in the blistering noonday sun. *"But one among them, who was named Marcian, carelessly composed himself to sleep; and while he lay there an eagle, with outspread wings, hovered over him, now rising, now falling, but always contriving to shelter him, and him only, from the sun by the shadow of her wings."*

Gaiseric observed this omen from the window of an upper room and interpreted it as meaning that Marcian would one day become emperor. Summoning the young man into his presence, he offered to release him in return for a pledge never to take up arms against the Vandal kingdom, Marcian had agreed, and kept his promise. While it is a nice story, Marcian needed no miracles to excuse staying his hand – coping with the Huns and then recovering the finances of the Eastern empire had fully occupied him. Leo's common-sense attitude had furthered the delay in dealing out revenge, and his early prudence was rewarded with the release in 462 of the empress Eudoxia and her daughter Galla Placidia the Younger; her second daughter, Eudocia, had to remain behind, since she was married to Gaiseric's son Huneric.

In the West, Ricimer's puppet emperor Severus had died, giving Leo the opportunity to mend fences by suggesting Anthemius, Marcian's son-in-law, as his successor. When Ricimer agreed to this solution in 467, the way was paved for both halves of the empire to combine against Gaiseric. The greater weight of expense and resources fell on the comparatively unexhausted empire of the East, with Anthemius probably contributing only a small number of men. The campaign was greeted with universal joy – heightened by news of Gaiseric's persecutions of orthodox Christians – and Leo mounted it on a vast

Leo's wife Aelia Verina would continue to have a profound effect on the affairs of the Eastern empire after her husband's death, both in concert with and against her brother Basiliscus.

scale. We are told that a thousand ships, a hundred thousand men, and a hundred and thirty thousand pounds of gold were amassed in Constantinople. The combined naval and military force was more than enough to wipe out the Vandal nation. That it did not do so was entirely the fault of the supremely incompetent Basiliscus.

The sole source for the campaign of the spring of 468 is Procopius. Although writing some sixty-five years later, his account is probably reliable because he accompanied Belisarius's campaign against Carthago that began in 533 and succeeded where Basiliscus failed. The war started promisingly, with Marcellinus, the lord of virtually independent Dalmatia, driving the Vandals from Sardinia, while a Byzantine general named Heraclius landed a small diversionary force in Tripolitania and advanced on Carthago from the southeast. Thus Basiliscus was able to land his main

The joint attack on Gaiseric, 468

Sardinia
Held by Vandals, temporarily lost to Marcellinus.

Caralis (Cagliari)

ITALIA

Neapolis (Napoli, Naples)

MARE TYRRHENUM

Byzantine secondary force under Marcellinus attacks Sardinia, driving out the Vandal occupying army. It proves to be only a temporary gain for the Roman empire.

0   50   100 miles
0   50   100 kilometers

Vandal territory

Panormus (Palermo)

Messana (Messina)

Rhegium (Reggio)

Lilybaeum (Marsala)

Sicilia

Hippo Diarrhytus (Bizerte)

Capo Hermaeum (Cap Bon)

(Pantelleria)

Syracusea (Siracusa)

Carthago

VANDAL KINGDOM

Neapolis (Nabeul)

Melita (Malta)

Hadrumentum (Sousse)

Gaiseric is drawn out to deal with Heraclius as Basiliscus lands to his rear. After buying time, Gaiseric burns the Byzantine fleet trapped in Mercurion harbour, ending the campaign.

Thysdrus (El Djem)

The main Byzantine army under Basiliscus lands at Mercurion near Neapolis, but Basiliscus fails to take the initiative and either advance on undefended Carthago or pincer Gaiseric between his own force and that of Heraclius. The delay is fatal.

MARE INTERNUM

Byzantine diversionary force under Heraclius storms Tripolitana, drawing Gaiseric away from Carthago.

Tacapae (Gabès)

Gigthis

Oea (Tripoli)

Leptis Magna

Sabratha

Tentheos (Zintan)

force on the North African coast at Mercurion, site of an old temple to Mercurius (Hermes), close to the town of Neapolis (Nabeul) on the south of Capo Hermaeum (Cap Bon), without resistance. This put him, undetected, barely thirty-five miles from Carthago and – more importantly – between Gaiseric and the city. With Gaiseric occupied by the Byzantine diversionary detachment, Basiliscus was in an advantageous position to march directly on the Vandal capital and take his enemy by surprise. But he did no such thing, Instead, he made camp near his beach-head and settled down. Procopius attributed this negligence to either cowardice or treachery. Later generations believed that Basiliscus was in the pay of Aspar and under orders not to press too hard his Arian fellow-believers. Human stupidity seems a better explanation. Gaiseric seized the opportunity to send Basiliscus envoys to say that he would do everything Leo wanted of him. He requested only five days' grace to make preparation for surrender.

Even a half-better general with a smattering of military history would have instantly rejected this mild-mannered approach from the fierce Vandal king, but not Basiliscus. Overjoyed at what appeared to be a bloodless victory, he was happy to agree. And then, using the time so cheaply purchased, Gaiseric organised a fire-ship fleet, and on the fifth day sailed it into the harbour at Mercurion. The Vandal sailors lit the fuses and released the blazing hulks into the densely packed Roman ships. As the fire advanced the Romans were thrown into confusion and the Vandals began ramming vessels and capturing any sailors who tried to escape. On land, the story was repeated.

The Roman defeat was complete and Basiliscus, who had fled the battlefield at an early stage, returned in disgrace to Constantinople. The rage of the people at his disastrous failure was so great that he sought refuge in St. Sophia, and only his sister Verina's entreaties to Leo saved him from certain execution. As the campaign's architect, Aspar found himself held in equal odium, and the rumours began circulating that he was in treacherous alliance with his fellow Arian. The gossip had no effect on his unassailable position, however, for within two years he persuaded Leo to betroth his younger daughter Leontia to his own second son Patricius (who was susceptible to conversion to orthodoxy), and proclaim the young man Caesar. And this occurred despite Aspar and his sons' involvement in a plot in 469 to kill Zeno, which almost succeeded. Matters finally came to a head in 471 after Aspar's elder son, Ardabur, was discovered intriguing with the Isaurian faction in an attempt to win its members over to his father's side. Leo stayed his hand no longer and his EXCUBITORII unsheathed their swords and cut down Aspar and Ardabur; Patricius was wounded, but may have recovered.

Given the divisions of the Byzantine court, it is hardly surprising that many thought the murders unjustifiable, and Leo earned the epithet Macellus (the butcher), a term derived from the meat-markets of Rome. It was, perhaps, an unfair nickname for an emperor who had, in comparison to the many who had sat the thrones of Rome, little blood on his hands, and who was a just and merciful ruler of his people. One engaging story involves the hermit Daniel the Stylite (409–93). On a visit to Simeon Stylites in Antiochia, Daniel had determined to adopt this strange form of penitential asceticism – which involved the hermit in living on top of a wooden or stone column. Returning to Constantinople, he erected his own pillar of modest height and lived on its top for some time. Leo was so impressed by Daniel's piety that at his own expense he had a much taller double-pillar erected for him. In order not to break his vow of touching the ground, Daniel crossed from one to the other over a makeshift bridge of planks. When he died he had remained aloft for a total of thirty-three years and three months. He did, however, come down to earth on one occasion, which is related in the following section.

With Aspar gone, there was a general purge of the Germanic element of the court and Leo completed his reconstruction of the army, almost no one happy to have Arians under arms. This was of benefit to the Isaurians and Zeno particularly, who now took an increasingly heavy hand in the government as his septuagenarian father-in-law's health began to fail him. By the same token, Verina's influence held more sway, and it was no doubt at her insistence that Julius Nepos, nephew by birth of Marcellinus of Dalmatia who had temporarily swept the Vandals from Sardinia, and by marriage nephew of the empress, be made the next Western emperor on the death of the incumbent, Glycerius. in the summer of 473. The new emperor was proclaimed in Constantinople in August of that year, but concerns over Leo's rapidly deteriorating health delayed his departure for Italia until the following spring. In September the emperor surprised his court by naming his heir, certainly not the ludicrous Basiliscus but neither the expectant Zeno. Leo instead nominated his seven-year old grandson, whom Zeno had named Leo after his grandfather. Five months later, Leo died on the third day of February 474, aged about seventy-three.

LEO II
Other names unknown (r.2/9/474–11/17/474)

ZENO
Tarasicodissa (Trascalissaeus) Rusumbladeotus
(co-Augustus 2/9/474;
sole 11/17/474–November 475;
restored July 477–4/9/491)

BASILISCUS
Other names unknown
(r.November 475–July 477)

No indication is left to tell us whether Leo I passed over Zeno because of personal animosity, or his feeling that no Isaurian was fit to rule, or whether he simply wanted to pass on the succession to one of his own line, however partly diluted by Isaurian blood. In the event, it hardly matters. Young Leo's mother Ariadne instructed the child to crown his father co-Augustus at the moment he came to make his formal obeisance, which happened on 9 February. Perhaps she was gifted with foresight – nine months later Leo II lay on his

Leo's son-in-law Zeno expected to be next in line but was passed over for his own son Leo II (top). However, through the offices of his mother Ariadne, infant Leo raised his father to be co-Augustus with him, as the lower coin indicates, with its simple inscription of LEO ET ZENO.

funeral bier, dead of natural causes, leaving Zeno the sole ruler of the Eastern empire.

Zeno began his untrammelled reign well by deciding to cut any further expenditure in warring against the Vandals. For a mission of peace to Gaiseric he appointed a distinguished senator called Severus, and gave him the rank of patrician to underline the importance of his embassy. It was a wise choice because the moderation, unselfishness and sense of fair-play of venerable Severus won over Gaiseric's barbarian heart. Yet the embassy almost foundered before it started as a result of a Vandal raid on the Epirote city of Nicopolis. Gaiseric explained this away by telling Severus that attacks such as this were only his way of telling Zeno he was still at war with the empire. And yet within a short space of time Severus persuaded the Vandal king to make peace and set free all the Roman prisoners in bondage. Gaiseric liberated all those prisoners in his own and his sons' keeping, and interceded with his chief nobles to arrange reasonable ransoms for those Romans in their hands. On his return to Constantinople, Severus sold off all his valuables to help raise the price for as many prisoners as he could manage.

And so in 475, the same year Orestes in Italia concluded his treaty with Gaiseric, peace finally existed between Romans and Vandals. Unfortunately, for Zeno this auspicious start was the best part of his reign. His main headache was caused by the Isaurians; never much liked in Constantinople, their recently objectionable behaviour had made them universally unpopular. Arrogant, rowdy and frequently violent, their actions reflected badly on their most distinguished representative, the emperor himself. And Zeno harboured two enemies in his own household: the dowager-empress Verina, and her brother Basiliscus. Although their goals were identical, their objectives were not. Basiliscus had kept his head down since the Carthaginian debacle, but this had not dampened his ardour for the imperial diadem. Verina, on the other hand, wanted it for her newly acquired lover Patricius, an ex-PRAEFECTUS PRAETORIO and the MAGISTER OFFICIORUM (and not the son of Aspar). Despite the divergence of their

Basiliscus (above) – an ineffective and clumsy ruler – was usually at loggerheads with his far more able but meddlesome sister, the empress-dowager Aelia Verina.

ambitions, Verina and Basiliscus joined forces to conspire against Zeno, and in this they were greatly aided by Illus, an Isaurian general who had turned against his benefactor and roused the sympathies of the Isaurian officers and soldiers. No reason for this change of loyalty is given, but it would not be hard to imagine that affection among the senior officers for their fellow Isaurian had been weakened by his pretensions as emperor. In return there was a cooling of the emperor's temper towards those who were staining his reputation with their drunken antics. In November 475, by means of a bluff that seems too obvious to be credible, Verina persuaded Zeno that the army, senate and people were united against him, and he must flee the city immediately. Amazingly, he gave no thought to any defence, and the same night slipped away with his wife and mother to hide away in his native Isauria.

Since only Verina supported the cause of Patricius, Basiliscus was proclaimed emperor and rapidly showed himself to be every bit as useless a ruler as he had been a general. First he ordered – or allowed – the slaughter of every Isaurian in Constantinople. The bloodshed did little shore up his hopeless position, entirely the creation of his own stupidity. He lost his sister's sympathy by having Patricius executed, earned the hatred of the populace through vicious taxation, and incurred the wrath of the Church by openly expressing his monophysite opinions and attempting to enforce them. The former bishop of Alexandria, known as Timotheus Ailouros (the suitably nicknamed Weasel), a staunch monophysite and ally of the emperor, had been expelled from his see in 460 after the Council of Chalcedon. Basiliscus now reinstated him. Timotheus insisted that Basiliscus abrogate the decrees of Chalcedon and abolish the patriarchate of Constantinople. According to the contemporary chronicles Basiliscus was only dissuaded from obeying these extraordinary demands by the astonishing arrival on the ground of Daniel, the city's famous stylite. He descended from his pillar for the first (and only) time in fifteen years to intercede by haranguing the emperor and terrifying him into withdrawing his edict.

As if to indicate that even the heavens wanted Basiliscus gone, a massive fire broke out in the city in 476 – the same year the Teuton warriors who had sworn to protect the Western Roman empire possessed it for their own. Among the tragic losses were Julian's library, said to contain a hundred and twenty thousand books, and the Palace of Lausus with its irreplaceable collection of antiques. At this point Illus, disgusted by the man he had helped to the throne, made overtures to Zeno to restore him to the purple. Verina also conspired against her brother, raising funds to help Zeno mount a rebellion. Basiliscus's cause completely collapsed as a result of his nephew Harmatius's simple-minded treachery. The well-known dandy was promoted by his uncle to the rank of MAGISTER MILITUM, and he dressed the part by appearing in the hippodrome as the Greek hero Achilles. Basiliscus dispatched him with an army to seek out Zeno and Illus who, reconciled to each other, had joined forces. We will never know whether the foppish Harmatius could actually fight, for he was easily persuaded by Zeno to negotiate, and happily turned against his uncle in return for a promise of the praetorian office of MAGISTER PRAESENTALIS for himself and the rank of Caesar for his son.

Unrest in Zeno's second reign

And so, in July 477, Zeno returned to Constantinople unopposed. Basiliscus, who had for the second time hidden away in St. Sophia, came out when he was promised his life. Zeno then banished him and his family to a wild region of Cappadocia, where – as probably intended – they perished for lack of food in the bitter winter. Verina had sought refuge in a church in Blachernae, but her nephew Harmatius came to her rescue, and she was saved; a clemency Zeno would come to regret bitterly. As to matters abroad, much had changed in his absence. The events that had led to the proclamation of the boy-emperor Romulus Augustulus, his overthrow and the seizure of Italia by Odoacer were irrelevant to Zeno, who was far more inclined to object strongly to the earlier dethronement of his own nominated co-Augustus, Julius Nepos. Nevertheless, it appears that he diplomatically washed his hands when Nepos wrote to congratulate him on his restoration to the purple and asked for Zeno's support in effecting a similar restoration to the Western throne for himself. For when Odoacer's envoys arrived in Constantinople requesting the title of Patrician for their king, Zeno pointed out that Nepos was the Western emperor, and their request should be directed to him in Dalmatia. However, he signed the letter prepared to go back with the envoys which had been addressed 'to the Patrician Odoacer' – a purposeful slip that indirectly gave recognition or a silly clerical error?

Nepos was not to receive the backing he craved, Zeno still had too many internal matters to settle. First among these was Harmatius, whose silly behaviour pointed to a break down in his sanity. Zeno appears to have suffered a crisis of conscience about this, but the outcome was never really in doubt. A suitable assassin was found – an Ostrogoth who was still in imperial service named Onoulf, and who happened to be Odoacer's brother – and Harmatius was swiftly dispatched. His son, named Basiliscus like his great-uncle, was spared. Zeno stripped him of his rank and title of Caesar and forced him into the Church. Since young Basiliscus later served in the imperial palace at Blachernae and ended his life as the bishop of Cyzicus, he may well have been much happier as a PRIVATUS than saddled with imperial burdens.

Having recovered from her fright at Zeno's return, Verina now turned her fury against her former co-conspirator Illus, who was by then serving as MAGISTER OFFICIORUM. An attempt was made on his life in 477, in which her hand was suspected, but never proved. However, in the following year, when Illus was consul and stationed in Isauria, another plot against his life was uncovered, and the assassin proven to be in the employ of Epinicus, one of Verina's officials. Illus was naturally reluctant to return to Constantinople unless Verina was removed. Zeno concurred, and sent her to a convent in Tarsus, from which she was later moved to Dalisandus, and then Cherreus in Isauria, where she was incarcerated. But even at this distance, the empress was still able to cause trouble for Zeno and Illus.

In 479 the emperor faced another insurrection, this time headed by Marcian, grandson of his imperial namesake, son of the Western emperor Anthemius and husband of Leontia, younger daughter of Leo I. (She had been betrothed to Aspar's son Patricius, but this was broken off after Aspar's fall.) Marcian had two reasons to stage a coup: the treatment of his mother-in-law Verina; and his claim that his wife, having been born in the purple, was of higher rank than her older sister Ariadne, Zeno's wife, who was born before the emperor Marcian had been elevated. In company with his brothers Procopius and Romulus, Marcian's forces stormed the palace and nearly succeeded in overthrowing Zeno. Only swift action by Illus, who brought a unit of Isaurian troops across the Bosphorus under the cover of night and took the rebels by surprise, saved Zeno's throne. Marcian was treated

After a seven-month 'sabbatical', Zeno returned to the throne in the summer of 477, only to find himself entangled in the political machinations of his mother-in-law Verina.

with clemency and sent into exile as a monk in Cappadocian Caesarea, from where he escaped and raised a second rebellion, but this also failed. Still unwilling to execute him, Zeno had Marcian ordained a presbyter, and sent his wife Leontia into a convent.

But the MAGISTER OFFICIORUM's problems were not over. In 482, while attending races at the hippodrome, an imperial life guardsman named either Spanicus or Sporacius attacked him. His own bodyguard managed to deflect the blow away from Illus, but the sword sliced through his right ear. The person behind this thwarted attempt turned out to be none other than the empress Ariadne, her motives perhaps being revenge for the treatment of her mother and sister. Events now rapidly moved towards the inevitable break between Illus and the emperor; it is unclear from the confused sources, but Illus had every reason in his own mind to suspect that Zeno was, if not conspiring against him, at least turning a blind eye to his possible assassination. Illus prudently took himself away from the court and retired to Anatolia, but this coincided with the rebellion of a certain Leontius. Again, the fragmentary sources make a degree of guesswork necessary to order any form of history. It seems that messengers rode after Illus carrying orders for him to take command of the Eastern armies and restore calm. Somewhat reassured by this trust placed in him by the emperor, Illus hastened to Syria, where he discovered none other than Zeno's incompetent brother Longinus in charge. The profligate Longinus was not amused to find his authority compromised and an argument ensued, in which Illus had him arrested and thrown into prison.

If this was a high-handed reaction, Zeno's was the more ill-judged. When news of his brother's arrest reached Constantinople, the emperor pronounced Illus a public enemy and ordered the confiscation of his properties. This inevitably drove Illus into the rebel's camp. He made common cause with Leontius, and the two of them released the empress Verina from her imprisonment at Cherreus. This fortress was also known by the name of its builder, a by then dead robber-baron named Papirius. In return for her freedom, she was happy to crown Leontius at Tarsus, and then they went to Antiochia, where on 27 June 484, Leontius established a rival court... or so goes one version. Another places a very different emphasis on the events. According to the alternative version Leontius, probably an Isaurian (though origins in Syria and Thracia also appear), who

had a successful military career, was sent by Zeno against Illus, who had gone into Anatolia in revolt and seized the emperor's brother Longinus as a hostage. However, Illus persuaded Leontius to desert Zeno, and then declared him Augustus on 19 July at Tarsus, with the support of Verina. Antiochia was occupied for twelve days (27 July to 8 August), during which time Leontius minted a few coins.

Regardless of which of these is to be believed (and a yet third version claims that Illus proclaimed the ordained Marcian emperor, not Leontius) the later events are generally clear. Illus and Leontius seemed content to remain where they were – probably for many weeks rather than the twelve days – which gave Zeno time to mount a second expedition. This included a young barbarian named Theodoric, prince of the Ostrogoths, under the overall command of Ioannes the Scythian (sometimes called John the Goth). The rebels were rapidly evicted from Antiochia and chased to Papirius in Isauria, where they were besieged for four years, and where Verina died unlamented. In 488 the fortress was betrayed, probably by the false promise of a pardon, and the rebels were all executed. The heads of Leontius and Illus were sent to Constantinople, there to be impaled above the city walls. Of Theodoric, who did not take part in the siege because of important occupations elsewhere, much more will be heard in the following chapter.

Schism between the two Churches

The monophysite controversy continued to dog Zeno, and he never managed to solve it. A little before the events recounted immediately above, in 482 the emperor together with Patriarch Acacius attempted to heal the breach between the dangerously disaffected monophysite eastern provinces and the Church through an edict known as the Act of Union, or *Henoticon*. It sought to mend the differences by affirming that Christ was both God and man, but it conspicuously avoided the delicate word 'nature'. As a compromise it was unsuccessful, predictably arousing the ire of all parties. In Rome, Pope Simplicius (p.468–83) and his successor Felix III (p.483–92) were particularly outraged. After the monophysite Alexandrian bishop Timotheus Ailouros (*see above, page 270*) had been expelled from his see, Constantinople had installed the orthodox Timotheus Solophaciolus. But, as has been related, Basiliscus returned Ailouros to the see in 475, to which he adhered until his death in 477. At this point there were two contenders, the orthodox John Talaia and the monophysite Peter Mongos (the Stammerer), but amid

Leontius, who is thought to be Isaurian in origin, managed to mint coins as a usurping Augustus in the 12 days he ruled in Antiochia, before being ousted by Zeno's forces and besieged for four years in the Isaurian fortress of Papirius.

the bickering Solophaciolus was given the vacant see, which he held until his death 481.

For years Zeno had held Talaia in esteem, but for some reason Acacius hated him. When the Alexandrian Catholics elected Talaia to the see, he announced his succession to Rome and Antioch, according to custom, but he sent no message to Acacius in Constantinople. Instead, he wrote to Illus, who had befriended him at court, but Illus was in Antioch and so word of mouth reached Constantinople before the announcement arrived. The patriarch seized his chance to poison Zeno against Talaia, championing instead Mongos. In the following year the unimpeachably orthodox Talaia refused to sign the *Henoticon*, whereas politically astute Mongos said he would. Zeno ordered Talaia expelled from Alexandria and replaced him with Peter Mongos. Talaia now fled to Rome and made his case to Pope Felix, who defended his rights to Acacius and refused to accept Mongos. Stubborn Acacius refused to accede to the pope's demands, and at a synod held in Rome in 484 Felix excommunicated the patriarch. So the story goes, there was no orthodox ecclesiastic courageous enough to read out the papal proclamation, so instead it was written out on a scrap of parchment and pinned to the back of the patriarch's cope when he was not looking, during a service in St. Sophia. When he discovered it a few minutes later, the fuming Acacius instantly excommunicated Felix in turn. This action declared that Constantinople now stood at the same hierarchical level as Rome, and the open schism between the two Churches was to last for thirty-five years. It was not the outcome that fumbling Zeno had hoped for.

By the end of the decade Zeno was failing mentally and physically. His second son was already dead, worn out by a life of homosexual excess and the ravages of venereal disease. Much of the government was in the hands of the Zeno's brother Longinus, rescued from Illus in 484, who was in his second consulship in 490. He no doubt anticipated his natural succession, but events transpired differently when Zeno took counsel from the well-known soothsayer Maurianus and was told, in typically oblique fashion, that Longinus would not succeed. 'Your successors,' Maurianus intoned, 'shall be your wife and one who has served as a SILENTARIUS.' The SILENTARII formed an elite corps of thirty picked officials whose duty was to watch over the emperor's private apartments to ensure he enjoyed undisturbed sleep. This somewhat mundane-sounding task disguised a very competent body of men, who ranked with senators and carried out many administrative and confidential tasks, including writing the official imperial history.

Quite why Zeno picked out one among the thirty, an eminent statesman named Pelagius, as the SILENTARIUS of the prophesy is not known. Perhaps to the emperor's senile mind the rebukes he had received from Pelagius over his misgovernment, and his sturdy resistance to Zeno making Longinus Caesar, were sufficient to condemn him.

The unfortunate Pelagius was given no chance to defend himself. His property was confiscated, he was thrown into prison, and soon after strangled to death. It was a mistake. Pelagius had been widely respected and well liked, and this arbitrary cruelty cost Zeno any last dregs of popular affection. Thus he died without lamentation on 9 April 491 after an epileptic seizure, and the prophecy of Mauranus came true. When the mob greeted the widowed empress Ariadne with cries to give them a real emperor, an orthodox emperor, a Roman emperor! their meaning was obvious: no more Isaurians and no more heretics. Ariadne did as she was asked, and bestowed the diadem, as well as her hand in marriage, to one Flavius Anastasius, a native of Dyrrachium, in his early sixties... and one of the college of SILENTARII.

Flavius Anastasius brought common sense to the government and a sometimes too-careful hand on the purse strings, but his suspect religious stance would lead to much civil unrest.

ANASTASIUS
Flavius Anastasius (r.[East] 11/4/491–9/7/518)

Anastasius was born at Dyrrachium on the Adriatic coast opposite Brundisium in 430. He was given the cognomen Dicorus ('two pupils') because his eyes were differently coloured: one blue one and one black one – a peculiarity which apparently only enhanced his handsome appearance. Anastasius had not been

ISAURIA, politically, was of very different extent at different periods. Its permanent nucleus lay directly south of Iconium. When the Romans first encountered the Isaurians early in the first century BC they regarded Cilicia Trachea as part of Isauria. Towards the end of the second century AD Diocletian detached Isauria, at first with Lycaonia, and then on its own. Later Pisidia was removed, and in compensation Isauria received the eastern part of Pamphylia. Its inhabitants, an independent mountain people, had always been predatory. Despite their apparent submission to the proconsul Publius Servilius in 75 BC, Isaurian pirates remained the bane of Roman merchant shipping until Pompeius Magnus defeated them in the last days of the Republic. Isauria's history extends beyond the scope of this book; in addition to Zeno, Isaurian Leo III became emperor in 718, reigned until 741, and founded a dynasty of three generations.

prominent at Zeno's court beyond gaining the position of a SILENTARIUS, but he had earned a reputation for honesty and uprightness. This was so well known in Constantinople that when the sixty-one-year-old emperor appeared for the first time wearing the purple and diadem the people acclaimed him with the cry, 'Reign, Anastasius, as you have lived!'

His accession and then his marriage to Ariadne on 20 April were marred by a rebellion caused partly by the oppressive conduct of an unpopular PRAEFECTUS and partly by disaffected Isaurians. Anastasius ordered the latter banished from the city, but they lingered around the nucleus of the Longinus faction. Stronger action was demanded, and Longinus was compelled to enter the priesthood and banished to Thebae (the sources do not make clear whether this was in Aegyptus or Boeotia), where after eight years he perished of hunger. His wife, daughter, and mother Lalis were sent to Brochti, a small oratory on the Bithynian shore, where for the remainder of their lives they existed on alms. Zeno's property was confiscated and everything, even his imperial robe, sold for the benefit of the FISCUS. This sale illuminates an aspect of the generally wise and peaceable Anastasius: he was obsessively mean when it came to money. As a consequence, Constantinople became a dull place to live, a city where puritanism ruled – although, as we shall see, not necessarily peace. The emperor immediately began a programme of cutting down on imperial expenditure, and so by the end of his long reign of

A coin of Kavadh, the Sassanian who broke the 60-year peace established by Stilicho and instituted almost continual hostilities from then on.

twenty-seven years, the treasury was richer by three hundred and twenty thousand pounds of gold than it had been on his accession. This figure, quoted by Procopius, compares interestingly with his estimate for the cost of Leo I's ill-fated African expedition of 468: a hundred and thirty thousand pounds.

Although the Isaurians' expulsion restored a temporary order in the capital, in their native province they continued the rebellion until 496, largely unchecked by the ineffectual forces sent against them. When a charge of feebleness was laid at his feet, a war-weary Anastasius considered his options, and chose to take a strong stance. With renewed energy, the imperial army prosecuted a bolder war and achieved complete victory by 498. The rebellion's leaders were decapitated and their heads sent to Constantinople to be displayed, 'a sweet sight to the Byzantines'. In the remainder of his reign, there was generally peace among his provincial subjects but many external threats. In 502 Kavadh (Cabades), king of Persia, broke the sixty-year-long peace, and invaded. In a four-year war that lasted until 505 several important Roman strongholds along the eastern frontier were lost, and hostilities only ceased when the Persians were promised a renewal of tribute. To the north, invasions of newly arrived Bulgars into Thraciae became endemic. Eventually, Anastasius was obliged to build a great wall across the thirty miles from Selymbria (Silivri) on the Propontis to the coast of the Euxinus to keep them away from the capital.

Perhaps the most dangerous threat to Anastasius was the insurrection of Vitalian. Although the son of an imperial army officer, Vitalian was of Gothic extraction; small in stature, he possessed all the fire and courage to lead a band of barbarians and mutineers. Vitalian championed a cause for which he can have had little real sympathy, that of the Chalcedonians. But it was a good pretext for rebellion against the emperor, whose monophysite leanings were never hidden. His real reason was less noble and stemmed from a grievance concerning his removal from the office of distributor of rations to the FOEDERATI. The mutinous soldiers alleged that they had been refused payment of arrears, and the Huns who made up the bulk of Vitalian's rag-tag army – well, they needed no excuse for rapine and pillage. Although Vitalian's ravaging took place mostly in the region of Odessus (Varna), he succeeded on three occasions in reaching the suburbs of Constantinople by sailing a fleet from the Euxinus into the Bosphorus. After the rebels retired from the second of these attacks in 514, Anastasius dispatched an army of eighty thousand troops under the command of his nephew Hypatius to bring Vitalian to heel. Unfortunately, Hypatius was no great general and near Odessus Vitalian's Huns dealt the Romans a terrible blow from which only twenty thousand survived. Hypatius himself was captured and Anastasius forced to treat with Vitalian. The terms were humiliating: Vitalian was appointed MAGISTER MILITUM PER THRACIAE and paid an enormous sum for Hypatius's ransom, and Anastasius was forced to promise the restoration of exiled Chalcedonian bishops.

However, the emperor's failure to keep this promise made Vitalian feel insecure, and in 515 he made a third amphibious advance on the capital. This time the rebel fared badly. A rough Thracian soldier named Justin, who was PRAEFECTUS EXCUBITORUM, took the Byzantine navy into the centre of Vitalian's fleet and struck such terror into the sailors that the rebels were scattered. On witnessing the collapse of the seaborne raid, Vitalian's land army dispersed and the arch-rebel troubled Anastasius no more. He was, however to remain a problem for the emperor's successor (*see chapter 17*).

The Blue and Green battle

By contrast with the provinces, Constantinople was continually shaken by outbreaks of violent rioting, almost always over religious matters. At Anastasius's accession Patriarch Euphemius had raised objections to Anastasius's monophysite adherence, and refused him coronation him unless he signed a declaration of orthodoxy, which Anastasius did without hesitation. Many viewed this as a sign that he was a man ready to sacrifice his principles for power, but Anastasius held only a sympathy for the heretical creed and believed he was a Chalcedonian at heart. Nevertheless, as his reign progressed the emperor showed a greater inclination towards monophysitism. At this time Constantinople was riven between two factions, the Blues and the Greens. These institutions, of course, originated from two of the several chariot-racing teams that dated back to before the beginnings of the imperial era. In the course of the passing decades, the other teams had disappeared and – while still supporting their respective charioteers on racing days – the two factions had long since expanded beyond the confines of the hippodrome and evolved into political parties. There is an earlier hint at this development. In 456, the emperor Marcian heavily censured the Greens throughout the Eastern empire for railing at his patronage of the Blues. When they refused to

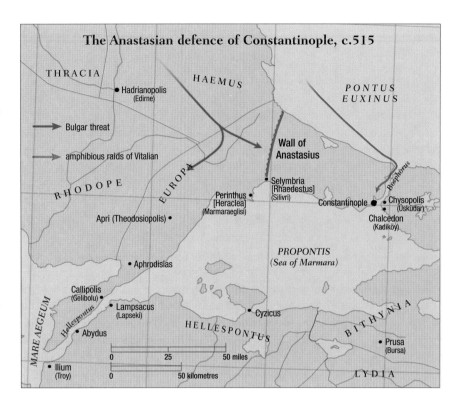

The Anastasian defence of Constantinople, c.515

desist in their jeering Marcian responded by banning the Greens from holding any administrative or public posts for three years. It is interesting to note that Chrysaphius – the chamberlain who had plotted to assassinate Attila – had patronised the Greens, and Marcian's favouritism of the Blues clearly had a political aspect to it.

At the time of Anastasius the political affiliation of the Blues tended towards the big landowners and the old Graeco-Roman aristocracy, therefore orthodoxy, while the Greens were on the side of tradesmen and the civil service. Since many of the latter came from the eastern provinces where heresy was more widespread, the Greens gradually became associated with monophysitism. Although at first Anastasius tried to act impartially, his economic policies – which favoured manufacturing industries over agrarian – and his leaning towards the monophysites drew him to the Greens. Throughout his reign, hostility between the two factions (or DEMES, as they had come to be known) increased, with many violent eruptions in the streets. In 510 the Greens attacked the Blues in the hippodrome, and in the ensuing fight the emperor's own illegitimate son was killed. Worse followed in the next year and Anastasius was largely responsible for the disturbance. To the important refrain in the Byzantine liturgy of 'Holy God, Holy and Mighty, Holy and Immortal' (the so-called TRISAGION) the monophysites added: '...who was crucified for us'.

This emphasised their belief that it was not the man Jesus but God himself who died on the cross.

When the heretics were heard loudly chanting this in the Chapel of the Archangel, which stood within the palace walls, orthodox tempers were roused. But they boiled over when, on the following Sunday, the heretics defiantly shouted them during mass in St. Sophia. The orthodox congregation shouted back, and the service dissolved into chaos as fighting broke out. Anastasius should have acted impartially, but instead he laid the blame at the feet of Euphemius's successor, the saintly Patriarch Macedonius II. The infuriated mob marched on the palace, threatening to remove the heretical emperor, and only Macedonius's imprecations for peace saved the terrified Anastasius from being manhandled from his throne. But the lesson went unlearned. Macedonius was quietly exiled soon after and the heretical chant was heard again. On 4 November 512 the violence was renewed in St. Sophia, until the great basilica's floor ran with the blood of dead and wounded. The fighting boiled over into the city and continued unabated for two full days before Anastasius acted. He went to the hippodrome and there, before twenty thousand of his angry subjects, offered to lay aside the imperial diadem and let them choose his successor; or, if they preferred, he would continue in office and solemnly promise to sin no more. The ploy worked; quiet returned.

The riots awakened in the emperor's mind the question of succession. There is a most probably apocryphal, though charming, story related in the source known only as the *Anonymous Valesii* that towards the end of his life Anastasius became curious about which of his three nephews would succeed him. Hypatius, the son of one of his sisters, we have already met; the other two were the brothers Probus and Pompeius, who may have been the sons of his brother. Accordingly, the emperor invited all three to dine with him and had three couches made ready on which they could take their rest after the meal. Under the cushion of one couch he placed a slip of paper inscribed with the word REGNVM. Whichever nephew chose that particular couch would reign after him. On the face of it this was a foolproof plan, but it still failed. Hypatius chose one couch and the two brothers, who appear to have held somewhat incestuous feelings for one another, chose to sleep together on another. Sadly, the couch secretly marked by the emperor remained unoccupied, and Anastasius knew then that none of his nephews would succeed him.

Consequently, he conceived of another method of divination, based on the concept that since God had moved in mysterious ways with his nephews, so He might again. This time he determined that the first person to enter his bed-chamber the very next day should be the anointed one. This should certainly have been his chamberlain, but it chanced that the Justin who had so soundly routed Vitalian, now COMES EXCUBITORUM, came to report the carrying-out of certain of his emperor's orders. Anastasius bowed before the will of God and recognised his successor. Justin's elevation to the purple was not as smooth as Anastasius might have hoped. When the emperor finally died, aged eighty-seven, after midnight on 9 July 518, his chief eunuch Amantius had his own preferred candidate for the throne, a certain Theocritus, and confided in Justin, giving him a sum of money with which to bribe the EXCUBITORII to support him. This was clearly an error of judgement. Justin kept the money, and warned his men to be ready. The next morning, as the crowds began to gather in the hippodrome to hear of the senate's choice of successor, fighting broke out. The EXCUBITORII were brought in to restore order and, apparently of their own accord, began calling on their COMES to take up the imperial mantle. In time-honoured tradition, Justin at first refused, but the senators, recognising a put-up job when they saw one, added their voices to that of the soldiers, and Justin allowed himself to be persuaded.

The events of Justin's reign are related in chapter 17, and at this point, it is necessary to go back in time to the moment when Odoacer deposed Romulus Augustulus in Italia. In time, Odoacer's successors would have to deal with Justin's nephew, the real power behind the throne of Byzantium after the death of Anastasius – and his name was Justinian.

Justin, his coin shown here – an illiterate from Thracia – was the right man in the right place at the right time, but it would be his nephew who would return true stability to the Eastern empire.

Organisation of the Eastern Roman empire, and the barbarian kingdoms, 490

More provinces have appeared, but the empire is now divided between only two dioceses: Illyrici (or Eastern Illyricum) and Orientis.

Eastern Roman empire

- Diocese Illyrici
- Diocese Orientis
- Ghassanid allies
- provincial border
- Vandal kingdom
- Ostrogothic kingdom
- Sassanian empire
- Lakhmid allies of Persia (kingdom of Hira)
- Bulgar migration, c.500
- kingdom of Odoacer
- Geppid kingdom

MARE CASPIUM

HUNNI

BULGARI

ALANI

AVARI

PALUS MAEOTIS (Sea of Azov)

MAEOTAE

AVARI

HERULI

HUNNI

GOTHS

ABASGI

Lazica

REGNUM GEPIDAE

Scythia

The Bulgars were to become a continual threat to the Eastern empire in the sixth and seventh centuries.

SCLAVENI

Iberia

PONTUS EUXINUS

Danuvius

Moesia I

Dacia Ripensis

Moesia II

Trapezus (Trabzon)

Armenia

Sinope (Sinop)

Pontus Polemoniacus

GEPIDAE

Dacia Mediterraneum

Thracia

Haemus

Pahplagonia

Helenopontus

Gentes (degree of power share with Sassanians)

evaliana

Dardania

Honorias

Armenia I

SASSANIAN EMPIRE

Rhodope

Europa

Constantinople

Galatia I

Cappadocia I

Macdonia Salutaris

Bithynia

Armenia II

Mesopotamia

MESOPOTAMIA

Macdonia I

Thessalonica

Galatia Salutaris

Caesarea

Augusta Euphratensis

Epirus Nova

Hellespontus

Phrygia I II

Cappadocia II

Osrhoene

Tigris

Pergamum

Lydia

Pisidia

Cilicia I II

Epirus Vetus

Thessalia

Asia

Lycaonia

Syria I

Euphrates

Athenae

Caria

Pamphylia

Antiochia

Syria Salutaris

REGNUM HIRAE

Achaea

Lycia

Isauria

Orontes

LAKHMIDAE

Insulae

Cyprus

Phoenicia Libanensis

Phoenicia

GHASSANIDAE

Creta

MARE INTERNUM

Palaestina II

Bostra (Busra)

Palaestina

Arabia

The rival Ghassanids (Byzantine allies) and Lakhmids (Sassanian allies) were in constant dispute at the conjunction of their desert territories. Ghassanid forces frequently supported Roman arms in the border wars with Sassanian Persia.

Cyrene

Alexandria

Palaestina Salutaris

Augustamnica

Aegyptus

Libya Superior

Libya Inferior

Heliopolis

Arcadia

Nilus

MARE ERYTHRAEUM

Thebais

Thebae

0   100   200   300 miles

0   100   200   300   400 kilometres

CHAPTER SIXTEEN   AD 476–534
BARBARIANS IN ITALIA

ODOACER THE HERULIAN
Flavius Odovacer (r.Italia 4/9/476–15/3/493)

The schism between the Churches of East and West caused by Constantinople's acquiescence in the matter of the monophysite heresy was introduced in the previous chapter, and how it enraged the popes Simplicius and Felix III. What is interesting from the West's point of view is that Felix was allowed to summon a synod in 484 and then free to excommunicate Patriarch Acacius. This suggests that, at least from the Church's perspective, not much had altered in Italia since Odoacer removd Romulus Augustulus and made himself *de facto* ruler of what was left of the Western Roman empire. Although this would be to underestimate how much the political situation had changed in respect of the traditional legality of the ruler, for the mass of people life went on as usual, and for the papacy the status of the Roman see was actually enhanced.

The abdication of young Romulus Augustulus early in September 476 is generally regarded as marking the end of the Roman empire in the West, although some historians have argued that this was not the case. Their position is that the empire was indivisible – whether it was ruled by one Augustus, or two, or even more, was a matter of administrative convenience. And since Odoacer still acknowledged the ultimate sovereignty of the emperor in Constantinople, it meant that the German was ruling the West as the emperor's viceroy – and what in that was so different to previous situations? Italians for almost a century, it is true, had also grown used to seeing barbarian war lords, the Patricians, as the real power, so was Odoacer very different? But Odoacer had caused a seminal change. Unlike his precursors Arbogast, Stilicho, Aëtius, and Ricimer, Odoacer wanted no Western puppet as a figurehead, and without the title of Augustus, no matter how hollow the title may have become in the recent decades, the symbol of imperial continuity had been banished. And although Odoacer was fobbed off by Zeno when he requested of the emperor the title of Patrician, he nevertheless

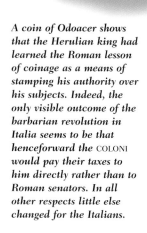

A coin of Odoacer shows that the Herulian king had learned the Roman lesson of coinage as a means of stamping his authority over his subjects. Indeed, the only visible outcome of the barbarian revolution in Italia seems to be that henceforward the COLONI *would pay their taxes to him directly rather than to Roman senators. In all other respects little else changed for the Italians.*

appears to have been content with Zeno's diplomatic slip in addressing his response to 'the Patrician Odoacer'. Besides, the title Odoacer preferred was to use was REX.

It was in the city of Rome that the Augustan vacuum was felt most keenly. Even though emperors may with only a few exceptions have made their courts in Mediolanum or Ravenna in preference to Rome, the old capital sensed its decline in prestige without an imperial presence anywhere within the realm. Therefore, it seemed to follow naturally that the Romans would seek a representative to look up to, a figure who possessed prestige and offered the prospect of continuity. And so the they turned to the pope and raised him up. Almost immediately, the papacy was offered extended temporal secular powers in addition to its ecclesiastical ones and the lavish ceremony normally only accorded to emperors. In the persons of Simplicius and Felix it is possible to see the medieval papacy of religious princes springing into existence.

Odoacer was the master of the Germanic Heruli and Sciri (Scythian) tribes, and these – as soldiers of Rome – were the men who had demanded Orestes give them one-third of Italia for their settlement. It is logical to assume that this donation was made, and that it probably affected the urban population very little, since the weight of loss must have fallen on the wealthy land-owning class, largely in the north. Indeed, for the great mass of Italians the old order of things hardly changed at all. What impoverished and almost always third-hand annals of the period survive, suggest that Odoacer employed the existing machinery of Roman government. No doubt the Teutonic subjects of the new ruler, living on Italian land assigned to them from their old possessors, adhered to their old tribal laws, but there is no indication that this became a barbarian land under the oppressing feet of German petty chieftains; indeed, the opposite. Roman administrators served Odoacer in all the major and traditional offices. The names that have come down through time include Liberius (in an unknown function), Cassiodorus as a PRAEFECTUS PRAETORIO, Peirius as COMES DOMESTICORUM, and Pelagius as another PRAEFECTUS PRAETORIO in Liguria. Justice was still administered according to Roman law, judged by Roman magistrates; taxes were still collected by the RATIONALES; the administrative and courtly hierarchy introduced by Diocletian and perfected under Constantine continued to work for the benefit of the state. Only the centre had changed, instead of an Augustus, there was a barbarian chieftain who refused the imperial diadem, wore not the purple (indeed, he sent these symbols of Roman authority to Zeno), and paid only lip service to the traditional legitimacy of his rule.

That he had a care for all his subjects – arbitrary as it may have been in the Germanic mould, rather than steadfastly Roman – is illustrated by his treatment of Ticinum (Pavia), the city that had suffered most during the overthrow of Orestes. When its saintly bishop Epiphanius appealed to Odoacer to relieve the citizens of their unbearable tax burden levied by Pelagius to replenish the bankrupt exchequer, his wish was granted. Despite the city's penurious state, Epiphanius desired to rebuild the two great churches that had been destroyed in the mercenary revolt that made Odoacer master of Italia. On seeing the bishop's worthy efforts, Odoacer decreed that Ticinum should be exempted from tribute for five years. A similar degree of wisdom is to be found in his attitude towards the pope in Rome, and his dealings with and support for the papacy in its battle with see of Constantinople contributed greatly to the increased eminence of papal dignity.

A back turned on the Mediterranean

Odoacer made his capital at Ravenna, not because this was the capital of the last Roman emperors, but because it was conveniently close to the northern borders. The Mediterranean seems to have held little interest for him. Corsica and Sardinia were in Vandal hands, and he was content with the peace Orestes had established with Gaiseric. In a formal treaty, probably the last act of the aged Vandal king, all but the western part of Sicilia around the town of Lilybaeum (Marsala) was ceded to Orestes, and thus in turn to Odoacer, in return for an annual tribute. Gaiseric went to the grave early in 477. It seems appropriate that the great scourge of Rome for more than fifty years should have expired only six months after the death of the Western empire, as though deprived of his ancient foe there remained no meaning to the Vandal king's life. It was soon apparent that the fearsome reputation of the Vandal nation was largely due to Gaiseric's destructive genius, for it rapidly declined under his son Huneric and grandson Hilderic, as indeed did Odoacer's willingness to continue paying tribute. Had Odoacer turned his attention across the Mediterranean with any serious intention, Italia might well have regained its African possessions, but he looked to the north instead.

Odoacer's dominions were almost unchanged from those of the Roman emperors of the West for the past twenty-five years. Gallia was lost to him, and the region comprised of Narbonensis II and Alpes Maritimae (Provence), Rome's first gained and last lost PROVINCIA, remained staunchly set against the barbarian king, and appealed to the East for protection. But as he had with the claim of Nepos, Zeno favoured Odoacer's simultaneous embassy over that of the Provençals'. In the event, Odoacer never made them submit to his rule, preferring instead to make his claim over to Euric, king of the Visigoths, whose power in Gallia was predominant. To the north of the Alps the old Italian province of Raetia, lost to the last emperors, was firmly in Odoacer's hands, and from there he could expand to the north against the Alamanni and Thuringii, northwest towards the Burgundi, and east to the other side of the MARE ADRIATICUM. A pretext for this expansion came when Julius Nepos, who still held precariously onto Dalmatia, fell to the swords of the COMITES Ovida and Viator in 480. Technically, Dalmatia belonged to the Western empire – although its possession had switched several times – and so Odoacer could argue the legitimacy of an invasion to revenge the murder of his technical superior. In the following year he transported an army into the province, conquered and slew Ovida (Viator appears to have already died), and added Dalmatia to his dominions.

Odoacer also took war into the region corresponding with Roman Noricum. This once densely populated and wealthy province had fallen on sad times, with its still largely Roman citizens falling prey to raids of Alamanni from the west and Thuringii from the northwest. The cities of Batavia Castra (Passau) and Noreia (Neumarkt in Styria) were attacked regularly, and their citizens carried off into slavery. The only semblance of government in the region was offered by the powerful monarchy of the Rugi, who occupied a territory north of the Danuvius. Their expansion into Noricum after 482 inevitably brought them close to Odoacer's borders. In 486, the Rugi made some movement against Odoacer, and he responded by invading in 487, carrying off prisoners to Ravenna and annexing the region (also making himself king of the Rugi). Frederick, the last prince of the Rugi, fled before the Gothic army commanded by Odoacer's brother Onoulf and sought refuge at the court of Theodoric, probably then residing at Novae (Sistova, Bulgaria). This insult to one who was certainly an Ostrogothic ally could certainly be seen as a CASUS BELLI, but Theodoric already had a more solid reason for his invasion of Italia.

THEODORIC

Flavius Theodoricus
(r.Italia 15/3/493–30/8/526)

Born in about 454, Theodoric was the son of the Ostrogothic chieftain Theodemir and his concubine Erelieva. It was said that the day of his birth was the same as the Ostrogoths' great victory over the Huns, won by Theodemir's brother and joint-ruler Walamir, and that this omen boded well for the baby prince's future. However, within seven years this was looking less rosy. The annual tribute paid to the Ostrogoths had fallen into arrears under the emperor Leo, and they began to ravage Moesia. Leo recognised his error in ignoring his FOEDERATI, and made peace, promising to honour the tributes and pay the arrears in return for sureties of good behaviour and the security of holding Theodemir's son hostage in Constantinople. For ten years, young Theodoric dwelt in the capital, where he appears to have benefited little from any formal education†, but gained tremendous insight into Byzantine politics. This served him well when, after successfully commanding an imperial conquest of the Sarmatae in 471, he succeeded his father in 474 as a leader of the Ostrogothic nation.

He was not alone, for another Theodoric, nicknamed Strabo (Squinter), challenged his position. Ten years of changing relationships between the two Ostrogoths, and between themselves and the emperor, ended with Strabo's death in 481, which left Theodoric in undisputed control. The main purpose of his early life was to secure a permanent home for his people, and in pursuit of this goal he spent twenty years engaged with the empire on its behalf and fighting against it, employing all his skills in diplomacy, bargaining, arguing, threatening and cajoling by turns. He assisted Zeno against Basiliscus in 477 and Illus in 484. He became a Patrician, a MAGISTER MILITUM in 477 and an adopted son of the emperor, and then a consul in 484. Yet he was also responsible for devastating Epirus and Macedonia in 479, laying waste Thessalia in 482 and he even marched on Constantinople itself in 487.

This constant vacillation in his relations with Zeno profited neither side, and by about 487 the emperor

Under Theodoric the Ostrogoth, Italia was to enjoy a peace and prosperity that few imperial Romans had managed for almost a hundred years. Images of the great German king were all erased on the orders of Justinian; however, a portrait of Theodoric survives on one of his coins.

† Theodoric never learned to read or write, and was said to have used a golden stencil for signing his name, and even then his secretary had to guide his hand to ensure the ink was correctly applied.

and his prodigal adopted son accepted that some resolution was necessary. According to the historian Procopius (the great chronicler of early Byzantium), the emperor, who was losing any sympathy he might have had for Odoacer, had the bright idea of sending Theodoric to Italia to retake it for the empire. Cassiodorus, chief minister to Theodoric and his chronicler, claimed it was the Ostrogoth's notion and that Zeno immediately saw the wisdom of such a suitable political settlement. Whoever was the campaign's real architect, at some point in late 487 or early 488, it was agreed between them that Theodoric should lead the entire Ostrogothic nation into Italia, overthrow Odoacer and rule the land as an Ostrogothic province-kingdom under imperial sovereignty.

The Gothic conquest of Italy

Before tackling Italia, Theodoric had to get his people across Illyricum. Had this been a purely military expedition, the journey across the war-ravaged and mountainous land would have posed little real problem, but conservative estimates put the non-combatants travelling with him well in excess of two hundred thousand. Progress was no faster than the slowest laden wagon, and the train included pack animals, cattle and sheep, fodder, and the usual paraphernalia of an ancient army. Soon, the food began to run out, and pestilence followed them. At a point when it seemed most hard to continue, the Ostrogoths encountered the unconquered Gepidae, who barred the forward route. In a battle that took place in the vicinity where Constantine fought his first battle against Licinius in 314, the Ostrogoths were victorious. The capture of the Gepid provisions came only just in time for the starving women and children (less fortunate, of course, for the Gepids). Thus it was that in August 489, Theodoric crossed the Julian Alps like so many conquerors and usurpers before him and descended into Italia.

However, the war proved tougher than Theodoric had anticipated. Odoacer fought back fiercely, ranging his army to the east of ruined Aquileia, on the banks of the Isonzo. The battle of the same name took place on August 28. Despite owning all the advantages, Odoacer was overcome, and fled the field to take up position on the banks of the Athesis (Adige). The outcome of this second battle of 30 September was also an Ostrogothic victory. Many of the Heruli and Scyrii were slain, and their king hastily retreated to close himself up in Ravenna. Theodoric proceeded to Mediolanum and received the surrender of its garrison in October.

At this point it must have seemed to the Ostrogoths

that they had all but succeeded in their mission, with only a mopping up campaign to pursue. But it was not to be so. Theodoric decided to place his faith in a surrendered Herulian commander named Tufa to organise the siege of Ravenna. This proved to be an unwise move, but in his defence it should be remembered that Theodoric knew little of the territory he was investing, and Ravenna, set in its spreading marshes, had a reputation as a treacherous place to attack. When Tufa began his blockade of the capital, Odoacer came out and persuaded his former subordinate to renew his allegiance. This Tufa did, even going so far as to hand over in chains several Ostrogothic nobles in his company to Odoacer. Their subsequent murder made even more bitter the contest between the two foes.

This reverse placed Theodoric in a difficult position. Mediolanum was sprawling, its defences were weak, and it was too close to Ravenna for comfort. The Ostrogoths, therefore, moved further west to Ticinum, better defended by its position in the crook of the Ticinus and Padus rivers. Here, Theodoric became acquainted with Bishop Epiphanius, and his good relations with the cleric did much to endear the Roman Church to the Ostrogoths. In the spring of 490, the appearance in Liguria of another contender tied up Theodoric's forces. This was Gundobad, king of the Burgundi, who had remained out of Italian politics for some sixteen years since his abandonment of Glycerus that had left the puppet emperor at the mercy of Julius Nepos. Gundobad feared that if Theodoric conquered Italia, he would turn on the Burgundi next.

However, a truce was arranged (which later ripened into an abiding friendship), and the Burgindi returned home. Unfortunately, as a consequence of this diversion, Odoacer issued forth from Ravenna and reoccupied much of the territory he had lost. By the time Theodoric was able to confront him again Herulian forces had assumed a threatening position around Ticinum. The Ostrogoths found themselves besieged, and only the timely arrival of a friendly Visigothic army averted disaster. Another battle was fought along the banks of the Addua (Adda), with great slaughter on both sides, and once again the Gothic cause prevailed.

In 491 Theodoric turned the tables and besieged Odoacer in Ravenna, where he was to remain penned in until 25 February 493. By this time, the state of the defenders was appalling, and stubborn Odoacer was forced to ask for an armistice. Theodoric agreed and John, bishop of Ravenna, arranged the terms, which included Odoacer's young son Thelane (sometimes given as Oclan) being handed over as a hostage.

On 5 March Theodoric triumphantly entered the city that was to become his home for the remaining thirty-three years of his life. Discussion of the settlement terms between the two Teutonic kings continued for several days, with a suggestion that Theodoric might even be prepared to share the throne. But this was certainly no part of the Ostrogoth's real plan. On the evening of 15 March 493, Theodoric invited Odoacer to a banquet. The Herulian king attended with his faithful COMITATUS, but was separated from them in order to take the guest of honour's seat. As he sat, two men came forwards and knelt, making some pretended request, and in so doing each clasped the king's arms. At this, soldiers – previously hidden in side alcoves – rushed up, raised their swords and prepared to strike, but the sight of the now silver-haired Odoacer, defenceless before them, stayed their hands. Greatly angered at this hesitancy, Theodoric himself strode forwards, his own sword unsheathed, and struck such a trenchant blow that he sliced Odoacer from the collar-bone to the loins, crying out his vengeance for those Ostrogoths treacherously delivered by Tufa that the Herulian king had murdered. Theodoric, himself surprised by the force of his blow, laughed and said: 'I think the wretch never had a bone in his body.'

The members of Odoacer's COMITATUS were swiftly dealt with by Theodoric's surrounding guard, while his brother Onoulf was shot down by arrows and killed trying to flee the palace gardens. Odoacer's wife Sunigilda was imprisoned and later died of hunger, and Prince Thelane was sent to Visigothic Gallia, but later executed on the king's orders. In short, the Heruli-Scyrian line was wiped out, and Theodoric had accomplished his ambition. Unlike his predecessor, the Ostrogoth discarded the furs and skins of his Germanic heritage and donned the imperial purple. However, he kept his promise to Zeno, and ruled Italia as a Patrician and MAGISTER MILITUM PRAESENTALIS, giving his allegiance to the emperor, and issuing coins in his own name but with the emperor's portrait on them. Within his own dominions, he styled himself REX GOTHORUM and DUX ITALIAE, and at Ravenna he established a recognisably medieval monarch's court.

To the Italians, who greatly outnumbered the emigrant Ostrogoths and the conquered Teutons, Theodoric's reign brought peace and prosperity to a degree Italia had not seen for ninety years, since before the days of Alaric the Visigoth. They were allowed to live as they had done, on their estates and in their villages, towns and cities. Indeed, there is reason to suppose that no further Italian land was taken for the settlement of the Ostrogoths, since they simply dispossessed the Heruli. Romans were barred from taking military service, but received the civil service as their exclusive preserve, and so good Roman administration continued and even flowered.

Despite beginning in bloodshed, Theodoric's reign was also one of moderation, stained only by the imprisonment and brutal execution by slow garrotting of the MAGISTER OFFICIORUM and philosopher Boethius in 524. His offence was to have defended his friend the ex-Consul Albinus, who had been wrongfully accused of treason. During the course of his confinement, Boethius wrote *The Consolations of Philosophy*, which became so popular in succeeding centuries that it was even translated into Anglo-Saxon vernacular by Alfred the Great. Theodoric was said to have bitterly regretted this action to the end of his days. And when he died on 30 August 526, Italia lost the greatest of her early medieval rulers. Theodoric was interred in his great mausoleum at Ravenna, a half-barbaric, half-classical building that symbolised the life of a man who bestrode two civilisations, and attempted to bring unity to both.

Theodoric's remarkable daughter, Amalasuntha, mother of the child Athalaric. Classically educated and ruthlessly ambitious, she assumed her son's regency the moment her father died.

ATHALARIC

Athalaricus (r.Italia 30/8/526–2/10/534)

Shortly before his death Theodoric, who had no son to follow him, summoned the leading Gothic chieftains and presented to them his eight-year-old grandson Athalaric as their future king. This child was the son of Theodoric's only daughter, Amalasuntha, a woman remarkable not only for her time, but also as a Goth. She had received a classical education, spoke Latin and Greek fluently, and revelled in intellectual pursuits. She also possessed a love of power for its own sake, and displayed a ruthless ambition. When her father died, she automatically assumed her son's regency. Among her first acts, she assured the Romans they would continue to be well treated, and to prove her good intentions the confiscated properties of Boethius were restored to his children. This all boded well, but the male-dominated Gothic society frowned on her – as a ruler her gender was an affront, and the chieftains objected to having their king raised as a classical aesthete when he should be a rowdy warrior. Before a year had passed, a body of influential Gothic nobles insisted on taking Athalaric away from Amalasuntha 's influence. It might be assumed that

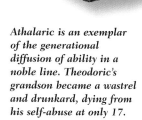

Athalaric is an exemplar of the generational diffusion of ability in a noble line. Theodoric's grandson became a wastrel and drunkard, dying from his self-abuse at only 17.

this meant his removal from the lap of luxury to a harsh regimen, but in fact it was the opposite. His mother's educational methods had been severe, and although the boy was immediately immersed in training to be a warrior-king, and given tough young male companions to accompany him, unfortunately in their lax and unbridled behaviour, they led him into a life of drunken debauchery. Before he was even of an age to begin properly ruling, a life of dissipation killed him in his eighteenth year, on 2 October 534.

By Gothic default, the throne now passed to Theodahad, Theodoric's nephew and the last surviving male member of his line. For Amalasuntha, who had been dispossessed of her authority when Athalaric was removed from her sphere, this presented an opportunity. She had been considering her choices for some

Brigantium (La Coruña)

VASCONI (Basques)

Gallicia

Legio (León)

Asturica Augusta (Astorga)

SUEVI

Portus Cale (Oporto)

Caesa (Zar

Cauca (Coca)

After the loss of Tolosa, Toletum became the Visigothic capital.

Tagus

Toletum (Toledo)

VISIGOTHIC KINGDOM

Olisipo (Lisbon)

Emerita Augusta (Mérida)

Anas (Guadiana)

Baetis (Guadalquivir)

Corduba

Hispalis (Sevilla)

Baetica

Carthago N (Cartag

Gades (Cadiz)

Malaca (Málaga)

time, and had concluded that an alliance with her cousin was the obvious answer. Now here he was, unexpectedly given the crown by her son's demise. However, her future intentions must be placed on hold because from this point on the tale of the Gothic kings of Italy becomes inextricably entwined with that of the Eastern Roman empire. To understand, it is necessary to go back sixteen years in time and move to Constantinople and the events that transpired there following the accession of Justin.

Western Europe in 534, at the outbreak
of the Ostrogothic war of Justinian

SALIAN FRANKS

Treveri (Trier)

Noviodunum (Soissons)

Remi (Reims)

RIPURARIAN FRANKS

Lutetia (Paris)

Durocatalauni (Châlons-sur-Marne)

Argentorate (Strabourg)

Rhenus

Danuvius

THURINGII

Vindobona (Vienna)

Brigetio (Szöny)

HERULI

LANGOBARDI (Lombards)

nabum Aureliani (Orléans)

KINGDOM OF CLOVIS

ALAMANNI

Arar (Saône)

GEPIDAE

Danuvius

Liger (Loire)

Virinum (Maria Saal)

Poetovio (Ptuj)

Dravus

OSTROGOTHIC

Augustonemetum (Clermont-Ferrand)

BURGUNDIAN KINGDOM

Aventicum (Avenches)

Aquileia

Siscia (Sisak)

Savus

SLAVONIANS

Singidunum (Beograd, Belgrade)

The many remaining
Romans, Gauls and Goths
are generally recognised
as being 'Franks'.

Lugdunum

Vienna (Vienne)

Mediolanum (Milan)

Verona

Padus (Po)

Dalmatia

Salonae (Solin)

Praevalitana

Naissus (Nis)

Rhodanus

Valentia (Valence)

Augusta Taurinorum (Turin)

Ticinum (Pavia)

Placentia (Piacenza)

Ravenna

KINGDOM OF

MARE ADRIATICUM (ADRIATIC SEA)

EASTERN ROMAN EMPIRE

Avennio (Avignon)

Arelate (Arles)

Nicaea (Nice)

Sinus Ligusticus

(Ligurian Sea)

Tiberis

Tolosa (Toulouse)

RENEES

Narbo (Narbonne)

Massilia (Marseilles)

ITALIA

Dyrrachium (Durrës, Durazzo)

EPIRUS

Corsica
to Vandal
kingdom

Aleria (Aléria)

Roma

Brundisium (Brindisi)

Apollonia (Pojan)

Tarraco (Tarragona)

Neapolis (Napoli, Naples)

Tarentum (Taranto)

Hydruntum (Otranto)

Sardinia
to Vandal
kingdom

MARE TYRRHENUM (TYRRHENIAN SEA)

Nicopolis

Balearic Islands
to Vandal kingdom

Caralis (Cagliari)

to Vandal
kingdom

Messana (Massina)

Rhegium (Reggio)

MARE IONIUM (IONIAN SEA)

Panormus (Palermo)

Lilybaeum (Marsala)

Sicilia

Agrigentum (Agrigento)

Syracusae (Siracusa)

ennae s)

Hippo Regius (Annaba)

Carthago

Caesarea (Cherchell)

VANDAL KINGDOM

Melita (Malta)

Hadrumetum (Sousse)

MARE INTERNUM

Oea (Tripoli)

Leptis Magna

Berenice (Banghazi)

Ostroogthic kingdom of Italia

Provence, ceded to Visigoths by Odoacer

Frankish kingdoms

Burgundian kingdom

Visigothic kingdom

Suevic kingdom (independent, but Visigothic client)

Vandal kingdom

Eastern Roman empire

capital city

| 0 | 100 | 200 | 300 miles |
| 0 | 100 | 200 | 300 | 400 kilometres |

CHAPTER SEVENTEEN AD 518–565
THE RECOVERY OF THE WEST

JUSTIN
(r.9/7/518–1/8/527)

Through the offices of his clever nephew, Justin was able to heal the long breach between the Churches of the East and West and bring a new era of 'Roman' glory to the Eastern empire.

Justin was born in about 452 in Dardania, a province of the diocese of Daciae. The region had suffered dreadfully at the hands of the Huns during the raids that reached as far south as Thermopylae in 447, and a decade later by the Ostrogoths. For the peasants living there life was harsh and short, and so at some moment during Leo I's reign three strapping Thracian peasant lads, tired of the constant struggle for existence, left home determined to better their lot in the imperial army. Zimarchus, Dityvistus and Justin departed Bederiana, a village some sixty miles south of Naissus and, according to Procopius, they went *'with their cloaks slung over their shoulders…and when they reached the city they had nothing more than the cooked biscuit that they had brought with them from home'*.

The man who was to step into Anastasius's worn shoes was, therefore, hardly imperial material. He never learned to read or write and, like Theodoric, required the use of a stencil to make his signature (though he was less grand, preferring good old wood to gold). Procopius sniffily dismissed Justin by comparing him to a donkey 'inclined to follow the man who pulls the rein, wagging his ears steadily the while'. His wife, Lupicina, was of even humbler origin, a slave who had been the concubine of the man from whom he purchased her. Despite the poor opinion of Procopius, Justin – we hear nothing further of his two companions – had little trouble in taking service and advancing through the ranks. In this he was a beneficiary of Leo's newly organised corps of palace guards,

the EXCUBITORII, and when Anastasius died in 518 Justin had risen to become COMES EXCUBITORUM in recognition of his defeat of Vitalian in 515.

As soon as the SILENTARII had assured themselves that the emperor had indeed expired they summoned the MAGISTER OFFICIORUM Celerianus (Celer), and Justin. Celer commanded the SCHOLAE, but they no longer had a military function; by comparison Justin's EXCUBITORII were tough fighters and this put him in the pivotal position on the morning of 9 July already described at the conclusion of chapter 15. The only other possible claimants were Anastasius's three discarded nephews. The brothers Probus and Pompeius seemed to have no stomach for a contest, and Hypatius – having been ransomed – had been posted to the eastern frontier as MAGISTER MILITUM and was too far away to affect the fast-moving events in the capital. Having been 'persuaded' to accept the purple, Justin offered the troops a donative, the same amount that Leo I in 457 and Anastasius in 491 had distributed: five NOMISMATA[†] and one pound of silver to each soldier. Justin's popularity with the army helped ensure his elevation, but the orthodox population of Constantinople also admired him, for he was a staunch Chalcedonian opposed to the Anastasian party with its monophysite leanings, and he openly championed the Blues against the highly unpopular Greens. The people also felt confident that he was the man to deal with Vitalian, who was sill at liberty and causing trouble along the Illyrian Danuvius.

Vitalian was actually an embarrassment for Justin the Chalcedonian, because on the surface they were of the same religious party, championing the same cause: the ending of the schism between the Churches of East and West. The restoration of Vitalian to the office he had held before falling out with Anastasius was an indispensable part of any reconciliation with the see of Rome, even though on the grounds of piety he hardly deserved the pope's championing his cause. Vitalian himself clearly held that, after the death of Anastasius, he also had a claim on the throne. He would have to be dealt with, but not until after Justin's cherished aim of reconciling the Churches was accomplished. The credit for this most important

---

† (sing. *nomisma*) The Greek word for the Latin gold *solidus* struck at 72 to the Roman pound (4.48gm). In the West it became known as the *besant* (*bisant*, from Byzantine)

achievement of Justin's reign must go to his clever nephew Justinian, who guided his uncle in all things. The regime swiftly moved to re-establish orthodoxy. On 16 July 518 Patriarch John, successor to Timotheus, bowed to the wishes of the people and pronounced anathema against Severus, the hated monophysite bishop of Alexandria. On 1 August Justin sent a letter to Pope Hormisdas (p.514–23), informing him of his accession – and, somewhat disingenuously, his unwillingness to accept the honour. This epistle was actually crafted by Justinian, whose talent for theological disputation had matured nicely at thirty-six. It took more than three months to reach Rome and the pope's cordial reply was not returned until the next year. Hormisdas declined the invitation to go to Constantinople in person, but he sent a delegation to set out Rome's non-negotiable position, which he made clear in his letter. The papal LEGATI had been provided with an INDICULUS, instructions on how far they were to go in negotiation (hardly anywhere, since they had been forbidden to enter into debate), and a LIBELLUS, or formula of submission to be signed by all who wished reunion with the see of Rome.

The embassy arrived at Constantinople on 25 March 519, having been met outside the city by a glittering delegation headed by Justinian himself and a reluctantly restored, eager-eyed Vitalian. On the following day the LEGATI presented their patents to the emperor. Patriarch John, who would not compromise his dignity by attending, like the pope sent his representatives, who pronounced the LIBELLUS true to the facts. At this, the impatient emperor and gathered senators demanded that John accede, which he did with some reluctance on 28 March. As a consequence Acacius (whose excommunication had been pinned to his back), author of the *Henoticon*, was posthumously condemned as a heretic. He was joined by the names of Timothy the Weasel, Paul the Stammerer, and the emperors Zeno and Anastasius. Sadly, Hormisdas insisted on the damnation of the patriarchs Euphemius and Macedonius, neither of whom had veered from orthodoxy, and who had even suffered exile for their beliefs. The accord was an unconditional surrender for Constantinople, but it was a price Justinian was willing to pay for a reunited Church.

The emperor was hailed by his people as their saviour, but Justin knew too well that his nephew had been the real architect of the reconciliation. For the remainder of his life, he was content to be Justinian's mouthpiece, and so it is the nephew and not the uncle who came to symbolise the glory of the new age.

JUSTINIAN

Flavius Petrus Sabbatius Justinianus
(r.co-Augustus 4/4/527;
Augustus 1/8/527–14/11/565)

In 482 Justinian was born in the small hamlet of Tauresium, close to the birthplace of his uncle. After his own assumption of the purple, he was to rebuild his native village and rename it Justiniana Prima, modern Caricin Grad. His mother-tongue was undoubtedly Thracian, but the region had been romanised for a long while and he probably spoke Latin from an early age but not Greek, the language by that time having barely impinged in Thracia. The date of his arrival in Constantinople – presumably at Justin's calling – is unrecorded, but he must have been still a child because, unlike his uncle, Justinian was extremely well educated. His grasp of affairs, his wide knowledge and his culture could not have been acquired anywhere else but in the capital. At the time of Anastasius's death, he was a member of the SCHOLAE, but it seems that he had also been adopted by Justin as his son, at which point he dropped his given names of Flavius Petrus Sabbatius and became simply Justinian.

On his elevation, Justin raised his nephew to the rank of Patrician, and appointed him COMES DOMESTICORUM, a position that gave him access to the highest levels of government. With the papacy and patriarchy once again unified in holy communion, there was no longer a need to put up with the insufferably stubborn Vitalian. Again, it was not the capable and affable soldier Justin who handled the matter, but wily Justinian. Vitalian had been persuaded to return to the capital in order to aid in negotiations with the papal embassy and, in typically Byzantine fashion, his suspicions were lulled by awarding him the rank of MAGISTER MILITUM. He was further gulled with a consulship in 520, and while he was quietly gloating over his success, Justinian had him quietly assassinated in the palace. With him fell Celer of the SCHOLAE, not only a henchman but also, Justinian suspected, another potential trouble-maker with independent imperial ambition.

In the following year Justinian celebrated his own consulship with the most lavish games Constantinople had ever seen. After the parsimony of Anastasius the contrast was dramatic. The spectacle was intended to say to the world that the empire was poised on the

For his regaining the empire's Italian, African and part of the Hispanic territories, and because – as a man of Thracian descent – Justinian spoke Latin not Greek, he is generally regarded as the last of the Roman emperors before the Eastern empire evolved into what is today called the Byzantine state.

The empress Theodora, seen here from a contemporary Byzantine mosaic, was a powerful woman of conflicting character, which was frequently assassinated in prose by the historian Procopius.

threshold of a new golden age, united under God, whose representative on earth was a noble emperor who would restore its lost territories and recapture its prestige in the eyes of all men. Justin, however, was an aged man approaching his seventies and it would be Justinian who would accomplish these noble goals.

Soon after 520 Justinian met his future empress – one of late antiquity's most famous women, although the supremely catty Procopius would have used the word 'infamous' to describe Theodora. The historian revelled in her character-assassination in his *Anecdota* (*see side panel below*). Regardless of Procopius's lurid tales of Theodora's debauchery, she was certainly not the woman a future emperor was supposed to marry. She was one of three daughters of a bear-keeper employed by the Greens at the hippodrome named Acacius. His

Last of the classical historians

Procopius (c.490/510–c.560s) is the most important historian of late antiquity. Not only have his works survived mostly intact, but for the first time since the Severan dynasty, the empire had produced a writer of merit, enormous curiosity and a talent for organising and then telling the events he witnessed. As related in the main text, he became the biographer of the great general Belisarius, and his accounts of the campaigns were variously grouped in *De Belli* (*Wars*). He wrote the 'official' and revoltingly sycophantic *De Aedifici* (*Buildings*, a record of the marvels of Justinian's reconstruction programme) and in his bitter later years *Anecdota* or *Historia Arcana* (*Secret History*). In keeping with most historians, Procopius wrote *Secret History* for posterity. Unlike them, he apparently wrote *only* for posterity, because publication during his lifetime would have led to almost certain disgrace and death. He hated the emperor and empress, painting her as a shameless prostitute and he as a genocidal tyrant. In *Secret History* even his benefactor and patron Belisarius – so praised in *Wars* – comes off badly, his return to Italia in 544 being described as a personal quest for booty. It is a strange and, at points, borderline-pornographic work, never more so than when he deals with Theodora:

'*...although she made use of the three apertures in her body, she was wont to complain that Nature had not provided her with larger openings in her nipples, so that she might have contrived another form of intercourse there.*' And he describes her nightly occupation: '*Many a time she would attend a banquet with ten young men or more, all with a passion for fornication and at the peak of their powers, and would lie with all her companions the whole night long; and when she had reduced them all to exhaustion she would go to their attendants – sometimes as many as thirty of them – and copulate with each in turn; and even then she could not satisfy her lust.*'

A formidable lady indeed. Is there not just a hint of jealousy in the man who would, through his detailed chronicles, make Justinian's general Belisarius world famous?

death left the family destitute and his widow, who was a professional dancer and actress, married another animal-keeper for whom she tried to retain her former husband's position. But when the Greens gave the job to another, the Blues were more accommodating. As a consequence, the young Theodora conceived an adoration of the Blues and an undying hatred of the Greens. While still a child she joined her elder sisters on the stage and developed into an accomplished mime and player of low comedy and farce. As Theodora grew into a beautiful young woman, she became one of the capital's most notorious courtesans, although surely not to the extent described by Procopius. At some point in her twenties she became the mistress of a civil servant and accompanied him to North Africa, where the two fell out. On her return journey – the fee earned, says Procopius, in the only way she knew; on her back – Theodora reached Alexandria, and spent some time there. It appears that she met with many churchmen and underwent a form of religious experience that altered her character, for when she finally returned to Constantinople she was not the same Theodora who had left it. She also brought with her a noticeable leaning towards Alexandrian monophysitism.

Theodora resumed her support of the Blues, and this is how she met Justinian. The beautiful woman, now in her thirties, immediately captivated him and he soon made her his mistress; then announced his intention to marry her. However, there were obstacles in his path. One was the law that forbade the marriage of senators to actresses; another was the opposition of the empress. Justin's low-born wife Lupicina had changed her name to Euphemia on his accession, but she retained her peasant attitude to one of baser extraction than herself, even though she was fond of her nephew, and supported him in most of his wishes. Against Theodora, however, she was implacable, and the marriage was impossible while she lived. But after Euphemia's death in 524, Justin was willing to clear the way. He issued a NOVELLA to extend the one formulated by the emperor Marcian. This allowed a contrite actress who abandoned her profession and should recover her pristine condition to marry whomsoever she chose. With the way clear, Justinian and Theodora were wed in due pomp by the patriarch in St. Sophia. Two years later, on 4 April 527, they were crowned jointly as co-Augustus and Augusta, and when Justin died on the first day of August in the same year, they found themselves the sole rulers of the Eastern Roman empire.

Justinian's law reforms

For all that there were to be glorious achievements during Justinian's reign, it cannot be said that he was a popular ruler. This was partly his own fault in having the tax system streamlined in order to produce the funds necessary for his lavish church-building programme, and in placing in charge a most disliked man known as John of Cappadocia. In part it was because of his court's aloofness from the people, although this was much more due to the empress than the generally affable Justinian. Some care is required here, for it is again Procopius who speaks loudest in description. Her monophysite tendencies were distrusted; she was extravagant, where Justinian was personally frugal; he worked long, hard hours, she slept all afternoon, and then after a night's banqueting until late into the next morning; he was merciful, she delighted in cruelty; he was inclined to talk to anyone, even those of low state, while Theodora surrounded herself with unapproachable magnificence. But at Justinian's door must be laid blame for the great unrest that followed his abandonment of the Blues once he no longer required their political support, and which is related later in this section.

John of Cappadocia was an able administrator, despite a lack of formal education, and Justinian appointed him PRAEFECTUS PRAETORIO in 531. In this capacity he made sweeping changes to the taxation system that fell on both rich and poor alike. He also did much to centralise the bureaucracy and reduce the powers of provincial officials. Unfortunately, although he was personally incorruptible, his morals were of a different standard, and matched his methods when he thought someone was hiding wealth from him. Suspects were frequently subjected to floggings or even torture; he was a glutton and a drunkard who, in his travels through the provinces 'left behind not a single vessel of any kind; neither was there any wife, any virgin or any youth free of defilement'.

Another of Justinian's appointees is associated with similar odium, but also with the emperor's most magnificent monument. The jurist Tribonianus (Tribonian), who became the highest law officer within the government in 529, was a Pamphylian from Side, an unapologetic pagan and completely corrupt in his legal dealings; a judge for whom the outcome of a court case was for sale to the highest bidder. However, he was also beguilingly charming, an expert on the law and astonished everyone who met him with his erudition. Almost a century had passed since publication of the CODEX THEODOSIANUS, but by comparison with Justinian's ambition, the work of Theodosius II represented a relatively simple exercise of compiling edicts. Justinian desired a total overhaul of the law, an entirely new code that would substitute clarity for confusion. Under the leadership of Tribonian, a special commission set about the task with unbelievable speed, and by 8 April 529, in less than fourteen months, produced the new *Codex*. It became the supreme authority for every court in the empire one week later. Tribonian did not stop at this point, and in 530 a second commission began to organise the major writings of all previous jurists, collectively known as the *Digest* or *Pandects*. In everything that was done in the recodifying, Justinian ensured that there was nothing incompatible with Christian teaching.

It would be easy to imagine that by this period pagan worship had been entirely eradicated, but Justinian's legislation gives the lie to this supposition. Pagans were barred from the civil service, and Christians who became apostate were condemned to death, as was any person discovered making a secret sacrifice to the old gods. As had occurred previously, classical scholars were expected to demonstrate their faith through baptism or be denied payment for their work and face banishment. Justinian also acted against Manichaeans and the Samaritans. In the early sixth century the Samaritans – hated by Christians and Jews alike – made up a large number of the farmers in the two northern provinces of Palaestina, with their centre at Neapolis (biblical Shechem). In early 529 Justinian ordered the Samaritan synagogues destroyed, and as a consequence the Samaritans revolted. There were some early Samaritan successes, but eventually imperial forces overwhelmed them, their leader was beheaded, and thousands of his followers sold into slavery. Even two decades later Propcopius commented on the devastation to the Palaestinian economy this disaster caused.

As has been related above, when Justin ascended the throne Anastasius's nephew Hypatius was MAGISTER MILITUM PER ORIENTEM, a peacetime posting that suited his poor abilities, but as war with Persia loomed Justinian replaced him in 529. The new MAGISTER MILITUM was Belisarius, a young Thracian soldier who had shown promising talent in the previous two years while commanding the fortress of Daras, which Anastasius had

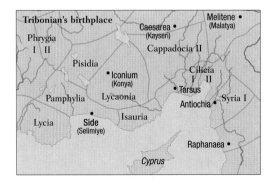

built on the frontier in violation of treaty obligations with the Persians. His appointment proved to be a good decision. In June 530 Belisarius won a spectacular victory at Daras over superior Persian forces. In the following year, however, the Persians fought Belisarius to a draw at Callinicum on the Euphrates and, perhaps as a consequence, he was recalled to Constantinople. Procopius laid the blame for this failure at the feet of the Arabic Ghassanid allies of the empire, but another account by John Malalas, a monophysite Antiochene who chronicled the reigns of Anastasius to Justin II, accused Belisarius of incompetence in his leadership. But Kavadh's death in September brought an unexpected peace to the frontier. His successor, Khosrow III (the first of the Sassanid dynasty), needed to consolidate his authority, for he was not his father's eldest son. In 532, Justinian and Khosrow agreed on the Endless Peace, which proved to be neither. The Romans paid eleven thousand pounds of gold, and within eight years Khosrow was ready to take to the field.

A younger son of Kavadh I, Khosrow III (r.531–579, and Khosrow I of the Sassanid dynasty) is revered by the Persians as the greatest of the Sassanian kings, an avid reformer, and patron of the arts and scholarship. He rebuilt many cities damaged by the Romans, reformed the system of taxation and stimulated commerce. But he was also a despotic ruler, and to the Romans a dedicated foe. By the end of his reign the Sassanian empire stretched from Armenia to the Indus valley.

The rebuilding of Constantinople

The oppression of John of Cappadocia and peculation of Tribonian contributed to a growing expression of grievance among the people, both in the capital and the provinces, but it was the Blues and Greens that brought Constantinople to its knees in 532. Angered by the slights and satires of the Blues, who felt keenly their abandonment by the emperor, Justinian began a repression of both factions, limiting their privileges and meting out sometimes harsh punishment for any excesses. When the two parties clashed in the hippodrome on 10 January he immediately sent in the EXCUBITORII to restore order. Seven ringleaders were subsequently condemned to death, although two, half-dead, were rescued and placed in sanctuary. One was a Blue, the other a Green; enemies with a common cause. Three days later as Justinian took his place in the hippodrome he was greeted by jeers from the Blues and the Greens, but not at each other. For the first time ever, the factions were united in their common anger. The mob shouted 'Nikā! Nikā!' – 'Victory! Victory!' the usual cry of support for their teams – in menacing unison at the emperor instead of raucously at each other as was usually the case.

Attempting to ignore the outcry, Justinian ordered the races to start, but when the spectacle failed to calm the rioters he cancelled the last few contests.

The mob – many of their number swelled by the recent influx of peasants dispossessed of their holdings through taxation – went wild and poured out of the hippodrome, bent on destruction. The home of the PRAEFECTUS URBI was attacked, the guards killed and the building set on fire. In rapid succession the rioters destroyed the PRAETORIUM, setting its prisoners free, the senate house, the Baths of Xeuxippus and Alexander, and even attacked St. Sophia. By the end of the day much of Constantinople was in flames; and so it continued for five terrifying days and nights.

On the second day of chaos, the mob demanded the removal of John of Cappadocia, Tribonian and Eudaimon, the PRAEFECTUS URBI, which in his panic Justinian agreed to. However, this was not enough and there came shouts for a new emperor. First named was Probus, the nephew of Anastasius who had chosen to share the couch with his brother Pompeius during the late-emperor's divination to discover his would-be successor. But Probus was (wisely?) absent from the city, so in frustration the mob burned his house down. On 18 January Justinian attempted what had worked well for Anastasius and faced a packed hippodrome, offering everyone amnesty if they would return to their homes. But the rioters would not have their fury disarmed, and again the emperor was forced to flee to the security of the palace, and there – for a reason of his own, but lost to us – he ordered Hypatius and his cousin Pompeius from his presence.

Both men, understandably alarmed for their safety in the riot-torn streets, slunk to their homes. But Hypatius was recognised and the mob's ringleaders set up a cry for his elevation. Now a man of advanced years and no imperial ambition, Hypatius tried to hide but chased down and taken to Constantine's forum, where – joined by his cousin Pompeius – he was roughly gowned in purple and crowned with a gold circlet. From here the mass of rioters surged towards the hippodrome so that their new emperor could mount to the PULVINATOR and address them before leading them in an assault on the palace.

Procopius says that Justinian now argued for flight to avoid certain death, but that in peremptory tones the empress confronted him. Wearing his official-historian's hat, Procopius paints Theodora in an admirable light he never allowed her in his *Anecdota*. *'If you, my lord, wish to escape, you will have no difficulty in doing so. Here is the sea; there are the ships. But consider first whether, when you reach safety, you will not regret that you did not choose death in preference. As for me, I stand by the ancient saying: "There is no grander sepulchre for any man than the kingship".'* This last line may also be translated as 'kingship is a good shroud' and is a misquotation of the famous maxim that was once ironically thrown at the tyrant of Syracusae, Dionysius the Elder: 'tyranny is a good shroud'. Contemporary readers would have known the quotation Procopius purposely misplaced on Theodora's lips and may have wryly considered the writer's emendation redundant.

Fortunately, due to his recent recall from the eastern frontier, Belisarius was present in the palace. So too was an Illyrian general named Mundus, who was only by chance passing through the capital with a unit of Heruli mercenaries on their way back from the eastern front (he had briefly replaced Belisarius there). These two were the empire's best generals, and although neither commanded a large force they had surprise on their side. They slipped out of the palace grounds and went by separate routes to surround the hippodrome.

At the same time a middle-aged Armenian named Narses, a eunuch who had attained the distinguished rank of grand chamberlain, took a sum of money to try to bribe any Blues he knew to the imperial cause. He also led sufficient men to guard the hippodrome exits and gave them orders to cut down any who tried to escape. Inside, the trained soldiers fell on the screaming mob without mercy. The two generals did their work relentlessly, slaughtering everyone, whether Green or Blue, citizen of Constantinople or newly arrived stranger, so that the arena ran with more blood than it ever had in the days of gladiatorial combat. By the evening, when silence finally settled over the city (and depending on which ancient authority is to be believed), between thirty and fifty thousand lay dead.

Justinian was typically inclined to be merciful towards Hypatius and Pompieus, but Theodora would have none of it. Hypatius is said to have faced his fate with courage, and said to the weeping Pompeius, 'Courage, my cousin, do not demean yourself. We perish as innocent men, for we could not resist the pressure of the people, and it was out of no ill-will to the emperor that we went into the hippodrome.' Justinian gave way to his wife's will, and the next day the two men were executed and their bodies thrown into the sea.

The Nika revolt (as it came to be called) taught Justinian a lesson, Although John of Cappadocia and Tribonian were soon restored to their offices, there was no return to the harsh taxation. In corollary, the emperor's subjects had learned that Justinian was not a ruler to mess with, and returned to normal life much chastened. The wreckage of the city also benefited Justinian's undampened enthusiasm for building, and in fact work began on St. Sophia just over a month after the riots, on 23 February 532, under the personal direction of the emperor. This was to be the third incarnation of the church, and the final one, in the shape we know it today: a massive square rising into a high dome and by far the largest building in Christendom for seven hundred years (until Seville Cathedral). The first had been built in the reign of Constantius and destroyed in the riots following the expulsion of St. John Chrysostom in 404. The second, dedicated by Theodosius II, was constructed along the lines of a standard basilica, and this Justinian must have been planning to rebuild because the revolutionary design of his architects Anthemius of Tralles and Isidore of Miletus could not have been prepared in under six weeks.

Belisarius in Africa

The important events in the remainder of Justinian's reign did not take place in Constantinople; it is two of the men who helped him in his hour of need that now take the concluding parts of this history forwards, in Africa and Italia – Belisarius the general and Narses the eunuch.

Belisarius was born in about 505, which made him barely out of his youth when he was given command in 527 of Daras, the newly built fortress standing on a hill above the once-proud Roman frontier city of Nisibis. And it was here that he made the appointment that was to ensure his fame throughout history, that of Procopius as his jurist and counsellor. It was probably shortly after his recall to Constantinople that Belisarius married Antonina, a close associate of the empress Theodora – albeit the women's relationship was frequently a stormy one. It is a matter for conjecture as to whether Belisarius was recalled to Constantinople in 531 because of his disappointment at Callinicum or because Justinian already had ambitious plans in mind for the young general following his success at Daras. In any event, little time was wasted in mounting a campaign to achieve what Basiliscus had so disastrously failed in: bringing down the North African Vandal kingdom and the restoration of its provinces to the empire.

The scheme had been brewing in Justinian's mind for some time, certainly since King Hilderic, son of Huneric and Eudocia, the daughter of Valentinian III, had been overthrown by his cousin Gelimer in June 531. Justinian had been engaged in friendly correspondence with Hilderic, who as a Roman on his mother's side espoused her orthodox Catholicism rather than the Arian creed of his father, and the emperor felt bound to insist on the Vandal king's restoration. Gelimer's response was not calculated to please Justinian. There was nothing more desirable, he told 'King Justinian', than that a monarch should mind his own business. The Endless Peace signed with Persia left Justinian free to invade Africa.

His closest advisors met this proposal with a cool reaction, especially John of Cappadocia, who cautioned against the waste, the enormous distance, either by land or sea, and the time two-way messages would take. But Gelimer's insult rankled; and during the summer of 533 the expedition set out, with Antonina at Belisarius's side (he was to take her with him on every campaign).

The army consisted of ten thousand infantry and five thousand cavalry, composed of regular Romano-Byzantine soldiers and a larger portion of FOEDERATI, mostly Huns, but also some Heruli. This force sailed in a fleet of five hundred transports manned by up to twenty thousand sailors, and accompanied by ninety-two DROMONES. The DROMON was the smallest ship of the Byzantine navy, light and built for speed, carrying a rowing crew of twenty and covered over to protect against missiles.

The army's general enthusiasm was dampened by an incident that Belisarius turned to his advantage. While temporarily becalmed in the Hellespontus he was obliged to hang two drunken Huns for murdering a comrade. Procopius noted that Huns were the most intemperate drinkers in the world and such an event was natural in their order of things, but Belisarius told the gathered soldiers that no man, whether Roman or FOEDERATI, should be allowed 'to plead drunkenness as an excuse for his crime, which was rather its exaggeration'. And he went on to berate them that they were a Christian army on a holy mission and should behave appropriately. Seeing his ferocious determination, even the Huns quieted down, but Belisarius was to remain rightly suspicious of their loyalty.

A second mishap befell off the Peleponnessus, when some five hundred soldiers fell seriously ill with food poisoning caused by eating rotten biscuit. Apparently John of Cappadocia, exercising imprudent economies, had sent the dough not to a proper bakery but to the furnace heating the baths of Achilles, where it had come out only half-baked. The outbreak forced

Hilderic (above) was the grandson of Gaiseric, but adhered to the orthodox Christian creed of his mother, the Roman princess Eudocia. Under his father Huneric and his own reign, the Vandals had lost much of their prowess in arms, and Hilderic fell foul of a coup by his cousin Gelimer (below), who intended war against Justinian.

a delay for reprovisioning, and then the fleet sailed on to Catana (Catania). Sicily was in Ostrogothic hands, and officially still friendly to Constantinople, so it made a useful base for gathering intelligence on the enemy's dispositions. It was quickly established through sailors recently returned from Carthago that Gelimer was completely unaware of the approaching fleet. In fact the Vandals were engaged in putting down an uprising in Sardinia, that had been fomented by AGENTES of Justinian to create a diversion. Belisarius gave the order to sail at once, and his army landed safely on the African coast to the north of Hadrumetum. From here the legions began a march of one hundred and forty miles towards the Vandal capital. But hindered by the baggage train, the five-day journey took twice that time, and the Romans had only reached AD DECIMUM (the tenth milestone from Carthago) when, on 13 September Gelimer struck.

The Vandal usurper had acted quickly as soon as the Roman ships had been spotted offshore keeping pace with the imperial army. His fleet and a part of his army were indeed in Sardinia, but he still had plenty of men to mount a dangerous ambush. He paused only to issue orders for the murder of Hilderic and his family, and then outlined his plan. His brother Ammatas was to attack the Roman vanguard, while his nephew Gibamund struck at the centre, and he himself dealt with the rear. Gelimer's strategy was admirable, and should have succeeded, but these were not the Vandals of Gaiseric. Grown lazy and complacent in the peaceful years of good living, the warriors were more likely to be found around martial campfires swapping stories of old rather than in training for war. The plan required careful timing, and Gelimer's communications failed him. Ammatas attacked too soon, and was killed by the prepared Roman foot. Gibamund hesitated to support Ammatas, and instead of advancing drew his men up in line of battle, at which point the Roman cavalry – mostly terrifying Huns – swept through their ranks. The Vandals turned and ran for their lives.

Gelimer fared little better. After an initial success, in which he managed to separate Belisarius and his staff officers from the bulk of the army, the Vandal king came across his brother's body. The sight unmanned him, and he refused to move further until the corpse had been safely removed from the field. Belisarius recognised the opportunity, and counterattacked, scattering the Vandal host in all directions. Gelimer fled with the remnant of his forces west into the Numidian desert, and on 15 September 532 Belisarius victoriously entered Carthago.

There was no sack or pillage. The army was under strict orders from Justinian to respect the property and lives of what were, even after a century of barbarian occupation, still Roman citizens. The emperor's proclamation, handed out at all the towns and villages on the march, most of whose inhabitants had joyously welcomed the invaders, stated that the army was not making war on civilians, but only removing the usurper Gelimer. But Gelimer was not finished. From his temporary base at Bulla Regia in Numidia, some hundred miles west of Carthago, he summoned back to Africa Tzazo, his surviving brother, from his command of the Sardinian expedition. Gelimer spent the few weeks waiting for Tzazo's arrival recruiting from among the local Berber tribes, offering a bounty for every Roman head taken. And so by mid-December he was ready to go back on the offensive.

When he was newly in occupation of the province, Gaiseric had ordered the tearing down of all town and city walls in order to discourage civil insurrection and make potential armed access for his warriors easier. While this policy had been a great aid to Belisarius during his advance, it also meant that Carthago was not easily defended in a siege. He also had a real cause to suspect the loyalty of the Huns under his command. It was known by his AGENTES that the Huns had been approached by Gelimer's spies making appeals to their common Arian bond. If they were to desert, Belisarius preferred that they did so in the open, rather than catch him out behind flimsy siege defences. He, too, gave the order to march, and the Romans met the Vandal army at Tricamarum, thirty miles west of Carthago, on 15 December.

This was no ambush situation as had been the case at AD DECIMUM, but a prepared battle on open ground, entirely suited to Roman arms and tactics. Nevertheless, there was fierce hand-to-hand combat amid the Vandals' ranks after repeated Roman charges; and in the fighting Tzazo was slain at the side of his brother. Once again Gelimer hesitated. Alarmed at his indecision, his men began to fall back, and at this point the Huns – who, as Belisarius had suspected, had been waiting to see which way the fortunes of war went – spurred their horses into a mighty charge, and swept away the Vandals. Belisarius advanced to Hippo Regius (Gaiseric's first capital) and seized the royal treasure stored there, before returning to Carthago. Gelimer escaped to wander the desultory Numidian hills for several months before surrendering. It is said that when he was brought into Belisarius's presence, he was openly laughing, and it was suspected that his sufferings had unhinged his mind. The war was over,

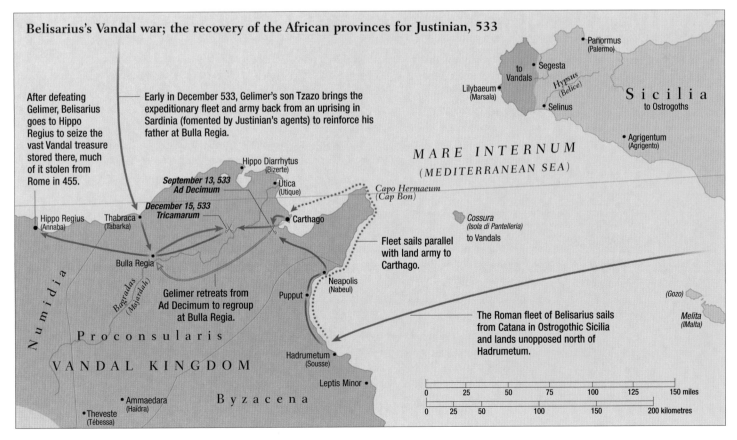

Belisarius's Vandal war; the recovery of the African provinces for Justinian, 533

After defeating Gelimer, Belisarius goes to Hippo Regius to seize the vast Vandal treasure stored there, much of it stolen from Rome in 455.

Early in December 533, Gelimer's son Tzazo brings the expeditionary fleet and army back from an uprising in Sardinia (fomented by Justinian's agents) to reinforce his father at Bulla Regia.

Panormus (Palermo)

Segesta

to Vandals

Lilybaeum (Marsala)

Hypsus (Belice)

Selinus

S i c i l i a
to Ostrogoths

Agrigentum (Agrigento)

MARE INTERNUM
(MEDITERRANEAN SEA)

Hippo Diarrhytus (Bizerte)

September 13, 533
Ad Decimum

Utica (Utique)

Capo Hermaeum (Cap Bon)

Cossura (Isola di Pantelleria)
to Vandals

Hippo Regius (Annaba)

Thabraca (Tabarka)

December 15, 533
Tricamarum

Carthago

Fleet sails parallel with land army to Carthago.

Bulla Regia

Bagradas (Majardah)

Gelimer retreats from Ad Decimum to regroup at Bulla Regia.

Pupput

Neapolis (Nabeul)

(Gozo)

Melita (Malta)

N u m i d i a

P r o c o n s u l a r i s

VANDAL KINGDOM

Hadrumetum (Sousse)

The Roman fleet of Belisarius sails from Catana in Ostrogothic Sicily and lands unopposed north of Hadrumetum.

Leptis Minor

Ammaedara (Haidra)

B y z a c e n a

Theveste (Tébessa)

0 25 50 75 100 125 150 miles

0 25 50 100 150 200 kilometres

although operations along the Mauretanian coast were to continue for a further seven years.

In the summer of 533, Belisarius left the continued pacification of Africa in the hands of the PRAEFECTUS PRAETORIO, although a mutiny was to force his temporary return two years later. In spite of this setback, the pacification of Africa was successful and returned it to imperial administration, also making it possible to contemplate the recapture of Hispania (*see side panel below*).

Justinian wanted his general back in Constantinople to brief him on even more ambitious scheme. But first the emperor, who loved Roman custom, wanted to award Belisarius a triumph. The last non-imperial recipient of this honour had been Lucius Cornelius Balbus in 19 BC, and in recent centuries the practice had almost died out, even for emperors. And so, for the massed and cheering spectators, it must have been an awesome sight to see this ancient ceremony enacted in the hippodrome, scene of so much recent misery. Even so, to emphasise his non-imperial status, Belisarius entered the stadium on foot rather than riding in the IMPERATOR's traditional QUADRIGA, and advanced to bow before Justinian and Theodora alongside the most important of his prisoners, Gelimer. The occasion was enhanced by the glittering array of Vandal treasures, paraded in a succession of groaning wagons. Among the booty was the *menorah*, the sacred seven-branched candelabra of the Jews that Titus had removed from the ruins of the Temple of Solomon in Jerusalem in AD 71, and which in turn Gaiseric had stolen from Rome in 455. Later, Justinian returned it to the small Jewish community which had reformed in Jerusalem, after he had been assured by the Jews in Constantinople that bad luck would follow its detention. Gelimer was pardoned, and set free with his family to settle in Galatia, but his fellow-prisoners were sent to the eastern front, there to survive in the wars as best they might.

The retaking of Africa was only a prelude to the much greater task of restoring the Western Roman empire, a dream of Justinian's from the moment he gained power. It was, however, a distinctly different prospect from the African campaign. Italia was, in theory, a vassal of the empire, and while it was Arian in creed, the Ostrogothic kings had done nothing to suppress the orthodoxy of the papal see, on the contrary Theodoric had done much to strengthen its position. Julian was also aware that the Roman citizens of Italia had enjoyed a settled and prosperous period under Theodoric, and might well resent an intrusion from the East, and especially rail at the increased tax burden that would inevitably follow.

However, after Theodoric's death, the loyalty of the Ostrogothic line was uncertain, and Justinian's advisors counselled that he would not be able to keep Africa while the lands of Sicilia and Italia were in alien, possibly in the future hostile, hands. It was clear that the Ostrogothic kingdom must go, but it was also obvious that Justinian needed a proper, legal pretext for invasion if he was to gain the support of the Roman populace. Fortunately, he was given one.

Portraits depicting Belisarius are rare, but this coin shows Justinian on the obverse (top) and the mounted Belisarius on the reverse, being guided by an angel in his holy mission of reconquest.

DUE TO THE IMPETUS given by Belisarius's effective North African campaign, Justinian was soon able to boast that one again the empire extended from Euxinus to Atlanticus. His dominions by the end of his reign included the recovered provinces of Mauretania (Tingitana and Caesariensis), Numidia, Africa Proconsularis, Tripolitania, the Balearic islands, Corsica, Sardinia and Sicilia. A decade later he was able to complete the boast by a reconquest of Hispania, although really only in part and only nominally.

For the Visigothic masters of Hispania, the first warning of danger came with Belisarius's recovery of Vandal North Africa and the eviction of a Visigothic garrison from Septem (Ceuta) in 534. King Theodis disastrously attempted to recapture it in 547, and died soon after at the hands of an assassin. In 551 Justinian was presented with an opportunity to strike at Hispania itself. A rebellion of Roman citizens at Corduba, and a simultaneous mutiny by Athnagild against his kinsman King Agila, led to a joint call for Byzantine help. Justinian ordered Narses, then commanding the Italian recovery, to detach a small force and send it to Hispania. With the Visigothic army divided in loyalty between the king and Athnagild, the Romans met with almost no resistance and soon occupied the whole area south of a line between Valentia-Corduba-Gades.

THEODAHAD
Theodahadus (r.Italia 2/10/534–August 536)

At the end of chapter 16, Athalaric, the youthful but entirely debauched grandson of Theodoric, had just died on 2 October 534, with the throne passing to Theodoric's nephew Theodahad, the last surviving male of his line. Some years before this point, Athalaric's mother Amalasuntha, having been removed from her son's regency by Gothic chieftains and fearing her exposed position, had entered into secret correspondence with Justinian. Aware how improved his cause would be among the Goths in Italia with the daughter of the great Theodoric at his side, the emperor greeted her advances cordially, and assured her that he was preparing a palace for her at Dyrrachium, ready for her to take asylum there. But before any further plans could be advanced, inconvenient Athalaric expired of excess.

The new king was not popular. His avarice and suspect dealings had made him the largest land-owner in Italia. Theodahad had created an enormous LATI-FUNDIUM from land in much of Tuscia and had extensive holdings in the Campania, to the very edge of Rome. As Procopius wryly put it: 'to have neighbours of any kind seemed a sad misfortune.' But for Theodahad ruling held little interest; he preferred the scholarly studies of a landed noble amid his vast solitude. Theodahad had also been in communication with Justinian, and also secretly for – as Amalasuntha did – he feared the animosity of the patriotic Gothic party in Ravenna. This, however, she could not have known when she saw her opportunity to retrieve some of that power lost to her. Theodahad received

Amalasuntha's approach favourably, and agreed to her suggestion that they should share the throne equally. In that way Theodahad could enjoy the privileges of kingship without the burden of its responsibilities, while she managed the government from Ravenna. She had no wish to marry him (anyway, he already was), it was to be simply a joint-monarchy. For a short while, therefore, Amalasuntha felt that she did not need Justinian's protection, which effectively put on hold his ambitions in Italia… however, not entirely.

Soon after Amalasuntha's pact with Theodahad, an embassy from Constantinople arrived at Ravenna with a complaint from Justinian regarding Lilybaeum. This western-most town in Sicilia had belonged to the Vandals as a part of that treaty signed between Gaiseric in his last year and Orestes, which in turn meant the Goths held almost all of the island. But when the Romans claimed Lilybaeum as part of their conquest of Gelimer's dominions, the Goths refused to yield it. There were a few other items of complaint, but none of significance, and indeed the question of Lilybaeum itself was of no real consequence. In public, Amalasuntha regally rejected Justinian's claim to the tiny promontory, while in private she entertained his ambassador in secret discussions that dealt with her handing over the whole of Sicilia and Italia.

How this intriguing situation might have developed, will never be known, for almost as soon as the proclamation of joint-monarchy had been announced Theodahad began to regret a decision that, with hindsight, appeared to have been made in haste. The restored Amalasuntha had many enemies in high places at Ravenna, and they were only too happy to enter into a plot with the king to remove the queen. In April 535 she was taken and imprisoned in a fortress on an island in the lake of Volsiniensis (Bolsena). On hearing of Amalasuntha's imprisonment, Justinian had a message passed on to Theodahad warning that if the queen were not immediately freed and restored to her throne, he would be forced to intervene (*see side panel*). The warning came too late. Shortly after her

Theodahad was to prove a poor ruler of Italia, more concerned with grabbing land for himself than with sound government. And by issuing coins with only his portrait on them in contravention of the imperial demand that Justinian should feature, he made war with the Eastern empire inevitable.

PROCOPIUS INFORMS us in *Anecdota* that the empress Theodora sent a second message to Theodahad telling him not to worry, that her husband was only posturing for form's sake, and that he could do with impunity what he liked with his prisoner. This, says the historian, was purely jealousy on Theodora's part; she had no wish to see a barbarian queen arriving in Constantinople to steal her glory. It could also, of course, be interpreted as the empress acting as an *agent provocateur*, to goad Theodahad into rash action and thus prompting a war.

incarceration, Amalasuntha was strangled to death in her bath, and although Theodahad vigorously disclaimed responsibility, the gifts he gave to her murderers were sufficient to damn him.

By the murder of his cousin, Theodahad had played straight into Justinian's hands, and given him the pretext he had been looking for. Mundus was made MAGISTER MILITUM PER ILLYRICUM and sent to occupy Dalmatia, which the Ostrogothic kingdom had inherited from Odoacer's invasion after the death of Julius Nepos. Belisarius, fresh from his triumph, was dispatched in 535 to Sicilia with an army of seven thousand five hundred men — a number hardly more than one of Julius Caesar's thirty legions.

Its composition is uncertain, but there were troops drawn from confederate Huns, Isaurians, some Berber Moors, and some four thousand drawn from the medley of Teutonic and Slavonic peoples now roaming the southern shores of the Danuvius. As Thomas Hodgkin points out in *The Barbarian Invasions of the Roman Empire*, it may have called itself Roman, its enemies may have derided it as Greek, but it was essentially a barbarian band. However, it fared well in Sicilia, where the Gothic forces, probably few in number, were easily overwhelmed. But before Belisarius could cross to the mainland, a mutiny in the army occupying Africa commanded his attention for several weeks. On his return, he found the temper of his own troops uncertain, and with winter approaching, decided to remain for the rest of the year in Sicilia raising his men's morale.

In Dalmatia events had not turned out as happily for Mundus. He encountered much stiffer resistance that had been anticipated, and after a few weeks the general was killed in battle. Meanwhile, Theodahad, panicked by Belisarius's swift reduction of Sicilia, had entered into private negotiations with Justinian. But the emperor's terms were humiliating: an annual tribute in gold and fighting men; the removal of the king's right to sentence senators or to enoble any citizen without Justinian's approval; and that Justinian's statues or images on coins should take preference over his own. With an uncharacteristic burst of courage, Theodahad rejected the terms, and in spite issued coins with only his own portrait on them. This petulant display soon crumbled, however, when Belisarius crossed the strait from Sicilia and landed his army at Rhegium (Reggio) in early May 536.

From this beach-head, meeting no resistance, Belisarius was soon outside Neapolis, whose citizens refused him entry and defended themselves for three weeks. The city fell after a band of Isaurians crawled

Belisarius (shown here on his own) appears in a mosaic from San Vitale in Ravenna standing next to his emperor Justinian. A copy of a contemporary mosaic first created in Constantinople, but since lost, the likeness is believed – within the iconic tradition – to be reasonably accurate.

along an ancient conduit that had been discovered, and attacked the defenders from the rear. Neapolis was subjected to days of pillage, rape and slaughter by the semi-savage barbarian horde; but Belisarius had fairly warned the Neapolitans in advance that resistance would certainly lead them to this fate.

As has been noted previously, Gothic interest in the south of Italia was scant, and while the advance of Belisarius would have caused alarm, it hardly harmed the Goths. But the fall of Neapolis was a different matter. The Roman army was now on the edge of the Campania, where even the king held lands. Inevitably, blame for the disaster was placed on Theodhad's shoulders, and the never-popular monarch was excoriated for failing to send a relief army to Neapolis. It was whispered at large that he was, in fact, in league with Belisarius to betray Italia, a reasonable assumption considering his secret dealings with Justinian.

A conclave of Gothic leaders met in assembly near Terracina, and declared Theodahad deposed. Sensing the end was near, Theodahad fled for the dubious sanctuary of ravenna. Since there was no surviving male of Theodoric's line – only Matasuntha, the young sister of Athalaric, remained – they raised up an elderly general named Witigis. The new king's first command was to execute the old one, and this task was eagerly taken up by a vengeful Goth named Optaris, whom Theodahad had at some point harmed through his venal dealings. Optaris caught up with his victim near Ravenna. He threw Theodahad to the ground and sliced open his throat.

WITIGIS
(r.Italia August 536–540)

Fearing that Belisarius was preparing to march on Rome, the second act of Witigis should have been to organise the city's defences. Instead, he announced a retreat to Ravenna in order to consolidate his forces and draw up a strategy. He had a second reason: the divorce of his wife so he could marry Matasuntha. To be fair, there were some sound reasons for this match. Witigis was of humble origins, and a royal marriage could only improve his status. Then there was the danger that if Matasuntha married another suitor, her husband would become a dynastic threat. Finally, Witigis hoped that with the granddaughter of Theodoric on the throne, Justinian could be persuaded to desist in his intervention in Italia. Alas, in the last he was to be disappointed, and the hasty divorce and marriage did more to

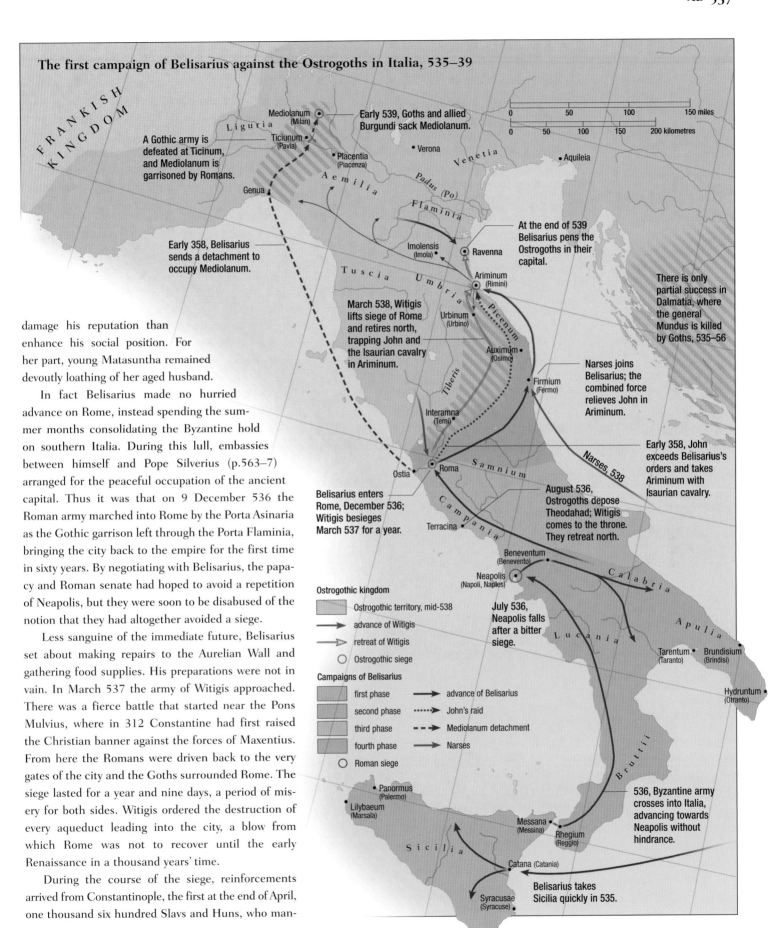

The first campaign of Belisarius against the Ostrogoths in Italia, 535–39

Early 539, Goths and allied Burgundi sack Mediolanum.

A Gothic army is defeated at Ticinum, and Mediolanum is garrisoned by Romans.

Early 358, Belisarius sends a detachment to occupy Mediolanum.

At the end of 539 Belisarius pens the Ostrogoths in their capital.

There is only partial success in Dalmatia, where the general Mundus is killed by Goths, 535–56

March 538, Witigis lifts siege of Rome and retires north, trapping John and the Isaurian cavalry in Ariminum.

Narses joins Belisarius; the combined force relieves John in Ariminum.

Early 358, John exceeds Belisarius's orders and takes Ariminum with Isaurian cavalry.

Belisarius enters Rome, December 536; Witigis besieges March 537 for a year.

August 536, Ostrogoths depose Theodahad; Witigis comes to the throne. They retreat north.

July 536, Neapolis falls after a bitter siege.

Ostrogothic kingdom

- Ostrogothic territory, mid-538
- advance of Witigis
- retreat of Witigis
- Ostrogothic siege

Campaigns of Belisarius

- first phase
- second phase
- third phase
- fourth phase
- Roman siege
- advance of Belisarius
- John's raid
- Mediolanum detachment
- Narses

536, Byzantine army crosses into Italia, advancing towards Neapolis without hindrance.

Belisarius takes Sicilia quickly in 535.

FRANKISH KINGDOM

Liguria
Mediolanum (Milan)
Ticinum (Pavia)
Placentia (Piacenza)
Verona
Aquileia
Venetia
Genua
Aemilia
Padus (Po)
Flaminia
Imolensis (Imola)
Ravenna
Ariminum (Rimini)
Tuscia
Umbria
Urbinum (Urbino)
Picenum
Auximum (Osimo)
Firmium (Fermo)
Interamna (Terni)
Tiberis
Narses, 538
Ostia
Roma
Samnium
Campania
Terracina
Beneventum (Benevento)
Calabria
Neapolis (Napoli, Naples)
Apulia
Lucania
Tarentum (Taranto)
Brundisium (Brindisi)
Hydruntum (Otranto)
Bruttii
Panormus (Palermo)
Lilybaeum (Marsala)
Messana (Messina)
Rhegium (Reggio)
Sicilia
Catana (Catania)
Syracusae (Syracuse)

damage his reputation than enhance his social position. For her part, young Matasuntha remained devoutly loathing of her aged husband.

In fact Belisarius made no hurried advance on Rome, instead spending the summer months consolidating the Byzantine hold on southern Italy. During this lull, embassies between himself and Pope Silverius (p.563–7) arranged for the peaceful occupation of the ancient capital. Thus it was that on 9 December 536 the Roman army marched into Rome by the Porta Asinaria as the Gothic garrison left through the Porta Flaminia, bringing the city back to the empire for the first time in sixty years. By negotiating with Belisarius, the papacy and Roman senate had hoped to avoid a repetition of Neapolis, but they were soon to be disabused of the notion that they had altogether avoided a siege.

Less sanguine of the immediate future, Belisarius set about making repairs to the Aurelian Wall and gathering food supplies. His preparations were not in vain. In March 537 the army of Witigis approached. There was a fierce battle that started near the Pons Mulvius, where in 312 Constantine had first raised the Christian banner against the forces of Maxentius. From here the Romans were driven back to the very gates of the city and the Goths surrounded Rome. The siege lasted for a year and nine days, a period of misery for both sides. Witigis ordered the destruction of every aqueduct leading into the city, a blow from which Rome was not to recover until the early Renaissance in a thousand years' time.

During the course of the siege, reinforcements arrived from Constantinople, the first at the end of April, one thousand six hundred Slavs and Huns, who managed to break through the Gothic lines. In November five thousand more infantry and cavalry arrived under the command of John, nephew of the rebellious Vitalian who had so plagued Anastasius. By this stage, the plight of the besiegers was as bad as that of the besieged; starving within, dying of disease without. With his increased garrison, Belisarius was able to order several sorties and, defeated in various encounters, the Goths finally asked for a three-month truce, during which they made peace overtures. Against his better judgement, Belisarius forwarded these to Justinian, but loathe to give Witigis time to recoup, he commanded John to harry the eastern slopes of the Appenines. However, John exceeded his orders, passing by Auximum (Osimo) and Urbinum (Urbino) to seize Ariminum (Rimini), only thirty-three miles from Ravenna, and occupied the city with his two thousand Isaurian cavalry.

John's dashing exploit, his sudden proximity to the capital, not to mention reports of his handsomeness, excited Matasuntha's interest, and she sent him an appeal to 'rescue' her. On learning that the enemy was now in control of an important centre two hundred miles to his rear, and that his wife was proposing to betray Ravenna to John, Witigis lifted the siege of Rome. The retreat began in the middle of March 538, but the Goths were not left alone. Belisarius led his men out of the gates and fell on their rearguard, leaving several hundred dead on the banks of the Tiberis or swept away in the spring flood.

Belisarius's main concern now was rash John, exposed in Ariminum, with the Gothic army falling back towards him. Two trusted officers were dispatched to order his return, but with a rebellious streak no doubt inherited from his uncle Vitalian, he refused. Suddenly, Witigis appeared with his retreating army and surrounded the town. John's position was perilous for, unlike Rome, Ariminum was not prepared. Belisarius, furious at his subordinate's disobedience, deliberated whether to leave him to his fate, though he could ill-afford to lose the two thousand Isaurians. At this critical point the eunuch Narses arrived from the East with an imperial army of five thousand men to join Belisarius at Firmium (Fermo). Eventually, Narses, who 'loved him [John] above all other men' according to Procopius, persuaded the general to go to John's rescue.

A superb strategist, Belisarius planned a two-pronged amphibious assault. Almost all his forces approached by sea, while a smaller land unit contrived to persuade the Goths outside Ariminum that they confronted a far larger army than really existed. The Goths were put to flight, and the Isaurians saved.

A coin of Theodebert, the Frankish king who sent troops to aid the Goths against Belisarius, shows how widespread the Byzantine stylistic influence was at the time among the barbarian states of western Europe.

John, however, ignored Belisarius, refused to thank him, and heaped praise instead on Narses.

Because of John's ingratitude and Narses' equanimity in accepting the undeserved honour, the mopping up operation began amid a new distrust among the commanders. At first things proceeded smoothly, the Romans taking Urbinum, Imolensis (Imola), and the province of Aemilia. But then came a disaster that arose entirely from the bad feeling between Narses and Belisarius. In the previous spring Belisarius had taken an uncharacteristically dangerous gamble in sending one thousand troops to Mediolanum at the request of the archbishop to save the city from Gothic Arianism. This small detachment had gone by sea to Genua and then crossed the Padus to defeat a Gothic army outside Ticinum. Several grateful towns opened their gates to the Byzantines, each requiring a small garrison to remain behind, so that on reaching Mediolanum, there were only three hundred men left.

When he heard of Mediolanum's betrayal Witigis reacted to this bitter blow by sending an army under the command of his nephew Uraias to recover it. At the same time Theodebert, the Frankish king, sent some ten thousand Burgundi to help the Goths. And so by mid-summer 538, Mediolanum – a city far larger than Rome – was surrounded by a massive enemy force, and defended by very few soldiers. Unaware of the Frankish intervention, Belisarius ordered north a detachment that he believed to be strong enough to relieve the city from the Goths, but when its commanders saw the swollen numbers of the enemy they refused to advance further without support from John and Justin, the recently arrived MAGISTER MILITUM PER ILLYRICUM and Mundus's successor. Belisarius issued the command only to be flatly refused by both men, who insisted that they would only take orders from Narses.

Even now Belisarius kept his temper, and sent messages to Narses, but by the time the eunuch confirmed the order in the first months of 539, Mediolanum had fallen. Uraias mercifully offered quarter to the small Byzantine garrison, but not to the treacherous citizens who had invited in the enemy. Every man in the city was put to the sword, perhaps as many as three hundred thousand were slaughtered, the women were taken into slavery or given as gifts to the Burgundi soldiers; and then the Goths sacked the city. Mediolanum was the largest, most populous, and most prosperous city in Italia, but by the time the Goths finished not one stone was left standing on another. The once-imperial tetrarchic capital had been erased from the face of the earth.

It was a ruinous disaster, but for Belisarius some good came of it. Using her influence with Theodora, Antonina sent letters that persuaded the emperor of her husband's innocence in the matter, and Justinian recalled Narses. The two thousand Heruli he had brought with him also left, refusing to serve under any other, but their defection was a price Belisarius was willing to pay to be back in sole command of the campaign again. He was now free again to concentrate his forces for the final push on Ravenna. Soon, the imperial fleet blockaded the seaward approach and his infantry surrounded the land walls. The position for Witigis was fearful. And then one day towards the end of 539 an embassy arrived from Constantinople offering the Goths a treaty. In return for capitulation they would be allowed to keep half their treasure and all of Italia north of the Padus.

This astonishing turn of events infuriated Belisarius, within inches of total victory, but its cause lay far to the east. Justinian had become increasingly concerned at the warlike preparations of the Persians. He could not afford to take risks with Khosrow, even if that meant abandoning the completion of his Italian dream. Justinian needed Belisarius on the eastern front. Witigis could not believe his luck, but he made a fatal error. Uncertain that the offer was not just a shabby diplomatic trick, he insisted that the treaty would only be valid if it was also signed by Belisarius as well as the imperial ambassadors. Smiling grimly, Belisarius refused to sign, unless he was so ordered to do by his emperor. The general had bought time.

During the stalemate that followed, Witigis made an extraordinary proposal: he would surrender his crown and throne if Belisarius would proclaim himself emperor of the West. How many soldiers during the course of this history would have given their right hands for such an open offer? Had there yet been such a general as this, having accomplished so much, who had not dreamed of claiming the purple in his own name? Belisarius did not disappoint. First dispatching those of his staff he distrusted (the party of John and Narses) to go foraging, he accepted the offer, and the Goths flung open Ravenna's gates to receive their new emperor. It was an astonishing sight. Row upon row of tall and martial Goths lined the streets, far outnumbering their Roman conquerors, all bowing before Belisarius. Procopius noted that their women failed to be impressed, either by the Romans or the spirit of their own men: '*Are these the mighty heroes,*' they cried, '*with whose deeds you have terrified us? Are these your conquerors? We can no longer call you men, who have been beaten by champions such as these!*'

At what point the Goths realised they had been cheated is not recorded. Belisarius probably kept the deceit going long enough that there was no chance for them to rally and fight back. Perhaps when they saw all – rather than half – of the royal treasure being loaded onto Byzantine ships ready for transport to Constantinople it sank in how low their state had fallen. It certainly must have done when King Witigis and the chief nobles were taken aboard loaded down in chains. Procopius insisted that Belisarius never for a moment considered taking Witigis at his word for 'he hated the name of usurper with perfect hatred'. And yet if that is the case, it might be prudent to wonder why Belisarius sent away those disaffected officers if he was only playing with the Goths?

HILDEBAD
Ildibadus (r.Italia 540–May 541)

ERARIC
Erarichus (r.Italia May–October 541)

TOTILA
Baduila (r.Italia October 541–552)

TEIAS
Theia (r.Italia 552)

Belisarius might have reasonably hoped for a second triumph for his even greater achievement than the reconquest of Africa, but it was not to be. For one, Justinian was growing jealous of his successful general and disinclined to heap more honours on him; for another, the situation on the eastern front was desperate, and his skills were required there urgently. The events of the Persian war are not really the concern of this history, but it is worth relating them briefly for the purpose of continuity. In March 540 Khosrow crossed the imperial frontier and captured Sura on the Euphrates. From there he marched on Antiochia, leaving burning towns behind him, and sacked the great Syrian city.

Justinian accepted a humiliating peace, but Khosrow returned the next year, annexing Lazica, a poor client kingdom, but strategically placed on the Pontus Euxinus, and a direct threat to Constantinople. Belisarius was sent to contend with the Persians, but it was a lacklustre campaign, ended by an epidemic of dysentery among the troops. The campaign of 542 was

Despite his youth, Totila was able to reunite all Italia, Romans and Germans, in a last blaze of Romanesque glory against the tide of Constantinople.

equally frustrated, when both sides were hit by a bubonic plague that rapidly spread to all parts of the empire, killing tens of thousands. The emperor himself was stricken, and for weeks his life hung in the balance before he made a slow recovery. Belisarius was only able to take the field again at the beginning of 544, but this time not against Persia. He was again given command of the army in Italia.

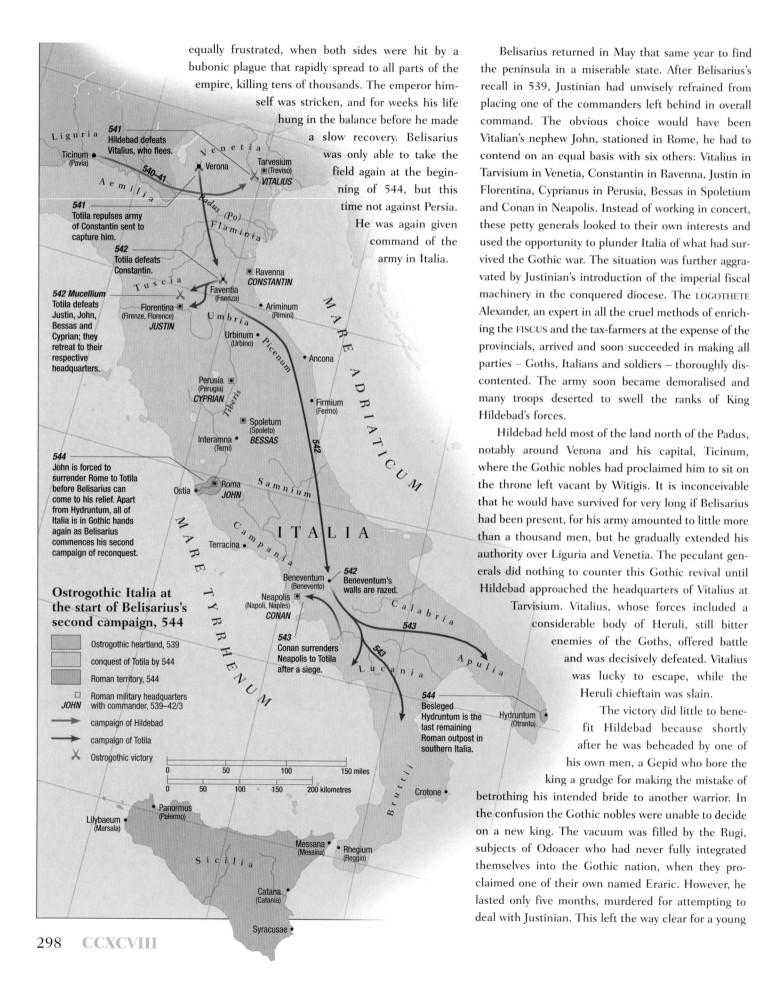

541
Hildebad defeats Vitalius, who flees.

541
Totila repulses army of Constantin sent to capture him.

542
Totila defeats Constantin.

542 Mucellium
Totila defeats Justin, John, Bessas and Cyprian; they retreat to their respective headquarters.

544
John is forced to surrender Rome to Totila before Belisarius can come to his relief. Apart from Hydruntum, all of Italia is in Gothic hands again as Belisarius commences his second campaign of reconquest.

Ostrogothic Italia at the start of Belisarius's second campaign, 544

- Ostrogothic heartland, 539
- conquest of Totila by 544
- Roman territory, 544
- □ Roman military headquarters with commander, 539–42/3
- *JOHN*
- → campaign of Hildebad
- → campaign of Totila
- ✗ Ostrogothic victory

542
Beneventum's walls are razed.

543
Conan surrenders Neapolis to Totila after a siege.

544
Besieged Hydruntum is the last remaining Roman outpost in southern Italia.

Belisarius returned in May that same year to find the peninsula in a miserable state. After Belisarius's recall in 539, Justinian had unwisely refrained from placing one of the commanders left behind in overall command. The obvious choice would have been Vitalian's nephew John, stationed in Rome, he had to contend on an equal basis with six others: Vitalius in Tarvisium in Venetia, Constantin in Ravenna, Justin in Florentina, Cyprianus in Perusia, Bessas in Spoletium and Conan in Neapolis. Instead of working in concert, these petty generals looked to their own interests and used the opportunity to plunder Italia of what had survived the Gothic war. The situation was further aggravated by Justinian's introduction of the imperial fiscal machinery in the conquered diocese. The LOGOTHETE Alexander, an expert in all the cruel methods of enriching the FISCUS and the tax-farmers at the expense of the provincials, arrived and soon succeeded in making all parties – Goths, Italians and soldiers – thoroughly discontented. The army soon became demoralised and many troops deserted to swell the ranks of King Hildebad's forces.

Hildebad held most of the land north of the Padus, notably around Verona and his capital, Ticinum, where the Gothic nobles had proclaimed him to sit on the throne left vacant by Witigis. It is inconceivable that he would have survived for very long if Belisarius had been present, for his army amounted to little more than a thousand men, but he gradually extended his authority over Liguria and Venetia. The peculant generals did nothing to counter this Gothic revival until Hildebad approached the headquarters of Vitalius at Tarvisium. Vitalius, whose forces included a considerable body of Heruli, still bitter enemies of the Goths, offered battle and was decisively defeated. Vitalius was lucky to escape, while the Heruli chieftain was slain.

The victory did little to benefit Hildebad because shortly after he was beheaded by one of his own men, a Gepid who bore the king a grudge for making the mistake of betrothing his intended bride to another warrior. In the confusion the Gothic nobles were unable to decide on a new king. The vacuum was filled by the Rugi, subjects of Odoacer who had never fully integrated themselves into the Gothic nation, when they proclaimed one of their own named Eraric. However, he lasted only five months, murdered for attempting to deal with Justinian. This left the way clear for a young man named Baduila to take the Gothic throne. Baduila is how he styled himself on his coins, but to the Greeks, and therefore to history, he was known as Totila, and he proved to be one of the greatest of all the Gothic rulers. He was Hildebad's nephew, in his middle twenties, and simply not considered much of a threat to the complacent Roman generals; they were too busy lining their own pockets to hear the call to all-out war.

Totila was a clever politician. He knew that to succeed in throwing out Justinian's soldiers and administrators he needed the support of all his people, not just the Goths but also the Italians. Since the Italian aristocracy had given its allegiance to the emperor and his plenipotentiaries, it was to the middle class, urban proletariat and tenant farmers that Totila turned. To many of these, the 'Roman' occupiers were really Byzantine Greeks, and the people were burdened by their new, vicious tax-gatherers. Totila promised freedom from oppression, the breaking up of the great LAT-IFUNDIA, the return of farm land to ordinary people and the abolition of taxes intended only to furnish fabulous palaces in far-flung lands. His cry to arms found listeners everywhere, and within months of his accession he was ready.

By this time, incensed at his generals' inactivity, Justinian issued orders to subdue the growing threat, and in the early winter of 541 it was decided that a detachment from the Ravenna garrison under Constantin and the LOGOTHETE Alexander should attack Totila at his capital of Verona. But the king was ready, and his army of five thousand repulsed the imperial force of some twelve thousand outside the city. Totila moved with speed to pursue them, and in a battle at Faventia annihilated Constantin's army. In the spring of 542 the Goths attacked Justin at Florentina. The combined armies of John, Bessas and Cyprian hurried to his relief, but in the locality of Mucellium (Mugello) Totila defeated and routed them. While John retreated to Rome, Totila took towns in Umbria and then – bypassing the strongly fortified urban centres around Rome – surged into the south of the peninsula, razed the walls of Beneventum and began collecting taxes in the provinces of Lucania, Brutti, Apulia and Calabria.

Justinian sent out several ineffective PRAEFECTI PRAETORIO to recover the situation, but none was able to prevent things from getting worse. In 543 Totila besieged Conan in Neapolis, who was soon forced to surrender to the Goths, where in stark contrast to Belisarius the king doled out grain to the starving inhabitants and enforced the good behaviour of his troops. By early 544 all of Italia was in his hands, with the exceptions of besieged Hydruntum (Otranto) in the furthest south, and Rome – under John's command – on which he was preparing to march. This, then was the situation facing Belisarius when he returned to Italia in the summer of 544. It was, however, to be a very different campaign from the first. Justinian had furnished him with no funds, few soldiers and limited IMPERIUM. But he did his best, recovering much of the south, although he was unable to prevent Rome from falling into Totila's hands.

In turn Belisarius regained the city, only to lose it shortly after. In all, during Justinian's reign, Rome changed hands five times, accurately reflecting the purposeless and desultory battle for Italia throughout the period. By 548 it was clear that neither side was strong enough to decisively defeat the other. Belisarius determined to appeal to Constantinople for proper funding and a real army, and sent as his ambassador his wife Antonina to speak not with Justinian but with her friend the empress. She left at the start of summer in 548 and arrived in the capital only to find that a few days before, on 28 June, Theodora had died. Antonina saw immediately that her mission was doomed. The emperor was inconsolable and no one was in any position to take decisions. She did, however, achieve one result, the recall of Belisarius. Antonina was determined that if anyone were to be blamed for the failure to retake Italia, it would not be her husband.

And so it was that early in 549 Belisarius returned to Constantinople, disillusioned, frustrated, politically impotent. But his efforts had at least held Italia to some degree for the empire, and his resolve laid the foundations for the final triumphant conquest by another. Belisarius now retired to semi-obscurity until Justinian once again called on his best general to save the empire in 559. This time the threat came from the north as a fearful new wave of invaders crossed the Danuvius, a Hunnish tribe known as the Kotrigurs. He accepted the command, defeated the Kotrigurs and drove the barbarian horde back across the mighty river. It was his last victory. In 562 he stood trial for a probably trumped-up charge of corruption, was declared guilty and imprisoned. But Justinian released him after a short time and restored him to the court. Belisarius died at the age of about sixty in March 565, barely eight months before the emperor whose name he had done so much to promote to posterity as the last emperor of the Romans.

EPILOGUE: ITALIA RESTORED (552–56)

To Belisarius's old enemy Narses went the glory of the final conquest of Ostrogothic Italy. The Armenian eunuch was now in his seventy-fifth year, hardly a likely candidate for such an onerous task. But the wily chamberlain was still possessed of good health, knew his emperor better than any man alive and had already proven his military skills. Moreover, the one Byzantine left in Italy of any worth, Vitalian's nephew John, was devoted to him. Narses was easily able to persuade the emperor to supply an army far greater than ever given to Belisarius: at least thirty-five thousand men, comprised mostly of barbarians: Gepids, Lombards, Heruli and Huns, together with a small number of captured Persians.

Since Belisarius had left Italy for the final time, Totila had lost Rome to the Byzantines, only to regain it again on 16 January 550. In response, Justinian had appointed his first cousin Germanus to command a relief army. The soldiers had marched across Illyricum as far as Serdica, where unfortunately Germanus was stricken by a fever and died. And so it was that in the early summer of 552, with his reinforcements, Narses collected Germanus's soldiers and continued the overland march across the Julian Alps into Italy. He can have had few illusions as to the task ahead, for the Byzantines now held only four cities in the peninsula: Ravenna and Ancona in the north, Otranto and Crotone in the south. Yet nor can he have had any idea as to how spectacular his success was to be.

On the army's arrival at Ravenna, Narses paid the demoralised garrison their pay arrears, and spent a few days in preparation for a southward advance, while Totila marched north to block him. The two armies met towards the end of June, at Taginae (Gualdo Tadino), where the eunuch general proved his martial skill by soundly defeating the Goths. Totila was mortally wounded in the battle, and fled with his scattered host in disorder, with the Byzantines in close pursuit. Totila died a few hours later in the small village of Caprae (Capara).

Yet the Goths, with all hope lost, did not give up. They raised up Teia, Totila's best general, to be their king. Teia attempted to renew the alliance with the Franks, but it came to nothing, and the Gothic remnant was forced further south towards Neapolis. Finally, in the valley of the Draco (Sarno), a scant few miles from buried and forgotten Pompeii, at the end of October 552, the Romans and Goths met for the final time. The battle was short and furiously fought, but its outcome was never in any doubt. Teia was struck by a javelin and died on the spot. Even then the Goths fought on, until only a few remained to negotiate terms. By these, they agreed to leave Italy and never again make war on the empire. Justinian's great dream had been fulfilled.

But was it worth it? Narses soon drove out any remaining pockets of resistance, mostly in the north (although Verona resisted him for another nine years), and completely reorganised the government of the Byzantine Italian state in 554 by a PRAGMATICA SANCTIO ('Pragmatic Sanction', a sovereign's solemn decree on a matter of primary importance and which has the force

Narses wins back Italy at the battle of Taginae

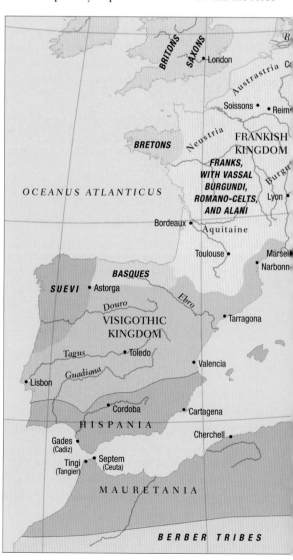

of law). But what was this new Italia? Years of warfare had reduced the once-prosperous peninsula to a smoking wasteland. Its greatest cities, formerly the pride of a powerful empire, had either been razed or left in such ruin as to be almost uninhabitable. Pestilence and famine stalked the hills and valleys, and the devastated populace had been left with no means of defending themselves from future raiders – and the Langobardi ('Long Beards', or Lombards), recently dismissed from imperial service by Narses, were just waiting to return. By his new social order, Narses obliterated the senatorial class of Rome, which had survived the fifth-century barbarian invasions, even to flourish under the Ostrogoth Theodoric. The new government, or EXARCHATE, made Ravenna into a resplendant Byzantine capital, but it had been done at the price of the impoverishment of Italia and Rome. How sad can it be, that Italia's latest period of prosperity, under the benign eye of a great Germanic king, should be ended by a Roman emperor's determination to repossess it as a damaged province of an empire now ruled from Constantinople?

Justinian died suddenly – of a heart attack or a stroke – on the night of 14 November 565, leaving the empire to Justin, the son of his sister Vigilantia. For his attempt to recreate the glory of the Roman empire, and because he spoke Latin not Greek, Justinian is regarded as the last of the Roman emperors, and the story of his nephew Justin II belongs to that of the Byzantine empire. When he died, Justinian was the effective ruler of more Roman territory than any of his predecessors since the early fifth century, but at the cost of the empire's defences along the Danuvius and the eastern frontier, where they were most needed. And within three years of his death Italy would again be lost, to the Langobardi, from which point on any connection with the greatness of the Roman empire was forever lost, and Italia plunged into the darkness of the early medieval period.

The recovered Roman empire at the death of Justinian, 565

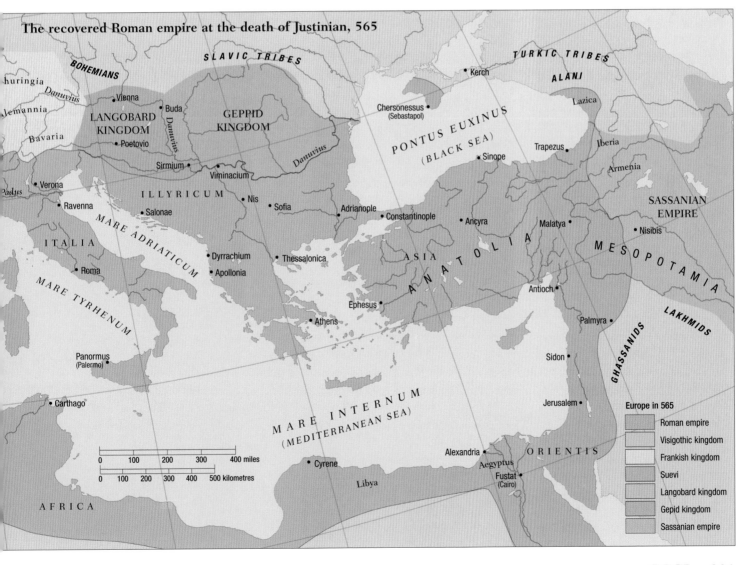

GLOSSARY

adlect A process of admitting a man of a lower rank, who possesses merit but insufficient finances, to a higher rank without his having held a traditionally required intermediate rank.

adsidui Roman citizens of the lowest class (see also *comitia*). They owned the minimum amount of property to be classed as land-owners. Dispossessed of his land, an *adsidui* became *infra classem* (beneath the class) and excluded from army service (see also *mob, the*).

aedile A second-level magistracy of the *cursus honorum* (q.v.) between quaestor (q.v.) and praetor (q.v.), whose duties were confined to the city of Rome. There were four: two plebeian and two curule aediles (see *sella curulis*). The plebeian aediles (created 493 BC) first assisted the *tribuni plebis* (q.v.) in their duties and protection of plebeian rights and were elected by the *comitia plebis tributa* (see *comitia*). The curule aediles (created 367 BC) were elected by the *comitia populi tributa* to give patricians a share in the custody of public buildings and records. From the fourth century BC, all four were responsible for Rome's streets, water supply, drainage, grain dole, civic buildings, markets and general facilities.

aerarium Treasury; the main treasury was the *aerarium Saturni*, sited in the temple of Saturn under the Capitol. Augustus founded the *aerarium militare* to provide pensions for discharged soldiers. Soon after the start of the imperial period control of the *aerarium Saturni* passed from the senate to the principate, and increasingly finances were funnelled through the emperor's personal treasury or 'privvy purse', the *fiscus*.

ager publicus Land in Roman public ownership usually acquired by right of conquest or confiscated as punishment for disloyalty. The censors (q.v.) leased out the land in a way that usually favoured the large estates (*latifundia*).

alae In the Republic the *alae sociorum* were two bodies of Roman allies, cavalry and infantry, which fought on the wings (*alae*) of the battle-line; also referred to as *auxilia* (auxiliaries). In the imperial era *alae* referred exclusively to cavalry, the men under the command of an equestrian *praefectus equitum*, frequently one of their fellow countrymen.

alimenta A welfare system for the feeding of poor children financed by the investment of capital in mortgage on land, the interest being paid to the city or state. It became state-sponsored when Nerva and Trajan began making gifts from the *fiscus* (see *aerarium*) to Italian cities. This inspired other wealthy men to contribute, and the *alimenta* spread throughout the empire. Evidence indicates that the *alimenta* survived into the third century.

Anatolia Not a country, but the region that approximates modern Turkey from the Black Sea to the Mediterranean north to south, and from the Aegean Sea to modern Armenia, Iran and Syria.

aqua Aqueduct; a channel for supplying water from a distant source. The *aqua* might be underground or carried on a bridge. By the time of the middle Republic, the *aquae* were leased by the censors (q.v.) to water companies which charged tariffs to those connected to the supply.

aquilifer The man in a legion who carried the legion's eagle standard. He wore a wolf or lion skin as a mark of his distinction. The rank was probably created by Marius during his army reforms.

armillae Bracelets of gold or silver, which were awarded for valour to legionaries, centurions (q.v.), and *tribuni militum* (q.v).

atrium The main reception room of a Roman house, usually located centrally, with an opening in the roof and a pool underneath. This was based on the archaic model, where the pool stored household water, but by later times had become ornamental.

auctoritas *lit.* 'authority', but in Latin the word meant much more, with overtones of eminence, public leadership and the ability to influence events through sheer personality.

augur A priest who divined the outcome of future events according to a manual of interpretation.

auxilia A legion incorporated into the Roman army without its troops having Roman citizenship; the term extended to the cavalry arm, and later referred exclusively to cavalry (see also *alae*).

basilica, basilicae A large building of Greek origin to house public facilities such as banking, law courts, stores and offices. The first, the Basilica Porcia, was built in Rome by Cato the Censor. Basilicae were usually lit by clerestory windows above, and became the standard model in the late Roman period for Christian churches.

biga A two-horse chariot.

Note to use of the glossary. Where appropriate the singular is given first, followed by the plural; cross-references are indicated by (q.v.).

bisextilis   The Roman equivalent to the extra day added in a leap year. The extra day was intercalated between 23 and 24 February and, because it did not appear to exist, was considered ill-omened; no business was conducted on any *bisextilis*.

Boni   *lit.* 'the good men'. Gaius Gracchus used the term to describe his supporters. Later it became widely used to describe ultra-conservative *opitmates* (q.v.), the men whom Julius Caesar loathed.

campus, campi   A wide, flat expanse of land, sometimes marshy. The words also described a plain.

Campus Martius   The flat area enclosed by a bend of the Tiberis in the west, the Capitol to the south, and the Pincian hill to the north. It was so named because the army did military exercises and cadet training there, although there were also parks and market gardens along the river bank. In later imperial times it was almost completely built over.

castra praetoria   see *cohortes praetorio*

casus belli   *lit.* 'cause for war'.

cella, cellae   *lit.* 'room'. Any room in a Roman house that did not have a name describing its function (which most did), or the main space inside a temple.

censor   The most senior Roman magistracy. Two were elected at the same time and held office for five years. A censor had to have been a consul previously. The censor regulated the the membership of the senate, the order of knights (*equites*), and conducted a census of Roman citizens throughout the empire. The censor lacked *imperium* (q.v.) and so was not escorted by lictors.

centurio, centuriones   Centurion; a regular professional non-commissioned officer of Roman legions. Half were elected by the troops, the other half appointed by the election winners. The centurion was the backbone of army organisation, since the senior officers were usually young aristocrats on attachment, and even the *legati* (q.v.) spent only a short time with their legions.

century   An archaic term that applies to any gathering of 100 men (originally, usually soldiers). By the later Republican and early imperial periods, the centuries of the *comitia centuriata* (see *comitia*) contained many more than 100 men and had no military significance.

circus   A place where chariot races were held, synonymous with Greek term 'hippodrome'. The most famous is the Circus Maximus in Rome.

cliens   Client; a free man who pledged himself to his *patronus* (q.v.) in return for various favours, usually financial or legal assistance. In his turn, a *cliens* could be a *patronus* to his own *clientes*, but these men were also automatically the *clientes* of his *patronus*. In this way a powerful Roman built blocks of supporters to increase his political clout. Clashes between rival supporters frequently led to street violence. In a similar way, colonies, towns or even allied kingdoms could be *clientes* of Rome itself. The title 'Friend and Ally of the Roman People' was a statement of clientship.

clivus   A hilly street or a street on a steep incline.

cloaca   A sewer or drain; Rome's system of *cloacae* were built in the city's archaic history, although they were repeatedly enlarged and improved.

cognomen, cognomina   A nickname. Roman naming conventions were very restrictive (see also *gens* and *praenomen*) and the *cognomen* helped a man distinguish himself from all his fellows having the same first and family name as he.

collegium   Association of a number of men having something in common: priestly, political, religious, work-related, military; there were many *collegia* that banded together. Among the trades the *collegium* acted similarly to a guild or a trades union. In the later empire many *collegia* were placed under military discipline to ensure compliance with the state's needs.

colonia   A self-administrating settlement or colony established by the state, often with a strategic defensive function. Most *coloniae* founded by Pompeius Magnus, Julius Caesar and Augustus had the joint function of providing settlement land to veteran soldiers and at the same time increasing the process of romanisation of foreign territories. With the right of full citizenship (*civitas optimo iure*) the inhabitants had voting rights, which gave a *colonia* a higher status than a *municipium* (q.v.).

cohortes praetorio   Praetorian guard, originally a bodyguard for a praetor (*cohors praetoria*), but later a separate arm of the military devoted to the safe-keeping of an emperor and his family. Augustus was the first to form them into a military elite of nine cohorts, camped in several towns around Rome. Sejanus concentrated the scattered cohorts in the *castra praetoria* immediately outside the Servian *pomerium* (q.v.). The guard was usually commanded by two joint-*praefecti* (see *praefectus praetorio*). Diocletian demoted the praetorians to Rome's garrison; Constantine finally disbanded the guard in favour of the *scholae* (q.v.).

cohortes urbanae   Three urban cohorts formed

Rome's city police, stationed in the *castra praetoria*. Further units were formed and sent to other towns in Italia and the provinces to guard harbours and mints. Each cohort was commanded by a *tribunus* under the overall command of the *praefectus urbi*.

colonus, coloni A tiller of the soil, a tenant farmer.

come, comes The title given in the Eastern empire to a small town or village which had no official status. Its equivalent in the West was *vicus, vici*.

comes, comites *lit.* 'companion' (of the emperor). In the fourth century smaller forces of mobile, usually mounted, troops (*comitatenses*) detached from an army were commanded by a *comes*, from which we derive the word 'count'. In Constantine's increasingly complex bureaucracy many new offices were given to *comites*. The most distinguished was the *magister officiorum* (q.v.) whose rank was *comes primi ordinis*. Next in line were the two officials in charge of financial administration. The count of sacred largesses (*comes sacrarum largitionum*) handled cash. As such, he ran the mines and mint, collected taxes in specie and distributed pay and donatives to the army (hence the title). The 'count of the personal property' (*comes rerum privatarum*) ran the emperor's large number of estates (the *res privata*).

comitatenses see *comes*

comitatus *lit.* 'the emperor's travelling court', derived from *comes, comites* (q.v.), the emperor's companions and commanders of mobile forces. The concept was devised by Diocletian to replace the outmoded *palatium*, or court officials who resided in the Palatine palace in Rome. Also attached to the *comitatus* were Diocletian's elite cavalry forces – the *scholae palatinae*, the *equites comites* and the *equites promoti* (see *schola*).

comitia Any assembly gathered to deal with legislative, governmental or electoral matters. By the late Republican era there were three main assemblies. The *comitia centuriata* organised the people into the Five Classes as defined by an economic means test – from the First (richest) to Fifth (poorest, or *adsidui*). It also elected consuls every year, and censors and praetors every five years. The *comitia populi tributa* (popular assembly) allowed participation of the patricians and met at the order of a consul or praetor in the 35 tribes into which all Roman citizens were divided. It elected the curule aediles, quaestors and *tribuni militum* (q.v.). The *comitia plebis tributa* (plebeian assembly) was convoked by a *tribunus*

plebis (q.v.) and had the right to enact plebiscites (*plebiscitum, plebiscita*, q.v.) and – like the other two *comitia* – conduct trials. It elected the plebeian aediles and *tribuni plebis*.

congiarum, congiara Originally a gift of food distributed to the plebs on the occasion of a festival. In the empire it became a cash largesse, exclusively the gift of the emperor to mark celebrations or to buy popularity.

consilium The advisory council, or cabinet, appointed by the emperor to help him govern. These men – of variable number – may have been either exclusively senators or exclusively equestrians, sometimes both, depending on the emperor. Jurists tended to be prominent, and the *praefecti praetorio* (q.v.) were invariably members. Constantine changed its name to the *sacrum consistorium* (he sat while all the others stood).

consul, consules The most senior magistrate with *imperium* (q.v.). The consuls' primary concerns were to command the military forces, preside over senate meetings and implement its decisions. Two were proposed each year by the senate but elected by the *comitia centuriata* (q.v.). Under the principate awarding the office became increasingly the emperor's prerogative. Consuls could not exercise supreme power because they shared it and served for only one year. In theory each consul was active for a month while his colleague looked on. When active, the consul was said to hold the *fasces* (q.v.) and was accompanied by 12 lictors (q.v.). In practice this alternate power-sharing was confused by the consul's military duties, especially in times of war, when both might be in the field with their legions at the same time. The extension of consular *imperium* was called prorogation and introduced in 326 BC to enable the retiring consul to complete a military campaign as proconsul (*lit.* 'in place of a consul'). This promagistracy was sometime extended to praetors (q.v.), who became propraetors, and this practice was increased during the imperial era, otherwise there would not have been enough men to manage the increased number of provinces. There was a proper age for a consul (42 after the first century BC), but this was increasingly ignored, as was the tradition that a consul should only serve once in his lifetime (see also *cursus honorum*). The nature of the consulship changed under the principate. Augustus introduced an abbreviated consulship of six months. After AD 69 it became normal for three, sometimes more,

Barbalissus: Mesken, Syria
Barcino: Barcelona, Spain
Beneventum: Benevento, Italy
Beroe (Augusta Traiana): Stara Zagora, Bulgaria
Beroea: Veroia, Greece
Beroea (Syria): Halab (Aleppo), Syria
Berytus: Beirut, Lebanon
Berzobis: Resita, Romania
Besontio: Besançon, France
Bibracte: Beuvray, France
Bilitio: Bellinzona, Switzerland
Bingium: Bingen, Germany
Blatobulgium: Birrens, Scotland
Bonna: Bonn, Germany
Bononia (Felsina): Bologna, Italy
Bononia (Gesoriacum): Boulogne, France
Borbetomagus: Worms, Germany
Bostra: Busra, Syria
Branodunum: Brancaster, England
Bravonium: Leintwardine, England
Brigantium: La Coruña, Spain
Brigetio: Szöny, Hungary
Brocolitia: Carrawburgh, England
Brotomagus: Brumath, Germany
Brundisium: Brindisi, Italy
Burdigala: Bordeaux, France
Byblus: Jubaïl, Lebanon
Byzantium (Constantinopolis): Istanbul, Turkey
Caesaraugusta: Zaragoza, Spain
Caesarea (also Mazaca, Cappadocia): Kayseri, Turkey
Caesarea (Mauretania): Cherchell, Algeria
Caesarea Maritima: Caesarea, Israel
Caesarodunum: Tours, France
Caesaromagus: Beauvais, France
Calleva Atrebates: Silchester, England
Callinicum: (also *Nicephorium*) Raqqa, Syria
Callipolis: (Gallipoli) Gelibolu, Turkey
Camboglanna: Birdoswald, England
Camulodunum: Colchester, England
Capraea: Isola Capri, Italy
Caralis: Cagliari, Sardinia
Carcaso: Carcasonne, France
Carnuntum: Petronell, Austria
Carrhae: Harran, Turkey
Cartennae: Ténès, Algeria
Carthago: Carthage, Tunis
Carthago Nova: Cartagena, Spain
Castra Batavia: Passau, Austria
Castra Regina: (Ratisbon) Regensburg, Germany
Catana: Catania, Sicily
Cauca: Coca, Spain
Cavillonum: Chalon-sur-Saône, France
Cenabum (Aureliani): Orléans, France

▶

▼

pairs of consuls to hold office in the same year. The pair that assumed office on 1 January were called *consules ordinarii* (ordinaries), and gave their names to the year. The later two consuls were called *consules suffecti* (suffect). In 190, under the emperor Commodus, the system reached its most extreme when 25 men held the consulship during the year. Modern usage is consul*ship*. not consul*ate*, as the latter is a diplomatic institution.

consular   The title given to a man who has been a consul; similarly for proconsular.

corona civica   Civic crown; awarded to a soldier for saving the lives of fellow soldiers or capturing enemy ground and holding it until the end of a battle. The crown was made from oak leaves, which were later rendered in gold for victorious emperors as a sign of supreme *imperium* (q.v.).

cura, curatores   Boards; Augustus established boards to take over the functions of many Republican magistracies, among them *curatores viarum* (keepers of roads), *curatores operus publicorum* (public works) and *curatores aquarum* (water supply). *Curatores* is also synonymous with 'commissioners', especially in connection with financial administration, such as developed by Trajan at the end of the first century AD.

curia   One of the 30 most ancient Roman clan divisions. The *curiae* gathered in a meeting hall (a *curia*) headed by a chief elected for life called a *curio*. The word eventually came to mean the hall itself rather than the meeting. Legal enactments, *lex curiata*, had fallen into disuse by the end of the Republic, other than for the adoption of a patrician into a plebeian family or the conferring of *imperium* on a senior magistrate, when the 30 original curiae were represented by the 30 lictors. Under the principate even this fell into disuse.

Curia Hostilia   The senate house, thought to have been built originally by King Tullus Hostilius.

cursus honorum   *lit.* 'way of honour'. The political route to becoming a consul. This was senator (aged 30), quaestor, and praetor. The ranks of aedile (q.v.) and *tribunus plebis* (q.v.) were not a legal part of the *cursus honorum*, but most candidates found it useful to serve in one or more of these capacities to attract electoral attention.

cursus publicus   *lit.* 'public way', this referred to the Roman postal system created by Augustus, a complex of way-stations along the numerous highways where couriers changed a tired horse for a fresh one and thus moved dispatches at great speed from one point to another. The *cursus publicus* was also synonymous with espionage, since its officers, frequently recruited from among the *speculatores* and *frumentarii* (q.v.), were well place in their travelling to make reports to the emperor on all aspects of his dominions.

damnatio memoriae   *lit.* 'damnation of the memory', the term applied to those whose names after death were to be erased from public record.

decennalia   tenth anniversary (*vicennalia*, twentieth anniversary).

delator   *lit.* 'denouncer', men employed to uncover treason and bring the guilty party to court. They were universally loathed because many emperors used *delatores* to bring false charges against wealthy citizens with a view to confiscating their estates; synonymous with *frumentarii* (q.v.).

dictator   *lit.* 'one who speaks', ie. 'orders'. In times of extreme danger to the state the active consul with the senate's approval could appoint a man of consular rank (often himself) dictator, also known as *magister populi*, master of the infantry – *populus* meaning those eligible to be soldiers. The period was for a maximum of six months, and he held supreme military and judicial authority, although other magistrates remained in office. The dictator appointed a *magister equitum* (q.v.) to be his second-in-command. The dictator received special indemnity so that when he stepped down he could not be held liable to prosecution for the consequences of any of his actions. The dictatorship was abolished after Caesar's murder in 44 BC.

dies imperii   The date counted by an emperor as that of his accession, which was not necessarily the same as the date on which his powers were conferred by the senate.

domus   A city or town house as distinct from an apartment (*insula* (q.v.)) or country villa.

Domus Publicus   A house owned by the state, usually given to senior priests as part of their remuneration.

dux, duces   *lit.* 'he [who] leads', commander of a cavalry unit in the reorganised army of Constantine. The term had probably come into common currency earlier, but Constantine gave it official status as a title. A *dux* may have been a relatively minor military officer or as distinguished as a *comes* (q.v.). We derive the modern word 'duke' from it.

emporium   A large waterfront building where importers and exporters had their offices; or a whole seaport concerned with maritime trade.

eques   *lit.* a 'horseman', from the Latin for horse (*equus*); its nearest modern equivalent is 'knight'. In the early Republic members of the *Ordo Equester* (Equestrian Order) were, by possessing sufficient wealth to own at least one horse, Rome's top non-senatorial citizens, at which time there were about 1,800 *equites*. By the second century BC, this had become a social class distinction with little military connection, since Rome's cavalry was recruited from among the allies. Under the early empire the *equites* came to represent the burgeoning middle class (senators were not allowed to earn money through trade), and eventually the core from which emperors selected their civil servants. There were several important offices usually the preserve of equestrians, the most distinguished being the *praefectus praetorio* (q.v.).

equites comites (Augusti)   Diocletian's title for the elite cavalry arm formerly referred to as the *equites singulares Augusti*, probably formed by the Flavians, when they had a strength of between 500–1,000 men recruited from the *auxilia* (q.v., also see *alae*).

equites promoti   Another elite cavalry arm created by Diocletian, so named because it was comprised of horsemen 'promoted' from barbarian tribes.

excubitorii   *lit.* 'sentinels', an imperial bodyguard formed by Leo I which pointedly excluded Germans from among its number.

fasces   Originally an emblem of the Etruscan kings, these were bundles of birch rods tied with red leather thongs and each carried by a lictor (q.v.) to precede a magistrate with *imperium*. Within Rome's *pomerium* (q.v.) only the rods were carried as a symbol that the magistrate had the right to chastise, but outside an axe was inserted to indicate he had the right to execute offenders. A curule aedile had two *fasces*, a praetor six, a consul 12, and a dictator 24.

fiscus   see *aerarium*

flame, flamines   A priest who served Rome's most ancient and most Roman deities. The most senior was the *flamen Dialis*, who served Jupiter.

flumen   A river.

foederatus, foederati   Derives from *foedus*, a treaty that established a peaceful alliance between Rome and another state in perpetuity. The term came to have a concrete meaning towards the end of the fourth century when it applied to the Visigoths who were allowed to settle in great numbers in the Balkans and Illyricum, and were expected to supply whole armies to the Romans in return.

forum, fora   An open-air meeting place. The most famous is the Forum Romanum. Other *fora* originally had specific purposes. The Forum Boarium (*boarium* means 'cattle') was the beef market. A *forum castrum* was the meeting place in a Roman military camp. The *forum frumentarium* was a fruit market, *forum holitorium* a vegetable market, *forum piscinum* a fish market.

frumentarii   Army quartermasters whose duties included the purchase and distribution of grain were called *frumentarii*. Because they constantly travelled on logistical assignments, the *frumentarii* were in a position to watch over the army, imperial bureaucracy and local population, and report back to the emperor. Caracalla, among other emperors, used the *frumentarii* as spies and they began to replace the *speculatores*, the agents of men like Julius Caesar. Constantine replaced the *frumentarii* with the *schola agentium in rebus* (see *schola*).

gens, gentes   A family (eg. Aemilius *Aemilii*, Cornelius *Cornelii*, or Julius *Julii*).

Hispania   Spain; in the late Republic the Romans held sway over two provinces, Hispania Citerior (Nearer Spain) and Hispania Ulterior (Further Spain). The northwestern corner remained beyond Roman hegemony until the time of Augustus, after which the territory was divided into three provinces: Tarraconensis, Baetica and Lusitania, corresponding roughly to northern Portugal-Castile-León-Aragon, Andalucia and southern Portugal. Under Diocletian it was combined with Mauretania Tingitana (Morocco) as the diocese Hispaniae (*lit.* 'The Spains').

imperator   Originally 'commander-in-chief' or 'general' but later a title given by his soldiers to a successful general after a victory but who had not yet entered Rome to celebrate a triumph. With the advent of the principate, Augustus appropriated the right to celebrate a triumph to himself, and by the time of Vespasian it was synonymous with 'emperor', the modern word being derived from *imperator*.

imperium   The degree of authority invested in a curule magistrate (see *sella curulis*). A man with *imperium* could exercise the power of his office freely without objection so long as he remained within the laws governing the position. He was preceded by lictors bearing the *fasces* (q.v.). There were degrees of *imperium*, Germanicus was sent to Syria with a *maius imperium*, implying a 'bigger' degree of authority than any other with *imperium* except the emperor.

▼

insula, insulae *lit.* 'an island', the word was also used to describe the tall apartment blocks in Rome and in other Roman cities.

interregnum *lit.* 'between kings', the term came to mean the period of time between the death or deposition of one emperor and the accession of another.

iugerum, iugera The basic Roman unit of land measurement, approximately equal to half an acre.

legatus, legati Originally senior officers of a general's staff, who had to be of senatorial rank to qualify. Augustus appointed senators of consular rank as *legati Augusti propraetore* to govern his imperial provinces (except Aegyptus, which had an equestrian *praefectus Aegypti*). In the early imperial period each legion stationed in an imperial province was commanded by a *legatus legionis*, a man of senatorial rank. The Severans began to divorce military posts from senators, and by the time of Diocletian all military officers were equestrians and the term had fallen into disuse.

lex Latin for 'law'. In the Republic a *lex* was decreed by the *comitia centuriata* (see *comitia*) and only became valid when its terms had been inscribed on bronze or stone, which is why so many, even in fragments, have survived. Under the principate the right of passing *leges* was abrogated by the emperor (see also *plebiscitum* and *senate*).

libellus *lit.* 'little book', it also meant a form of judicial paperwork certifying that its bearer had sworn an oath. Under Decius, *libelli* were issued to Christians who had recanted.

lictor, lictores A public servant who carried the *fasces* (q.v.) and accompanied a magistrate holding *imperium*. By imperial times there were some 300.

limes, limites Originally a Roman surveyor's term for the path(s) that marked the boundaries of centuriated land and gave access between the plots. Later it described the military roads that penetrated enemy territory and, as forts and even walls and ditches were added, the entire defensive structure of a frontier boundary.

limitanei Permanent frontier garrisons so called because they occupied stations on the *limites* (q.v.).

litus A coast (*Litus Saxonicum*, Saxon Coast).

macellum An open-air market with booths (originally for butchers). The Roman *fora* started out this way, but were distinguished by the buildings that sprang up around them, whereas the *macellum* remained a simple market space.

magister, magistri *lit.* 'master', from which we derive the word 'magistrate'. During the Republic he was an elected executive of the senate and people. The hierarchy went: *tribunus militum*, quaestor, *tribunus plebis*, plebeian aedile, curule aedile (all q.v.), praetor, consul. In times of emergency the senate was allowed to appoint an extraordinary *magister* called a dictator (q.v.). By the end of the third century the term was applied to many military and administrative functionaries.

magister equitum *lit.* 'master of the horse'. In the middle and late Republic this office held great *imperium*, since a *magister equitum* was appointed only by a dictator (q.v.) as his second-in-command. By the end of the third century the office had declined somewhat in prestige, and Constantine made the rank subordinate to the *magister militum* (q.v.). After this point each military province might expect to have its own *magister equitum* in command of the cavalry, an equal colleague to the *magister peditum* (q.v.)

magister memoriae, epistularum, libellorum (see *scrinia*)

magister militum *lit.* 'master of military'. This office was created by Constantine to take overall command of an army in the absence of either an Augustus or a Caesar. Their immediate subordinates were the *magister equitum* (q.v) and *magister peditum* (q.v.).

magister officiorum *lit.* 'master of offices' (civil service). Another of Constantine's creations, he was the chief of the government departments and a permanent member of the emperor's *sacrum consistorium* (see *consilium*). He was assigned a number of the functions previously the preserve of the *praefectus praetorio* (q.v.). He commanded the *scholae palatinae* (see *schola*); he held a general direction over the provision of arms to the military; he was minister for foreign affairs; he commanded the newly formed *schola agentium in rebus* (see *schola*) which had replaced the *frumentarii* (q.v.) to act as dispatch-bearers, supervise the transport of troops and act as spies. With these duties, the *magister officiorum* became the most powerful man in the empire after the emperor.

magister peditum *lit.* 'master of foot" (infantry). Unlike the *magister equitum* (q.v.), this was a new post created by Constantine. Although theoretically equal to the *magister equitum*, the greater reliance on cavalry in the later empire meant that infantry commanders were less regarded in the military hierarchy.

magister populi (see *dictator*)

magister praesentalis Commander of the entire field army in the very late empire, e.g. Stilicho.

magister utriusque militiae Commander of *both* arms of the army, cavalry and infantry, ie synonymous with *magister equitem et peditum*.

manumission *lit.* 'send from the hand', making a slave a freedman.

mare sea (see also *oceanus*, *pontus*, *sinus*)

minim A red pigment that triumphant generals painted on their faces, apparently to look like the terracotta statue of Jupiter Optimus Maximus.

mob, the A convenient appellation for what was known in the Republic as *capite censi* (head count), those who were too poor to belong to one of the Five Classes; also known as *proletarii* because they were too poor to contribute anything to the state except *proles* (children). A dispossessed *adsidui* (q.v.) could fall into this *infra classem* (beneath the classes) position. In the late Republic and early imperial periods, this increasingly overwhelming, unstable and frequently riotous section of the Roman populace was only controlled through the cheap or even free distribution of grain or bread, the so-called corn dole, and plenty of free, lavish entertainment.

modius, modii The Roman basic measure of grain, weighing approximately 13 pounds (5.9 kg).

municipium, municipia The title originally given to Italian towns whose inhabitants had been granted Roman 'half' citizenship (*civitas sine suffragio*, citizenship without suffrage), which meant they had all the obligations (taxes, etc.) of citizenship without the right to vote. This meant that a *municipium* had a lower status than a *colonia* (q.v.) In the early first century BC citizens of Italian *municipia* became full citizens (*civitas optimo iure*). As the empire expanded charters of *municipium* were granted to towns outside Italia whose inhabitants were not Roman citizens. However, the rights of citizenship were usually only given to the local aristocracy, magistrates and town councillors until Caracalla's *constitutio antoniniana* (212) gave citizenship to all free men.

nobilis *lit.* 'nobility', the term that described a man of consular rank and his descendants. It was coined by plebeians after they were permitted to the consulship to reduce the distinction of being a patrician by birth.

nomen, nomina Family name or *gens* (q.v.).

notarius, notarii (see *schola*)

novella, novellae An amendment or addition to an existing law.

oceanus A sea without perceivable end.

oppidum A Celtic (Gaulish) hill fort or fortified settlement.

Optimates Senatorial political party of conservatives during the late Republic. They placed the rule of the senate above all other forms of government. Its members were also known as the *Boni* (q.v.)

Ordo *lit.* 'order', a social grouping with a similar family background and amount of wealth. The best known is the *Ordo Equester* (see *eques*).

palatium see *comitatus*.

pantheon The array of all Roman gods.

patronus Patron, a man of rank who held the allegiance of *clientes* (q,v,) in return for favours of money, legal assistance or political promotion opportunities.

patrician The Roman aristocracy from the archaic period. They lost their special rights as plebeian power increased, and by the later Republic were frequently 'genteelly' impoverished. By the end of Nero's reign the patricians had all been wiped out. In the mid-fifth century the term was reintroduced to mean 'father of the emperor' – not to be taken literally since it was more equivalent to 'protector of the emperor', or first minister.

pilum, pilae The Roman infantry spear introduced by Marius with a barbed iron head. A weakness where the shaft joined the head meant it would break on contact, rendering the weapon useless to the enemy but easily repairable by Roman armourers.

plebeian, plebs Any Roman citizen of one of the Five Classes who was not of patrician rank. Originally the plebs were forbidden election to any magisterial post, but this changed rapidly during the Republican period until plebs occupied almost all senior posts.

plebiscitum, plebiscita A plebiscite enacted in the *comitia plebis tributa* (see *comitia*) had the same force of law as a *lex* passed by the *comitia centuriata*. Originally a plebiscite was separately distinguished from a law, but later the two merged in the records, and all were called a *lex*.

pomerium The sacred boundary of the city of Rome. In the religious sense, Rome existed within the boundary and everything outside it was Roman territory. The *pomerium* is said to have been created by King Servius Tullus, but it did not exactly follow the course of the Servian Wall.

▶

The *pomerium* could only be enlarged by a man who substantially increased the size of Roman territory, as Augustus did considerably.

pontifex   A priest, which may have been derived from the notion that a *pontifex* was a bridge builder – bridges (*pons*, *pontes*) being considered structures with magical or mysterious properties.

Pontifex Maximus   The most senior of all Roman priests, who supervised the members of the various priestly *collegia*. The ancient kings held the title *Rex Sacrorum* (holy king). Despite the universal loathing of the kings, the young Republic kept the title because it was sacred, but created the *Pontifex Maximus* to be superior. The *Pontifex Maximus* was elected, which made him a statesman and head of the state religion.

pontus   an enclosed sea, such as the Black Sea (*Pontus Euxinus*).

Populares   The political party of radical reformers during the late Republic that believed in legislation through the force of popular (public) will rather than that of the senate. Julius Caesar was one of the party's luminaries.

porta   A gateway, usually in a defensive wall.

porticus   A colonnade with a roof above, either as a straight arcade or enclosing a square (*peristylus*). Porticoes were frequently used as places of business and for meetings of the senate.

praefectus fabrum   *lit.* 'prefect of making' (quartermaster in modern parlance). He was responsible for every aspect of supplying and maintaining the Roman armies, although usually a civilian not a soldier. Like his modern counterpart he was able to enrich himself through the lucrative contracts he handled (see also *frumentarii*).

praefectus praetorio, praefecti   Commander(s) of the *cohortes praetorio* (q.v.). With some exceptions, it was the custom to appoint two in joint-command. The office was the most distinguished an *eques* (q.v.) could aspire to, and many praetorian prefects were in a position to affect the accession of an emperor. Hadrian altered the prefect's status, making him a judicial administrator, while Diocletian appointed four prefects, one for each tetrarch, to take supreme command of the military in each division of the empire, but limited their power of each by giving his second-in-command, the *vicarius* (q.v.), direct access to himself.

praefectus urbi   see *cohortes urbanae*

praefectus vigilum   *see vigiles*

praenomen, praenomina   The first or given name of a Roman man. There were not many in use, which complicates distinguishing between members of the same *gens* or family, hence the importance of the *cognomen* (q.v.) or nickname.

praeses   Under the Severan dynasty in some provinces the title of governor was no longer *procurator* (q.v.), but *procurator agens vices praesides*, or just simply *praeses*. Although an equestrian rank, in the reign of Caracalla *praesides* became recognised as the appellation for all governors, both of senatorial and imperial provinces. Diocletian also used the term, when every province except Africa Proconsularis and Asia were governed by *praesides*. These had consular governors reporting directly to the emperor.

praetor   *lit.* 'one who leads'. The second most senior rung on the *cursus honorum* (q.v.) of magistrates. Originally, it was the highest rank until the Republic introduced the consuls. At first there were two, the *praetor urbanus* administered laws in the city of Rome, and the *praetor peregrinus*, administered lawsuits concerning foreigners at Rome, and was also in charge of supervising the games. With acquisition of overseas territories, the number increased to four and then six praetors.

primicerius domesticorum   Commander of the *scholae palatinae* (see *schola*) in Constantine's reign and thereafter.

potestas tribunicia   see *tribunus plebis*

praepositus sacri cubiculi   A eunuch officer whose duties were looking after the emperor's bedchamber, a position first created by Diocletian. In time he ranked with highest officials in the empire, with control of the imperial wardrobe (*sacra vestis*), the *primicerius sacri cubiculi*, who was the emperor's personal equerry, and the *silentarii* (q.v.).

praetorian guard   see *cohortes praetorio*

princeps   The 'first citizen', a title assumed by Augustus. Previously, the *princeps senatus* was the chosen leader of the senate, but in the imperial period the simpler *princeps* was used to describe the emperor, hence the use of the word 'principate' to describe the early imperial era. The modern word 'prince' is derived from it.

privatus, privati   *lit.* 'private person', a citizen holding no magisterial or imperial rank.

procurator   An agent or, in legal proceedings, representative. Under the principate the term came to mean an employee of the emperor in the civil service, and *procurators* fulfilled a wide range of duties from legal to fiscal. They may have been men of the emperor's own household, probably freedmen, but were more usually *equites* (q.v.).

propraetor   (see *consul*)

pulvinator   The imperial box at the theatre, amphitheatre or circus; derived from *pulvinar*, a cushioned couch on which offerings were left to the gods in front of a temple.

quadriga   A four-horse chariot.

quaestor   Lowest rung on the *cursus honorum* (q.v.), and generally a fiscal role (treasury, port customs, provincial finances). Quaestors were regularly attached to a propraetor or proconsul's provincial administration.

quattuorviri consulares   The four 'circuit judges' appointed by Hadrian to see that the law was efficiently administered in Italia, and to relieve citizens of the previous necessity of bringing appeals to Rome for judgement. Because their appointment appeared to downgrade the status of Italia to a mere province, they were unpopular among senators.

res publica   *lit.* 'thing' or 'affair of the public'. A republic is a government that constitutes the people as a whole and describes the Roman constitution after the abolition of the kings.

rex   king

saepta   *lit.* 'sheepfold', which describes the way the open space on the Campus Martius was divided by temporary fences so that the Five Classes could vote in their centuries at an assembly. Buildings such as the Saepta Julia borrowed the term.

scrinia   *lit.* 'file holder', this term described the administrative bureau of Constantine and refers to the fact that the actual files were dragged around with the *comitatus* (q.v.). There were three departments in the *scrinia*, controlled by the *magister memoriae* (issuer of imperial memoranda in response to petitions), the *magister epistularum* (letter-writing and dealing with embassies), and the *magister libellorum* (petitions and judicial matters). Time has obscured how these various functions actually worked or the real scope of their duties.

senate   *senatus populusque Romanus* (S.P.Q.R.) was the senate and people of Rome. Originally an advisory council of 100 patricians under the kings, the senate expanded to 300 patricians at the start of the Republic. By the middle Republic plebeians had earned the right to be senators. At first entry was *adlection* (q.v.) by the *censors* (q.v.), but by the middle Republic admittance was automatically

given for life once a man had been elected by his *comitia* (q.v.) to his first magistracy. It had its own meeting house, the Curia Hostilia (later replaced by Diocletian), but frequently met in temples and other sites such as the Porticoes of Pompeius, where Julius Caesar was murdered. Its permanent chief was the senior patrician, the *princeps senatus*. The senate remained an advisory body in the Republic, never empowered to make laws, only recommend them to the *comitia* (see *senatus consultum*). Augustus amended the body's powers to include law-making, but later emperors severely reduced the senate's prerogatives and gave many senatorial offices to those of equestrian rank.

sella curulis   The ivory chair reserved for the exclusive use of *magistri* (q.v.) with *imperium* (q.v.); a curule aedile sat in one, but a plebeian aedile did not. Praetors and consuls used curule chairs.

senatus consultum   Resolutions of the senate passed to magistrates and the *comitiae* as recommendations for the promulgation of a *lex* (q.v.) or *plebiscitum* (q.v). In the late Republic they were rarely ignored and therefore acquired the force of law. In the principate many emperors preferred to issue their legislation in the form of *senatus consulta* rather then their own *edicta in perpetuum*, which perpetuated the fabrication that it was actually the senate passing the laws.

schola   Originally the meeting place near the main gate of a Roman army camp for the first cohorts of the legion. During the reign of Septimius Severus *scholae* came to mean the clubs formed by junior officers of a legion. Apart from providing social amenities, these clubs were insurance societies. In return for regular contributions of pay, if a soldier was discharged or fell ill he received a lump sum from the society's bank, which was controlled by a *quaestor* (q.v.). By the time of Constantine the name had come to refer to the crack cavalry units which were housed in instant readiness near the camp's main gate. Constantine replaced the *cohortes praetorio* (q.v.) with the *scholae palatinae*, under the overall command of the *magister officiorum* (q.v.). Each *schola* numbered 500 cavalrymen recruited from Germania, and they were better paid and equipped than the cavalry of the field army. The *schola agentium in rebus* replaced the *frumentarii* (q.v.) as dispatch-bearers, logistics supervisors and spies. The *schola notarorium* was composed of men with the rank of *tribunus*. These *notarii* acted as secretaries to the *sacrum consistorium* (see *consilium*), emissaries to the provinces, and drew up letters of patent for lower military ranks. They also kept a register containing the names of the higher state officials called the *laterculum maius.*

silentarii A body of thirty men responsible for maintaining quiet and decorum in the court of Diocletian and onward (especially in the East).

sinus In the geographical context, a gulf, such as Sinus Ligurius (the Gulf of Genoa).

suffect consul (see *consul*)

therma, thermae The public baths of Roman cities; a private bath was called a *balineum.*

toga Made from a single piece of lightweight woollen cloth, only a full citizen of Rome was permitted to wear the toga. Its extreme length (about 15 feet, 4.6m) and the complex of folds it created when draped makes it unlikely that a togate man wore anything else under it. There were several types of toga: *toga alba*, ordinary white garment; *toga candida*, specially whitened to look smart when canvassing for election; *toga picta*, all purple for triumphing generals; *toga praetexta*, purple-bordered for curule magistrates; *toga pulla*, black mourning toga; *toga trabea*, particoloured in strips for augurs; *toga virilis*, toga of manhood, actually a *toga alba.*

Transtiberim *lit.* 'across the Tiberis', the district on the opposite bank of the Tiberis (Tiber) from the city of Rome. Modern-day Trastevere.

tribunus militum Each of the middle officers in the chain of command of a Roman army was classed as a military tribune.

tribunus plebis Tribune of the plebs; originally a man representing one of the three Roman *tribus* (tribes). The magistracy came into being in the early Republic when the plebeians were confronting the power of the patricians. Elected by the *comitia plebis tributa* (see *comitia*), *tribuni* swore an oath to defend lives and property of the plebs. The office held no *imperium* (q.v.) but the tribunician power (*potestas tribunicia*) lay in the right to exercise a veto against the actions of any other magistrate, or the holding of an election, or the passing or a law or plebiscite, or decrees of the senate, even in war or foreign affairs. Only a dictator was above the tribunician veto. This was the power that when it was vested in Augustus made him the absolute ruler of the empire; soon thereafter the office fell into disuse.

vexillum Flag or banner. In the Republic it was the standard of the legionary cavalry. The standard bearer was called the *vexillarius*. It also came to represent a detached unit (*vexillatio*) and so eventually to mean the unit itself (see next entry).

vexillationes Originally a detachment of Roman infantry, in the later empire it came to mean units of cavalry (implying how more important mounted soldiers had become).

via A road or main highway.

vicarius, vicarii Originally a substitute for a *procurator* (q.v.), or equestrian provincial governor, generally when the *procurator* was forced to be absent from his province. Under the Severan dynasty equestrian *vicarii* were more frequently appointed as governors in their own right. Diocletian's twelve dioceses of the empire were largely administered by *vicarii*, who reported to one of the four *praefecti praetorio* of the tetrarchs. However, they had the right of direct access to the senior Augustus, which was an effective check and balance to the enormous power wielded by the *praefecti*. The modern word 'vicar' (and still associated with a diocese) is derived from it.

vigiles The third of Rome's garrison after the *cohortes praetorio* and *urbanae*, the *vigiles* formed a permanent fire brigade, first established by Augustus. Each of the seven cohorts was commanded by a *tribunus* under the equestrian *praefectus vigilum*. In addition to fire-fighting, they acted as the city's night watch; there was also a detachment stationed at Ostia.

vigintivirate Although not an official step in the *cursus honorum* (q.v.), this post was a useful entry point, and loosely translates as 'the twenty', since this body of government officers consisted of 20 men, the *vigintiviri*. Their duties, usually under the supervision of an aedile (q.v.), split into four categories: ten assigned to the courts; four to look after Rome's streets; three in charge of criminal trials; three, called moneyers, to attend to the coinage.

viri Generic title for the most distinguished officers of the later empire. There were generally four classes of *viri*: *vir clarissimus* (most distinguished gentleman), a senatorial officer; *vir eminentissimus* (eminent gentleman) belongs only to an equestrian *praefectus praetorio*; *vir egregius* (honourable gentleman), an equestrian in the civil service; *vir perfectissimus* (most perfect gentleman) other *praefecti* and *procurators.*

TABLE OF EMPERORS

Bold italics indicates senior or elder colleague

JULIO–CLAUDIAN DYNASTY

27 BC–AD 14	Augustus
14–37	Tiberius
37–41	Gaius Caligula
41–54	Claudius
54–68	Nero

YEAR OF THE FOUR EMPERORS

68–69	Galba
69	Otho
69	Vitellius

FLAVIAN DYNASTY

69–79	Vespasian
79–81	Titus
81–96	Domitian

NERVO–TRAJANIC AND ANTONINE DYNASTIES

96–98	Nerva
97–117	Trajan (97–98 with Nerva)
117–38	Hadrian
139–61	Antoninus Pius
161–69	Lucius Verus (with *Marcus Aurelius*)
161–80	Marcus Aurelius
180–92	Commodus

EMPERORS OF THE CIVIL WAR AND THE SEVERAN DYNASTY

193	Pertinax
193	Didius Julianus
193–211	Septimius Severus
211–12	Geta (with *Caracalla*)
211–17	Caracalla
217–18	Macrinus
218	Diadumenian (with *Macrinus*)
218–22	Elagabalus
222–35	Severus Alexander

PERIOD OF MILITARY ANARCHY AND CIVIL DISORDER

235–38	Maximinus Thrax
238	*Gordian I* and II (in Africa)
238	Balbinus & Pupienus (In Italia)
238–44	Gordian III
244–49	Philip the Arab
247–49	Philip II (with, *Philip the Arab*)
249–51	Decius
251–53	Trebonianus Gallus
251–53	Volusian (with *Trebonianus Gallus*)
251	Hostilian (with *Trebonianus Gallus*)
253	Aemilianus
253–60	Valerian
253–68	Gallienus (253–60 with *Valerian*)

USURPERS

88	Saturninus (Germania)
235	Quartinus (Germania)
238	Capellianus (Africa)
240	Sabinianus (Africa)
248	Pacatianus (Illyricum)
248–53	Antonius (Syria)
248–?	Iotapianus (Syria)
248–?	Sponsianus (Syria)
248–?	Silbannacus (Gallia)
250–51	Julius Valens Priscus (Moesia)
258–59	Ingenuus (Illyricum)
259–60	Regalianus (Illyricum)

IMPERIUM GALLORUM

259–69	Postumus
268	Laelianus
268	Marius
269–71	Victorinus
c.270	Domitianus
271–74	Tetricus

RECOVERY OF THE EMPIRE

268–70	Claudius II Gothicus
270	Quintillus
270–75	Aurelian
275–76	Tacitus
276–82	Probus Bonosus (*usurper*, Germania)
282–83	Carus
283–84	Carinus and Numerian

EAST AND PALMYRA

260–62	Macriani (2, Asia)
260–67	Odenath (Palmyra)
267–72	Zenobia & Vabalathus (Palmyra)
285	M. Aurelius Julianus (*usurper*, Illyricum)

THE TETRARCHY AND HOUSE OF CONSTANTINE

WEST		EAST	
287–305	Maximian Aug.	284–305	Diocletian Aug.
287–93	Carausius (*usurper*, Britannia)		
293–96	Allectus (*usurper*, Britannia)		
	(*usurper*)	296–97	Domitianus (Aegyptus)
	(*usurper*)	297–98	Achilleus (Aegyptus)
293–305	Constantius Caes.	293–305	Galerius Caes.
305–06	Constantius Aug.	305–11	Galerius Aug.
305–06	Severus II Caes.	305–09	Maximinus Daia Caes.
306–07	Severus II Aug.	309–13	Maximinus Daia Aug.
306–12	Maxentius (in Italia with *Maxentius* reinstated 307–08)		
306–07	Constantine Caes.		
307–24	Constantine Aug. (joint)	308–324	Licinus Aug.
316–17	A. Valens (appointed by *Licinius* in opposition to Constantine)		
324	Martianus (appointed by *Licinius* in opposition to Constantine)		
	324–37 Constantine Aug. (sole ruler)		
337–40	Constantine II Aug.	337–61	Constantius II Aug.
	337–40 Constans Aug.		
340–50	Constans Aug.		
350–53	Magnentius (*usurper*)	350	Vetranio Caes.
350	Nepotianus (*usurper*, Rome)		(with *Constantius II*)
		351–54	Gallus Caes.
			(with *Constantius II*)
355–61	Julian Caes. (with *Constantius II*, Aug. from 360)		
	361–63 Julian Aug. (sole ruler)		
	363–64 Jovian Aug. (sole ruler)		

VALENTINIAN AND THEODOSIAN DYNASTY

364–75	Valentinian Aug.	364–78	Valens Aug.
375–83	Gratian Aug.	365–66	Procopius (*usurper*)
375–92	Valentinian II Aug. (Italia)	379–92	*Theodosius Aug.*
	392–95 Theodosius Aug. (sole ruler)		
383–88	Magnus Maximus (*usurper*, with son Flavius Victor, 384–88)		
392–94	Eugenius (*usurper*)		
395–423	Honorius	395–408	Arcadius
	(Stilicho as regent 395–408)		
406	'Marcus' (*usurper*, Britanniae)		
406–07	Gratianus (*usurper*, Britanniae)		
408–11	Constantine III (*usurper* Britanniae/Galliae; co-Aug. from 409)		
409–10	Priscus Attalus (Rome, with *Honorius*; restored 414, exiled)		
409–11	Maximus, son of Gerontius (*usurper* Hispaniae)		
411–13	Jovinus (*usurper* Galliae)		
412–13	Sebastianus, brother of *Jovinus* (co-usurper)		
413	Heraclianus (*usurper* Africa)		
421	Constantius III (with *Honorius*)	408–50	Theodosius II
423–25	Joannes (*usurper*)		
425–55	Valentinian III	450–57	Marcian

TABLE OF EMPERORS, POPES AND PATRIARCHS

FALL OF THE WEST

455	Petronius Maximus
455–56	Avitus
457–61	Majorian
461–65	Libius Severus
467–72	Anthemius
472	Olybrius
473	Glycerius
473–75	Julius Nepos
475–76	Romulus Augustulus

BARBARIAN KINGS OF ITALIA

476–93	Odoacer
493–526	Theodoric
526–34	Athalaric
534–36	Theodahad

BYZANTINE RECONQUEST

536–40	Witigis
540–41	Hildebad
541–52	Totila
552–53	Teias

EASTERN EMPIRE

457–74	Leo I
474	Leo II
474–75	Zeno (deposed)
475–77	Basiliscus
477–91	Zeno (restored)

EASTERN EMPIRE

484–88	Leontius (*usurper* Syria)
491–518	Anastasius
518–27	Justin
527–65	Justinian

POPES OF ROME (*ex. anti-Popes*)

d.AD 64	St. Peter
c.66–c.68	St. Linus
c.79–c.91	St. Anacetus
c.91–c.101	St. Clement I
c.100–c.101	St. Evaristus I
c.109–c.116	St. Alexander I
c.116–c.25	St. Sixtus I
c.125–36	St. Telesphorus
c.138–c.42	St. Hyginus
c.142–c.55	St. Pius I
c.155–66	St. Anicetus
c.166–74	St. Soter
c.174–89	St. Eleutherius
189–98	St. Victor I
198/9–217	St. Zephyrinus
217–22	St. Callistus I
222–30	St. Urban I
230–35	St. Pontian I
235–36	St. Anterus
236–50	St. Fabian
251–53	St. Cornelius
253–54	St. Lucius I
254–57	St. Stephen I
257–58	St. Sixtus II
260–68	St. Dionysius
269–74	St. Felix I
275–83	St. Eutychian
283–96	St. Gaius
296–?304	St. Marcellinus
306–08	St. Marcellus I
310	St. Eusebius
311–14	St. Miltiades
314–35	St. Silvester I
336	St. Mark
337–52	St. Julius I
352–66	Liberius
366–84	St. Damasus I
384–99	St. Siricius
399–401	St. Anastasius I
401–17	St. Innocent I
417–18	St. Zosimus
418–22	St. Boniface I
422–32	St. Celestine I
432–40	St. Sixtus III
440–61	St. Leo I
461–68	St. Hilarius I
468–83	St. Smplicius I
483–92	St. Felix III (II)
492–96	St. Gelasius I
496–98	Anastasius II
498–514	St. Symmachus
514–23	St. Hormisdas
523–26	St. John I
526–30	Felix IV (III)
530–32	Boniface II
533–35	John II
535–36	St. Agapitus I
536–37	St. Silverius
537–55	Vigilius
556–61	Pelagius I
561–74	John III

PATRIARCHS OF BYZANTIUM

38–54	Stachys the Apostle
54–68	Onesimus
69–89	Polycarpus I
89–105	Plutarch
105–14	Sedecion
114–29	Diogenes
129–36	Eleutherius
136–41	Felix
141–44	Polycarpus II
144–48	Athendodorus
148–54	Euzois
154–66	Laurence
166–69	Alypius
169–87	Pertinax
187–98	Olympianus
198–211	Mark I
211–17	Philadelphus
217–30	Ciriacus I
230–37	Castinus
237–42	Eugenius I
242–72	Titus
272–84	Dometius
284–93	Rufinus I
293–306	Probus
306–14	Metrophanes
314–37	Alexander
337–39	Paul I (341–42; 346–51)
339–41	Eusebius of Nicomedia
342–46	Macedonius I (351–60)
360–70	Eudoxius of Antioch
370–79	Demophilus
379	Euagrius
380	Maximus
379–81	Gregory I the Theologian
381–97	Nectarius
398–404	John I Chrysostom
404–05	Arsacius of Tarsus
406–25	Atticus
426–27	Sisinius I
428–31	Nestorius
431–34	Maximianus
434–46	Proclus
446–49	Phlabianus
449–58	Anatolius
458–71	Gennadius I
471–88	Acacius
488–89	Phrabitas
489–95	Euphemius
495–511	Macedonius II
511–18	Timotheus I
518–20	John II of Cappadocia
520–35	Epiphanius
535–36	Anthimus I
536–52	Menas
552–65	Eutychius (577–82)

PATRIARCHS OF ALEXANDRIA

43–63	Mark the Evangelist
61–82	Anianus
83–95	Avilius
96–106	Kedron
106–18	Primus
118–29	Justus
131–41	Eumenes
142–52	Mark II
152–66	Celadion
167–78	Agrippinus
178–89	Julian
189–232	Demetrius
232–48	Heraclas
248–64	Dionysius
265–82	Maximus
282–300	Theonas
300–11	Peter I
312–13	Achillas
313–28	Alexander I
328–39	Athanasius I (346–73)
339–46	Gregory of Cappadocia
373–80	Peter II
380–85	Timothy I
385–412	Theophilus I
412–44	Cyril I
444–51	Dioscorus I
452–57	Proterius
457–60	Timothy II
477	Peter III
477–82	Timothy III
482	John I
482–89	Peter III
489–96	Athanasius II
496–505	John II
505–16	John III
516–17	Dioscorus II
517–35	Timothy IV
535–36	Theodosius
537–40	Paul
541–51	Zoilus
551–69	Apollinarius

PATRIARCHS OF ANTIOCH

c.37–c.53	St. Peter the Apostle
c.53–68	Euodius
68–107	St. Ignatius
107–27	Hero
127–54	Cornelius
154–69	Eros
169–82	Theophilus
182–91	Maximus I
191–211	Serapion
211–20	Ascelpiades
220–31	Philetus
231–37	Zebinnus
237–53	Saint Babylas
253–56	Fabius
256–60	Demetrius
260–72	Paul of Samosata
268–73	Domnus I
273–82	Timaeus
283–303	Cyril
304–14	Tyrannos
314–20	Vitalis
320–23	Saint Philogonus
323–24	Paulinus of Tyre
324–37	St. Eustathius
331–33	Eulalius
333–34	Euphornius
334–42	Philaclus
342–44	Stephanus I
344–57	Leontius
358–59	Eudoxius
360	Euzoius
361–81	St. Meletius
381–404	Flavian I
404–12	Porphyrus
412–17	Alexander
417–28	Theodotus
428–42	John I
442–49	Domnus II
449–55	Maximus II
456–58	Basil
458–61	Acacius
461–65	Martyrius
465–66	Peter the Fuller (476–88)
466–76	Julian
488–90	John II
490–95	Stephanus II
495–96	Callandion
496–98	Palladius
498–512	Flavian II
512–38	Severus of Antioch*
518–21	Paul I
521–28	Euphrosius
528–46	Ephrem of Amid

* Severus was deposed by the Greek Orthodox Church in 518; while in exile in Aegyptus, he was recognised by many Syriac Christians as the lawful Patriarch until his death in 538.

BIBLIOGRAPHY

In compiling this narrative history I have read or re-read many books on the topic, and attempted to weave a reasonable path between frequently conflicting opinions. One title in this list is not strictly speaking a history but a novel. However, Robert Graves' magnificent *Count Belisarius* deserves to be considered as historically accurate in its greater part, and the words he puts into the mouths of his characters – while obviously imagined for the sake of the tale – may well be considered as authentic as, say, those of Procopius, the recognised historian of the period. The list could be enormous; here are the titles I found most useful.

ADKINS, LESLEY AND ADKINS, ROY A. *Handbook to Life in Ancient Rome* Oxford University Press, 1998, US edition by Facts On File, Inc. ISBN 0195123328

AMMIANUS MARCELLINUS. *Works: Vol 1 (Res Gestae) – Ammianus Marcellinus* Rolfe J.C. translator, Loeb Classical Library, 1935. ISBN 0674993314

CONSTABLE, NICK. *Historical Atlas of Ancient Rome* Checkmark Books, New York, 2003. ISBN 0816053316

CORNWELL, T. AND MATTHEWS, J. *Atlas of the Roman World* Phaidon Press, 1982

DIO, CASSIUS COCCEIANUS. *The Roman History* Cary, E. translator, Loeb Classical Library, 1914. ISBN 0674990595
 and
The Roman History: Reign of Augustus I. Scott-Kilvert editor, Penguin Books, 1987. ISBN 0140444483

GIBBON, EDWARD. *The History of the Decline and Fall of the Roman Empire* The Folio Society, 8 vols., 1983, 1995, 14th reprint 2004.

GRANT, MICHAEL. *The History of Rome* Faber and Faber, 2002. ISBN 057111461X
 and
The Fall of the Roman Empire Weidenfeld & Nicholson, 1997. ISBN 1857999754

GRAVES, ROBERT. *Count Belisarius* Penguin Books, 1975. ISBN 0140010254

HODGKIN, THOMAS. *The Barbarian Invasions of the Roman Empire (Italy and her Invaders)* (8 vols.) Clarendon Press, 1880–99; Folio Society, 2000.

HORNBLOWER, SIMON AND SPAWFORTH, ANTONY. *The Oxford Classical Dictionary, Third Revised Edition* Oxford University Press, 2003. ISBN 0198606419

LACTANTIUS. *On the Deaths of the Persecutors* W. Fletcher translator, Ante-Nicene Library, Edinburgh, 1871.

NORWICH, JOHN JULIUS. *Byzantium – The Early Centuries* Viking, 1988; Penguin Books, 1990. ISBN 0140114475

PARKER, H. M. D. *A History of the Roman World* AD 138–337 Methuen & Co. Ltd., 1958.

PROCOPIUS. *The Secret History (Anecdota or Historia Arcana)* G. A. Williamson translator, Penguin Books, 1981. ISBN 0140441824
 and
History of the Wars (De Belli) B. H. Dewing translator, Loeb Classical Library, in various volumes, 1914–1938 ISBNs 0674990544, 0674991915, 0674991192, 0674990900, (1989) 0674992393
 and
On Buildings (De Aedifici) B. H. Dewing and G. A. Williamson translators, Loeb Classical Library, 1940. ISBN 0674993780

SALMON, E. T. *A History of the Roman World 30 BC to AD 138* Methuen University Paperback, 1968. ISBN 416295703

Scriptores Historiae Augustae Loeb Classical Library, 1921, 1924, 1932 (the new Folio Society edition is particularly good)

SUETONIUS, GAIUS TRANQUILLUS. *The Twelve Caesars* Robert Graves translator, Penguin Books, 1957.

TACITUS, CORNELIUS. *The Annals* Michael Grant translator, Penguin Books, 1971. ISBN 0140440607

Background map shows the archaeological sites of the Imperial Fora, Forum Romanum, Palatine and Colosseum area.

And two internet sites…

The Catholic Encyclopedia,
www.newadvent.org/cathen

Roman Numismatic Gallery, www.romancoins.info/

A few of these sources deserve a special mention. Hodgkin's *The Barbarian Invasions of the Roman Empire* is not only an enlightening work, but one that remains highly readable, even though these huge volumes were published between 1880–99. It is fortunate for the researcher that, while a great deal of archaeological work has changed our view of the ancient Romans considerably during the later 20th century, the sphere of Hodgkins' scholarship is largely unaffected. It is also interesting to read his Latin translations and compare them – when they coincide – with other standard interpretations. His personable descriptions of the time, the places and the people make these volumes a must-read for anyone with a passion for the later Roman empire. And it is a testament to the depth of his detail that Hodgkin refuses to be eclipsed by the monolithic Edward Gibbon.

Of *The Decline and Fall*, there are many editions available, but it is always best to refer to those that are unabridged, although footnotes by modern experts are a useful way to avoid the occasional pitfalls of Gibbon's personal, often partisan view.

Of Internet sources, I really only found two that provided a rounded compendium of useful background information. The Roman Numismatic Gallery was invaluable for its large collection of portraits, which often help the researcher to imagine the human behind the imperial mask. Many of the better quality coin portraits offer a real insight into personalities, thanks to the Roman propensity for (often cruelly) accurate representation.

The Catholic Encyclopedia is one of the best historical information sites on the web, for its organisation, detail, information and refreshingly non-partisan approach to all matters relating to the early Church. (Of course it also covers a vastly greater caucus of religious matters beyond the period with which this book deals.)

Getting it right

The problems encountered when authenticating the likeness of an historical figure are demonstrated by the bust above. Its owner, the Museum of Antalya in Turkey, claims it shows the AD 238 co-Augustus Balbinus, but if one compares the portrait on the coin struck by him (bottom), a distinctly closer semblance can be found with the Balbinus bust in the Vatican Museums (below) – so our choice was made.

Colouring a Roman
Traces of colour pigment found on Roman statues indicate that the 'noble' white marble busts we know today were never intended to be such, and were in fact covered in paint. Clearly, this was to add to the realism of the sculptor's vision, and would have been particularly evident in details like the eyes – alive with colour and, perhaps, intelligence, rather than the disconcertingly blank gaze we see today. The example above shows how Lucius Verus – so proud of his gold-dusted blond hair – might have appeared when the bust was spanking new.

Comparison of coin sizes
As explained in the preface on page 9, the coins depicted in this book are used as portraiture. As a result, they are shown considerably larger than their real size. This can be seen from the comparison of Trajan's coin, shown left, as it appears on page 76, and its real size (11mm), to be found in the Museo Nazionale di Roma, Rome.

INDEX